INTRODUCTION

This richly illustrated full-colour guide to Historic Houses Castles and Gardens has been completely revised. It has now been published annually for some 40 years and contains information on some 1500 beautiful properties and gardens open to the general public.

Properties listed are privately owned or in the care of the National Trust, English Heritage, National Trust for Scotland, Scottish Border Heritage, CADW - Welsh Historic Monuments and Irish Heritage.

Civil wedding ceremonies in historic properties have become more and more fashionable. For this reason a list of properties who have been licensed for the great day has been included towards the end of the book. Couples can now marry in places of their own choosing, and oh what a choice! Five possible venues explain what they can do to make this important day memorable in our article on page v.

Number One, London, once described as 'the most renowned mansion in the capital' has been home to the Dukes of Wellington since 1817. It has been the subject of a three-and-a-half-year programme of renovation and repair. Our article explains the care and skills which have gone into the 're-making' of Apsley House.

Champagne breakfast, taking in the sights of the English countryside whilst travelling in style in time for 'Lunch in the Garden of England' is a mouth-watering thought. This can become a reality with The Orient Express excursions to Historic Properties described in our article 'The Art of Travelling Graciously.'

Visit an historic village, walk down the streets of Lacock and take ale in The Red Lion, the Old Coaching Inn where Elizabeth Bennett first encountered Mr Darcy in the television dramatisation of 'Pride and Prejudice'. John Hodgson reminisces about his years of village life in our article on page xxv.

Taking children from the classroom and allowing them to 're-live' history is as exciting for a child as for a Sandford Award judge. Eric Steed explains 'The Joys of Judging' on page xxxii.

Levens Hall in Cumbria was the winner of the Historic Houses Association/Christie's Garden of the Year Award and is featured on our title page. More information about Levens Hall can be found on page 24.

All admission charges quoted are subject to change without notice. All dates are inclusive, i.e. May to September. Opening times and dates apply to 1996 only. Please note that the proposed new county boundaries are not reflected in this publication but will be in future editions.

CONTENTS

Cover picture: Mapledurham House and Watermill, Oxfordshire

Title Page picture: Levens Hall, Cumbria. Winner Christie's/HHA Garden of the Year Award presented in 1995

ISBN 0 948056 28 2

"The loveliest Castle in the world."

LORD CONWAY

LEEDS CASTLE

Maidstone in Kent

ROMANCING WITH HISTORY

"Here Comes the Bride", the traditional entrance music, can now be heard in many more venues than the writer of this well-known music could ever have imagined.

We are used to the Hollywood movie which has its stars being married in all sorts of strange locations, from the bottom of the ocean to ceremonies in the sky. In this country we probably expected our marriage ceremonies to be restricted to either church or registry office. Now it has all changed. Suddenly, couples can marry in places of their own choosing, and what a choice! Five of these choices explain what they can do to make this important day even more memorable.

Tabley House - The magnificence and memory of that special day.

Arley Hall and Gardens

Your wedding day should always be a day to remember. Imagine a private country estate, in the heart of the Cheshire countryside, and the exclusive use of the magnificent Hall.

At Arley Hall near Northwich, we can offer you all this and more.

We have long been popular for wedding receptions, held in the beautiful family home of Lord and Lady Ashbrook. Since 1995 we have been able to offer a civil wedding ceremony in addition to wedding receptions: enjoy your day in the panelled splendour of the Hall for both your wedding and reception.

The estate has been owned by the family, originally the Egerton-Warburtons, for over 500 years and retains all its charm, originality, peace and beauty. Opening the magnificent gardens to the public in the 1960s gave the owners the opportunity to share their love of gardening. Since those early days, the Hall too has welcomed visitors from all over the world, entertained dignitaries and consulates, held summer balls and masques, corporate dinners, seminars and conferences, parkland leisure pursuits and wedding receptions.

'Arley Hall has always been a beautiful place and very popular for receptions, and we are delighted to welcome couples who now wish to be married here.'

With the advantage of being privately owned and therefore flexible, each enquiry is handled personally by expert, understanding staff who know what is required to organise a wedding. Coupled to that, our caterer also has vast experience and gently guides you through the canapes and petit-fours to champagne and oysters.

The Hall can seat up to 100 guests for the wedding ceremony in the delightful Drawing Room. For a smaller, more intimate wedding, the panelled Front Dining Hall is offered with guests toasting the health of the couple in the adjoining Gallery.

Arley Hall's magnidicent staircase.

Arley Hall - Wedding party outside the hall.

In addition to the Hall, Arley can also offer the atmospheric, heavily beamed Tudor Barn for a larger formal meal or dance/reception.

Whatever you choose, come and visit Arley and see for yourself. For further information, please contact Eric Ransome at the Arley Estate Office on 01565 777353.

Chiddingstone Castle

The release of the Civil Marriage Ceremony from the confines of the Registry Office instantaneously brought into being a new social occasion, a wedding with all the panoply of a church ceremony without the religion. Brides of all ages appeared, sumptuously dressed, often in traditional white, with bridesmaids and pageboys, friends and relations round them. It soon became clear that the favourite wedding venue would be the historic country house. Large and small, each of them unique, they confer their own grace on a wedding as no commercial establishment can.

Chiddingstone Castle is one of the smaller mansions. We can take up to only about eighty guests, but this has advantages. The place is compact, grouped around three courtyards, where guests can sit in fine weather. There is room enough, and they do not get scattered. We do not open to the general public on Wedding Days, so the bride can regard the place as her home for the day. The Great Hall, our Marriage Room, is in late Georgian Gothic style, which gives it faint overtones of sanctity that appeal to brides, strangely, as they have rejected a real church. The other rooms officially required for the ceremony are nearby, and the adjacent Drawing Room can be hired for the reception of guests.

The Great Hall, Chiddingstone Castle - Where grandeur welcomes romance.

These rooms are furnished as they usually are, only the more fragile objects are removed. We know we have a problem here. Overuse can easily damage the essential peace of a house, so we have always limited activities to a size and type compatible with its nature.

Quality is what attracts guests, though they do not always understand the damage done by misuse, often unintentional. At our first wedding, I was peering down from the Great Hall Gallery and was startled to see that a careful mother had placed her infant in its cot on the lid of the grand piano. The pianist played on, unperturbed. We learned a lesson, always to keep the lid of the piano right open. 'DON'T' notices are unpleasing, better to make sure they 'CAN'T'.

If a wedding breakfast is required, our excellent appointed caterers will provide this in the Buttery or Assembly Room of the Conference Wing. Numbers of over fifty can be accommodated in a marquee, as we have done for years, just in front of William Atkinson's romantic south entrance. We do not allow outside caterers. The uninitiated are baffled by the intricate arrangements of an old house.

For music, Sue Casson, the composer, who lives here, will play the piano, sing her wedding song, even compose a special one to commission, and arrange other suitable musical entertainments. We also have our resident printer and Estates Manager, Ron Vernon, who supplies wedding stationery, printed on his own Victorian press in the coachyard workshop.

Arrangements for booking are no light task. After the couple have inspected the place come tours by the relatives, but their problems are all sorted out by the friendly patience of our tireless Functions Manager, Rene Vernon.

The Castle is fortunately well-placed to meet its new responsibilities. The ten-year programme of refurbishment has been completed, the thirty-five acre grounds, with their matchless view over the Weald, have recovered from the 1987 storm. Old houses need new life, and we welcome this new activity, by its nature directed to the future.

Penshurst Place and Gardens

Situated in the picturesque village of Penshurst, surrounded by unspoilt country-side, 135 acres of parkland and tudor gardens, stands Penshurst Place, a magnificent medieval manor house providing an idyllic setting for hospitality of all kinds. In fact, as long ago as 1832 John Britten wrote of Penshurst, 'This House has been the natal home of poetry, romance, patriotism - the theatre of sumptuous hospitality - the abode of chivalry and the resting place of virtue and honour'.

Continuing that tradition today, Penshurst offers excellence in cuisine from one of the two appointed caterers, the attention of an experienced, dedicated team to assure the success of every sort of function or event and that extra ingredient the 'spirit of place' - not easily defined - but which perhaps is due to the intricacies of the lives of those who have spent their days in this historic manor house.

The home of Viscount De L'Isle and his forbears for over 450 years, Penshurst was approved by Kent County Council as a venue for civil marriages in July 1995. It would be difficult to find a more beautiful and romantic setting for a wedding ceremony or reception: the ancient sandstone building which has a golden hue to it in the sunshine, emanates a feeling of peace and tranquility and the formal gardens, with their fountains, flowers, lily ponds, apple blossom and yew hedges, form the perfect backdrop for photographs.

Down the centuries Penshurst has played host to many famous people including Kings and Queens. Whilst wooing Anne Boleyn, Henry XVIII used it as his base and in 1519 the Duke of Buckingham hosted a sumptuous

The Italian Garden, with the Baron's Hall as backdrop, provides the perfect setting for wedding photographs.

Signing the register, after a civil marriage ceremony in the Sunderland Room.

The 14th Century Sunderland Room, arranged for wedding breakfast.

programme of entertainment for the King which set him back £870,000 in today's money.

The massive trestle tables at which King Henry dined are still standing today on either side of the Barons Hall - each of them over twenty foot long. 'One of the grandest rooms in the world' is how John Julius Norwich described the Baron's Hall, one of the two original 14th century rooms approved as premises for civil marriages at Penshurst Place. Whilst waiting for the bride, wedding guests can admire the original 60' high chestnut roof towering above their heads and wonder about the identity of the carved wooden figures that appear to be supporting the roof. The original octagonal fireplace can be used to give added atmosphere to receptions, and

when used with the four candelabra standing in the arched windows, make a magical setting in the evenings.

The more intimate Sunderland Room is also available for wedding ceremonies and receptions. At one time it formed the private apartments of Lady Dorothy Sidney, who lived at Penshurst while her husband was away fighting in the Civil War. It is furnished with antiques and portraits of the period and can seat up to eighty people for a wedding breakfast.

Music can be arranged, in keeping with the atmosphere, such as minstrels playing reproduction medieval instruments in authentic costumes or string quartets playing early music. Jesters, jugglers and fire-eaters and torch-lit pathways can add to the excitement.

Knebworth

Picturesque formal gardens of Knebworth House form a romantic backdrop for bridal receptions and photographs.

Knebworth, home to the Lytton Cobbold family, has been the centrepoint for many exciting and historical events in its 500-year-old history. The recent decades have brought major concerts, rallies, and regular corporate hospitality, but the social dinner dances, events and wedding receptions have long been a mainstay of Knebworth business. Lord and Lady Cobbold have now added wedding ceremonies to the exciting list of activities organised by their family-run Lytton Catering event management team.

Weddings are a wonderful part of Knebworth life. The sunken lawns beckon bridal Champagne receptions, the formal gardens and herbaceous borders form beautiful backdrops for bride's photographs, and the spectacular rooms of Knebworth House and the 16th Century Barns Conference and Banqueting Centre echo the memories of innumerable wedding receptions, banquets and breakfasts.

One of the hardest parts of planning a wedding is booking the ceremony, and now with the recent extension of civil wedding venues,

Knebworth can solve that problem too. The licensed Knebworth Barns Conference and Banqueting Centre is an especially beautiful and tranquil setting.

The wedding party arrives within Knebworth Park through the ancient Chestnut Avenue, to be welcomed by the distant site of the turrets, flags and heraldic beasts of Knebworth House. Surrounded by 250 acres of deer park, Knebworth House and the Knebworth Barns Conference and Banqueting Centre are within walking distance of one another, separated by the formal gardens, newly re-planted maze, fountains, lake and wilderness walkways.

There is an incredible choice of photographic settings both indoors and out. There are floral colour schemes to suit every bride's fancy, historical charm to touch every guest, and a true sense of family warmth and welcome throughout the estate. A perfect example of which can be found painted around the eves of the Jacobean Banqueting Hall, a poem of welcome, written by Edward Bulwer Lytton, Victorian ancestor, novelist and statesman.

Weddings can be organised any day of the week, in fact Friday and Sunday are becoming

Autumnal wedding ceremony in the Manor Barn, Knebworth Park.

almost as popular as the traditional Saturday. The atmosphere of the Manor Barn in the Knebworth Barns Conference and Banqueting Centre can be altered and decorated to suit the couple's wishes or maintained in its traditional appearance. The open-beamed structure is fully restored, carpeted, and has an avenue of heraldic flags running down the ceiling centre.

Themed weddings are very popular where not only is the room dressed in, for example the Tudor period, but the Bride, Groom, attendants, flowers, catering staff, and menus are as well. Lytton Catering is highly experienced in organising themed events, and can advise on entertainment, decorations, menus and hotel accommodation, among many other aspects of this special day.

The Lytton Catering event management team is proficient in organising wedding ceremonies of all sizes, themes, and character. The team is in consistent contact with the Registry Office and would be pleased to advise a prospective couple about their Knebworth wedding and reception.

And what a spectacularly memorable day in history it will be!

Tabley House

Tabley House, set in delightful parkland, is a very atmospheric mansion which lends itself beautifully to Civil Wedding Ceremonies. To date two rooms have been licensed, reached via a magnificent sweep of steps overlooking the lake.

The calm and elegant Portico Room, with its superb plaster reliefs, is ideal for those who prefer the more formal setting for their marriage, whereas the adjacent great Gallery, with its magnificent wallpaper, pictures and flamboyance is equally suitable as a venue for the very small or a larger wedding.

Tabley can undertake small Receptions at the House, or large Marquee Receptions on the lawns. To keep costs down as low as possible, all aspects of the Reception are arranged between the couple and the suppliers direct (from catering to tentage and everything in between) giving complete freedom of

Tabley - Grace and Splendour.

choice. This is a very different outlook, because many other venues are happy to hold the ceremonies to gain the Receptions, whereas Tabley is somewhat the other way round!

The hire of each area and the use to which it is put is charged for separately, which makes the costing system as fair as it can possibly be. There is a large free car park, where cars can be left for the day at owner's risk if the wedding party wish to go on to a Reception at another venue. The House is perfectly situated for access at Junction 19 on the M6 Motorway and is an easily reached unusual venue. With privacy and appeal, magnificent rooms with a special atmosphere, lots of excellent indoor and outdoor photographic locations, access for the disabled, and with a fair pricing structure, Tabley must be hard to beat as a most lovely setting for that special Civil Wedding.

Tabley's Portico Room, a photographic location for brides.

A day out

BLICKLING HALL, N.T.P.L.

SOUTER LIGHTHOUSE, N.T.P.L.

with the National Trust

captivating views of Stowe Landscape Gardens - widely regarded as Britain's largest work of art - rival anything a gallery has to offer.

In fact, with over 300 historic properties, 547 miles of coastline and over half a million acres of countryside, we have something for everyone.

From proud stately homes to

The towering perspectives of Souter, the country's first reliable working lighthouse, are an imposing sight.

Impressive, yet no more outstanding than Blickling Hall in

all shapes

Norfolk, the first major country house to come to the National Trust. A property whose medieval origins date back to Anne Boleyn, Henry VIII's ill-fated second wife.

And, whilst English landscape art is celebrated the world over, the

modest country cottages, celebrated works of art to working industrial heritage sites, the National Trust cares for properties great and small.

Each different from the last.

Each significant in its own right. And each offering the visitor a vastly different experience and endless ways to spend their days.

For further information telephone **0181-315 1111.**

can come in

FELBRIGG HALL, N.T.P.L.

and sizes.

The National Trust

APSLEY HOUSE
'NUMBER ONE, LONDON'

While Londoners sweltered through the hottest summer for centuries, a small army of museum creators, conservators and craftsmen was putting the finishing touches to one of the most famous historic residences in the capital. Apsley House opened its doors once again in June 1995, after a three-and-a-half-year programme of essential renovation and repair work costing £6 million.

Located at the junction of Knightsbridge and Park Lane, Apsley House is a building of unique architectural and cultural significance, and has been the London home of the Dukes of Wellington since 1817. Once described as 'the most renowned mansion in the capital', Apsley House contains a magnificent collection of paintings, silver, porcelain, sculpture and furniture. Its rich interiors have now been returned to their former glory as the private palace of the Iron Duke. Today, Apsley House is the last great London town-house with its collections and its family still in residence.

The house, originally built between 1771 and 1778 for Baron Apsley, Second Earl of Bathurst, acquired the popular name 'Number One, London' because it was the first building encountered upon entering the capital from the west. Following his dazzling military career in India, Spain and Portugal and

Reguilding in the Waterloo Gallery

Apsley House in 1810. View of Hyde Park Corner.

Orders of the Duke of Wellington.

culminating in his famous victory over Napoleon at the Battle of Waterloo, Arthur Wellesley, the First Duke of Wellington, bought the house from his brother for £42,000. At that time, Apsley House was the last property in a terrace designed by the celebrated neo-classical architect Robert Adam (the rest of the terrace was demolished as late as 1961, to improve the flow of traffic between Hyde Park Corner and Park Lane).

Wellington needed a London base to make into a 'Waterloo Palace'; he wanted to celebrate his prestige as the most powerful military commander in Europe, and to use his enormous popularity with the British people to support his entry into politics. The Iron Duke also had advanced tastes in the fine and decorative arts. Wellington engaged the services of the architect Benjamin Dean Wyatt and together they embarked on an ambitious programme of rebuilding, enlarging and redecorating. Wyatt extended the original Adam brick construction and encased the whole in Bath stone, adding the Corinthian portico. He created the great 90ft long Waterloo Gallery in the Louis XIV style, evoking the Galerie des Glaces at Versailles. From 1830 till the death of the First Duke in 1852, annual banquets were held here for the officers who had served under

Wellington at Waterloo. Wyatt's alterations incorporated the Iron Duke's State and private apartments and contained interior decorations and collections that reflected Wellington's personal taste as well as the fashion of the period.

The project was to last for nearly all of Wellington's life. He would undertake more work when funds became available, although he complained bitterly over the cost - by 1831 he had spent £64,000 on improvements to the house. However, he succeeded in creating a great London residence suitable as a setting for his remarkable collections and appropriate to his status as a (short-lived) Prime Minister, a national figurehead of heroic stature.

The contents of Apsley House include the First Duke's magnificent collection of the fine and decorative arts and many original furnishings. Many of the two hundred paintings originally came from the Spanish Royal Collection, and were captured by Wellington when his forces overtook Joseph Bonaparte's baggage train after the Battle of Vitoria in 1813. In addition to outstanding seventeenth century Spanish pictures, there is a considerable group by seventeenth century Dutch and Flemish masters and by the nineteenth century British School. The collection also includes important works by Velasquez, Murillo, Goya, Rubens, Correggio, Steen, De Hooch, Brueghel, Wilkie and Lawrence.

The Piccadily Drawing Room.

Of particular interest to visitors is the collection of porcelain and silver from the most important factories in Europe; the Sèvres

Egyptian Service was commissioned by Napoleon as a divorce present for the Empress

Marble statue of Napoleon by Antonio Canova, 1806.

Josephine, who rejected it. Outstanding examples of presentation plate include a twenty-six foot long Portuguese silver centrepiece which graces the Dining Room. The romantic Lawrence portrait of the First Duke inspired the design of the old £5 note, while a colossal nude statue by Canova of Wellington's old adversary, Napoleon (which displeased its subject, who thought it was '...too athletic...') dominates the ornate flying staircase.

Apsley House survived where other great houses did not, due to the generosity and foresight of the Seventh Duke of Wellington, a founder member of the Georgian Group and a pioneer of the Regency Revival, who gave the house and most of its contents to the nation in 1947. The Eighth Duke and his eldest son, the

Best Loved Hotels of the World 1996 Directory

20% saving to readers of *Historic Houses*

There is only one directory with such a wide range of hotels in Britain and Ireland presented with such a depth of information

There is only one hotel directory that combines all the stars, crowns, rosettes and ribbons awarded to hotels by the tourist boards and motoring organisations in Britain and Ireland.

There is only one hotel directory that gives first hand, verbatim reports from guests about the quality of comfort, cuisine and atmosphere they experienced at their best-loved hotels.

There is only one hotel directory that neatly presents all the pertinent information about an hotel from its room rates

and on-site facilities to its local attractions and proximity to airports, railway stations, ports of entry and golf courses.

There is only one hotel directory that makes every hotel look interesting and inviting by relating its location to local events and the wealth of heritage that exists nearby.

There is only one Best Loved Hotels of the World 1996 Directory, a pleasure to browse through, very easy to use and so easy to get hold of - just send us the order form below.

The easiest way to find the hotel you are looking for

Only the Best Loved Directory does all this:

- **The 1996 Best Loved Directory** features 405 hotels each the best of its kind within various price ranges in its region. Inns dating back to the 10th century, restaurants with rooms, hotels with their own golf courses (17 of them), castles with Royal connections, leisure resorts, health farms, country houses (many listed buildings) and city centre hotels and apartments.

- Beautifully designed pages, one to each hotel, with full colour pictures, words of recommendation from a previous guest PLUS the facts column, shown here: all the information you need researched from many different sources. Now you can tell at a glance which hotel suits you best - from its location (see top of column) to price, facilities and local attractions ➤

- The Directory is divided into eight regions and a special section for islands. Each is introduced with a character sketch of the region and its people and a list of 400 heritage sites.

- A calendar of 176 local, national and international events for 1996: from the Oyster Festival in Galway to the Flower Show in Chelsea; from the Military Tattoo in Edinburgh to Cricket at Lords; Eisteddfods, Highland Gatherings and the Promenade Concerts all included.

- A facilities index: hotels with swimming pools and tennis; those which offer health/beauty facilities; hotels offering riding and fishing; nearest quality golf courses and their proximity to the hotel.

- Other indexes show Ports of Entry with all the Best Loved Hotels within a 30 mile radius. Also an index of meeting facilities. Whether its a business conference or a wedding reception, this Directory will help with some ideas.

Get the facts. All the relevant facts for each of 405 hotels are clearly presented like this so you can find the hotel you are looking for quickly and easily

Tear along here

Marquess of Douro, retain private apartments in the building to this day. Apsley House opened to the public as the Wellington Museum in 1952; the Department of National Heritage are responsible for the care and upkeep of the building while the Victoria and Albert Museum cares for the contents and runs the building as a museum.

The need to close Apsley House to carry out essential repairs was seen by both the Department of National Heritage and the V&A as the ideal opportunity to refurbish the public areas of the building. The intention was to return those areas of the House, as far as possible, to the condition in which they were known by the First Duke. The inevitable wear and tear of two centuries was exacerbated by the location of the house on Hyde Park Corner, probably one of the busiest road junctions in Western Europe. Similarly, the proximity of Underground lines and the demolition of the rest of the ter-

The Waterloo Gallery.

race in the 1960s had had a detrimental effect on the structure.

Apsley House closed to the public in January 1992. Before essential repairs could begin in July 1992, all moveable objects from the 2,500 strong collection were removed from the House, a complex and delicate task given the fragility and the great age of some of the objects. Eleven of the most famous paintings

from the collection of two hundred were loaned to the National Gallery for display; others went to the V&A for conservation where necessary. Some objects were immoveable, such as Canova's 11ft high marble nude statue of Napoleon, which would have been too large to take from the building - indeed it had not been moved since being placed in situ by the First Duke in 1817. Similarly the 23ft long Egyptian Centrepiece and the Adam and Wyatt decorations were protected during the extensive rebuilding work. The crystal chandeliers and lanterns were taken away for specialist cleaning and restoration. An intensive programme of conservation work then began.

While work commenced on overhauling the roof and replacing the electrical, heating, fire and security systems and installing a new air plant to improve the environment for the priceless collection, extensive redecoration of the interiors was carefully planned. Over 300 metres of special fabric for the wall-hangings, curtains and banquettes in the Striped and Yellow Drawing Rooms were handwoven on wooden looms from the 1820s, to match a fragment of original silk found behind a bell-pull during the restoration programme and to correspond exactly with Victorian renderings of the rooms. Similarly, a fragment of the original carpet was found in the attic at the Duke of Wellington's country house, Stratfield Saye; it was identified as being the same carpet depicted in early watercolours of the interior of Apsley House, and has been faithfully copied to match the original. Fortunately, examples of curtain rails, French pulley rods, windows and door handles and all other brass accessories had survived, and exact copies were made where items were missing.

Numerous paint sections were taken to enable specialists to match exactly the colour and finish of the walls; the entrance halls were remarbled and the gilding was cleaned and restored where necessary. Great care was taken to retain and conserve original decorative surfaces and, wherever possible, to reproduce exactly the arrangement of pictures adopted by the First Duke. The paintings so avidly collected and carefully displayed by Wellington were rehung on great gilded metal chains, which had been stored on the premises in tea-chests since this method of displaying paintings fell from fashion in the last century. In this respect, the Curator of Apsley House, Jonathan Voak, was greatly assisted by bills and documentary material relating to the original decorations during the lifetime of the

First Duke, and a set of contemporary watercolours by Thomas Shotter Boys, along with detailed inventories, all undertaken just after the death of the First Duke in 1852. Of particular assistance in the refurbishing of the Waterloo Gallery was the 1836 painting of The Waterloo Banquet, by William Salter. It has been lent to Apsley House by the present Duke of Wellington, having been at Stratfield Saye for many years.

Apsley House re-opened in June 1995 to great critical and popular acclaim; '...a palace of gilt and satin with a significant history and a notable collection of paintings' was the verdict of The Independent on Sunday, while The Times called it '...one of the most lavish and meticulous restorations ever undertaken in Britain.' More than 40,000 visitors queued for admission in the first 20 weeks that the house was open, an increase of 33% on the annual attendance figure for the last year that Apsley House was open before the restoration and refurbishment programme commenced. Restored to its former magnificence, Apsley House is living up to its affectionate epithet of 'Number One, London'.

Equestrian statue of 1st Duke facing Apsley House.

THE ART OF TRAVELLING GRACIOUSLY

The Pullman train of the Venice Simplon-Orient-Express offers travellers an extensive programme of luxury day excursions and weekend breaks to romantic castles and ancient cities, as well as to a number of special events. Also included in the train's programme are luncheon trips to celebrate special occasions such as St Valentine's Day, Mother's Day and Christmas. The revival of the Golden Arrow in 1996 will enable the original Pullman carriages to be hauled by steam through the English countryside, reminiscent of the golden era of travel.

Passengers are seated in Pullman dining carriages, originally built in the 1920s and 1930s, which have been restored to their former glory. Each carriage has its own name and history. Intricate wooden marquetry patterns, mirrors, and brass luggage racks adorn the inside of the carriages; the lavatories have mahogany fittings and fascinating mosaic floors. Passengers are looked after by uniformed stewards who offer an old-fashioned and courteous style of service.

Pullman destinations include a visit to the spa town of Bath, founded by the Romans; or Bristol, home to Harvey's Sherry and the magnificent Clifton suspension bridge which spans the River Avon. Alternatively, leave the train at Salisbury for a tour of the Cathedral and Wilton House, home of the Earl of Pembroke. Other great houses visited are Sandringham, country house in Norfolk of Her Majesty the Queen and Chatsworth House in Derbyshire, belonging to the Duke of Devonshire.

Excursions created around events such as the Grand National and Royal Ascot make

A British Pullman steward ready to greet passengers.

unforgettable days out. In addition to racing events, new additions to the train's programme include visits to the Open Golf Championships at Lytham St. Anne's,

Leeds Castle.

Henley Regatta, Cowes and the International Festival of the Sea at Bristol.

Trips to Leeds Castle are offered throughout the year. Still impregnably surrounded by water, Leeds Castle is considered to be one of the most beautiful in the country. It was the royal palace of six medieval Queens and has been immaculately restored to its former splendour.

Sudeley Castle, home to Henry VIII's widow, also figures in the British Pullman's itinerary. The castle has eight spectacular walled gardens and over one thousand years of history. As well as visiting the castle, its

Sudeley Castle.

neighbouring villages and countryside, Orient-Express passengers will be given a falconry display at Sudeley.

The British Pullman visits Warwick Castle on a number of occasions during the year. Home to the notorious Kingmaker of the Wars of the Roses, Warwick Castle was built on Roman foundations. Although partially destroyed by fire, much of the medieval castle walls and dungeons remain. The tour of the castle includes the State Rooms, dungeons, gardens and the well-known Kingmaker exhibition.

Introduced into the Pullman programme during the last couple of years are British Pullman weekends. Departing Victoria Station on a Friday, passengers may choose between Stratford-upon-Avon and the Cotswolds; the city of Chester; or the Roman city of Bath.

A romantic dinner for two on the British Pullman.

On all three weekends accommodation for two nights is offered at a choice of hotels. The Pullman leaves London mid-morning and a three-course lunch is served during the journey. Having reached the destination of their choice, passengers are free to spend their time as they wish. However, an optional sightseeing programme is available. After a leisurely trip back to London, during which lunch is served, passengers are back in London by Sunday evening.

Whether travelling for business or pleasure, the Pullman's 'Lunch in the Garden of

England' excursion is an original choice. The Pullman departs Victoria just before midday and passengers are served a five-course luncheon as the train makes a circular tour of the Kent countryside and coast, arriving back in London just before four o'clock.

For train enthusiasts based in Birmingham, Manchester, Chester, Bristol or Cardiff, luncheon or dinner trips departing from all five cities are also available.

On dates when the Pullman connects with the Continental train, there is the option for day excursion passengers to take the train to Folkestone, having lunch on the way down.

After spending a couple of hours in Folkestone, visiting the town or taking a bracing walk along the cliffs, they may rejoin the train for tea on the journey back to London.

Pullman day excursions are ideal for celebrating a special occasion or entertaining in style. Depending upon the trip, passengers enjoy a champagne breakfast, luncheon or dinner, accompanied by wine and champagne, or a traditional English afternoon tea.

Whatever the destination, a day excursion on the Pullman recreates the heyday of luxury train travel and is a memorable experience.

Welcoming passengers on board.

A CHAPTER IN THE HERITAGE OF THE BRITISH ISLES

Best Loved Hotels of the World reveals some gems from the past

In 978 AD, the 18 year-old King Edward was murdered by his stepmother at Corfe Castle in Dorset. In 1646, the castle was sacked in the Civil War. All that is left after a thousand years is one of the most striking relics of British history. Much of the village at the foot of the castle was built of its scattered stones, some of which were used to expand an elegant Elizabethan house known as *Mortons House Hotel* which now features in the Best Loved Directory.

SAVOURING THE ATMOSPHERE

It is easy to believe that the heritage of a nation is vested in documents and monuments listed in official archives; a case of look but don't touch. Nothing could be further from the truth; the heritage of the British Isles (geographically speaking, this includes Ireland) is a living thing to be enjoyed by all who have the wit to appreciate it. The 1996 edition of **Best Loved Hotels of the World - England, Scotland, Wales & Ireland** brings together a collection of places you can stay and savour the atmosphere of centuries.

INNS AND TAVERNS

Humble though they may be, inns and taverns have made an enormous contribution to the history books. The oldest recorded inn in England is *The Royalist*, dating from 947 AD. Behind the 17th Century facade is the original structure. The Knights of St John Hospitaliers ran it as a hospice and alms house. Today, it is a Best Loved hotel. The Best Loved Directory has many others that bring history vividly to life: *The Oxenham Arms* in Okehampton is a 12th Century inn built around a 5000 year-old monolith; *The Three Cocks* at Brecon, 15th Century, is built around a tree. Some of the ancient inns have become the centre-piece of picturesque towns and villages: *The Angel Hotel,* Bury St Edmunds (1452 AD), *The Spread Eagle* in Midhurst (1430 AD), *The Shaven Crown* in Shipton-under-Wychwood (14th Century) - all steeped in history. The *Lygon Arms* in Broadway, said to be the prettiest village in Britain, started life in the 16th Century as a coaching inn. Today it is an internationally acclaimed hotel owned by the Savoy Group.

FIT FOR A KING

Interestingly, the concept of an *hotel* is relatively new. Until the end of the 19th Century, travellers stayed at an inn or tavern. It was the French, with their well-known penchant for good-living, who invented the hotel - a place to stay that was like home, not just a bed. One of the first hotels in Britain was started by Richard D'Oyly Carte in 1889, with Caesar Ritz as manager and Escoffier as Chef des Cuisines. The hotel was *The Savoy* - also in the Best Loved Directory.

Many of the hotels in the Best Loved Directory make the home-from-home concept an art form; within the mature fabric of the building, the facilities are right up-to-date, the service impeccable and the food fit for a king. Indeed, many of the hotels have hosted royalty - but quite some time ago. The 60ft walls of Amberley Castle near Arundel, built 900 years ago, welcomed Henry VIII, Elizabeth I and Charles II; Charles II's favourite hunting lodge is now called *New Park Manor* and stands near Brockenhurst; Elizabeth I held court at *Seckford Hall* near Woodbridge, a fine example of Tudor architecture; Henry VIII stayed with his wife Ann Boleyn at *Thornbury Castle*, built by the third Duke of Buckingham in 1511. *Hartwell House* near Aylesbury, virtually a palace, was once the home of Louis XVIII of France whilst in exile.

RESTAURANT WITH ROOMS

Providing good food has a been a part of our inn-keeping tradition but there is a discernible new trend - the Restaurant with Rooms. *The Old Library* is a 200 year-old converted stable on the Inverness-shire coast; *Old Beams* at Waterhouses, Staffordshire, puts food first and a comfortable night a close second. *Ahernes*, near Cork, is famous for its fish. Hotel du Vin & Bistro is a Grade II listed building in Winchester. Though described as a town house hotel, one surely goes there for its cuisine which is decidedly haute.

PLENTY OF CHOICE - MADE EASY

These are 405 establishments in the Best Loved Directory. Each with its own character that stems as much from its history and location as from its proprietor. Don't think for a moment that eccentricity is the prerogative of the guest!

The Directory divides the country into eight regions and a section on Islands. There are route planning maps highlighting places of interest and pin-pointing the hotels with price-coded rosettes. Unusually, the directory combines the ratings of the tourist boards, motoring organisations and the Good Hotel Guide to help you find what you want.

To make this directory unique: every hotel displays a word or two from a past guest and some of them can be quite amusing; for example: 'A charming place, I hope you didn't mind me bringing my own wine, your food compliments it perfectly' - enough to raise the hackles but, then, look who said it: Baron de Rothschild.

As a reader of this publication, you can get the 1996 edition of the Best Loved Hotels of the World at 20% off the recommended retail price. See the insert on page xvi.

HISTORY IN YOUR LIVING ROOM
by John Hodgson

We should not underestimate the debt we owe to television.

It was quite a shock. Sitting comfortably by the fire, enjoying the recent dramatisation of 'Pride and Prejudice', I found myself staring at a street scene that was strangely familiar. I searched my mind to place that particular sequence of old houses, some stone, some brick and timber, all with heavy stone roofs. Was it, could it be, Lacock, my home village of past years? I didn't remember the wide grass verges and I was confused by the hurrying and colouful crowds. For a time I forgot the story and concentrated on efforts to recognise shopfronts and doorways. Then I saw "The Red Lion" , the old coaching inn where the Elizabeth Bennet first encountered Mr Darcy at the Meryton assembly.

Life in a Heritage Village

Church Street, Lacock Village, The 14th century Cruck House is one of the oldest houses in Lacock.

Lacock is a remarkably unspoiled village now protected by the National Trust, and as a staff member of the Trust I had the privilege of living there for some nine years. In 1944, when it came to the Trust, little had changed for almost a century. There were no modern street lamps, few overhead electric cables, and television aerials had not yet arrived to disfigure every town and village rooftop. Wisely the trust decided to keep it as it was. When television did arrive, a communal aerial was built on a nearby hill out of site of the village - though this has disadvantages: if anything goes wrong every screen in the village is blank! While the street scene hardly changed, the interiors of the cottages were gradually modernised: bathrooms and indoor lavatories!

In general Lacock is a delightful place to live. The village people, almost all descended from generations of local families, are exceptionally friendly and welcoming, despite the problems that inevitably arise from the popularity of the place as a tourist attraction. One problem was partially solved when I was living there: every street was marred by lines of cars - the Trust had opted to have no yellow lines. Now there is a good car-park within easy strolling distance. A continuing problem is the occasional inquisitive visitor, given to nose-pressing against sitting room windows, even on occasion walking in as if the cottages were open to the public. They are of course all private homes, and the villagers like their privacy respected as much as anyone.

My National Trust work took me out of the village most of the time, and I often wished I could spend more time there. There is much to see and do. Apart from the lovely village itself with its houses and cottages dating from the thirteenth century to the eighteenth, the beautiful 15th century church decorated with many grotesque carvings, outside and in, and the Abbey, a happy mixture of styles from true gothic to Georgian Gothick, there is the remarkable photographic museum which commemorates the work of the former squire and pioneer photographer, William Fox Talbot, and his successors.

What was more, something always seemed to be happening - Photographers' Day, when the villagers all turned out in period clothes so

Lacock Abbey's Oriel Window, South Gallery, with early cameras.

that visiting photographers could attempt to emulate the Victorian founder of the art; dancers and singers invading the village from the Chippenham Folk Festival; performances by the Young National Trust Theatre in which hordes of Wiltshire schoolchildren dressed as medieval peasants relived the life of shepherds and drovers. Not the least of these diversions were the visits of film crews because the village is such a perfect setting for period films. 'Pride and Prejudice' has provided but the latest of a long line of star roles for the village - and walk-on parts for many villagers.

Coping with the Demands of Television

The National Trust, like many private owners, after some initial reluctance, now makes properties available for filming. It is a sensitive business. Historic houses are very delicate and easily damaged. Busy film crews, with other priorities, need careful watching, not least because there are invariably dozens of actors, extras, camera-, lighting- and sound-

technicians milling about, not to mention all the other staff who seem essential for any film or television production. It can be a security nightmare for the administrator of the property and his staff. Nevertheless there is an enormous demand for new locations and both sides have become more sensitive and understanding. Gone, I suspect, are the days when one house was used to advertise a certain toilet product, and the owner's wife walked into the Long Gallery to discover a very beautiful young woman, her nakedness barely covered with a flimsy towel, admiring the portraits.

Some years ago I was responsible for opening the Trust's Sudbury Hall in Derbyshire to the public, and creating the Museum of Childhood there. This house with its stunningly beautiful

South front of Lyme Park from across the lake.

Caroline interiors also featured in 'Pride and Prejudice', providing some of the rooms of Mr Darcy's great house, Pemberley (The exterior shots were of Lyme Park in Cheshire). Here the film's researchers and designer transformed lightly furnished rooms into the elegant magnificence of a typical early nineteenth century great house interior. The effect was totally convincing, and this brings me - at last - to the art of Time Shifting - an art of which BBC researchers and designers have become masters.

Pauses in Time

A growing number of people now visit historic houses with a well-informed eye, thanks in no small part to the period plays and programmes about antiques that we see on television. Knowledge certainly adds to appreciation, especially if it is used creatively. Of course we feel a sense of achievement if we are able to identify a period chair or porcelain figure with some certainty. It is satisfying to be able to date a painting by the costume style of the sitters. And many of us can now confidently recognise a cellaret or dressing case unaided by the guidebook or room steward.

The day nursery at Wightwick Manor.

There is a much greater pleasure, in my view, if we can bring it all together with our own or borrowed knowledge to reinhabit the place as it was at some time in the past. Knowledge - and a good deal of it - is essential if you are to accomplish this magical transformation successfully, but two other things are of equal importance: a creative imagination and authenticity. Of course this is what the television researcher and designer has to strive for all the time but, given the will, it is something that any keen country house visitor can do.

The effect on one's mind can be transporting. I can recollect several occasions when I have enjoyed this delightful experience. After studying the original family photographs on display at Wightwick Manor in Staffordshire I was

The smoking room at Lanhydrock.

walking alone in the garden one day, and turned to look at the house. Suddenly I was imaginatively carried back to 1898 and quite expected to see and hear the Mander children come running round the corner of the house to play on the terrace.

Every time I visit Lanhydrock in Cornwall, a house particularly rich in period atmosphere, I especially enjoy the Smoking Room where one can almost smell the cigar smoke and the whisky, and can catch whispers of elderly men reliving their youthful triumphs at school and college. In the late Victorian and Edwardian years, the great public schools, Eton especially, despite all the brutality of the school life at that time, had an extraordinarily powerful hold on the memories and affections of their Old Boys. Some of that atmosphere still remains in

The night nursery at Wightwick Manor.

the buildings of Eton, Harrow and Winchester. Powis Castle has quite a different atmosphere. For me it epitomises the classic French fairy tales of such as Charles Perrault and Mme Leprince de Beaumont. This entrancing castle might well have once housed the Sleeping Beauty or the sad and kindly Beast.

Country houses such as these, and gardens like those at Stowe and Stourhead, have the magical ability to carry the informed imagination into other worlds, not least because they are not faked-up re-creations but because they are

Powis Castle.

totally genuine, inspirations from long ago that have successfully survived the meddling of later days.

The National Trust is sometimes criticised for preserving its properties at a particular moment as in aspic, attempting to halt the nat-

ural evolution of a home or garden. There are of course good arguments for allowing a place to go on changing as any normal home does. Some would say that to halt the continuing development kills the spirit of the place. Unfortunately, however, if we do this we destroy the opportunity to be inspired by the past, for once destroyed it cannot be created. Many museums have tried to re-create the past by putting together period room displays. Everything is genuine, yet I have yet to see one that successfully recaptured the true spirit of a moment in past time.

Time Shifting

The threefold secret of the magical art of Time Shifting is first, to be well-informed - by visiting genuine survivors of the past and imbuing the atmosphere. Also by reading literature of the time - especially contemporary novels and newspapers. The very style of writing will give you a far stronger feel for the period than any text book can, however well-informed the writer.

Which takes me to the second factor: the 'magic' of transformation requires original objects. Reproductions, however carefully made, will not do. This was brought home to me many years ago at Sudbury. I had often seen people dressed in reproduction period costume walking the rooms for one reason or another. One day a group of art students persuaded me to let them wear garments from a collection of real Victorian dresses and suits for a charity event in the house. Of course they took great care to copy the hairstyles and mannerisms of the period, but it was the costumes that transformed the presentation: the audience (and I) were quite overawed by the effect they had on us. Our spines tingled: it was as if ghosts walked before us. I am convinced that this could not have happened if the students had worn re-creations, however clever.

The third part of the secret is to revive and cultivate your creative imagination. We were all endowed with this at birth, and children show plenty of evidence of it. Unfortunately

The Temple of the British Worthies,
Stowe Landscape Gardens.

The Oxford Bridge at Stowe Landscape Gardens.

schools and parents do their best to destroy it. The very busyness of our time does little to help too. The creative imagination can best be cultivated in solitude, a rare commodity these days, but it is worth the effort to find time for uninterrupted quiet reading, and visiting historic houses when you can experience genuine rooms without crowd of other visitors.

Time Shifting adds an inspiring extra dimension to visits to historic houses, castles and gardens. Initially it demands some effort but once you experience the magical transformation that it can bring to your mind you will want to go on, assured that future visits offer the promise of

exciting surprises, deeper understanding, and greater enjoyment of these beautiful places.

Editor's Note

John Hodgson worked for the National Trust for 20 years, first as Curator of Sudbury Hall and Museum of Childhood, then as the Trust's Education Advisor - he initiated the Trust's educational activities. He now works freelance in schools and at National Trust properties providing programmes that encourage children to 're-story' natural landscapes with the help of myth and legend.

Sandford Award Holders
1995

The following properties received Sandford Awards in the years in brackets after their names in recognition of the excellence of their educational services and facilities and their outstanding contribution to Heritage Education. Two or more dates indicate that the property has been reviewed and received further recognition under the system of quinquennial review introduced by the Heritage Education Trust in 1986. Any property which wishes to retain its listing must apply for review of its educational services and facilities five years after the date of its last award.

Sandford Award holders may now apply jointly with a school for the Reed Award for children with special educational needs. Under this award the Heritage Education Trust will also be able to make financial grants to selected Reed Award winners deemed by the Directors of the Trust to be of exceptional merit. The annual closing date for both awards is 31st January.

THE ARGORY, Co. Tyrone, Northern Ireland **(1995)**
ASTON HALL, Birmingham **(1993)**
*AVONCROFT MUSEUM OF BUILDINGS, Bromsgrove, Worcestershire **(1988) (1993)**
*BASS MUSEUM VISITOR CENTRE AND SHIRE HORSE STABLES, Burton upon Trent, Staffordshire **(1990)**
BEAULIEU ABBEY, Nr. Lyndhurst, Hampshire **(1978) (1986) (1991)**
BEWDLEY MUSEUM, Worcestershire **(1992)**
BICKLEIGH CASTLE, Nr. Tiverton, Devon **(1983) (1988)**
BLAKESLEY HALL MUSEUM, Birmingham **(1993)**
BLENHEIM PALACE, Woodstock, Oxfordshire **(1982) (1987) (1992)**
BODIAM CASTLE, East Sussex **(1995)**
BOUGHTON HOUSE, Kettering, Northamptonshire **(1988) (1993)**
BOWHILL HOUSE & COUNTRY PARK, Bowhill, Nr. Selkirk, Borders, Scotland **(1993)**
BRONTË PARSONAGE MUSEUM, Haworth, Nr. Keighley, West Yorkshire **(1993)**
BUCKFAST ABBEY, Buckfastleigh, Devon **(1985) (1990)**
CANTERBURY CATHEDRAL, Canterbury, Kent **(1988) (1993)**
*CASTLE MUSEUM, York, North Yorkshire **(1987) (1993)**
CASTLE WARD, County Down, Northern Ireland **(1980) (1987) (1994)**
CATHEDRAL & ABBEY CHURCH OF ST. ALBAN, St. Albans, Hertfordshire **(1986) (1991)**
*THE CECIL HIGGINS ART GALLERY AND MUSEUM & *THE BEDFORD MUSEUM, Bedford, Bedfordshire **(1989) (1993)**
CHILTERN OPEN AIR MUSEUM, Chalfont St. Giles, Buckinghamshire **(1994)**
CHIRK CASTLE, Chirk, Clwyd, Wales **(1994)**
CLIVE HOUSE MUSEUM, Shrewsbury, Shropshire **(1992)**
COLDHARBOUR MILL, Working Wool Museum, Cullompton, Devon **(1989) (1994)**
COMBE SYDENHAM, Nr. Taunton, Somerset **(1984) (1989) (1994)**
CRATHES CASTLE AND GARDENS, Kincardineshire, Scotland **(1992)**
CROXTETH HALL AND COUNTRY PARK, Liverpool, Merseyside **(1980) (1989) (1994)**
CULZEAN CASTLE AND COUNTRY PARK, Ayrshire, Scotland **(1984) (1989) (1994)**
*DOVE COTTAGE AND THE WORDSWORTH MUSEUM, Grasmere, Cumbria **(1990)**

DRUMLANRIG CASTLE AND COUNTRY PARK, Dumfriesshire, Scotland **(1989)**
DULWICH PICTURE GALLERY, London **(1990)**
DUNHAM MASSEY, Altrincham, Cheshire **(1994)**
ERDDIG HALL, Nr. Wrexham, Clwyd, Wales **(1991)**
EXETER CATHEDRAL, Devon **(1995)**
FLORENCE COURTHOUSE, Co. Fermanagh, Northern Ireland **(1995)**
GAINSBOROUGH OLD HALL, Gainsborough, Lincolnshire **(1988) (1993)**
GEORGIAN HOUSE, Edinburgh, Lothian, Scotland **(1978)**
GLADSTONE'S LAND, Edinburgh **(1995)**
GODOLPHIN, Helston, Cornwall **(1993)**
HAREWOOD HOUSE, Leeds, West Yorkshire **(1979) (1989) (1994)**
SIR HAROLD HILLIER GARDENS AND ARBORETUM, Ampfield, Nr. Romsey, Hampshire **(1993)**
HOLDENBY HOUSE, Northampton, Northamptonshire **(1985) (1991)**
HOPETOUN HOUSE, South Queensferry, Lothian, Scotland **(1983) (1991)**
MUSEUM OF KENT LIFE - COBTREE, Kent **(1995)**
KINGSTON LACY HOUSE, Wimborne, Dorset **(1990)**
LAUNDRY COTTAGE, Normanby Hall Country Park, South Humberside **(1994)**
LICHFIELD CATHEDRAL AND VISITORS' STUDY CENTRE, Lichfield, Staffordshire **(1991)**
LLANCAIACH FAWR MANOR, Nelson, Mid Glamorgan **(1994)**
*MACCLESFIELD MUSEUMS, Macclesfield, Cheshire **(1988) (1993)**
MOSELEY OLD HALL, Wolverhampton, West Midlands **(1983) (1989) (1994)**
NATIONAL WATERWAYS MUSEUM, Gloucester, Gloucestershire **(1991)**
NORTON PRORY, Cheshire **(1992)**
*OAKWELL HALL COUNTRY PARK, Birstall, West Yorkshire **(1988) (1993)**
PENHOW CASTLE, Nr. Newport, Gwent, Wales **(1980) (1986) (1993)**
*THE PRIEST'S HOUSE MUSEUM, Wimborne Minster, Dorset **(1993)**
*QUARRY BANK MILL, Styal, Cheshire **(1987) (1992)**
THE QUEEN'S HOUSE, Greenwich **(1995)**
ROCKINGHAM CASTLE, Nr. Corby, Northamptonshire **(1980) (1987) (1992)**
ROMAN BATHS MUSEUM, Bath, Avon **(1994)**
ROWLEY'S HOUSE MUSEUM, Shrewsbury, Shropshire **(1993)**

RYEDALE FOLK MUSEUM, Hutton le Hole, North Yorkshire **(1993)**
THE SHUGBOROUGH ESTATE, Stafford, Staffordshire **(1987) (1992)**
SPRINGHILL, Co. Londonderry **(1995)**
TATTON PARK, Knutsford, Cheshire **(1979) (1986) (1991)**
*TOWER OF LONDON, Tower Bridge, London **(1978) (1986) (1991)**

*WIGAN PIER, Wigan, Lancashire **(1987) (1992)**
WIGHTWICK MANOR, Wolverhampton, West Midlands **(1986) (1991)**
*WILBERFORCE HOUSE AND GEORGIAN HOUSES,
Hull, Humberside **(1990)**
WIMPOLE HALL, Near Cambridge, Cambridgeshire **(1988) (1993)**

1995 Results
Full Sandford Awards

THE ARGORY
BODIAM CASTLE
EXETER CATHEDRAL
FLORENCE COURT HOUSE

GLADSTONE'S LAND
MUSEUM OF KENT LIFE - COBTREE
NATIONAL MARITIME MUSEUM
SPRINGHILL

Quinquennial Review
1995
Full Sandford Awards

At Quinquennial review Full Awards are made where the educational services and facilities are deemed to have been developed or improved since the date of the previous Award.

BASS MUSEUM
BUCKFAST ABBEY
DOVE COTTAGE

DULWICH PICTURE GALLERY
HOLDENBY HOUSE
KINGSTON LACY

The National Maritime Museum, Greenwich.

The Sandford Awards and the Reed Awards are both administered by the Heritage Education Trust and sponsored by Reed Information Services.

Application forms and full details of the two Awards and details of the work of the Heritage Education Trust from: David Hill, Heritage Education Trust, Pickwick, Badley, Daventry, NN11 3AD telephone 01327 77943.

*For details of museums shown above listed with a star, please refer to Museums & Galleries in Great Britain and Ireland, 1996 edition.

HERITAGE EDUCATION TRUST

Sandford Awards
The Joys of Judging
by Eric Steed

Editor's Introduction

As sponsor of the annual Sandford Awards, details of which I have included for a number of years, I have often been intrigued by the whole process of judging. What actually makes a winner? I have had the great pleasure of meeting Eric Steed and in the following article he shares with us his thoughts and experiences on which he bases his recommendations.

It is quite probable that my enthusiasm for the ideals of the Heritage EducationTrust, and my own role as a Sandford Award judge, arise directly from my personal experience of active participant heritage education whilst I was at school. In the years preceding this experience, I had accompanied my fellow pupils to cinemas to watch films about the 1948 Olympic Games, Olivier's 'Hamlet' and 'The Ascent of Everest'. All very enjoyable but always second-hand events. Only as I entered the sixth form was I taken outside the confines of the campus to take part in a heritage-based lesson which took me across the ground on which the events under study occurred. This single experience happened on a warm day in the Autumn of 1954; over forty years ago, but it is a day which can be brought at will to the forefront of my mind. I am able to see again the sites of the 1651 Battle of Worcester, renew my understanding of how the day was both won and

lost; feel once more the fatigue at the end of the day's walking and, best of all, remember what a truly splendid day it had been and how it helped to bring about a life-long interest in history. In my experience, those properties which have proved worthy of receiving a Sandford Award, have shown themselves to possess an education staff which is equally

The Wordsworths' Living Room, Dove Cottage. Starting point for visitors to the house.

capable of providing days of parallel enjoyment, memory and, perhaps, life-long interests. Additionally, they also provide the opportunity for young children to enjoy the kind of day for which I had to wait until I was sixteen.

Following my appointment as a Sandford Award judge, I was fortunate to be inducted into the role by accompanying two experienced fellow judges around properties which each was considering for an award. During these visits, I quickly came to understand that the worries and apprehensions that I had felt whilst a property with which I was associated was being judged had been misplaced. Judging is certainly rigorous and very thorough, but it is also fair and open. The application forms and the reports from referees are read before the judging visit takes place - as is the literature supplied prior to, during or following the visit - in order to make the judge as aware as is possible of the strengths, aims and beliefs of the property.

Judging is undertaken in an extremely property-

Loxdale Primary School in the garden of Moseley Old Hall.

friendly manner. No anonymous visits are undertaken, no attempts are made to catch the education staff unprepared and unaware, indeed, every attempt is made by the judges to make arrangements for a visit to the property which

Dove Cottage, Grasmere

my benefit. In this respect I have always had my hopes fulfilled by those properties that have received an award. I am happiest when teachers have been informed of the reason for my presence and are confident that everything has been so well-planned that I will not interfere with the children's learning. Whilst the children usually have no idea who I am or why I am there, I find the majority of groups friendly and pleased to share the day's experiences with me once their teachers have informed them that I am to be one of their party for a portion of the visit. Such ad

Charles II "entertaining" children at Moseley Old Hall.

hoc arrangements clearly indicate that the education staff is confident in its ability to deliver a day's programme which has been planned with the primary aim of informing and satisfying the needs of the visiting groups. Where this qual-

is fully acceptable to all persons concerned with the day. The watchword in arranging the date of the judge's visit is partnership: in my own case, it has usually been the education staff at the property which has largely called the tune in deciding the date of my visit.

When I make a visit, my hope is that I am going to be able to witness a normal day's proceedings which do not include seeing groups of children which have been especially trained for

ity of planning is in place, the achievement of a Sandford Award is (almost) incidental. As a judge, I want to see worthwhile educational experiences being offered, which are based firmly on the strengths of the property, and which can be sustained day-in and day-out. In such properties there is no place for the specially-arranged day to impress a judge; I venture to suggest that the judges would be aware of any special arrangements from the moment that the performance started!

An important facet of the judging procedure is the interviews carried out with selected individuals from amongst the persons associated with the visit. These will always include representatives of the property's education staff, teachers and pupils. Equally important, and sometimes holding firm opinions about the day, are the AOTTS (adults other than teachers) who sometimes accompany groups and members of the property's staff who also come into contact with the children. From the totality of informal contact with these people the judge can form an opinion regarding how each has viewed the visit. From the two sets of educationalists, I expect an analysis of what has taken place together with some thoughts on possible improvements and/or follow-up activities to reinforce the things learned by the children.

Re-enactment of Victorian life in Tatton Park Mansion.

planned activities. I want to listen to focused questions and considered answers; to hear discussion and controlled argument which has arisen from received stimulation; to see children handling artefacts and hypothesising on their usage and comparing and contrasting life in past times with their own lives. In such situations, children will be totally engrossed, oblivious to their own world as they lose themselves in the everyday chores and pastimes of a bygone age. In truth, I have witnessed these things in great measure, for if there is a common feature between Sandford Award holders it is that in their various ways they display the ability to afford children personal pleasure by providing activities which unlock new areas of knowledge, understanding and skills.

From the children comes individual perceptions of their day; each may well be different and in some manner contradictory but, whatever is said, I look and seek out their excitement, news of what they have done which has been new, interesting and worthwhile. The adults will often share things told to them by children during the visit which illuminate the children's attitudes and values in a way which straightforward observation often fails to pick up.

I wish to see children interacting with aspects of the property and enjoying taking part in

When a judge is present to witness successful teaching and interaction, images stick in the mind; from my own pleasurable experiences I offer a few examples which have made my role as a Sandford Award judge so worthwhile. At Moseley Old Hall I saw comprehension dawn on the faces of children, who had been happily engaged in making rush lights, when they came to understand exactly what is meant by the phrase 'burning the candle at both ends'. Similarly, I was fortunate to be present when children, who had been busily working with flails to thresh wheat in the barn at Tatton Park, discovered just where the word 'threshold' originated. Again, I have waited, in hungry anticipation, in the Victorian kitchen areas of several properties for children to sit down with their teachers (with myself as guest) to eat buttered bread rolls which, to their own satisfaction - and no little amazement - have been made made and cooked by themselves. These examples are culled from practical activities, but, equally, where the opportunity is available a number of properties are able to present uplifting experiences of a different, spiritual kind. At Dove Cottage, for example, few children can fail to gain an insight into the poetic imagery of William Wordsworth after spending a day in the company of the education staff.

For me, the most successful interactions occur in rooms or areas which have been conserved (or carefully reconstructed) to appear, smell and sound as they did during a given historic period. Such areas provide a learning atmosphere and environment which is beyond the scope of even the most heritage-conscious school classroom or hi-tech lecture theatre. Here interaction must mean children handling artefacts and being encouraged to interrogate them in various ways; to hypothesise on their function and come to decisions rather than standing passively whilst objects are held aloft and their usage explained. As a judge, I look for children to be

encouraged to play an active part in their own education and for this to happen in a natural way the children must be excited and involved in what is going on around them.

Information about the eligibility of properties to apply for the Sandford Award is clearly set out on the application form - as is information regarding the period during which judging takes place. With regard to eligibilty, I have recently submitted a paper for consideration by the directors of the Heritage Education Trust, in which I suggest an extension of the categories of eligibility. Over the years, the directors have acknowledged the desirability of broadening the eligibilty list, for example to include industrial heritage sites, and my paper proposed further extension. My additional suggestions were 'large historical artefacts' and 'replica historical buildings - the originals of which are no longer extant'. An example of each includes historic ships and replica Iron-Age roundhouses. Each of these examples would involve interesting problems for the judges, but I believe that both can deliver heritage education experiences as worthwhile and as exciting for children as has proved the case in the properties currently eligible for the award. I was pleased to receive the news that the directors have decided to offer Historic Ships as a new category for this year. I look forward with pleasure to judging within this category.

The south front of Tatton Park Mansion, from the Italian Garden.

CHATSWORTH, DERBYSHIRE
Home of the Duke and Duchess of Devonshire

SCOTLAND'S BORDER

HERITAGE

TRAQUAIR · NEAR PEEBLES
OLDEST INHABITED HOUSE IN SCOTLAND

BOWHILL · NEAR SELKIRK
INTERNATIONALLY RENOWNED ART COLLECTION

ABBOTSFORD · NEAR MELROSE

HOME OF SIR WALTER SCOTT

THIRLESTANE CASTLE · LAUDER
UNSURPASSED 17TH CENTURY CEILINGS

FLOORS CASTLE · KELSO
SCOTLAND'S LARGEST INHABITED CASTLE

Spectacular Houses, Castles, Parks and Gardens, all within a 50 mile radius in one of the most scenic areas of Scotland.

PAXTON HOUSE · NEAR BERWICK UPON TWEED
BUILT FOR A KING'S DAUGHTER

THE HIRSEL · COLDSTREAM
COUNTRY PARK, MUSEUM AND CRAFTS

MELLERSTAIN · NEAR GORDON

SCOTLAND'S FINEST ADAM MANSION

MANDERSTON · DUNS

THE SWAN-SONG OF THE GREAT CLASSICAL HOUSE

HISTORIC HOUSES
Castles and Gardens 1996

The Premier Guide to Britain's National Heritage

This colourful publication is an essential guide to historic properties, gardens and other places of interest. With comprehensive details on opening times, locations and admission costs, it is a perfect companion for visitors to historic houses and gardens.

Historic Houses Castles and Gardens is the essential guide to over 1,300 properties and places of interest open to the public. This publication is beautifully illustrated with colour photographs throughout making it the ideal guide for anyone with an interest in Britain's National Heritage.

To order, simply complete the attached order form and post it to:

Specialist Marketing Department
Reed Information Services
Windsor Court
East Grinstead House
East Grinstead
West Sussex, RH19 1XA

Alternatively, call us on **01342 335872,** or fax us on **01342 335948.**

ISBN 0 948056 28 2

Order Form

Please supply _____ copy/ies of Historic Houses Castles and Gardens 1996 at £7.99 plus £2.80 p&p.

Name

Job Title

Company Name

Company Address

Postcode

Telephone   Fax

Signed _____ Date _____

☐ Cheque enclosed (payable to Reed Information Services)
☐ Please invoice my company
☐ Please debit my Access/Visa/Diners Club/Amex/Mastercard

Account No: **Expiry Date**   /

Cardholder's Name

Cardholder's address if different from above

Postcode

Telephone

Signed _____ Date _____
All orders are subject to our usual terms and conditions

VAT registration No. _____
(EU Companies only)

Historic Houses Castles and Gardens
in Great Britain and Ireland

 The National Trust — Denotes properties in the care of the National Trust

 ENGLISH HERITAGE — Denotes properties in the care of English Heritage

 Denotes properties in the care of the National Trust for Scotland

 Denotes property owned and administered by a member of the Historic Houses Association

Denotes property in the care of CADW - Welsh Historic Monuments

 Denotes guided tours of the building

 Denotes the major part of the property is suitable for wheelchairs

 Denotes educational services recognised by the Heritage Education Trust

 Denotes that the property is a recipient of the Sandford Award

 Denotes property is open all year round

Denotes property under the auspices of Irish Heritage

AVON

BARSTAPLE HOUSE (TRINITY ALMSHOUSES)
(Bristol Municipal Charities)
Bristol   map **14** U17   ENGLISH HERITAGE
Telephone: (0117) 9265777 (Warden)

Victorian almshouse with garden courtyard.

Location: Old Market Street, Bristol; ½ m from City centre on A420.
Station(s): Bristol Temple Meads (¾ m).
Open: GARDEN & EXTERIOR OF BUILDINGS ONLY, now extensively renovated. All the year week-days 10-4.
Admission: Free.
The Almshouse is occupied mainly by elderly residents & their rights for privacy should be respected.

BECKFORD'S TOWER
(The Beckford Tower Trust)
Bath   BA1 9BH   map **14** U18
Telephone: (01225) 338727

Built 1827 by William Beckford of Fonthill. A small museum (first floor) illustrating Beckford's life; fine views from Belvedere (156 easy steps).

Location: 2 m from Bath Spa Station via Lansdown Road.
Station(s): Bath Spa (2 m).
Open: Mar-end Oct Sat Sun & Bank Hol Mon 2-5. Parties other days by arrangement.
Admission: Adults £1.50 children/OAPs 75p.

BLAISE CASTLE HOUSE MUSEUM
(City of Bristol)
Henbury, Bristol   BS10 7QS
Telephone: (0117) 950 6789

Everyday life-childhood, schooldays, washing and cooking and cleaning-in a fine late 18th-century house. Blaise Castle Estate, the site of an Iron Age settlement and a Roman garrison, is now surrounded by suburban Bristol; it was once the home of the Harford family. John Harford had the present house built in the 1790's, and engaged Humphry Repton to landscape his garden. Repton's Red Book for Blaise is now one of the museum's treasures, alongside children's toys, mangles and washtubs, and elegant Victorian gowns. Access to upper floors is restricted.
Open: Tues-Sun 10-1 and 2-5.
Admission: Free.

BRACKENWOOD WOODLAND GARDEN AND GARDEN CENTRE
Portishead, Bristol   BS20 8DU
Telephone: (01275) 843484

Woodland garden (8 acres), Camellias, Rhododendrons, Acers and Pieris plus rare trees and shrubs. Superb views across the Bristol Channel.

Location: 1m from Portishead on Nore Road (coast road); M5 junction 19, 3 m.
Open: Garden open Apr-Sept. Garden Centre open every day.
Admission: Adults £1.50 party rate for 20+.
Refreshments: Tea room/café.

CLAVERTON MANOR
(The American Museum in Britain)
nr Bath   map **14** U18   △ Ⓔ
Telephone: (01225) 460503

A Greek Revival House high above the valley of the River Avon. Completely furnished rooms showing American decorative arts from the late 17th to the mid 19th centuries. Galleries of special exhibits. Paintings, furniture, glass, textiles, miniature rooms and Folk Art. Dallas Pratt Collection of Historical Maps, Special Exhibitions, American gardens.

Location: 2½ m from Bath Station via Bathwick Hill; 3¼ m SE of Bath via Warminster Road (A36) & Claverton village. Bus 18 (to University) from bus station - alight The Avenue, 10 mins walk to Museum.
Station(s): Bath Spa (2½ m).
Open: Mar 23-Nov 3 every day (except Mons) 2-5. Gardens open throughout the season 1-6 (except Mon).
Admission: House and Grounds £5 children £2.50 and OAPs £4.50. Grounds and Galleries only £2 children £1. Adult and Educational parties by previous arrangement with the Secretary.
Refreshments: Teas with American cookies. Light lunches at weekends.
Events/Exhibitions: Candace Bahouth: Colours: Needlepoint, Weaving, Mosaic. Events throughout the Season, apply the Secretary.

CLEVEDON COURT 🦡 The National Trust
Tickenham Road, Clevedon   BS21 6QU   map 14 U18
Telephone: (01275) 872257
Location: 1½ m E of Clevedon on the Bristol Road B3130.

DYRHAM PARK 🦡 The National Trust
nr Bristol and Bath   SN14 8ER   map 14 U18   ℳ
Telephone: (0117) 9372501
Location: 12 m E of Bristol approach from Bath/Stroud Road (A46), 2 m S of Tormarton interchange with M4, 8 m N of Bath.

ENGLISHCOMBE TITHE BARN
(Dr Jennie Walker)
Englishcombe   BA2 9DU   map 14 U18   ℳ
Telephone: (01225) 425073
Fax: (01225) 425073

Early 14th century cruck framed tithe barn recently restored.

Location: Adjacent to Englishcombe Village church 1 m S.W. of Bath.
Open: Suns and bank hols from Easter-Sept 2.30-6pm.
Admission: Adult £2 child £1. Wheelchairs free.
Refreshments: Cream teas.
Events/Exhibitions: Telephone for confirmation.
Car park. Toilets.

THE GEORGIAN HOUSE
(City of Bristol)
7 Great George Street, Bristol   BS1 5RR
Telephone: (0117) 921 1362

No.7 Great George Street was built between 1787 and 1791 for John Pinney, a Bristol merchant. Here you can explore upstairs and down, from the fine drawing room with its elegant furniture, to the basement kitchen complete with roasting spit, oven and pots and pans. A house of substance, from an age of prosperity and quiet self-confidence.

Open: Tues-Sat 1-5.
Admission: Adults £1 concessions 50p. Free to children under 16 and full-time students.

HORTON COURT 🦡 The National Trust
Horton   BS17 6QR   map 14 U18   ℳ
Location: 3 m NE of Chipping Sodbury, 3/4m N of Horton, 1 m W of Bath/Stroud Road (A46).

NUMBER ONE, ROYAL CRESCENT
(Bath Preservation Trust)
Bath   map 14 U18
Telephone: (01225) 428126

Number 1 was the first house to be built in the Royal Crescent, John Wood the Younger's fine example of Palladian architecture. The crescent was begun in 1767 and completed by 1774. The house was given to the Bath Preservation Trust in 1968 and both the exterior and interior have been accurately restored. Visitors can see a grand town house of the late 18th century with authentic furniture, paintings and carpets. On the ground floor are the Study and Dining Room and on the first floor a Lady's Bedroom and Drawing Room. A series of maps of Bath are on the second floor landing. In the basement is a Kitchen and a Museum Shop.

Location: Bath, upper town close to Assembly rooms.
Open: 13 Feb-27 Oct Tues-Sun 10.30-5 Oct 29-1 Dec Tues-Sun 10.30-4 last adm. half an hour before closing. Private tours out of hours with refreshments if required by arrangement with Administrator. Open Bank hols and Bath Festival Mon. Closed Good Fri.
Admission: Adults £3.50 children/students/OAPs/adult groups £2.50 school groups £2 family ticket £8.
Museum. Shop.

Sir Joshua Reynolds
Portrait painter (1723-1792)
First President of the Royal Academy, knighted in 1769

His work can be seen in the following properties included in Historic Houses Castles and Gardens:-

Arundel Castle	*Knole*
Dalmeny House	*Petworth House*
Parham Park	*Rockingham Castle*
Elton Hall	*Saltram*
Goodwood House	*Shalom Hall*
Ickworth House, Park & Garden	*Wallington House*
Kenwood, The Iveagh Bequest	*Weston Park*

Lancelot 'Capability' Brown

Born 1716 in Northumberland, Capability Brown began work at the age of 16 in the vegetable gardens of Sir William and Lady Loraine at Kirharle Tower. He left Northumberland in 1739, and records show that he worked at Stowe until 1749. It was at Stowe that Brown began to study architecture, and to submit his own plans. It was also at Stowe that he devised a new method of moving and replanting mature trees.

Brown married Bridget Wayet in 1744 and began work on the estate at Warwick Castle in 1749. He was appointed Master Gardener at Hampton Court in 1764, and planted the Great Vine at Hampton Court in 1768. Blenheim Palace designs are considered amongst Brown's finest work, and the technical achievements were outstanding even for the present day.

Capability Brown died in February 1783 of a massive heart attack. A monument beside the lake at Croome Court was erected which reads "To the memory of Lancelot Brown, who by the powers of his inimitable and creative genius formed this garden scene out of a morass". There is also a portrait of Brown at Burghley.

Capability Brown was involved in the design of grounds at the following properties included in Historic Houses Castles and Gardens:

Audley End	*Longleat*
Berrington Hall	*Luton Hoo*
Bowood	*Moccas Court*
Burghley House	*Petworth House*
Burton Constable	*Sledmere House*
Charlecote Park	*Stowe (Stowe*
Chilham Castle Gardens	*School)*
(reputed)	*Syon House*
Clandon Park	*Warwick Castle*
Claremont	*Weston Park*
Chillington Hall	*Wimpole Hall*
Corsham Court	*Wrest Park and*
Fawley Court	*Gardens*
Highclere Castle	

THE RED LODGE
(City of Bristol)
Park Row, Bristol   BS1 5LJ
Telephone: (0117) 921 1360

An Elizabethan lodge, hidden amidst the bustle of modern Bristol. Completed in about 1590, the Red Lodge was home to a succession of local families and more recently, the first girls' reformatory in this country. Now furnished as a family home, the panelling in the Great Oak Room is magnificent, and the smaller bedroom next door is a place in which to ponder past lives. A knot garden offers tranquility, a place to sit and wonder.

Open: Tues-Sat 1-5.
Admission: Adults £1 concessions 50p. Free to children under 16, full time students.

SHERBORNE GARDEN (PEAR TREE HOUSE)
(Mr & Mrs John Southwell)
Litton   BA3 4PP   map 14 U18
Telephone: (01761) 241220

4 acre garden of considerable horticultural interest with collections of hollies, ferns, hostas, hemerocallis, and species roses. Picnic area.

Location: Litton, 7 m north of Wells, Somerset, on B3114 off A39.
Open: Suns & Mons June through September. Also for National Garden Scheme Mar 31 June 16 July 14 Sept 15 11-6. Other times by appointment.
Admission: £1.50 Chd free. Parties by arrangement. Free car parking.
Refreshments: Tea/coffee available, other refreshments by arrangement.
Suitable for the disabled. Dogs on leads.

BEDFORDSHIRE

CECIL HIGGINS ART GALLERY & MUSEUM
(Gallery jointly owned and administered by Bedford Borough Council and the Trustees of the Cecil Higgins Art Gallery)
Castle Close, Bedford   MK40 3NY   map 5 S22   ♿ ⓢ
Telephone: (01234) 211222
Fax: (01234) 221606

Re-created Victorian Mansion, originally the home of the Higgins family, wealthy Bedford brewers. Rooms displayed to create a 'lived-in' atmosphere, including many items from the Handley-Read Collection, and a bedroom with furniture designed by William Burges (1827-1881). Adjoining Gallery with changing displays of watercolours, prints and drawings from own outstanding collections, and permanent displays of English and Continental ceramics and glass. Situated in pleasant gardens leading down to the river embankment.

Location: Centre of Bedford, just off The Embankment.
Station(s): Bedford Midland (1 m). Bus Station: (½ m).Trains from London (St.Pancras), and King's Cross Thameslink - fast trains 36 mins. United Counties X4 Bedford/Milton Keynes - Buckingham - Bicester - Oxford; X3 Northampton - Bedford - Cambridge; Coach link from London Marylebone Station.
Open: Tues-Sat 11-5 Sun 2-5 closed Mon (except Bank Hol Mons) Christmas Day Boxing Day and Good Fri.
Admission: Free. Group bookings by prior arrangement.
Refreshments: By prior arrangement.
Events/Exhibitions: Phone for current details.
Facilities for the disabled.

LUTON HOO - WERNHER COLLECTION
(The Luton Hoo Foundation)
Luton   LU1 3TQ   map **5** S22
Telephone: (01582) 22955
Fax: (01582) 34437

The works of Carl Fabergé, the Russian Court jeweller which are on view at Luton Hoo, are part of the finest private Collection of works of art in Great Britain, which includes continental treasures rarely seen in English Country Houses. There are many paintings, costume and other personal possessions of the Russian Imperial Family Romanov, complemented by the acquisition of memorabilia of Father Gibbes who was tutor to the Tsarevitch. All the Russian Collection has been redesigned and redisplayed in and around the beautiful Chapel - extensively restored to its original decorative splendour, and in 1991, consecrated into the Russian Orthodox Church and dedicated to the memory of Tsar Nicholas II and the Imperial Family. Other treasures in the House are Old Master paintings, magnificent Tapestries, English and French Porcelain, European Ceramics, Furniture, Byzantine and Medieval Ivories, Sculpture, Bronzes and renaissance Jewellery.

Location: Signposted from J10 of M1.
Open: 1 Apr-13 Oct '96 Tues Wed Thurs pre-booked groups only either morning or afternoon by arrangement. Groups on these days will have a guided tour. Fri Sat Sun general public viewing. Gardens & Restaurant open at 12 Wernher Collection at 1.30pm (last entries 5). House *closed* Mon except bank hols when house & garden opens at 10.30.
Admission: Group rates £5 adults, £4.50 sen citizens/students £2.50 children. House & Gardens £5.50 adults £5 sen citizens/students £2 children.
Refreshments: Restaurant.
Disabled facilities. Coaches welcome, picnic area, gift shop. Ample parking.

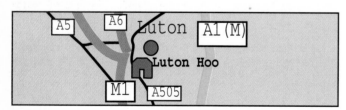

WOBURN ABBEY
(The Marquess of Tavistock and Trustees of the Bedford Estates)
Woburn   map **5** S21
Telephone: (01525) 290666; Antiques Centre (01525) 290350
Fax: (01525) 290271

Home of the Dukes of Bedford for over 350 years, the Abbey contains one of the most important private art collections in the world, including paintings by Canaletto, Van Dyck, Cuyp, Teniers, Rembrandt, Gainsborough, Reynolds, Velazquez and many other famous artists. French and English 18th century furniture, silver and the fabulous Sèvres dinner service presented to the 4th Duke by Louis XV of France. The 3,000 acre Deer Park has lots of wildlife, including nine species of deer, roaming freely. One of these, the Père David, descended from the Imperial Herd of China, was saved from extinction at Woburn and is now the largest breeding herd of this species in the world. In 1985 twenty two Père David were given by the Family to the People's Republic of China with the hope that the species may become re-established in its natural habitat. The Marquess of Tavistock visited Beijing to release the herd at Nan Haizi, the former Imperial hunting ground outside Beijing. The tour of the Abbey covers three floors including the Crypt. It is regretted that wheelchairs can only be accommodated in the House by prior arrangement with the Administrator but unfortunately the Crypt area is not accessible. The 40 shop Antiques Centre is probably the most unusual such centre outside London - the shop fronts having been rescued from demolition sites in various parts of Britain. All catering is operated by ourselves with banqueting, conferences, receptions and company days out our speciality, in the beautiful setting of the Sculpture Gallery, overlooking the private gardens. There is a Pottery and summer weekend events are arranged. Extensive picnic areas with ample coach and car parking. Gift shops and Pottery.

Location: In Woburn 8½ m NW of Dunstable on A4012. 42 m from London off M1 at junctions 12 or 13.
Station(s): Leighton Buzzard and Bletchley (Euston) and Flitwick (Kings Cross Thameslink). The three local stations are between 6 and 7 miles from Woburn village, which is 1½ m from the Abbey.
Open: HOUSE AND GARDENS 30th Dec-23rd Mar Sat & Bank Hols Sun only House 11-4 Park 10.30-3.45. Mar 24-Oct 3 daily House weekdays 11-4 Sun 11-5 Park weekdays 10-4.30 Sun 10-4.45. Last admissions as closing time.
Admission: House including Private Apartments Adults £6.80, group rate £5.80 (exc Private Apartments £6.40 group rate £5.40). Senior Citizens £5.80, group rate £4.80 (exc Private Apartments) £4.80 group rate £4.40. Children (over 12) £2.50 group rate *£2.50. *School parties are to be charged for children over 7 and under 16. Deer Park only charge is for the vehicle including its passengers. Coaches & Minibuses (incl of passengers) is free of charge. Visitors from the Safari Park is free of charge. Antiques Centre All visitors weekdays suns and Bank Hols 20p. For further information telephone (01525) 290666.
Refreshments: Flying Duchess Pavilion Coffee Shop. Larger groups may pre-book the Sculpture Gallery, Lantern or Long Harness Room.
Events/Exhibitions: There is a full programme of events throughout the summer.
Conferences: Facilities available at the Sculpture Gallery. Licensed for Civil Weddings.

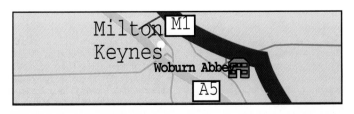

WREST PARK HOUSE AND GARDENS

Silsoe   map **5** S22

ENGLISH HERITAGE

Telephone: (01525) 860152

Here is a history of English gardening in the grand manner from 1700-1850, which would not, of course, be complete without some designs by 'Capability' Brown. Every whim of fashion is represented, whether it be for a Chinese bridge, artificial lake, classical temple or rustic ruin. The present house was built about 1839 by the Earl de Grey, whose family had lorded over the Manor of Wrest for 600 years. The State Rooms and gardens are open to the public.

Location: ¾ m (1 km) east of Silsoe.
Open: Apr 1-30 10-6 Sat Sun & Bank Hol only.
Admission: April 1-Sept 30 Adults £2.50 concessions £1.90 children £1.30.
Refreshments: Available.

William Kent (1685 - 1748)
Painter, architect, garden designer

His work can be seen in the following properties included in Historic Houses Castles and Gardens:-

Chiswick House
Ditchley Park (decoration of Great Hall)
Euston Hall
Rousham House
Stowe (Stowe School)

BERKSHIRE

BASILDON PARK   The National Trust

Lower Basildon, Reading   RG8 9NR   map **3** T20
Telephone: (01734) 843040

Classical house built 1776. Unusual Octagon room; fine plasterwork; important paintings and furniture, Garden and woodland walks.

Location: 7 m NW of Reading between Pangbourne and Streatley on A329. Leave M4 at junction 12.
Station(s): Pangbourne (2½ m); Goring and Streatley (3 m).
Open: 30 Mar-end Oct Wed-Sat 2-6 Sun & Bank Hol Mon 12-6. Grounds open 9 Mar-29 Mar Sat & Sun 12-5 30 Mar-end Oct as house but open 12-6 on Sat. Last adm to house half-hour before closing. Closed Good Fri & Wed following BH
Admission: House & Grounds £3.70 Park & Garden only £1.50 Children half price. Reductions (except Suns and Bank Hol Mons) to House and Grounds for parties of 15 or more (Booking essential). Family ticket house and garden £9. Family ticket Park and Garden £3.75.
Refreshments: Tea-room in house accessible to wheelchairs.
Events/Exhibitions: Same months as house: Wed-Fri 2-5.30 Sat Sun & BH Mon 12-5.30. Nov-15 Dec Sat &Sun 12-4.
Shop 30 March-end Oct Wed-Sat 2-5.30; Sun & BH Mon 12.30-5.30; Nov to 15 Dec Fri 12-4; Sat & Sun 11-5. Dogs in grounds only on leads. House unsuitable for wheelchairs.

DORNEY COURT

(Mr & Mrs Peregrine Palmer)
nr Windsor   SL4 6QP   map 3 T19
Telephone: (01628) 604638
Fax: (01628) 665772

'One of the finest Tudor Manor Houses in England' - Country Life. A visit to Dorney is a most welcome, refreshing and fascinating experience. Built about 1440 and lived in by the present family for over 400 years, this enchanting, many gabled pink brick and timber house is a joy to behold. The rooms are full of the continuing atmosphere of history: early 15th and 16th century oak, beautiful 17th century lacquer furniture, 18th and 19th century tables, 400 years of family portraits and stained glass and needlework. Charles II came here to seek the charms of Barbara Palmer, Countess of Castlemaine - 'the most intelligent beautiful and influential of ladies'. The 14th century church of St. James next door, is a lovely, cool, cheerful and very English Church.

Location: 2 m W of Eton & Windsor in village of Dorney on B3026. Signposted from M4, exit 7.
Station(s): Burnham (2 m).
Open: Easter weekend Fri-Mon, May Suns & Bank Hol Mons, also June-Sept Sun, Mon & Tues 2-5.30. Last admission and last orders for teas at 5.
Admission: Adults £4 children over 9 £2 10% discount for National Trust and NADFAS members and OAPs. Parties at other times by arrangement.
Refreshments: Home-made cream teas.
Outstanding collection of plants for sale at Bressingham Plant Centre. PYO fruit from June-middle August.

ENGLEFIELD HOUSE GARDEN
Theale, Reading   RG7 5DU   map **5** U20
Telephone: (01734) 302504
Fax: (01734) 303226

A seven acre garden, herbacious and rose borders.

FROGMORE HOUSE
Windsor   map **3** T19
Telephone: (01753) 831118

One of the least known royal residences Frogmore House is situated within the private Home Park at Windsor Castle.

MAPLEDURHAM HOUSE AND WATERMILL
See under Oxfordshire.

SAVILL GARDEN
(Crown Property)
Windsor Great Park   map **3** T19
Telephone: (01753) 860222
Fax: (01753) 859617

World renowned woodland garden of 35 acres with adjoining area of herbaceous borders, rose gardens, alpine raised beds, an extensive dry garden and the new Queen Elizabeth Temperate House. The whole garden offering much of great interest and beauty at all seasons.

Location: To be approached from A30 via Wick Road & Wick Lane, Englefield Green.
Station(s): Egham (3 m).
Open: Open daily Mar-Oct 10-6. Nov-Feb 10-4. (closed 25/26 Dec)
Admission: Adults £3.50 OAPs £3. Parties of 20 and over £3. Accompanied children (under 16) free.
Refreshments: Licensed self-service restaurant.

SWALLOWFIELD PARK
(Country Houses Association)
Swallowfield   RG7 1TG   map **12** U21
Telephone: (01734) 883815

Built by the Second Earl of Clarendon in 1678.

Location: In the village of Swallowfield 6 m SE of Reading.
Open: May-September Weds & Thurs 2-5. Last entry 4.00.
Admission: £2.50 Children £1.
Free car park. No dogs admitted.

WELFORD PARK
(Mrs A.C. Puxley)
nr Newbury   RG16 8HU   map **3** U20 △
Telephone: (01488) 608203

Queen Anne house with later additions. Attractive gardens and grounds.

Location: 6 m NW of Newbury and 1 m N of Wickham village off B4000.
Station(s): Newbury.
Open: Spring and Summer Bank Hols and July 31-Aug 25 inclusive from 2.30-5.
Admission: Adults £3 OAPs and under 16s £2.
Interior by prior appointment only.

WINDSOR CASTLE
(Official residence of H.M. The Queen)
Windsor   SL4 1NJ   map **4** U21
Telephone: (01753) 831118 (24 hr information line)

Perhaps the largest fortress of its kind in the world, Windsor Castle has belonged to the Sovereigns of England for over 900 years.

BUCKINGHAMSHIRE

ASCOTT   🦌 The National Trust
Wing, nr Leighton Buzzard   LU7 OPS   map **5** T21   △
Telephone: (01296) 688242
Location: ½ m E of Wing; 2 m SW of Leighton Buzzard, on the S side of Aylesbury/Leighton Buzzard Road (A418).

CHENIES MANOR HOUSE
(Lt Col & Mrs MacLeod Matthews)
Chenies   WD3 6ER   map **12** T21   △
Telephone: (01494) 762888

15/16th century Manor House with fortified tower. Original home of the Earls of Bedford, visited by Henry VIII and Elizabeth I. Home of the MacLeod Matthews family. Contains contemporary tapestries and furniture. Hiding places, collection of antique dolls; medieval undercroft and well. Surrounded by beautiful gardens which have featured in many publications - a Tudor sunken garden, a white garden, herbaceous borders, a fountain court, a physic garden containing a very wide selection of medical and culinary herbs, a parterre and two mazes. The kitchen garden is in the Victorian style with unusual vegetables and fruit. Special exhibitions. Flower drying and arrangements. Plants and unique ivy topiary for sale.

Location: Off A404 between Amersham & Rickmansworth (M25 - junction 18).
Station(s): Chorleywood (1½ m).
Open: First week in April to end of Oct Weds and Thurs 2-5. Also open Bank Hol Mons 2-5. Last entry to house 4.15pm.
Admission: £4 Gardens Only £2 children (under 14) half price. Parties throughout the year by prior arrangement - min charge £50.
Refreshments: Home-made teas. Corporate events welcome.
Events/Exhibitions: Spectacular tulip display open days 2 Apr-mid May.
Conferences: Welcome.
Free parking. No dogs.

CHILTERN OPEN AIR MUSEUM
(Chiltern Open Air Museum Ltd)
Newland Park, Gorelands Lane, Chalfont St Giles   HP8 4AD   map 12 T21
Telephone: (01494) 871117
Fax: (01494) 872163

A museum of historic buildings, rescued from demolition, and which reflect the vernacular heritage of the Chilterns region. You can explore barns, granaries, cartsheds and stables, a blacksmith's forge, a toll house, vicarage room, Edwardian cast-iron public conveniences, a pair of 18th century thatched cottages, a 1947 prefabricated bungalow, a reconstruction of an Iron Age House and a 19th century Mission Room - and the collection is growing all the time. Several of the buildings incorporate displays illustrating their original use, or house exhibitions on Chiltern life and landscape. The Museum occupies 45 acres of beautiful parkland and woodland which has an attractive Nature Trail running through it.

Location: At Newland Park, Chalfont St Giles; 4½ m Amersham, 8 m Watford, 6 m Beaconsfield; 2 m A413 at Chalfont St Peter, 4 m from junction 17 on the M25 via Maple Cross and the Chalfonts.
Station(s): Chorleywood, Chalfont and Latimer.
Open: Apr-Oct Tues-Fri 2-6. Sat & Sun & Bank Hols 11-6. Tues-Sun during Aug 11-6. Parties and school parties by arrangement weekdays all year round.
Admission: Adults £3.50 OAPs £3 children under 16yrs £2 under 5 free family ticket (2 adults 2 children) £10. For special event weekends special admission costs apply.
Refreshments: Tea-rooms located in historic building.
Events/Exhibitions: Various special event weekends throughout the season.

CLAYDON HOUSE   ✤ The National Trust
Middle Claydon, nr Buckingham   MK18 2EY   map 5 T21
Telephone: (01296) 730349/730693

The most perfect expression of Rococo decoration in England, in a series of great rooms with woodcarvings in the Chinese and gothic styles. Relics of the Civil War and a museum with memorabilia of Florence Nightingale and the Verney family.

Location: In the village of Middle Claydon, 13m NW of Aylesbury, 3½ m SW of Winslow. Signposted from A413, A421 and A41.
Open: 30 Mar-end Oct Sat-Wed 1-5 Bank Hol Mons 1-5. Last adm 4.30. *Closed Thurs & Fri (inc Good Fri).*
Admission: £3.70 Children £1.85. Family ticket £9. Parties write to Custodian.
Refreshments: Tea Room 2-5
Dogs in park on leads only. Wheelchairs provided (access to ground floor only, half price adm.)

CLIVEDEN   ✤ The National Trust
Taplow, Maidenhead (1851)   SL6 OJA   map 12 T21   △
Telephone: (01628) 605069
Location: 3 m upstream from Maidenhead; 2 m N of Taplow on Hedsor Road. Main entrance opposite Feathers Inn.

COWPER & NEWTON MUSEUM
(Trustees)
Orchard Side, Market Place   MK46 4AJ   map 5 S21
Telephone: (01234) 711516

Personal belongings of eighteenth century poet, William Cowper, and Rev. John Newton, (author of 'Amazing Grace'). Exhibitions of Bobbin Lace. Two gardens, one contains Cowper's Summerhouse.

Location: Market Place, Olney; N of Newport Pagnell via A509.
Station(s): Milton Keynes.
Open: 1st Nov-31 Mar 1-4. 1st Apr-31 Oct 10-1 & 2-5 Tues-Sats. Open Bank Hol Mons. Closed 15 Dec-31 Jan and Good Fri.
Admission: £1.50 adults, £1.00 over 65's 50p children.

HUGHENDEN MANOR   ✤ The National Trust
High Wycombe   HP14 4LA   map 12 T21
Telephone: (01494) 532580

Home of Benjamin Disraeli, Earl of Beaconsfield (1847-1881). Small formal garden set in parkland.

Location: 1½ m N of High Wycombe on W side Gt Missenden Road (A4128).
Station(s): High Wycombe (2 m).
Open: House & Garden 2 Mar-31 Mar Sat & Sun only 3 Apr-end Oct Weds-Sun 1-5 BH Mon. *Closed Good Fri.* Last admissions 4.30. Shop open as House and pre-Christmas Nov to Dec 15 Wed-Sun 11-3. *Parties must book in advance.* Parties Wed-Fri only if booked in advance. Park open all year.
Admission: £3.70 Children half price. Family ticket £9. Garden only £1
Refreshments: Tea-room in stableblock 12-5, open same days as house.
Dogs in Park & car park only. Wheelchair provided.

MILTON'S COTTAGE
(Milton Cottage Trust)
Chalfont St Giles   HP8 4JH   map 12 T21
Telephone: (01494) 872313

The Cottage where John Milton completed 'Paradise Lost' and wrote 'Paradise Regained', contains many Milton relics and a library including first and early editions. Free car park for visitors. Three museum rooms and charming cottage garden open to the public.

Location: ½ m W of A413; on road to Seer Green and Beaconsfield.
Station(s): Gerrards Cross L.T. to Amersham or Chalfont and Latimer.
Open: Mar-Oct Wed-Sun 10-1 and 2-6 Spring & Summer Bank Hol Mons 10-1 and 2-6 closed Mon and Tues (except Bank Hols) & Jan, Feb, Nov and Dec.
Admission: Adults £2 children (under 15) 60p parties of 20 or more £1.50.
Refreshments: By prior arrangement with Milton's restaurant (opposite).

NETHER WINCHENDEN HOUSE

(Trustees of Will Trust of J.G.C. Spencer Bernard Dec'd)
Aylesbury   HP18 0DY   map **12** T21   △ &
Telephone: (01844) 290101

Medieval and Tudor manor house with 18th century Gothic additions. Home of Sir Francis Bernard, Governor of New Jersey and Massachusetts, 1760.

Location: 1 m N of A418 Aylesbury/Thame Road, in village of Lower Winchendon, 6 m SW Aylesbury.
Station(s): Aylesbury (7½ m). Haddenham and Thame Parkway (2½ m).
Open: May 1-May 28 and Aug 25 & 26 2.30-5.30. Last party each day at 4.45. Parties at any time of year by written appointment.
Admission: Adults £2.50 children (under 12) and OAPs £1.50 (not weekends or Bank Hols).
Refreshments: By arrangement.
Correspondence to Administrator, R.V. Spencer Bernard Esq.

PRINCES RISBOROUGH MANOR HOUSE

 **The National Trust**
Princes Risborough   HP17 9AW   map **12** T21   &
Location: Princes Risborough (1 m).

STOWE LANDSCAPE GARDENS    **The National Trust**

nr Buckingham   MK18 SEH   map **5** S20
Telephone: (01280) 822850

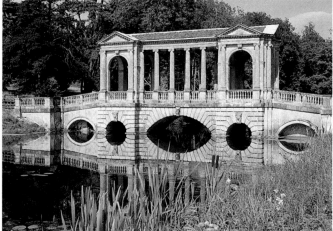

Splendid landscape gardens with buildings and temples by Vanbrugh, Kent and Gibbs. One of the supreme creations of the Georgian era. (N.B. the main house is in the ownership of Stowe School).

Location: 3 m NW of Buckingham, via Stowe Avenue off the A422 Buckingham/Banbury Road.

Open: Gardens: Mar 23-Apr 14 daily; 15 Apr-5 July Mon Wed Fri Sun; 7 July-8 Sept daily. 9 Sept-3 Nov: Mon Wed Fri Sun; closed Christmas Eve, Christmas Day & Boxing Day; 27 Dec-5 Jan 1997: daily 10-5 or dusk if earlier. Last admissions 1 hour before closing.
Admission: Entry to Gardens £4 Family ticket £10. The main house belongs to Stowe School and may be open during Stowe School holidays at an additional charge of £2 (inc NT members).
Refreshments: Light refreshments and teas as above 11-5 (11-4 during Dec and Jan). Dogs on lead only. Batricar available for disabled visitors, telephone Administrator for details. Shop in menagerie; open as gardens MON-FRI 10-5; SAT & SUN 11-5

STOWE (STOWE SCHOOL)

Buckingham   MK18 5EH   map **12** T21
Telephone: (01280) 813650 house 822850 gardens

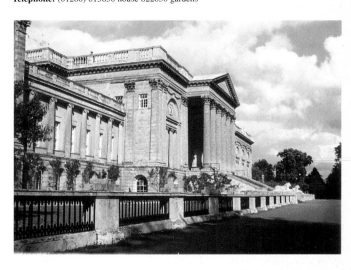

Stowe is one of the most majestic English Houses of the eighteenth century. Formerley the home of the dukes of Buckingham it is a house adorned with the traditions of aristocracy and learning. For over one and a half centuries up to the great sale of 1848, the temples and Grenvilles almost continuously rebuilt and refurbished it in an attempt to match their ever growing ambitions with the latest fashions. Around the mansion is one of Britains most magnificent landscape gardens now in the ownership of the National Trust.

Location: 4 m N of Buckingham town.
Station(s): Milton Keynes.
Open: House Only Sat 23 Mar-Sun 14th Apr. Sun 7th July-Sunday 8th Sept daily 2-5pm Suns 12 noon-5pm. **Please note** it may be necessary to close the house for private functions. Please check before visiting. Tel - House (01280) 813650 National Trust Gardens (01280) 822850.
Admission: Adults £2 children £1.
Conferences: Licensed for Civil Weddings.
Guide books, postcards, souvenirs and prints available from the Stowe Bookshop situated in the Menagerie on the South Front - opening times 10am-5pm.

Sir Peter Lely - portrait painter

His paintings can be seen at the following properties included in Historic Houses Castles and Gardens:-

Aynhoe Park
Belton House
Breamore House
Browsholme Hall
Dalmeny House
Euston Hall
Goodwood House
Gorhambury

Kedleston Hall
Knole
Petworth House
Ragley Hall
Rockingham Castle
St Osyth Priory
Stanford Hall
Weston Park

WADDESDON MANOR

(Rothschild Waddesdon Ltd/The National Trust)
nr Aylesbury   HP18 OJH   map **12** T21   △ &

Telephone: (01296) 651211
Fax: (01296) 651293

Waddesdon Manor, designed in the style of a French Renaissance château, was built in the 1870's by Baron Ferdinand de Rothschild. The interior evokes 18th century France and is furnished with panelling, furniture, carpets and porcelain, many of which have a royal French provenance. There is an important collection of English 18th century portraits by Gainsborough and Reynolds and of Dutch 17th century Old Masters. In addition to the State Reception rooms and the bedrooms there are rooms devoted to Sèvres porcelain, an exhibition on the Rothschild family, and important rooms on the first floor recently restored with more of Baron Ferdinand's 18th century panelling. The family's long association with wine is represented in the Wine Cellars. Set in the garden is a rococo style aviary housing exotic birds. In the recently restored formal parterre, the elaborate raised ribbon bedding is typically Victorian. The shrubberies have been revived around the garden in the style of the 19th century. Daffodil valley boasts a display of daffodils in March followed by a mass of wild flowers. Many magnificent trees can be seen throughout the garden.

Location: At W end of Waddeson village; 6 m NW of Aylesbury on Bicester Road (A41).
Station(s): Aylesbury (6 m). Buses: Red Rover 1, 15, 16, from Aylesbury. (Tel: (01296) 28686).
Open: Garden, Aviary, Wine Cellars, Shops & Restaurant: 28 Feb-22 Dec, Wed-Sun, 11-5. House: 28 Mar-13 Oct, Thrus-Sat, 12.30-6, Suns, Bank Hol Mon & Good Fri, 11.30-6.30. (NB Whole property closed 14-18 Oct inc. preparing the Christmas Shop).
Admission: Grounds, Aviary, Shops, Licensed Restaurant & Parking: £3 children £1.50. House State Reception Rooms: £6 children over 5 only £4.50. First Floor Exhibition Rooms: £6 children over 5 only £4.50. Combined ticket £8 children over 5 £6.50. Additional charge to ~House on Sun, Bank Hol Mon & Good Fri: Adults & children £1.
Conferences: Licensed for Civil Weddings.

Dogs not admitted apart from guide dogs. For further information please call: (01296) 651211 (recorded info) or The Events Office for details of special tours, wine tastings, weddings and banqueting: (01296) 651282.

WEST WYCOMBE PARK (1750)   🌿 The National Trust

West Wycombe   HP14 3AJ   map **12** T21   △
Telephone: (01494) 524411

Palladian house with frescoes and painted ceilings. 18th century landscape garden with lake and various classical temples.

Location: At W end of West Wycombe, S of Oxford Road (A40), 2½ m W High Wycombe.
Station(s): High Wycombe (2½ m).
Open: Grounds only Apr & May Sun & Wed 2-6 and Easter, May and Spring Bank Hols. Sun & Mon 2-6. Closed Good Fri. House and Grounds June July & Aug Sun-Thurs 2-6 (last adm 5.15). Entry to house by timed tickets on weekdays.
Admission: House & Grounds £4 Grounds only £2.50 Children half price. *No reduction for parties.* Family ticket £10.
Dogs in car park only. House unsuitable for wheelchairs.

WINSLOW HALL

(Sir Edward & Lady Tomkins)
Winslow   MK18 3HL   map **5** S21   △
Telephone: (01296) 712323

Built 1698-1702. Almost certainly designed by Sir Christopher Wren. Has survived without major structural alteration and retains most of its original features. Modernized and redecorated by the present owners. Good eighteenth century furniture, mostly English. Some fine pictures, clocks and carpets. Several examples of Chinese art, notably of the Tang period. Beautiful gardens with many unusual trees and shrubs.

Location: At entrance to Winslow on the Aylesbury road (A413).
Station(s): Milton Keynes or Aylesbury (both 10 miles).
Open: Open all Bank Holiday weekends except Christmas 2-5. July and Aug Wed and Thurs 2.30-5.30 or by appointment throughout the year.
Admission: £4.50 Children free.
Refreshments: Catering by arrangement.

CAMBRIDGESHIRE

ANGLESEY ABBEY AND GARDEN   🍂 The National Trust
Lode   CB5 9EJ   map **7** S23
Telephone: (01223) 811200
Location: In village of Lode 6 m NE of Cambridge on B1102, signposted off A45.

ELTON HALL 🏛
(Mr & Mrs William Proby)
nr Peterborough   PE8 6SH   map **7** R22 △
Telephone: (01832) 280 468
Fax: (01832) 280584

Spanning five centuries, this romantic house has been the home of the Proby family for over 300 years. The house, with its mixture of mediaeval, gothic and classical styles, reflects the family's passion for collecting, and this is shown in the remarkable contents to be seen today - excellent furniture and outstanding paintings by Gainsborough, Reynolds, Constable, Alma Tadema, Millais and other fine artists. There are over 12,000 books, including Henry VIII's prayer book. Wonderful gardens, including restored Rose Garden, new knot and sunken gardens and recently planted Arboretum. Bressingham Plant Cantre in walled Kitchen Garden.

Location: On A605, 5 m W of Peterborough.
Open: Easter Mon May and Aug bank hols - Sun and Mon July - Weds and Suns Aug - Weds, Thurs and Suns 2-5.
Admission: House and Garden: Adults £4 children £2. Garden only: Adults £2 children £1. Private parties by arrangement with House Manager.
Refreshments: Home-made teas. Lunches by arrangement.
Events/Exhibitions: Contact administration.
Conferences: By arrangement. Please apply to office for details
Souvenirs, Loch Fyne Oyster Bar Restaurant, Bressingham Plant Centre, Garden Shop.

ISLAND HALL
(Mr Christopher & The Hon Mrs Vane Percy)
Godmanchester   PE18 8BA   map **7** S22
Telephone: 0171-491 3724

An important mid 18th century mansion of great charm owned and restored by an award winning Interior Designer. This family home has lovely Georgian rooms, with fine period detail, and interesting possessions relating to the owners' ancestors since their first occupation of the house in 1800. A tranquil riverside setting with formal gardens and ornamental island forming part of the grounds in an area of Best Landscape. Octavia Hill, the Victorian reformer, and a founder of the National Trust, who stayed at Island Hall at least twice in 1859 and 1865, would instantly recognise the house and grounds, and she says in a letter to her sister "This is the loveliest, dearest old house, I never was in such a one before".

Location: In centre of Godmanchester next to the car park. 1 m south of Huntingdon. 15 m north west of Cambridge (A14).
Station(s): Huntingdon 2m. Good bus routes.
Open: June 30, July 7/14/21/28 Sundays only 2.30-5.00pm.
Admission: Parties by arrangement (May-Sept). Adm House and Grounds £3 child 13-16 £2; under 13 grounds only.
Refreshments: Light refreshments.

KIMBOLTON CASTLE
(Governors of Kimbolton School)
Kimbolton   map **7** S22
Telephone: (01480) 860505
Fax: (01480) 861763

Tudor manor house associated with Katherine of Aragon, completely remodelled by Vanbrugh (1708-20); courtyard c. 1694. Fine murals by Pellegrini in chapel, boudoir and on staircase. Gatehouse by Robert Adam. Parkland.

Location: 8 m NW of St Neots on B645; 14 m N of Bedford.
Station(s): St Neots (9 m).
Open: Easter Sun & Mon, Spring Bank Hol Sun & Mon, Summer Bank Hol Sun & Mon also Sun only late July and Aug 2-6pm.
Admission: Adults £1.50 children & OAPs 50p.
Conferences: By negotiation.

THE MANOR OR GREEN KNOWE
(Mr and Mrs Peter Boston)
Hemingford Grey PE18 9BN map **14** T18
Telephone: (01480) 463134

Built about 1130 and recreated by the author Lucy Boston as Green Knowe this is reputedly the oldest continuously inhabited house in the country. It contains Lucy Boston's patchworks. The garden has old roses and topiary.

Open: All year by appointment.
Admission: £3 adults £1.50 children or £1.50 adults and £1 children to garden only.

OLIVER CROMWELL'S HOUSE
29 Mary Street, Ely CB7 4HF
Telephone: (01353) 665555 ext 294
Fax: (01353) 668518

Oliver Cromwell and his family moved here in 1636 and remained in Ely for some ten years. The 13th century house has been beautifully restored and in 1995 the first floor rooms also opened to the public. Period rooms, sets, exhibitions and videos give insight into 17th century domestic life, the fascinating character of Oliver Cromwell and the Fen Drainage story.

Open: 1st Oct to 31st Mar 10 - 5.15 Mon to Sat. 1st Apr-30 Sept 10-6 daily.
Admission: Charge of £2.30 per person, £1.80 concessionary rates. Family ticket £5. Group prices on request. Guides can be booked to show parties around the house.

PECKOVER HOUSE AND GARDEN   🍂 The National Trust
North Brink PE13 1JR map **7** R23 △ ♿
Telephone: (01945) 583463
Location: Centre of Wisbech town on N bank of River Nene (B1441).

PRIOR CRAUDEN'S CHAPEL
(The Bursar, The King's School)
The College, Ely map **7** S23
Telephone: (01353) 662837
Fax: (01353) 662187

Built as a private chapel in 1324/1325 for Prior Crauden, the Prior of the Mediaeval Benedictine Monastery from 1321 to 1341. Recently restored to show glimpses of coloured walls, painted glass and wall paintings.

Location: In the precincts of Ely Cathedral.
Station(s): Ely 5 mins walk.
Open: Mon-Fri 9-5 excluding statutory and Bank Hols. Key available from Chapter Office in Firmary Lane.
Admission: Free.
Parking in Cathedral Car Park. Not suitable for disabled visitors.

UNIVERSITY BOTANIC GARDEN
(University of Cambridge)
Cory Lodge, Bateman Street, Cambridge CB2 1JF map **5** S23 ♿
Telephone: (01223) 336265
Fax: (01223) 336278

Owned by the University of Cambridge. Laid out by Henslow in 1846. Forty acres of outstanding gardens with lake, glasshouses, winter garden, chronological bed and other special features. Incorporates nine National Collections, including Geranium and Fritillaria.

Location: 1½ m south of Cambridge centre. Entrance on Bateman Street.
Station(s): Cambridge Railway Station ½ m (Bateman Street entrance).
Open: Open all year except Christmas Day and Boxing Day 10-6 (summer) 10-5 (autumn & spring) 10-4 (winter).
Admission: Charged weekends and Bank Hols throughout the year and weekdays Mar 1-Oct 31. All parties must be pre-booked. Pre-booked school parties and registered disabled people free. No reductions for parties.
Refreshments: Tea-room and gift shop in Gilmour Building; picnic area.
No dogs except guide dogs for the visually impaired. All parties must pre-book. Guided tours by the Friends of the Garden available by arrangement.

WIMPOLE HALL   🍂 The National Trust
Arrington SG8 0BW map **7** S22 ⓢ
Telephone: (01223) 207257
Location: 8 m SW of Cambridge; signposted off A603 at New Wimpole.

Grinling Gibbons (1648-1721)
Sculptor and wood carver. His work can be seen at the following properties included in Historic Houses Castles and Gardens:-

Blenheim Palace   *Lyme Park*
Breamore House   *Petworth House*
Dunham Massey   *Somerleyton Hall*
Fawley Court   *Sudbury Hall*
Kentchurch Court

CHESHIRE

ADLINGTON HALL

(Mrs C.J.C Legh)
Macclesfield   SK10 4LF   map **15** Q18   ♿
Telephone: (01625) 829206
Fax: (01625) 828756

Adlington Hall is a Cheshire Manor and has been the home of the Leghs since 1315. The Great Hall was built between 1450 and 1505, the Elizabethan 'Black and White' in 1581 and the Georgian South Front in 1757. The Bernard Smith Organ was installed c 1670. A 'Shell Cottage', Yew Walk and Lime Avenue are features of the gardens. Recently restored follies include a chinese bridge, Temple to Diana and Tig House.

Location: 5 m N of Macclesfield on the Stockport/Macclesfield Road (A523).
Station(s): Adlington (½ m).
Open: Throughout the year, by prior arrangement only.
Admission: Hall And Gardens Adults £4 Children £1.50 (over 25 people £3.50).
Refreshments: At the Hall.
Events/Exhibitions: Craft Fairs 5 6 May 11 12 Aug 1996.
Gift Shop. Car park free.

ARLEY HALL AND GARDENS

(The Hon Michael and Mrs Flower)
nr Great Budworth and midway between Warrington and Northwich   CW9 6NA   map **15** Q18
Telephone: (01565) 777353
Fax: (01565) 777465

Arley Hall, built about 1840, stands at the centre of an estate which has been owned by the same family for over 500 years. An important example of the early Victorian Jacobean style, it has fine plaster work and oak panelling, a magnificent library, and interesting pictures, furniture and porcelain. There is a private Chapel designed by Anthony Salvin and a fifteenth century cruck barn. The old established gardens overlooking beautiful parkland, and providing great variety of style and design, won the Christies/HHA Garden of the Year Award in 1987. Features include the Double Herbaceous Border established in 1846, a unique avenue of Quercus Ilex clipped to the shape of giant cylinders, a pleached Lime Avenue, fine Yew Hedges, a good collection of Shrub Roses, a Herb Garden and a Woodland Garden which has been developed over the last 20 years with an interesting collection of exotic trees and shrubs including over 200 varieties of Rhododendron.

Location: 5 m N of Northwich; 6 m W of Knutsford; 7 m S of Warrington; 5 m off M6 at junctions 19 & 20; 5 m off M56 at junctions 9 & 10. Nearest main roads A49 and A50.
Open: Apr-Sept incl Tues-Suns & Bank Hol Mons 12-5. Guided Tours and Parties by arrangement. June, July, Aug. 11-5. Hall dates and times may vary.
Admission: GARDENS £3.30 HALL £2.30. C oncessions and group bookings.
Refreshments: Lunches and light refreshments in converted Tudor barn.
Events/Exhibitions: Antique fairs, Garden Design Show Craft Show Firework & Laser Concert etc.
Conferences: Facilities available. Corporate activities, Product Launches, Filming, weddings, Themed Events, Countryside Days etc.
Shop and Plant Nursery. Woodland Walk. Facilities for disabled. Dogs allowed in gardens on leads. Picnic area.

BEESTON CASTLE

ENGLISH HERITAGE

map **6** Q17
Telephone: (01829) 260464

Built on an isolated crag, Beeston Castle is visible for miles around. The view across the Cheshire plain extends to the Pennines in the east and westwards to Wales. Begun about 1220 by Ranulf de Blundeville, the castle was further fortified by Edward I. The ditch alone can have been no small task, as it is hewn from the solid rock. There is an exhibition on the history of the castle in the museum.

Location: 2 m (3.2 km) west of Bunbury. 11m (18 km) south east of Chester.
Open: Apr 1-Sept 30 10-6 daily Oct 1-Mar 31 10-4 daily.
Admission: Adults £2.30 concessions £1.70 children £1.20.

Sir Edwin Landseer Lutyens Architect

His work can be seen at the following properties included in Historic Houses Castles and Gardens:-

Castle Drogo
Goddards
Great Dixter
Great Maytham Hall
Hestercombe House and Gardens
Knebworth
Lindisfarne Castle

BRAMALL HALL

(Stockport Metropolitan Borough Council)
Bramall   SK7 3NX
Telephone: 0161-485 3708
Fax: 0161-486 6959

This magical Tudor Manor House is set in 70 acres of parkland, with lakes, woods and gardens. The House contains 16c wall paintings, Elizabethan fine plaster ceilins, Victorian kitchens and Servant's quarters. Excellent Stables Tea Room and Gift Shop.

Location: 4 m S of Stockport off the A5102.
Station(s): Cheadle Hulme.
Open: Good Fri-Sept 30, Mon-Sat 1-5. Sun 11-5. Oct 1-Jan 1. Tues-Sat 1-4. Sun 11-4. (Closed Christmas Day & Boxing Day). Jan 2-Apr 4, Sat & Sun 12 noon-4. Parties by arrangement including out of hours bookings.
Admission: Adults £2.95 child/senior citizen £2.
Refreshments: In the Stables Tea Room.
Events/Exhibitions: Full events programme.
Conferences: Available for civil marriages and corporate entertaining.

CAPESTHORNE

(Mr and Mrs William Bromley-Davenport)
Macclesfield   SK11 9JY   map **6** Q17
Telephone: (01625) 861221
Fax: (O625) 861619

Capesthorne has been the home of the Bromley-Davenport family and their ancestors the Capesthornes and Wards since Domesday times. The family were originally Chief Foresters responsible for the law and order in the King's Forests of Macclesfield and Leek. The family crest, a felon's head with a halter of gold around his neck, denoted the power of life and death without trial or appeal. Later members of this same family were to serve as Speakers to the House of Commons and in the last and present centuries, as Members of Parliament. Recent research has revealed that Francis and William Smith of Warwick were almost certainly the original architects of this Jacobean style house built in 1722. Later alterations were made by Blore and Salvin. Pictures, furniture, Capesthorne collection of vases, family muniments and Americana. The extensive grounds include an arboretum, nature trail and delightful woodland walk. Other amenities include a Touring Caravan Park, fishing and souvenir shop. Capesthorne is available for Corporate entertaining and a brochure outlining the many advantages of using the hall and grounds is available on request. Enquiries to: Administrator, Capesthorne Hall, Macclesfield, Cheshire SK11 9JY. Telephone: Hall (01625) 861221 Caravan Park (01625) 861779. Fax: (01625) 861619.

Location: 7 m S of Wilmslow, on Manchester/London Road (A34); 6½ m N of Congleton, Junction 18 (M6).
Station(s): Chelford (3 m).
Open: PARK, GARDENS AND CHAPEL 12-6 HALL 1.30-3.30. March through to Oct: Wed & Sun. *Open* All Bank Hols (except xmas and new year). Caravan Park open Mar-Oct inc. We strongly advise that you telephone to check details.
Admission: PARK, GARDENS & CHAPEL £2.25 Chd (5-16 years) £1 OAPs £2. PARK, GARDENS, CHAPEL & HALL £4 OAPs £3.50 Chd £1.50 Budget Family ticket £8.50 Visitors £2.50 Chd £1 at the desk in the Hall entrance. Chd under 5 years accompanied by an adult free. Organised parties are welcome on any open day by appointment (please send for booking form and brochure). Special reductions for parties of 25 or more at £3 per person to Hall, Park, Gardens & Chapel. Evening parties are also welcome by appointment. Evening party rate £3.50 per person, Chd £1 minimum number 25. Guided tours from 50p.
Refreshments: Bromley Rooms.
Coach and Car Park free. Dogs (exempt from government control regulations) are permitted in the Park area only.

CHOLMONDELEY CASTLE GARDENS

(The Marchioness of Cholmondeley)
Malpas   SY14 8AH   map 6 Q17
Telephone: (01829) 720383

Extensive pleasure gardens dominated by romantic Gothic Castle built in 1801 of local sandstone. Imaginatively laid out with fine trees and water gardens, it has been extensively replanted from the 1960's with rhododendrons, azaleas, cornus, acer and many other acid loving plants. As well as the beautiful water garden, there is a rose and lavender garden and herbaceous borders. Lakeside picnic area, rare breeds of farm animals including Llamas. Ancient private chapel in park.
Location: Off A41 Chester/Whitchurch Road and A49 Whitchurch/Tarporley Road.
Station(s): Crewe.
Open: Gardens & Farm only Good Fri & Easter Sun Apr 7-Sept 29. Suns and Bank Hol Mons 12-5.30. Wed and Thurs 12-5. Other days by prior arrangement. Enquiries to: The Secretary, Cholmondeley Castle, Malpas, Cheshire. (House not open to public.)
Admission: Adults £2.50 OAPs £2 children 75p. Other days for coach parties of 25 and over by prior arrangement at reduced rates.
Refreshments: Excellent tea-room open for light lunches.
Gift Shop. Plants for sale.

DORFOLD HALL

(R.C. Roundell, Esq)
Nantwich   CW5 8LD   map 6 Q17 △
Telephone: (01270) 625245
Fax: (01270) 628723

Jacobean country house built 1616. Beautiful plaster ceilings and panelling. Interesting furniture and pictures. Attractive gardens including spectacular sprng garden and newly planted herbaceous borders (1991). Guided tours.
Location: 1 m W of Nantwich on A534 Nantwich/Wrexham Road.
Station(s): Nantwich (1½ m).
Open: Apr-Oct Tues & Bank Hol Mons 2-5. At other times by appointment only.
Admission: Adults £3 children £2.

> ## *Sir Christopher Wren - architect*
> ## *(1632-1723)*
>
> *Fawley Court*
> *Old Royal Observatory*
> *Winslow Hall*

DUNHAM MASSEY   🌿 The National Trust

Altrincham   WA14 4SJ   map 15 Q18
Telephone: 0161-941 1025
Fax: 0161-929 7508

Fine 18th century house with Georgian and Edwardian interiors. Outstanding collection of furniture, paintings and Huguenot silver. Large garden, extensively replanted with shade-loving and waterside plants, with attractive woodland. Deer park and water mill.

Location: 3 m SW of Altrincham off A56; junction 19 off M6; junction 7 off M56.
Station(s): Altrincham 3 m Hale 3 m.
Open: 30 Mar-27 Oct. House Sat-Wed 12-5 last audio tour 4 last adm 4.30. Garden 30 Mar-27 Oct daily 11-5.30. Outside normal hours guided tours of house by arrangement at an extra charge. Shop daily throughout the year 12-5 (or dusk if earlier) closed 23 Dec-3 Jan. Park open until 7.30pm or dusk if earlier.
Admission: House and Garden incl free audio tour £4.50 children £2. House only incl free audio tour £3 children £1.50. Garden only £2.50 children £1. Family ticket incl audio tour £11.
Refreshments: Licensed, self-service restaurant on first floor with wide variety of lunches and teas: vegetarian choice. Open daily throughout the year, 11-5 or dusk if earlier, closed 23 Dec-3 Jan 1997. Reduced menu weekdays Nov-Mar. Seating for 120. Functions and parties welcome by arrangement. The Piers Davenport Room available for booked parties. All enquiries Tel 0161-941 2815.
Events/Exhibitions: For details of concerts, walks and other events send sae.
Conferences: Please contact the Administrative Assistant.
Dogs in park only on lead. Wheelchairs provided: access to shop, garden and park. Limited access to house. Information from the Property Manager, Dunham Massey Hall, Altrincham, Cheshire. WA14 4SJ.

GAWSWORTH HALL

(Mr & Mrs Timothy Richards)
Macclesfield   SK11 9RN   map 6 Q18
Telephone: (01260) 223456
Fax: (01260) 223469

Tudor half-timbered manor house with tilting ground. Former home of Mary Fitton, Maid of Honour at the Court of Queen Elizabeth I, and the supposed 'Dark Lady' of Shakespeare's sonnets. Pictures, sculpture and furniture. Open air theatre with covered grandstand - June/July/August. Situated half-way between Macclesfield and Congleton in an idyllic setting close to the lovely medieval church. Open Air Theatre: Shakespeare's Twelfth Night - 20th June-30th June, Gilbert & Sullivan - 4th July-13th July, Heroic Brass Band Evenings - 25-27th July, Plays - 17-21st July and 31st July-3 Aug. Also various concerts up to 11th Aug. Telephone or fax for details.
Location: 3 m S of Macclesfield on the A536 (Congleton/Macclesfield Road).
Station(s): Macclesfield.
Open: 30th Mar-6th Oct daily 2-5.30. Evening parties by arrangement.
Admission: Adults £3.60 children £1.80. Groups of 20 or more £2.80.
Refreshments: In the Pavilion.
Events/Exhibitions: Craft Fairs Spring and Aug Bank Holidays.

HANDFORTH HALL

(Dr & Mrs J.C. Douglas)
Handforth, nr Wilmslow   SK9 3AE   map **15** Q18

Small 16th century half-timbered manor house.

HARE HILL GARDEN   ❧ The National Trust
Over Alderley, nr Macclesfield   SK10 4QB   map **6** Q18

Walled garden with pergola, rhododendrons and azaleas; parkland.

Location: Between Alderley Edge and Prestbury off B5087 at Greyhound Road. Link path to Alderley Edge 2 m in each direction. Free parking at Alderley Edge.
Station(s): Alderley Edge (3½ m); Prestbury (2½ m).
Open: 3 Apr-31 Oct Wed Thurs Sat Sun and Bank Hol Mons 10-5.30. Special opening for rhododendrons and azaleas May 13-June 2 daily 10-5.30.
Admission: £2.50 Entrance per car £1.50 refundable on entry to the garden. Parties by appointment to the Head Gardener, Garden Lodge, Oak Road, Over Alderley, Macclesfield SK10 4QB. Unsuitable for school parties.
Wheelchair access - some assistance needed. Wheelchair available.

LITTLE MORETON HALL   ❧ The National Trust
Congleton   CW12 4SD   map **6** Q18   &
Telephone: (01260) 272018
Location: 4 m SW of Congleton off Newcastle-under-Lyme/Congleton Road (A34).

LYME PARK   ❧ The National Trust
Disley, Stockport   SK12 2NX   map **15** Q18   △ & Ⓔ
Telephone: (01663) 762023
Fax: (01663) 765035

Legh family home for 600 years. An Elizabethan house survives with C18th and C19th additions. Four centuries of period interior - tapestries, carvings, unique English clock collection. Historic gardens with orangery, a lake and 'Dutch' garden. 1,400 acre park, home to red and fallow deer. Exterior featured as 'Pemberley' in BBC's Pride & Prejudice.

Location: Entrance on A6 between Stockport and Buxton.
Station(s): Disley ½ m from Park entrance. Bus: Stockport to Park entrance. Park entrance to Hall 1m.
Open: Park daily Apr-Oct 8-8.30. Nov-Mar 8-6. Gardens 30 Mar-31 Oct 11-5 daily. Nov-Mar 12 noon-4 weekends, closed Dec 23, 24, 30, 31. House 30 Mar-4 Sept, Sat-Wed 1.30-5 last entry 4.30.

Admission: House & Garden £3; children half price; family £7. Garden only £1. Park only £3 per car. (NT members free).
Refreshments: Park Shop Coffee and Gift Shop: Apr-Oct 11-5 daily, Nov-Mar 12 noon-4 weekends and local school holidays. Hall Tea Room and Gift Shop: 30 Mar-4 Sept Sat-Wed 11-5, Sept-Mar Sat and Sun only 11-4. Closed Dec 23,24,30,31.
Dogs under close control in park, no dogs in house or garden. Wheelchairs provided on prior request.

NETHER ALDERLEY MILL   ❧ The National Trust
Congleton Road, Nether Alderley   map **15** Q18
Telephone: (01625) 523012
Location: 1½ m S of Alderley Edge on E side of A34.

NORTON PRIORY MUSEUM
(Norton Priory Museum Trust)
Runcorn   WA7 1SX   & Ⓢ
Telephone: (01928) 569895
The beautiful woodland gardens covering 30 acres with an 18th century award winning walled garden were the setting for the now demolished mansion of Sir Richard Brooke, built on the site of a former Augustinian priory. Excavated remains of the priory, the atmospheric 12th century vaulted undercroft, can be found with displays on the mediaeval priory, and the later houses and gardens in the museum. A collection of contemporary sculpture is sited throughout the grounds.
Location: From M56 (junction 11) turn towards Warrington and follow Norton Priory road signs.
Open: Open daily all year. Apr to Oct - Sats, Suns & Bank Hols 12-6; Mons to Fris 12-5. Nov to Mar - Daily 12-4. Walled Garden open Mar to Oct. *Closed* Dec 24, 25 & 26, Jan 1. Special arrangements for groups.
Admission: Adults £2.60 Concessions £1.40 family ticket £6.95
Shop, including specialist plants, picnic area and easy parking

PECKFORTON CASTLE
(Graybill Ltd)
Stonehouse Lane , Peckforton   CW6 9TN   map **6** Q17
Telephone: (01829) 260930
Fax: (01829) 261230

The only intact medieval style castle in Britain. Location for "Robin Hood" film 1991.

PEOVER HALL
(Randle Brooks)
Over Peover, Knutsford   map **6** Q18

An Elizabethan House dating from 1585. Fine Caroline stables. Mainwaring Chapel. 18th century landscaped park. Large garden with Topiary work, also Walled and Herb gardens.

Location: 4 m S of Knutsford off A50 at Whipping Stocks Inn.
Open: Beginning of May-end of Sept (except Bank Holidays).
Admission: House Stables & Gardens Mons 2.30-4.30 adults £2.50 children £1.50 Stables & Gardens Only Thurs 2-5 adults £1.50 children 50p. Enquiries: J.Stocks (01565) 722656.
Refreshments: Teas in the Stables on Mons.

QUARRY BANK MILL   🦋 The National Trust

(The National Trust & Quarry Bank Mill Trust Ltd)
Styal   map **15** Q18   Ⓢ
Telephone: (01625) 527468
Location: 1½ m N of Wilmslow off B5166. 1 m from M56 exit 5. 10 m S of Manchester
(log: SJ 35835).

RODE HALL

(Sir Richard Baker Wilbraham, Bt)
Scholar Green   map **6** Q18
Telephone: (01270) 873237
Fax: (01270) 882962

18th century country house with Georgian stable block. Later alterations by L. Wyatt and Darcy Braddell.

Location: 5 m SW of Congleton between A34 & A50.
Station(s): Alsager (2¼ m).
Open: Apr 3-Sept 25 Wed and Bank Hols 2-5.
Admission: House, Garden & Kitchen Garden £3.50 Garden & Kitchen Garden £2.
Refreshments: Bleeding Wolf Restaurant, Scholar Green.

STAPELEY WATER GARDENS LTD

London Road, Stapeley, Nantwich   CW5 7LH   map **6** Q17
Telephone: Gdn Centre (01270) 623868; The Palms (01270) 628628

See under Specialist Growers Section.

TABLEY HOUSE COLLECTION

(Victoria University of Manchester)
Tabley House   WA16 0HB   map **6** Q18
Telephone: (01565) 750151
Fax: (01565) 653230

Fine Palladian mansion designed by John Carr of York for the Leicester family. The state rooms show family memorabilia, furniture by Gillow, Bullock and Chippendale, and the first collection of English paintings ever made.

Location: 2 m W of Knutsford, entrance on A5033 (M6 Junction 19, A556).
Open: Apr to end Oct: Thurs, Fri, Sat, Sun and Bank Hols 2-5.(Last entry 4.30). Free car park. Main rooms and the Chapel suitable for the disabled.
Admission: £3.50 Child/Student with card £1.00.
Refreshments: Tea room and shop facilities. ALL ENQUIRIES TO THE ADMINISTRATOR.
Conferences: Civil Wedding Licence.

TATTON PARK
Knutsford   WA16 6QN
Telephone: (01565) 654822

Tatton is England's most complete country estate with an important portfolio of historic buildings, contents, archaeological sites, formal gardens and parkland. The jewel in Tatton's crown is the late Georgian **Mansion** home to the Egerton family paintings, porcelain and furnishings including the largest collection of Gillow furniture in Britain. Maurice the 4th and last Baron Egerton left Tatton to the nation in 1958, but fresh flower arrangements, letters half written and the occasional presence of the Tatton Living History Society portray Tatton's opulent Victorian heyday. In contrast the stark servants workrooms and cellars are reminders of the rigid social hierarchy. To the south and the east of the great house are the 50 acres of **Gardens**, ranked amongst the finest in the country. Filled with fine specimens and unusual features from around the world, the Gardens promise a surprise round every corner, including the newly restored Orangery and Fernery, the famous Japanese Garden, redwoods, unique rhododendrons and azaleas. A Greek monument, Italian Garden and African hut complete the microcosm. Immaculate lawns, colourful borders and a rose garden satisfy enthusiasts of the English horticultural scene. The atmosphere of the **Old Hall** touches all the senses. A guided tour and audio show starts a vivid journey through five centuries when Old Hall was the home of both the mighty and the humble. Farming was the lifeblood of Tatton and little has changed at **Tattondale Home Farm** for 70 years. Cattle, poultry and pigs provide a picture of the past. At the stables, the vital role of the horse is brought to life.800 deer roam the 1000 acre **Parkland** which includes two lakes and a landscape history trail, with boards describing Tatton's history going back to the times of prehistoric man. The needs of the modern visitor are catered for with a new outdoor and sailing centre, adventure playground, gift shop, garden sales area and the Housekeeper's Store where there is a supply of estate and local produce.

Open: SUMMER: 1 Apr-30 Sept and Oct half term. Closed Mon except Park. Park: 10-7 Gardens: 10.30-6. Last adm 5. Mansion & Farm 12-5. Old Hall: weekends 12-5 weekday tours at 3 and 4. WINTER: 1 Oct-31 Mar. Closed Mon. Park 11-5 Gardens 11-4 Farm 12-4 Shops 11.30-4.
Admission: All Attractions: Adult £8 group £6.40 Child £5 group £4. Any two attractions Adult £4 group £3.20 Child £2.50. Mansion, Garden Farm or Old Hall Adult £2.50 group £2 Child £1.50 group £1.50. Park per car £2.50 coaches free. Mansion & Garden only £4. OAP as adult rate. Group - 12 people Children 5-15
Refreshments: Home made food and snacks available in the self service restaurant.
Events/Exhibitions: June 1-2 Classic Car Spectacular tel. 01565 723863, July 27 Halle' Orchestra with Fireworks tel. 01565 654822, Nov 17 (Provisional) Network Q RAC Rally tel. 01565 750260. Please telephone property for full events calender.

WOODHEY CHAPEL
(The Trustees of Woodhey Chapel)
Faddiley, nr Nantwich   map **6Q17**
Telephone: (01270) 74215

'The Chapel in the Fields.' A small private chapel, recently restored, dating from 1699.
Location: 1 m SW of Faddiley off A534 Nantwich/Wrexham Road.
Station(s): Nantwich (4 M)
Open: Apr-Oct Sats & Bank Hol Mons 2-5 at other times by appointment.
Admission: Adults 50p children 25p.

CLEVELAND

THE CASTLE, CASTLE EDEN
Hartlepool

ORMESBY HALL   The National Trust
nr Middlesbrough   map **9** O20   △
Telephone: (01642) 324188
Location: 3 m SE of Middlesbrough.

CORNWALL

ANTONY   The National Trust
Torpoint   PL11 2QA   map **2** W14   △
Telephone: (01752) 812191
Location: 5 m W of Plymouth via Torpoint car ferry. 2 m NW of Torpoint, N of A374.

ANTONY WOODLAND GARDEN
(Carew Pole Garden Trust)
Torpoint, Cornwall   map **2** W14   △
Telephone: (01752) 812364

A woodland garden and natural woods extending to 100 acres in an area designated as one of Outstanding Natural Beauty and a Site of Special Scientific Interest. The Woodland Garden established in the late 18th century with the assistance of Humphry Repton features over 300 types of Camellias and a wide variety of Magnolias, Rhododendrons, Hydrangeas, Azaleas and other flowering shrubs together with many fine species of indigenous and exotic hardwood and softwood trees. Adjoining and contrasting with this long established woodland garden an additional 50 acres of natural woods bordering the River Lynher, featuring a 'Fishful' Pond, many wild flower species and birds make this an area to delight botanists, ornothologists, or those who merely enjoy peaceful woodland walks.

Location: 5 m W of Plymouth via Torpoint Car Ferry. 2 m NW of Torpoint off A374.
Station(s): Plymouth.
Open: Antony Woodland Garden and Woodland Walk Mar 1-Oct 31 Mon-Sat 11-5.30 Sun 11.30-5.30.
Admission: Adults £2 children under 14 free special openings in aid of Charities by arrangement.
Refreshments: Available at adjoining Antony House during its opening times.
Car parking available. No dogs allowed.

BOSVIGO HOUSE (GARDENS)
(Wendy and Michael Perry)
Bosvigo Lane, Truro   TR1 3NH
Telephone: (01872) 75774

A series of enclosed and walled gardens.

CAERHAYS CASTLE GARDENS
St. Austell   PL26 6LY   map **2** W13   △
Telephone: (01872) 501310
Fax: (01872) 501870

Informal 60 acre woodland garden created by J. C. Williams who sponsored plant hunting expeditions to China at the turn of the century. Noted for Camellias, Magnolias and Rhododendrons.

Location: South coast of Cornwall between Mevagissey and Portloe.
Open: House open Mon 25 Mar- Fri 3 May. Mon-Fri 2-4 excluding Bank Hols. Gardens Mon 18 Mar- Fri 3 May. Mon-Fri 11-4.30. Charity events - gardens only Sun 7 Apr Sun 21 Apr Mon 6 May 11-4.30.

Admission: House Mar 25-May 3 £3 guided tours only. Gardens Mar 18-May 5 adults £2.50 children £1.50. Combined House/Garden admission £5. Charity events adults £1.50 children free (Gardens only).
Refreshments: Tea-room.
Guided Tours by Head Gardener £3.50 (prior booking). Ample free parking at Beach Car park.

COTEHELE   The National Trust
St. Dominick   PL12 6TA   map **2** W14
Telephone: (01579) 50434 Restaurant (01579) 50652
Location: On W bank of the Tamar, 1 m W of Calstock by footpath, (6 m by road). 8 m SW of Tavistock; 14 m from Plymouth via Saltash Bridge.

GLENDURGAN GARDEN   The National Trust
Mawnan Smith   TR11 5JZ   map **2** W12
Telephone: (01326) 250906 (Opening hours only)
Location: 4 m SW of Falmouth ½ m SW of Mawnan Smith on road to Helford Passage.

GODOLPHIN HOUSE
(Mrs. Schofield)
Helston   TR13 9RE   map **2** W12
Telephone: (01736) 762409

A Former home of the Earls of Godolphin and the birthplace of Queen Anne's famous Lord High Treasurer - Sidney, first Earl of Godolphin. Parts of the house are of early Tudor date and additions were made in Elizabethan and Carolean times. The unique front was completed shortly before the Civil War and rests on massive columns of local granite. The fine 'Kings Room' is traditionally said to have been occupied by Charles II (then Prince of Wales) at the time of his escape from Pendennis Castle to the Scilly Islands. Pictures include 'The Godolphin Arabian' by John Wootton. Display of Farm Waggons and Reproduction maps, prints and documents. Five acres of recently identified 17th century gardens, undergoing clearance, £1.

Location: 5 m NW of Helston; between villages of Townshend and Godolphin Cross.
Open: Bank Hol Mons May & June Thurs 2-5. July & Sept Tues 2-5 Thurs 2-5 Aug Tues 2-5 Thurs 10-1 2-5.
Admission: £3 Children 50p and £1. Open at other times for pre-booked parties.
Plants and old roses for sale.

LANHYDROCK   The National Trust
nr Bodmin   PL30 5AD   map **2** W13   &
Telephone: (01208) 73320 Restaurant (01208) 74331
Location: 2½ m SE of Bodmin on Bodmin/Lostwithiel Road (B3268).

LONG CROSS VICTORIAN GARDENS
(D.J. Crawford)
Long Cross Victorian Hotel & Gardens, Trelights   map **2** V13
Telephone: (01208) 880243

A late Victorian garden constructed in a maze layout to provide shelter for the borders. The only public garden on the N. Cornwall Coast and is a demonstration of what can be achieved on the coast with salt wind problems. The garden incorporates many granite and water features, as well as a pets corner. Many plants found in the garden can be purchased.

Station(s): Bus service from Wadebridge.
Open: 10.30 until dusk all year.
Admission: Adult £1.25. Children 25p.
Accommodation: 10 spacious ensuite rooms many with panoramic views of the garden and coastline. Bargain Gardeners breaks in Spring/Autumn
The gardens contain a Free House Tavern with an exceptional Beer/Tea Garden.

MOUNT EDGCUMBE HOUSE & PARK
(City of Plymouth & Cornwall County Council)
Cremyll, Nr. Plymouth   PL10 1HZ   map **2** W14
Telephone: (01752) 822236
Fax: (01752) 822199

Mount Edgcumbe House, a Tudor mansion restored (after 1941 bombing) by the architect Adrian Gilbert Scott, was the home of the Mount Edgcumbe family for 400 years. The house and furniture have been refurbished to reflect the 18th century. Stretching along 10 miles of spectacular coastline from Plymouth to Whitsand Bay the park contains one of only three Grade I listed gardens in Cornwall. The garden was designed 240 years ago with views, woodland walks, follies, garden buildings and includes formal gardens in English, French and Italian styles and now has New Zealand and American plantations. It holds the National Camellia Collection. In the park are ancient trees, wild fallow deer, and fortifications of Iron age, Tudor and Victorian date.

Location: On Rame Peninsula, 12 m from Torpoint, Cornwall, or by Cremyll (pedestrian) Ferry from Plymouth (Stonehouse) to Park entrance.
Station(s): Plymouth; Liskeard.
Open: Park including Landscaped Park and Formal Gardens open every day all year round Free. House and Earls Garden open Apr 3-Oct 27 11-5 Wed-Sun and Bank Hol Mons.
Admission: Adults £3.50 children £1.70 concessions £2.50 family (2+2) £8 season ticket £6.50. Group rate £3 per head.
Refreshments: Lunches, teas and light refreshments available in the Orangery Restaurant/Cafe, Apr 1 to Oct 31 daily. Cedar Tearoom in the house during opening hours. Reservations and enquiries telephone Plymouth (01752) 822586.
Events/Exhibitions: Mar 16/17 Camellia Show; June 21-23 Floral Celebration; Aug 13-14 Open Air Theatre Sept 7-8 Wood Fair.
Visitor Centre and Shop selling guides and souvenirs open Apr 1 to Oct 31 every day. Gifts produced in Devon and Cornwall a speciality.

Robert Adam - architect

His work can be seen at the following properties included in Historic Houses Castles and Gardens:-

Audley End   *Mellerstain*
Bowood House & Gardens   *Moccas Court*
Culzean Castle   *Newby Hall & Gardens*
Hatchlands Park   *Nostell Priory*
Kedleston Hall   *Osterley Park*
Kenwood, The Iveagh Bequest   *Papplewick Hall*
Killerton   *Saltram House*
Kimbolton Castle   *Syon House*
Luton Hoo

PENCARROW

(The Molesworth - St Aubyn Family)

Bodmin map **2** V13 △ ♿

Telephone: (01208) 84369

Georgian house and listed gardens, still owned and lived in by the family. A superb collection of 18th century pictures, furniture and porcelain. Mile long drive and Ancient British Encampment. Marked walks through beautiful woodland gardens, past the great granite Victorian Rockery, Italian and American gardens, Lake and Ice House. Approx 50 acres in all. Over 600 different species and hybrid rhododendrons and also an internationally known specimen conifer collection.

Location: 4 m NW of Bodmin off A389 & B3266 at Washaway.

Open: House Tea-rooms and Craft Centre Easter-Oct 15 every day (except Fri and Sat) 1.30-5 (Bank Hol Mon and from 1 June-10 Sept 11am-). Gardens open daily.

Admission: House and Gardens adults £3.80 children £1.80 Gardens Only adults £1.50 children free. Coaches £3 (1995 prices) Guided tours.

Refreshments: Light lunches and cream teas.

Car park and toilet facilities for disabled. Dogs very welcome in grounds. Plant shop. Picnic area. Small children's play area, and pets corner. Self pick soft fruit in season.

PENDENNIS CASTLE

ENGLISH HERITAGE

Falmouth map **2** W12

Telephone: (01326) 316594

Henry VIII's reply to the Pope's crusade against him was to fortify his coastline. Two castles guarded the Fal Estuary, Pendennis and St Mawes. Built high on a promontory, Pendennis saw action in the Civil War when 'Jack-for-the-King' Arundell held the castle for five terrible months. It continued in military use until 1946. 1588 Gundeck tableau, exhibition, views and refreshments.

Location: Pendennis Head 1 m (1⅔ km) south east of Falmouth.

Open: Apr 1-Sept 30 10-6 daily Oct 1-Mar 31 10-4 daily.

Admission: Adults £2.50 concessions £1.90 children £1.30.

PRIDEAUX PLACE

(The Prideaux-Brune Family)

Padstow PL28 8RP map **2** V13

Telephone: (01841) 532411 and 532945

An Elizabethan Mansion set in extensive grounds above the fishing port of Padstow.

ST. MAWES CASTLE

ENGLISH HERITAGE

map **2** W12

Telephone: (01326) 270526

Shaped like a clover leaf, this small 16th century castle, still intact, nestles among rock plants and tropical shrubs. During the Civil War the Governor capitulated without gunfire or bloodshed, unlike Pendennis on the opposite shore.

Location: St Mawes.

Open: Apr 1-Sept 30 10-6 daily Oct 1-31 10-4 daily Nov 1-Mar 31 Wed-Sun 10-4.

Admission: Adults £2 concessions £1.50 children £1.

ST. MICHAEL'S MOUNT

The National Trust

Marazion, nr Penzance TR17 OHT map **2** W12

Telephone: (01736) 710507

Location: ½ m from the shore at Marazion (A394), connected by causeway. 3 m E Penzance.

TINTAGEL CASTLE

ENGLISH HERITAGE

map **2** V13

Telephone: (01840) 770328

Amazing that anything has survived on this wild, windswept coast. Yet fragments of Earl Reginald's great hall, built about 1145, and Earl Richard's 13th century wall and iron gate still stand in this incomparable landscape. No wonder that King Arthur and his Knights were thought to have dwelt here. Site exhibition.

Location: ½ m (0.8 km) north west of Tintagel.

Open: Apr 1-Sept 30 10-6 daily Oct 1-Mar 31 daily 10-4.

Admission: Adults £2.80 concessions £1.90 children £1.30.

TINTAGEL - THE OLD POST OFFICE

The National Trust

Tintagel PL34 ODB map **2** V13 ♿

Telephone: (01840) 770024 (opening hours only)

Location: Nos 3 & 4 in the centre of Tintagel.

TREGREHAN

(Mr T.C. Hudson)

Par PL24 25J map **2** W13

Telephone: (01726) 814389 or (01726) 812438

Woodland garden created since early 19th century by Carlyon family concentrating on species from warm-temperate regions. Fine glasshouse range in walled garden. Small nursery, also open by appointment, specialising in wild source material, and camellias bred by the late owner.

Location: 2 m E of St Austell on A390. 1 m W of St. Blazey on A390.

Station(s): Par.

Open: Mid Mar-end of June and Sept 10.30-5 closed Easter Sun.

Admission: Adults £2.50 children free. Guided tours for parties by prior arrangement.

Refreshments: Teas available.

Accommodation: Self catering cottages available.

Parking for cars and coaches. Access for disabled to half garden only. No dogs.

TRELISSICK GARDEN

The National Trust

nr Truro TR3 6QL map **2** W12 ♿

Telephone: (01872) 862090; Restaurant (01872) 863486

Location: 5 m S of Truro on both sides of B3289 overlooking King Harry Ferry.

TRELOWARREN HOUSE & CHAPEL

(Sir Ferrers Vyvyan, Bt)

Mawgan-in-Meneage, Helston map **2** W12

Telephone: (01326) 221366

Home of the Vyvyan family since 1427 part of the house dates from early Tudor times. The Chapel, part of which is pre-Reformation, and the 17th century part of the house are leased to the Trelowarren Fellowship, an Ecumenical Christian Charity. The Chapel and main rooms containing family portraits are open to the public and Sunday Services are held in the Chapel during the holiday season. Exhibitions of paintings.

Location: 6 m S of Helston off B3293 to St Keverne.

Open: House & Chapel open from Apr 3-Sept 25 Weds & Bank Hol Mons always 2.15-4.30. Organised tours by arrangement.

Admission: Adults £1.50 children 50p (under 12 years free) including entry to various exhibitions of paintings.

Ground floor only suitable for disabled.

TRENGWAINTON GARDEN   🍃 The National Trust
Penzance   TR20 8RZ   map **2** W11   ♿
Telephone: (01736) 63021
Location: 2 m NW of Penzance ½ m W of Heamoor on Morvah Road (B3312).

TRERICE   🍃 The National Trust
nr. Newquay   TR8 4PG   map **2** W12   ♿
Telephone: (01637) 875404; Restaurant (01637) 879434
Location: 3 m SE of Newquay A392 & A3058 (turn right at Kestle Mill).

TREWITHEN HOUSE AND GARDENS
(A.M.J. Galsworthy)
Probus   TR2 4DD   map **2** W13
Telephone: (01726) 882763/882764 (nurseries) (01726) 883794 (garden shop)

'Trewithen' means 'House of the Trees' which truly describes this exceptionally fine early Georgian house in its magnificent setting of wood and parkland. The origins of the house go back to the 17th century but it was the Architect Sir Robert Taylor, aided by Thomas Edwards of Greenwich, who were responsible for the splendid building and interiors we see today. Philip Hawkins bought the property in 1715 and began extensive rebuilding. The house has been lived in and cared for by the same family since that date. The magnificent landscaped gardens have an outstanding collection of magnolias, rhododendron and azaleas which are well known throughout the world. The gardens are particularly spectacular between March and the end of June and again in Autumn, although there is much to see throughout the year. A wide variety of shrubs and plants from the famous nurseries are always on sale. Other attractions include a children's playground and a 25-minute video of the house and gardens. The gardens are one of only two in this county to be awarded 3 stars by the Michelin Guide to the South West.

Location: On A390 between Probus and Grampound, adjoining County Demonstration Gardens.
Open: GARDENS: Open Mar 1-Sept 30 Mon-Sat 10-4.30. Sun Apr-May only. Nurseries: Open throughout the year Mon-Sat 9-4.30.
Admission: Gardens:Adults £2.80 Group adult (over 12) £2.50 children (under 15) £1.50. HOUSE: Guided tours Mon and Tues only Apr-July and Aug Bank Hol Mon (2-4) £3.20 children (under 15) £1.50. Parties by arrangement please.
Refreshments: Tea shop for light refreshments.

CUMBRIA

ABBOT HALL ART GALLERY & MUSEUM OF LAKELAND LIFE & INDUSTRY
(Lake District Art Gallery & Museum Trust)
Kirkland, Kendal   LA9 5AL   map **9** O17   ♿
Telephone: (01539) 722464

Impressive Georgian House.

ACORN BANK GARDEN   🍃 The National Trust
Temple Sowerby, Penrith   map **9** N17
Telephone: (017683) 61893
Location: Just N of Temple Sowerby, 6 m E of Penrith on A66.

BRANTWOOD
(Brantwood Educational Trust)
Coniston   LA21 8AD   map **9** O16
Telephone: (015394) 41396

The most beautifully situated house in the Lake District with the best lake and mountain views in England.

CARLISLE CASTLE
Carlisle   map **9** N17
Telephone: (01228) 591922

ENGLISH HERITAGE

Twenty-six years after the Battle of Hastings. Carlisle remained unconquered. In 1092 William II marched north, took the city and ordered the building of a stronghold above the River Eden. Since William's time the castle has survived 800 years of fierce and bloody attacks, extensive rebuilding and continuous military occupation. A massive Norman keep contains an exhibition on the history of the castle. D'Ireby Tower now open to the public, containing furnishings to authentic medieval design, an exhibition and shop. Guided tours are given by a local group of volunteers.

Location: North of town centre.
Open: Apr 1-Sept 30 daily 9.30-6, Oct 1-Mar 31 daily 10-4.
Admission: Adults £2.50 concessions £1.90 children £1.30.

CASTLETOWN HOUSE
(Giles Mounsey-Heysham, Esq)
Rockcliffe, Carlisle   CA6 4BN   map **9** N17
Telephone: (01228) 74792
Fax: (01228) 74464

Georgian House set in attractive gardens and grounds.

Location: 5 m NW of Carlisle on Solway coast, 1 m W of Rockcliffe village and 2 m W of A74.
Open: HOUSE ONLY by appointment only.

Gertrude Jekyll
writer and gardener
(1843-1932)

Her designs were used at the following properties included in Historic Houses Castles and Gardens:-

> *Barrington Court*
> *Castle Drogo*
> *Goddards*
> *Hatchlands Park*
> *Hestercombe House and*
> *Gardens*
> *Knebworth*
> *Lindisfarne Castle*

A collection of her tools can be found at Guildford Museum

CONISHEAD PRIORY
Ulverston   LA12 9QQ
Telephone: (01229) 584029

Victorian Gothic mansion, under restoration, on 12th century site.

DALEMAIN
(Robert Hasell-McCosh Esq)
nr Penrith   CA11 0HB   map **9** N16
Telephone: (017684) 86450
Fax: (017684) 86223

Mediaeval, Tudor and Georgian house and gardens occupied by the same family for over 300 years. Interesting garden as featured on TV and in various publications. Fine furniture and portraits. Countryside and Agricultural Museum, Westmorland and Cumberland Yeomanry Museum. Fell Pony Museum. Plant Centre, gift shop, picnic area, ample parking.

Location: 3 m from Penrith on A592. Turn off M6 exit 40 onto A66 (A592) to Ullswater.
Station(s): Penrith.
Open: 31 Mar-6 Oct daily 11-5.15 except Fri and Sat.
Admission: Charged. Entry to car park and picnic area, shop, and restaurant free.
Refreshments: Licensed Restaurant. Coffee from 11.15. Lunches 12-2.30. Home made teas from 2.30. High teas by arrangement.
Events/Exhibitions: Rainbow Craft Fair July 20th and 21st.
Accommodation: Bed & breakfast, Parkhouse Farm, Dalemain Telephone (017684) 86212.
Conferences: Group visits by arrangement with the Administrator, Mr B McDonald.
Old fashioned Rose Collection on view, and for sale in conjunction with Stydd Nurseries. No dogs please. Pleasant country walk to Dacre Church where there is a fine Laurence Whistler window.

DOVE COTTAGE & THE WORDSWORTH MUSEUM
(The Wordsworth Trust)
Grasmere   LA22 9SH   △ Ⓔ Ⓢ
Telephone: (015394) 35544

Dove Cottage, Wordsworth's home 1799-1808. Visitors are offered guided tours. The garden is oen weather permitting. The award winning Wordsworth Museum houses permanent exhibition and a programme of special exhibitions.

Location: On A591 Kendal-Keswick Road next to Dove Cottage Tea shop.
Station(s): Windermere, bus service 518,555,556,557.
Open: 9.30-5.30. Closed Jan 9-Feb 5 & Dec 24-26 1995.
Admission: Adults £4 children £2 special rates for families & groups - family ticket (1 adult & 1-3 children) £6 (2 adults and 1-3 children) £10 and group rate adults £3.10.
Refreshments: Dove Cottage Tea-rooms serve meals and snacks throughout the day. Groups should book in advance, tea-rooms can take group bookings (pre-arranged) (015394) 35268

HOLKER HALL AND GARDENS
(Lord and Lady Cavendish)
Cark-in-Cartmel, nr Grange-over-Sands   LA11 7PL   map **6** O11   △ ♿ Ⓔ Ⓢ
Telephone: (015395) 58328
Fax: (015395) 58776

Cumbria's premier Stately home has 25 acres of National Award winning gardens with water features, rare plants and shrubs, 'World Class...not to be missed by foreign visitors' (Good Gardens Guide '95). Also exhibitions, Deer Park, Adventure Playground, Motor Museum. Home of the spectacular Great Garden and Countryside Festival held first weekend in June annually. (Show Office (015395) 58838).

Location: ½ m N of Cark-in-Cartmel on B5278 from Haverthwaite; 4 m W Grange-over-Sands.
Station(s): Cark-in-Cartmel.
Open: Apr 1-Oct 31 everyday excluding Sat 10-6 last admissions 4.30.
Admission: ('95) from £3 reduction for groups of 20 or more.
Refreshments: Home made cakes, sandwiches, salads in the Clock Tower Cafe.
Events/Exhibitions: Hawk events. The Great Garden & Countryside Festival May 31, 1/2nd June.
Dogs on leads in Grounds only. Free parking.

HUTTON-IN-THE-FOREST
(Lord and Lady Inglewood)
Penrith map **9** N17
Telephone: (017684) 84449
Fax: (017684) 84571

One of the ancient manors in the Forest of Inglewood, and the home of Lord Inglewood's family since the beginning of the 17th century. Built around a medieval pele tower with 17th, 18th and 19th century additions. Fine English furniture and pictures, ceramics and tapestries. The outstanding gardens and grounds include a lovely walled garden established in 1730 which has an ever increasing collection of herbaceous plants against a backdrop of wall trained fruit trees and topiary. Also terraces, dovecote, lake and woodland walk through magnificent specimen trees.

Location: 7 m NW of Penrith on B5305 Wigton Road (3 m from M6 exit 41).
Station(s): Penrith.
Open: House 1-4pm Easter 7-11 Apr. Thurs, Fri and Sun from May 2-Sept 29 with Bank Holiday Mons and Aug Weds. Gardens 11-5 every day except Sat. Private groups by arrangement from Apr 1.
Admission: House & gardens adults £3.50 children £1.50 family £9. Gardens only adults £1.50 children free.
Refreshments: Home-made light lunches & teas in Cloisters tea-room when house is open. Group catering by arrangement.

19/20 IRISH STREET
(Copeland Borough Council)
Whitehaven map **8** N15
Telephone: (01946) 693111 Ext 285

1840-50 Italianate design, possibly by S. Smirke. Stuccoed 3-storey building now occupied by the Council Offices.

Location: In town centre.
Station(s): Whitehaven.
Open: All the year during office hours. For details and appointments telephone Mr J. A. Pomfret.
Refreshments: Hotels and restaurants in town centre.
Ground floor only suitable for disabled.

ISEL HALL
(The Administrator)
Cockermouth, Cumbria   CA13 0QG   map **9** N16   △

Pele Tower with domestic range and gardens set on north bank of River Derwent. The house is small so groups limited to 30.

Location: 3½ miles N.E. of Cockermouth.
Station(s): Aspatria 9 miles; Penrith 32 miles.
Open: Mondays 8 Apr-14 Oct 2-4. Other times by written arrangement.
Admission: £2.50.
No dogs. No photography inside. It is regretted there is no disabled access upstairs.

Butterfly Houses

can be found at the following properties included in Historic Houses Castles and Gardens:-

Berkeley Castle
Elsham Hall - Wild butterfly walkway
Syon House

LEVENS HALL
(C.H. Bagot, Esq)
Kendal, Cumbria   LA8 0PD   map **9** O17   &
Telephone: (015395) 60321

This magnificent Elizabethan home of the Bagot family, with its famous topiary garden (c.1694) is a must for visitors to the Lake District. The garden is unique in age and appearance, beautifully maintained in its original design with colourful bedding and herbaceous borders and was a winner of the prestigous HHA/Christie's Garden of the Year Award for 1994. The house contains a superb collection of Jacobean furniture, fine plaster ceilings, panelling, paintings and needlework, including the earliest English patchwork (c.1708). A collection of working model steam engines shows the development of steam power from 1820 to 1920, with full-sized traction engines in steam on Sundays and Bank Holiday Mondays.

Location: 5 m S of Kendal on the Milnthorpe Road (A6); Exit 36 from M6.
Station(s): Oxenholme.
Open: Apr 1-Sept 30 House, Garden, Gift Shop, Tea-rooms, Plant Centre, Play Area and Picnic Area Sun Mon Tues Wed & Thurs 11-5; House open from noon Mon-Thurs. Steam Collection 2-5 closed Fri & Sat.
Admission: Charge. Group rates for 20 or more.
Refreshments: Home-made light Lunches and teas.
Regret house not suitable for wheelchairs.

MIREHOUSE
(Mr & Mrs Spedding)
Keswick   CA12 4QE   map **9** N16   &
Telephone: (017687) 72287
Fax: (017687) 72287

First built in 1666 Mirehouse was last sold in 1688 and remains a private family home: an unusually literary house with an interesting picture collection and live classical music. The grounds stretch to Bassenthwaite Lake. French, German and Spanish spoken. Children welcome.

Location: 3½ m N of Keswick on A591. Regular Stagecoach bus service.
Open: Apr-Oct. Grounds and adventure playgrounds daily 10.00-5.30. House Sun Wed (also Fri in Aug) 2-last entries 4.30. Parties welcome at other times by appointment.
Refreshments: Old Sawmill Tearoom specialises in generous Cumbrian home-cooking. Parties please book. (017687) 74317
Conferences: A small hall is available for wedding parties which opens into the Rose Garden which has a covered victorian collonade.

MUNCASTER CASTLE
(Mrs P. Gordon-Duff-Pennington)
Ravenglass   CA18 1RQ   map **9** O16   △ &
Telephone: (01229) 717614
Fax: (01229) 717010

Home of the Pennington family from 1208 to the present day. The Pele Tower stands on Roman foundations. Set in superb gardens with magnificent views of the Lakeland Fells. Owl Centre with daily talk and flying display.

Open: Gardens and Owl Centre daily all year. Castle 24 Mar-3 Nov Tues-Sun 1-4 (last entry) plus all Bank Holidays.
Admission: Rates available on request. Party rates available.
Refreshments: Stable Buttery serves light refreshments to full meals 11am to 5pm and is licensed.
Cafeteria, Gift Shops, Plant Centre, Children's Play Area, Nature Trail, Free Parking.

NAWORTH CASTLE

(Philip Howard)
Brampton Castle, Brampton   CA8 2HE   map 9 O17
Telephone: (016977) 3229
Fax: (016977) 3679

Naworth Castle is a historic Border fortress, built by the Dacre family in 1335. Originally a stronghold for the wardens of the West March and subsequently an impressive residence for the powerful Earls of Carlisle. Now owned by Philip Howard. Much pre-Raphaelite restoration by Philip Webb and Burne-Jones following the 1844 fire. Dungeons and 17th century walled garden. Rooms include the Great Hall, 100ft in length with Gobelin Tapestries and four healdic Beasts, the Philip Webb Library for conferences, lectures and corporate functions. The Drawing Room for dining parties up to 50. The Old Library with a Marriage Licence and corporate function use. The Long Gallery for art exhibitions and Lord Williams Tower with a Bridal Suite, Old Library and Chapel. The Castle is in its second year of being a functions venue. We pride ourselves on being able to offer an exceptional standard of service. Guided tours available from 15-100 people.

Location: ½ m off main A69 Carlisle-Newcastle road. Carlisle 12 m. Newcastle 46 m. M6 is 9 m.
Station(s): Carlisle, Brampton junction 2 m.
Open: Throughout the year by appointment. Groups only: minimum party size 15 people.
Events/Exhibitions: Recitals and concerts, charity events, antique sales and fairs.
Accommodation: There are 10 bedrooms available for overnight parties.
Conferences: Conferences, fashion shoots, charity balls, dinners and dances. Game and clay pigeon shooting and fishing and horse riding. The Great Hall seats up to 200. Licenced for Civil Marriage Ceremonies. There is an excellent retained caterer available.
Up to 40 cars in the car park and 10 acres of field available.

RYDAL MOUNT

(The Trustees of Rydal Mount)
Ambleside   LA22 9LU   map 9 O17
Telephone: (015394) 33002

Wordsworth home from 1813-1850. Family portraits and furniture, many of the poet's personal possessions, and first editions of his works. The garden which was designed by Wordsworth has been described as one of the most interesting gardens to be found anywhere in England. Two long terraces, many rare trees and shrubs. Extends to 4½ acres.

Location: Off A591, 1½ m from Ambleside, 2 m from Grasmere.
Station(s): Windermere
Open: Mar 1-Oct 31 daily 9.30-5 Nov 1-Mar 1 10-4 (closed Tues in winter). Evening groups by arrangement with curators: Mr & Mrs P. Elkington.
Admission: House & Gardens £3 children £1 parties £2.50. Reciprocal discounts with Dove Cottage and Wordsworth House.

SIZERGH CASTLE AND GARDEN   🍂 The National Trust
Sizergh, Kendal   LA8 8AE   map 9 O17
Telephone: (015395) 60070
Location: 3½ m S of Kendal NW of interchange A590/A591 interchange; 2 m from Levens Hall.

TOWNEND   🍂 The National Trust
Troutbeck   LA23 1LB   map 9 O17
Telephone: (015394) 32628
Location: At S end of Troutbeck village, 3 m SE of Ambleside.

WORDSWORTH HOUSE   🍂 The National Trust
Cockermouth   CA13 9RX   map 9 N16   △
Telephone: (01900) 824805
Location: In Main Street.

DERBYSHIRE

BAKEWELL OLD HOUSE MUSEUM
(Bakewell & District Historical Society)
Bakewell   DE45 1DD   map 4 Q19
Telephone: (01629) 813165

An early Tudor house with original wattle & daub screen and open chamber. Costumes and Victorian kitchen, children's toys, craftsmen's tools and lacework.

Location: Above the church in Bakewell. ¼ m from centre.
Open: House Only Apr 1-Oct 31 daily 2-5 parties in morning or evening by appointment (Telephone Bakewell (01629) 813647).
Admission: 1994 rates £2 children £1.
Events/Exhibitions: Exhibitions- call for details.

CALKE ABBEY AND PARK   🍂 The National Trust
nr Derby   map 4 R20
Telephone: (01332) 863822
Location: 9m S of Derby on A514 at Ticknall between Swadlincote and Melbourne.

Sir Anthony Van Dyck
Portrait and religious painter
Born in Antwerp 1599, died in London 1641
First visited England in 1620, knighted by Charles I in 1633

His work can be seen in the following properties included in Historic Houses Castles and Garden:-

Alnwick Castle
Arundel Castle
Boughton House
Breamore House
Eastnor Castle
Euston Hall
Firle Place
Goodwood House
Holkham Hall
Kingston Lacey
Petworth House
Southside House
Sudeley Castle
Warwick Castle
Weston Park
Wilton House
Woburn Abbey

CHATSWORTH
(Chatsworth House Trust)
Bakewell   DE45 1PP   map **4** Q19
Telephone: (01246) 582204
Fax: (01246) 583536

Built by Talman for 1st Duke of Devonshire between 1687 and 1707. World famous collection of pictures, drawings, books and furniture. Garden with elaborate waterworks surrounded by a 1000 acre park. **House impossible for wheelchairs, but they are most welcome in the garden.**

Location: ½ m E of village of Edensor on A623, 4 m E of Bakewell, 16 m from junction 29, M1. Signposted via Chesterfield.
Open: HOUSE & GARDEN Mar 20-Nov 3 Daily 11-4.30 FARMYARD & ADVENTURE PLAYGROUND Mar 20-29 Sept Daily 10.30-4.30.
Admission: Charges not available at time of going to press.
Refreshments: Licensed self service restaurant. Coach Drivers' Rest Room.
Events/Exhibitions: May 11-12 96 Chatsworht Angling Fair. Aug 31 & 1 Sept Chatsworth Country Fair. International Sheepdog Trials 12-14 Sept.
Gift shops. Baby Room. All details subject to confirmation. Two electric wheelchairs available for use in the Garden only.

Sir John Van Brugh (1664-1726)

Architect. His work can be seen at the following properties included in historic Houses Castles and Gardens:-

Blenheim Palace
Castle Howard
Claremont
Grimsthorpe Castle
Seaton Delaval Hall

EYAM HALL
(R.H.V. Wright)
Eyam   S30 1QW   map **4** Q19   △
Telephone: (01433) 631976
Fax: (01433) 631976

Seventeenth century manor house situated in the famous 'plague village' of Eyam. Built and still occupied by the Wright family. A glimpse of three centuries through the eyes of one family. Great variety of contents, including family portraits, tapestries, clocks, costumes, and toys. Jacobean staircase and spectacular old kitchen.

Location: 100 yds W of church. Eyam is off A623, 12 m W of Chesterfield, 15 m SW of Sheffield.
Open: Sun 31 Mar-Sun 3 Nov, Weds, Thurs, Suns and Bank Hol Mons. Tues for schools only. Opens 11am. Last tour 4.30.
Admission: Adults £3.25 children £2.25 concessions £2.75 family ticket (2 adults + 4 children) £9.50. Advance booking essential for parties, reductions available.
Refreshments: Eyam Hall Buttery: Home-made teas, cakes and light lunches. Open daily except Mons during House opening season plus all Bank Holiday Mons 10.30-5.30. Also open weekends from 2 Mar. Gift shop and Craft Centre open same hours as Buttery.
Eyam Hall may be booked outside normal opening hours for private tours and for exclusive conferences, seminars and a wide range of other small events.

HADDON HALL
(His Grace the Duke of Rutland)
Bakewell   DE45 1LA   map **4** Q19
Telephone: (01629) 812855
Fax: (01629) 814379

One of our few remaining 12th century manor houses, perfectly preserved. Noted for its tapestries, wood carvings and wall paintings. Standing on a wooded hill overlooking the fast flowing River Wye, Haddon is totally unspoiled. The beautiful terraced gardens dating from the middle ages are famous for roses, old fashioned flowers and herbs. Banqueting and clay pigeon facilities available in Hall and Park. The House is extremely difficult for disabled visitors.

Location: 2 m SE Bakewell & 6½ m N of Matlock on Buxton/Matlock Road (A6).
Station(s): Matlock 5 m Chesterfield 11m.
Open: Apr 1-Sept 30 Mon-Sun 11-5.45 closed Sun in July and Aug except Bank Hol weekends.
Admission: Adults £4.50 children £2.80 party rate £3.50 OAPs £3.50 family ticket £12.50 NB: These prices may vary - please ring to check for details.
Refreshments: Morning coffee, lunches, afternoon teas at Stables Restaurant.
Events/Exhibitions: Flower Festival 15-19 May; Craft Show 29-30 June.
Conferences: Functions.

CHATSWORTH, DERBYSHIRE
Home of the Duke and Duchess of Devonshire

HARDWICK HALL 🍂 The National Trust

Nr Chesterfield   map **4** Q20
Telephone: (01246) 850430
Location: 2 m S of Chesterfield/Mansfield Road (A617) 6½ m NW of Mansfield and 9½ m SE of Chesterfield. Approach from M1 exit 29.

KEDLESTON HALL 🍂 The National Trust

Derby   map **4** Q19
Telephone: (01332) 842191
Location: 4 m NW of Derby on Derby/Hulland Road via the Derby Ring Road Queensway.

LEA GARDENS

(Mr & Mrs J. Tye)
Lea, Matlock, Derbyshire   DE4 5GH   map **7** Q19   ♿
Telephone: (01629) 534380.

LOSEHILL HALL

(Peak National Park)
Peak National Park Centre, Castleton   map **15** Q19
Telephone: (01433) 620373
Fax: (01433) 620346

A residential study centre which organises holiday weeks and special interest weekends.

MELBOURNE HALL AND GARDENS

(Lord Ralph Kerr)
Melbourne   DE73 1EN   map **7** R20
Telephone: (01332) 862502
Fax: (01332) 862263

This beautiful house of history is the home of Lord and Lady Ralph Kerr. In its picturesque poolside setting, Melbourne Hall was once the Home of Victorian Prime Minister William Lamb who as 2nd Viscount Melbourne gave his name to the famous city in Australia. This delightful family home contains an important collection of pictures and antique furniture. One of the most famous formal gardens in Britain featuring Robert Bakewell's wrought iron 'Birdcage'.

Location: 9 m S of Derby off the A453 in village of Melbourne.
Station(s): Derby.
Open: HOUSE open every day of Aug only (except first 3 Mons) 2-5. Garden open: Apr to Sept: Weds, Sats, Suns, Bank Hol Mons 2-6.
Admission: Pre-booked parties in House - Aug only.
Refreshments: Melbourne Hall Tearooms - open throughout the year Tel: (0332) 864224/863469. Craft Centre & Gift Shop open at various times throughout the year. Car parking limited - none reserved. Suitable for disabled persons.

PEVERIL CASTLE

ENGLISH HERITAGE

map **15** Q19
Telephone: (01433) 620613

The castle was built to control Peak Forest, where lead had been mined since prehistoric times. William the Conqueror thought so highly of this metal - and of the silver that could be extracted from it - that he entrusted the forest to one of his most esteemed knights, William Peveril.

Location: In Castleton on A625, 15 m west of Sheffield.
Open: Apr 1-Sept 30 10-6 daily Oct 1-Mar 31 daily 10-4, Nov 1-Mar 31 Wed-Sun 10-4.
Admission: Adults £1.50 concessions £1.10 children 80p.

SUDBURY HALL AND NATIONAL TRUST MUSEUM OF CHILDHOOD 🍂 The National Trust

nr Derby   map **4** Q19   Ⓢ
Telephone: (01283) 585305
Location: At Sudbury, 6 m E of Uttoxeter off A50 Road.

WINSTER MARKET HOUSE 🍂 The National Trust

nr Matlock   map **4** Q19
Telephone: (0133 529) 245
Location: 4 m W of Matlock on S side of B5057.

DEVON

A LA RONDE 🍂 The National Trust

Exmouth   EX8 5BD   map **3** V16
Telephone: (01395) 265514
Location: 2 m N of Exmouth on A376.

ARLINGTON COURT 🍂 The National Trust

Barnstaple   map **3** U15   ♿
Telephone: (01271) 850296
Location: 8 m NE of Barnstaple on E side of A39.

AVENUE COTTAGE GARDENS

(R.J. Pitts, Esq, R.C.H. Soans, Esq)
Ashprington, Totnes   TQ9 7UT   map **3** W15
Telephone: (01803) 732 769

11 acres of garden and woodland walks. Part of 18th century landscape garden under going recreation by Designers/Plantsmen.

Location: 3 m SE of Totnes 300 yds beyond Ashprington Church (Sharpham Drive).
Open: Apr 1-Sept 30 Tues-Sat inclusive 11-5. Parties by arrangement.
Admission: Adults £1.50 children 25p. Collecting box.
Refreshments: At Durant Arms in the village
Accommodation: Bed and breakfast available telephone for details
No coaches. Limited access for disabled persons. No wheelchairs available. Dogs on leads only.

BICKLEIGH CASTLE

(Mr O.N. Boxall)
nr Tiverton   EX16 8RP   map **3** W15   △ Ⓔ Ⓢ
Telephone: (01884) 855363

A Royalist Stronghold with 900 years of history and still lived-in. The 11th c detatched Chapel, the Armoury featuring a Civil War display including Cromwellian arms and armour, the Guard Room with Tudor furniture and pictures, the Great Hall, Elizabethan bedroom, and the 17th c farmhouse - all are shown. Museum of 19th c domestic and agricultural objects and toys. Maritime Exhibition showing Bickleigh Castle's connection with the 'Mary Rose' and the 'Titanic'. World War 11 original spy and escape gadgets: picturesque Moated garden, 'Spooky' tower (57 steps). Spinning. Heritage Education Trust Award winner. Full of interest for all the family.

Location: 4 m S of Tiverton A396. At Bickleigh Bridge take A3072 and follow signs.
Open: Easter Week (Good Fri-Fri) then Weds, Suns & Bank Hol Mons to late Spring Bank Hol; then to early Oct daily (except Sats) 2-5.30 (last admission 5) *parties of 20 or more by prior appointment (preferably at times other than above) at reduced rates.*
Admission: Adults £3.50 children (5-15) £1.80 family tickets. Free coach & car park.
Refreshments: Devonshire Cream Teas in the thatched Barn.
Souvenir shop. Popular for Wedding Receptions etc. For further details, group booking discounts, and booking of functions, receptions etc throughout the year please telephone the Administrator.

BICTON PARK GARDENS

(Bicton Park Trust Co)
nr Exeter   map **3** V16
Telephone: (01395) 568465

Bicton Park, regarded by many as one of the finest old gardens in England, is set in the beautiful wooded countryside of East Devon just 8 miles from Exeter. Sixty acres of formal gardens. Ornamental lakes and fountains are complemented with a fine display of statuary. Specialist glasshouses are a particular feature at Bicton (the best known of these being the famous Palm House, a magnificent glass domed structure) and include displays of Fuchsias, Geraniums, Temperate and Tropical plants. 25 minute steam/diesel train ride, Museum, Shops, Garden Centre, Indoor/outdoor play areas.

Location: 8 m S of Exeter near Budleigh Salterton. Signed of M5 Jct.30.
Open: Apr-Oct, 10-6pm (4pm Oct). Nov-Mar (weekends only) 10-4pm.
Refreshments: Restaurant/licensed bar.
Good disabled facilities. Dogs welcome on leads.

BOWDEN HOUSE

(Mr & Mrs C V Peterson)
Totnes   TQ9 7PW
Telephone: (01803) 863664

Part Tudor with Queen Anne facade. 1740 costume guides with ghost stories, photographic museum (Christmas tours by appointment).

Open: 2 weeks before Easter until end Oct. Mon-Tues afternoons plus Bank Hol Suns.
Admission: Adults £4.50 (House & Museum) children £1.50 and £2.50 (under 6 free).

BRADLEY MANOR   🌿 The National Trust
Newton Abbot   TQ12 6BN   map **3** V15
Telephone: (01626) 54513
Location: W end of town, 7½ m NW of Torquay. On W side of A381.

BUCKLAND ABBEY   🌿 The National Trust
(The National Trust jointly managed with Plymouth County Council)
Yelverton   PL20 6EY   map **2** W14
Telephone: (01822) 853607
Location: 11 m N of Plymouth 6 m S of Tavistock between the Tavistock/Plymouth Road (A386) & River Tavy.

CADHAY
(Lady William-Powlett)
Ottery St Mary   EX11 1QT   map **3** V16   △
Telephone: (01404) 812432

Cadhay is approached by an avenue of lime-trees, and stands in a pleasant listed garden, with herbaceous borders and yew hedges, with excellent views over the original mediaeval fish ponds. Cadhay is first mentioned in the reign of Edward I, and was held by a de Cadehaye. The main part of the house was built about 1550 by John Haydon who had married the de Cadhay heiress. He retained the Great Hall of an earlier house, of which the fine timber roof (about 1420) can be seen. An Elizabethan Long Gallery was added by John's successor at the end of the 16th century, thereby forming a unique and lovely courtyard. Some Georgian alterations were made in the mid 18th century. The house is viewed by conducted tour. Photography is permitted outside.

Location: 1 m NW of Ottery St Mary on B3176.
Station(s): Feniton (2½ m) (not Suns.)
Open: Spring (May 26 & 27) & Summer (Aug 25 & 26) Bank Hol Suns & Mons, also Tues Wed & Thurs in July & Aug 2-6 (last adm 5.30).
Admission: Adults £3 children £1.50 parties by arrangement.

CASTLE DROGO   🌿 The National Trust
nr Chagford   EX6 6PB   map **2** V15   ♿
Telephone: (0164 743) 3306
Location: 4 m NE of Chagford; 6 m S of A30.

COLETON FISHACRE GARDEN   🌿 The National Trust
Coleton   TQ6 0EQ   map **3** W15   ♿
Telephone: (01803) 752466
Location: 2 m from Kingswear; take Lower Ferry Road, turn off at tollhouse & follow 'Garden Open' signs.

COMPTON CASTLE   🌿 The National Trust
nr Paignton   TQ3 1TA   map **3** W15
Telephone: (01803) 872112
Location: 1 m N of Marldon off A381.

DARTMOUTH CASTLE
Dartmouth   map **3** W15
Telephone: (01803) 833588

Boldly guarding the narrow entrance to the Dart Estuary this castle was among the first in England to be built for artillery. Construction began in 1481 on the site of an earlier castle which was altered and added to over the following centuries.

Victorian coastal defence battery with fully equipped guns, a site exhibition and magnificent views can all be seen at the castle.

Location: 1 m (1⅔ km) south east of Dartmouth.
Open: Apr 1-Sept 30 10-6 daily Oct 1-31 10-4 daily Nov 1-Mar 31 Wed-Sun (closed for lunch 1-2) 10-4.
Admission: Adults £2.20 concessions £1.70 children £1.10.

ENDSLEIGH HOUSE
(The Endsleigh Charitable Trust)
Milton Abbot, Nr Tavistock   PL19 OPQ   map **2** V14
Telephone: (01822) 87248
Fax: (01822) 87502

Arboretum, Shell House, Flowering Shrubs, Rock Garden.

Location: 4 m W of Tavistock on B3362.
Open: House and Gardens Apr-Sept weekends 12-4 Tues and Fris by appointment 12-4 Bank Hols 12-4.
Admission: Honesty Box in Aid of Trust.
Refreshments: Lunches and teas at Endsleigh House by appointment. No dogs.
Limited car parking. No coaches. No dogs. Not suitable for the disabled. No wheelchairs.

FLETE
(Country Houses Association)
Ermington, Ivybridge   PL21 9NZ   map **2** W15
Telephone: (01752) 830308

Built around an Elizabethan manor with alterations in 1879 by Norman Shaw.

Location: 11 m E of Plymouth at junction of A379 and B3121.
Station(s): Plymouth (12m), Totnes (14m). Bus Route: No 93 Plymouth-Dartmouth.
Open: May-Sept Weds & Thurs 2-5. Last entry 4.30.
Admission: £2.50 Children £1. Free car park.
No dogs admitted.

FURSDON   🏛
(E.D. Fursdon, Esq)
Cadbury, Thorverton, Exeter   EX5 5JS   map **3** V15   △
Telephone: (01392) 860860

Fursdon is set in a beautiful rural landscape and the Fursdons have lived here for over 700 years. It remains primarily a family home. There is a Regency library, oak screen from the mediaeval hall, family portraits and annual displays from the family costume collection including some fine 18th century examples. Attractive developing garden.

Location: 9 m N of Exeter, 6 m SW of Tiverton; ¾ m off A3072.
Open: Easter Mon-end Sept Thurs and Bank Hol Mon only 2-4.30 Tours at 2.30 and 3.30. Parties over 20 by arrangement please.
Admission: House & Gardens £3 children £1.50. Under 10 yrs free.
Refreshments: Home made teas in Coach Hall on open days.

THE GARDEN HOUSE
(The Fortescue Garden Trust)
Buckland Monachorum, Yelverton   PL10 7LQ   map **2** W14
Telephone: (01822) 854769

Romantic, terraced, walled garden, 2 acres, with mediaeval gatehouse; enhanced by new, excitingly planted 6-acre development. Wide range of herbaceous and woody plants; of interest throughout the opening season.

Location: 1½ m W of Yelverton. Follow signs off A386 Plymouth to Yelverton.
Station(s): Plymouth.
Open: Mar 1-Oct 31 daily 10.30-5 including Bank Holidays.
Admission: Adults £3.00 children £1 OAPs £2.50 parties £2.50 if pre-booked.
Refreshments: Tea-room open 11.30-5 in house, Apr-Sept.
Plants for sale. Parking for cars. Coaches by arrangement.

HARTLAND ABBEY   🏛
(Sir Hugh Stucley, Bt)
Bideford   map **2** V13
Telephone: (012374) 41264

Abbey founded in 1157. Dissolved in 1539 and descended to the present day through a series of marriages. Major architectural alterations in 1705 and in 1779. Unique document exhibition dating from 1160 AD. Pictures, furniture and porcelain collected over many generations. Victorian & Edwardian photographic exhibition. Shrub gardens of rhododendrons, azaleas and camellias. Magnificent woodland walk to a remote atlantic cove with spectacular cliff scenery. Set in a designated area of outstanding natural beauty.

Location: NW Devon (Hartland Point); 15 m from Bideford; 5 m approx from A39.
Open: Wed May-Sept incl. Thur and Sun June-Sept incl. Sun and Mon on Bank Hols from Easter-Aug. 2.00-5.30.
Admission: £3.50 Children £1.50. Parties welcomed £3. Shrub garden and grounds only £2.
Refreshments: Teas provided at house.
Ample car parking close to house.

HEMERDON HOUSE

(J.H.G. Woollcombe, Esq)
Plympton map **2** W14 ♿ △
Telephone: (01752) 841410 (office hours);(01752) 337350 (weekend & evenings)
Fax: (01752) 331477

Regency house containing West country paintings and prints, with appropriate furniture and a Library.

Location: 2 m from Plympton.
Station(s): Plymouth.
Open: 30 days including May and August Bank Holidays 2-5.30. For opening dates please contact the Administrator.
Admission: £2.50.

HIGH CROSS HOUSE

Dartington Hall, Totnes TQ9 6ED map **2** W15
Telephone: (01803) 864114 ext.250
Fax: (01803) 867057

The first International Modernist House in Britain to be open to the public. Built in 1932, set in a most beautiful 800 acre medieval estate, **High Cross** contains unique private collection of early Twentieth Century paintings and Ceramic belonging to the **Dartington Hall Trust**.

Location: Between Exeter & Plymouth, 2 m from Totnes on A385.
Open: 13 Feb-31 Oct. Tues-Fri 10.30-4.30 Sat and sun 2-5. Admission out of season by arrangement.
Admission: Adults £2.50, concessions £1.50. Pre-booked parties special rates. Free admission to cafe only.
Refreshments: Terrace cafe with licence.
Events/Exhibitions: Permanent and temporary exhibitions, lecture programme, details on application.
Conferences: Facilities for small meetings and private functions.

KILLERTON ⚘ The National Trust

nr Exeter EX5 3LE map **3** V16 ♿
Telephone: (01392) 881345
Location: 7 m NE of Exeter on W side of Exeter - Cullompton road (B3181 - formerly A38); from M5 s'bound exit 28/B3181; from M5 n'bound exit 29 via Broadclyst & B3181.

KNIGHTSHAYES COURT ⚘ The National Trust

nr Tiverton EX16 7RQ map **3** V16 ♿
Telephone: (01884) 254665
Location: 2 m N of Tiverton; turn off A396 (Bampton/Tiverton Road) at Bolham.

OVERBECKS MUSEUM & GARDEN ⚘ The National Trust

Sharpitor, Salcombe TQ8 8LW map **2** W15
Telephone: (0154 884) 2893 or (0154 884) 3238
Location: 1½ m SW of Salcombe signposted from Malborough & Salcombe.

POWDERHAM CASTLE

(Lord and Lady Courtenay)
nr Exeter EX6 8JQ map **3** V16
Telephone: (01626) 890243
Fax: (01626) 890729

Originally built as a medieval castle by Sir Philip Courtenay (1390), the Castle is still lived in by his descendants. The siege of Powderham in the Civil War led to substantial alterations and restoration in the 18th and 19th centuries. A guided tour of the State Rooms brings alive the history of this lived in family home.

Location: 8 m S of Exeter off A379 in Kenton Village.
Station(s): Starcross 1½ m.
Open: Mar 31-Oct 27 everyday except Sat.
Admission: Adults £4.40 Children £2.95. Reduced rates for groups. Please contact General Manager for details.
Refreshments: Light lunches and cream teas available in the Courtyard. Tea-room.
Events/Exhibitions: Special events incl Classic Car Rallies, Open Air Classical Concert, Outstanding Leisure Shows and Country Fairs. Ring for details.
Conferences: The Castle is fully and exclusively available for corporate meetings, entertainment, private parties, cicil weddings and receptions, filming, product launches.

RHS GARDEN ROSEMOOR

(The Royal Horticultural Society)
Great Torrington, N. Devon EX38 8PH map **2** V14 ♿
Telephone: (01805) 624067
Fax: (01805) 624717

A stunning new National Garden often seen on TV, situated in the breathtaking setting of the Torridge Valley just south of Great Torrington. Rosemoor is designed to delight and inspire all gardeners from novice to professional. Its 40 acres contain a wide range of features: the mature planting in Lady Anne's magnificent garden and arboretum around Rosemoor House; a winding rocky gorge with bamboos and ferns along the stream towards the lake; and the more formal area which contains one of the longest herbaceous borders in the country and a wide range of individual gardens; herbs, roses (2000 plants, 200 varieties), a potager and cottage, colout theme, foliage and winter. There is also a very popular fruit and vegetable garden. Exciting trails for children a picnic area and an award winning Visitor's Centre with licensed restaurant, shop and plant centre.

Location: 1 m SE of Great Torrington on B3220 to Exeter.
Open: Garden open all year. Visitor's Centre 2 Jan-24 Dec. 10-6pm (5pm Oct-Mar).
Admission: Adults £3 children £1. Groups (10 or over) £2.50. Shop, plant centre free.
Refreshments: A restaurant provides home-made lunches and Devon Cream teas.
Coaches by appointment. Guide dogs only. Disabled facilities.

SALTRAM HOUSE ⚘ The National Trust

Plymouth PL7 3UH map **2** W14 ♿
Telephone: (01752) 336546
Location: 2 m W of Plympton 3½ m E of Plymouth city centre, between A38 & A379 main roads.

SAND

(Lt Col P.V. Huyshe)
Sidbury, nr Sidmouth EX10 OQN map **3** V16 △
Telephone: (01395) 597230

Lived in Manor house owned by Huyshe family since 1560, rebuilt 1592-4, situated in unspoilt valley. Screens passage, panelling, family documents, heraldry. Also **Sand Lodge** roof structure of late 15th century Hall House.

Location: ¾ m NE of Sidbury; 400 yds from A375, Grid ref 146925.
Open: Suns & Mons Easter Sun & Mon Apr 7 8 May 5 6 26 27 July 28 29 Aug 25 26 from 2-5.30. Last tour 4.45.
Admission: Adults £3 children/students 60p. Sand Lodge and outside of Sand by written appointment £1.
Refreshments: Light teas in house.

SHUTE BARTON ⚘ The National Trust

Shute, nr Axminster EX13 7PT map **3** V16
Telephone: (01297) 34692
Location: 3 m SW of Axminster, 2 m N of Colyton on Honiton-Colyton road (B3161) [177(193): SY253974].

TIVERTON CASTLE
(Mr and Mrs A.K. Gordon)
Tiverton EX16 6RP map **3** V15
Telephone: (01884) 253200

Historically important mediaeval castle commissioned by Henry I in 1106; magnificent mediaeval gatehouse and tower containing important Civil War armoury, notable clock collection, fine furniture and pictures.

Location: Next to St. Peter's Church. The Castle is well signposted in Tiverton.
Station(s): Tiverton Parkway.
Open: Easter Sun-end June, and Sept Suns Thurs and Bank Holiday Mons July Aug Suns to Thurs 2.30-5.30. Open at other times to private parties of more then 12 by prior arrangement.
Admission: Adults £3 children 7-16 £2 children under 7 free. Free parking inside.
Accommodation: 3 superb self-catering holiday apartments inside Castle available weekly, short breaks, or winter lettings. Graded 4 Keys Highly Commended.
Conferences: Castle available for business conferences, wedding receptions, filming or photographic location.
Coach parties by appointment only.

TORRE ABBEY
(Torbay Borough Council)
Torquay TQ2 5JX map **3** W15
Telephone: (01803) 293593

Torbay's most historic building. Founded in 1196 as a monastery and later adapted as a private residence. Contains historic rooms, Cary family chapel, mementoes of crime writer Agatha Christie, and mainly 19th century paintings, sculpture, antiques and Torquay terracotta pottery. The medieval monastic remains - including the great barn, guest hall, gatehouse, church and undercrofts - are the most complete in Devon and Cornwall. Gardens include tropical palm house, rockeries and spring bulbs. Special 'Quest' leaflet available for children and exhibitions by local artists are held throughout the summer. The enormously popular flower festival takes place in mid September. Rooms may be hired.

Location: On Torquay sea front, behind Torre Abbey sands and next to the Riviera Centre.
Station(s): Torquay (¼ m).
Open: House Apr-Oct daily 9.30-6 (last admissions 5) other times by appointment. Gardens all the year daily.

Admission: (1995 rates) House adults £2.50 students/OAPs £2 children over 8 years £1.50 younger children free family ticket £5.95 (2 adults and up to 3 children). Gardens free.
Refreshments: Victorian tea-room serving refreshments, teas and light lunches.
Events/Exhibitions: Festival of Flowers Sept 13-16.
Conferences: Facilities available including Christian services, barn dances etc.

TOTNES CASTLE
map **3** W15
Telephone: (01803) 864406

The Normans also built a stronghold here to overawe the townspeople. But they surrendered without a blow, as they did again in the Civil War. The remains date largely from the 14th century, although the huge earth mound on which the castle rests is Norman.

Location: Totnes.
Open: Apr 1-Sept 30 10-6 daily Oct 1-31 10-4 daily Nov 1-Mar 31 Wed-Sun 10-4.
Admission: Adults £1.50 concessions £1.10 children 80p.

UGBROOKE HOUSE
(Lord Clifford)
Chudleigh TQ13 0AD map **3** V15
Telephone: (01626) 852179
Fax: (01626) 853322

Set in beautiful scenery and quiet parkland in the heart of Devon. The original House and Church built about 1200, redesigned by Robert Adam. Home of the Cliffords of Chudleigh, Ugbrooke contains fine furniture, paintings, beautiful embroideries, porcelain, extremely rare family military collection. Capability Brown landscaped Park with lakes, majestic trees, scenic views to Dartmoor. Guided tours relate stories of Clifford Castles, Shakespeare's 'Black Clifford', Henry II's 'Fair Rosamund' Lady Anne Clifford who defied Cromwell, The Secret Treaty, the Cardinal's daughter, Charles II's Lord High Treasurer Clifford of the CABAL, and many more tales of intrigue, espionage and bravery.

Location: Chudleigh.
Open: July 16-Sept 7 on Sun Tues Wed and Thurs. Grounds 1-5.30. Guided tours of House at 2 and 3.45.
Admission: Adults £4 children (5-16) £2. Groups (over 20) £3.60. Private party tours/functions by arrangement.
Refreshments: Afternoon teas at The Orangery 2-5.

YARDE
(John and Marilyn Ayre)
Malborough, nr Salcombe TQ7 3BY map **2** W15
Telephone: (0154 884) 2367

Grade 1 Listed. An outstanding example of the Devon farmstead with a Tudor Bakehouse, Elizabethan Farmhouse and Queen Anne Mansion under restoration. Still a family farm.

Location: On A381 ½ m E of Malborough. 4 m S of Kingsbridge.
Open: Easter-Sept 31 Sun Wed and Fri 2-5.
Admission: Adults £2 children 50p.
Refreshments: Country teas.

DORSET

ATHELHAMPTON HOUSE & GARDENS
(Patrick Cooke)
Athelhampton, Dorchester   DT2 7LG   map **3** V18
Telephone: (01305) 848363

Five centuries of history in a family home built in 1485 on the site of King Athelstan's Palace. Great Hall with unique timber roof, oriel window, heraldic glass and linenfold panelling. Other rooms include the Great Chamber, Wine Cellar, Dining Room, Green Parlour, State and Yellow Bedrooms. Surrounded by one of the Great Gardens of England with massive topiary pyramids, pavillions, fountains, rare plants and trees.

Open: 31 Mar-27 Oct everyday (except Sat) 11-5.
Refreshments: Restaurant.

CHETTLE HOUSE
(J.P.C. Bourke)
Chettle, Blandford   DT11 8DB   map **3** V18
Telephone: (01258) 830209
Fax: (01258) 830380
Location: 6 m NE of Blandford on A354 & 1 m W.

CHIFFCHAFFS
Chaffeymoor, Bourton   map **3** U18
Telephone: (01747) 840841

A wonderful colourful garden around a 400 year old Dorset stone cottage and an idyllic woodland garden with glorious views across the Bladmoor Vale.

CLOUDS HILL   ❦ The National Trust
nr Wool   BH20 7NQ   map **3** V18
Location: 1 m N of Bovington Camp, ½ m E of Waddock crossroads (B3390), 9 m E of Dorchester.

CORFE CASTLE   ❦ The National Trust
nr Wareham   BH20 5ES   map **3** V18
Telephone: (01929) 481294
Location: In the village of Corfe Castle: on A351 Wareham-Swanage road.

CRANBORNE MANOR GARDEN
(The Viscount and Viscountess Cranborne)
Cranborne   BH21 5PP   map **3** V19
Telephone: (01725) 517248
Fax: (01725) 517248

Walled gardens, yew hedges and lawns; wild garden with spring bulbs, herb garden, Jacobean mount garden, flowering cherries and collection of old-fashioned and specie roses. Beautiful and historic garden laid out in the 17th century by John Tradescant and much embellished in the 20th century.

Location: 18 m N of Bournemouth, B3078; 16 m S of Salisbury, A354, B3081.
Open: Garden Centre open Tues-Sat 9-5 Sun 10-5 closed Mon except Bank Holidays. Something for every gardener, but specialising in old-fashioned and specie roses, herbs, ornamental pots and garden furniture. Gardens Only Mar-Sept Wed 9-5 South Court occasionally closed. Free car park.

DEANS COURT
(Sir Michael & Lady Hanham)
Wimborne   map **3** V19   ♿

Thirteen acres of partly wild garden, in a peaceful setting on the River Allen. Specimen trees, monastery fishpond. Peacocks. Herb garden with over 200 varieties. Chemical free herb plants for sale; also kitchen garden produce (also chemical free) as available. Free parking. Wheelchair available.

Location: A few mins walk South from Wimborne Minster & Square.
Station(s): Poole and Bournemouth (30-45 mins. by bus).
Open: Daffodil Weekends with teas Sat & Sun 16/17th & 23/24th Mar, 2-5. Easter Sun 2-6. Bank Hol Mons 10-6. First and last Sun, May to Sept 2-6. Last opening: Sun 6 Oct 2-6. Organic Gardens Weekend 22/23rd June 2-6.
Admission: Adults £1.50 children 70p. Regret guide dogs only and no unaccompanied children.
Refreshments: Wholefood teas & morning coffee.

EDMONDSHAM HOUSE AND GARDENS
(Mrs J.E. Smith)
Cranborne, nr Wimborne   BH21 5RE   map **3** V19   △ ♿
Telephone: (01725) 517207

A family home since the 16th century, and a fine blend of Tudor and Georgian architecture, with a Victorian stable block and dairy, interesting furniture, lace and other exhibits. The Gardens include an old-fashioned walled garden, cultivated organically, with an excellent display of spring bulbs, shrubs, lawns and herbaceous border.

Location: Between Cranborne and Verwood, off the B3081.
Open: HOUSE AND GARDENS Easter Sun all Bank Hol Mons all Weds in Apr and Oct 2-5. Groups by arrangement at other times. GARDENS Open at all times when the House is open and on all Wed and Suns Apr to Oct 2-5.
Admission: House and Garden: Adult £2.50 children £1 under 5 free. Garden only: Adult £1 children 50p under 5 free.
Refreshments: Teas village hall on house open days. Teas for groups.

FORDE ABBEY AND GARDENS

(Trustees of Forde Abbey)
nr Chard TA20 4LU map **3** V17 △ &
Telephone: (01460) 220231

Award winning garden 1992. Cistercian monastery, founded 1140. Converted to private house mid 17th c. and unaltered since. Thirty acres of outstanding gardens - trees and shrubs, herbaceous borders, rock garden, bog garden and kitchen garden. Plants on sale.

Location: 1 m E of Chard Junction, 4 m SE of Chard signposted off A30.
Open: Gardens open daily throughout the year 10-4.30. House Apr-end Oct Sun Wed & Bank Hol 1-4.30.
Admission: Our charges for 1996: House and Gardens adults £4.50 OAPs £4. Gardens only £3.25 OAPs £3.
Refreshments: Undercroft open for light lunches and teas 11-4.30 daily Apr-end of Oct.

HARDY'S COTTAGE   The National Trust

Higher Bockhampton DT2 8QJ map **3** V18 &
Telephone: (01305) 262366
Location: 3 m NE of Dorchester; ½ m S of Blandford Road (A35).

HIGHBURY

(Stanley Cherry Esq.)
West Moors
Telephone: (01202) 874372

Small Edwardian house (Listed, 1909) in half acre garden.

HORN PARK

(Mr & Mrs John Kirkpatrick)
Beaminster map **3** V17
Telephone: (01308) 862212

Large and beautiful garden, house built 1910 by pupil of Lutyens - unique position, magnificent view to sea. Plantsman's garden, unusual trees, shrubs and plants in Rock, water gardens, terraces and herbaceous borders. Woodland Garden, Bluebell Woods, Wild flower meadow with over 140 species including orchids. Plants for sale.

Location: 1½ m N. of Beaminster on A3066.
Station(s): Crewkerne.
Open: Apr 1-Oct 31. Every Sun, Tue, Wed 2-6 and Bank Hols Mon.
Admission: £2.50 (under 16 and wheelchair users free).

ILSINGTON HOUSE

(Mr & Mrs P. Duff)
Puddletown, Dorchester map **3** V18
Telephone: (01305) 848454

This family home, set in the picturesque village of Puddletown (Thomas Hardy's Weatherbury). A classical William and Mary mansion built by the 7th Earl of Huntingdon. Home of George III's illegitimate grandson, born to HRH Princess Sophia in 1800, kept a secret until the Royal Scandal of 1829. Ilsington was visited by many members of the Royal Family during George III's reign. Fine furniture and present owners' private collection of pictures and sculpture. A fully guided house tour given. Formal and landscape gardens with probably the longest haha in Dorset. Large collection of beautiful bearded irises and unusual peonies.

Location: 4 m from Dorchester on the A35.
Open: Ilsington House Tours May 1-Sept 29 1996 Wed and Thurs 2-6 last tour 5. **Also Sundays and Bank Hol Mon in Aug.**
Admission: House and Gardens £4.
Refreshments: Lunch, supper or tea for parties by arrangement in the House, teas available in the village.

Conferences: Suitable for small conferences.
Free car parking. Unfortunately not suitable for disabled persons. No dogs. Ideal location for small specialised conferences. Also available for film locations.

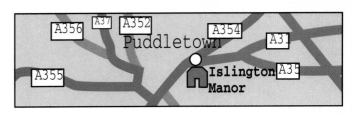

KINGSTON LACY   The National Trust

nr Wimborne Minster BH21 4EA map **3** V18 Ⓢ
Telephone: (01202) 883402
Location: On B3082 - Blandford-Wimborne Road, 1½ m W of Wimborne.

MAPPERTON

(Earl and Countess of Sandwich)
Beaminster DT8 3NR map **3** V18 △
Telephone: (01308) 862645
Fax: (01308) 863348

Terraced gardens with Italianate fountain court. Modern orangery in classical style, 17th century fish ponds. Tudor manor house, enlarged 1660s. Magnificent walks and views.

Location: 1 m off B3163, 2 m off B3066.
Station(s): Crewkerne..
Open: Mar-Oct daily 2-6.
Admission: Adults £2.50 under 18 £1.50 under 5 free. House open to group tours by appointment, adults £3.50 or £6 for house and gardens.

MAX GATE   The National Trust

Dorchester DT1 2AA map **3** V17
Telephone: (01305) 262538
Location: 1 m E of Dorchester.

MILTON ABBEY

(The Council of Milton Abbey School Ltd)
Milton Abbas, nr Blandford DT11 0BP map **3** V18
Telephone: (01258) 880489 Organising Secretary

A fine Abbey Church (Salisbury Diocese) partially completed 15th century on site of 10th century Abbey. The magnificent Abbot's Hall, completed 1498, with fine hammerbeam roof and carved screen, is incorporated in the Georgian Gothic mansion (now Milton Abbey School). Architect Sir William Chambers with ceilings and decorations by James Wyatt. The ancient St. Catherine's Chapel looks down on this unique group set in secluded valley seven miles SW of Blandford. The little town of Milton, swept away in the late 18th century by the imperious owner of the house, in order to improve his park, was rebuilt as a charming model village nearby.

Location: 7 m SW of Blandford, just N of A354 from Winterborne Whitechurch or Milborne St Andrew.
Open: House and Grounds mid July-end Aug daily 10-6 ABBEY CHURCH Church throughout the year.
Admission: Adults £1.75 children free. ABBEY CHURCH voluntary donations except for above dates.
Refreshments: Abbey Tea-rooms open Easter and main summer season only.
Events/Exhibitions: Easter - Crafts Fair at Milton Abbey.

MINTERNE

(The Lord Digby)

Dorchester   DT2 7AU   map **3** V18
Telephone: (01300) 341370

Important rhododendron and shrub garden, many fine and rare trees, landscaped in the 18th century with lakes, cascades and streams.

Location: On A352 2 m N of Cerne Abbas; 10 m N of Dorchester, 9 m S of Sherborne.
Open: Apr 1-Nov 10 daily 10-7.
Admission: Adults £2 accompanying child free. Free car park.

PRIEST'S HOUSE MUSEUM OF EAST DORSET LIFE AND GARDEN

(Priest's House Museum Trust)

23 High Street, Wimborne Minster   BH21 1HR   map **3** V19   △ Ⓔ Ⓢ
Telephone: (01202) 882533
Fax: (01202) 882533

A fascinating historic town house of medieval origin with many Tudor and Georgian features. Set in an exquisite walled garden, the displays include an 18th century parlour, Victorian stationer's shop and working kitchen plus regular special exhibitions. An award winning museum!

Location: Centre of Wimborne Minster.
Station(s): Poole or Bournemouth.
Open: Apr 1-Oct 31 Mon-Sat 10.30-5. Plus Bank Holiday Suns and every Sun June 2-Sept 29 2-5. Special Christmas exhibition.
Admission: Includes entrance to garden. Group bookings welcome.
Refreshments: Tea-room in summer season and museum gift shop.
Disabled access ground floor and garden only. Free quizzes. Several special events are planned.

PURSE CAUNDLE MANOR

(Michael de Pelet, Esq)

nr Sherborne   DT9 5DY   map **3** V18
Telephone: (01963) 250400

Interesting 15th/16th century Manor House. Lived in as a family home. Great Hall with minstrel gallery; Winter Parlour; Solar with oriel; bedchambers; garden. Not commercialised! Come and visit us.

Location: 4 m E of Sherborne; ¼ m S of A30.
Open: Easter Mon and May-Sept '94 Thurs Sun & Bank Hol Mon 2-5 showing every half hour. Coaches welcomed by appointment.
Admission: £2.50. Children free. Free car park.
Refreshments: Home-made cream teas by prior arrangement at £2 each for coach parties.

SANDFORD ORCAS MANOR HOUSE

(Sir Mervyn Medlycott, Bt)

Sandford Orcas, Sherborne   map **3** V17   △
Telephone: (01963) 220206

Tudor Manor House with gatehouse, fine panelling. furniture, pictures. Terraced gardens, with topiary, and herb garden. Personal conducted tour by owner.

Location: 2½ m N of Sherborne, ent. next to Church.
Open: Easter Mon 10-6 then May-Sept Suns 2-6 & Mons 10-6.
Admission: Adults £2 children £1. Pre-booked parties (of 10 or more) at reduced rates on other days if preferred.

SHERBORNE CASTLE

Sherborne   DT9 3PY   map **3** V18
Telephone: (01935) 813182
Fax: (01935) 816727

Built by Sir Walter Raleigh in 1594. Home of the Digby family since 1617. The House contains fine furniture, porcelain and pictures. Set in 20 acres of lawns and pleasure grounds planned by 'Capability' Brown around the 50 acre lake.

Location: 5 m E of Yeovil off A30 to S.
Station(s): Sherborne.
Open: Easter Sat-end Sept Thurs Sat Sun and Bank Hol Mons. House 1.30-5. Grounds and Tea-room 12-30.
Admission: Charges on request. parties by arrangement.
Refreshments: Tea-room.
Events/Exhibitions: Various telephone for details.
Gift Shop. Car parking on site.

WOLFETON HOUSE

(Capt. N.T.L.L. Thimbleby)

Dorchester   DT2 9QN   map **3** V18
Telephone: (01305) 263500

A fine mediaeval and Elizabethan Manor House lying in the water-meadows near the confluence of the rivers Cerne and Frome. It was much embellished around 1580 and has splendid plaster ceilings, fireplaces and panelling of that date. To be seen are the Great Hall, stairs and chamber; parlour; dining room, chapel and cyder house. The mediaeval gatehouse has two unmatched and older towers. There are good pictures and furniture.

Location: 1½ m from Dorchester on Yeovil road (A37); indicated by Historic House signs.
Station(s): Dorchester South and West 1¾ m.
Open: May 1-Sept 30 Tues Thur and Bank Hol Mons 2-6. At other times throughout the year parties by arrangement.
Admission: Charges not available at time of going to press.
Refreshments: Ploughman's lunches, teas and evening meals for parties, by prior arrangement. Cyder for sale.

Robert Adam - architect

His work can be seen at the following properties included in Historic Houses Castles and Gardens:

Audley End
Bowood House & Gardens
Culzean Castle
Hatchlands Park
Kedleston Hall
Kenwood, The Iveagh Bequest
Killerton
Kimbolton Castle
Luton Hoo

Mellerstain
Moccas Court
Newby Hall & Gardens
Nostell Priory
Osterley Park
Papplewick Hall
Saltram House
Syon House

COUNTY DURHAM

AUCKLAND CASTLE
(The Church Commissioners)
Bishop Auckland   map **9** N19
Telephone: (01388) 601627

Principal country residence of the Bishops of Durham since Norman times and now the official residence of the present day Bishops. The Chapel, reputedly the largest private chapel in Europe, was originally the 12th century banquet hall. Chapel and State Rooms, including the Throne Room, Long Dining Room and King Charles Dining Room are open to the public. Visitors are also able to see the exhibition in the medieval kitchens dedicated to the life of St Cuthbert and the history of the Durham diocese. There is also access to the adjacent Bishop's park with its 18th century deer house.

Location: In Bishop Auckland, at the end of Market Place.
Station(s): Bishop Auckland.
Open: Castle: May-Sept Sun, Tues, Wed and Thurs 2pm-5pm. Also Bank Holiday Mon's and Sat's in Aug.(Last admission 30 mins before closing time). Arrangements can be made for group bookings and school visits throughout the year. Bishop's park open daily, 7am-Sunset.
Admission: Adults £2.50 Children & over 60s £1.50. Concessions available for group bookings. Bishop's park: Admission free.
Conferences: Excellent venue for concerts, exhibitions, conferences and meetings.

BARNARD CASTLE
Durham   map **9** O19
Telephone: (01833) 38212

ENGLISH HERITAGE

Named after it's founder, Bernard de Baliol, the castle overlooks the River Tees from a craggy cliff-top. It's ownership was disputed by the Bishops of Durham, one of whom seized it in 1296. He added a magnificent hall and refortified the castle. Part of the castle has recently been excavated to discover more of it's complex building history.

Location: In Barnard Castle.
Open: Apr 1-Sept 30 10-6 daily Oct 1-31 10-4 daily Nov 1-Mar 31 Wed-Sun 10-4.
Admission: Adults £2 concessions £1.50 children £1.

BOTANIC GARDEN, UNIVERSITY OF DURHAM
(University of Durham)
Durham   DH1 3TN
Telephone: 0191-3742671

18 acres of trees and shrubs, set in mature woodland.

DURHAM CASTLE
(The University of Durham)
Durham map **9** N19 △
Telephone: 0191-374 3863
Fax: 0191-374 7470

Durham Castle, the former home of the Prince Bishops of Durham, was founded in the 1070's. Since 1832 it has been the foundation College of the University of Durham. With the Cathedral it is a World Heritage Site. Important features include the Norman Chapel (1072), the Great Hall (1284), the Norman Doorway (1540's). With its 14th century style Keep it is a fine example of a Motte and Bailey Castle. In vacations the Castle is a conference and holiday centre and a prestige venue for banquets etc.

Location: In the centre of the city (adjoining Cathedral).
Station(s): Durham (½ m).
Open: Guided tours only July-Sept 10-12 noon and 2-5pm. Oct-June 2-4pm.
Admission: £1.75 Children £1.20 Family ticket £4. Guide book £2.50.
Events/Exhibitions: Contact conference and accommodation secretary.
Accommodation: Contact conference and accommodation secretary 0191-374 3863.
Conferences: Contact conference and accommodation secretary 0191-374 3863.

RABY CASTLE
(The Lord Barnard, T.D.)
Staindrop, Darlington DL2 3AH map **9** O19 ♿
Telephone: (01833) 660202

Principally 14th century, alterations made 1765 and mid-19th century. The Castle is one of the largest 14th century castles in Britain and was built by the Nevills although one of the towers probably dates back to the 11th century. Interior mainly 18th and 19th century; medieval kitchen and Servants' Hall. Fine pictures of the English, Dutch and Flemish Schools and good period furniture. Collection of horse-drawn carriages and fire engines. Large walled Gardens.

Location: 1 m N of Staindrop village, on the Barnard Castle/Bishop Auckland Road (A688).
Station(s): Bishop Auckland/Darlington.
Open: Easter weekend (Sat-Wed) closed remainder of Apr then May 1-June 30 Wed & Sun; July 1-Sept 30 daily (except Sat); May Spring and Aug Bank Hols Sat-Tues Castle 1-5 Park & Gardens 11-5.30.
Admission: Castle, Park and Gardens £3.50 Senior Citizens £3.20 children £1.50. Family ticket (2 adults, 3 children) £9. Park and Gardens only £1, Senior Citizens and children 75p. Separate adm charge for Bulmer's Tower when open. Rates may vary when charity events are held. Special terms for parties over 25 on above days by arrangement (Tel Curator).
Refreshments: Tea at the Stables.
Picnic area.

ROKEBY PARK
nr Barnard Castle DL12 9RZ map 9 N19
Telephone: (01833) 637334 - Curator

Palladian House built by Sir Thomas Robinson in 1735. Fine rooms, furniture and pictures (including exceptional collection of 18th century needlework pictures by Anne Morritt). Fine print room.

Location: Between A66 (signposted Barnard Castle and Bowes Museum) and Barnard Castle.
Open: May 6 then each Mon & Tues from May 27-Tues Sept 10 2-5 (last adm 4.30). Parties of 25 or more will also be admitted on other days if a written appointment is made with the Curator.
Admission: Adult £3.50 child/concessions £1.50.

ESSEX

AUDLEY END HOUSE AND PARK
Saffron Waldron map 5 S23
Telephone: (01799) 522399

James I is said to have remarked that Audley End was too large for a king but not for his Lord Treasurer, Sir Thomas Howard, who built it. The house was so large in fact that early in the 18th century about half of it was demolished as being unmanageable, but this still leaves a very substantial mansion. The interior contains rooms decorated by Robert Adam, a magnificent Jacobean Great Hall, a picturesque 'Gothic' chapel and a suite of rooms decorated in the revived Jacobean style of the early 19th century.

Location: ¾ m (1 km) west of Saffron Walden off B1383.
Open: Apr 1-Sept 30 12-6 Wed-Sun (and Bank Hols) Last admission 5.
Admission: House & Grounds adults £5.50 concessions £4.10 children £2.80. Grounds only adults £3.30 concessions £2.50 children £1.70.
Refreshments: Restaurant.

BETH CHATTO GARDENS
(Mrs Beth Chatto)
Elmstead Market

5-acre garden, attractively landscaped with many unusual plants in wide range of conditions.

THE COTTAGE GARDEN
Langham Road, Boxted, Colchester, Essex   CO4 5HU &
Telephone: (01206) 272269

Over 400 varieties of hardy perennials, alpines, herbs, trees, shrubs, conifers and hedging.

GOSFIELD HALL
(Country Houses Association)
Halstead   CO9 1SF   map 5 S24
Telephone: (01787) 472914

Very fine Tudor gallery.

Location: 2½ m SW of Halstead on Braintree/Haverhill Road (A1017).
Station(s): Braintree. Bus route 310 Braintree-Halstead.
Open: May-Sept Weds & Thurs 2-5. House tours 2.30 and 3.15.
Admission: £2.50 Children £1. Free car park.
Conferences: By arrangement
No dogs admitted.

HARWICH REDOUBT

(The Harwich Society)
Harwich Harbour, Harwich   CO12 3TE   map 5 T25
Telephone: (01255) 503429

Commanding Harwich Harbour this substantial circular fort was built to keep Napoleon out. Now being restored by volunteers of The Harwich Society, with 11 different guns on the battlements and a variety of small museums in the casemates.

Location: Opposite 42A Main Road, Harwich.
Station(s): Harwich Town.
Open: 1 May-31 Aug 10-5 daily. 1 Sept-30 Apr Suns only 10-12 and 2-5. Parties at any time by arrangement. Annual Fete 27 May 2-5.
Admission: Adults £1 accompanied children free (no unaccompanied children).
Refreshments: Light drinks only.
Not suitable for disabled. Photograph by courtesy of ECC.

Sir Christopher Wren - architect (1632-1723)

Fawley Court
Old Royal Observatory
Winslow Hall

INGATESTONE HALL
(Lord Petre)
Ingatestone   CM4 9NR   map 13 T24
Telephone: (01277) 353010
Fax: (01245) 248979

Tudor mansion in 11 acres of grounds, built by Sir William Petre, Secretary of State to four monarchs. The house continues to be the home of his descendants and contains furniture, pictures and memorabilia accumulated over the centuries. The house retains its original form and appearance including two priests' hiding places.

Location: From London end of Ingatestone High Street take Station Lane. House is half a mile beyond the level crossing.
Open: Apr 6-Sept 29 Sat Sun and Bank Holidays. Plus July 18-Aug 30 Wed and Thurs and Fri 1-6.
Admission: Adults £3.50 OAPs/students £3 children 5-16 £2 (under 5s free) parties 20 or more 50p per head reduction.
Refreshments: Tea-room.
Car park adjacent to gates. 200m. walk to house. Gift shop. No dogs (except guide dogs). The upper floor and some rooms downstairs are inaccessible to wheelchairs.

LAYER MARNEY TOWER
(Mr Nicholas Charrington)
nr Colchester   CO5 9US   map 13 T24   △ Ⓔ &
Telephone: (01206) 330784
Fax: (01206) 330784

Lord Marney's 1520 masterpiece is the tallest Tudor gatehouse in the country. Visitors may climb the tower for excellent views of the Essex countryside and the Blackwater estuary, explore the formal gardens and visit the Long Gallery. The adjoining Church has 3 effigy tombs of the Marney's and an original wallpainting of St. Christopher. There is a collection of rare breed farm animals and deer. A Farm walk starts from the Mediaeval Barn. Guided Tours are available by arrangement (minimum number 25 people). The Long Gallery and Carpenters Shop can be hired for Receptions, Banquets and Concerts and Weddings.

Location: 6 m S of Colchester, signpost off the B1022 Colchester/Maldon Road.
Station(s): Kelvedon.
Open: Apr May Jun July Aug and Sept every day except Sat 2-6 July and Aug open Suns 12-6. Bank Hols 11-6. Parties other days by prior arrangement throughout the year.

Admission: Adult £3.25 Child £1.75 Family (2A + 2C) £9.00. Guided tour (20 people+) £4.50.
Refreshments: Teas.
Events/Exhibitions: Small exhibition on farming, rare breeds & food chain. History of Tower and past owners. Special events through the year.
Conferences: 2 rooms available, a/u, overhead. Licensed for Civil Weddings. Carpenters shop - 150 theatre style Long Gallery 220 theatre.

LOWER DAIRY HOUSE GARDEN

(Mr & Mrs D.J. Burnett)
Water Lane, Nayland, Colchester   CO6 4JS
Telephone: (01206) 262220

1¾ acre plantsman's garden.

MOOT HALL

Maldon Town Castle, 1st Floor, 50 High Street   CM9 5PN   map 13 T24
Telephone: (01621) 857373
Fax: (01621) 850793

Built c.1440, the old Courthouse and Council Chamber are well preserved, latter is still used by the Town Council. The Millennium Tapestry is housed on the lower floor and depicts 1000 years of Maldon's history.

Location: 18 miles SW of Colchester, 12 miles E of Chelmsford, situated on the northern end of the Town's High Street.
Open: Mon-Sat 10-4 (some Bank Hols) guided tours only in main part of building- prior booking with Maldon Town Council 01621 857373.
Admission: Free to main building (donations welcome) to Millennium Tapestry £1 Adult 50p Chd/OAP.

THE SIR ALFRED MUNNINGS ART MUSEUM

Castle House, Dedham, Colchester   CO7 6AZ   map 5 T25   &
Telephone: (01206) 322127

Large collection of paintings and other works by the late Sir Alfred Munnings, KCVO, PRA 1944-1949.

Location: ¾ m Dedham village, 7 m NE Colchester 2 m E of Ipswich Road (A12).
Station(s): Colchester, Manningtree, Ipswich.
Open: May 5-Oct 6 Wed Sun & Bank Hol Mons also Thurs & Sats in Aug 2-5.
Admission: Adults £3 children 50p OAPs £2. Private parties by arrangment. Free car park.

PAYCOCKE'S   🌿 The National Trust

West Street   CO6 1NS   map 5 T24
Telephone: (01376) 561305
Location: On A120; S side of West St. Coggeshall next to Fleece Inn; 5½ m E of Braintree.

RHS GARDEN HYDE HALL

(The Royal Horticultural Society)
Rettendon, Chelmsford   CM3 8ET   map 13 T24   &
Telephone: (01245) 400256

The most recent addition to the RHS Gardens, Hyde Hall occupies a delightful hilltop site with fine views across the surrounding area. The Garden has been developed over the last 36 years and hosts a wide variety of plants including a large selection of roses. The plantsman's garden extends to 8 acres and includes the national collections of **Malus** and **Viburnum**. Among other features are fine heathers and many willows that have been incorporated for winter colour.

Open: The garden is open on Wed Thurs Sat Sun and Bank Hols from 24 Mar-27 Oct (inclusive) 11-6. (11am-5pm in Sept & Oct).
Admission: Adults £2.70 children under 6 years free children 6-16 70p. Groups of more than 20 £2.20. One person accompanying a blind or disabled visitor free. Dogs are not admitted (except guide dogs).
Refreshments: Light refreshments, hot and cold lunches are available and there are plants for sale during opening hours.

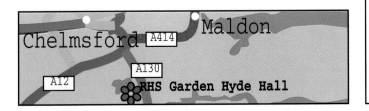

SHALOM HALL

(Lady Phoebe Hillingdon)
Layer Breton, nr Colchester   map 13 T24

19th century house containing a collection of 17th and 18th century French furniture and porcelain and portraits by famous English artists including Thomas Gainsborough, Sir Joshua Reynolds etc.

Location: 7 m SW of Colchester; 2 m from A12.
Open: Aug Mon-Fri 10-1 and 2.30-5.30.
Admission: Free.

ST. OSYTH PRIORY

(Lady Juliet de Chair)
St.Osyth   map 13 T25
Telephone: (01255) 820492

'Constable' Country. Within 12 miles of Dedham and the Stour Valley. The Great gatehouse c 1475, ('unexcelled in any monastic remains in the country',*Country Life*), was built 20 years before Christopher Columbus sailed. A unique group of buildings dating from the 13th, 15th, 16th, 18th and 19th centuries, surrounding a wide quadrangle like an Oxford or Cambridge college. Gardens include Rose garden, Topiary garden, Water garden etc. Peacocks. Art collection in Georgian wing includes world-famous paintings by George Stubbs ARA.

Location: 65 m from London via A12, A120; A133 12 m from Colchester; 8 m from Frinton.
Open: Easter and May-end Sept. Daily except Sat from 11-4.30. Gardens 10-5 daily. Art collection Easter w/e 1 May-30 Sept Sun-Fri 11-4.30. Closed. Sat. Gardens & Ancient Monuments Easter w/e 1 May-30 Sept daily 10-5.
Admission: Adults £3.50 Children £1 OAPs £2.00. Free car parking adjacent to The Priory. Dogs allowed in grounds if kept on a lead.
Refreshments: 2-3 mins walk to the village from entrance.
Gardens suitable for disabled persons. Gardens overlook but do not include deer park on the estuary of the River Cole. Contact Mrs Colby, Tel (01255) 820242 (9-10 am)

GLOUCESTERSHIRE

BARNSLEY HOUSE GARDEN

(Rosemary Verey)
Barnsley, nr Cirencester   GL7 5EE   map 3 T19   &
Telephone: (01285) 740281
Fax: (01285) 740281

Garden laid out 1770, trees planted 1840. Re-planned 1960. Many spring bulbs. Laburnum avenue (early June). Lime walk, herbaceous and shrub borders. Ground cover. Knot garden. Autumn colour and winter interest. Gothick summerhouse 1770. Classical temple 1780. House 1697 (not open). Vegetable garden laid out as decorative potager.

Location: 4 m NE of Cirencester on Cirencester to Bibury and Burford Road (B4425).
Station(s): Kemble.
Open: Garden Only, all the year Mon Wed Thurs Sat 10-6 (or dusk if earlier).
Admission: (Mar-Nov inc) adults £2.50 OAPs £1.50 season tickets £4 guided parties entrance plus £50 by R. Verey £25 by another guide. Dec & Jan free to Barnsley, Bilbury and Winson . **Refreshments:** Morning coffee, lunch, supper and tea by appointment (01285) 740421, The Village Pub.
Plants and R.Verey books, antiques and garden furniture for sale

---

"Playgrounds for the Children"

Belton House
Bowood
Drumlanrig (woodland playground)
Hever Castle
Kelburn (Secret Forest adventure course and stockade)
Longleat
Ragley Hall (adventure wood)
Weston Park
Wilton House

BATSFORD ARBORETUM
(The Batsford Foundation - registered charity 286712)
Moreton-in-Marsh   GL56 9QF   map **3** T19
Telephone: (01608) 650722

Designed and planted as a wild garden, the 50 acres of arboretum contain over 1500 species of trees and shrubs. Set in delightful Cotswold countryside, the arboretum is a place of peaceful tranquility and enjoys wonderful views over-looking the Vale of Evenlode. Spring colour is provided by carpets of bulbs, mag-nolia blossom, flowering cherries and the spectacular "Handkerchief" tree in May. The autumn season brings on a change that sets the arboretum on fire with a vibrancy of colour; the large collection of Acers and Sorbus provide an explo-sion of autumn reds and golds. Picnic area, Tea Rooms, Garden Centre and Falconry.

Location: 1½ m NW of Moreton-in-Marsh on A44 to Evesham road.
Station(s): Moreton-in-Marsh (1½ m).
Open: GARDEN ONLY: 1 Mar to 5 Nov daily 10-5 .
Admission: Adults £2.50 increase to £3 on 1 October. OAP's and Children aged 5-15 £2. Coach parties by prior arrangement only.
Refreshments: Tea-room serves coffees, light lunches and teas. Picnic area. Free car parking. Dogs welcome, on leads please.

Thomas Gainsborough (1727-1787)

His paintings can be seen at the fol-lowing properties included in Historic Houses Castles and Gardens:-

Arundel Castle
Bowhill
Christchurch Mansion
Dalmeny House
Elton Hall
Gainsborough's House
Ickworth Park & Garden
Firle Place
Kenwood, The Iveagh Bequest

Knowle
Parham House & Gardens
Petworth House
Shalom Hall
Upton House
Waddesdon Manor
Weston Park
Woburn Abbey

BERKELEY CASTLE
(Mr & Mrs R.J. Berkeley)
Gloucestershire   GL13 9BQ   map **14** T18   △
Telephone: (01453) 810332

BERKELEY CASTLE
Gloucestershire

England's most Historic Home and Oldest Inhabited Castle

Completed in 1153 by Lord Maurice Berkeley at the command of Henry 11 and for nearly 850 years the home of the Berkeley family. 24 generations have gradually transformed a savage Norman fortress into a truly stately home.

The castle is a home and not a museum. Enjoy the castle at leisure or join one of the regular one-hour guided tours covering the dungeon, the cell where Edward 11 was murdered, the medieval kitchens the magnificent Great Hall and the State Apartments with their fine collections of pictures by primarily English and Dutch masters, tapestries, furniture of an interesting diversity, silver and porcelain.

Splendid Elizabethan Terraced Gardens and sweeping lawns surround the castle, Tropical Butterfly House with hundreds of exotic butterflies in free flight - an oasis of colour and tranquillity.

Facilities include free coach and car parks, picnic lawn and two gift shops. Tea rooms for refreshments, light lunches and afternoon teas.

Opening times and admission charges - see editorial reference. Evening parties by arrangement. Further information from the Custodian, Berkeley Castle, Glos. GL13 9BQ. Telephone 01453 810 332.

Location: Midway between Bristol and Gloucester, just off A38. M5 junctions 13 or 14.
Open: Apr - Daily (exc Mons) 2-5, May to Sept - Tues to Sats 11-5, Suns 2- 5; *closed Mons.* Oct - Suns only 2-4.30, also Bank Hol Mons 11-5. Grounds open same day as House, until 6 pm (5.30 in Oct).
Admission: Adults £4.50 Children £2.25 OAPs/Students £3.50 Group rate (parties of 25 or over) £4 Children £2 OAPs/Students £3.30.
Refreshments: Light lunches (May to Sept) and teas at Castle. Evening parties by arrangement. Further information from the Custodian.

BOURTON HOUSE GARDEN
(Mr. & Mrs. Richard Paice)
Bourton on the Hill, Gloucestershire   GL56 9AE   map **3** T19
Telephone: (01386) 700121

An imaginatively planted garden, largely created under the present ownership, enhances a handsome c.18th century Cotswold Manor House (not open). Unusual plants for sale.

Location: 2 m west of Moreton-in-Marsh on A44.
Station(s): Moreton-in-Marsh
Open: From 23 May-27 Sept. Bank Hol Monday 27 May and Aug Bank Hol Monday 26, noon-5.
Admission: £2.50 children free.
Refreshments: Tea in c.16th century Tithe barn.
For charity in conjunction with village gardens Bank Holiday Sunday May 26 1-6 & Aug 25 £3.

CHAVENAGE

(David Lowsley-Williams, Esq)
Tetbury   map **14** T18   △
Telephone: (01666) 502329
Fax: (01453) 836778

Elizabethan House (1576) set in the tranquil Cotswold countryside with Cromwellian associations. 16th and 17th century furniture and tapestries. Personally conducted tours, by the owner or his family.

Location: 2 m N of Tetbury. Signposted off A46 (Bath-Stroud) or B4014.
Open: Easter Sun & Mon then May-end Sept Thurs Sun & Bank Hols 2-5.
Admission: Adults £2.50 children half-price. Parties by appointment as above or other dates and times to suit.
Refreshments: Catering for parties by arrangement.
Conferences: Wedding receptions, dinners, corporate hospitality, also available for film and photographic location.

CHEDWORTH ROMAN VILLA   🌾 The National Trust

Yanworth, nr Cheltenham   GL54 3LJ   map **3** T19   ċ
Telephone: (01242) 890256
Fax: (01242) 890544

One of the best exposed Romano-British villa in Britain. It was built about AD120 and extended and occupied until about AD400. There are good fourth century mosaics in the bath suits and triclinium (dining room). The villa was excavated in 1864, and a museum has a useful range of artefacts.

Location: 3 m NW of Fossebridge on Cirencester-Northleach Road (A429).
Station(s): Cheltenham Spa 9 m.
Open: 6 Feb-1 Mar: Tue to Fri 10-4 site open for pre-booked parties. 5 Mar-3 Nov: Tues-Sun & Bank Hol Mon 10-5. (Closed Mons open Bank Hol Mon & Good Fri). Also 5 Nov-1 Dec: Tues-Sun 10-4; also 7 & 8 Dec.
Admission: £3 Children £1.50 Family £7.50. Parties by prior written arrangement only. Disabled - all parts accessible but some with difficulty. Disabled WC. Shop open on site - introductory film.

FRAMPTON MANOR

(Mr & Mrs P. R. H. Clifford)
Frampton-on-Severn, Gloucester   map **14** T18
Telephone: (01452) 740698

Medieval/Elizabethan timber-framed Manor House with walled garden. Reputed 12th century birthplace of 'Fair Rosamund' Clifford mistress of King Henry II. 15th century Wool Barn and Granary with dovecote.

Location: 3 miles J 13, M5.
Open: House and Garden open year by written appointment. Garden opens Mons Apr 22-July 8 1996 incl 2-5; also open in aid of Red Cross.
Admission: House and Garden £2.50 Garden only £1.50.

HARDWICKE COURT

(C.G.M. Lloyd-Baker)
nr Gloucester   map **14** T18
Telephone: (01452) 720212

Late Georgian house designed by Robert Smirke, built 1816-1817. Entrance Hall, Drawing Room, Library and Dining Room open.

Location: 5 m S of Gloucester on A38 (between M5 access 12 S only and 13).
Open: Easter Mon-end Sept Mon only 2-4 other times by prior written appointment.
Admission: £1, parking for cars only.
Not suitable for disabled.

HIDCOTE MANOR GARDEN   🌾 The National Trust

Hidcote Bartrim, nr Chipping Campden   GL55 6LR   map **3** T19
Telephone: (01386) 438333

One of the most beautiful English gardens.

Location: 4 m NE of Chipping Campden, 1 m E of A46 (re-designated B4632) off B4081.
Open: Apr-end of Sept daily except Tue & Fri 11-7. Closed Good Fri. Also open Tues in June & July only. Oct daily except Tues & Fri 11-6. Last admission 1 hour before closing.
Admission: £5.20 children £2.60 Family ticket £13. *Parties by prior written arrangement only. No party concessions*
Refreshments: Coffee, lunches 11-2. Teas 2.15-5. Light refreshments available in plant sales centre adjacent to car park Apr-30 Sept 10.30-5.45
No dogs. No picnics. No games in the Garden. Liable to serious overcrowding on Bank Hol weekends and fine Suns. Access: for the less able is limited in parts due to the nature of some informal stone paved paths. Wheelchair access to part of garden only. Wheelchairs available.

HODGES BARN GARDENS

Shipton Moyne, Tetbury   GL8 8PR   map **14** T18   ċ
Telephone: (01666) 880202
Fax: (01367) 718096

One of the finest private gardens in England. Spring bulbs, Magnolias and flowering trees are followed by a superb collection of old fashioned and climbing roses with many mixed shrub and herbaceous beds.

Open: Apr 1-Aug 19 Mon Tues Fri 2-5.
Admission: Adults £2.50 Children free. Weekends £3.50. Wed,Thur £3.
Refreshments: Teas by appointment. Lunches nearby.

KIFTSGATE COURT

(Mr & Mrs J.G. Chambers)
nr Chipping Campden   map **3** S19
Telephone: (01386) 438777
Fax: (01386) 438777

Garden with many unusual shrubs and plants including tree paeonies, abutilons etc, specie and old fashioned roses.

Location: 3 m NE of Chipping Campden.
Open: Apr May Aug Sept Wed Thur and Sun 2-6pm. June July Wed Thur Sat and Sun 12-6pm. Bank Hols Mons 2-6pm.
Admission: Adults £3 children £1.
Refreshments: Whit Sun to Sept 1.
Coaches by appointment only.*Unusual plants for sale on open days.*

LITTLE DEAN HALL

(D.M. Macer-Wright, Esq)
Littledean, Nr Cinderford   GL14 3NR   map **14** T18
Telephone: (01594) 824213

Little Dean Hall is reputedly England's oldest inhabited hosue (Guiness Book of Records) and also has the reputation for being "one of the most haunted houses in the British Isles" as quoted by Simon Marsden in The Journal of a Ghosthunter. There are remains in the grounds of a major cult shrine to Sabrina, goddess of the river Severn and the site is steeped in the myth and legend of the Celtic west and the Arthurian Age. The house has Saxon and Celtic remains in the cellars dated to before the 11th century and believed to originate in the 5th or 6th centuries. From 1996 visitors will be able to join an ongoing survey to study the paranormal effects as a research programme which we hope to link to a University Parapsychology Department. The Hall is sparsely furnished and is presented as a low key museum depicting its remarkable archaeological, structural and supernatural history. The informal grounds and ancient chestnut trees provide an atmospheric setting for this unusual house.

Location: 12 m W of Gloucester; 2m E of Cinderford; 400 yds from A4151 on Littledean/Newnham-on-Severn Road, turn at King's Head.
Open: Apr 1-Oct 31. Suns-Fri 2-5.30. Other times for parties by appointment only.
Admission: Charged.

LYDNEY PARK GARDENS
(Viscount Bledisloe)
Lydney   GL15 6BU   map **14** T17
Telephone: (01594) 842844 (office)

Extensive Woodland Garden with lakes and a wide selection of rhododendrons and azaleas fine shrubs and trees. Museums and Roman Temple Site. Deer Park (picnics).

Location: ½ m W of Lydney on A48 (Gloucester to Chepstow).
Station(s): Lydney
Open: Suns, Wed and Bank Hol from Easter 7 Apr-9 June 11-6. Everyday 27 May-2 June.
Admission: Car park and accompanied children free. Adults £2 Wed £1.
Refreshments: Teas in house (house not otherwise open). Picnics in Deer Park. Taurus Café/Restaurant. Craft shop and Pottery at Old Park.
Open all year. Free car park. Dogs on lead.

MISARDEN PARK GARDENS
(Major M.T.N.H. Wills)
Miserden, Stroud   map **14** T18   &
Telephone: (01285) 821303
Fax: (01825) 821530

Spring flowers, shrubs, fine topiary (some designed by Sir Edwin Lutyens) and herbaceous borders within a walled garden, roses and fine specimen trees. 17th century Manor House (not open), standing high overlooking Golden Valley.

Location: Miserden 7 m from Gloucester, Cheltenham, Stroud & Cirencester; 3 m off A417 (signed).
Open: Every Tues, Wed & Thurs from 1 Apr-30 Sept 9.30-4.30. Nurseries adjacent to garden open daily except Mons.
Admission: £2.50 (includes leaflet) Children (accompanied) free. Reductions for parties (of 20 or more) by appointment. (Guided tour extra)

NEWARK PARK   🍂 The National Trust
Ozleworth   GL12 7PZ
Telephone: (01453) 842644
Location: 1½ m E of Wotton under Edge, 1½ m S of junction of A4135 and B4058.

OWLPEN MANOR
(Mr & Mrs Nicholas Mander)
Uley, nr Dursley   GL11 5BZ   map **14** T18
Telephone: (01453) 860261
Fax: (01435) 860819

Romantic Tudor manor house in 16th/17th century formal terraced gardens. Picturesque Cotswold manorial group - including Jacobean Court House and Watermill dated 1728 (now holiday cottages), Victorian church and medieval tithe barn - enclosed in its own lovely wooded valley. 'The epitome of romance' (Pevsner). The mellow stone manor dates from 1450-1616, with small improvements of 1719; uninhabited for over 100 years before 1925, when it was restored by Cotswold Arts & Crafts architect, Norman Jewson. Tudor Great Hall and Jacobean Oak Parlour. Contents include unique series of 17th C painted-cloth wall hangings in Queen Margaret of Anjou's bedroom, family and Cotswold Arts & Crafts furniture and pictures, and textiles, wallpaintings and panelling. One of the oldest complete gardens in England, with parterres, topiary yews and mill pond. 'Owlpen, in Gloucestershire - ah, what a dream is there!' Vita Sackville-West.

Location: 3 m E of Dursley off B4066, 1 m E of Uley at Green by Old Crown pub.
Station(s): Stroud
Open: 2-5 Apr 1-Sept 30 incl. Tues, Thur, Suns and Bank Hol Mons. Also Weds in July and August. No dogs.
Admission: £3.50 children £2. Tours for pre-booked groups of 30 or more.
Refreshments: Light lunches from 12.00, cream teas. Pre-booked evening meals for groups in Cyder House Restaurant.
Accommodation: Nine period cottages, including listed buildings, available on the Owlpen Estate.
Conferences: Facilities available including filming and corporate entertaining.

PAINSWICK ROCOCO GARDEN
(Painswick Rococo Garden Trust)
Painswick   map **3** T18
Telephone: (01452) 813204

This beautiful six acre garden, set in a hidden combe, is a rare and complete survivor of the brief eighteenth century taste for the Rococo in garden design.

Sir Joshua Reynolds
Portrait painter (1723-1792)
First President of the Royal Academy, knighted in 1769

His work can be seen in the following properties included in Historic Houses Castles and Gardens:-

Arundel Castle	*Parham Park*
Dalmeny House (Roseberry Collection of	*Pencarrow House*
Political Portraits)	*Petworth House*
Elton Hall	*Rockingham Castle*
Goodwood House	*Saltram*
Ickworth House, Park & Garden	*Shalom Hall*
Kenwood, The Iveagh Bequest	*Wallington House*
Knole	*Weston Park*

THE PRIORY GARDENS
(The Hon. Mrs. Healing)
Kemerton, Nr. Tewkesbury, Gloucestershire   GL20 7JN   map **3** S18   &
Telephone: (01386) 725258

4 acre garden with a collection of rare trees and shrubs, long herbaceous borders planned in colour groups. Stream, fern and suncken garden, raised beds planted with alpine and many other unusual and interesting plants. Remains of 16th Century ruins with large clipped yew of same date.

Location: 5m north of Tewkesbury B4080 Evesham Road.
Open: Fris May 31-Sept 27 Suns May 26 June 23 July 14 Aug 4 and 25 Sept 8. 2-6pm.
Admission: £1.50 June. £2 July-Sept. Children under 7 free. Parties by arrangement £2.
Refreshments: Suns only.
Gardens open only.

RODMARTON MANOR
(Mr & Mrs Simon Biddulph)
Cirencester   GL7 6PF   map **14** T18
Telephone: (01285) 841253

Rodmarton Manor was one of the last great country houses to be constructed entirely by hand with local materials between 1909 and 1929. Built for Claud and Margaret Biddulph by Ernest Barnsley the house stands today as a superb example of the Arts and Crafts Tradition. Most of the furniture was specially made for the house and there are also fine examples of decorated pottery, appliques, rugs and curtains. We do conducted tours of the house for groups. The gardens were laid out as the house was being built and consist of a series of outdoor rooms each with its own character. There are hedges, topiary, a troughery, a rockery, lawns, recently replanted herbaceous borders, kitchen garden and 'leisure garden'. A wide selection of plants, shrubs and trees have been planted over three generations. Although there is interest all year round in the garden the season of greatest impact is June but we are extending the flowering range now well beyond that through August. Over 80 different kinds of snowdrops are grown here.

Location: Off A433 6 m west of Cirencester.
Open: The house is open to groups by prior written appointment throughout the year. The garden is open Sats 11 May-31 Aug 2-5pm and by appointment throughout the year. Also see NGS book.
Admission: Conducted tour of the house with unconducted tour of the garden £4.50 (child £2.20). Minimum group charge £31.50. Garden only £2.00 Sat 2-5 and £2.50 any other time (accompanied children free).

SEZINCOTE
(Mr & Mrs D. Peake)
Moreton-in-Marsh   GL56 9AW   map **3** T19   △

Oriental water garden by Repton and Daniell with trees of unusual size. House in 'Indian' style inspiration of Royal Pavilion, Brighton.

Location: 1½ m W of Moreton-in-Marsh on A44 to Evesham; turn left by lodge before Bourton-on-the-Hill.
Station(s): Moreton-in-Marsh.
Open: Garden Thurs Fri & Bank Hol Mons 2-6 (or dusk if earlier) throughout year, except Dec. House May June July & Sept Thurs & Fri 2.30-6 parties by appointment. Open in aid of *National Gardens Scheme* Sun 7 July 2-6.
Admission: House & Garden £4 Garden only £3 children £1 under 5's free.
Refreshments: Hotels & restaurant in Moreton-in-Marsh.
No dogs.

SNOWSHILL MANOR   ❦ The National Trust
nr Broadway   WR12 7LU   map **3** T19   &
Telephone: (01386) 852410

A Tudor house with c1700 facade; 21 rooms containing interesting collection of craftsmanship, including musical instruments, clocks, toys, bicycles and Japanese armour, with small formal garden.

Location: 3 m SW of Broadway off A44.
Open: Daily except Tues Apr & Oct 1-5 Closed Good Fri. May to end Sept daily except Tues 1-6 Grounds & Visitor facilities open from 12: Last admissions to house & restaurant½ hour before closing. Timed tickets will be issued for the house. Liable to serious overcrowding on Sun & Bank Hol Mons.
Admission: £5.20 children £2.60 Family ticket £13. Grounds restaurant and shop £2. School Parties by prior written arrangement only. The Manor is a 10 minute walk (500 yds) along an undulating countryside path.
Refreshments: Open for coffees, lunches & teas Apr-Oct 12-4.30: May-end Sept 12-5.30: also 2 Nov-8 Dec Sat & Sun 12.30-4.30.
Coach & school parties by prior written appointment. No dogs. Liable to serious overcrowding on Suns and Bank Hol Weekends. Disabled access to visitor facilities but house and grounds unsuitable. Shop.

STANWAY HOUSE
(Lord Neidpath)
nr Broadway   GL54 5PQ   map **3** T19
Telephone: (01386) 584469

This jewel of Cotswold Manor houses is very much a home rather than a museum and the centre of a working landed estate which has changed hands once in 1275 years. The mellow Jacobean architecture, the typical squire's family portraits, the exquisite Gatehouse, the old Brewery, mediaeval Tithe Barn, the extensive gardens, arboretum pleasure grounds and formal landscape contribute to the timeless charm of what Arthur Negus considered one of the most beautiful and romantic houses in England.

Location: 1 m off B4632 Cheltenham/Broadway road; on B4077 Toddington/Stow-on-the-Wold road; M5 junction 9.
Open: June-Sept Tues and Thurs 2-5.
Admission: Adults £3.50 OAPs £3 children £1.
Refreshments: Teas in Old Bakehouse in village (Stanton 204).

SUDELEY CASTLE AND GARDENS
(Lord and Lady Ashcombe)
Winchcombe GL54 5JD map **3** T19 △
Telephone: (01242) 603197/602308
Fax: (01242) 602959

Nestling among the rolling Cotswold Hills, Sudeley Castle, the home of Lord and Lady Ashcombe, is one of England's great historic houses. Sudeley has royal connections stretching back 1000 years. Once the property of King Ethelred the Unready, Sudeley was later the magnificent palace of Queen Katherine Parr, Henry VIII's sixth wife, who is buried in the Castle Church. Henry VIII, Anne Boleyn, Lady Jane Grey and Elizabeth I stayed at the Castle. Charles I resided here while Prince Rupert established his headquarters during the Civil War. During the Victorian era a sympathetic programme of reconstruction enhanced Sudeley's earlier magnificence. Among a wealth of history on show is an impressive collection of treasures including masterpieces by Turner, Van Dyck and Rubens. Surrounding the Castle are seven enchanting gardens which have gained recognition for their floral displays and topiary. Famous for its fine collection of old-fashioned roses, the Queen's Garden is well worth a visit. New for the 1996 season is a Tudor Knot Garden, with intricate patterns, mosaics and water features. The design has been inspired by the pattern of the cloth taken from a dress worn by Queen Elizabeth I in a painting by Lucas de Heere, "An Allegory of the Tudor Succession", which hangs in the Castle. Group tours of the gardens may be booked. There is an interesting exhibition illustration the diaries of Emma Dent and her lace collection, Picnic Area, Adventure Playground, Castle Shop, Specialist Plant Centre and fully-licensed Restaurant and Tea Rooms.

Location: 7 m NE of Cheltenham on B4632 (A46). Access A40, A38, A417, M5 (junction 9, Tewkesbury).
Station(s): Cheltenham Spa.
Open: Mar 1-31 Gardens, Plant Centre and Shop 10.30-4.30 daily. Apr 1-Oct 31 Gardens, Exhibition Centre, Restaurant and Tea-rooms, Shop and Plant Centre 10.30-5.30 daily. Church 10.30-5 daily. Castle Apartments 11-5 daily.
Admission: Adults £5.40, Adult party £4.10, Adult gardens £4, Senior Citizens £4.70, Sunior Citizens party £3.80, Senior Citizens gardens £3.20, Children £3, Child party £2.20, Child gardens £1.80, Family £14, Friends of Sudeley Local & Founder members Family Season £25, Adult Season £12. Other Friends Family Seaon £30, Adult Season £15. Adventure Playground (only) 75p per person.
Refreshments: Fully licensed Restaurant and tea rooms open for morning coffee, lunches and afternoon tea. Adjacent pavilion available for group bookings.
Events/Exhibitions: Lace and the Times of Emma Dent, The English Table and History of the Knot Garden. Special events are also held during the year.
Accommodation: 14 romantic Cotswold Cottages on Castle Estate. Private guided tours of Castle Apartments and Gardens by prior arrangement. Schools educational pack available.
Conferences: Sudeley Castle is suitable for corporate events all year including conferences, entertaining, fine dining, medieval dinners and product launches. Also a location for management training courses, filming, photography and various activities.
Regretfully the Castle and Gardens are not suitable for the disabled. Sudeley Castle reserves the right to close all or part of the Castle and Gardens and to amend information in the leaflet as necessary.

WESTBURY COURT GARDEN ❧ The National Trust
Westbury-on-Severn GL14 1PD map **3** T18 ♿
Telephone: (01452) 760461

A formal Dutch water-garden with canals and yew hedges, laid out between 1696 and 1705; the earliest of its kind remaining in England.

Location: 9 m SW of Gloucester on A48.
Station(s): Nearest Gloucester, bus from Gloucester Red & White 31 & 73.
Open: Apr to end Oct Wed to Sun & Bank Hol Mons 11-6. *Closed* Good Fri. Other times by appointment only.
Admission: £2.50 children £1.25. Parties by prior written arrangement only. Picnic area. No dogs. Wheelchairs provided. Braille guide.

WHITTINGTON COURT
(Mrs J L Stringer)
Whittington, nr Cheltenham GL54 4HF map **3** T19
Telephone: (01242) 820556

Small Elizabethan stone-built manor house with family possessions.

Location: 4½ m E of Cheltenham on A40.
Open: Apr 6-21 Aug 10-26. Daily 2-5.
Admission: £2 OAPs £1.50 Children £1. Open to parties by arrangement.

WOODCHESTER MANSION
(Woodchester Mansion Trust)
Nympsfield map **3** T18
Telephone: (01453) 860661 Visitor information (01453) 750455 (Trust office)

Hidden in a secret wooded valley near Stroud is one of the most intriguing houses in the country. Woodchester Mansion was started in 1856 but abandoned, incomplete, in 1870. Designed in the Gothic style by the brilliant young architect, Benjamin Bucknall, it is an unfinished masterpiece of golden Cotswold stone. Like a Victorian building site caught in a timewarp, it offers a unique insight into traditional building techniques. It is now leased by the Woodchester Mansion Trust, whose repair programme includes training courses in stonemasonry and building conservation. Open days and private visits are organised by volunteers from the local community.

Location: By Coaley Peak Picnic Site on B4066 Stroud-Dursley, ½ m from Nympsfield village.
Station(s): Stroud 3 m.
Open: First weekend in each month from Easter-Oct (Sat/Sun) and Bank Holiday weekends (Sat/Sun/Mon). Gates open 11-4. Regular guided tours. Free minibus service or walk down .75 mile wooded track. Gift shop.
Admission: Adults £3 students £2 children £1. Private group visits by arrangement (01453) 860531.
Refreshments: Teas and snacks.
No dogs, please.

Sir Peter Lely - portrait painter

His paintings can be seen at the following properties included in Historic Houses Castles and Gardens:-

Aynhoe Park	*Kedleston Hall*
Belton House	*Knole*
Breamore House	*Petworth House*
Browsholme Hall	*Ragley Hall*
Dalmeny House	*Rockingham Castle*
Euston Hall	*St Osyth Priory*
Goodwood House	*Stanford Hall*
Gorhambury	*Weston Park*

SUDELEY CASTLE

A Thousand Years of History in the Heart of the Cotswolds
Open every day April to October

Winchcombe, Gloucestershire.
Telephone: Cheltenham (01242) 602308

HAMPSHIRE

AVINGTON PARK
(Mr and Mrs J.B. Hickson)
Winchester   SO21 1DD   △ &
Telephone: (01962) 779260
Fax: (01962) 779715

Avington Park is an old house enlarged in 1670 by the addition of two wings.

BASING HOUSE
(Hampshire County Council)
Basingstoke   RG24 7HB   map **3** U20
Telephone: (01256) 467294
Fax: (01256) 26283

Basing House ruins were once the country's largest private house, the palace of William Paulet, 1st Marquess of Winchester who was Lord Treasurer of England under three Tudor monarchs. The Civil War brought disaster to Basing which fell to Oliver Cromwell in person after 2.5 years of siege in 1645. The ruins, which cover about 10 acres, contain Norman earthworks, the remains of Tudor kitchens, cellars, towers, a 300 foot long tunnel, a spectacular barn, Civil War defences designed by Inigo Jones and a recently re-created 16/17th century formal garden.

Location: 2 m from Basingstoke Town Centre & 2 m from Junction 6 of M3.
Station(s): Basingstoke.
Open: Apr 3-Sept 29 Wed-Sun and Bank Hols 2-6. Parties any time by prior arrangement.
Admission: £1.50 Children and OAPs 70p.
Refreshments: Meals can be obtained at two public houses near main entrance.
Car parking. Suitable for disabled persons (please telephone in advance for easier parking).

BEAULIEU
(The Lord Montagu of Beaulieu)
Beaulieu   map **3** V20   Ⓢ
Telephone: (0159) 061 2345

'Beaulieu's Palace House is the ancestral home of the Montagu Family. The house was once the Gatehouse to the Beaulieu Abbey (ruins of which can be seen today along with an Exhibition of Monastic Life) and has many unusual architectural features that make it stand out from other historic houses. Beaulieu is of course famous for its National Motor Museum featuring more than 250 exhibits including motor cars, commercial vehicles and motorcycles. There is 'Wheels' a futuristic ride on space age pods through 100 years of motoring; Monorail and Veteran Bus rides, plus a Driving Simulator and many other rides and drives for the whole family'.

Location: In Beaulieu 7 m SE of Lyndhurst; 14 m S of Southampton; 6 m NE of Lymington.
Station(s): Brockenhurst.
Open: All facilities open throughout the year. Easter to Sept - Daily 10-6; Oct to Easter - Daily 10-5. *Closed Christmas Day.*
Admission: Inclusive charge. Reduced rates for Chd and OAPs. *Parties at special rates.*
Refreshments: Lunches and teas at licensed Brabazon Restaurant.
Events/Exhibitions: A variety of special events is held each year including:- Autojumble, Boat Jumble, Outdoor Symphony Concert, Fireworks Fair and a number of Car Club Rallies. Tel: (01590) 612345 for details.
Conferences: A unique range of facilities is on offer for conference and corporate hospitality including a tiered seating theatre for up to 200 people, the Brabazon Catering Centre which can accomodate up to 300, a 13th century Banqueting Hall, outdoor Exhibition Arena and Rally Field. Licensed for Civil Weddings.

BRAMDEAN HOUSE
(Mrs H. Wakefield)
Bramdean, nr Alresford
Telephone: (01962) 771214

Carpets of Spring bulbs.

BREAMORE HOUSE
(Sir Westrow Hulse, Bt)
nr Fordingbridge   SP6 2DF   map **3** V19   △
Telephone: (01725) 512468

Elizabethan Manor House (1583) with fine collection of paintings, tapestries, furniture. Coutryside Museum takes the visitor back to when a village was self sufficient. Exhibition of Rural Arts and Agricultural machinery. Carriage Museum. 'The Red Rover', and other coaches.

Location: 3 m N of Fordingbridge off the main Bournemouth Road (A338) 8 m S of Salisbury.
Station(s): Salisbury.
Open: Easter Hol Apr - Tues Wed Sun, May June July & Sept - Tues Wed Thurs Sat Sun and all Bank Hols, Aug daily. House 2-5.30 Countryside Museum 1-5.30. Other times by appointment.
Admission: Combined ticket adults £4.50 children £3 reduced rate for parties and OAPs.
Refreshments: Home-made snacks and teas available from midday.

BROADLANDS
(Lord and Lady Romsey)
Romsey   SO51 9ZD   △ &
Telephone: (01794) 516878

Fine example of Palladian architecture set in Capability Brown parkland on the banks of the River Test.

EXBURY GARDENS
(E.L. de Rothschild, Esq)
nr Southampton   SO45 1AZ   map **3** V20
Telephone: (01703) 891203
Fax: (01703) 243380

Described as "Heaven with the gates open" this 200 acres garden, created by Lionel de Rothschild, contains magnificent displays of rhododendrons, azaleas and other woodland shrubs. Free 'Trail Guides' in Spring, Summer and Autumn encourage the visitor to see newly planted areas, making this a beautiful day out any time.

Location: Exbury village, south drive from Jct. 2 M27 west of Southampton. Turn W off A326 at Dibden Purlieu towards Beaulieu.
Open: Daily 10-5.30pm (dusk if earlier). Gardens: End 17 Feb-end Oct. July and Aug 53 acres remain open; ideal for picnics. Free entry to Gift Shop and Plant Centre, open until Christmas Eve anf re-opens in January.
Admission: £4.50, OAPs and parties £4, Chd (10-16) £3.50 for main season. Early and late season discounts. Season tickets available.
Refreshments: Licensed refreshments.
Events/Exhibitions: Marquee hospitality end Apr/beginning June.
Free parking for all and excellent toilet facilities.

FURZEY GARDENS
Minstead, Nr. Lindhurst   SO40 7GT
Telephone: (01703) 812464

A garden of great peace and beauty featuring a lake and extensive views of the Isle of Wight. There is also a restored 16th Century cottage and large gallery stocked with different types of crafts.

GILBERT WHITE'S HOUSE & GARDEN AND THE OATES MUSEUM
(Charitable Trust)
The Wakes, High Street, Selborne   GU34 3JH   map 12 U21
Telephone: (01420) 511275

Historic 18th century house & glorious garden, home of famous naturalist REV. GILBERT WHITE, author of 'THE NATURAL HISTORY OF SELBORNE'. Furnished rooms & original manuscript. Also fascinating museum on Frank Oates, Victorian explorer and Capt. Lawrence Oates who accompanied Scott on the ill-fated Antarctic expedition of 1911/1912.

Location: In main high street of Selborne village.
Station(s): Liss or Alton.
Open: 11-5 DAILY from END MAR-CHRISTMAS then WEEKENDS ONLY during WINTER. Day, evening & winter opening for groups by arrangement.
Admission: £3 OAPs £2.50 Children £1. Free admission to shop.
Refreshments: Three venues along High Street in village and tea parlour in house.
Events/Exhibitions: Unusual plants fair 22/23 June: Picnic to 'Jazz in June' 22 June: Mulled wine day 24 Nov.
Conferences: Charming room for up to 20 people.
Excellent gift shop. Plant sales.

HIGHCLERE CASTLE
(The Earl of Carnarvon KCVO, KBE)
nr Newbury   RG15 9RN   map 3 U20
Telephone: (01635) 253210

Designed by Charles Barry in the 1830s at the same time as he was building the Houses of Parliament. This soaring pinnacled mansion provided a perfect setting for the 3rd Earl of Carnarvon one of the great hosts of Queen Victoria's reign. The extravagant interiors range from church Gothic through Morrish flamboyance and rococo revival to the solid masculinity on the long Library. Old master paintings mix with portraits by Van Dyck and 18th century painters. Napoleon's desk and chair rescued from St. Helena sits with other 18th century furniture. The 5th Earl of Carnarvon, discovered the Tomb of Tutankhamun with Howard Carter. The castle houses a unique exhibition of some of his discoveries which were only rediscovered in the castle in 1988. The current Earl is the Queen's Horseracing Manager. In 1993 to celebrate his 50th year as a leading owner and breeder "The Lord Carnarvon Racing Exhibition" was opened to the public, and

offers a fascinating insight into a racing history that dates back three generations. The magnificent parkland with its massive cedars was designed by Capability Brown. The walled gardens dated from an earlier house at Highclere but the dark yew walks are entirely victorian in character. The glass Orangery and Fernery add an exotic flavour. The Secret Garden has a romance of its own with a beautiful curving lawn surrounded by densely planted herbaceous gardens. A place for poets and romantics. Guided tours are often provided, free of charge, to visitors.

Location: 4½ m S of Newbury on A34, junction 13 of M4 about 2 m from Newbury. M3. Basingstoke junction 15 m. Heathrow via M4 1 hr. Rail from London (Paddington station) 1 hr.
Station(s): Newbury
Open: Tues-Suns inclusive, 1 May-29 Sept from 11-5. Last admissions at 4pm. The Castle will be closed on Mons - except for the Bank Hol Mons during May and Aug. The Castle will not be open over the Easter Bank Holiday.
Admission: House and Grounds: Adults £5 OAP's £4 children £2.50. Gardens and Exhibitions only adults £3 children £1.50. Annual VIP Season Ticket - 2 adults and up to 3 children (from date of joining) and allows 10% off in Shop 10% off in Tea-rooms, free admission to all daytime special events, discounted tickets for Concert tickets. Also 10% off the Stubbs Restaurant at the Newbury Hilton Hotel. Group rate £4 adults and OAP's (children ½ price).
Refreshments: Lunches, teas, ices, soft drinks. Parties by prior arrangement.
Conferences: Business conferences, management training courses, film and photographic location. Licensed for Civil Weddings.
Ample car park and picnic area adjacent to Castle. Suitable for disabled persons on ground floor only. One wheelchair available. Visitors can buy original items in Castle Gift Shop. No dogs are permitted in the house or gardens except guide dogs. No photography in the house.

THE SIR HAROLD HILLIER GARDENS AND ARBORETUM
(Hampshire County Council)
Ampfield, nr Romsey   SO51 0QA   map 5 V20   Ⓔ
Telephone: (01794) 368787
Fax: (01794) 368027

Begun by the famous nurseryman Sir Harold Hillier in 1953, and gifted to Hampshire County Council in 1977, the Gardens and Arboretum now extend to more than 160 acres and contain the largest collection of different hardy plants in the British Isles. With this diversity in plants, the Gardens provide something of interest throughout the seasons, from the magnificent floral displays in spring and the pastel shades of summer, to the riot of autumnal hues in October and the highly-scented winter flowering Witch Hazels.

Location: 3 m north east of Romsey, off A31.
Station(s): Romsey.
Open: Every day Apr-Oct 10.30-6 every day Nov-Mar 10.30-5 (or dusk if earlier). *Closed* Public and Bank Hols over Christmas.
Admission: Apr-Oct £4 adults £3.50 OAPs £1 children. Nov-Mar £3 adults £2.50 OAPs £1 children.
Refreshments: Teas and light meals at weekends November to March and every day from April to October.
Regret NO DOGS.

HINTON AMPNER GARDEN   🌿 The National Trust
nr Alresford   SO24 0LA   map 3 U20   &
Telephone: (01962) 771305

The garden, set in superb countryside, combines formal and informal design and planting, producing delightful walks and unexpected vistas. The house was rebuilt by Ralph Dutton following a fire in 1960, and re-furnished with fine Regency furniture, 17th century Italian pictures and porcelain.

Location: 1 m W of Bramdean Village on A272; 8 m E of Winchester.
Station(s): Alresford 4 m; Winchester 9 m.
Open: 30 Mar-end Sept GARDEN Sat Sun Tues and Wed and Bank Hol Mons 1.30-5.30. HOUSE Tues & Wed only and Sat & Sun in Aug 1.30-5.30 (last adm 5). Car park open at 1.15.
Admission: House and Garden £3.90; Garden only £2.50. Reduction for parties £3.40 (advance booking only). No groups in August.
Refreshments: Tea-room same days as garden 2-5. Picnics in grass car park only.
No dogs. Most of garden accessible by wheelchair.

HOUGHTON LODGE GARDENS

(Captain & Mrs M.W. Busk)
Stockbridge   SO20 6LQ   map **3** U19
Telephone: (01264) 810177 or (01264) 810502
Fax: (01794) 388072

Landscaped pleasure grounds surround unique 18th C 'Cottage Ornee' beside the River Test with lovely views over the tranquil and unspoilt valley. Featured in BBC's TV series "The Buccaneers". Within the traditional kitchen garden surrounded by rare chalkcob walls is the HAMPSHIRE HYDROPONICUM where flowers, fruits, herbs and vegetables grow WITHOUT SOIL. Believed to be the first Hydroponicum in England primarily intended to delight and inform the visitor. The ease of Hydroponic Gardening (no weeding, or digging, no soil borne pests) makes it an ideal method for the handicapped.

Location: 1½ m S of A30 at Stockbridge on minor road to Houghton village.
Station(s): Winchester, Andover.
Open: Mar-Sept incl. Sat, Sun & Bank Holidays 10-5. Mon Tues and Fri 2-5. House open for groups by appointment.
Refreshments: By prior arrangement.
Telephone for details. Free parking.

HURST CASTLE

map **3** V20   ENGLISH HERITAGE
Telephone: (01590) 642344

Built by Henry VIII to defend the Solent, Hurst Castle was completed in 1544, and had a garrison of 23 men. During the Civil War it was occupied by Parliamentary forces and Charles I was imprisoned here for a short time. A longer incarceration was that of an unfortunate priest called Atkinson, who was a prisoner here for 29 years in the 18th century. The castle was considerably modernised in the mid-19th century, under the fear of a French invasion, and was still useful in the Second World War. Café open during summer season.

Location: Approach by ferry from Keyhaven.
Open: 10-5.30 Apr/May/June, 10-6 July/Aug, 10-5.30 Sept/Oct.
Admission: Adults £2 concessions £1.50 children £1.
Refreshments: Café open during summer season.

JANE AUSTEN'S HOUSE

(Jane Austen Memorial Trust)
Chawton   map **12** U21
Telephone: (01420) 83262
Location: In Chawton, 1 m SW of Alton, sign-posted off roundabout at junction of A31 with A32.

JENKYN PLACE

(Mrs G E Coke)
Bentley, Nr. Farnham   GU10 5LU
Telephone: (01420) 23118

Beautifully designed garden with large collection of rare plants.

MOTTISFONT ABBEY GARDEN   🌿 The National Trust

Mottisfont   SO51 0LP   map **3** U19
Telephone: (01794) 340757

A country estate of timeless beauty. A tributary of the River Test flows through the garden forming a superb and tranquil setting for a 12th-century Augustinian priory, which, after the Dissolution of the monastries, became a house. In the

Abbey you can visit the drawing room, superbly decorated by Rex Whistler, and the Cellaruim of the Old Priory. The maginificent trees, walled gardens and the national collection of old-fashioned roses combine to provide interest throughout the seasons.

Location: 4½ m NW Romsey ¾ m W of A3057.
Station(s): Mottisfont Dunbridge (¾ m).
Open: GARDEN 24 & 31 Mar 1 Apr-30 Oct Sat-Wed 12-6 (or dusk if earlier). June all week daily. Last admissions one hour before closing.
Admission: GARDEN £3, £4 during rose season. No reduction for parties. Coaches please book in advance. Rose season varies according to the weather. Check with the property in June.
Shop; open same time as garden. Dogs in car park only. Wheelchairs and powered buggy available. Special parking area for disabled people for shop and use garden only.

PORTCHESTER CASTLE

map **5** V20   ENGLISH HERITAGE
Telephone: (01705) 378291

A Roman fortress, a Norman castle and a Romanesque church share this same site on the north shore of Portsmouth harbour. The outer walls were built in the 3rd century when Britain was the vulnerable north-west frontier of a declining Roman Empire. Today they are among the finest Roman remains in northern Europe. Eight centuries - and very little repair work - later, the walls were sound enough to encompass a royal castle. Portchester was popular with the medieval monarchs but by the 15th century royal money was being spent on Portsmouth instead. The last official use of the castle was as a prison for French seamen during the Napoleonic wars. An exhibition tells the story of Portchester.

Location: South side of Portchester.
Open: Apr 1-Sept 30 10-6 daily Oct 1-Mar 31 daily 10-4.
Admission: Adults £2.50 concessions £1.90 children £1.30.

SANDHAM MEMORIAL CHAPEL   🌿 The National Trust

Burghclere, nr Newbury   map **5** U20
Telephone: (01635) 278394

A small chapel built to house the paintings of the distinguished 1st World War artist Stanley Spencer. The huge canvases which cover the chapel walls depict the lives of the ordinary men Spencer met while working as a hospital orderly at Salonica. A moving experience.

Location: In village of Burghclere 4 m S of Newbury ½ m E of A34.
Station(s): Newbury 4m.
Open: Mar and Nov, Sat & Sun only 11.30-4. 3 Apr-end Oct, 11.30-6, Wed-Sun & Bank Hol Mons (closed Wed following Bank Hol Mon) Dec-Feb by appointment only.
Admission: £1.50 children 75p. Parties must book. No reduction for parties. Wheelchair access via ramp.

SPINNERS

(P. Chappell)
Boldre, Lymington, Hampshire   SO14 5QE.   map **3** V19
Telephone: (01590) 673347

Woodland garden. Rare plant, shrub and tree nursery.

Location: Signed off A337 btw Lymington and Brockenhurst.
Admission: £1.50. Tue-Sat 10-5.

STRATFIELD SAYE HOUSE
(The Duke of Wellington)
Reading   RG7 2BT   map **5** U20   &
Telephone: (01256) 882882
Fax: (01256) 882345

Homes of the Dukes of Wellington since 1817, Stratfield Saye is a living exam-ple of the classic English Country House tradition with the present Duke and Duchess in residence for much of the year. The house and exhibition pay tribute to Arthur Wellesley, the first and Great Duke - soldier, statesman and victor of the Napoleonic wars. THE HOUSE: Gift of a grateful nation, the house contains a unique collection of paintings, prints, furniture and personal effects belonging to the Great Duke. THE WELLINGTON EXHIBITION: Depicts the life and times of the Great Duke and features his magnificent funeral carriage. THE GROUNDS: Include gardens and the grave of Copenhagen, the Duke's favourite charger that carried him throughout the battle of Waterloo.

Location: 1 m W of A33 between Reading & Basingstoke (turn off at Wellington Arms Hotel); signposted. Close to M3 & M4. The house and associated Wellington Country Park are situated on the Hampshire/Berkshire borders.
Open: House and Gardens open daily (except Fri) May 1-last Sun in Sept 11.30-4. Available for private and corporate functions by arrangement with The Wellington Office (Tel 01256 882882). Wellington Country Park (3 m from house) - nature trails, adventure playground, animals, boating, windsurfing, fishing, deer park, miniature railway, National Dairy Museum, Thames Valley Time Trail Mar-Oct daily 10-5 Nov-Feb Sat & Sun only. (Tel 01734 326444).
Admission: Please telephone for charges to House and Park.
Refreshments: Tea and snacks, licensed restaurant.

UPPARK   🌿 The National Trust
South Harting, Petersfield   GU31 5QR   map **12** V21   &
Telephone: (01730) 825415

Fine late 17th century house situated high on the South Downs with magnificent views towards the Solent. Important collection of paintings and decorative art formed by members of Fetherstonhaugh family; interesting below stairs servants' rooms, links with H.G. Wells whose early years were spent here. Extensive exhi-bition in Sun Alliance Visitor Centre, fully detailing restoration of house and con-tents.

Location: 5 m SE of Petersfield on B2146. 1½ m S of South Harting (197:SU775177)
Station(s): BR (Petersfield 5½ m) Petersfield-Midhurst alight South Harting, 1½ m (tel 01962 868944. Bus: Hants & Sussex 61 Stagecoach Coastline 73/5.
Open: 31 Mar-31 Oct: Sun-Thurs. House: 1-5; Car Park and Woodland Walk: 11-5.30. Garden & Exhibition 12-5.30. Last admissions to house 4-4-15. Print room open on a limit-ed basis first Mon each month. Tickets might sell out early on each day and the whole prop-erty, including the car park may have to close once its visitor capacity has been reached. Visitors wanting to be assured of admission are encouraged to pre-book. Some tickets avail-able for pre-booking for each open day. A small charge will be made (tel 01730 825317 pre-booking only). Booking open 1 Mar 10-1 Mon -Fri.
Admission: House, Garden and Exhibition: £5 family ticket £12.50. Parties (no reduction) must be pre-booked weekdays only.
Refreshments: Light lunches and afternoon teas. Open 12-5.30 same days as house. Picnic area near car park and in woodland. Kiosk near car park serving sandwiches, hot and cold drinks 11-5 (tel 01730 825256).
Braille guide to house. Baby Front Carriers available for loan at house (**No Back Carriers please** pushchairs not allowed in the house; changing facilities, highchairs, children's guide, hands-on exhibits in exhibition. Exhibition, (Stannah stairlift to upper floor) shop, garden and house accessible; lift to basement show-rooms. Wheelchairs available. WC. Disabled visitors are advised to telephone before visiting as house is likely to be full. Woodland walk and car park only, dogs on leads please (no shade in car park). NB: The property re-opened in 1995 after restoration, following a major fire in 1989 and is likely to continue to be extremely busy. The house has been fully restored and the garden re-planned and re-planted. Conservation requirements in the house, and the limited capacity of the whole property will restrict the number of visitors that can be accommodated. All entry by timed ticket.

THE VYNE   🌿 The National Trust
Sherborne St John, nr Basingstoke   RG26 5DX   map **5** U20   &
Telephone: (01256) 881337

Woodland walks and lawns sloping to the lake provide a magnificent setting for this early Tudor house. The panelled gallery and chapel with Renaissance glass are some of the finest examples in Britain. Outstanding collections of ceramics, textiles and furniture within a warm, historic atmosphere. The house will close earlier in the year to allow essential services and retoration work to begin. The house will be closed throughout 1997 and will re-open mid 1998. The grounds are planned to remain open.

Location: 4 m N of Basingstoke between Bramley & Sherborne St John (1½ m from each). *Station(s):* Bramley (2½ m).
Open: House: 19 Mar-1 Sept, 1.30-5.30, daily except Mon and Fri. Grounds: 19 Mar-end Oct, 12.30-5, daily except Mon & Fri. Also open Good Fri and Bank Hol Mons (11-5.30) but closed Tues following. Last admission ½ hour before closing.
Admission: House and Grounds £4. Grounds only £2 *Children half-price. Reduced rates for pre-booked parties Tues Wed & Thurs only £3.*
Refreshments: Light lunches and teas in the Old Brewhouse, same days as grounds, 19 Mar-end Oct 12.30-2 and 2.30-5.30.
NT Shop. Dogs in car park only. Wheelchair available.

HEREFORD & WORCESTER

ABBERLEY HALL
(Mrs Bishop)
nr Worcester   WR6 6DD   map **14** S18
Telephone: (01299) 896634 (office hours only)
Fax: (01299) 896875

Five principal rooms show ornate decoration of mid-Victorian period.

Location: 12 m NW of Worcester on A443.
Open: House only. June 10 July 17-19 22-26 29-31 Aug 1-2 5-9 12-16 19-23 and 27. 1.30-4.00
Admission: £1.
Unsuitable for wheelchairs. No dogs.

BERNITHAN COURT
(Bernithan Court Farm Partnership)
Llangarron   map **3** T17

House 1692: fine staircase, walled gardens.

Location: 1½ m from A40 Ross-Monmouth road.
Open: By prior appointment, Mrs James (01989) 770772. Admission £2.
Accommodation: On application.1

BERRINGTON HALL   🌿 The National Trust

Leominster   HR6 0DW   map **3** S17   △ &
Telephone: (01568) 615721

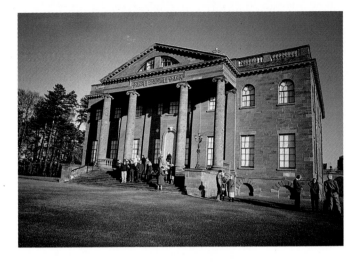

Built 1778-1781,designed by Henry Holland, the architect of Carlton House. Painted and plaster ceilings.'Capability' Brown laid out the park.

Location: 3 m N Leominster, 7 m S of Ludlow, W of A49.
Station(s): Leominster 4 m.
Open: 29 Mar-end Apr & Oct: Fri, Sat & Suns (open Bank Hol Mon, but closed Good Fri) 1.30-5.30. (4.30 in Oct). May-end June & Sept: Wed-Sun & Bank Hol Mon 1.30-5.30. July & Aug: open 7 days a week 1.30-5.30.
Admission: £3.80 Children £1.90 grounds only £1.70. Family ticket £9.50. Parties by prior written arrangement only.
Refreshments: Licensed restaurant in the Servants' Hall, serving homemade lunches and teas. Restaurant 12.30-2 (lunch), 2.30-5.30 (teas) last orders 5. Open same days as house and also Nov 2 to Dec 15, Sats and Suns 12.30-4.30. Park walk open July, August, September & October, same days as house.
Events/Exhibitions: Please contact the Property Manager for details.
No dogs. Wheelchair available. Wheelchair access grounds only. No photography.

BROBURY HOUSE GARDEN

(Leonora Weaver)

Brobury, nr. Hereford   HR3 6BS
Telephone: (01981) 500229

Victorian Gentlemans Country House set in 8 acres of magnificent gardens, with stunning view over the Wye Valley. Overnight accommodation available. Art gallery with antique maps & prints on site.

Open: All year except Christmas and New Year Mon-Sat 10-4.30.

BURTON COURT 🏛

(Lt-Cmdr & Mrs R.M. Simpson)

Eardisland   HR6 9DN   map **3** S17   &
Telephone: (01544) 388231

A typical squire's house, built around the surprising survival of a 14th century hall. The East Front re-designed by Sir Clough Williams-Ellis in 1912. An

extensive display of European and Oriental costume, natural history specimens, and models including a working model fairground. Pick your own soft fruit in season.

Location: 5 m W of Leominster signposted on A44.
Open: Spring Bank Hol-end Sept Wed Thurs Sat Sun & Bank Hol Mons 2.30-6.
Admission: Adults £2.50 children £2 coach parties £2
Refreshments: Coach parties catered for. Teas.
Accommodation: Holiday flat (first floor) self contained - sleeps 7.
Conferences: Conferences (Oct-Apr only).

CROFT CASTLE   🌿 The National Trust

nr Leominster   HR6 9PW   map **3** S17   &
Telephone: (01568) 780246

Welsh Border castle mentioned in Domesday Book. Inhabited by the Croft family for 900 years. Fine 18th century Gothic interior. Extensive wooded parkland.

Location: 5 m NW of Leominster just N of B4362 signposted from Ludlow/Leominster road (A49), and from A4110 at Mortimers Cross.
Station(s): Leominster 7 m.
Open: Apr & Oct Sat & Sun 1.30-4.30 Easter Sat Sun & Mon 1.30-4.30 Closed Good Fri May to end Sept Wed to Sun & Bank Hol Mons 1.30-5.30. Last admission 30 mins before closing.
Admission: £3.20 children £1.60 family ticket £8.00. Car park charge £1.50 per car; £10 per coach. Parties by prior written arrangement.
Refreshments: Picnics allowed in car park only.
Events/Exhibitions: Contact the Administrator for details.
Access for disabled to ground floor and part of grounds. Wheelchair available.

CWMMAU FARMHOUSE, BRILLEY   🌿 The National Trust

Brilley   HR3 6JP   map **3** S16
Telephone: (01497) 831251

Early 17th century timber-framed and stone tiled farmhouse.

Location: 4 m SW of Kington between A4111 and A438. Approached by a narrow lane.
Open: Easter May Spring & Summer Bank Hol weekends **only** (Sat Sun & Mon) 2-5.30. Also open Aug 7,14,21,28th 2-5.30. *At other times by prior appointment with the tenant Mr D Joyce.*
Admission: £2, chd £1.*No reduction for parties.*
No dogs. Unsuitable for wheelchairs and coaches.

DINMORE MANOR

(R.G. Murray)

nr Hereford   HR4 8EE   map **3** S17   &
Telephone: (01432) 830322

Spectacular hillside location. A range of impressive architecture dating from 14th to 20th century. Chapel, Cloisters, Great Hall (Music Room) and extensive roof walk giving panoramic views of the countryside and beautiful gardens below. Large collection of stained glass. Interesting and unusual plants for sale in plant centre.

Location: 6 m N of Hereford on (A49).
Open: All the year daily 9.30-5.30.
Admission: Adults £2.50 children (under 14) free when accompanied.
Refreshments: Available in the Plant Centre most afternoons.

EASTNOR CASTLE

nr Ledbury, Hereford & Worcester   **HR8 1RD**   map **3** T18
Telephone: (01531) 633160/632302
Fax: (01531) 631776

Splendid Norman Revival Castle built in 1812 in a dramatic setting within the Malvern Hills, Eastnor Castle captures the spirit of medieval chivalry and romance. The lavish interiors, in Italianate, Norman and Gothic style, display a unique collection of armour, tapestries, fine art, furniture and pictures by Van Dyck, Kneller, Romney, Watts and others. Castellated terraces descend to a lake. There is a renowned arboretum in the pleasure grounds, and a 500 acre park with red deer.

Location: 5 m from M50 (exit 2) 2 m E of Ledbury on Hereford/Tewkesbury Road A438.
Station(s): Ledbury (2 m).
Open: Sun from Easter-end Sept Bank Holiday Mon Sun-Fri during July & Aug 11.30-4.30. Group bookings at other times throughout the year by appointment.
Admission: Adults £4 children £2 reduced rates for parties and for grounds only.
Refreshments: Light lunches and home made cream teas.
Accommodation: Luxury accommodation for select groups.
Conferences: Conference activity days, exclusive 'Land-Rover' off road driving tel. Portcullis Office (01531) 633160. Licensed for Civil Weddings.
Dogs on lead allowed.

GOODRICH CASTLE

map **3** T17
Telephone: (01600) 890538

ENGLISH HERITAGE

The castle was built to command the ancient crossing of the Wye by the Gloucester/Caerleon road. Among the extensive remains of the original castle the keep survives, which largely dates from the late 13th century. For almost 300 years from the mid-14th century it was held by the Earls of Shrewsbury.

Location: 3 m (4.8 km) south west of Ross-on-Wye.
Open: Apr 1-Sept 30 10-6 daily Oct 1-Mar 31 daily 10-4.
Admission: Adults £2.20 concessions £1.70 children £1.10.

Anthony Salvin (1799-1881)
Architect - trained under John Nash

His work can be seen in the following properties included in Historic Houses Castles and Gardens:-

Helmingham Hall Gardens
Muncaster Castle
Petworth House

THE GREYFRIARS   The National Trust

Worcester   **WR1 2LZ**   map **14** S18   △
Telephone: (01905) 23571

A richly timber-framed house built c. 1480, was rescued from demolition at the time of World War II. Carefully restored and refurbished; interesting textiles and furnishings add character to panelled rooms; an archway leads through to a delightful garden.

Location: In Friar Street, Worcester.
Station(s): Worcester, Foregate Street (½ m).
Open: Apr-end Oct Wed & Thurs and Bank Holiday Mons 2-5. Other times adult parties by written application only.
Admission: £2.20 Children £1.10 Family ticket £5.50. Parties of children (inc schools) not admitted.
Events/Exhibitions: Three Choirs Festival 17,19,24 Aug 11-1 & 2-5. Closed Sun.
No dogs. Unsuitable for wheelchairs.

HANBURY HALL   The National Trust

nr Droitwich   map **14** S18   &
Telephone: (01527) 821214

William and Mary style red brick house built c. 1700 for a wealthy barrister. Outstanding painted ceilings and staircase by Sir James Thornhill. The Watney Collection of porcelain; Orangery c. 1740. 18th century formal garden reinstatement.

Location: 4½ m E of Droitwich, 1 m N of B4090.
Station(s): Droitwich Spa 4 m.
Open: 31 Mar-30 Oct: Sun-Wed 2-6. Last admission 5.30 or dusk if earlier.
Admission: House & garden £4 Children £2 Garden only £2.50 Family ticket £10. *Parties by prior written arrangment only.*
Refreshments: Teas in the house.
Events/Exhibitions: Details from the Property Manager.
Conferences: House is available for private and commercial functions and licensed for civil wedding ceremonies.
Shop. No dogs. Wheelchair available.

HARTLEBURY CASTLE

(The Church Commissioners)
nr Kidderminster   **DY11 7XX**   map **14** S18
Telephone: (01299) 250410

Historic home of the Bishops of Worcester for over 1,000 years. Fortified in 13th century, rebuilt after sacking in the Civil War and Gothicised in 18th century. State Rooms include medieval Great Hall, Hurd Library and Saloon. Fine plaster-work and remarkable collection of episcopal portraits. Also County Museum in North Wing.

Location: In village of Hartlebury, 5 m S of Kidderminster, 10 m N of Worcester off A449.
Station(s): Kidderminster 4 m.
Open: 1996: State Rooms Easter Mon-Sept 1 first Sun in every month but please telephone to check also Bank Holidays and Tues following Bank Holidays 2-5. Also every Wed Easter during this period 2-4. County Museum Mar-Nov Mon-Thurs 10-5 Fri and Sun 2-5 closed Sat and Good Friday. Open Bank Holidays 10-5.
Admission: State Rooms adults 75p children 25p OAPs 50p guided tours for parties of 30 or more on weekdays by arrangement. County Museum £1.90 OAPs/students/children 90p family tickets (2 adults and up to 3 children) £5 (1995 prices). School parties please telephone for information.(Museum tel: (01299) 250416).
Refreshments: Available but no refreshments in the State Rooms.
Events/Exhibitions: Museum tells story of life throught the ages in Hereford and Worcester. Picnic area.

HARVINGTON HALL
(The Roman Catholic Archdiocese of Birmingham)
nr Kidderminster   DY10 4LR   map **14** S18
Telephone: (01562) 777846

Moated medieval and Elizabethan manor-house containing secret hiding-places and rare wall-paintings. Georgian Chapel in garden with 18th century altar, rails and organ.

Location: 3 m SE of Kidderminster, ½ m from the junction of A448 and A450 at Mustow Green.
Station(s): Nearest Kidderminster.
Open: Mar 3-Oct 31, Suns, Tues, Weds and Thurs from 11.30-5.30. Closed at other times except by appointment.
Admission: Adults £3.50, OAP's £2.50, children £2. Private tours, wedding receptions etc, by arrangement. Free car parking.
Refreshments: The licensed restaurant is open when the Hall is open, for both lunches and light refreshments. Bookings can be made for Sunday lunch, evening functions and wedding and other receptions.
Events/Exhibitions: Harvington Festival 12th-21st July 1996. Other events throughout the year.

HELLEN'S
(The Pennington-Mellor-Munthe Trust)
Much Marcle   HR8 2LY   map **3** T17   △
Telephone: (01531) 84668
Fax: (01531) 660668

Built as a stone fortress in 1292 by Mortimer, Earl of March, this manorial house has been lived in since then by descendants of original builder. Visited by Black Prince and Bloody Mary.

Location: In village of Much Marcle on Ledbury/Ross Road. Entrance opp church.
Open: Good Fri-Oct 2 Wed Sat Sun and Bank Hol Mons 2-6 guided tours hourly. Last entry 5pm. *Other times by written appointment with the Administrator.*
Admission: Adults £3 children (must be accompanied by an adult) £1.

HERGEST CROFT GARDENS
(W.L. & R.A. Banks, Esq)
Kington
Telephone: (01544) 230160
Fax: (01544) 230160

From spring bulbs to autumn colour, this is a garden for all seasons. Four distinct gardens extend over 50 acres, with over 4,000 rare shrubs and trees, 59 of which are the champions of the British Isles. Hergest Croft Gardens is one of the finest collections in the British Isles assembled over the last 100 years by the Banks family containing the National Collections of birches, maples and zelkovas. The Azalea Garden has spectacular azaleas shaded by magnificent birches and maples. An avenue of ancient apple trees shades a riot of spring bulbs in the old-fashioned kitchen garden as well as a 120 foot double herbaceous flowering all summer. Park Wood is a hidden valley with rhododendrons up to 30ft tall.

Location: On outskirts W of Kington off Rhayader Road (A44) *(signposted to Hergest Croft at W end of bypass).*
Station(s): Leominster - 14 miles.
Open: Daily - 5 Apr-27 Oct 1.30-6.
Admission: Adult £2.50, children under 15 free. Reduced rate £2 for parties over 20 by appointment anytime. Season tickets £9 access permitted from Apr-Mar.
Refreshments: Home-made light lunches and afternoon teas and for parties over 20 by arrangement served in the old Dining Room of Hergest Croft.
Events/Exhibitions: Centenary Flower Fair on Monday May 6th 1996 - celebrating 100th anniversary.
Accommodation: Self-catering house - The Nursery sleeps 7.
Conferences: Not available.
Gift shop in the old Hall has a wide selection of attractive gifts. Plant sales of rare and unusual trees and shrubs some raised from wild collected seed.

HILL COURT GARDENS & GARDEN CENTRE
(Mr J C Rowley)
Hom Green, Ross on Wye   &
Telephone: (01989) 763123

Set in the beautiful grounds of a William and Mary Mansion.

HOW CAPLE COURT GARDENS
(Mr & Mrs P.L. Lee)
How Caple   HR1 4SX   map **3** T17
Telephone: (01989) 740612
Fax: (01989) 740611

11 acres overlooking the River Wye. Formal terraced Edwardian gardens, extensive plantings of mature trees and shrubs, water features and a sunken Florentine garden undergoing restoration. Norman church with 16th century Diptych. Specialist nursery plants and old variety roses for sale. Teas and light snacks.

Location: B4224, Ross on Wye (4½ m) to Hereford (9 m).
Open: All year Mon-Sat 9-5. Sunday Apr 1-Nov 9-5.
Admission: Adults £2.50 children £1.25. Parties welcome by appointment.
Events/Exhibitions: Open air Opera Sat June 29. Jazz concert Fri June 28. Shakespearean Play Thur June 27.
Fabric Shop and Menswear. Open all year- Car parking. Toilets.

KENTCHURCH COURT

(Mrs JC Lucas-Scudamore)
Hereford   map **3** T17
Telephone: (01981) 240228

Fortified border manor house altered by Nash. Gateway and part of the original 14th century house still survives. Pictures and Grinling Gibbons carving. Owen Glendower's tower.

Location: Off B4347, 3 m SE of Pontrilas; 12 m Monmouth; 14 m Hereford; 14 m Abergavenny, on left bank River Monnow.
Open: May-Sept. *All visitors by appointment.*
Admission: £3, chd £1.50.
Refreshments: At Kentchurch Court by appointment.
Accommodation: By appointment.

KINNERSLEY CASTLE

(Katherina Henning)
Kinnersley   map **3** S17
Telephone: (01544) 327407
Fax: (01544) 327663

Medieval Welsh border Castle, reconstructed about 1588. Little changed since then, retaining fine plasterwork and panelling, leaded glass and stone tiled roof. Yew hedges, walled garden and fine trees including probably the largest example of a Ginkgo tree in the United Kingdom. Art and other exhibitions. Still a family home, used out of season for courses and conferences. Early home of the De Kinnardsley and De le Bere families, remodelled by Roger Vaughan and later home of parliamentary General Sir Thomas Morgan.

Location: 4 m W of Weobley on A4112 (Black and White Village Trail).
Station(s): Hereford or Leominster.
Open: Dates and times of opening will be available from local tourist information offices (Hereford, Leominster, Hay-on-Wye etc) from Easter 1996 or phone enquiry (01544) 327407. Coach parties by arrangement throughout the year.
Admission: £2 children £1 OAPs/Student/UB40 £1.50 Groups £1.50 (by arrangment throughout the year).
Refreshments: By arrangement.
Events/Exhibitions: Traditional French Music festival in Summer and Shakespeare outside performance.
Accommodation: Accommodation for residential groups by arrangement, retreats etc.
Conferences: Day facilities for up to 100 persons.
Plant sales from organic gardens.

LANGSTONE COURT

(R.M.C. Jones Esq.)
Llangarron   HR9 6NR
Telephone: (01989) 770254

Mostly late 17th century house with older parts. Interesting staircases, panelling and ceilings.

Location: Ross on Wye 5m, Llangarron 1m.
Open: May 22-Aug 22 Wed and Thurs 11-3.
Admission: Free.

LITTLE MALVERN COURT AND GARDENS

(The Trustees of the late T.M. Berington esq.)
nr Great Malvern   WR14 4JN   map **3** S18   △
Telephone: (01684) 892988

14th century Prior's Hall once attached to 12th-century Benedictine Priory, with Victorian addition by Hansom. Family and European paintings and furniture. Collection of 18th and 19th century needlework. Home of the Berington family by descent since the Dissolution. 10 acres of former monastic grounds. Magnificent views, lake, garden rooms, terrace. Wide variety of spring bulbs, old fashioned roses, shrubs and trees.

Location: 3 m S of Great Malvern on Upton-on-Severn Road (A4104).
Open: Apr 19-Jul 20 Wed and Thurs 2.15-5 parties by prior arrangement. Guided tours - last adm 4.30.
Admission: Adults: House & Garden £3.80; House or Garden only £2.80. Children: House & Garden £2; House or Garden only £1.
Refreshments: Home made teas only available for parties by arrangement. Unsuitable for wheelchairs.

LOWER BROCKHAMPTON   The National Trust

Bringsty   WR6 5UH   map **3** S18   ⓰
Telephone: (01885) 488099

Small half-timbered manor house c. 1400 with unusual detached 15th century gatehouse and ruins of 12th century chapel.

Location: 2 m E of Bromyard N of A44 Bromyard/Worcester Road. Hall reached by narrow road through 1½ m woods and farmland.
Open: Medieval Hall, Parlour, Gatehouse & Chapel open Apr to end of Sept Wed to Sun & Bank Hol Mons 10-5. *Closed* Good Fri. Oct Wed to Sun 10-4.
Admission: £1.60 Children 80p Family ticket £4. Parties by prior written arrangement only. No dogs. Wheelchair access.

MOCCAS COURT 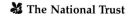

(Trustees of the Baunton Trust)
Moccas   HR2 9LH   map **3** S17   △
Telephone: (01981) 500381

'Built by Anthony Keck in 1775 overlooking the River Wye, decoration by Robert Adam including the round room and oval stair. Scene of famous 17th century romance and destination of epic night ride from London. Set in 'Capability' Brown parkland with an attractive walk to The Scar Rapids.'

Location: 10 m E of Hay on Wye and 13 m W of Hereford on the River Wye. 1 m off B4352.
Station(s): Hereford.
Open: House and Gardens Apr-Sept Thurs 2-6.
Admission: £1.95.
Refreshments: Food and drink available at the Red Lion Hotel, Bredwardine, by pre-booking only.
Accommodation: Available at the Red Lion Hotel, Bredwardine. Picnics in garden allowed.

SPETCHLEY PARK
(Mr & Mrs R J Berkeley)
Worcester   WR5 1RS   map **3** S18
Telephone: (01905) 345213/345224

This lovely 30 acre garden is a plantsman's delight, with a large collection of trees, shrubs and plants, many of which are rare or unusual. There is colour and interest throughout the months that the garden is open to visitors. The park contains red and fallow deer.

Location: 3 m E of Worcester on Stratford-upon-Avon Road (A422).
Station(s): Worcester.
Open: Gardens Apr 1-Sept 30 Tues Wed Thurs Fri 11-5 Sun 2-5 Bank Hol Mons 11-5 closed other Mons and all Sats.
Admission: Adults £2.50 children £1.20 reduced rates for pre-booked parties of 25 or more.
Refreshments: Tea in the garden.
Events/Exhibitions: A new formal and sunken garden within the existing garden will be open in 1996.
Regret no dogs. House not open.

THE WEIR   The National Trust
Swainshill, nr Hereford   map **3** S17

Delightful riverside garden, particularly spectacular in early spring. Fine views of the river Wye and Black Mountains.

Location: 5 m W of Hereford on A438.
Open: Feb 14-end Oct Wed-Sun & Bank Hol Mon 11-6. (incl Good Fri).
Admission: £1.50. No reductions for parties.
Unsuitable for coaches. No dogs. Unsuitable for wheelchairs or visually handicapped. No WCs.

WITLEY COURT
map **14** S18
Telephone: (01299) 896636

This is one of the most spectacular country house ruins. Cast in the Victorian Italian style of the 1860s, it is on a huge scale, with a glorious facade. Looking from the house to the gardens, a view enjoyed by Edward VII, who as Prince of Wales often stayed at the house, the scene is dominated by the immense Perseus Fountain.

Location: 10 m NW of Worcester on the A443.
Open: Apr 1-Sept 30 10-6 daily, Oct 1-31 10-6 or dusk if earlier, Nov 1-Mar 31 (closed 1-2) Wed-Sun 10-4.
Admission: Adults £2.50 concessions £1.90 children £1.30.

WORCESTER CATHEDRAL
(The Dean and Chapter of Worcester)
Worcester   map **3** S18   △ &
Telephone: (01905) 28854

Beside the River Severn opposite the Malvern Hills. Built between 1084 and 1375. Norman Crypt and Chapter House. Early English Quire, Perpendicular Tower. Monastic buildings include refectory (now College Hall and open on request during August), cloisters, remains of guesten hall and dormitories. Tombs of King John and Prince Arthur. Cloister herb garden, Elgar memorial window, misericords. Edgar Tower gatehouse.

Location: Centre of Worcester. Main roads Oxford and Stratford to Wales. 3 m junction 7 (M5).
Station(s): Foregate Street (easier) and Shrub Hill (taxi).
Open: Every day 7.30-6. Choral Evensong daily (except Thurs and school hols).
Admission: No admission charge but donations of £2 accepted. Charges for guided tours £2 adults £1 senior citizens £1 children. Visits Officer (01905) 28854. Tower (Summer only) Sats & Bank Hols £2 & £1.
Refreshments: Light refreshment in Cloister Tea-Room. Special arrangements made for parties.
Events/Exhibitions: Three Choirs Festival Aug 1996.
No cathedral car parking - City centre parking. Disabled visitors most welcome - some steps, but help and wheelchair available. Information Desk, shop and toilets.

Grinling Gibbons (1648-1721)

Sculptor and wood carver. His work can be seen at the following properties included in Historic Houses Castles and Gardens:-

Blenheim Palace
Breamore House
Dunham Massey
Fawley Court
Kentchurch Court

Lyme Park
Petworth House
Somerleyton Hall
Sudbury Hall

HERTFORDSHIRE

ASHRIDGE

(Governors of Ashridge Management College)
Berkhamsted   HP4 1NS   map **12** T21
Telephone: (01442) 843491

150 acres of both Parkland and intimate smaller gardens. The landscape influenced by Humphrey Repton. Mature trees combined with unique features e.g. Beech Houses with Windows and doors, in a Pink and Grey Garden, Grotto - Ferns planted between Herts Pudding Stone.

Location: 3½ m N of Berkhamsted (A4251), 1 m S of Little Gaddesden.
Station(s): Berkhamsted
Open: Gardens open Apr-Oct Sat & Sun 2-6.
Admission: Gardens adults £2 children/OAPs £1.
Conferences: For information on our facilities please contact Carol Johnston, Conference Manager (01442) 841027.
The House is not open to the public.

CAPEL MANOR

(Capel Manor Charitable Corporation)
nr Enfield   EN1 4RQ   map **12** T22   ♿
Telephone: 0181-366 4442
Fax: (01992) 717544

Capel Manor is Greater London's only specialist College of Horticulture and Countryside studies with the 30 acres of richly planted and diverse gardens, which surround the Georgian manor, fully open to the public. A comprehensive self-guided tour starts from the new visitor's centre with information boards and free leaflets to help visitors get the most from their visit at all times of the year. There are many 'themed' areas within the garden including for example, historical, modern, rock, and water, a sensory and disabled persons garden, an Italianate maze and Japanese garden. Gardening Which? manage a large site with demonstrations and model gardens and The National Gardening Centre includes more exhibits of gardens and associated products. A small range of rare breeds of farm animals are being introduced around the old stable buildings. Unfortunately, the house is only open for use by Capel Manor students.

Location: 3 mins from M25 junction M25/A10 S and turn right at traffic lights. Nearest station Turkey Street/Liverpool Street line. (Not Sun)
Open: Gardens daily 10-5.30. (Check for winter times)
Admission: Normal rates - adults £3 concessions £2 children £1.50. Please check for dates and charges at special shows. Special rates for coaches, garden tours. All parking free.
Refreshments: Available.
Further details from Capel Manor, Bullsmoor Lane, Enfield, Middlesex EN1 4RQ Tel 0181-366 4442.

CROMER WINDMILL

(Hertfordshire Building Preservation Trust)
Ardeley, Stevenage   SG2 7QA   map **5** T22
Telephone: (01438) 861662

Hertfordshire's unique 17th century Post Windmill, under restoration to working order. Static display, guided visits.

Location: Adjoins the B1037 between Walkern and Cottered, 4 m NE of Stevenage.
Open: Sun May 12 'National Mill Day'. Second and fourth Sat and Suns, Sat 11 May-Sun 8 Sept 2.30-5.
Admission: £1.00, chd 25p. Individual and groups by appointment with Mr. Simon Bennett (01438) 861662.

Ghosts are in residence at the following properties included in Historic Houses Castles and Gardens:-

Blickling Hall - *Anne Boleyn*

Breamore House - *Haunted picture - if touched, death on the same day*

East Riddleden Hall - *5 ghosts including lady in Grey Hall Lady's Chamber*

Fountains Abbey & Studley Royal - *Choir of monks chanting in Chapel of Nine Altars*

Hinton Ampner - *Nocturnal noises*

Ightham Mote - *Supernatural presence*

Lindisfarne Castle - *Monk, and group of monks on causeway*

Lyme Park - *Unearthly peals of bells and lady in white, funeral procession through park*

Malmesbury House - *Ghost of a cavalier*

Overbecks Museum & Garden - *'Model' ghost in the Children's room (for them to spot)*

Rockingham Castle - *Lady Dedlock*

Rufford Old Hall - *Elizabeth Hesketh*

Scotney Castle Garden - *Man rising from the lake*

Sizergh Castle & Garden - *Poltergeist*

Speke Hall - *Ghost of woman in tapestry room*

Springhill - *Ghost of a woman*

Sudbury Hall - *Lady in Green, seen on stairs*

Tamworth Castle - *Haunted bedroom*

Treasurer's House - *Troop of Roman soldiers marching through the cellar*

Wallington House - *Invisible birds beating against the windows accompanied by heavy breathing*

Washington Old Hall - *Grey lady walking through corridors*

THE GARDENS OF THE ROSE
(Royal National Rose Society)
Chiswell Green, St Albans AL2 3NR map **12** T22 ♿
Telephone: (01727) 850461
Fax: (01727) 850360

The Showgrounds of the R.N.R.S. containing some 30,000 roses of over 1,650 different varieties and many companion plants.

Location: Off B4630 (formerly A412) St Albans/Watford Road.
Station(s): St Alban's City (2 m).
Open: June 8-Oct 13 Mon-Sat 9-5 Sun & Bank Hols 10-6.
Admission: £4. Discount for pensioners and disabled. Accompanied children free.
Refreshments: Licensed cafeteria.
Events/Exhibitions: A series of musical and other entertainments are held during the season. The National Miniature Rose show is held in the garden 27/28th July.
Facilities for the disabled.

GORHAMBURY - See Page 58.

HATFIELD HOUSE
(The Marquess of Salisbury)
Hatfield map **12** T22 △
Telephone: (01707) 262823

This celebrated Jacobean house, which stands in its own great park, was built between 1607 and 1611 by Robert Cecil, 1st Earl of Salisbury and Prime Minister to King James I. It has been the family home of the Cecils ever since. The Staterooms are rich in world-famous paintings, fine furniture, rare tapestries and historic armour. The beautiful stained glass in the chapel is original. Within the delightful gardens stands the surviving wing of the Royal Palace of Hatfield (1497) where Elizabeth I spent much of her girlhood and held her first Council of State in November 1558. She appointed William Cecil, Lord Burghley as her Chief Minister. Some of her relics can be seen in the house. Further particulars from The Curator, Hatfield House.

Location: In Hatfield, Junction 4 A1(M), 7 m M25.
Station(s): Hatfield. 25 minutes by regular fast train service from Kings Cross to Hatfield (station faces Park gates). The Moorgate to Hatfield electric train service has direct Underground links; Victoria Line at Highbury, Circle Line at Moorgate, Piccadilly Line at Finsbury Park. Hatfield House Lodge is opposite the station.
Open: Mar 25-Oct 13 1996. Hatfield House open daily except Mon and Good Fri weekdays from 12 guided tours only (last tour 4). Sun 1-4.30 no guided tours - guides in each room. Also open on Easter, May Day, Spring and Aug Bank Hol Mon 11-5 no guided tours - guides in each room. Park 10.30-8 daily except Good Fri West Gardens 11-6 daily except Good Fri East Gardens 2-5 Mon only (except Bank Hol Mons). Guided Tour (Tues-Sat) takes about 1 hour.
Admission: Reductions for pre-booked parties of 20 or more. Coach and car park free.
Refreshments: Available in adjacent restaurant - coffee shop. ELIZABETHAN BANQUETING IN THE OLD PALACE THROUGHOUT THE YEAR. Telephone: (01707) 262823 (Curator); Banqueting and Restaurant (01707) 262055/262030. FAX: (01707) 275719.
Events/Exhibitions: Living crafts 9-12 May 10-6. Festival of gardening 22-23 June 10-5.
Conferences: Licensed for Civil Weddings. Old Palace and Riding School (01707) 262055.
Dogs not admitted to House or garden.

GORHAMBURY
(The Earl of Verulam)
St Albans   AL3 6AH   map **12** T22   △
Telephone: (01727) 854051
Fax: (01727) 843675

Mansion built 1777-84 in classical style by Sir Robert Taylor. 16th century enamelled glass and historic portraits.

Location: 2 m W of St Albans. Entrance off A4147 at St. Michael's by Roman Theatre.
Station(s): St. Albans.
Open: May-Sept Thurs 2-5. Gardens open with the house.
Admission: Adults £4 children £2.50 OAPs £2. Guided tours only. Parties by prior arrangement Thurs £3.50 other days £5.

KNEBWORTH
(The Lord Cobbold)
Knebworth House   map **5** T22
Telephone: (01438) 812661
Fax: (01438) 811908

Home of the Lytton family since 1490. The original Tudor Manor House was transformed 150 years ago with spectacular High Gothic decoration by Victorian novelist and statesman Sir Edward Bulwer-Lytton. There are many beautiful rooms, important portraits and furniture, and a fine collection of manuscripts and letters associated with many famous visitors to the house. Charles Dickens acted here in private theatricals, and Winston Churchill painted at his easel in the superb Jacobean Banqueting Hall. It was the home of Constance Lytton, the suffragette, and Robert Lytton, Viceroy of India. Lord Lytton's Viceroyalty and the great Delhi Durbar of 1877 are commemorated in a fascinating exhibition and audio-visual display. The formal gardens by Sir Edwin Lutyens include a unique pattern Jekyll herb garden - a new feature is the reinstated maze. The house stands in a 250 acre country park with herds of Red and Sika deer. For children, hours of pleasure in Fort Knebworth, a large adventure playground with Miniature Railway.

Location: Knebworth 28 m N of central London. Own direct access off the A1 (M) junction 7 (Stevenage South A602) 12 m N of M25.
Station(s): Stevenage (2 m).
Open: PARK, GARDENS AND FORT KNEBWORTH Mar 29-Apr 15 inclusive, and May 25-Sept 3 inclusive. Plus weekends and Bank Hols from Apr 20-May 19 and weekends only

from Sept 7-29. HOUSE open as above except closed Mon. Open Bank Hol Mons. HOURS Park, Gardens and Fort Knebworth 11-5.30. House 12-5.
Admission: HOUSE, GARDENS, PARK, FORT KNEBWORTH £4.50 (not inc. miniature railway) children/sen cits £4. GARDENS, PARK & FORT KNEBWORTH ONLY £3.50 family ticket (four persons) £12 (no reductions for children/sen cits) Reductions for pre-booked parties of 20 or more (29 Mar-29 Sept). Opening times and prices subject to special events. Coach and car park free.
Refreshments: Licensed cafeteria in 16th Century Tithe Barn close to House & Gardens (Tel:(01438) 813825). Oakwood Restaurant in hotel at Park entrance. (Tel:(01438) 742299).
Conferences: Licensed for Civil Weddings at The Manor Barn, Knebworth Park.
Dogs admitted to Park only on leads. Telephone above number for further details.

SCOTT'S GROTTO
(East Hertfordhire District Council)
Ware   SG12 9SQ   map **12** T23
Telephone: (01920) 464131

Grotto, summerhouse and garden built 1760-73 by Quaker poet, John Scott. Described by English Heritage as 'one of the finest grottos in England.' Now extensively restored by The Ware Society.

Location: Scott's Road, Ware (off A119 Hertford Road).
Station(s): Ware/Liverpool Street line.
Open: New extended opening times. Every Sat beginning of Apr-Sept and Easter, Spring and Summer Bank Hol Mons 2-4.30.
Admission: Free but donation of £1 requested.
Please park in Amwell End car park by level crossing (300 yds away) and walk up Scott's Road. Advisable to wear flat shoes and bring a torch. Parties by prior arrangement.

WIMPOLE HOME FARM   The National Trust
Arrington   SG8 0B6   map **5** S22
Telephone: (01223) 207257
Fax: (01223) 207838
Location: 8 m S of Cambridge; signposted off A603 at New Wimpole.

HUMBERSIDE

BEVERLEY GUILDHALL
(East Yorkshire Borough of Beverley Borough Council)
Beverley
Telephone: (01482) 3867430

Beverley's heritage spans a period of 1300 years which is reflected in its fine old buildings and outstanding Market Square.

BLAYDES HOUSE
(The Georgian Society for East Yorkshire)
Hull
Telephone: (01482) 326406

Mid-Georgian merchants house, fine staircase and panelled rooms.

BURNBY HALL GARDENS
(Stewart's Burnby Hall Gardens & Museum Trust)
Pocklington, The Balk   YO4 2QF   map **4** P21   &
Telephone: (01759 30) 2068

Large gardens with 2 lakes. Finest display of hardy water lilies in Europe - 80 varieties, **designated National Collection.** Museum housing Stewart Collection - sporting trophies, ethnic material. Picnic area, rose garden. Sales kiosk. Large variety of fish in lakes.

Location: 13 m E of York on A1079.
Open: Fri 5 Apr-Sun 29 Sept 1996 daily 10-6.
Admission: Adults £2.10 party rate (over 20) £1.30 Accompanied children (under 5) free (5-16) 75p OAPs £1.60 party rate (over 20) £1.30.
Refreshments: Teas in the garden.
Events/Exhibitions: Sunday band concerts fortnightly.
Free coach and car park. Disabled facilities.Guide Dogs only.

BURTON AGNES HALL
(Preservation Trust Ltd)
nr Bridlington   YO25 0ND   map **4** P22
Telephone: (01262) 490324
Fax: (01262) 490513

The Hall is a magnificent example of late Elizabethan architecture - still lived in by descendants of the family who built it in 1598. There are wonderful carvings, lovely furniture and fine collection of modern French and English paintings of the Impressionist Schools - Renoir, Pissaro, Corot, Utrillo, Gauguin, Augustus John, etc. The recently redeveloped walled garden contains a potager, maze, herbaceous borders, campanula collection, jungle garden and giant games set in coloured gardens. Also woodland gardens and walk, children's corner, Norman manor house, donkey wheel and gift shop.

Location: In village of Burton Agnes, 6 m SW of Bridlington on Driffield/Bridlington Road (A166).
Open: Apr 1-Oct 31 daily 11-5.
Admission: Adults £3.50 OAPs £3 children £2. Group rates on application. Garden only adults £1.80 OAPs £1.50 children 80p. *The management reserves the right to close the house or part thereof without prior notice; adm charges will be adjusted on such days.*
Refreshments: Licensed cafeteria. Teas, light lunches & refreshments.
Events/Exhibitions: Gardener's Fair 8-9 June.

BURTON CONSTABLE
(Burton Constable Foundation)
nr Hull HU11 4LN map **4** P22
Telephone: (01964) 562400
Fax: (01964) 563229

Magnificent Elizabethan House, built c 1570.

THE CHARTERHOUSE
(Charterhouse Trustees)
Hull map **4** P22
Telephone: (01482) 320026

Charterhouse, was founded in 1384 by Michael de la Pole, Earl of Suffolk.

Open: Chapel & Gardens open daily during July and on Good Friday Easter Day Easter Mon Spring and Summer Bank Holidays 10-8.

ELSHAM HALL COUNTRY AND WILDLIFE PARK AND ELSHAM HALL BARN THEATRE
(Capt J Elwes and Robert Elwes)
Brigg DN20 0QZ map **4** P22 △ ㄴ Ⓔ Ⓢ
Telephone: (01652) 688698
Fax: (01652) 688738

Beautiful lakes and gardens; Miniature zoo; Giant Carp; Falconry Centre; Wild Butterfly walkway; Adventure playground; Garden and Craft Centre; Granary Tea-rooms; Animal farm; Art Gallery; Caravan site; Ten National Awards. Also excellent New Theatre.

Location: Near Brigg M180 Jct 5. Near Humberside Airport.
Station(s): Barnetby.
Open: Times and Prices on application. Contact Manager.
Refreshments: Granary Tea-rooms, Ice Cream Parlour, Restaurant, Banqueting.
Conferences: Conference facility. Licensed for Civil Weddings.

MAISTER HOUSE 🍂 The National Trust
Hull map **4** P22
Telephone: (01482) 324114
Location: 160 High Street, Hull.

SEWERBY HALL AND GARDENS
(Borough of East Yorkshire)
Bridlington map **7** O22
Telephone: Hall: (01262) 677874 Estate Office: (01262) 673769
Fax: (01262) 674265

Built 1714-20 by John Greame with additions 1808. Sewerby Hall occupies a dramatic setting overlooking Bridlington Bay. The 50 acres of gardens of great beauty and botanical interest include fine old English walled garden and small zoo and aviary. There is also an art gallery and a museum which includes the Amy Johnson Trophy Room dedicated to the pioneer woman aviator.

Location: In Bridlington on the cliffs, 2 m NE from centre of town.
Station(s): Bridlington (2½ m); Bempton (2 m).
Open: Gardens open all year daily 9-dusk. Art Gallery open 1-14 Jan, 2 Mar-2 Apr, 30 Sept-31 Dec Sat-Tues 11-4.
Admission: From May-Sept adults £2.50, OAP £2, children £1.
Refreshments: Traditional tea-room in the Grounds.
Events/Exhibitions: Temporary exhibition programme of East Yorkshire art, photography and history.
Conferences: Facilities available.
Childrens play area.

Sir Joshua Reynolds

Portrait painter (1723-1792)
First President of the Royal Academy, knighted in 1769

His work can be seen in the following properties included in Historic Houses Castles and Gardens:-

Arundel Castle
Dalmeny House (Roseberry Collection of Political Portraits)
Elton Hall
Goodwood House
Ickworth House, Park & Garden
Kenwood, The Iveagh Bequest

Knole
Petworth House
Rockingham Castle
Saltram
Shalom Hall
Wallington House
Weston Park

SLEDMERE HOUSE
(Sir Tatton Sykes, Bart)
Driffield   YO25 OXG   map 7 P21
Telephone: (01377) 236637

A Georgian house begun in 1751 with important additions attributed to Samuel Wyatt in conjunction with Sir Christopher Sykes, containing superb library 100ft long. The entire building was burnt to the ground in 1911 and splendidly restored with an Edwardian feeling for space by York architect Walter Brierley during the first world war. The latter copied Joseph Rose's fine ceilings and inserted a magnificent Turkish room. The House contains much of its original furniture and paintings. An unusual feature is the great organ, which is played Sun & Weds 2-4pm. Capability Brown Park. 18th century walled rose garden. Main garden under reconstruction.

Location: 24 m E of York on main York/Bridlington Road; 8 m NW of Driffield at junction of B1251 & B1253.
Open: Fri 5 Apr-Tues 9 Apr Suns in Apr and then open daily from 5 May-29 Sept. Closed Mon and Fri but open Bank Hol Mons. House open 1-4.30pm. Organ played Wed & Sun 2-4pm.
Admission: Adults £3.50 OAP's £3 children £1.75. Special rates for parties of more than 20 people. Park and Gardens only, adults £1.50 children £1.
Refreshments: Excellent self service licensed restaurant, Driffield (01377) 236637.
Illustrated brochure from The House Secretary, Sledmere House, Driffield, East Yorkshire.

WILBERFORCE HOUSE
(Hull City Council)
Hull   map 4 P22 Ⓢ
Telephone: (01482) 593902
Fax: (01482) 593710
17th century Merchant's house, now a local history museum with period furniture.

ISLE OF WIGHT

BARTON MANOR GARDENS AND VINEYARDS
East Cowes, Isle of Wight PO32 6LB   map 3 V20 ♿
Telephone: (01983) 292835
Fax: (01983) 293923
Admission: The Manor is not open to the public - only the grounds and farm buildings.

CARISBROOKE CASTLE
map 3 V20
Telephone: (01983) 522107

ENGLISH HERITAGE

Here are seven acres of castle and earthworks to explore. The oldest parts of the castle are 12th century, but the great mound - 71 steps high - bore a wooden castle before that, and there are fragments of Roman wall at its base. Fortified against the French, then the Spaniards, the castle is best known as the prison of Charles I in 1647/8. A bold escape plan failed when the King became wedged between the bars of the great chamber window. The castle contains the island's museum. A personal stereo guided tour is available.

Location: 1¼ m (2 km) south west of Newport.
Open: Apr 1-Sept30 10-6 daily Oct 1-Mar 31 daily 10-4.
Admission: Adults £3.80 concessions £2.90 children £1.90.

THE NEEDLES OLD BATTERY   ❦ The National Trust
West Highdown, Totland Bay   map 3 V19
Telephone: (01983) 754772

Victorian Coastal fort built in 1862, 77m above sea level; 60m tunnel to spectacular view of the Needles. Exhibition on history of the Needles Headland. in its defence of the Realm.

Location: At Needles Headland. W of Freshwater Bay and Alum Bay.
Open: 24 Mar-31 Oct, Sun-Thurs (but open Easter week-end and daily in July & Aug) 10.30-5 last admission 4.30. Conducted school and special visits 24 Mar 31-Oct (but not Aug) by written appointment.
Admission: £2.40 Children half-price. Family ticket £6. No reductions for parties.
Refreshments: Tea-room open same days as Battery 10.30-4.30.

NEWTOWN OLD TOWN HALL   ❦ The National Trust
Newtown   map 3 V20
Telephone: (01983) 741052

A charming 18th century building that was once the focal point of the 'rotten borough of Newtown'. An exhibition tells the story of the famous 'Ferguson's Gang'.

Location: In Newtown, midway between Newport and Yarmouth.
Open: 1 Apr-31 Oct Mon Wed & Sun 2-5 (also open Good Fri Easter Sat and Tues and Thurs in July and Aug) last adm 4.45. *Closed Oct-end March.*
Admission: £1.10 Children half-price. No reduction for parties.
No dogs. Unsuitable for wheelchairs.

NUNWELL HOUSE AND GARDENS   ⌂
(Colonel & Mrs J A Aylmer)
Brading   map 3 V20
Telephone: (01983) 407240

Nunwell with its historic connections with King Charles I is set in beautiful gardens and parkland with channel views. A finely furnished home with Jacobean and Georgian wings. Home Guard museum and family military collection.

Location: 1 m from Brading, turning off A3055; 3 m S of Ryde.
Station(s): Brading.
Open: House and Gardens July 7-Sept 25 Sun 1-5 Mon-Wed 10-5 closed Thurs Fri and Sat.
Admission: Adults £2.80 OAPs £2.30 accompanied children 60p school parties £1.40.
Refreshments: Large parties may book catering in advance. Picnic areas.
Parties welcome at all times if booked. No dogs.

Thomas Gainsborough (1727-1787)

His paintings can be seen at the following properties included in Historic Houses Castles and Gardens:-

Arundel Castle
Bowhill
Christchurch Mansion
Dalmeny House
Elton Hall
Gainsborough's House
Ickworth Park & Garden
Firle Place
Kenwood, The Iveagh Bequest

Knowle
Parham House & Gardens
Petworth House
Shalom Hall
Upton House
Waddesdon Manor
Weston Park
Woburn Abbey

OSBORNE HOUSE

East Cowes   map **3** V20
Telephone: (01983) 200022

This was Queen Victoria's seaside residence built at her own expense, in 1845. The Prince Consort played a prominent part in the design of the house, it was his version of an Italian villa, and the work was carried out by Thomas Cubitt, the famous London builder. The Queen died here in 1901 and her private apartments have been preserved more or less unaltered. Crowded with furniture and bric-a-brac they epitomise the style we call 'Victorian'. Also see the Queen's bathing machine. There is a carriage drawn by horse running from House to the Swiss Cottage Gardens and Museum. This is included in the adm price, see below for details.

Location: 1 m SE of East Cowes.
Station(s): Ferry terminal East Cowes (1 m).
Open: Apr 1-Sept 30 10-5 (Grounds 6pm). Last admission 4.30 (Grounds 5pm) Oct 1-Oct 31 10-5. Last admission 4 (Grounds 4.30pm).
Admission: House and Grounds adults £5.80 concessions £4.40 children £2.90. Grounds only adults £3 concessions £2.30 children £1.50.

KENT

BEDGEBURY NATIONAL PINETUM

(Foresty Enterprise)
nr Goudhurst   map **3** U23
Telephone: (01580) 211044
Fax: (01580) 212523

The most comprehensive collection of conifers in Europe. Conifers from all continents are planted in generic groups within 160 acres. Landscaped with grass avenues, paths, stream valleys, ridges and a lake. Rhododendrons, azaleas, maples and uncommon oak species add colour in spring and autumn.

Location: On B2079, 1 m from A21 London to Hastings travelling towards Goudhurst.
Open: Daily 10-dusk. Visitor centre daily 10-5 April 1- Christmas Weekends in March.
Admission: Adults £2.00, OAPs £1.50, Children £1.20.
Refreshments: Tea rooms new for 1996.
Events/Exhibitions: Orchestra Concert June 23rd. Craft Fair July 7th.
Car parking, difficult for wheelchairs.

BLACK CHARLES

(Mr & Mrs Hugh Gamon)
nr Sevenoaks   map **13** U23
Telephone: (01732) 833036

Charming 14th century home of John de Blakecherl and his family. A hall house with beautiful panelling, fireplaces and many other interesting features.

Location: 3 m S of Sevenoaks off A21; 1 m E in the village of Underriver.
Open: Open to groups by appointment (minimum of 10).
Admission: £3.50.

BELMONT

(Harris (Belmont) Charity)
nr Faversham   ME13 0HH   map **13** U24   △ &

Telephone: (01795) 890202

Belmont was built in the late 18th century to the design of Samuel Wyatt, in a splendid elevated position with commanding views over the attractive and unspoilt countryside. It has been the seat of the Harris family since it was acquired in 1801 by General George Harris, the victor of Seringapatam. The Mansion remains in its original state and contains interesting mementos of the family's connections with India and the finest collection of clocks in any English country house open to the public.

Location: 4 m SSW of Faversham. 1½ m W of A251 follow brown signs from Badlesmere.
Station(s): Faversham.
Open: Easter Sun-end Sept Sat Sun and Bank Hol Mons guided tours 2-5 last adm 4.30. Telephone (01795) 890202 to confirm availability. Groups (minimum 20) by prior arrangement only Tues and Thurs.
Admission: Mansion, Grounds and Clock Museum £4.50 children £2.50.
Refreshments: Teas in the Stables Tea-room Sat, Sun and Bank Hol Mons. Pre-booked parties by arrangement.
Events/Exhibitions: Telephone for details.
Car parking. Shop.

BOUGHTON MONCHELSEA PLACE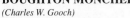

(Charles W. Gooch)
nr Maidstone   ME17 4BU   map **13** U24 △
Telephone: (01622) 743120

Battlemented Elizabethan Manor of Kentish ragstone built in 1567, with interesting Regency alterations still a family home. Dramatically situated with breathtaking view over its own landscaped park, in which fallow deer have roamed for at least 300 years, and beyond, to the whole Weald of Kent. The beautiful interior is still that of an intimate and inhabited home to which successive generations have added new treasures. Edwardian ladies bedroom and nursery, dress display and early farm implements. Manor records. Walled flower gardens with interesting plants. Tudor kitchen tearoom. House and Grounds are available for private hire all year. Corporate Days, civil marriage ceremonies, wedding receptions, private dining, small meetings, Conference and Exhibitions. Clay Shooting, Quad Biking, Pilots etc. Contact (01622) 743120.

Location: On B2163. In village of Boughton Monchelsea 5 m S of Maidstone. Junction 8 off M20. Ten minutes from Leeds Castle.
Open: Good Fri-early Oct Sun & Bank Hols (also Wed during June July & Aug) 2-6.
Admission: House and Grounds: family ticket (2 adults 2 children) £10, adult £4 children (under 14) £2.75 child under 5 free, students/OAPs/disabled £3.75. Grounds Only: adult £3.25 children (under 14) £1.75 students/OAPs/disabled £2.75. Groups rates: Housr & Grounds adults £3.50 children (under 14) £2.50 students/OAPs/disabled £3.50. Grounds only: adults £2.50 children (under 14) £2 students/OAPs/disabled £2.50.
Refreshments: Afternoon Teas always available. Lunch or supper for groups can be arranged.
Conferences: Licensed for Civil Marriage Ceremonies.
St. Peter's Church, claiming one of the oldest Lych Gates in the country, and is situated next door to the house. Guide Book for church available in Gift Shop at house.

CHARTWELL   The National Trust
Westerham   map **13** U23   ♿
Telephone: (01732) 866368

The home for many years of Sir Winston Churchill. Exhibition. Garden.

Location: 2 m S of Westerham off B2026. Signed off M25 junction 6 or 5.
Open: Mar & Nov: House only, Sat, Sun & Wed 11-4.30pm. Last admission 4pm. 30 Mar-2 Nov: House, garden & Studio, daily (except Mon & Fri) 11-5.30pm. Open Bank Hol Mon 11-5.30pm. Last admission 4.30pm. Closed Mon, Fri & Tues following Bank Hol Mon.
Admission: House & Garden £4.50 Children £2.25 Family ticket £11.25. Garden only £2 Chd £1. House only £2.50 Children £1.25 Studio 50p extra (Children no reduction). Pre-booked parties by arrangement.
Refreshments: Restaurant open from Apr-end Oct 10.30-5 (Mar & Nov 10.30-4) on days when house is open. Self-service, licensed (no spirits).
Events/Exhibitions: Exhibition on Churchill's life during the years he lived at Chartwell. 1940s dance 15th June.
Car park. Lavatory for disabled. Small lift to first floor. Shop.

CHIDDINGSTONE CASTLE

(Trustees of the Denys Eyre Bower Bequest)
nr Edenbridge   TN8 7AD   map **13** U23   ♿ ®
Telephone: (01892) 870347

The dream-child of two romantics. Squire Henry Streatfeild, who c.1805 had his family seat transformed into a fantasy castle, and whose money ran out; and Denys Bower, eccentric and inspired art collector, who never had any money at all. Entranced with the (by then) semi-derelict Castle, he made it his home in 1955. He died in 1977 leaving the Castle and its fascinating contents to the Nation. Untouched by commercialism, lovingly restored and cherished, it remains a home, with its fine furnishings, personal collections of Japanese lacquer and swords, Egyptian antiquities, Stuart and Jacobite relics. Landscaped grounds, listed as one of the historic gardens of Kent, in course of restoration.

Location: In Chiddingstone village, off the B2027 at Bough Beech about 10 m Sevenoaks, Tonbridge and Tunbridge Wells.
Station(s): Penshurst 2½ miles, Edenbridge 4 miles.
Open: Apr 1-Oct 31. Easter and PH. Apr, May and Oct: Suns only. 1 June-30 Sept: Wed-Sun Booked parties (min 20) at any time of year. Hours: weekdays 2-5.30; Sun 11.30-5.30. Last admission 5pm.
Admission: Adults £3.50 children 5-15 (with adult) £1.50 under 5 free. Booked parties of 20 or more (normal hours) £3 (Special fee at other times). Fishing dawn till dusk £8 one onlooker per fisherman £3.50.
Refreshments: Tea-room serves tea, coffee and cakes. Cream teas and light meals for parties by arrangment. Picnics allowed adjacent car park, not in grounds.
Events/Exhibitions: Programme for summer events available later. Xmas Fair: Sun Dec 1.
Conferences: The Goodhugh Wing (off coachyard) provides elegant Assembly Room (capacity 50) seminar rooms and tea kitchen for business and social meetings. Meals supplied to order by recommended caterer, in 17c Buttery (with access to inner courtyard). Marquee in grounds (adjacent Castle) for larger receptions. Civil Marriage Ceremony: licensed by Kent County Council, Information from Rene Vernon, Functions Manager. The gothic Great Hall (opening on to courtyard) is available at any time for the ceremony. The adjacent drawing room may be hired for the reception of guests. 17c. changing room for bride. Arrangements can be made for the provision of live music and a specially composed wedding song. Special wedding stationery supplied.
School visits may be arranged at any time. Egyptian collection recommended for use with National Cirriculum. Teacher packs available for all collections and for study of social and economic importance of house. Picnics in grounds or under cover. A no-hassle visit. Teachers free, prices for children by arrangement.

CHILHAM CASTLE GARDENS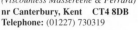
(Viscountess Massereene & Ferrard)
nr Canterbury, Kent   CT4 8DB
Telephone: (01227) 730319

25 acre garden with formal terraces.

COBHAM HALL
Cobham, nr. Gravesend, Kent   DA12 3BL   map **13** U23   △
Telephone: (01474) 824319/823371
Fax: (01474) 822995

Cobham Hall is an outstandingly beautiful, red brick mansion in Elizabethan, Jacobean, Carolian and 18th century styles. This former home of the Earls of Darnley is set in 150 acres of parkland. The Gardens, landscaped for the 4th Earl of Darnley by Humphry Repton, are gradually being restored by the Cobham Hall Heritage Trust. Extensive tree planting and clearing have taken place since the hurricanes of the 1980's. The Gothic Dairy and some of the classical garden buildings are being renovated. Charles Dickens used to walk through the grounds from his house in Higham to the Leather Bottle Pub in Cobham Village. Visitors to the house should not miss the many fine 17th century marble fireplaces and the 18th century historic Snetzler organ in the magnificent Gilt Hall. The grounds yield many delights for the lover of nature, especially in Spring, when the gardens and woods are resplendent with displays of Spring bulbs including many rarities. Cobham Hall is now an independent, international boarding and day school for girls aged 11-18 years.

Location: Cobham Hall is adjacent to the A2/M2 between Gravesend and Rochester, 8 miles from Junction 2 on the M25. 27 miles from London.
Station(s): Meopham and Sole Street via London Victoria. Gravesend via London Charing Cross and Waterloo.
Open: Apr most Weds Thurs Suns and Easter Weekend, July & Aug most Weds Thurs and Suns Aug most Weds Thurs and Suns. Please telephone (01474) 823371 to check opening dates. 2-5 each day. All tours guided.
Admission: Adults £2.50 OAPs and children £2.
Refreshments: Tea, coffee.Lunches and dinner for parties by arrangement.
Events/Exhibitions: Mar 24: National Garden Scheme Day. Apr 5,6,7,8 The Medway Craft Fair (House open). July 13 British Red Cross Open Air Concert.Aug 18 'Prom in the Park' - The Royal Philharmonic Concert & Fireworks. Aug 25-26 - The Medway Flower and Garden Show (House open). Sept 1 - National Garden Scheme Day (House open). Oct 19-20 The Medway Craft Fair (House Open).
Accommodation: The House, grounds, accommodation (250 beds) and sports facilities are available for private hire, wedding receptions, business conferences, residential and non-residential courses and film and photographic location.
Conferences: Excellent in-house catering team for private and corporate events (cap. 200).
Historical guided tours of the house. Pre-booked guided tours of the garden. Party bookings and coach parties welcomed. Souvenir shop. Ample free parking. For further information contact The Development Director, Sue Anderson, Cobham Hall, Cobham, Kent DA12 3BL. Tel: (01474) 824319. (24hr ansaphone) or (01474) 823371. **New:** In 1995 Cobham Hall was granted its Civil Marriage Licence, couples can now get married in the magnificent Gilt Hall.

DEAL CASTLE
map **13** U25
Telephone: (01304) 372762

ENGLISH HERITAGE

When Henry VIII divorced Catherine of Aragon he defied the Pope and broke with Catholic Europe. Deal and Walmer were built under the threat of a 'crusade' against Henry - an invasion which never came. Deal contains an exhibition on the coastal defences of Henry VIII. At Walmer the atmosphere is country house rather than martial, for this has long been the official residence of the Lords Warden of the Cinque Ports. One of the best remembered is the Duke of Wellington (the original 'Wellington boot' may be seen here), and one of the best loved, Queen Elizabeth the Queen Mother.

Location: Deal Castle is near the town centre.
Open: Apr 1-Sept 30 10-6 daily Oct 1-31 10-4 daily Nov 1-Mar 31 Wed-Sun 10-4.
Admission: Adults £2.80 concessions £2.10 children £1.40.

> *Sir Christopher Wren - architect*
> *(1632-1723)*
>
> *Fawley Court*
> *Old Royal Observatory*
> *Winslow Hall*

DODDINGTON PLACE GARDENS

(Mr Richard Oldfield)
Doddington   ME9 0BB   map **13** U25
Telephone: (01795) 886101

Landscaped gardens in the grounds of a Victorian country house (not open)with good views over surrounding parkland and countryside. Edwardian rock garden and formal garden, rhododendrons and azaleas in a woodland setting, fine trees and yew hedges.

Location: 4 m from A2 and A20. 5 m from Faversham. 6 m from Sittingbourne. 12 m from Canterbury.
Station(s): Sittingbourne, Faversham.
Open: May to Sept: Suns 2-6 Weds and Bank Hol Mons 11-6. (In aid of the National Gardens Scheme Sun 7, 14, 21 May). Groups also on other days by prior arrangement.
Admission: Adults £2 children 25p group rate £1.50 coaches by prior arrangement only.
Refreshments: Restaurant serving morning coffee, lunches, afternoon teas.
Present shop.

DOVER CASTLE

Dover   map **13** U25
Telephone: (01304) 201628

Castle Hill dominates the shortest passage between Britain and the Continent, and has been the scene of military activity from the Iron Age to the present day. Here is extensive proof from every age of man's ingenuity in devising ways to repel invaders. Dover Castle had its narrowest escape in 1216 when in an heroic siege it just managed to hold out against the French. There is much to see, including the Roman lighthouse (now the bell tower of a fine Saxon church) and the great keep itself and a spectacular exhibition 'Live and Let Spy'. The secret war tunnels of the castle are now open to the public including the underground field dressing station. The evacuation of the troops from Dunkirk was planned by Vice-Admiral Ramsay from this once secret base. Entry is by guided tours only.

Location: East side of Dover.
Open: Apr 1-Sept 30 10-6 daily Oct 1-Mar 31 daily 10-4. Last tours begin at 5pm (summer) and 3pm (winter).
Admission: Adults £6 concessions £4.50 children £3.
Refreshments: In the Keep Yard.

EMMETTS GARDEN   🍂 The National Trust

nr Brasted   map **13** U23   ♿
Telephone: (01732) 750367 or 750429

Hillside shrub garden 18 acres open to the public. Lovely spring and autumn colours, rock garden, formal garden and roses.

Location: 1½ m S of A25 on Sundridge/Ide Hill Road.
Open: Garden only Mar weekends only 30 Mar-2 Nov Wed-Sun Good Fri Bank Hol Mon 1-6. Last adm 5. Guided tours by prior arrangement with Head Gardener.
Admission: £3 Children £1.50 family ticket £7.50. Pre-booked parties £2 Children £1 (15 or more).
Refreshments: Tea-room 2-5, 30 Mar-2 Nov.
Events/Exhibitions: Country fair 17-18 Aug. Jazz Concert 10 Aug.
Dogs admitted on lead. Wheelchair access to level parts of garden only. Small Shop.

FINCHCOCKS

(Mr & Mrs Richard Burnett)
Goudhurst   map **13** U23
Telephone: (01580) 211702
Fax: (01580) 211007

Finchcocks, dated 1725, is a fine example of Georgian baroque architecture, noted for its brickwork, with a front elevation attributed to Thomas Archer. It is set in beautiful gardens and parkland near the village of Goudhurst. The house contains a magnificent collection of historic keyboard instruments which are restored to full playing condition, and provides a unique setting where visitors can hear music performed on the instruments for which it was written. Demonstration tours and music whenever the house is open.

Location: 1½ m W of Goudhurst, 10 m E of Tunbridge Wells off A262.
Station(s): Marden (6 m) no taxi, Paddock Wood (8 m) taxi, Tunbridge Wells (10 m) taxi.
Open: Easter-end of Sept Suns also Bank Hol Mon & Wed-Sun in Aug: 2-6. Demonstrations & Music on instruments of the collection on Open Days.
Admission: £5 children £3.50 Family ticket £12.50. Garden only £1.80. Free parking.
Refreshments: Facilities available morning, afternoon & evening by arrangement.
Events/Exhibitions: Also private visits by appointment with music April to October. Festival: September Festival. Fairs: End of May and 2nd weekend of October. Exhibitions of prints and costumes: 18th century Pleasure Gardens etc.
Conferences: Suitable for conferences, wedding receptions and other functions. Licensed for civil marriages.

GAD'S HILL PLACE

(Gads Hill School Ltd)
Rochester   map **13** U23   △
Telephone: (01474) 822366

Grade 1 listed building, built in 1780. Home of Charles Dickens from 1857 to 1870.

Location: On A226; 3 m from Rochester, 4 m from Gravesend.
Station(s): Higham (1½ m).
Open: 1st Sun in month Apr-Sept and Bank Hol Suns 2-5pm. During Rochester Dickens Festivals (June and Dec) 11-4pm. At other times by arrangement.   Parties welcome. Rooms including newly restored conservatory can be hired for functions. Refreshments during Dickens Festivals, other catering by arrangement.
Admission: £2, Chd £1, parties by arrangement. Proceeds to restoration fund.
Refreshments: Food & Drink available.

"Playgrounds for the Children"

Belton House
Bowood
Drumlanrig (woodland playground)
Hever Castle
Kelburn (Secret Forest adventure course and stockade)
Longleat
Ragley Hall (adventure wood)
Weston Park
Wilton House

GODINTON PARK
(Godinton House Preservation Trust, Alan Wyndham Green, Esq)
Ashford   TN23 3BW   map **13** U24   △

The existing house belongs mostly to Jacobean times though there are records of another house being here in the 15th century. The interior of Godinton contains a wealth of very fine panelling and carving, particularly in the Hall and on the Staircase. The house contains interesting portraits and much fine furniture and china. The gardens were originally laid out in the 18th century and were further extended by Sir Reginald Blomfield with topiary work and formal gardens giving a spacious setting to the house.

Location: 1½ m W of Ashford off Maidstone Road at Potter's Corner (A20).
Station(s): Ashford (2 m).
Open: Easter Sat Sun & Mon then June-Sept Sun & Bank Hols only 2-5.
Admission: House & Gardens £2 children (under 16) £1 Weekdays by appointment only. Parties of 20 or more £1.50.

GOODNESTONE PARK
(The Lord & Lady FitzWalter)
nr Canterbury   map **13** U25
Telephone: (01304) 840107

The garden is approximately 14 acres, with many fine trees, a woodland garden and the walled garden with a large collection of old roses and herbaceous plants. Jane Austen was a frequent visitor, her brother Edward having married a daughter of the house.

Location: 8 m SE of Canterbury; 4 m E of A2; ¼ m SE of B2046; S of A257.
Station(s): Adisham (2 m).
Open: GARDEN ONLY **Weekdays** Mar 25-Oct 25 (incl Bank Holidays) Mon-Fri (NOT TUES OR SAT) 11-5. **Suns** Mar 31-Oct 20. House open by appointment for parties of not over 20.
Admission: £2.30 OAPs £2 Children (under 12) 20p. Wheelchairs £1. Parties (25 & over) £2 if guided £2.50. Parties, by appointment, not over 20 for house £1.50.
Refreshments: Teas Apr & May Sun & Wed June July Aug Sun Wed-Fri Pre-booked parties anyday.
Coach parties welcome but please book in advance. Rates on application. *No Dogs Allowed in the Garden.*

GREAT COMP GARDEN
(The Great Comp Charitable Trust)
nr Borough Green   map **12** U23
Telephone: (01732) 882669/886154

This outstanding garden of seven acres has been expertly developed by Mr and Mrs Cameron since 1957 to provide interest throughout the year. In a setting of well maintained lawns the carefully designed layout and good use of plants allows the visitor to wander through areas of different character. Around the 17th century house are formal areas of paving, terraces, old brick walls and hedges. These are surrounded by less formal planting providing winding paths, vistas and woodland glades with occasional ornaments and constructed 'ruins' for additional interest. A wide variety of trees, shrubs, herbaceous plants and heathers offer inspiration and pleasure and include many which are rarely seen. Good Autumn colour. Nursery open daily with wide range of plants from garden for sale. Music festival and other events in July & September. S.A.E. to The Curator Great Comp, Borough Green, Sevenoaks, Kent TN15 8QS.

Location: 2 m E of Borough Green B2016 off A20. First right at Comp crossroads ½ m on left.
Station(s): Borough Green & Wrotham (1½ m).
Open: Garden and Nursery Only Apr 1-Oct 31 daily 11-6. Free parking. Parties by prior arrangement (coaches welcome) guided tours and lectures by arrangement.
Admission: Adults £2.50 children £1 guide book available. Annual tickets £7.50 OAPs £5 annual ticket holders may visit any day Apr-Oct and out of season in Nov Feb and Mar.
Refreshments: Teas on Sun and Bank Hols and for parties by arrangement.
Events/Exhibitions: Garden party in July.
Conferences: Facilities available.
No dogs.

GREAT MAYTHAM HALL
(Country Houses Association)
Rolvenden   TN17 4NE   map **13** U24
Telephone: (01580) 241346

Built in 1910 by Sir Edwin Lutyens.

Location: ½ m S of Rolvenden village, on road to Rolvenden Layne.
Station(s): Headcorn (10 m) Staplehurst (10 m).
Open: May-Sept Weds & Thurs 2-5. Last entry 4.30.
Admission: £2.50 Children £1. Free car park.
No dogs admitted.

Robert Adam - architect

His work can be seen at the following properties included in Historic Houses Castles and Gardens:-

Audley End	*Mellerstain*
Bowood House & Gardens	*Moccas Court*
Culzean Castle	*Newby Hall & Gardens*
Hatchlands Park	*Nostell Priory*
Kedleston Hall	*Osterley Park*
Kenwood, The Iveagh Bequest	*Papplewick Hall*
Killerton	*Saltram House*
Kimbolton Castle	*Syon House*
Luton Hoo	

GROOMBRIDGE PLACE GARDENS AND ENCHANTED FOREST

Groombridge   map **12** U23   &

Telephone: (01892) 863999

Fax: (01892) 863996

Discover the most inspiring attraction in the Kingdom, with 164 acres of breathtaking gardens and parkland - the setting for Peter Greenaway's acclaimed film, "The Draughtsman's Contract". *17th Century Formal Gardens *Medieval Moat *Birds of Prey *The Enchanted Forest - a major new garden in the making *Canal Boat and Tractor - Trailer rides*.

Location: On B2110 (off A264), 4 m south west of Tunbridge Wells and 9 m east of East Grinstead.

Station(s): Rail - Charing Cross - Tunbridge Wells (55 minutes).

Open: Daily 1 Apr-31 Oct 10-6.

Admission: Adults £5 Seniors/Students £4.50 Children £3.50 (includes complimentary rides on canal boat and tractor-trailer).

Refreshments: Enjoy a light snack or meal in our new garden restaurant.

Events/Exhibitions: We host a range of events throughout the year, including: The Battle of Groombridge 15th and 16th June, Kent and Sussex Craft Show 20th and 21st July, Weald of Kent Country Show 21st and 22nd Sept.

Conferences: Groombridge place offers the perfect venue for civil wedding ceremonies, receptions, meetings, conferences and functions.

For enquiries and event details please contact: The Estate Office, Groombridge Place. Tel: (01892) 863999.

HEVER CASTLE & GARDENS

(Broadland Properties Limited)
nr Edenbridge, Kent   TN8 7NG   map **12** U23
Telephone: (01732) 865224
Fax: (01732) 866796

Hever Castle is a romantic 13th century moated castle best known as the childhood home of Anne Boleyn, Henry VIII's second wife and mother of Elizabeth I. At the beginning of this century William Waldorf Astor bought the estate and spent time, money and imagination in restoring the castle and creating one of the most beautiful gardens in England. He filled the castle with wonderful furniture, tapestries, paintings and other works of art and built the unique Italian Garden to display his collection of antique statuary. Today's visitor can wander around this delightfully intimate castle learning about the great love affair between Henry VIII and Anne Boleyn and then enjoy the magnificent grounds which include a maze, topiary, lake, herb garden and walled rose garden.

Location: Hever Castle is 30 miles from central London and 30 minutes from Gatwick. 3 miles south-east of Edenbridge, Kent, off the B2026. Exit junctions 5 or 6 of the M25 or junction 10 of the M23.
Station(s): Hever Station 1 m, no taxis available. Edenbridge Town Station 3 m, taxis available.
Open: Daily Mar 1-Nov 30 1996 Gardens open 11am Castle 12 noon - last entry 5pm and final exit 6pm (11am-4pm winter time). Dogs on lead in gardens only. Facilities for disabled. Special pre-booked private tours available all year round. Gift, book and garden shops and an adventure play-ground.
Admission: Family ticket available and discounts for groups of 15 or more.
Refreshments: Two licensed self-service restaurants in grounds serving hot and cold food throughout the day. Picnics welcome. Henry VIII public house opposite the main entrance.
Events/Exhibitions: Miniature model houses exhibition featuring 'Life in English Country Houses through the Ages'. Special events for 1996: Jousting Tournaments, Longbow Archery Demonstrations, Summer Concert Festival and Patchwork & Quilting Exhibition.
Conferences: The Tudor Village adjoining the Castle is available all year round for residential and day conferences, incentive travel, product launches, private dining and receptions.

HOLE PARK GARDEN
(D.G.W. Barham)
Hole Park, Rolvenden, Cranbrook
Telephone: (01580) 241251

Beautiful parkland with distant views of the Weald.

IGHTHAM MOTE   🍃 The National Trust
Ivy Hatch   map **12** U23
Telephone: (01732) 810378
Fax: (01732) 811029

One of the most complete remaining examples of a medieval moated manor house. Major exhibition of building conservation in action.

Location: 3 m S of Ightham, off A227, 4½ m E of Sevenoaks off A25.
Open: 31 Mar-1 Nov Mon Wed Thur Fri 12-5.30 Sun and Bank Hol Mon 11-5.30 (last adm 5) pre-booked guided tours 11-12 weekdays no reduction open Good Fri.
Admission: £4 adult, £2 child, family ticket £10, £3 for Pre-booked parties. (No reduction for pre-booked guided tour). 1995 prices.
Refreshments: Tea pavilion in car park. Open half an hour before house, may close early in bad weather.
Events/Exhibitions: 5 & 6 July Orchestral Concert. Exhibition on building conservation. Shop open as house. Disabled access to ground floor only. No dogs.

KNOLE   🍃 The National Trust
Sevenoaks   map **12** U23   △
Telephone: (01732) 450608
Fax: (01732) 465528

The largest private house in England dating from 15th century, with splendid Jacobean interior and world renowned collection of Stuart furniture, including three state beds and the prototype of the Knole settee. Paintings by Van Dyck, Lely, Kneller, Hoppner, Wootton, Reynolds and Gainsborough.

Location: At the Tonbridge end of Sevenoaks, just E of A225; 25 m from London, just off M25 London orbital.
Station(s): Train ½ hour from London (Charing Cross) to Sevenoaks and bus to house. Special all inclusive rail/bus/admission ticket available.
Open: House 30 Mar-2 Nov, Wed, Fri, Sat, Sun & Bank Hol Mon 11-5pm. Thurs 2-5pm. Lat admission 4pm. Pre-booked groups welcome on Wed, Fri & Sat 11-4pm, Thurs 2-4pm. Garden May-Sept first Wed in each month only by courtesy of Lord Sackville.
Admission: Car park £2.50 (NT members free). House: £4.50 chd £2.25 Family ticket £11.25. Garden: 50p, chd 30p (1995 prices). Pre-booked parties Wed-Sat (Thurs am pre-booked guided tours, no reductions) £3.50 child £1.50.
Refreshments: Restaurant/tea-room open as house.
Events/Exhibitions: Promoted locally.
Shop open as house. Picnics welcome in 1000 acre deer park open by courtesy of Lord Sackville. No dogs in house.

LADHAM HOUSE
(Betty, Lady Jessel)
Goudhurst   map **13** U23
Telephone: (01580) 211203

10 acres of rolling lawns, fine specimen trees, rhododendrons, azaleas, camellias, shrubs and magnolias. Newly planted arboretum. Spectacular twin mixed borders. Fountain garden and bog garden. Fine view. Reserected Old Rock garden with waterfall.
Refreshments: Teas served and homemade ploughmans.

Lancelot 'Capability' Brown

Born 1716 in Northumberland, Capability Brown began work at the age of 16 in the vegetable gardens of Sir William and Lady Loraine at Kirharle Tower. He left Northumberland in 1739, and records show that he worked at Stowe until 1749. It was at Stowe that Brown began to study architecture, and to submit his own plans. It was also at Stowe that he devised a new method of moving and replanting mature trees.

Brown married Bridget Wayet in 1744 and began work on the estate at Warwick Castle in 1749. He was appointed Master Gardener at Hampton Court in 1764, and planted the Great Vine at Hampton Court in 1768. Blenheim Palace designs are considered amongst Brown's finest work, and the technical achievements were outstanding even for the present day.

Capability Brown died in February 1783 of a massive heart attack. A monument beside the lake at Croome Court was erected which reads "To the memory of Lancelot Brown, who by the powers of his inimitable and creative genius formed this garden scene out of a morass". There is also a portrait of Brown at Burghley.

Capability Brown was involved in the design of grounds at the following properties included in Historic Houses Castles and Gardens:

Audley End	*Longleat*
Berrington Hall	*Luton Hoo*
Bowood	*Moccas Court*
Burghley House	*Petworth House*
Burton Constable	*Sledmere House*
Charlecote Park	*Stowe (Stowe*
Chilham Castle Gardens	*School)*
(reputed)	*Syon House*
Clandon Park	*Warwick Castle*
Claremont	*Weston Park*
Chillington Hall	*Wimpole Hall*
Corsham Court	*Wrest Park and*
Fawley Court	*Gardens*
Highclere Castle	

LEEDS CASTLE

(Leeds Castle Foundation)
nr Maidstone   ME17 1PL   map **13** U24   △ &
Telephone: (01622) 765400
Fax: (01622) 735616

Leeds Castle stands as one of the most beautiful and ancient Castles in the Kingdom, rising from its two small islands in the middle of a lake and surrounded by 500 acres of magnificent parkland and gardens. Dating back to the 9th century and rebuilt by the Normans in 1119, Leeds Castle was then a Royal Palace for over three centuries. It now contains a superb collection of mediaeval furnishings, French and English furniture, tapestries and paintings. You can wander down through the Duckery into the Wood Garden, where peacocks and swans roam free. Visit the aviaries with rare tropical birds and the Culpeper Garden full of old fashioned flowers and fragrance. See a fascinating underground grotto at the centre of the maze and visit the greenhouses and vineyard. There's also a museum of Medieval Dog Collars in the 13th century Gate Tower. Or, come and play our 9-hole golf course. Now owned by the Leeds Castle Foundation, a private Charitable Trust, the Castle is also used as a high level residential conference centre.

Location: 4 m E of Maidstone; access on B2163 at junction 8 of the M20 and well signposted.
Station(s): Bearsted (2 m). Inclusive ticket schemes combining admission with rail and coach travel operate all year round on Castle open days from Victoria Station or Charing Cross to Bearsted.
Open: Every day 10-5* Mar-Oct and 10-3* in winter (* last admission to grounds). Closed Christmas Day also 29 June and 6 July before Open Air Concerts and 2 Nov for Fireworks Display (The Trustees reserve the right to close all or parts of the Castle as necessary).
Admission: Fully inclusive Castle and Park adults £8 senior citizens/students £6.30 children £5.20 disabled visitors £4 family ticket (2 adults and up to 3 children) £22. Park and attractions £6, senior citizens/students £4.80, children £3.70, disabled visitors £3 family ticket (2 adults and up to 3 children) £18. Significant discounts for groups (min 20 persons) and school parties. Also a great value Season Pass, "The Castle Card".
Refreshments: Licenced self-service restaurant in the Fairfax Hall and waitress service in the Terrace Restaurant provide a full range of hot and cold meals, plus cream teas. Also barbecues and fast food outlets in the Stable Courtyard.
Events/Exhibitions: Mon Jan 1; **New Year's Day Treasure Trail:** Sat Mar 23-Sun Mar 31; **Spring Garden's Week:** Sat Apr 6-Mon 8; **Celebration of Easter:** Sat May 18-Sun 19 May; **Festival of English Food & Wine:** Sat June 8-Sun 9; **Balloon and Vintage Car Fiesta:** Sat June 29 and Sat July 6; **Annual Open Air Concerts:** Wed Sept 18-Sat 21 Sept; **Flower Festival:** Sat Nov 2; **Grand Firework Spectacular:** Wed Nov 1-Sun Dec 24; **Special Christmas Shop:** Throughout Dec; **Christmas at the Castle.**
Conferences: Residential conferences or day meetings in the Castle itself; or in the Culpeper Conference Centre (12-50 delegates). Wide choice of historic venues for special functions.
Other Details: Picnic area. Car park. Fully accessible minibus provides shuttle service to and from car and coach parks, for disabled and elderly visitors. Good facilities for disabled. Regret no dogs. Castle shop, Park shop, book shop, plants for sale from greenhouses.

LULLINGSTONE CASTLE

(Guy Hart Dyke, Esq)
Eynsford   DA14 0JA   map **12** U23   △ &
Telephone: (01322) 862114

Family portraits, armour, Henry VII gatehouse, Church, Herb garden.

Location: In the Darenth valley via Eynsford on A225.
Station(s): Eynsford (½ m).
Open: Castle and Grounds Apr-Sept Sat Sun Bank Hols 2-6 Wed Thur and Fri by arrangement (2-6). Telephone for enquiries or bookings.
Admission: Adults £3.50 children £1.50 OAPs £3. Free car parking.
Refreshments: In the gatehouse tea-rooms.
Events/Exhibitions: June 16 National Gardens Scheme. July 11-14 and 17-20 Open Air Production of "The Wind in The Willows".
No dogs.

LULLINGSTONE ROMAN VILLA

ENGLISH HERITAGE

map **12** U23
Telephone: (01322) 863467

The ancient Romans understood the art of gracious living. In this country villa they walked on mosaic floors, dined off fine tableware and commissioned elaborate wall paintings to decorate one of the earliest churches in Britain.

Location: ½ m (0.8 km) south west of Eynsford.
Open: Apr 1-Sept 30 10-6 daily Oct 1-Mar 31 daily 10-4.
Admission: Adults £2 concessions £1.50 children £1. Price includes a Personal Stereo Guided Tour.

LYMPNE CASTLE
(Harry Margary, Esq)
nr Hythe   CT21 4LQ   map 13 U25
Telephone: (01303) 267571

This romantic medieval castle with an earlier Roman, Saxon and Norman history was once owned by the Archdeacons of Canterbury. It was rebuilt about 1360, and restored in 1905, 300 feet above the well known Roman Shore Fort - Stutfall Castle. Four miles from the ancient Cinque Port of Hythe, it commands a tremendous view across Romney Marshes to Fairlight over the great sweep of the coast from Dover to Dungeness and across the sea to France. Terraced gardens with magnificent views out to sea.

Location: 3 m NW of Hythe off B2067, 8 m W of Folkestone.
Station(s): Sandling (2½ m).
Open: Easter-Sept 30 daily 10.30-6 *Parties by appointment* closed occasionally on Sat.
Admission: Adults £2 children 50p.
Conferences: Conferences, licensed for civil weddings. Reception facilities.

MARLE PLACE GARDENS
(Mrs Lindel Williams)
Marle Place Road, Brenchley, Tonbridge   TN12 7HS   map 12 U23   △ &
Telephone: (01892) 722304
Fax: (01892) 724099

Marle Place is a romantic privately owned Wealden Garden of 10 acres close to Scotney and Sissinghurst Castles. A plantsmans garden with many interesting trees and shrubs. Featuring a Victorian gazebo and Edwardian rockery (now a herb garden). Walled, fragrant garden and ornamental ponds. Yew hedges and herbaceous border. Architecturally important listed,17th century house.Unusual plant nursery.

Location: Off the B2162 1 m south of Horsmonden, and 1½ m north west of Lamberhurst, turn west on Marle Place Road for ½ m or follow brown and white tourist signs from Brenchley Village.
Station(s): Paddock Wood B.R. Bus from Tunbridge Wells.
Open: Apr 1-Oct 31 9.30-5.30.
Admission: Adults £2 Groups by arrangement.
Refreshments: Tea-room, self-service tea, coffee & cake.
Coach parties are most welcome, but must be booked in advance. Car parking.

NEW COLLEGE OF COBHAM
(Presidents of the New College of Cobham)
Cobham   map 13 U24   &
Telephone: (01474) 814280

Almshouses based on medieval chantry built 1362, part rebuilt 1598. Originally endowed by Sir John de Cobham and descendants.

Location: 4 m W of Rochester; 4 m SE of Gravesend; 1½ m from junction Shorne-Cobham (A2). In Cobham rear of Church of Mary Magdalene.
Station(s): Sole St (1 m).
Open: Apr-Sept daily (except Thurs) 10-7 Oct-Mar Mon Tues Wed Sat & Sun 10-4.
Admission: Free.
Refreshments: Afternoon teas by prior arrangement.

"GHOSTS"

Ghosts are in residence at the following properties included in Historic Houses Castles and Gardens:-

Blickling Hall - *Anne Boleyn*

Breamore House - *Haunted picture - if touched, death on the same day*

East Riddleden Hall - *5 ghosts including lady in Grey Hall Lady's Chamber*

Fountains Abbey & Studley Royal - *Choir of monks chanting in Chapel of Nine Altars*

Hinton Ampner - *Nocturnal noises*

Ightham Mote - *Supernatural presence*

Lindisfarne Castle - *Monk, and group of monks on causeway*

Lyme Park - *Unearthly peals of bells and lady in white, funeral procession through park*

Malmesbury House - *Ghost of a cavalier*

Overbecks Museum & Garden - *'Model' ghost in the Children's room (for them to spot)*

Rockingham Castle - *Lady Dedlock*

Rufford Old Hall - *Elizabeth Hesketh*

Scotney Castle Garden - *Man rising from the lake*

Sizergh Castle & Garden - *Poltergeist*

Speke Hall - *Ghost of woman in tapestry room*

Springhill - *Ghost of a woman*

Sudbury Hall - *Lady in Green, seen on stairs*

Tamworth Castle - *Haunted bedroom*

Treasurer's House - *Troop of Roman soldiers marching through the cellar*

Wallington House - *Invisible birds beating against the windows accompanied by heavy breathing*

Washington Old Hall - *Grey lady walking through corridors*

OWL HOUSE GARDENS
(Maureen, Marchioness of Dufferin & Ava)
Lamberhurst   map **12** U23
Telephone: (01892) 890963/890230

13 acres of romantic gardens surround this 16th century timber framed wool smuggler's cottage. Spring flowers, roses, rare flowering shrubs and ornamental fruit trees. Expansive lawns lead to leafy woodland walks graced by English and Turkish oaks, elm, birch and beech trees. Rhododendrons, azaleas, camellias encircle peaceful informal sunken water gardens.

Location: 8 m SE of Tunbridge Wells; 1 m from Lamberhurst off A21.
Station(s): Tunbridge Wells or Wadhurst.
Open: GARDENS ONLY. All the year - daily and weekends including all Bank Hol weekends 11-6.
Admission: £3 children £1 (Proceeds towards Lady Dufferin's charity, Maureen's Oast House for Arthritics). Free parking.
Events/Exhibitions: May 19: Spring Plant Fair; National council for the conservation of plants and gardens.
Dogs on lead. Coach parties welcome.

PATTYNDENNE MANOR
(Mr. & Mrs. D.C. Spearing)
Pattyndenne Manor, Goudhurst   TN17 2QU   map **13** U27
Telephone: (01580) 211361
Location: 1 m south of Goudhurst on W. side of B2079.

Sir Joshua Reynolds
Portrait painter (1723-1792)
First President of the Royal Academy, knighted in 1769

His work can be seen in the following properties included in Historic Houses Castles and Gardens:-

Arundel Castle
Dalmeny House (Roseberry Collection of
Political Portraits)
Elton Hall
Goodwood House
Ickworth House, Park & Garden
Kenwood, The Iveagh Bequest

Knole
Petworth House
Rockingham Castle
Saltram
Shalom Hall
Wallington House
Weston Park

PENSHURST PLACE

(The Rt Hon Viscount De L'Isle, MBE)
Tunbridge Wells   TN11 8DG   map **12** U23   △
Telephone: (01892) 870307
Fax: (01892) 870866

One of England's finest family-owned stately homes with a history going back six and a half centuries. Unique mediaeval Baron's Hall with splendid 60 foot-high chestnut beamed roof, paintings, furniture, and tapestries from 15th, 16th and 17th centuries. Other highlights include Toy Museum, Venture Playground, Nature trail, and magnificent gardens dating back to the 14th century, recently restored to their former glory.

Location: Penshurst, near Tonbridge. From M25, junction 5, follow A21 to Tonbridge, leaving at Tonbridge (North) exit; then follow brown tourist signs to Penshurst Place. From M26 Junction 2a. Follow A25 (Sevenoaks) and the A21 for Tonbridge; further directions as above.

Station(s): Penshurst (2 m). Regular services operate from BR Charing Cross to Hildenborough (4 miles) or Tonbridge (6 miles); then taxi.

Open: Sat and Suns in Mar and Oct. Open seven days a week from 1 Apr-29 Sept. Gardens and venture playground 11-6pm. House 12 noon-5.30pm (last entrance 5pm). Toy museum 12 noon-5pm.

Admission: House and Grounds adults £5.50 OAP's/students £5.10 children £3 family ticket £14.50 adult party (20 plus) £5.10 Grounds only adults £4 OAP's/students £3.50 children £2.75 family ticket £10.50. Garden Season Ticket £20. Pre-booked guided tours mornings only. Group rates of 20+ guided house tours adults and OAPs £5.50 children £2.75. Guided garden tours adults and OAPs £6.50 children £3.75. Combined guided tours adults and OAPs £6.50 children £3.75. Non-guided group visit adults and OAPs £5.10 children £2.75.

Refreshments: Light luncheons and teas available in Restaurant.

Events/Exhibitions: Featured regularly Home Design Exhibition, Craft Fairs, Wool Race, Balloon Fiesta, Falconry Displays, Classic Car Show, Theatre, and Concerts - please ask for our special events leaflet.

Conferences: Conferences/Banqueting: The Buttery, The Sunderland Room and Barons Hall, all part of the original 14th century manor house, are available for corporate hospitality, private functions, licensed for civil wedding ceremonies, receptions. Marquees for up to 450 people may be erected on the South Lawn, overlooking the Italianate Garden and Home Park is the setting for company activity days, clay pidgeon shoots and product launches.

No dogs admitted. Wheelchair visitors welcome. (Disabled access limited by age/architecture of House. For enquiries and group bookings, contact Penshurst Place, Penshurst, Tonbridge, Kent TN11 8DG. (01892) 870307

PORT LYMPNE WILD ANIMAL PARK, MANSION & GARDENS
(John Aspinall, Esq)
Lympne, Hythe   CT21 4PD   map **13** U25
Telephone: (01303) 264647
Fax: (01303) 264944
Location: 3 m W of Hythe; 6 m W of Folkestone; 7 m SE of Ashford exit 11 off M20.

QUEBEC HOUSE   The National Trust
Westerham   map **12** U23
Telephone: (01959) 562206
Location: At junction of Edenbridge & Sevenoaks Roads (A25 & B2026).

QUEX HOUSE, QUEX PARK
(Trustees of the Powell-Cotton Museum)
Birchington   map **13** U25
Telephone: (01843) 42168
Fax: (01843) 846661

Wander through the period rooms of P.H.G. Powell-Cotton's mansion, Quex House, the only stately home in Thanet, with its superb woodcarving and panelling, beautiful plasterwork and an air of mellow maturity. The rooms are arranged much as they were in his lifetime and contain fine 17th and 18th century English furniture and many family treasures. The unique Chinese Imperial porcelain collection, however, has been moved into its own gallery in the Powell-Cotton Museum as have the English and Continental porcelain collections. This purpose-built museum, adjoining the Mansion, now extends to nine large galleries; here Powell-Cotton created huge dioramas showing 500 African and Asian animals, all mounted by Rowland Ward, in scenes re-creating their natural habitats. He assembled the world's finest collection of African ethnography gathered on his 28 expeditions, and displayed it at Quex, together with superb weapons collections, cannon, local archaeological material and outstanding fine arts from many countries of the Orient. Enjoy the Pleasure Gardens and see the Victorian Walled Kitchen Garden presently under restoration.

Location: In Birchington, ½ m S of Birchington Square (signposted). SW of Margate; 13 m E of Canterbury.
Station(s): Birchington (1 m).

Open: Open regularly in summer (times on request) please telephone for brochure.
Admission: Adults £2.50 children/OAPs £1.80 (Summer) adults £2 children/OAPs £1.30 (Winter) Gardens only adults £1 children/OAPs 60p Summer and Winter.
Refreshments: The newly-built licensed restaurant can accommodate up to 150 guests and the front hall/dining hall in Quex House can accommodate a maximum of 60 guests.
Events/Exhibitions: Quex Prom July 1996 - outdoor event with Royal Philharmonic Orchestra. Also probably, popular concert with leading artist due to be announced.
Conferences: Licensed for Civil Weddings. Two rooms available.
Ground floor rooms and museum only suitable for disabled. Free car and coach parking. New museum shop in recently completed Visitor Centre. Registered Charity. The information above was correct at time of going to press but could be altered without prior warning.

RIVERHILL HOUSE
(The Rogers Family)
Sevenoaks   TN15 0RR   map **12** U23   △
Telephone: (01732) 458802/452557

Small Ragstone house built in 1714 and home of the Rogers family since 1840.

ROCHESTER CASTLE   ENGLISH HERITAGE
Rochester   map **13** U24
Telephone: (01634) 402276

Built in the 11th century to guard the point where the Roman road of Watling Street crossed the River Medway, the size and position of this grand Norman bishop's castle, founded on the Roman city wall, eventually made it an important royal stronghold for several hundred years. The keep is truly magnificent - over 100 feet high and with walls 12 feet thick. At the top you will be able to enjoy fine views over the river and surrounding city of Rochester.

Location: By Rochester Bridge (A2).
Open: Apr 1-Sept 30 10-6 daily Oct 1-Mar 31 daily 10-4.
Admission: Adults £2.50 concessions £1.90 children £1.30.

SCOTNEY CASTLE GARDEN   The National Trust
Lamberhurst   map **13** U24   &
Telephone: (01892) 891081
Fax: (01892) 890110

Romantic landscape garden framing moated castle.

Location: 1m SE of Lamberhurst (A21).
Open: Garden 30 Mar-2 Nov Wed-Fri 11-6 or sunset if earlier *(closed Good Fri)* Sat & Sun 2-6 or sunset if earlier. Bank Hols and Sun preceeding Bank Hol. Mon 12-6. Old Castle May-Sept 15 days and times as for garden. Last adm one hour before closing.
Admission: £3.50 (pre-booked parties £2.20 weekdays only) Children £1.70 Family ticket £8.70.
Events/Exhibitions: 11-14 July & 18-20 July Opera.
No dogs. Picnic area next to car park. Shop. Wheelchairs available. (Steep entrance to garden).

SISSINGHURST CASTLE GARDEN   The National Trust
Sissinghurst   map **13** U24
Telephone: (01580) 712850
Location: 2 m NE of Cranbrook; 1 m E of Sissinghurst village (A262).

SMALLHYTHE PLACE   The National Trust
Tenterden   map **13** U24
Telephone: (01580) 762334
Location: 2½ m S of Tenterden on E side of Rye Road (B2082).

SOUTH FORELAND LIGHTHOUSE   🍂 The National Trust
map **13** U25
Telephone: (01892) 890651
Location: 1½ m SW of St. Margaret's at Cliffe village. Visitors are advised to park in village car park (2 miles).

SQUERRYES COURT 🏛
(J St A Warde, Esq)
Westerham   TN16 1SJ   map **12** U23
Telephone: (01959) 562345 or 563118
Fax: (01959) 565949

Beautiful manor house built in 1681. Warde family home since 1731 (still lived in today). Important Italian, 18c English and 17c Dutch paintings; furniture, porcelain and tapestries all collected by the family in the 18c Memorabilia of General Wolfe of Quebec. Landscaped garden lovely all seasons. Lake, borders, recently restored formal garden, 18c dovecote.

Location: Western outskirts of Westerham signposted from A25. Junctions 5 & 6 M25 10 mins.
Station(s): Oxted or Sevenoaks.
Open: During Mar Sun only 2-6 Apr 1-Sept 30 Wed Sat Sun and Bank Hol Mons 2-6 (last adm 5.30).
Admission: Adults £3.70 OAPs £3.40 children (14 and under) £1.80 Grounds only £2.20 OAPs £2 children (14 and under) £1.20. Parties over 20 (any day) by arrangment at reduced rates.
Refreshments: Homemade teas served in Old Library. Catering for Groups (light lunches, teas, suppers) by prior arrangement. Restaurant licence.
Conferences: House and Grounds are available for private hire all year i.e Marquee Wedding Receptions, Small Conferences, Luncheons, Dinners, Promotions, Launches, Clay Pigeon Shoots.
Dogs on leads in grounds only. Free parking at house.

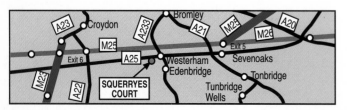

STONEACRE   🍂 The National Trust
Otham   map **13** U24
Telephone: (01622) 862871
Location: In Otham, 3 m SE of Maidstone; 1 m S of A20.

TONBRIDGE CASTLE
(Owned and Managed by Tonbridge & Malling Borough Council)
Tonbridge   TN9 1BG   map **12** U24   △ Ⓔ
Telephone: (01732) 770929
Fax: (01732) 770449

Reputedly England's finest example of the layout of a Norman Motte and Bailey Castle with 13th century Gatehouse set in landscaped gardens overlooking the River Medway. The site is clearly interpreted for your enjoyment. Superb exhibition in Castle Gatehouse depicting life as it was 700 years ago. Tours are available from the Tourist Information Centre.

Location: In town centre off High Street.
Station(s): Tonbridge (Main line Charing Cross).
Open: Apr-Sept Mon-Sat 9-5 Sun & Bank Hol 10.30-5 Oct-Mar Mon-Fri 9-5 Sat 9-4 Sun 10.30-4 closed Christmas Day and New Year's Day (last tours leave 1 hr before closing time) guided tours by arrangement.
Admission: Adults £3 children/OAPs £1.50 family £7.50 10% discount for groups.
Refreshments: Available nearby.
Events/Exhibitions: New exhibition for 1996.
Accommodation: Available nearby.
Conferences: Room available for hire. Annually approved for Civil Marriages.

WALMER CASTLE
ENGLISH HERITAGE
Kingsdown Road, Walmer, Deal
CT14 7LJ   map **13** U25
Telephone: (01304) 364288

One of the coastal castles built by Henry VIII and the official residence of The Lords Warden of The Cinque Ports, including Queen Elizabeth, the Queen Mother and the Duke of Wellington who died at Walmer and whose furnished rooms have been preserved unaltered. (The original 'Wellington Boot' may be seen here).

Location: On coast at Walmer 2 m S of Deal off the Dover/Deal Road.
Station(s): Walmer (1½ m).
Open: Apr 1-Sept 30 10-6 daily Oct 1-31 10-4 daily Nov 1-Mar 31 Wed-Sun 10-4. Closed Jan & Feb, Lord Warden in residence.
Admission: Adults £3.80 concessions £2.90 children £1.90. Price includes a Personal Stereo Guided Tour.

WILLESBOROUGH WINDMILL
(Willesborough Windmill Trust)
Ashford   TN24 0GQ   map **13** U24
Telephone: (01233) 625643/629165

Willesborough Windmill, built in 1869, has now been restored as a working smock mill. Visitors can view the turn-of-the-century miller's cottage, enjoy guided tours of the mill which is not suitable for the disabled.

Location: 2 m E of Ashford town centre, just off A292 and approx ¼ m from Junction 10 of the M20.
Station(s): Ashford 2 miles.
Open: Easter-Oct 31 Sat Sun and Bank Hols 2-5 (or dusk if earlier).
Admission: Adults £1 children/OAPs 50p. Group rates available on application.
Refreshments: Tea-room and shop in restored barn adjacent to the mill. Light refreshments available. Suitable for disabled.
Events/Exhibitions: Bank Holiday Monday.
Limited parking.

LANCASHIRE

ASTLEY HALL

(Chorley Borough Council)
off Hallgate, Astley Park, Chorley   PR7 1NP   map **6** P17
Telephone: (01257) 262166
Fax: (01257) 232441

The Hall dates back to Elizabethan times with major additions in the 1660s and 1820s. Interiors contain elaborate plaster ceilings and fine furniture.

Location: 5 mins SW from J8 of M61, 10 mins SE of J28 and NE of J27 of M6. Follow signs for Chorley and brown tourist signs. 10 mins walk through park from town centre.
Station(s): In town. Bus route near to Hall.
Open: Apr-Oct Tue-Sun 12-5 open Bank Hol Mons Nov-Mar Fri-Sun 12-4.
Admission: Adults £2.50 Concessions £1.50 Family ticket £4.50
Refreshments: Adjacent Cafe in park.
Conferences: Licensed for Civil Weddings.

BROWSHOLME HALL

nr Clitheroe   BB7 3DE   map **6** P17
Telephone: (01254) 826719
Fax: (01254) 826739

Home of the Parker family, Bowbearers of the Forest of Bowland. Tudor with Elizabethan front, Queen Anne Wing and Regency additions. Portraits furniture and antiquities.

Location: 5 m NW of Clitheroe; off B6243; Bashall Eaves - Whitewell signposted.
Open: 2-5 Easter (Good Friday-Mon) late May Bank Hol weekend, July every Sat, Aug every Sat & Sun and Aug Bank Hol weekend.
Admission: £3 Reductions for booked parties at other times by appointment with A. Parker, Tel. as above.
Refreshments: For booked parties by arrangement.

GAWTHORPE HALL   The National Trust

Padiham, nr Burnley   BB12 8UA   map **15** P18
Telephone: (01282) 778511
Location: On E outskirts of Padiham (¾ m drive to house is on N of A671).

RUFFORD OLD HALL   The National Trust

Rufford, nr Ormskirk   L40 1SG   map **6** P17
Telephone: (01704) 821254
Location: 7 m N of Ormskirk at N end of Rufford village on E side of A59.0

STONYHURST COLLEGE

Hurst Green   map **15** P18 △
Telephone: (01254) 826345

The original house, (situated close to the picturesque village of Hurst Green in the beautiful Ribble Valley) dates from the late 16th century. Set in extensive grounds which include ornamental gardens. The College has an impressive approach down a long avenue flanked by man made rectangular ponds constructed in the 17th century. The Parish Church of St. Peters built in 1832, is linked to the main building which is a Catholic boarding 2 day school, founded by the Society of Jesus in 1593.

Location: Just off the B6243 (Longridge - Clitheroe) on the outskirts of Hurst Green. 10 m from junction 31 on M6.
Station(s): Preston.
Open: House weekly July 22-Aug 26 Sat-Thurs only (inc Aug Bank Hol Mon) 1-5 Grounds & Gardens weekly July 2-Aug 26 Sat-Thurs only (inc Aug Bank Hol Mon) 1-5.
Admission: House and Grounds £3.50 children (4-14) £2.50 (under 4 free) Senior Citizens £2.50 Grounds only £1.
Refreshments: Refreshments/Gift Shop: Limited facilities for disabled. Coach parties by prior arrangement.
Conferences: Facilities available.
No dogs permitted.

TOWNELEY HALL ART GALLERY & MUSEUM AND MUSEUM OF LOCAL CRAFTS & INDUSTRIES

(Burnley Borough Council)
Burnley   BD11 3RQ   map **15** P18
Telephone: (01282) 424213
Fax: (01282) 36138

The House dates from the 14th century, with 17th and 19th century modifications. The furnished rooms include an Elizabethan Long Gallery, and a fine entrance hall with plasterwork by Vassali completed in 1729. Collections include oak furniture, 18th and 19th century paintings and Zoffany's painting of Charles Towneley. Loan exhibitions are held throughout the summer. There is a Museum of Local Crafts and Industries in the old Brew House, and the Natural History Centre, with an aquarium in the grounds. Guided tours: Weds afternoon.

Location: ½ m SE of Burnley on the Burnley/Todmorden Road (A671).
Station(s): Burnley Central (1¾ m).
Open: All the year Mon-Fri 10-5 Sun 12-5 closed Sat throughout year and Christmas-New Year.
Admission: Free.
Refreshments: At cafe in grounds.

TURTON TOWER

(Lancashire County Council)
Chapeltown Road, Turton   BL7 OHG   map **15** P18
Telephone: (01204) 852203
Fax: (01204) 853754

Medieaval Tower extended by Tudors, Stuarts and Victorians.

LEICESTERSHIRE

BELGRAVE HALL

(Leicestershire Museums, Arts and Records Service)
Church Road, off Thurcaston Road, Belgrave, Leicester
Telephone: (0116) 2666590

Small Queen Anne house of 1709-13, with period room settings from late 17th to late 19th century.

BELVOIR CASTLE
(His Grace the Duke of Rutland)
nr Grantham   map **7** R21
Telephone: (01476) 870262

Seat of the Dukes of Rutland since Henry VIII's time, and rebuilt by Wyatt in 1816. A castle in the grand style, commanding magnificent views over the Vale of Belvoir. The name dates back to the famous Norman Castle that stood on this site. Many notable art treasures, and interesting military relics. The Statue gardens contain many beautiful 17th century sculptures. Flowers in bloom throughout most of the season. Medieval Jousting Tournaments. Conference and filming facilities. Banquets, school visits, private parties.

Location: 7 m WSW of Grantham, between A607 (to Melton Mowbray) and A52 (to Nottingham).
Open: Apr 1-Oct 31 Tues Wed Thurs Sat 11-5 Sun and Bank Hols 11-6. Other times for groups by appointment.
Admission: Adults £4.25 children £2.65 OAPs £3. All coach tours and excursions £3.25 (coach driver free) parties of 20 or more adults £3 (organiser free) school parties £2.20 (teacher free). On Jousting Tournament days an extra charge of 50p per person will apply. Ticket office and catering facilities in the Castle close approximately 30 mins before the Castle. Guide books are on sale at the ticket office or inside the Castle, or by post (£2.50) incl. post and packing.
We regret that dogs are not permitted (except Guide dogs).

BOSWORTH BATTLEFIELD VISITOR CENTRE & COUNTRY PARK
(Leicestershire County Council)
Sutton Cheney, nr Market Bosworth   &
Telephone: (01455) 290429

Exhibition, shops, battle trail, T.I.C. Adjacent to "Battlefield Line" steam railway and two miles from classic market town of Market Bosworth. A series of medieval themed special events throughout summer Sundays. Telephone Warden (01455) 290429.

KAYES GARDEN NURSERY
(Mrs Hazel Kaye)
1700 Melton Rd, Rearsby, Leicester, Leicestershire   LE7 4YR   map **14** R20
Telephone: (01664) 424578

Hardy herbaceous perennials and good selection of climbers and shrubs. The garden and nursery are in Rearsby, in the Wreake Valley countryside of Leicestershire. Once an orchard, the one acre garden houses an extensive selection of hardy herbaceous plants. Mixed borders and a fine pergola provide year-round interest, while the nursery offers an excellent range of interesting plants.

Location: Just inside Rearsby village, N of Leicester on A607, on L.H. side approaching from Leicester.
Open: Mar-Oct inclusive Wed-Sat 10-5 Sun 10-12. Nov to Feb inclusive Fri and Sat 10-4.30. *Closed* Dec 25-Jan 31 inclusive.

THE MANOR HOUSE
(Leicestershire Museums, Arts and Records Service)
Donington-le-Heath
Telephone: (01530) 831259

Fine medieval manor house circa 1280 with 16th to 17th century alterations.

OAKHAM CASTLE
(Leicestershire Museums, Arts and Records Service)
Market Place, Oakham
Telephone: (01572) 723654

12th century Great Hall of Norman castle in castle grounds with earlier motte. Unique collection of horseshoes presented by visiting Peers of the Realm.

Location: In Oakham.
Station(s): Oakham.
Open: Castle Grounds: Apr to Oct - daily 10-5.30. Nov to Mar - daily 10-4. Sun 2-4. Great Hall: Apr to Oct - Tues to Sat and Bank Holiday Mon 10-1, 2-5.30. Sun 2-5.30. Nov to Mar - Tues to Sat 10-1, 2-4. *Closed* Good Friday, Christmas Day and Boxing Day. Access for disabled to Great Hall. Parking for disabled visitors **only** on request.
Admission: Free.

STANFORD HALL
(The Lady Braye)
Lutterworth   LE17 6DH   map **14** R20   △
Telephone: (01788) 860250
Fax: (01788) 860870

William and Mary house, fine pictures (including the Stuart Collection), furniture and family costumes. Replica 1898 flying machine, Motorcycle Museum, Rose Garden, Nature Trail. Craft Centre (most Sundays)

Location: M1 exit 18, M1 exit 19 (from/to North only); M6 exit at A14/M1 (N) junction, 7½ m NE of Rugby; 1¼ m from Swinford.

Open: Easter-end Sept, Sats, Suns, Bank Hol Mons & Tues following 2.30-5.30 (last adm 5). On Bank Hol and Event Days open 12 noon (House 2.30).
Admission: House and Grounds adults £3.50 children £1.70. Grounds Only adult £1.90 child 80p. Parties (min 20) adult £3.20, OAP £3, child £1.50. Prices subject to increase on some Event Days. Museum adult £1 child 30p.
Refreshments: Home-made teas. Light lunches most Suns. Suppers, Teas, Lunches for pre-booked parties any day during season.

WYGSTON'S HOUSE, MUSEUM OF COSTUME

(Leicestershire Museums, Arts and Records Service)
Applegate, St Nicholas Circle, Leicester   ♿
Telephone: (0116) 2473056

Important late medieval building, with later additions housing costume from 1750 to present day.

LINCOLNSHIRE

AUBOURN HALL

(Sir Henry Nevile)
nr Lincoln   LN5 9DZ   map **7** Q21   △
Telephone: (01522) 788270

Late 16th century house attributed to J. Smythson (Jnr). Important carved staircase and panelled rooms. New rose garden.

Location: In Aubourn village 7 m S of Lincoln.
Open: July and Aug Wed 2-5 also Sun May 19, and June 2, June 30 or by appointment.
Admission: Adults £2.50 OAPs £2.

BELTON HOUSE   The National Trust

nr Grantham   map **7** R21   ⑤
Telephone: (01476) 66116
Location: 3 m NE of Grantham on A607 Grantham/Lincoln Road; easily accessible from A1.

BELVOIR CASTLE

See under Leicestershire.

BURGHLEY HOUSE

(Burghley House Trustees)
Stamford   map **7** R22   △
Telephone: (01780) 52451
Fax: (01780) 480125

The finest example of later Elizabethan architecture in England, built (1565-1587) by William Cecil, the most able and trusted adviser to Queen Elizabeth I.

Eighteen magnificent state rooms are open to visitors. Those painted by Antonio Verrio in the late 17th century form one of the greatest decorated suites in England. Burghley is a sumptuous Treasure House and contains one of the finest private collections of 17th century Italian paintings in the world. There are superb collections of English and Continental tapestries and furniture, many of which have been recently conserved. Burghley also houses the earliest inventoried collection of Oriental porcelain in the West. Works of art, silver, marbles and wood-carving fill the state rooms. The house is surrounded by a large and beautiful deer park, landscaped by 'Capability' Brown in the late 18th century. Car parking and entry to the Park is free.

Location: 1 m SE of Stamford, clearly signposted from the A1 and all approaches.
Station(s): Stamford (1 m), Peterborough (10 m).
Open: Apr 5-Oct 6 daily 11-4.30 closed Sept 7.
Admission: Adults £5.50 OAPs £5.20 accompanied children free (1 per adult, otherwise £2.50 per child). Party rates available.
Refreshments: Snacks, lunches and teas in the 'Capability' Brown Orangery. Enquiries for bookings party rates & menus tel: (01780) 52451.
Conferences: Contact the House Manager.

DODDINGTON HALL

(Mr & Mrs A. G. Jarvis)
Doddington   map **7** Q21   △ ⑤
Telephone: (01522) 694308

One of the Elizabethan gems of England. A romantic house set in 5 acres of superb gardens, with beautiful contents which reflect 400 years of unbroken family occupation. Fine furniture, porcelain, tapestries and pictures, and still very much a family home.

Location: 5 m W of Lincoln on the B1190 & signposted off the A46 Lincoln by-pass.
Open: Spring Garden Days Suns in Mar and Apr. House & Gardens Weds, Suns and Bank Hol Mons 2-6. Restaurant open from 12 noon on open days. Parties at other times by appointment.
Admission: Adults £3.70 Gardens £1.85 Children £1.85 Gardens 90p. Family ticket £10.50. Group bookings minimum £74 (20 people).
Refreshments: The Littlehouse Restaurant.

FULBECK HALL

(Mrs M. Fry)
Grantham   NG32 3JW   map **7** Q21   ♿ △
Telephone: (01400) 272205
Fax: (01400) 272205

Home of the Fane family since 1632. Mainly 18th century with 17th century service wing. 11 acres Edwardian formal and wild garden. Arnhem Museum. Fulbeck Hall and Manor open for groups by prior arrangement.

Location: On A607 between Lincoln and Grantham.
Open: Easter, May and Aug Bank Hol Mons. Daily 30 June-28 July inc. 2-5pm.
Admission: £3.50 OAPs £3.00 Children £1.50 Family £9.50. Garden only £1.50 Children £1.
Refreshments: Cream teas Sat and Sun. Lunches/teas/suppers for group visits.
Conferences: Conference and private banqueting facilities available.
Guided tours for pre-booked groups only.

GRANTHAM HOUSE   🌿 The National Trust

Grantham   map **7** R21
Location: In Castlegate, immediately E of Grantham Church.

GRIMSTHORPE CASTLE
(Grimsthorpe & Drummond Castle Trust)
Bourne   map **7** R22
Telephone: (01778) 591205
Fax: (01778) 591259

The home of the Willoughby de Eresby family since 1516. Examples of early 13th century architecture, the Tudor period of the reign of Henry VIII and work by Sir John Vanbrugh. State Rooms and Picture Galleries open to the Public.

Location: 4 m NW of Bourne on A151 Colsterworth/Bourne Road, SE of Grantham.
Open: Sundays, Thursdays and Bank Holidays from Easter Sunday (7 April) until 30 September. Also daily in August except Fridays and Saturdays. Park and Gardens open 11-6. Castle open 2pm (last admission 5).
Admission: Park: Adults £2 concessions £1. Additional separate charge for Castle - Adults £3 concessions £1.50. Combined ticket or Party Rate (20 or more) Adults £4 concessions £2.
Refreshments: The Coach House cafeteria serves lunches, teas & light refreshments - licensed.
Events/Exhibitions: CLA Game Fair 26-28 July. For this and other special major events, alternative charges will operate.
Conferences: Conference room.
Nature Trails, Adventure Playground.

GUNBY HALL   🌿 The National Trust
Burgh-le-Marsh   map **7** Q23
Location: 2½ m NW of Burgh-le-Marsh; 7 m W of Skegness on S side of A158.

LINCOLN CASTLE
(Recreational Services Dept, Lincolnshire County Council)
Castle Hill
Telephone: (01522) 511068

Built by William the Conqueror in 1068, the Castle with its towers, walls and gatehouses, dominates the bail, alongside Lincoln's great Cathedral. The 1215 Magna Carta sealed by King John at Runnymede is set in an informative exhibition. The Westgate, recently opened after 400 years, is another major architectural feature available to the visitor. The administration of law and order is well established here with a history stretching back over 900 years. Visitors may attend Crown Court sittings on most weekdays. Encompassed within the walls is

a unique Victorian prison chapel where incarceration can be 'experienced'. Events throughout the summer.

Location: Opposite west front of Lincoln Cathedral in the centre of Historic Lincoln.
Station(s): Lincoln Central Station, St. Marks Bus Station.
Open: BST: Sat 9.30-5.30. Sun 11-5.30. GMT: Mon-Sat 9.30-4. Sun 11-4. Last admission 30 minutes before closing. Closed Christmas Day, Boxing Day, and New Year's Day.
Admission: Adults £2; concessions £1.20; family £5.50 children under 5 and wheelchairs free. Children's group rate £1, accompanying adults free. Pre-booking recommended.

MARSTON HALL
(The Rev Henry Thorold, FSA)
Grantham   map **7** R21
Telephone: (01400) 250225

Tudor manor house with Georgian interiors, held by Thorold family since 14th century; interesting pictures and furniture. Romantic garden with long walks and avenues, high hedges enclosing herbaceous borders and vegetables. Gothick gazebo and ancient trees.

Open: Suns June 16, June 23, June 30, August 11 and by appointment.
Admission: House & Garden £2.50.
Refreshments: Home-made teas.

TATTERSHALL CASTLE   🌿 The National Trust
Lincoln   map **7** Q22
Telephone: (01526) 342543
Location: 12 m NE of Sleaford on Louth Road (A153); 3½ m SE of Woodhall Spa.

WOOLSTHORPE MANOR   🌿 The National Trust
nr Grantham   map **7** R21
Telephone: (01476) 860338
Location: 7 m S of Grantham, ½ m NW of Colsterworth; 1 m W of A1 (not to be confused with Woolsthorpe, nr Belvoir).

LONDON

THE BLEWCOAT SCHOOL   🌿 The National Trust
Westminster   **SW1H 0PY**   map **12** T22
Telephone: 0171-222 2877
Location: No 23 Caxton Street, Westminster, SW1.

BOSTON MANOR

(London Borough of Hounslow)
Brentford   map **12** T22
Telephone: 0181-570 0622

Boston Manor House is a fine Jacobean Manor built in 1623, extended in 1670 when the Clitherow family bought the house. It was their family home until 1924. Boston Manor is renowned for its fine English Renaissance plaster ceilings in the State Rooms on the first floor. In 1996 the ground floor rooms will be open to visitors.

Location: In Boston Manor Road. Tube 10 mins walk - Boston Manor - (Piccadilly Line).
Open: Sats, Suns and Bank Hol Mons from first Sat in Apr to last Sun in Oct 2.30-5pm.
Admission: Free.

BUCKINGHAM PALACE

(Official residence of Her Majesty The Queen)
London SW1A 1AA map **12** T22
Telephone: 0171-799 2331

The official London residence of Her Majesty The Queen.

BURGH HOUSE

(Burgh House Trust)
Hampstead NW3 1LT map **12** U22
Telephone: 0171-431 0144

Built 1703. Used for art exhibitions, concerts. Hampstead Museum. Terrace Garden.

Location: New End Sq E of Hampstead Underground Station.
Station(s): Hampstead (Underground). Hampstead Heath (BR North London Link).
Open: Wed-Sun 12-5 Good Fri and Bank Hol Mons 2-5.
Admission: Free.
Refreshments: Coffee, lunches and Teas. Licensed Buttery (for reservations and enquiries about catering for functions at the House Tel: 0171-431 2516).
Events/Exhibitions: Held throughout year, telephone for details.
Conferences: Licensed for Civil Weddings.

CAREW MANOR AND DOVECOTE

(London Borough of Sutton)
Church Road, Beddington SM6 7NH map **12** U22 △
Telephone: 0181-770 4781
Fax: 0181-770 4666

The Grade I listed late-medieval Great Hall, with its arch-braced hammer-beam roof, is now accessible on Suns and Bank Hol Mons from Easter until Oct, together with the restored early 18th century Dovecote, with its 1,288 nesting boxes and potence, which is a scheduled ancient monument. Guided tours available of the Dovecote, the Great Hall and the cellars of the house which contain medieval, Tudor, and later features (cellars accessible on guided tours only). Carew Manor stands on the edge of Beddington Park, the landscaped home park of the Carews, through which a Heritage Trail has been established. Guide book, trail leaflet and other publications and souvenirs available.

Location: Church Road, Beddington. Off A232 ¾ m E of junction with A237.
Station(s): WADDON, then bus 407 or 408.
Open: Suns & Bank Hol Mons from Easter to Oct 1 (phone Sutton Heritage Service 0181-773 4555).
Admission: Charge.
Short tours at 2pm 3pm and 4pm.

CARLYLE'S HOUSE 🍀 The National Trust

Chelsea SW3 5HL map **12** U24
Telephone: 0171-352 7087

Home of Thomas and Jane Carlyle 1834-1881 and full of the writer's books and possessions. *Note: Certain rooms have no electric light, visitors wishing to make a close study of the interior should avoid dull days.*

Location: At 24 Cheyne Row, Chelsea SW3 (off Cheyne Walk on Chelsea Embankment).
Station(s): Sloane Sq (Underground 1 m); Victoria (BR 2m). South Kensington (Underground 1 m).
Open: 30 Mar-end of Oct Wed-Sun & Bank Hol Mons 11-5. Last adm 4.30. *Closed Good Fri.*
Admission: £3 children £1.50. No reductions for parties which should not exceed 20 and must book.
No dogs. Unsuitable for wheelchairs.

CARSHALTON HOUSE

(London Borough of Sutton/Daughters of the Cross)
St. Philomena's School, Pound Street, Carshalton SM5 3PN map **12** U22 △
Telephone: 0181-770 4781/0181-773 4555
Fax: 0181-770 4666

An important listed building, built by about 1707 around the core of an older house and with grounds laid out originally by Charles Bridgeman, Carshalton House is open on a limited number of occasions each year. Its garden buildings include the unique 18th century Water Tower, now in the care of the Carshalton Water Tower Trust. The house contains principal rooms with 18th century decoration, including the 'Adam' or Blue Room and the Painted Parlour (attributed to Robert Robinson). Openings are organised by Sutton Heritage Service in conjunction with the Water Tower Trust. Tours of the house and grounds and a programme of short talks on the house and its people are given during the day (included in entrance fee). Refreshments and publications are available. Carshalton House is close to Sutton's Heritage Centre at Honeywood, in the Carshalton conservation area.

Location: Pound Street, Carshalton, at junction with Carshalton Road, on A232.
Station(s): Carshalton (¼ m).
Open: 1996 Mon 8 Apr (Easter Mon) Bank Hol Mon 26 Aug 10-5 (last admission 4.15).
Admission: £2.50 adults £1.50 children under 16 yrs.
Refreshments: Sandwiches, tea, coffee and home made cakes available.
For further details telephone Sutton Heritage Service on 0181-770 4781 or 0181-773 4555.

CHAPTER HOUSE AND PYX CHAMBER OF WESTMINSTER ABBEY

map **12** T22   ENGLISH HERITAGE
Telephone: 0171-222 5897   🏛

Described as 'incomparable' when it was finished in 1253, with some of the finest of English medieval sculpture, the Chapter House was one of the largest in England and could seat 80 monks around its walls. It was converted to a record office in the 16th century, but by 1740 the roof had decayed and been removed. Restoration of the whole building took place in 1865 and again after it was bombed in 1941. The 11th century Pyx Chamber now houses the Abbey Treasures. A joint ticket admits to the Abbey Museum.

Location: East side of the abbey cloister.
Open: Apr 1-Sept 30 10-6 daily Oct 1-Mar 31 daily 10-4.
Admission: Adults £2.50 concessions £1.90 children £1.30.
Liable to be closed at short notice on state occasions.

CHELSEA PHYSIC GARDEN

Chelsea SW3 4HS
Telephone: 0171-352 5646
Fax: 0171-376 3910

The second oldest Botanic garden in the country, founded 1673 including notable collection of medicinal plants, comprises 4 acres densely packed with c. 7,000 plants, many rare and unusual.

Location: Swan Walk, off Royal Hospital Road, Chelsea; nr junction of Royal Hospital Road & Chelsea Embankment.
Station(s): Sloane Square (Underground).
Open: Apr 7 to Oct 27-Suns 2-6 and Weds 2-5. Also Mon 20 to Fri May 24 (Chelsea Flower Show Week) and Mon 3-Fri 7 June (Chelsea Festival Week) 12-5. Open at other times for subscribing Friends and groups by appointment.
Admission: (1996 prices) £3.50, Chd/unemployed/students (with cards) £1.80. Garden accessible for disabled and wheelchairs via 66, Royal Hospital Road. Parking in street Suns and other days across Albert Bridge in Battersea Park.
Refreshments: Home-made teas.
No dogs (except guide dogs).

COLLEGE OF ARMS

(The Corporation of Kings, Heralds & Pursuivants of Arms)
City of London EC4V 4BT map **12** T22 △
Telephone: 0171-248 2762
Fax: 0171-248 6448

1670's mansion housing English Officers of Arms, their records and Earl Marshal's Court.

Location: On N side of Queen Victoria Street; S of St Paul's Cathedral.
Station(s): Blackfriars or St. Paul's.
Open: Earl Marshal's Court open all the year (except Public holidays & on State & special occasions) Mon-Fri 10-4 group visits (up to 10) by arrangement only. Record Room open for tours (groups of up to 20) by special arrangement in advance with the Officer in Waiting.
Admission: Free (parties by negotiation).
No coaches, parking, indoor photography or dogs. Shop - books, souvenirs.

DE MORGAN FOUNDATION
(De Morgan Foundation)
Old Battersea House, 30 Vicarage Crescent, Battersea   SW11 3LD   map 12 U22
△ &
Telephone: (01344) 25142

A substantial part of the De Morgan Foundation collection of ceramics by William De Morgan and paintings and drawings by Evelyn De Morgan (nee Pickering), her uncle Roddam Spencer Stanhope, J. M. Strudwick and Cadogan Cowper are displayed in the ground floor rooms of elegantly restored Old Battersea House - a Wren style building which is privately occupied. Works from the Foundation's collection may also be seen at Cardiff Castle, Cragside (Northumbria), Knightshayes (Tiverton), The St. John portraits are at Lydiard Park, Swindon.

Location: 30 Vicarage Crescent, Battersea.
Station(s): Clapham Junction.
Open: Admission by appointment only usually Wed afternoons. All visits are guided.
Admission: £1 (optional catalogue £1.50) no special reductions. Parties - max 30. (split into two groups of 15).
Refreshments: No catering at house. Many facilities in Battersea/Wandsworth.
Car parking in Vicarage Crescent. Suitable for disabled, (no special facilities for wheelchairs) front steps are the only obstacle. Adm by writing in advance to De Morgan Foundation, Heyho Place, Windlesham, Surrey GU20 6LP.

THE DICKENS HOUSE MUSEUM
(The Trustees of the Dickens House)
48 Doughty Street, London   WCIN 2LF   map 12 T22
Telephone: (01710 4052127

House occupied by Charles Dickens and his family from 1837 to 1839 where he produced Pickwick Papers, Oliver Twist, Nicholas Nickleby and Barnaby Rudge. Contains the most comprehensive Dickens library in the world, as well as numerous portraits, illustrations and signed letters.

Location: 48 Doughty Street, near Grays Inn Road/Guildford Street.
Station(s): Underground- Russell Square.
Open: Mon-Sat 10-5
Admission: £3. Children £1.

Giovanni Antonio Canale
- known as Canaletto
Born in Venice 1697, died 1768
Lived in England 1746 - 1755

His work can be seen in the following properties included in Historic Houses Castles and Gardens:-

Alnwick Castle
Bowhill
Goodwood House
Upton House

FENTON HOUSE   🍂 The National Trust
Hampstead   NW3 6RT   map 12 T22
Telephone: 0171-435 3471

Late 17th century house, walled garden. Fine collection of porcelain, pottery and Benton Fletcher collection of early keyboard musical instruments.

Location: On W side of Hampstead Grove.
Station(s): Hampstead (Underground 300 yards); Hampstead Heath (BR 1 m).
Open: Mar Sat & Sun only 2-5 Apr-end Oct Sat Suns and Bank Hol Mon 11-5.30; Wed, Thurs & Fri 2-5.30. Last adm ½ hour before closing time.
Admission: £3.60 Children half-price. No reductions for parties, which must book. Family ticket £9.
No dogs. Suitable for wheelchairs on ground floor only.

FULHAM PALACE (MUSEUM OF FULHAM PALACE)
(London Borough of Hammersmith and Fulham)
Bishops Avenue, Fulham, London   SW6 6EA   map 12 U22   △ &
Telephone: 0171-736 3233 ((Museum & tours) 0181-748 3020 x4930 (Hire of rooms)

The former residence of the Bishop of London (Tudor with Georgian additions and a Victorian chapel). Three rooms available for functions incl. receptions. The museum (in part of the Palace) tells the story of this ancient site. The displays include paintings, archaeology, garden history, and architecture. The gardens, famous in the C17th century when many American species were introduced to Europe through Fulham Palace, now contian specimen trees and a knot garden of herbs.

Location: In Bishop's Ave, ½ m N of Putney Bridge underground station (District Line).
Open: Grounds, Botanic Garden and herb collection open daily during daylight hours. Museum Mar-Oct Wed-Sun 2-5 and BH Mons, Nov-Feb Thurs-Sun 1-4.
Admission: Grounds and Botanic Garden Free. Museum 50p concessions 25p children free. Tour of 4 rooms and gardens every second Sun throughout the year at 2 costing £2. Private tours at other times by arrangement (£4 per head incl. tea). School visits including sessions with replica costume by appointment.
Refreshments: Tea available on tour days or by arrangement.
Events/Exhibitions: Lectures, concerts and exhibitions (ring for details).
Conferences: Function rooms available.
Audio tour available including versions for visually impaired and people with learning difficulties. Quizzes and trails for children.

GUNNERSBURY PARK MUSEUM
(London Boroughs of Ealing & Hounslow)
Gunnersbury Park   W3 8QL   map **12** T22   &
Telephone: 0181-992 1612
Fax: 0181-752 0686

Large mansion built c.1802 by architect owner Alexander Copland. Fine rooms by Sydney Smirke and painted ceilings by E. T. Parris for N. M. Rothschild c.1836. Now a local history museum which includes Rothschild carriages. Original Victorian kitchens open summer. Large park with other buildings of interest, and sporting facilities.

Location: Mansion at NE corner of Park; alongside North Circular (A406); N of Great West Road & M4; Kew Bridge 1¼ m; Chiswick Roundabout ½ m. Bus: E3 (daily), 7 (Suns only).
Station(s): Acton Town (Underground ¼ m).
Open: House & Museum Apr-Oct Mon-Fri 1-5 Sat Sun & Bank Hols 1-6 Nov-Mar Mon-Fri 1-4 Sat Sun & Bank Hols 1-4 closed Christmas Eve, Christmas Day, Boxing Day New Years Day & Good Friday. Gardens daily dawn till dusk. Special facilities for school parties by arrangement with Interpretative Officer.
Admission: Free.
Refreshments: Cafeteria in Park (daily, winter weekends according to weather).
Vehicle access Popes Lane (ample car parking). Pedestrians - many entries to Park. Ground floor displays with ramp access, toilets (including disabled-user) nearby in park.

HALL PLACE
(Bexley London Borough Council)
Bourne Road, Bexley   DA5 1PQ   map **12** U23   △
Telephone: (01322) 526574
Fax: (01322) 522921

Historic mansion (1540) with additions c.1640. Museum and other exhibitions. Outstanding Rose, Rock, Herb gardens and Floral bedding displays, Conservatories, Parkland, Topiary.

Location: Near the junction of A2 and A223.
Station(s): Station: Bexley (½ m).
Open: MANSION. Mon-Sat 10-5 (or dusk if earlier) Suns 2-6 (British Summertime only). PARK & GROUNDS. Daily during daylight throughout the year.
Admission: Free.
Refreshments: At cafe & restaurant.

HAM HOUSE   The National Trust
Ham, Richmond   TW10 7RS   map **12** U22   &
Telephone: 0181-940 1950

Overlooking the River Thames, Ham is one of the finest 17th century houses in Europe and contains rare Stuart survivals including exquisite closets, fine furniture, textiles and paintings. The gardens have been returned to the original plan of 1671, with formal grass platts, a Cherry Garden and a Widerness. Work is continuing to fulfil the decorative scheme.

Location: On South bank of the river Thames, W of A307 at Petersham.
Station(s): Richmond 2 m by road. Kingston 2 m. Bus: LT 65 Ealing Broadway-Kingston. 371 Richmond-Kingston (both passing BR Richmond and Kingston).
Open: House 24; 30 Mar-end Oct. Mon-Wed 1-5 Sat & Sun 12-5.30 open Good Fri 1-5 closed Tues following. 2 Nov-15 Dec Sat & Sun 1-4. Last admission half hour before closing. Garden all year daily except Fri 10.30-6 (or dusk if earlier) open Good Fri.*Closed Christmas & New Year*
Admission: Garden free. House £4 children £2 pre booked parties on application. Family ticket £10.
Refreshments: Orangery Restaurant (licensed) Sun 12.30-2.30, waitress service. Garden room counter service only open Apr-end Oct daily except Fri (open Good Fri) 11-5.30. Restaurant available for booked parties and functions 0181-940 0735.
Disabled visitors may park near entrance. Lavatory for disabled in garden.

HERITAGE CENTRE, HONEYWOOD

(London Borough of Sutton)
Honeywood Walk, Carshalton SM5 3NX map **12** U22 △
Telephone: 0181-773 4555
Fax: 0181-770 4666

HERITAGE CENTRE
Honeywood Walk, Carshalton, Surrey
The history of the borough and its people plus a chamging programme of exhibitions, presented in a 17th cent. listed building. Features include Edwardian Billiard Room & Tudor Gallery. Tearooms and Gift Shop.

LITTLE HOLLAND HOUSE
40 Beeches Avenue, Carshalton, Surrey
The home of Frank Dickinson (1874-1961) follower of the Arts an Crafts Movement, who designed and built the house and its contents himself. Interior listed Grade II* Guide book and other publications on sale.

London Borough of Sutton Heritage Service

For information call 0181-773 4555

CARSHALTON HOUSE
Pound Street, Carshalton, Surrey
Built c. 1707 with grounds originally laid out byCharles Bridgeman, the principal rooms contain 18th century decoration. Garden buildings include the unique Water Tower. Publications, souvenirs and home-made refreshments available.

Open Days 1996: Please ring for information.

WHITEHALL
1 Maiden Road, Cheam, Surrey
A timber-framed continuous-jetted house built c.1500. Features revealed sections of original fabric plus displays on Cheam Pottery, Nonsuch Palace, Cheam School and timber-framed buildings. Tea Room.

CAREW MANOR & DOVECOTE
Church Road, Beddingon, Surrey
Grade I late medieval Great Hall, with hammer beam roof, and 18th cent. brick Dovecote with 1288 nesting boxes and restored potence (circular ladder). Guided tours include cellars of Manor. Gift Shop.

Discover the fascinating history of the area now within the London Borough of Sutton (which includes Beddington, Carshalton, Cheam, Sutton and Wallington). Based in 'Honeywood', a listed building of 17th century origin, with permanent displays plus a changing programme of exhibitions covering many aspects of local life. Areas of particular interest include a magnificent Edwardian billiard room, a Childhood Room, a Tudor Gallery, a display about the Wandle River, and an Art Gallery. A wide range of unusual gifts, souvenirs and local history publications are on sale in the shop. 'Honeywood' overlooks Carshalton's picturesque town ponds, in the heart of a conservation area.

Location: Honeywood Walk, Carshalton. By Carshalton Ponds, opp. the Greyhound Inn. (off A232).
Station(s): Carshalton (¼ m).
Open: Heritage Centre: Wed-Fri 10-5 Sat Sun & Bank Hol Mons 10-5.30. Tea-rooms: Tues-Sun 10-5.15.
Admission: Adults 85p children 45p.
Refreshments: Tea-rooms with separate non-smoking area.
Events/Exhibitions: Changing programme, inc local history and relatd subjects. Craft fairs, trails & quizzes for children.
Free entry to the shop and tearooms which serve a tempting array of hot and cold food. Art Gallery and rooms available for hire. Telephone the Heritage Centre on 0181-773 4555 for further information and details of current exhibitions.

Lancelot 'Capability' Brown

Born 1716 in Northumberland, Capability Brown began work at the age of 16 in the vegetable gardens of Sir William and Lady Loraine at Kirharle Tower. He left Northumberland in 1739, and records show that he worked at Stowe until 1749. It was at Stowe that Brown began to study architecture, and to submit his own plans. It was also at Stowe that he devised a new method of moving and replanting mature trees.

Brown married Bridget Wayet in 1744 and began work on the estate at Warwick Castle in 1749. He was appointed Master Gardener at Hampton Court in 1764, and planted the Great Vine at Hampton Court in 1768. Blenheim Palace designs are considered amongst Brown's finest work, and the technical achievements were outstanding even for the present day.

Capability Brown died in February 1783 of a massive heart attack. A monument beside the lake at Croome Court was erected which reads "To the memory of Lancelot Brown, who by the powers of his inimitable and creative genius formed this garden scene out of a morass". There is also a portrait of Brown at Burghley.

Capability Brown was involved in the design of grounds at the following properties included in Historic Houses Castles and Gardens:

Audley End	*Berrington Hall*	*Fawley Court*	*Highclere Castle*
Bowood	*Burghley House*	*Longleat*	*Luton Hoo*
Burton Constable	*Charlecote Park*	*Moccas Court*	*Petworth House*
Chilham Castle Gardens (reputed)		*Sledmere House*	*Stowe (Stowe School)*
Clandon Park	*Claremont*	*Syon House*	*Warwick Castle*
Chillington Hall	*Corsham Court*	*Weston Park*	*Wimpole Hall*

Wrest Park and Gardens

HOGARTH'S HOUSE
(London Borough of Hounslow)
Chiswick   map **12** U22   △
Telephone: 0181-994 6757
Fax: 0181-862 7602

Just 50 yards from the busy Hogarth Roundabout lies this charming early 18th century house which was once the country home of William Hogarth, the famous painter and engraver. It is now a gallery where most of his well known engravings are on display. These include: 'Harlot's Progress', 'Rake's Progress', 'Marriage a la mode', and also 'Gin Lane' and 'Beer Street' both of which can be bought at the house, together with books and postcards of Hogarth's works.

There is a restoration programme beginning for both the house and garden. In nearby Chiswick Mall are houses of a similar period, and in the graveyard around St. Nicholas' Church, is Hogarth's tomb. World famous Chiswick House is only 10 minutes walk away.

Location: In Hogarth Lane, Great West Road, Chiswick W4 2QN 50yds west of Hogarth roundabout.
Station(s): Chiswick (½ m) (Southern Region); Turnham Green (1 m) (District Line).
Open: Apr-Sept Mon-Sat 11-6 Sun 2-6 Oct-Mar Mon-Sat 11-4 Sun 2-4 closed Tues, Good Friday, first 2 full weeks in Sept, last 3 weeks in Dec & New Year's Day.
Admission: Free. Parties by arrangement.
Parking: Chiswick House car park and in named parking bays in Axis Business Centre - behind house.

KEATS HOUSE
(London Borough of Camden)
Wentworth Place, Keats Grove, Hampstead   NW3 2RR   map **12** T22   △
Telephone: 0171-435 2062
Fax: 0171-431 9293

Keats House was built in 1815-1816 as Wentworth Place, a pair of semi-detached houses. John Keats, the poet, lived here from 1818 to 1820; here he wrote 'Ode to a Nightingale', and met Fanny Brawne, to whom he became engaged. Keats' early death in Italy prevented the marriage. Keats House was completely restored in 1974-1975. It houses letters, books and other personal relics of the poet and his fiancee.

Location: S end of Hampstead Heath nr South End Green.
Station(s): (BR Hampstead Heath). Underground: Belsize Park or Hampstead. Bus: 24, 46, 168, C11, C12 (alight South End Green). 268 (alight Downshire Hill).
Open: All the year Apr 1-Oct Mon-Fri 10-1 and 2-6 Sat 10-1 and 2-5 Sun and Bank Holidays 2-5 Nov-Mar Mon-Fri 1-5 Sat 10-1 and 2-5 Sun 2-5 closed Christmas Eve Christmas Day Boxing Day New Year's Day Good Friday Easter Eve & Mayday. Please check times on 0171-435 2062.
Admission: Free.

KENWOOD, THE IVEAGH BEQUEST

ENGLISH HERITAGE

Hampstead   map **12** T22
Telephone: 0181-348 1286

Standing in splendid grounds on the edge of Hampstead Heath, Kenwood contains the most important private collection of paintings ever given to the nation. There is a selection of Old Masters, among the finest a Self Portrait of Rembrandt and paintings by British artists such as Turner, Reynolds and Gainsborough. The outstanding neoclassical house itself was remodelled by Robert Adam, 1764-73 who created the magnificent Library. Many rooms contain displays of English neoclassical furniture. Outside, the historic landscaped park, with sloping lawns and a lake, form a perfect setting to the lakeside concerts held here in the summer.

Location: Hampstead Lane, NW3.
Station(s): Archway or Golders Green Underground (Northern Line), then Bus 210.
Open: Apr 1-Sept 30 10-6 daily Oct1-Mar 31 daily 10-4.
Admission: Free.
Refreshments: At the Coach House.

LEIGHTON HOUSE MUSEUM AND ART GALLERY

(Royal Borough of Kensington and Chelsea)
12 Holland Park Road   W14 8LZ   map **12** T22
Telephone: 0171-602 3316
Fax: 0171-371 2467

Adjacent to Holland Park in Kensington lies the Artists' Colony, a group of remarkable Studio Houses, built by some of the leading figures of the Victorian Art World. Leighton House Museum was the first of these to be built, and is today a museum of High Victorian art. The opulent fantasy of Frederic Lord Leighton, President of the Royal Academy, the house was designed by George Aitchison. Leighton lived here from 1866 until his death in 1896. His unique collection of Islamic tiles is displayed in the walls of the Arab Hall, and the Victorian interiors, restored to their original splendour, are hung with paintings by Leighton, Millais, Watts, Burne-Jones and others. Sculpture is displayed in the house and garden. The study collection of Leighton drawings may be seen by appointment. Temporary exhibitions of modern and historic art throughout the year.

Location: Kensington.
Station(s): High Street, Kensington.
Open: All year Mon-Sat 11-5.30 (closed Sun & Bank Holidays) Garden Apr-Sept. Parties by arrangement with the Curator. Children under 16 must be accompanied by an adult.
Admission: Free.

LINLEY SAMBOURNE HOUSE

(The Victorian Society)
18 Stafford Terrace   W8 7BH   map **12** U22
Telephone: 0181-994 1019
Fax: 0181-995 4895

The home of Linley Sambourne (1844-1910), chief political cartoonist at 'Punch'. A unique survival of a late Victorian town house. The original decorations and furnishings have been preserved together with many of Sambourne's own cartoons and photographs, as well as works by other artists of the period.

Location: 18 Stafford Terrace, W8 7BH.
Station(s): (Underground) Kensington High Street. Bus: 9, 10, 27, 28, 31, 49, 52, 70 & C1.
Open: 1 Mar-31 Oct Wed 10-4 Sun 2-5 parties at other times by prior arrangement. Apply to The Victorian Society, 1 Priory Gardens, London W4 Telephone: 0181-742 3438.
Admission: £3 Senior Citizens   £2.50 under 16 £1.50.

LITTLE HOLLAND HOUSE

(London Borough of Sutton)
40 Beeches Avenue, Carshalton   SM5 3LW   map **12** U22   △
Telephone: 0181-770 4781
Fax: 0181-770 4666

The home of Frank Dickinson (1874-1961), follower of William Morris and the Arts and Crafts movement: artist, designer and craftsman in wood and metal who built the house himself to his own design and in pursuance of his philosophy and theories. Features his interior design, paintings, hand-made furniture and other craft objects.

Location: 40 Beeches Avenue, Carshalton. On B278 (off A232).
Station(s): Few minutes from Carshalton Beeches BR.
Open: First Sun in the month plus Bank Hol Suns & Mons 1.30-5.30. Closed January.
Admission: Free.
Further information from Sutton Heritage Service on 0181-770 4781 or 773 4555. Guided tours for groups available outside normal opening hours.

MUSEUM OF GARDEN HISTORY

(The Tradescant Trust (Registered Charity No 273436)
Lambeth   map **12** U22
Telephone: 0171-261 1891
Fax: 0171-401 8869

Fascinating permanent exhibition of the history of gardens, collection of ancient tools, re-creation of 17th century garden displaying flowers and shrubs of the period, the seeds of which may be purchased in the Garden Shop. Also tombs of the Tradescants and Captain Bligh of the 'Bounty'. Lectures, courses, concerts, fairs and art exhibitions are held regularly throughout the year. Knowledgeable staff; a shop selling books and gifts; light refreshments all combine to make a visit both pleasurable and worthwhile.

Location: Lambeth Palace Road.
Station(s): Waterloo or Victoria, then 507 Red Arrow bus, alight Lambeth Palace.
Open: Mon-Fri 10.30-4 Sun 10.30-5. *Closed Sat. Closed from second Sun in Dec to first Sun in Mar.*
Admission: Free. Donation requested.
Refreshments: Tea, coffee, light lunches; parties catered for but prior booking essential. Literature sent on request with SAE.

NATIONAL MARITIME MUSEUM

Greenwich, London   SE10   map **12** U23
Telephone: (0181) 8584422
Fax: (0181) 3126632

The National Maritime Museum tells the story of Britain and the Sea.

Open: 10-5.
Admission: Adults £5.50 OAP's/students £4.50 Children £3.
Limited access for wheelchairs ring for further information.

THE OCTAGON, ORLEANS HOUSE GALLERY

(London Borough of Richmond upon Thames)
Riverside Twickenham, Middlesex   TW1 3DJ   map **12** U22   &
Telephone: 0181-892 0221
Fax: 0181-744 0501

The magnificent Octagon built by James Gibbs in c.1720 for James Johnston, Joint Secretary of State for Scotland under William III. An outstanding example of baroque architecture. In 1729 it was the setting of a grand banquet in the honour of Queen Caroline, wife of George II. The adjacent wing houses an art gallery showing a varied exhibition programme, including the Borough Art Collection comprising mostly 18th and 19th century topographical oil paintings, watercolours and prints. The Octagon and Gallery are situated in a picturesque woodland garden on the bank of the River Thames.

Location: Access from Richmond Road (A305).
Station(s): St Margaret's (½ m); Twickenham (½ m); Richmond (underground 2 m)
Open: Tues-Sat 1-5.30 (Oct-Mar 1-4.30) Sun 2-5.30 (Oct-Mar 2-4.30) Easter, Spring and Summer Bank Hols 2-5.30. Closed Christmas Day, Christmas Eve, Boxing Day. & 31 Dec. Other times by appointment.
Admission: Free, but donations to the Octagon Appeal gratefully received. Free parking.
Refreshments: Upon request for group bookings (small charge).
Events/Exhibitions: For 1996 this includes Making 4 Changes, a contemporary craft show (Mar-May) and Mapping Values, a site specific installation by Those Environmental Artists (Jun-Aug).
Conferences: Octagon, maximum 70 seated.
Shop, WCs. Access for disabled visitors: W,S.

OLD ROYAL OBSERVATORY

(National Maritime Museum)
Greenwich   SE10   map **12** U23
Telephone: 0181-858 4422
Fax: 0181-312 6632

Following a major restoration and reinterpretation the Old Royal Observatory re-opened in March 1993. It includes Flamsteed House, designed by Sir Christopher Wren, the Meridian Building and the Greenwich Planetarium.

Location: In Greenwich Park, N side of Blackheath off A2.
Station(s): Maze Hill (short walk).
Open: Daily 10-5. *Closed* Dec 24/25/26.
Admission: Combined ticket to three attractions adult £5.50 OAPS/students £4.50 children £3.
Refreshments: In Park cafeteria and museum main buildings.
Partial wheelchair access.

OSTERLEY PARK   ❦ The National Trust

Isleworth, Middlesex   TW7 4RB   map **12** U22   △ &
Telephone: 0181-560 3918

Elizabethan mansion transformed by Robert Adam 1760-80 into an elegant neo-classical villa; with Adam decorations and furniture; 140 acres of parkland and lakes.

Location: ¾ m E of Osterley Underground station (Piccadilly Line) and ½ m W of Gillette Corner, access from Thornbury Road, N side of Great West Road (A4). M4 junction 3
Station(s): Syon Lane (1.50m); Underground: Osterley (¾ m). Bus: LT 91 Hounslow-Wandsworth (½ m)
Open: House 30 Mar-end Oct Wed-Sun 1-5 Bank Holiday Mon 11-5. House closed Good Fri. Last admission 4.30. Park and Pleasure grounds all year 9-7.30 or sunset if earlier. Car park closed Dec 25, 26. Shop open as house 1-5.30 and pre-Christmas Nov-Dec 15 Wed-Sun & BH Mon inc. Good Fri 12-4
Admission: £3.70 Family ticket £9. Parties must book Wed-Sat, rates on application to Administrator. Park free. Car park 250 yds £1.50. Guided tours may be arranged in advance with the Administrator.
Refreshments: Teas and light lunches in stable Tea Room Wed to Sun and Bank Holiday Mon, Mar 30 to end Oct 11.30-5. Also open Good Friday open Nov-15 Dec 12-4. .
Park suitable for disabled courtesy vehicle to the house, but steps at house. Lavatory for disabled. Dogs in park only; On leads except in certain areas as specified at the property.

PITSHANGER MANOR MUSEUM
(London Borough of Ealing)
Mattock Lane, Ealing   W5 5EQ   map **12** T22
Telephone: 0181-567 1227
Fax: 0181-567 0595

Set in an attractive park, Pitshanger Manor was built 1800-04 by the architect Sir John Soane (1753-1837) as his family home. The house incorporates a wing of the late 1760s by George Dance. The interiors are being restored. A Victorian room holds a changing and extensive display of Martinware pottery including a unique chimney-piece of 1891. Exhibitions and cultural events are held regularly.

Location: 5 mins from Ealing Broadway Tube Station (Central and District Lines). On the A3001 (Ealing Green). Limited parking for disabled.
Station(s): Ealing Broadway underground/BR.
Open: Tues-Sat 10-5. *Closed Sun & Mon. Also closed Christmas, Easter and New Year. All rooms are open to the public after 1pm. Please enquire in advance as to which rooms are open in the mornings.*
Admission: Free. Parties by arrangement in advance.
Refreshments: Tea and coffee vending machine.
Events/Exhibitions: Telephone for details.
Limited disabled access - further details available on request.

THE QUEEN'S HOUSE
(National Maritime Museum)
Greenwich   SE10   map **12** U23
Telephone: 0181-858 4422
Fax: 0181-312 6632

Royal Palace designed by Inigo Jones for Anne of Denmark, wife of James I, and Henrietta Maria, wife of Charles I.

ROYAL BOTANIC GARDENS, KEW
Kew, Richmond   TW9 3AB   map **12** U22   △ 𝕘 Ⓔ Ⓢ ▯
Telephone: 0181-940 1171
Fax: 0181-332 5197

Few attractions offer the variety and spectacle of Kew Gardens, 300 acres - six of them under glass - containing a collection of plants unique in the world.

Rhododendrons from the Himalayas, roses from Europe and the Far East, brilliant formal flower beds, a wild woodland covered in bluebells. At every season of the year, Kew presents a lasting memory. the extensive, world famous glass houses mean that even in the winter a visit is full of fascination. The Princess of Wales Conservatory contains ten climatic zones under one roof - from steamy rain forest with wild orchids, to arid desert with giant cacti. Many new features have been added to Kew in the past five years: the Evolution House showing how plants have changed over time, the Marine display of plants from the sea, swamp and river estuary under the Palm House, and the Victoria Gate visitor centre which contains a splendid shop, and where hour-long tours of the Garden are available.

Location: South circular (A205) car and coach parking. Underground Kew Gardens: District Line. British Rail Kew Bridge plus Kew Gardens.
Open: Gardens open everyday except Christmas and New Years day 9.30-sunset. Galleries and Glass Houses open 9.30.
Admission: Adults £4.50 children £2.50 concessions £3 family ticket (2+4) £12 (1996 prices).
Refreshments: Refreshment Pavilion (open Apr-Oct), Orangery Restaurant (open all year), Picnic Box (open Apr-Oct), Kew Bakery (open Apr-Oct). Tel: 0181-332 5157
Events/Exhibitions: Summer jazz festival July-programme of exhibitions in Kew Gardens Gallery. For details telephone 0181-332 5611.
Conferences: Licensed for Civil Weddings.
Easy access for disabled, W.C., wheelchairs available. Guided tours (Victoria Gate Visitor Centre) 11 and 2. Educational visits including topic days Tel: 0181-940 1171. Enquiry Unit: address as above Tel: 0181-940 1171.

ROYAL INSTITUTE OF BRITISH ARCHITECTS: DRAWINGS COLLECTION AND HEINZ GALLERY
(Royal Institute of British Architects)
London   W1   map **12** T22
Telephone: 0171-580 5533
Fax: 0171-486 3797

Changing architectural exhibitions throughout most of the year.
Location: 21 Portman Square W1H 9HF.
Open: Weekdays 11-5 Sats 10-1 Study room open weekdays by appointment only.
Admission: Free (exhibitions).
Unsuitable for disabled persons. No car parking.

RSA (THE ROYAL SOCIETY FOR THE ENCOURAGEMENT OF ARTS, MANUFACTURES AND COMMERCE)
8 John Adam Street, London   WC2N 6EZ   map **12** T22
Telephone: 0171-930 5115
Fax: 0171-839 5805

Founded in 1754, the RSA moved to its bespoke house, designed and built by Robert Adam, in 1774. The most interesting features of the Society's premises are its Great Room, a lecture hall, capacity 200, with murals by James Barry, and the recently restored vaults.

Location: 8 John Adam Street, London WC2N 6EZ.
Station(s): Charing Cross, Embankment.
Open: Mon-Fri 10-1 visitors who wish to see any of the Society's rooms are requested to telephone Susan Bennett in advance in order to avoid disappointment if the rooms are in use and therefore inaccessible.
Admission: Free.
Conferences: The RSA's room are available to hire for conferences, dinners, licensed for civil weddings, receptions. Catering is supplied by our in-house staff.

SIR JOHN SOANE'S MUSEUM
(Trustees of Sir John Soane's Museum)
13 Lincoln's Inn Fields   WC2A 3BP   map **12** T22
Telephone: Information line (0171) 4300175
Fax: (0171) 8313957

Built by the leading architect Sir John Soane, RA, in 1812-13 as his private residence. Contains his collection of antiquities and works of art.

Station(s): Holborn Tube.
Open: Tues-Sat 10-5 (lecture tours Sat 2.30 maximum 22 people free ticket on a first come first serve basis from 2pm. No groups). Groups welcome at other times but must book in advance. Late evening opening on the first Tues of each month 6-9. Also library and architectural drawings collection access by appointment. Closed Bank Holidays.
Admission: Free.
Events/Exhibitions: Changing exhibitions of drawings in the 'Soane Gallery' to Mar 96: 'Buildings in Progress: Soane's Views of Contruction' Mar-Sept 96, 'Soane Revisited' - recent re-discoveries of Soane work.

SOUTHSIDE HOUSE
(The Pennington-Mellor-Munthe Charity Trust)
Wimbledon Common   SW19 4RJ   map **12** U22   △
Telephone: 0181-947 2491 or 0181-946 7643

Built by Robert Pennington as a safe retreat for his family after his little son died in the London Plague in 1665. Still lived in by his descendants today. Much original furnishing remains. Family portraits by Van Dyke and Hogarth. Personal possessions of Ann Boleyn - whose sister married into this family - are shown. Also a bedroom prepared for the Prince of Wales in 1750 and gifts to John Pennington - the family 'Scarlet Pimpernel' - by those he helped to escape from the guillotine - including a pearl necklace which fell from Marie Antoinette when her head was cut off. Also the Dining Room where Admiral Lord Nelson dined with Sir William and Lady Hamilton and the Music Room where she performed her 'attitudes'. In 1907 the heiress of this house, Hilda Pennington Mellor married Axel Munthe the Swedish Doctor and Philanthropist who wrote part of his 'Story of San Michele' here.

Location: On S side of Wimbledon Common (B281), opposite The Crooked Billet Inn.
Station(s): Wimbledon (British Rail & Underground) 1 m. Buses: No 93, alight Rose & Crown Inn, Wimbledon High Street - six minutes walk along Southside of Common to Crooked Billet Inn and Southside House.
Open: From Oct 1-May 31. Guided tours only on Tues, Thurs, Sat & Bank Holiday Mons (*Closed Christmas*) on the hour from 2-4 (last admission), lasting approximately 1½ hrs. Other times by special agreement with Administrator. Organised school groups accompanied by responsible teachers free by appointment in writing.
Admission: Adults £5 (children accompanied by adult £3).

SPENCER HOUSE
27 St.James's Place, London   SW1A 1NR   map **12** T22
Telephone: 0171-409 0526

Spencer House, built 1756-66 for the first Earl Spencer, an ancestor of HRH The Princess of Wales, is London's finest surviving 18th - century townhouse. This magnificent private palace, overlooking Green Park, has regained the full splendour of its 18th century appearance after a painstaking ten year restoration. Eight state rooms are open to the public for viewing on Sundays and are available for private and corporate entertaining during the rest of the week.

Location: 27 St.James's Place, London SW1A 1NR.
Station(s): Green Park.
Open: Every Sun (except during Jan and Aug) from 10.30-4.45. Tours last approx. 1 hr. Tickets available at door from 10.30 on day. Advance reservation for groups of more than 20: please apply in writing to The Administrator at Spencer House.
Admission: Adults £6 concessions £5 (students/Friends of the Royal Academy/Tate and V&A all with cards/children 10-16; under 10 not admitted). Prices valid until end July 1996. Accessible for wheelchair users. All images are copyright of Spencer House Limited and may not be used without the permission of Spencer House Limited.

ST. JOHN'S GATE
(The Order of St. John)
Clerkenwell   EC1M 4DA   map **12** T22   △
Telephone: 0171-253 6644
Fax: 0171-336 0587

Headquarters of the Order in England, the 16th century gatehouse contains the most comprehensive collection of items relating to the Order of St John outside Malta. Together with the nearby Priory Church and 12th century Crypt it now forms the headquarters of the modern Order of St. John, whose charitable foundations include St. John Ambulance and the Ophthalmic Hospital in Jerusalem. The collection includes Maltese silver, Furniture, paintings, coins, pharmacy jars and collectors relating to the history and work of St. John Ambulance and the St. John Opthalmic Hospital in Jerusalem.

Location: In St John's Lane, EC1M 4DA.
Station(s): (Underground) Farringdon, Barbican.
Open: Mon-Fr 10-5 Sat 10-4. Tours of the building including the Grand Priory Church and Norman crypt on Tues Fri and Sat 11 & 2.30.
Admission: Free (donations requested).

STRAWBERRY HILL
(St. Mary's University College)
Waldegrave Road, Twickenham   TW1 4SX   map 12 U22
Telephone: 0181-240 4141
Fax: 0181-744 1947

Horace Walpole bought Strawberry Hill in 1749 and converted the modest house into his own vision of a 'gothic' fantasy. It is widely regarded as the first substantial building of the gothic revival and as such is internationally known and admired. A century later, Lady Frances Waldegrave addeed a magnificent wing to Walpole's original structure. It is only recently that Strawberry Hill is open more widely to the public for guided tours by professional trained guides.

Location: Twickenham.
Station(s): Strawberry Hill BR, No. 33 bus.
Open: Easter-Oct 2-3.30 for guided tours otherwise by pre-arrangement.
Admission: £4 concessions for OAPs & Students.
Refreshments: Strawberry cream teas available on request for pre-booked tours.
Tours can be arranged for groups of 10+ people any day throughout the year Sun-Fri by telephoning the Conference Office. Not suitable for children under 14 years. Unfortunately no disabled access.

SUTTON HOUSE   ❧ The National Trust
2 & 4 Homerton High Street, Hackney   E9 6JQ   map 12 T22
Telephone: 0181-986 2264

In London's East End; a rare example of a Tudor red-brick house, built in 1535 by Sir Rafe Sadleir, Principal Secretary of State for Henry VIII, with 18th century alterations and later additions. The recent restoration has revealed many 16th century details which are displayed even in rooms of later periods. Notable features include original linenfold panelling and 17th century wall paintings. The Edwardian chapel contains an audio-visual presentation and there is a craft workshop in the Old Tudor Kitchen.

Location: At the corner of Isabella Road and Homerton High Street.
Station(s): Hackney Central ¼ m; Hackney Downs ½ m. Frequent local bus services (tel: 0171-222 1234).
Open: 4 Feb to 27 Nov & 5 Feb 1997 onwards: Wed, Sun & Bank Hol Mon 11.30-5.30 (closed Good Fri). Last admissions 5.
Admission: Adults £1.60. Group visits by prior arrangement. Guided tours available. Rates on application. Public car park in Morning Lane and St.John's Churchyard ¼ m.
Refreshments: Cafe bar open all year except 22 Dec to 15 Jan, Wed-Fri 11-11, Sat, Sun and Bank Hol Mon 11-5.
Events/Exhibitions: For full programme of concerts, exhibitions, fairs, lectures, and other events, please contact Project Manager on 0181-986 2264.
Conferences: Contact Project Manager on 0181-980 2264.
Ground floor only accessible to wheelchairs. No lift. WC. Braille guide. Baby changing facilities. Family trails.

SYON HOUSE

(His Grace the Duke of Northumberland)
Brentford   TW8 8JF   map **12** U22   △
Telephone: 0181-560 0881
Fax: 0181-568 0936

Noted for its magnificent Adam interior and furnishings, famous picture collection, and historical associations dating back to 1415, 'Capability' Brown landscape.

Location: On N bank of Thames between Brentford & Isleworth.
Station(s): Gunnersbury (District line), Kew Bridge (BR). Buses 237, 267.
Open: For charges and times of entry please telephone 0181-560 0881.
Refreshments: Cafeteria and coffee shop. Telephone 0181-568 0778/9.

SYON PARK GARDENS

(His Grace the Duke of Northumberland)
Brentford   TW8 8JF   map **12** U22
Telephone: (0181) 560 0881
Fax: (0181) 568 0936

Includes the Great Conservatory by Charles Fowler and Miniature Steam Railway (operates weekends and Bank Holiday Mondays April to October and other times by arrangement). Within the Estate is the Garden Centre, The Butterfly House, Brit Koi Aquatic Centre, Art Centre, Needlecraft Centre, Gift Shop, Wholefood Shop. Pet care centre and pine furniture / Gift shop.

Location: On N bank of Thames between Brentford & Isleworth.
Station(s): Waterloo to Kew Bridge, nearest tube Gunnersbury. Buses: 267 or 237 to Brentlea.
Open: All the year daily 10-6 or dusk. Last adm 1 hour before closing. *Closed Christmas Day & Boxing Day.* Adm charges not available at time of going to press. Free car park. Telephone (0181)560 0881. London Butterfly House opening times & adm charges Telephone (0181)560 7272.
Admission: For admission charges telephone 0181 560 0881.
Refreshments: Cafeteria and coffee shop. Telephone 0181 568 0778/9. Enquiries to Administrator, Syon Park.

THE TRAVELLERS CLUB
Pall Mall SW1Y 5EP map **12** T22 △
Telephone: 0171-930 8688 (by prior appointment)

Built in 1829-33 by Sir Charles Barry.

Location: 106 Pall Mall.
Station(s): Piccadilly Circus Underground.
Open: By prior appointment Mon-Fri only from 10-12 and 3-5.30 weekends by negotiation. Closed Bank Hols, Aug and Christmas.
Admission: £6.
Refreshments: Included.

WHITEHALL
(London Borough of Sutton)
1 Malden Road, Cheam SM3 8QD map **12** U22 △
Telephone: 0181-643 1236
Fax: 0181-770 4666

A unique timber-framed house built c 1500. A feature is the revealed sections of original fabric. Displays include medieval Cheam pottery; Nonsuch Palace; timber-framed buildings and Cheam School. Changing exhibitions and a variety of events and fairs throughout the year.

Location: On A2043 just N of junction with A232.
Station(s): Cheam (¼ m).
Open: Apr-Sept Tues-Fri,Sun 2-5.30 Sat 10-5.30 Oct-Mar Wed Thurs Sun 2-5.30 Sat 10-5.30. Also open Bank Hol Mons 2-5.30. *Closed Dec 24-Jan 2 inclusive* Further information from Sutton Heritage Service on 0181-770 4781. Party bookings, guided tours by prior arrangement.
Admission: 1995 prices adults 85p children 45p.
Refreshments: Tea-room with home made cakes.
Events/Exhibitions: Changing programmes of events and exhibitions.
Gift Shop. Rooms and Exhibition space available for hire.

GREATER MANCHESTER

DUNHAM MASSEY
See under Cheshire.

HALLI'TH'WOOD
(Bolton Metropolitan Borough)
Greenway, off Crompton Way, Bolton BL1 8UA map **15** P18
Telephone: (01204) 301159

Dating from latter half of the 15th century and furnished throughout in the appropriate period. The Hall, built in the post and plaster style, dates from 1483, a further extension was added in 1591, the last addition being made in 1648. Home of Samuel Crompton in 1779 when he invented the Spinning Mule. House contains Crompton relics.

Location: In Green Way, off Crompton Way; 2 m NE of town centre off A58 (Crompton Way); signposted. Hall i' th' Wood (½ m).
Station(s): Bolton (2½ m); Bromley Cross (1¼ m). Hall i' th' Wood (½ m).
Open: Apr-Sept Tues-Sat 11-5 Sun 2-5 closed Mons except Bank Holidays Oct-Mar closed to general public. Open to pre-booked parties and evening party tours.
Admission: Adults £1.55 concessions 75p groups £1.05.

HEATON HALL 🏛
(Manchester City Council)
Heaton Park, Prestwich, Manchester M25 5SW △ &

Designed from 1772 by James Wyatt in the neo-classical style for Sir Thomas Egerton.

SMITHILLS HALL
(Bolton Metropolitan Borough)
Bolton map **15** P18
Telephone: (01204) 841265

One of the oldest manor houses in Lancashire, a house has stood on this site since the 14th century. The oldest part of Smithills, the Great Hall, has an open timber roof. Smithills has grown piece by piece over the centuries and such irregularly planned buildings, with the cluster of gables at the west end, give the hall its present day picturesque effect. Furnished in the styles of the 16th and 17th centuries. Withdrawing room contains linenfold panelling. Grounds contain a nature trail.

Location: Off Smithills Dean Road; 1½ m NW of town centre off A58 (Moss Bank Way); signposted.
Station(s): Bolton.
Open: Apr-Sept Tues-Sat 11-5 Sun 2-5. *Closed* Mons except BHs. Oct-Mar *Closed* to general public. Open to pre-booked educational parties and to evening party tours.
Admission: Adults £1.55 concessions 75p groups £1.05.

Gertrude Jekyll
writer and gardener
(1843-1932)

Her designs were used at the following properties included in Historic Houses Castles and Gardens:-

Barrington Court
Castle Drogo
Goddards
Hatchlands Park
Hestercombe House and Gardens
Knebworth
Lindisfarne Castle

A collection of her tools can be found at Guildford Museum

MERSEYSIDE

BLUECOAT CHAMBERS
(Bluecoat Arts Centre)
Liverpool
Telephone: 0151-709 5297

CROXTETH HALL & COUNTRY PARK
(Liverpool City Council)
Liverpool   L12 0HB   map **6** Q17   △ Ⓔ Ⓢ
Telephone: 0151-228 5311
Fax: 0151-228 2817

500 acre Country Park centred on the ancestral home of the Molyneux family, Earls of Sefton. Hall rooms with character figures on the theme of an Edwardian houseparty. Victorian Home Farm and Walled Garden both with quality interpretive displays; superb collection of farm animals (Approved Rare Breeds Centre). Miniature Railway. Special events and attractions most weekends. Picnic areas and adventure playground.
Location: 5 m NE of Liverpool City Centre; Signposted from A580 & A5088 (ring road).
Open: Parkland open daily throughout the year, adm free. Hall, Farm & Garden open 11-5 daily in main season, please telephone to check exact dates.
Admission: (Inclusive) Hall, Farm and Gardens £3.00 Children/OAPs £1.50. Reduced rates for parties. Free car parking.
Refreshments: 'The Old Riding School' cafe during season.
Wheelchair access to Farm, Garden and Cafe but to ground floor only in Hall. Leisure Services Directorate, Liverpool City Council.

MEOLS HALL
(R.F. Hesketh, Esq)
Southport   PR9 7LZ   map **6** P17
Telephone: (01704) 29826
Fax: (01704) 29826

A 17th century house, with subsequent additions, containing an interesting collection of pictures, furniture, china etc.
Location: 1 m N of Southport; 16 m SW of Preston; 20 m N of Liverpool; near A565 & A570.
Station(s): Southport
Open: All of Aug 2-5.
Admission: £3 children £1 those under 10 accompanied by adult free.
Refreshments: Available in local village 200 yds.
Events/Exhibitions: Maybe available 1995/6.

SPEKE HALL   ❧ The National Trust
The Walk, Liverpool   L24 1XD   map **6** Q17
Telephone: 0151-427 9860
Location: On N bank of Mersey. 1 m off A561 on W side of Liverpool Airport. Follow airport signs from M62; M56 junction 12.

NORFOLK

BILLINGFORD MILL
(Norfolk County Council)
Billingford, Nr. Diss
Telephone: (01746) 785225

Brick tower corn mill fully repaired with cap and sails.

BLICKLING HALL   ❧ The National Trust
Blickling   NR11 6NF   map **4** R25   ♿
Telephone: (01263) 733084
Fax: (01263) 734924
Location: 1½ m NW of Aylsham on N side of B1354 (which is 15 m N of Norwich on A140).

CASTLE RISING CASTLE   ENGLISH HERITAGE
map **4** R23
Telephone: (01553) 631330

The long and distinguished history of Castle Rising began in 1138. It was then that William de Albini started to build a grand castle to mark the upturn in his fortunes which followed his marriage to Henry I's widow. Later owners were no less notable and included Isabella 'The She-Wolf of France', wife of Edward II, the Black Prince, Prince Hal and the Howard Dukes of Norfolk. The 12th century keep, reached through a handsome decorated doorway is the finest part of the castle. Outside, there is a gatehouse of the same date and the remains of a church.
Location: 4 m (6.4 km) north of King's Lynn.
Open: Apr 1-Sept 30 10-6 daily Oct 1-31 10-4 daily Nov 1-Mar 31 Wed-Sun 10-4.
Admission: Adults £2 concessions £1.50 children £1

DENVER MILL
(Norfolk Mills and Pumps Trust)
Denver Mill, Nr. Downham Market
Telephone: (01603) 222709

A very tall cornmill now fully repaired with cap and sails.

THE FAIRHAVEN GARDEN TRUST
(G.E. Debbage (Reg. Charity No. 265686)
South Walsham, Nr. Norwich   map **4** R25   ♿
Telephone: (01603) 270449

A delightful natural woodland and water garden in the heart of broadland. Primroses, bluebells, candelabra primulas, azaleas, rhododendrons, giant lilies, rare shrubs and plants, native wild flowers, 900 year old King oak, private inner broad, tree lined walks, separate bird sanctuary for bird watching. "The Lady Beatrice" a vintage style river boat will be running trips every half hour on the two South Walsham broads from within the gardens on all open days.
Location: 9 m NE of Norwich on the B1140.

Open: Good Friday to 1 Oct Tue-Sun. Closed Mon except Bank Hols. 11-5.30 (Sat 2-5.30). Primrose Week 13-21 Apr. Candelabra Primula Week 18-27 May. Autumn Colours Week 20-31 Oct.
Admission: Adults £3, OAPs £2, Chd £1, Under 5's free. Bird Sanctuary £1, Season Ticket £7, Family Season £20. Parties by arrangement. Group discount. Enquiries 01603 270449.
Refreshments: Morning coffee, light lunches, afternoon teas.
Free parking. Plants for sale. The Fairhaven Garden Trust is a registered charity which exists to preserve this unique natural attraction. Charity No. 265686.

FELBRIGG HALL   ❧ The National Trust
Felbrigg   NR11 8PR   map **4** R25   ♿
Telephone: (01263) 837444 Restaurant:(01263) 838237
Location: 2 m SW of Cromer on S side of A148.

GRIME'S GRAVES   ENGLISH HERITAGE
map **4** S24
Telephone: (01842) 810656

This is an intricate network of pits and shafts sunk by our neolithic ancestors some 4000 years ago. The purpose of all this industriousness was to find flints for the world's first farmers - flints to make axes to fell trees so that the cleared ground could be sown with seed. Between 700 and 800 pits were dug, some of them to a depth of 30 or 40ft (9-12m). Two of the 16 excavated shafts have been left open; they give an idea of those early miners' working conditions.
Location: 2¾ m (4.4 km) north east of Brandon.
Open: Apr 1-Sept 30 10-6 daily Oct 1-31 10-4 daily Nov 1-Mar 31 Wed-Sun 10-4. (Last visit to pit 20 mins prior to closing).
Admission: Adults £1.50 concessions £1.10 children 80p.

HOLKHAM HALL
(The Earl of Leicester)
Wells   NR23 1AB   map **4** R24
Telephone: (01328) 710227
Fax: (01328) 711707

One of Britain's most majestic stately homes, situated in a 3,000 acre deer park at the centre of a great agricultural estate, on the beautiful north Norfolk coast. The celebrated Palladian style mansion was built between 1734 and 1762 by Thomas Coke, 1st Earl of Leicester, with his architect William Kent and compatriot Lord Burlington. Holkham is still the home of the Earls of Leicester. The magnificent alabaster entrace hall of the mansion rises the full height of the building and in the richly and splendidly decorated State Rooms are Greek and Roman statues, brought back by the 1st Earl from his grand tour of Europe, fine furniture by William Kent and paintings by Rubens, Van Dyck, Poussin and Gainsborough. In addition to the Hall there is a Bygones Museum in the original stable block, Garden Centre in the 18th century walled kitchen garden.

Location: 2m W of Wells; S off the Wells/Hunstanton Road (A149).
Open: Suns-Thurs (inc) 26 May-30 Sept 1.30-5. Easter, May, Spring and Summer Bank Hols, Sun & Mon 11.30-5 (last admission 4.40).
Admission: Adults £3 children £1.50. Bygones: adults £3 children £1.50. All inclusive adults £5 children £2.50. Reductions on parties of 20 or more.
Refreshments: Served in tea-rooms.
Events/Exhibitions: History of Farming Exhibition.
Pottery and Gift Shop.

HOUGHTON HALL
(The Marquess of Cholmondeley)
Kings Lynn   map **7** R24   ♿
Telephone: (01485) 528569

The Home of the Marquess of Cholmondeley, Houghton Hall was built in the 18th century for Sir Robert Walpole by Colen Campbell and Thomas Ripley, with interior decoration by William Kent, and is regarded as one of the finest examples of Palladian architecture in England. Houghton was later inherited by the 1st Marquess of Cholmondeley through his grandmother, Sir Robert's daughter. Situated in beautiful parkland, the house contains magnificent furniture, pictures and china. Pleasure grounds. A private collection of 20,000 model soldiers and militaria.

Location: 13 m E of King's Lynn; 10 m W of Fakenham off A148.
Open: Suns, Thurs and Bank Hol Mons from Easter Sun to last Sun in Sept. 2pm-5,30pm last admission 5pm.
Admission: House, park and grounds: (incl soldier museum, walled garden, tea room and gift shop) adults £5.50 children (5-16 incl) £3. Party rates (20+) adults £5 children (5-16

incl) £2.50. Excluding house: adults £3 children (5-16 incl) £2. Party rates (10+) adults £2.50 children (5-16 incl) £1.50.
Refreshments: Tea room.
Car park near House, toilets and lift to State floor for the disabled. Free parking for coaches and cars.

MANNINGTON GARDENS AND COUNTRYSIDE
(Lord and Lady Walpole)
Saxthorpe, Norfolk   map **4** R25   △
Telephone: (01263) 584175
Fax: (01263) 761214

15th century moated house and Saxon church ruin set in attractive gardens. Outstanding rose gardens. Extensive walks and trails around the estate.

Location: 2 m N of Saxthorpe, nr B1149; 18 m NW of Norwich. 9 m from coast.
Open: Garden Apr-Oct Sun 12-5 Also June-Aug Wed Thurs and Fri 11-5.
Admission: Adults £3 children (accompanied children under 16) free OAPs/students £2.50 House open by prior appointment only.
Refreshments: Coffee, salad lunches and home-made teas.

NORFOLK WINDMILL'S TRUST
Telephone: (01603) 222705

Why not visit some of Norfolks more unusual Historic Buildings in 1996? The County is famous for its windmills and many are open to the public on specified days courtesy of Norfolk Windmill's Trust. **Old Buckingham Mill** reputedly the largest mill in Great Britain, will be opening for the first time in 1996. Extensive restoration of **Denver Mill** continues to full working order, is underway. For full details of opening times and location or leaflet "Mill Open days 1996" contact the trust on the above telephone number.

NORWICH CASTLE MUSEUM
(Norfolk Museum Service)
Norwich   NR1 3JU   map **4** R25
Telephone: (01603) 223624
Fax: (01603) 765651

The world's largest collection of British cermaic teapots.

OXBURGH HALL The National Trust
Oxborough **PE33 9PS** map **4** R24 &
Telephone: (0136 621) 258
Location: 7 m SW of Swaffham on S side of Stoke Ferry Road.

RAVENINGHAM HALL GARDENS
(Sir Nicholas Bacon, Bt)
Norwich **NR14 6NS** map **4** R26
Telephone: (01508) 548222
Fax: (01508) 548958

An extensive garden laid out at the turn of the century surrounding original Georgian house. In the last thirty years a large number of new areas have been designed and brought into cultivation, many in the traditional style, with plantings of unusual shrubs, herbaceous plants and roses. An Arboretum planted in March 1990 contains many unusual trees. In recent years an important and extensive Nursery and Plant Centre has developed, to include many rare and exotic plants that can be seen in the garden. (Catalogue 3 x first class stamps). Also Victorian Conservatory and walled vegetable garden. The house is not open to the public.

Location: 4 m from Beccles off the B1136 between Beccles and Loddon.
Open: Plant Centre Mon-Fri 9-5 all year Sat 9-5 and Sun 2-5. Mid Mar-Mid Sept. Garden Sun and Bank Hol Mon 2-5 Wed 1-4. Mid Mar-Mid Sept.
Admission: £2 Children free in aid of local charities. Free car park.
Refreshments: Home-made teas served when gardens open.

SANDRINGHAM HOUSE, GROUNDS & MUSEUM
(Her Majesty The Queen)
Sandringham map **4** R24
Telephone: (01553) 772675

Sandringham is the charming country retreat of Her Majesty The Queen hidden in the heart of sixty acres of beautiful wooded grounds. All the main ground floor rooms used by The Royal Family, full of their treasured ornaments, portraits and furniture, are open to the public. More Royal possessions dating back more than a century are displayed in the Museum housed in the old stable and coach houses. Glades, dells, lakes and lawns are surrounded by magnificent trees and bordered by colourful shrubs and flowers. A free Land Train from within the entrance will carry passengers less able to walk through the grounds to the House and back. All areas are fully accessible by wheelchair.

Location: 8 m NE of King's Lynn (off A148).
Open: House: 4th Apr-22 July and 8th Aug-6th Oct daily 11-4.45pm. Grounds and Museum: 4th Apr-27th July and 7th Aug-6th Oct daily 10.30 (Museum 11am)-5pm.
Admission: House, Grounds and Museum adults £4, Seniors/Students £3, Chd (5-15) £2. Grounds & Museum £3 Seniors/Students £2.50, Chd (5-15) £1.50.
Refreshments: Air-conditioned Restaurant and waitress-service Tea Room open daily Easter-Oct. Gift shop and plant stall.

WALSINGHAM ABBEY
(Walsingham Estate Company)
Estate Office, Walsingham **NR22 6BP** map **4** S26 &
Telephone: (01328) 820259
Fax: (01328) 820098

The grounds contain the remains of the Augustinian Priory founded in 1153 on a site next to the Holy House, the Shrine of our Lady built in 1061.

Location: On B1105 between Wells and Fakenham.
Station(s): Light railway from Wells-Next-The-Sea.
Open: 2-5 Apr May June July & Sept Wed Sat & Sun, Aug Mon Wed Fri Sat & Sun. Also all Bank Holidays from Easter-Sept. Usual office hours through Estate office (01328) 820259.
Admission: Adults £1.50 children under 16 and OAP's 75p. Parties over 100 by arrangement.
Refreshments: Wide range available in the village.
Accommodation: Also available in the village (Hotel, B&B etc).
Walsingham is a picturesque village containing fine examples of 15th-18th century architecture with half timbered houses and medieval pump house. Ruins of Franciscan Friary, court house museum, Anglican shrine, R.C. Slipper Chapel. Guided tours, accommodation and catering available.

WOLTERTON PARK
(Lord and Lady Walpole)
Erpingham map **4** S25 △
Telephone: (01263) 584175
Fax: (01263) 761214

Extensive historic park with lake.

Location: Nr Erpingham, signposted from A140 Norwich to Cromer road.
Station(s): Gunton.
Open: Park open all year daily 9-5 or dusk if earlier.
Admission: £2 per car. See local press for details of special events and garden and Hall tours.
Refreshments: Pub at drive gate.
Events/Exhibitions: Yes.
Accommodation: Limited.
Conferences: Yes.

NORTHAMPTONSHIRE

AYNHOE PARK
(Country Houses Association)
Aynho **OX17 3BQ** map **5** S20
Telephone: (01869) 810636

17th century mansion. Alteration by Soane.

Location: Junction 10 M40 then 3 m west on B4100.
Station(s): Banbury (7½ m), Bicester (8 m).
Open: May-Sept Weds & Thurs 2-5. Last entry 4.30.
Admission: £2.50 Children £1. Free car park.
No dogs admitted.

BOUGHTON HOUSE

(His Grace the Duke of Buccleuch & Queensberry, KT. and The Living Landscape Trust)
map **4** S21   △ & ⑤
Telephone: (01536) 515731
Fax: (01536) 417255

Northamptonshire Home of The Duke of Buccleuch and Queensberry K.T., and his Montagu ancestors since 1528. A 500 year old Tudor monastic building gradually enlarged around 7 courtyards until the French style addition of 1695. Outstanding collection of 17/18th century English and other European furniture, tapestries, porcelain, 16th century carpets - notable works by El Greco, Murillo, Caracci and 40 Van Dyck sketches - celebrated Armoury and Ceremonial Coach. *Boughton House was the Silver Award Winner of the first Historic Houses awards, given by the AA and NPI, in co-operation with the Historic Houses Association, for the privately owned historic house open to the public, which has best preserved its integrity and the character of its architecture and furniture, while remaining a lived-in family home.* The surrounding parkland has historic avenues and lakes - picnic area - gift shop - exciting adventure woodland play area - garden centre - tea-room.Boughton House is administered by The Living Landscape Trust, which was created by the present Duke of Buccleuch to show the relationship between the historic Boughton House and its surrounding, traditional, but modern run, working estate.For details of our specialist Fine Art Courses run in conjunction with Sotheby's and our Schools Education Facilities (Sandford Award Winner 1988 and 1993), please telephone The Living Landscape Trust at Kettering (01536) 515731. BOUGHTON HOUSE 'The English Versailles'.

Location: 3 m N of Kettering on A43 at Geddington; 75 m N of London by A1 or M1, on northern spur from A14.
Station(s): Kettering (direct London St.Pancras 50 minutes)
Open: HOUSE AND GROUNDS-daily Aug 1-Sept 1. Grounds 1-5 House 2-5 (last entry 4.30). Staterooms strictly by prior appointment. The Living Landscape Trust welcomes educational groups at other times, strictly by prior arrangements.GROUNDS ONLY May 1- Sept 15 daily except Fri 1-5. Garden Centre open daily throughout year; Adventure Playarea and tea-rooms open 1-5 at weekends and public holidays May-Sept and daily throughout Aug for House opening, at other times by appointment.
Admission: House and Grounds adults £4 OAPs/students £3. Grounds adults £1.50 OAPs/students £1.
Refreshments: Tea-rooms: weekends, public holidays and daily in August.

CANONS ASHBY HOUSE   🌿 The National Trust
Canons Ashby   map **5** S20
Telephone: (01327) 860044
Location: Easy access from either M40 junction 11 or M1 junction 16. From M1 signposted from A5 2 m S of Weedon crossroads, along unclassified road (13 m) to Banbury. From M40 at Banbury take A422 exit, then left along unclassified road.

COTON MANOR GARDEN
(Mr & Mrs Ian Pasley-Tyler)
Nr Guilsborough   NN6 8RQ   map **4** S20   &
Telephone: (01604) 740219
Fax: (01604) 740838

Traditional old English garden set in Northamptonshire countryside, with yew and holly hedges, extensive herbaceous borders, rose garden, water garden, herb garden, woodland garden, famous bluebell wood (early May) and exotic wildfowl collection. Recently featured in the RHS Garden Magazine and Country Living.

Location: 10 m N of Northampton & 11 m SE of Rugby. Follow tourist signs on A428 and A50.
Station(s): Northampton, Long Buckby.
Open: Easter-end of Sept daily Weds-Sun and Bank Hol Mons 12-6.
Admission: £2.70 OAPs £2.20 Children £1.
Refreshments: Restaurant serving home-made lunches and teas.
Events/Exhibitions: Plant sale Sun 31 Mar '96-7 Apr '96.
Unusual plants for sale, propagated from the garden.

COTTESBROOKE HALL AND GARDENS

(Captain & Mrs John Macdonald-Buchanan)
nr Northampton   map **4** S21   △
Telephone: (01604) 505808
Fax: (01604) 505619

Architecturally magnificent Queen Anne house commenced in 1702. Renowned picture collection, particularly of sporting and equestrian subjects. Fine English and Continental furniture and porcelain. Main vista aligned on celebrated 7th century Saxon church at Brixworth. House reputed to be the pattern for Jane Austen's 'Mansfield Park'. Notable gardens of great variety including fine old cedars and specimen trees, herbaceous borders, water and wild gardens.

Location: 10 m N of Northampton (A14 - A1/M1 Link Road) nr Creaton on A50, nr Brixworth on A508.
Open: House and Gardens - from 8th April to 29th Sept - Thurs. and Bank Holiday Mon. afternoons, plus all Sun. afternoons in Sept. 2-5.30pm. Last admission 5pm. Gardens: from 8th April to 29th Sept. -Wed, Thurs, Fri and Bank Holiday Monday afternoons, plus all Sunday afternoons in Sept 2-5.30pm. Last admission 5pm.
Admission: Adults £4. Gardens only £2.50. Children half-price.
Refreshments: In the Old Laundry 2.30-5.
Parties accommodated by appointment on other days. Car parking. Gardens but not house suitable for disabled. No dogs.

"GHOSTS"

Ghosts are in residence at the following properties included in Historic Houses Castles and Gardens:-

Blickling Hall - *Anne Boleyn*

Breamore House *- Haunted picture - if touched, death on the same day*

East Riddleden Hall *- 5 ghosts including lady in Grey Hall Lady's Chamber*

Fountains Abbey & Studley Royal *- Choir of monks chanting in Chapel of Nine Altars*

Hinton Ampner *- Nocturnal noises*

Ightham Mote *- Supernatural presence*

Lindisfarne Castle *- Monk, and group of monks on causeway*

Lyme Park *- Unearthly peals of bells and lady in white, funeral procession through park*

Malmesbury House - *Ghost of a cavalier*

Overbecks Museum & Garden *- 'Model' ghost in the Children's room (for them to spot)*

Rockingham Castle - *Lady Dedlock*

Rufford Old Hall *- Elizabeth Hesketh*

Scotney Castle Garden *- Man rising from the lake*

Sizergh Castle & Garden *- Poltergeist*

Speke Hall *- Ghost of woman in tapestry room*

Springhill *- Ghost of a woman*

Sudbury Hall *- Lady in Green, seen on stairs*

Tamworth Castle *- Haunted bedroom*

Treasurer's House *- Troop of Roman soldiers marching through the cellar*

Wallington House *- Invisible birds beating against the windows accompanied by heavy breathing*

Washington Old Hall *- Grey lady walking through corridors*

DELAPRE ABBEY

(Northamptonshire Borough Council)

nr Northampton

HOLDENBY HOUSE AND GARDENS

(Owners Mr & Mrs Lowther - Administration Barbara Brooker)

Northampton   NN6 8DJ   map **14** S20   Ⓢ

Telephone: (01604) 770074

Fax: (01604) 770962

Once the largest house in Elizabethan England, Holdenby secured its place in history when it became the prison of Charles I during the Civil War. Today Holdenby's Falconry Centre and collection of rare farm animals complement the beauty and history of the grounds with their Elizabethan and fragrant borders. As buzzards and other birds of prey capture the attention in the sky above, an authentic armoury and reconstructed 17th century homestead add historical interest on the ground. And for the children, a 'cuddle farm' and play area ensure an enjoyable day. The house, with its collection of rare pianos, is open Bank Hol Mons (except May Day) and by appointment.

Location: 7 m NW of Northampton, off A428 & A50; approx 7 m from M1 exit 15a, 16 or 18.

Station(s): Northampton.

Open: Apr-end Sept GARDENS Thurs in 12 July 8 Aug 1-5. Sun 2-6 Bank Hol Suns and Mons 1-6. HOUSE Bank Hol Mons (except May Day) 1-6.*HOUSE Open by arrangement to pre-booked parties Mon-Fri.*

Admission: GARDEN £2.75 Children £1.75 OAPs £2.25 HOUSE & GARDENS £3.75 Children £2 Enquire for special rates for school parties and business conferences throughout the year.

Refreshments: Home-made teas in Victorian Kitchen.

Accommodation: A range of good quality accommodation is available locally.

Conferences: Holdenby is well known for its use as a corporate hospitality and conference venue. Open year round.

Souvenir shop selling Holdenby branded goods and craft items.

KELMARSH HALL

(Kelmarsh Hall Estate Preservation Trust)

Nr. Northampton   NN6 9LU   map **7** S21

Telephone: (01604) 686543

Fax: (01604) 686543

1732 Palladian house by Gibbs. Chinese Room with wallpaper from 1740's. Entrance lodges by Wyatt. Interesting gardens with lake and woodland walks. Herd of British White Cattle.

Location: 12 m N of Northampton 5 m S. of Market Harborough on A508/A14.

Open: Suns and Bank Hols between 7 Apr and 26 Aug 2.30-5.

Admission: Adults £3 OAP's £2 children £1. Gardens only £2. Group bookings by arrangement.

Refreshments: Home-made teas. Private parties, wedding receptions.

LAMPORT HALL AND GARDENS

(Lamport Hall Trust)

Northampton   NN6 9HD   map **4** S21   Ⓢ

Telephone: (01604) 686272

Fax: (01604) 686224

Lamport Hall was the home of the Isham family from 1560 to 1976. The South West front is a rare example of the work of John Webb, pupil and son-in-law of Inigo Jones and was built in 1655 (during the Commonwealth) with wings added in 1732 and 1740. High Room with plaster ceiling by John Woolston, an outstanding library, and thirteen other fine rooms containing the Ishams' collections of superb paintings, furniture and china. The Hall is set in spacious wooded parkland with tranquil gardens including a remarkable rock garden. Teas in Victorian dining room. Now run by the Lamport Hall Trust, school visits, group and private bookings are especially encouraged and a programme of fairs, music, art and craft events is put on throughout the season - details from the Director.

Location: 8 m N of Northampton on A508 to Market Harborough. M1 J15/16/18/20.

Station(s): Northampton.

Open: Easter-Oct 1 every Sun and Bank Holiday Mon 2.15-5.15 (Aug every day with one tour at 4.30 or 5) Oct 28-29 2.15-5.15 Dec 2-3 tour at 2.15.

Admission: Prices to be confirmed.

Refreshments: Home-made teas at the house.

Events/Exhibitions: Most months through the year, telephone for free brochure.

Conferences: The Hall and Grounds are available for conferences and corporate hospitality throughout the year.

Dogs on leads in picnic area only.

LYVEDEN NEW BIELD   🌼 The National Trust

Oundle   map **4** S21

Telephone: (01832) 205358

Location: 4 m SW of Oundle via A427. 3 m E of Brigstock (A6116) (½ m walk from roadside parking).

THE MENAGERIE, HORTON

(The Executors of the late Gervase Jackson-Stops)
Horton, Northampton　NN7 2BX　map **4** S21
Telephone: (01536) 418205
Fax: (01536) 418419

A garden in the making, designed by Ian Kirby, and surrounding a folly built by Thomas Wright of Durham for the 2nd Earl of Halifax, c1754-57. Spiral mount, lime and hornbeam allees, formal ponds with fountains and wetlands, thatched arbours in the classical and gothic styles. Plant sales.

Location: 6 m S of Northampton and 1 m S of Horton on B526 turn left immediately after lay-by.
Open: April-end Sept. Garden only Thurs 10-4. House Garden and Shell Grotto open to groups of 20 or more by appointment at other times.
Admission: Garden adults £2.50 children £1.

THE PREBENDAL MANOR HOUSE

Nassington　map **4** R22　△
Telephone: (01780) 782575

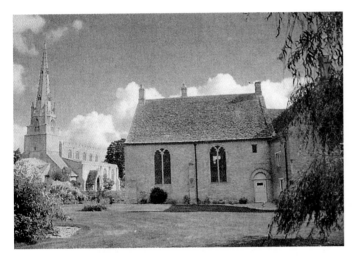

The earliest surviving Manor in Northamptonshire dating from the early 13th century. The present stone manor overlays one of the royal manors of the Danish King Cnut who once ruled England. The existing stone manor is of significant architectural and historical interest and forms the focus of a group of stone buildings which include a fine 16th century Dovecote. The Museum in the tithe barn depicting medieval life in the manor is an added attraction. The manor has lovely gardens and medieval fish ponds.

Location: 6 m N of Oundle. A605-C14, 7 m S of Stamford. A1 to Wansford C14. 9 m E of Peterborough. A47-C14.
Open: Wed and Sun 2-5.30 from May 1-Sept 29 Easter Mon 2-5.30 Bank Hol Mons 2-5.30. Closed Christmas.
Admission: Adults £3 children £1.50. Parties at other times by arrangement. Free car parking Tel (01780) 582575.
Refreshments: Home made teas. Lunches to order.
Events/Exhibitions: Telephone for information.
Accommodation: Bed & Breakfast in the 15th C Lodgings building.
Conferences: Licensed for Civil Weddings.
Gardens and Museum accessible to the disabled. House not suitable.

PRIEST'S HOUSE　　The National Trust

Easton-on-the-Hill　map **4** R21
Telephone: (01780) 62506
Location: 2 m SW of Stamford off A43.

Sir Christopher Wren - architect (1632-1723)

Fawley Court
Old Royal Observatory
Winslow Hall

ROCKINGHAM CASTLE

(Commander Michael Saunders Watson)
nr Corby　map **4** R21　△ Ⓔ Ⓢ
Telephone: (01536) 770240
Fax: (01536) 771692

Built by William the Conqueror, used by the early Kings of England until the 16th century when granted to Edward Watson whose family live there today. The house itself is memorable, representing a procession of periods. The dominant influence is Tudor within the Norman walls, but most centuries have left their mark in the form of architecture, furniture or works of art. There is a fine collection of English 18th, 19th and 20th century paintings. Dickens a frequent visitor used the Castle as a model for Chesney Wold in Bleak House. The Castle stands in 12 acres of formal and wild gardens. Special exhibition: 450 Years a Royal Castle, 450 Years a Family Home.

Location: 2 m N of Corby; 9 m from Market Harborough; 14 m from Stamford on A427; 8 m from Kettering on A6003.
Open: Easter Sun-Sept 30 Sun & Thurs also Bank Hol Mons & Tues following and Tues during Aug 1pm-5pm. Any other day by previous appointment for parties. Grounds open 11.30am Bank Hol Sun/Mon & Suns May-Aug.
Admission: Adults £3.80 OAPs £3.30 children £2.40. Gardens only £2.40 (variable for special events) family ticket (2+2) £10.50.
Refreshments: Teas: home-made at Castle.

SOUTHWICK HALL

(Christopher Capron, Esq)
nr Oundle　map **4** R22
Telephone: (01832) 274064

A family home since 1300, retaining medieval building dating from 1300, with Tudor re-building and 18th century additions. Exhibitions:- Victorian and Edwardian life; collections of agricultural and carpentry tools, named bricks and local archaeological finds and fossils.

Location: 3 m N of Oundle 4 m E of Bulwick.
Open: Bank Holidays, Sun & Mon (Apr 7,8 May 5,6,26,27 Aug 25,26) Wed May 3-Aug 30 2-5. Parties at other times (Easter-Aug) by arrangement with Secretary at Southwick Hall, Peterborough PE8 5BL.
Admission: Adults £3 OAPs £2.50 children £1.50.
Refreshments: Teas available.

STOKE PARK PAVILIONS
(A.S. Chancellor, Esq)
Towcester map **5** S21 &♿
Telephone: (01604) 862172

Two pavilions and colonnade. Built in 1630 by Inigo Jones.

Location: Stoke Bruerne village; 7 m S of Northampton just W of Stony/Northampton Road A508.
Open: June July & Aug Sat Sun & Bank Hols 2-6. *Exterior only on view.*
Admission: £1. Car park free.

SULGRAVE MANOR
(The Sulgrave Manor Board)
Banbury OX17 2SD map **5** S20 △
Telephone: (01295) 760205

The Home of George Washington's Ancestors. A delightful 16th Century Manor House presenting a typical wealthy man's home and gardens in Elizabethan times. Restored with scholarly care and attention to detail. "A perfect illustration of how a house should be shown to the public" - Nigel Nicholson, Great Houses of Britain.

Location: Sulgrave Village is off Banbury/Northampton Road (B4525); 5 m from Banbury junction of M40, 12 m from Northampton junction of M1. 7 m NE of Banbury; 28 m SE of Stratford-upon-Avon; 30 m N of Oxford; 70 m NW of London.
Open: Weekdays open every day except Weds. 1 Apr-31 Oct 2-5.30. Bank Hols and the month of Aug 10.30-1 and 2-5.30. Dec 27-31 10.30-1 and 2-4.30. Weekends Apr-Oct 10.30-1 and 2-5.30. Mar, Nov and Dec 10.30-1 and 2-4.30. Please note: Last admissions are one hour before closing times. All visitors on non-event days are taken round the Manor House in regularly organised guided tours. Closed: Christmas Day, Boxing Day and the whole of January and Sun 16 June.
Admission: Adults £3.50 children £1.75 group rates available.
Refreshments: At Thatched House Hotel opposite, Tel Sulgrave (01295) 760232. Light refreshments in Brewhouse.
Events/Exhibitions: Please telephone for details of Special Events Programme for 1996.

Butterfly Houses

can be found at the following properties included in Historic Houses Castles and Gardens:-

Berkeley Castle
Elsham Hall - Wild butterfly walkway
Syon House

NORTHUMBERLAND

ALNWICK CASTLE
(His Grace the Duke of Northumberland)
Alnwick map **9** M19
Telephone: (01665) 510777
Fax: (01665) 510876

Described by the Victorians as 'The Windsor of the North', Alnwick Castle is the main seat of the Duke of Northumberland whose family, the Percys, have lived here since 1309. This border stronghold has survived many battles, but now peacefully dominates the picturesque market town of Alnwick, overlooking landscape designed by Capability Brown. The stern, medieval exterior belies the treasure house within, furnished in palatial Renaissance style, with paintings by Titian, Van Dyck and Canaletto, fine furniture and an exquisite collection of Meissen china. The Regiment Museum of Royal Northumberland Fusiliers is housed in the Abbot's Tower of the Castle, while the Postern Tower contains a collection of early British and Roman relics. Other attractions include the Percy State Coach, the dungeon, the gun terrace and the grounds, which offer peaceful walks and superb views over the surrounding countryside. Gardens, childrens play ground.

Location: Just off the town centre on the northern side of Alnwick.
Station(s): Alnmouth (5 m)
Open: Daily (except Fri) 4 Apr-13 Oct 11-5 (last admission 4.30pm). Open All Bank Hols inc Good Fri.
Admission: Address: Estate Office, Alnwick Castle, Alnwick, Northumberland NE66 1NQ. Free parking for cars and coaches.
Refreshments: Tea-room serving home-made fare. Gift Shop.
Events/Exhibitions: For details, contact Castle Administrator.
Gift Shop. Special party rates. Guide service if required. Enquiries to the Administrator, Alnwick Castle, Alnwick, Northumberland, NE66 1NQ. Tel (01665) 510777 Mon-Fri and weekends only during season only. (01665) 603942.

BAMBURGH CASTLE

(Lady Armstrong)
Bamburgh ME69 7DF map **9** L19 △
Telephone: (01668) 214208
Fax: (01669) 21236

Fine 12th century Norman Keep with its setting upon The Crag, and referred to as a Royal Centre by AD 547, is certainly one of the most dramatic of all Castles in Britain. Remainder of the Castle considerably restored. Magnificent seascapes including Holy Island and the Farne Islands, the landscapes extending to the Cheviot Hills. Public rooms with exhibition of porcelain, china, paintings, furniture and items of interest. The Armoury includes loan collections from HM Tower of London, The John George Joicey Museum, Newcastle upon Tyne and others. Fine paintings, including some from the Duke of Cambridge's collection.

Location: Coastal - 16 m N of Alnwick 6 m from Belford; 3 m from Seahouses.
Open: Easter-last Sun of Oct daily (incl Suns) open at 12 noon parties may be booked out of normal hours. For closing times enquire The Custodian.
Admission: Adults £2.50 children £1.20.
Refreshments: Clock Tower tea-rooms.

Aviaries and Birds of Prey Centres

can be found at the following properties in Historic Houses Castles and Gardens:-

Drumlanrig Castle & Country Park
Elsham Hall Country and Wildlife Park
Holdenby House & Gardens
Leeds Castle
Leighton House Museum & Art Gallery
Sewerby Hall & Gardens
Sion Hill Hall
Waddesdon Manor
Muncaster Castle

BELSAY HALL CASTLE AND GARDENS
ENGLISH HERITAGE

map **9** M19
Telephone: (0166 181) 636

19th-century Neo-Classical mansion lies at the entrance to 30 acres of exciting gardens, which in turn lead on to the 14th-century castle and ruined manor. Important collections of rare and exotic flowering trees grow in the meandering, deep ravines of the 'picturesque' Quarry Gardens. Massed plantings of rhododendrons. Large heather garden. Spring bulbs. Exhibition of Belsay's architectural and landscape history in stable block.

Location: 14 m (22.4 km) north west of Newcastle upon Tyne.
Open: Apr 1-Sept 30 10-6 daily Oct 1-Mar 31 daily 10-4 daily.
Admission: Adults £3 concessions £2.30 children £1.50.
Events/Exhibitions: 'Living at Belsay' exhibition 1996.

BERWICK UPON TWEED BARRACKS
ENGLISH HERITAGE

map **9** L18
Telephone: (01289) 304493

The barracks were designed in 1717 to accommodate 36 officers and 600 men, first being occupied in 1721. The buildings consist of three blocks of accommodation around a square, the fourth side having a splendidly decorated gatehouse. The barracks' exhibition, the award winning 'Beat of Drum' traces the history of the British infantryman from 1660 to the end of the 19th century. The regimental museum of the King's Own Scottish Borderers and Borough Museum of Berwick on Tweed are also housed here.

Location: On the Parade, off Church St, Berwick town centre.
Open: Apr 1-Sept 30 10-6 daily Oct 1-31 10-4 daily Nov 1-Mar 31 10-4 Wed-Sun.
Admission: Adults £2.30 concessions £1.70 children £1.20.

CHERRYBURN   🦋 The National Trust
Mickley   NE43 7DB   map **9** N19   ♿
Telephone: (01661) 843276
Location: 11 m W of Newcastle on A695 (200 yards signed from Mickley Square).

CHESTER'S ROMAN FORT AND MUSEUM   <small>ENGLISH HERITAGE</small>

map **9** M18
Telephone: (01434) 681379

An impressive bath-house, buildings of great interest inside the fort, the remains of the bridge carrying Hadrian's Wall across the Tyne, a museum full of Roman inscriptions and sculptures, all set in one of the most beautiful valleys in Northumberland - these are among the attractions of Chesters, once garrisoned by a regiment of Roman cavalry.

Location: ½ m (0.8 km) south west of Chollerford.
Open: Apr 1-Sept 30 daily 9.30-6, Oct 1-Mar 31 daily 10-4.
Admission: Adults £2.50 concessions £1.90 children £1.30.

CHILLINGHAM CASTLE AND GARDENS   🏛
(Sir Humphry Wakefield, Bt)
Alnwick   NE66 5NJ   map **9** L19
Telephone: (01668) 215359

This medieval family fortress remains home since the 1200's, to the Earls Grey and their relations. Complete with jousting course, alarming dungeon and even a torture chamber, the Castle displays many remarkable restoration techniques in action, alongside antique furnishings, paintings, tapestries, arms and armour. The Italian ornamental garden, landscaped avenues and gate lodges were created by Sir Jeffrey Wyatville, fresh from his triumphs at Windsor Castle. There are attractive woodland walks and a lake, tea room, gift shop and antique shop, and some holiday lets.

Location: 12 m N of Alnwick, signposted from the A1 and A697.
Open: Good Fri-Easter Mon 1 May-30 Sept 12-5.30. (closed Tues) Open seven days a week July and Aug.
Admission: Adults £3.50 OAPs £3 children FREE when accompanied. Parties (over 10) £2.50 per head. Coaches welcome.

Refreshments: Tea room serving light refreshments available within the Castle during opening hours. Nearest restaurant - Percy Arms, Chatton (2 m). Restaurant facilities available by arrangement.
Accommodation: Private family suites of rooms available.
Access for disabled difficult due to number of stairs. Wheelchairs available only by arrangement. Holiday apartments available withing Castle. Fishing and Clay pigeon shooting by arrangement. Musical and Theatrical events regularly planned.

CHIPCHASE CASTLE & GARDENS
Wark On Tyne   map **9** M18
Telephone: (01434) 230203

An imposing 17th and 18th Century Castle with 14th Century Pele Tower set in formal and informal gardens. A chapel stands in the park. One walled Garden is now a Nursery specialising in unusual perennials.

Location: 2 m south of Wark on the Barrasford road.
Open: Castle: 1-28 June, daily 2-5. Tours by arrangement at other times. Gardens & Nursery: Easter 31 July, Thurs and Sun + Bank Hol 10-5.
Admission: Castle £3 Gardens £1.50 Nursery Free.

CORBRIDGE ROMAN SITE   <small>ENGLISH HERITAGE</small>
map **9** N18
Telephone: (01434) 632349

For nearly a century this was the site of a sequence of Roman forts, since Corbridge was an important junction of roads to Scotland, York and Carlisle. It developed into a prosperous town and supply base for Hadrian's Wall, with shops, temples, houses, granaries and an elaborate fountain. Among the rich collection of finds in the museum is a remarkable fountainhead - the Corbridge Lion.

Location: ½ m (0.8 km) north west of Corbridge.
Open: Apr 1-Sept 30 10-6 daily Oct 1-31 10-4 daily Nov 1-Mar 31 Wed-Sun 10-4.
Admission: Adults £2.50 concessions £1.90 children £1.30.

CRAGSIDE HOUSE, GARDEN AND GROUNDS
🦋 The National Trust
Rothbury   NE65 7PX   map **9** M19   ♿
Telephone: (01669) 620333/620266
Location: ½ m E of Rothbury; 30 m N of Newcastle-upon-Tyne. Entrance off Rothbury/Alnwick Road B6341; 1 m N of Rothbury at Debdon Burn Gate.

DUNSTANBURGH CASTLE   <small>ENGLISH HERITAGE</small>
map **9** M19
Telephone: (0166576) 231

Isolated and unspoilt, the ruins stand on a large, rocky cliff top rising steeply from the sea. Begun by Thomas, Earl of Lancaster, in 1313, the castle was attacked by the Scots and besieged during the Wars of the Roses. The keep gatehouse is still impressive and the south wall an enduring memorial to the workmanship of Earl Thomas's masons.

Location: 8 m (13 km) north east of Alnwick.
Open: Apr 1-Sept 30 10-6 daily Oct 1-31 10-4 daily Nov 1-Mar 31 (closed 1-2) Wed-Sun 10-4.
Admission: Adults £1.50 concessions £1.10 children 80p.

HOUSESTEADS ROMAN FORT   <small>ENGLISH HERITAGE</small>
map **9** N18
Telephone: (01434) 344363

This is the best-preserved Roman troop-base on Hadrian's Wall. In the museum, a model shows the layout of barracks, headquarters buildings, commandant's house and granaries. Also displayed are relics from the fort and the settlement that grew up outside the walls in the 3rd and 4th centuries.

Location: 2¾ m (4.4 km) north east of Bardon Mill.
Open: Apr 1-Sept 30 10-6 daily Oct 1-Mar 31 daily 10-4.
Admission: Adults £2.50 concessions £1.90 children £1.30.

HOWICK HALL GARDENS   🏛
(Howick Trustees Ltd)
Alnwick   NE66 3LB   map **9** M19
Telephone: (01665) 577 285
Fax: (01665) 577 285

Extensive grounds including a natural woodland garden in addition to the formal gardens surrounding the Hall.

Location: 6 m NE of Alnwick, nr Howick village.
Open: Apr-Oct daily 1-6.
Admission: £1.50 (OAPs 75p). 1995 prices-may increase 1996.

KIRKLEY HALL GARDENS

(Dr R. McParlin)
Ponteland   NE20 0AQ   map **9** M19
Telephone: (01661) 860808
Fax: (01661) 860047

Prestigious gardens, Greenhouses, Plantsman's paradise. All plants labelled, Plant sales, Sculptures, Conducted tours (prior arrangement).

Location: 3 m N of Ponteland off A696.
Open: Every day throughout the year 10-5.
Admission: £1.50 per person £3 per family parties of 20 or more (prior notice) £1.20 per person. Group guided tours (min no 13 prior notice) £2.50 per person. Free parking.
Refreshments: Available.
Conferences: Licensed for Civil Weddings.
No dogs.

LINDISFARNE CASTLE   🦂 The National Trust

Holy Island   TD15 2SH   map **9** L19
Telephone: (01289) 89244
Location: 5 m E of Beal across causeway.

LINDISFARNE PRIORY

map **9** L19
Telephone: (01289) 89200

Roofless and ruined, the priory is still supremely beautiful, its graceful arches and decorated doorways commemorating the craftsmanship of their Norman builders. This has been sacred soil since 634 when the missionary Bishop Aidan was sent from Iona, to spread Christianity through northern England. There is also a visitor centre with atmospheric exhibition and shop.

Location: On Holy Island, which can be reached at low tide across a causeway. Tide tables are posted at each end of the causeway.
Open: Apr 1-Sept 30 10-6 daily Oct 1-Mar 31 10-4 daily.
Admission: Adults £2.50 concessions £1.90 children £1.30.

PRESTON TOWER 🏛

(Major T.H. Baker-Cresswell)
Chathill   map **9** L19

One of the few survivors of 78 Pele Towers listed in 1415. The tunnel vaulted rooms remain unaltered and provide a realistic picture of the grim way of life under the constant threat of 'Border Reivers'. Two rooms are furnished in contemporary style and there are displays of historic and local information.

Location: 7 m N of Alnwick; 1 m E from A1. Follow Historic Property signs.
Open: All year Daily during daylight hours.
Admission: £1 children/OAPs 50p. Free car park.
No dogs (except those left in car).

SEATON DELAVAL HALL 🏛

(The Lord Hastings)
Seaton Sluice, Whitley Bay   map **9** M19
Telephone: 0191-237 3040/1493

Palladian House designed by Sir John Vanbrugh for Admiral George Delaval 1718-1728 and beautiful gardens.

Open: May-Sept Wed Sun and Bank Holidays 2-6.
Admission: £2.50 Children 50p.
Refreshments: Tea-room.

WALLINGTON HOUSE, WALLED GARDEN AND GROUNDS
🦂 The National Trust

Cambo   NE61 4AR   map **9** M19   ⚲
Telephone: (01670) 774283 (House)
Location: Access from N, 12 m W of Morpeth on B6343. Access from S, A696 from Newcastle; 6 m NW of Belsay B6342 to Cambo.

WARKWORTH CASTLE AND HERMITAGE

map **9** M19
Telephone: (01665) 711423

From 1332 the history of Warkworth was the history of the Percy family. In 1399 this became the history of England, when the third Percy lord of Warkworth and his son Harry Hotspur put Henry IV on the throne. Three scenes from Shakespeare's Henry IV Part 1 are set at Warkworth. Norman in origin, the castle has some very fine medieval masonry. Part of the keep was restored and made habitable in the 19th century. The hermitage and chapel of Holy Trinity is situated in a peaceful, retired place, overshadowed and surrounded by trees upon the left bank of the River Coquet half a mile above the castle.

Location: 7½ m (12 km) south of Alnwick.
Open: Castle: 1 Apr-30 Sept 9.30-6, Oct 1-31 10-6 or dusk, 1 Nov-31 Mar 10-4 Wed-Sun. Hermitage: 1 Apr-30 Sept Wed & Sun & Bank Hol Mon 11-5.
Admission: Adults £2 concessions £1.50 children £1.

NOTTINGHAMSHIRE

CARLTON HALL

(Trustees of G H Vere-Laurie dec'd)
Carlton-on-Trent, Newark   NG23 6NW   map **7** Q21   △
Telephone: (01636) 821421
Fax: (01636) 821554

George III house built c.1765 by Joseph Pocklington of Newark, banker, 1736-1817. Beautiful drawing room. Magnificent ancient cedar in grounds. Stables attributed to Carr of York.

Location: 7 m N of Newark just off A1.
Station(s): Newark.
Open: Any day. Telephone (01636) 821421. Written confirmation required.
Admission: House and Garden £3 per head. Minimum charge per party £30.
Refreshments: By arrangement
Accommodation: Self catering by arrangement.
Conferences: By arrangement.

CLUMBER PARK   🦂 The National Trust

nr Worksop   map **7** Q20   ⚲
Telephone: (01909) 476653
Location: Clumber Park 4½ m SE of Worksop; 6½ m SW of East Retford.

HODSOCK PRIORY GARDENS

(Lady Buchanan)
Blyth, nr Worksop   map **4** Q20
Telephone: (01909) 591204
Fax: (01909) 591578

We invite you to share the beauty and peace of a remantic traditional 5-acre private garden on the historic Domesday site bounded by a dry moat and Grade 1 listed brick gatehouse c.1500. Sensational snowdrops and woodland walk *Massed daffodils *Bluebell wood *Fine trees *Summer borders *Roses *Lilies.

Location: Less than 2 m from A1 at Blyth, off B6045 Blyth to Worksop road.
Open: Daily in February, Sats & Suns 10-4, weekdays 12-4 for winter borders & 'Snowdrop Spectacular'. Also Tues, Weds & Thurs 1 Apr-31 Aug, plus 2nd Suns in Apr, May & June, all 2-5.
Admission: Adult £2. No charge for accompanied children & visitors in wheelchairs.
Refreshments: Winter: Hot refreshments & light lunches daily. Summer: Teas in Priory conservatory Suns - At farmhouse (50yds from car park) weekdays.
No dogs in garden or wood.

HOLME PIERREPONT HALL

(Mr & Mrs Robin Brackenbury)
Radcliffe-on-Trent, nr Nottingham   NG12 2LD   map **7** R20   △
Telephone: (0115) 9332371

Medieval brick manor house. Historic Courtyard garden with box parterre, 1875. Regional 17th, 18th, 19th and 20th century furniture, china and pictures. Quiet and free from crowds. Jacob sheep. Shop with Jacob wool products.

Location: 5 m SE from centre of Nottingham by following all signs to the National Water Sports Centre and continue for 1½ m.
Open: June Suns 2-5.30. July Thurs and Suns 2-5.30. Aug Tues Thurs Fri Suns 2-5.30. Easter, Spring and Summer Bank Hol Suns, Mons and Tues 2-6. Groups by appointment throughout the year, including evenings.
Admission: Adults £3 children £1 subject to alteration.
Refreshments: Home-made teas. Other refreshments by arrangement.
Available for corporate and private dinner parties, 100 maximum.

NEWARK CASTLE
Newark, Notts   map **4** Q21
Telephone: (01636) 611908

Newark Castle stands proudly on the River Trent in the pretty market town of Newark-on-Trent. Built in the early 12th Century, the Castle has the finest Norman gatehouse in England. 'The Castle Story' exhibition, in the nearby Gilstrap Heritage Centre, unlocks the 800 year history of this historic monument.
Admission: Grounds and the Gilstrap Centre are free, and open daily. Please tel for further details.

NEWARK TOWN HALL
(Newark Town Council)
Newark   NG24 1DU   map **7** Q21   △ &
Telephone: (01636) 640100   **Fax:** (01636) 640967

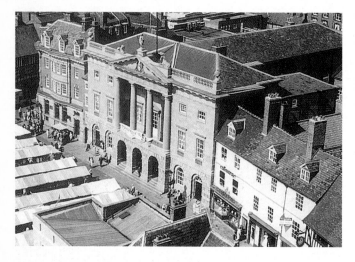

One of the finest Georgian Town Halls in the country, the building has recently been refurbished in sympathy with John Carr's original concept. On display is the Town's collection of Civic Plate, silver dating generally from the 17th and 18th century, including the 'Newark Monteith' and the Newark Siege Pieces. Other items of interest are some early historical records and various paintings including a collection by the artist Joseph Paul.
Location: Market Place, Newark; located on A1 and A46.
Station(s): Newark Castle; Northgate (½ m).
Open: All the year Mon-Fri 10-12 2-4. Open at other times for groups by appointment. *Closed* Sat Sun Bank Hol Mons and Tues following and Christmas week.

NEWSTEAD ABBEY HOUSE AND GROUNDS
(Nottingham City Council)
Newstead Abbey Park   NG15 8Ge   map **4** Q20
Telephone: (01623) 793557 Enquiries. (01623) 797136 Curators Office
Fax: (01623) 797136

Newstead Abbey is best known as the home of the poet Lord Byron who made the house and its ghostly legends famous. Visitors can see Byrons apartments and mementos of the poet including letters, manuscripts and first editions. 30 splendid 19th century rooms bring the lives of later Victorian residents of the house to life. The early history of Newstead as a religious building can be seen in the remains of the medieval priory. The cloisters of the priory surround a secret garden, in the centre is an ancient stone fountain carved with fantastic beasts. The grounds at Newstead Abbey are magnificent in all seasons and include waterfalls, lakes and ponds. There are delightful rose, iris and Japanese gardens to explore.
Location: 12 m N of Nottingham on A60 (Mansfield Rd). Close to junction 27 of the M1. By Bus: (Trent no's 63 and x2) from Nottingham Victoria Coach Station, drops off at Abbey gates (1 m from house).
Station(s): Newstead Village Station 1 mile w/days on hr Sat on ½ hr Sun no service.
Open: House 1 Apr-last w/end Sept daily 12-6. Gardens all year 10-dusk (except last Fri in Nov)
Admission: House and Gardens: £3.50, Reductions £2, Gardens only: £1.70, Reductions £1.
Refreshments: Tea room and licensed restaurant in grounds, tel (01623) 797392.
Conferences: Corporate hospitality- Ring Kevan Jackson. Nott. (01159) 483500 ext.14016

PAPPLEWICK HALL
(Dr R.B. Godwin-Austen)
Near Nottingham   NG15 8FE   map **7** Q20   △
Telephone: (0115) 9633491

Fine Adam house built 1784 with lovely plasterwork ceilings. Park and woodland garden, particularly known for its rhododendrons.
Location: 6 m N Nottingham off A60. 2 m from exit 27 M1.
Open: By appointment only, all year.
Refreshments: By arrangement
Events/Exhibitions: 3rd Sat June annual fête and Maypole dancing.
Accommodation: Country House hospitality, full breakfast and dinner, prices on request.
Conferences: Up to 30 people.

THRUMPTON HALL
(Mrs George Seymour)
Nottingham   NG11 0AX   map **7** Q20   △ &
Telephone: (0115) 9830333

Fine Jacobean house, built 1607, incorporating earlier manor house. Priest's hiding hole, magnificent Charles II carved staircase carved and panelled saloon and other fine rooms containing beautiful 17th and 18th century furniture and many fine portraits. Large lawns separated from landscaped park by ha-ha and by lake. This house retains the atmosphere of a home, being lived in by owners who will show parties around.
Location: 7 m S of Nottingham; 3 m E of M1 at junction 24; 1 m from A453.
Open: By appointment for parties of 20 or more persons. Open all year including evenings.
Admission: House and Gardens £4 children £2. Minimum charge of £80.
Refreshments: By prior arrangement.
Events/Exhibitions: To be arranged.
Conferences: Up to 50, also business lunches.

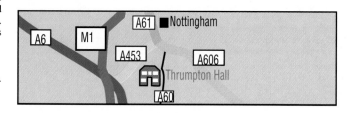

WOLLATON HALL
(City of Nottingham)
Nottingham   map **7** R20
Telephone: (0115) 9281333 or 281130

Fine example of late Elizabethan Renaissance architecture. Natural History Museum.
Location: 2½ m W of City centre.
Station(s): Nottingham (2¾ m).
Open: All the year. Apr to Sept: weekdays 10-7, Suns 2-5; Oct to Mar: weekdays 10-dusk, Suns 1.30-4.30.*Closed Christmas Day.*
Admission: Free (Small charge Suns and Bank Hols). Conducted tours by arrangement £1, Chd 50p (Subject to alteration).
Refreshments: Tea at refreshment pavilion all year.

OXFORDSHIRE

ARDINGTON HOUSE
(Mrs Desmond Baring)
nr Wantage   OX12 8QA   map **5** T20   △ Ⓔ
Telephone: (01235) 833244

Early 18th century of grey brick with red brick facings. Hall with Imperial staircase, panelled dining room with painted ceiling. Attractive Stable Yard.
Location: 12 m S of Oxford; 12 m N of Newbury; 2½ m E of Wantage.
Station(s): Didcot (8 m).
Open: May-Sept Mons & all Bank Hols 2.30-4.30 parties of 10 or more welcomed any day by appointment.
Admission: House & Grounds £2.50
Refreshments: Coffee & Teas by arrangement.

BLENHEIM PALACE

(His Grace the Duke of Marlborough)
Woodstock   OX20 1PX   map **5** T20   △ Ⓢ
Telephone: (01993) 811325 (24 hr information)
Fax: (01993) 813527

Blenheim Palace is the home of the Duke of Marlborough and birthplace of Sir Winston Churchill was built for John Churchill, 1st Duke of Marlborough, by Vanbrugh. A gift from Queen Anne, and a grateful nation to the victor of the Battle of Blenheim, 1704, the Palace, which is in the Baroque style, is set in 2100 acres of parkland landscaped by 'Capability' Brown who also created Blenheim's lake and significantly altered the original gardens of Henry Wise. Close to Oxford and next to the historic town of Woodstock, the Palace is easily accessible by car, train and coach. An inclusive ticket covers the Palace tour, Park, Gardens, Butterfly House, Motor Launch, Train, Adventure Play Area, Nature Trail and Car Parking. The Marlborough Maze and Rowing Boat Hire (on Queen Pool) are optional extras. 1996 events include the annual Charity Cricket Match (June 9), the International Horse Trials (Sept 19-22), Craft Fairs on the May Day and August Bank Holiday weekends Outdoor Concerts on 22 June and 9/10 August and various other events which will be publicised in the local press. For further details apply to Administrator's Office, Blenheim Palace, Woodstock, Oxon. OX20 1PX.

Location: SW end of Woodstock which lies 8 m N of Oxford (A44).
Station(s): Oxford
Open: Mid Mar-Oct 31 daily 10.30-5.30 (last adm 4.45)
Admission: Charges not available at time of going to press.
Refreshments: Licensed Restaurant & Self Service Cafeteria at the Palace. Self Service Cafeteria at Pleasure Gardens.
Events/Exhibitions: See above.
Conferences: The Orangery and Spencer Churchill Rooms are available for Conferences and Corporate Hospitality. Tel (01993) 813874.
Education Service. A Sandford award holder since 1982. The right to close the Palace or Park without notice is reserved.

BROUGHTON CASTLE
(The Lord Saye & Sele)
Banbury   OX15 5EB   map **5** S20
Telephone: (01295) 262624

Broughton Castle is essentially a family home lived in by Lord and Lady Saye and Sele and their family. The original medieval Manor House, of which much remains today was built about 1300 by Sir John de Broughton. It stands on an island site surrounded by a 3 acre moat. The Castle was greatly enlarged between 1550 and 1600, at which time it was embellished with magnificent plaster ceilings, splendid panelling and fine fireplaces. In the 17th century, William 8th Lord Saye and Sele, played a leading role in national affairs. He opposed Charles I's efforts to rule without Parliament and Broughton became a secret meeting place for the King's opponents. During the Civil War, William raised a regiment and he and his 4 sons all fought at the nearby Battle of Edgehill. After the battle, the Castle was beseiged and captured. Arms and armour from the Civil War and other periods are displayed in the Great Hall. Visitors may also see the Gatehouse, Garden and Park together with the nearby 14th century Church of St. Mary in which there are many family tombs, memorials and hatchments. The garden consists of mixed herbaceous and shrub borders containing many old roses. In addition, there is a formal walled garden with beds of roses surrounded by box hedging and lined by more mixed borders.

Location: 2 m SW of Banbury on the Shipston-on-Stour Road (B4035).
Station(s): Banbury.
Open: May 18- Sept 14 Weds & Suns 2-5 also Thurs in July & Aug 2-5 Bank Hol Suns & Bank Hol Mons including Easter 2-5.
Admission: Adults £3.50 OAPs/students £3 children £2 (1996). Groups on other days throughout the year by appointment (reduced rates).
Refreshments: Buffet teas on open days; by arrangement for groups.
Conferences: For Corporate Events the Park is available for private hire.
Castle and Gardens available for product launches, film and T.V. location work.

BUSCOT OLD PARSONAGE   🌿 The National Trust
Buscot, Faringdon   SN7 8DQ   map **5** T19   △
Location: 2 m SE of Lechlade; 4 m NW of Faringdon on A417.

BUSCOT PARK   🌿 The National Trust
nr Faringdon   SN7 8BU   map **5** T19   △
Telephone: (01367) 242094 (not weekends)
Location: 3 m NW Faringdon on Lechlade/Faringdon road (A417).

DITCHLEY PARK
(Ditchley Foundation)
Enstone   OX7 4ER   map **5** T20   △
Telephone: (01608) 677346
Fax: (01608) 677399

Third in size and date of the great 18th century houses of Oxfordshire, Ditchley is famous for its splendid interior decorations (William Kent and Henry Flitcroft). For three and half centuries the home of the Lee family and their descendants - Ditchley was frequently visited at weekends by Sir Winston Churchill during World War II. It has now been restored, furnished and equipped as a conference centre devoted to the study of issues of concern to the people on both sides of the Atlantic.

Location: 1½ m W of A44 at Kiddington; 2 m from Charlbury (B4437).
Station(s): Charlbury (2 m).
Open: Group visits by prior arrangement with the Bursar, Mon, Tues and Thurs afternoons only. Closed July-mid Sept.
Admission: House opening fee £30. Entry fee £4 per person.

FAWLEY COURT - MARIAN FATHERS HISTORIC HOUSE & MUSEUM

(Marian Fathers)
Henley-on-Thames   RG9 3AE   map **12** T21
Telephone: (01491) 574917

Designed by Sir Christopher Wren, Fawley Court was built in 1684 for Colonel William Freeman as a family residence. The Mansion House, decorated by Grinling Gibbons and later by James Wyatt, is situated in a beautiful park designed by Lancelot 'Capability' Brown. The Museum consists of a library, various documents of the Polish kings, a very rare and well preserved collection of historical sabres and many memorable military objects of the Polish Army. There are classical sculptures, and paintings from Renaissance and later times. Fawley Court also serves nowadays as a seat of religious community, and from 1953 has been cared for, maintained and restored by the Congregation of Marian Fathers.

Location: 1 m N of Henley-on-Thames via A4155 to Marlow.
Station(s): Henley-on-Thames (1½ m).
Open: Mar-Oct Wed Thurs Sun 2-5 closed Easter and Whitsuntide weeks. Nov and Feb open to groups by pre-booked appointment.
Admission: Adults £3 OAPs £2 children £1.
Refreshments: Tea, coffee & home-made cakes available.
Car park. No dogs.

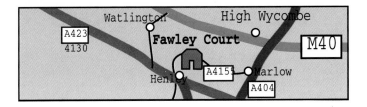

Sir Peter Lely - portrait painter

His paintings can be seen at the following properties included in Historic Houses Castles and Gardens:-

Aynhoe Park   Kedleston Hall
Belton House   Knole
Breamore House   Petworth House
Browsholme Hall   Ragley Hall
Dalmeny House   Rockingham Castle
Euston Hall   St Osyth Priory
Goodwood House   Stanford Hall
Gorhambury   Weston Park

KELMSCOTT MANOR

Kelmscott, nr Lechlade   GL7 3HJ   map **5** T19
Telephone: (01367) 252486
Fax: (01367) 253754

Kelmscott Manor was the country home of William Morris, poet, craftsman and socialist from 1871 until his death in 1896. The house contains a collection of the possessions and works of Morris and his associates including furniture, textiles carpets and ceramics.

Location: 2 miles south east of Lechlade off the Lechlade/Faringdon Rd.
Open: April-Sept: Wed 11am-1pm 2pm-5pm & the third Sat in each month 2-6pm. Thurs and Fri by appointment.
Admission: Adult £6 Child £3 Students £3.
Refreshments: Restaurant serving light refreshments.
Events/Exhibitions: 1996 Centenary exhibition: "William Morris at Kelmscott". Giftshop and bookshop.

KINGSTON BAGPUIZE HOUSE

(Mr and Mrs Francis Grant)
Kingston Bagpuize, Abingdon   OX13 5AX   map **5** T20   △ ㄴ (garden only)
Telephone: (01865) 820259

Beautiful Charles II manor House with cantilevered staircase, well proportioned panelled rooms and some good furniture and pictures. Surrounded by mature parkland the gardens, including shrub border and woodland garden, contain many interesting and unusual trees, shrubs, perennials and bulbs.

Location: 5½ m W of Abingdon (A415 near A420 interchange).
Station(s): Oxford or Didcot.
Open: 2.30-5.30 (last adm 5pm) Apr 6/7/8/17/20/21 May4/5/6/25/26/27 June12/15/16 July 17/20/21 Aug 7/10/11/24/25/26 Sept 4/7/8/18/21/22
Admission: House and Garden adults £3 OAPs £2.50 children £2. Garden only £1. (children not admitted to House). Gardens only: £1 (children under 5 free). Groups welcome by written appointment Feb-Nov rates on request.
Refreshments: Teas.
Wheelchairs garden only. No dogs. Small gift shop. Car parking.

MAPLEDURHAM HOUSE AND WATERMILL

(J J Eyston and Lady Anne Eyston)
Mapledurham   RG4 7TR   map **5** U20   △
Telephone: (01734) 723350
Fax: (01734) 724016

Late 16th century Elizabethan home of the Blount family. Original plaster ceilings, great oak staircase, fine collection of paintings and private chapel in Strawberry Hill Gothic added in 1797. Interesting literary connections with Alexander Pope, John Galsworthy's Forsyte Saga and Kenneth Graham's Wind in the Willows. Unique setting in grounds running down to the Thames. The 15th century Watermill is fully restored and producing flour and bran which are sold in the gift shop. Film set for "Eagle has Landed" and "Class Act".

Location: 4 m NW of Reading on North Bank of Thames. Signed off A4074.
Open: Sat Sun and Bank Hols 12.30-5. Midweek parties by arrangement. Easter to end Sept.
Admission: House & Mill £4 House only £3 Mill £2.50. Children under 14 half price. Weekend parties £3.80.
Refreshments: Tea-rooms serving cream teas.
Events/Exhibitions: By arrangement.
Accommodation: Eleven self catering holiday cottages.
Conferences: By arrangement.
Wedding receptions by arrangement. Car parking and picnic area.

NUFFIELD PLACE

(Nuffield College, Friends of Nuffield Place)
Nettlebed   map **5** T20
Telephone: (01491) 641224

The home from 1933-1963 of Lord Nuffield, founder of Morris Motors, Nuffield Place is a rare survival of a complete upper-middle class home of the 1930s. Built in 1914, the house was enlarged in 1933 for Lord Nuffield. Several rooms are still decorated in the 30's style, and all rooms contain furnishings acquired by Lord and Lady Nuffield when they took up residence. Clocks, rugs and some tapestries are of fine quality. Some of the furniture is antique but much was custom made by Cecil A. Halliday of Oxford, and is of skilled craftsmanship. The gardens, with mature trees, stone walls and rockery, were laid out during and just after the First World War. Lady Nuffield's Wolseley car is also on display.

Location: Approximately 7 m from Henley-on-Thames, just off A4130 formerly A423 to Oxford.
Station(s): Henley-on-Thames 6m. Well served by 390 Thames Transit coach service Victoria-Witney.
Open: May-Sept every 2nd and 4th Sun 2-5.
Admission: Adults £3.00 concessions £2.00 children 50p. Garden only £1. Parties by arrangement. Tel: (01491) 825556.
Refreshments: Home-made teas.
Ground floor and garden suitable for disabled, but no disabled lavatory.

George Stubbs
Portrait, animal and rural painter

(1724-1806)

His work can be seen in the following properties included in Historic Houses Castles and Gardens:-

Mount Stewart House
St Osyth Priory
Upton House

ROUSHAM HOUSE

(C Cottrell-Dormer, Esq)
Steeple Aston   map **5** T20   △
Telephone: (01869) 347110 or (0860) 360407

Rousham House was built by Sir Robert Dormer in 1635 and the shooting holes were put in the doors while it was a Royalist garrison in the Civil War. Sir Robert's successors were Masters of Ceremonies at Court during eight reigns and employed Court artists and architects to embellish Rousham. The house stands above the River Cherwell one mile from Hopcrofts Holt, near the road from Chipping Norton to Bicester. It contains 150 portraits and other pictures and much fine contemporary furniture. Rooms were decorated by William Kent (1738) and Roberts of Oxford (1765). The garden is Kent's only surviving landscape design with classic buildings, cascades, statues and vistas in thirty acres of hanging woods above the Cherwell. Wonderful herbaceous borders, pigeon house and small parterre. Fine herd of rare Long-Horn cattle in the park. Wear sensible shoes and bring a picnic, and Rousham is yours for the day.

Location: 12 m N of Oxford east of A4260 south of B4030.
Station(s): Heyford (1 m).
Open: Apr-Sept inclusive Wed Sun & Bank Hols 2-4.30. Gardens only every day all year 10-4.30. No children under 15. No dogs. Groups by arrangement on other days.
Admission: House adults £2.50. Garden £2.50.

STANTON HARCOURT MANOR
(Mr Crispin & The Hon Mrs Gascoigne)
Stanton Harcourt   map **5** T20   &
Telephone: (01865) 881928

Unique medieval buildings in tranquil surroundings - Old Kitchen, Pope's Tower and Domestic Chapel. House maintained as family home, contains fine collection of pictures, furniture, silver and porcelain. 12 acres of Garden with Great Fish Pond and Stew Ponds.

Location: 9 m W of Oxford; 5 m SE of Witney; off B4449, between Eynsham & Standlake.
Open: Apr 7 8 18 21 May 2 5 6 16 19 26 27 June 6 9 20 23 July 4 7 18 21 Aug 1 4 15 18 25 26 Sept 5 8 19 22 open 2-6 pm.
Admission: House and Gardens adults £4 children (12 and under)/OAPs £2. Gardens only adults £2.50 children (12 and under)/OAPs £1.50. Coaches by arrangement.
Refreshments: Teas on Suns and Bank Hols in aid of Parish Church.
Disabled visitors welcome. Home container-grown shrubs and pot plants for sale.

STONOR PARK
(Lord & Lady Camoys)
nr Henley-on-Thames   RG9 6HF   map **12** T21
Telephone: (01491) 638587
Fax: (01491) 638587

Ancient home of Lord and Lady Camoys and the Stonor family for over eight hundred years, and centre of Catholicism throughout the Recusancy Period, with its own medieval Chapel where mass is still celebrated today. Sanctuary for St. Edmund Campion in 1581. An exhibition features his life and work. The house is of considerable architectural interest, built over many centuries from c.1190, and the site of prehistoric stone circle, now recreated within the grounds. A family home containing fine family portraits and rare items of furniture, paintings, drawings, tapestries, sculptures and bronzes from Britain, Europe and America. Peaceful hillside gardens with magnificent roses and ornamental ponds. Now featuring exhibition of stone sculpture from Zimbabwe. Souvenir gift shop and afternoon tearoom serving home-made cakes. Parties welcome, lunches available by prior arrangement.

Location: On B480; 5 m N of Henley-on-Thames, 5 m S of Watlington.
Station(s): Henley-on-Thames.
Open: Apr - Suns and Bank Hol Mons only; May - Weds, Suns and Bank Hol Mons; June - Weds and Suns; July - Weds, Thurs and Suns; Aug Weds, Thurs, Sats, Suns and Bank Hol Mons; Sept - Weds and Suns 2-5.30 on each occasion - last admissions at 5pm. Parties by prior arrangement in addition to the above times on Tues, Weds and Thurs throughout the season morning or afternoons. Minimum number 12 on public days, 20 for private visits.
Admission: House and Gardens adults £4 children (under 14 with adult) free. Gardens and Chapel only £2. Group rate £3.50 subject to group payment on arrival. Private tours are charged at the full rate of £4 per person.
Refreshments: Tea-room. Group lunches and suppers by arrangement.

WALLINGFORD CASTLE GARDENS

Castle Street, Wallingford   map **5** T20
Telephone: (01491) 835373
Fax: (01491) 826550

These Gardens are situated on part of the site of Wallingford Castle, which was built by William the Conqueror and demolished by Oliver Cromwell in 1652. The remains of St Nicholas Priory are a feature of the Gardens, which is a haven of beauty and tranquillity.

Location: Bear Lane, Castle Street.
Open: Apr-Oct 10-6 Nov-Mar 10-3.
Admission: Free.
Events/Exhibitions: Band concerts somer summer Sundays. Telephone for details. Britain in Bloom winner 1993.
Car parking in the town.

WATERPERRY GARDENS

nr Wheatley   map **5** T20
Telephone: (01844) 339226/339254
Fax: (01844) 339883

Spacious and peaceful ornamental gardens of 6 acres. Church of Saxon origin and historical interest in grounds with famous old glass, brasses and woodwork. Many interesting plants. Shrub, Herbaceous and Alpine Nurseries.

Location: 2½ m from A40, turn off at Wheatley. 50 m from London, 9 m from Oxford. 62 m Birmingham M40, junction 8. Well signposted locally with Tourist Board Rose' symbol.
Station(s): Oxford & Thame Parkway.
Open: All the year. Daily Mar-Oct 10-5.30 (weekdays) 10-6 (weekends) Nov-Feb 10-5 (Tea-shop closes 30 mins earlier) closed for Christmas and New Year Hols. Open only to visitors to ART IN ACTION (enquiries 0171-381 3192) July 18-21. Parties and coaches at all times by appointment only. High quality Plant Centre and Garden Shop, telephone: (01844) 339226. In aid of National Gardens' June 9 & Aug 11.
Admission: Ornamental Gardens & Nurseries Mar-Oct £2.30 Nov-Feb 85p.
Refreshments: The Pear Tree Tea-shop for morning coffee, light lunches and teas. Wine licence. Tel (01844) 338087.
Gallery: A new Art and Crafts Gallery exhibiting and selling quality ceramics, glass and jewellery etc. Tel (01844) 338085.

SHROPSHIRE

ADCOTE

(Adcote School Educational Trust Ltd)
Little Ness, nr Shrewsbury   SY4 2JY   map **6** R17
Telephone: (01939) 260202
Fax: (01939) 261300

'Adcote is the most controlled, coherent and masterly of the big country houses designed by Norman Shaw' (Mark Girouard, 'Country Life' Oct 1970).

Location: 7 m NW of Shrewsbury off A5.
Open: Apr 23-July 12 (except May 24-28 inclusive) 2-5pm re-open Sept 9-Oct 18. All other times by appointment.
Admission: Free but the Governors reserve the right to make a charge.
Refreshments: For large parties by prior booking only

ATTINGHAM PARK   ⚘ The National Trust

nr Shrewsbury   SY4 4TP   map **6** R17   ⅙
Telephone: (01743) 709203
Fax: (01743) 709352

An imposing neo-classical house, built for the 1st Lord Berwick by George Steuart in 1785. The elegant interiors are furnished with the Regency collections of two brothers, the 2nd and 3rd Lords Berwick, one a bankrupt and the other a diplomat. The painted boudoir and the top-lit picture gallery by John Nash are outstanding in a house full of memorable interiors. Attractive walks through the park, landscaped by Humphry Repton in 1797.

Location: At Atcham; 4 m SE of Shrewsbury, on B4380.
Station(s): Shrewsbury 5 m.
Open: Mar 30-Sept 30 Sat-Wed 1.30-5pm (Bank Hol Mons 11-5). Oct Sat & Sun 1.30-5. Last adm 4.30. Tea-room: open same days as house, 12.30-5, Bank Hol Mon 11-5. Shop open as tea-room. Guided tours and pre-booked parties, including evening opening, by arrangement. Park open daily (except Christmas Day) Mar-Oct 8-8; Nov-Feb 8-5.
Admission: House & Grounds £3.50 children £1.75 Family ticket £8.70. Deer Park & Grounds £1.40.
Refreshments: Light lunches 12.30-2.30 and home-made teas 2.30-5 Bank Holiday Mon 11-5. Licensed. Lunches and suppers at other times for pre-booked parties.
Events/Exhibitions: "The 1796 Election: Policies or Pints?".
Conferences: Small groups, up to 50, by arrangement.
Dogs in grounds only (Not in deer park). Wheelchairs available and lift in house. Battery vehicle available for use in grounds. Gift shop. Baby changing room.

BENTHALL HALL   ⚘ The National Trust

Broseley   TF12 5RX   map **6** R17
Telephone: (01952) 882159
Location: 1 m NW of Broseley; 4 m NE of Much Wenlock; 6 m S of Wellington, (B4375).

BURFORD HOUSE GARDENS

(Treasures of Tenbury Ltd)
Tenbury Wells   WR15 8HQ   map **6** S17   △ ⅙
Telephone: (01584) 810777
Fax: (01584) 810673

In the 1950's the late John Treasure transformed the setting of this Georgian House by the River Teme into a garden of quiet serenity and fascination. Four acres of sweeping lawns and serpentine beds display over 2,000 varieties of plants, including the National Collection of Clematis, many of which are for sale in Treasure Plant Centre adjacent. Also on site is the Burford House Gallery, Craft Shop and Craft Workshops.

Location: 8m from Ludlow, 1 m W of Tenbury Wells on the A456.
Open: All year daily 10-5. Evening by arrangement.
Admission: £2.50, Children £1, Groups of 10+ £2 per person.
Refreshments: Burford Buttery serving hot and cold meals, homemade cakes and soups, specialist coffees and traditional teas; licensed.
Two wheelchairs available for use.

CARDING MILL VALLEY & LONG MYND
⚘ The National Trust

Church Stretton   SY6 6JG   map **6** R17
Telephone: (01694) 722631
Location: 15 m S of Shrewsbury; W of Church Stretton Valley & A49.

CASTLE GATES LIBRARY

Shrewsbury   SY1 2AS   map **6** R17
Telephone: (01743) 241487
Fax: (01743) 368576

Former premises of Shrewsbury Grammar School.

CONDOVER HALL

(Royal National Institute for the Blind)
nr Shrewsbury

DUDMASTON   ⚘ The National Trust

Quatt, Bridgnorth   WV15 6QN   map **14** S18   ⅙
Telephone: (01746) 780866

Late 17th century house; collections of Dutch flower paintings, modern art, botanical paintings and family history. Extensive grounds, woodlands and lakeside garden. Estate walks open all year.

Location: 4 m SE of Bridgnorth on A442.
Station(s): Bridgnorth (Severn Valley Railway) 4 m Kidderminster 10 m.
Open: Mar 31-Sept 29 Wed & Sun 2-5.30 (last adm 5). Special opening for pre-booked parties Thur 2-5.30.
Admission: House and Gardens £3.50 Child £1.50 Family £8. Garden only £2.50 Party £2.90.
Refreshments: 1-5.30 (light lunches 1-2). Light lunches for booked parties by arrangement on Wed & Thurs.
Dogs in Dingle, Park and Estate only, on leads. Shop. Electric mobility vehicle available for use in garden.

HAWKSTONE HALL AND GARDENS
(The Redemptorists)
Weston-U-Redcastle   SY4 5LG   map **6** R17   &
Telephone: (01630) 685242
Fax: (01630) 685565

Grade 1 Georgian Mansion and Gardens set in spacious parkland. From 1556 to 1906 Hawkstone was the seat of the distinguished HILL family of Shropshire. The principal rooms include the Venetian Saloon, the Ballroom, the Drawing Room and the Winter Garden. The Gardens comprise terraces and lawns, rose garden, lily pool and extensive woodland with a magnificent collection of trees.

Location: Entrance at MARCHAMLEY, on A442, 2 m N of HODNET.
Open: 5-31 Aug 2-5pm.
Admission: £2.50.

HAWKSTONE PARK
(Hawkstone Park Leisure Ltd)
Weston-under-Redcastle   SY4 5UY   map **6** R17
Telephone: (01939) 200300/200611
Fax: (01939) 200311
Location: 10 m N of Shrewsbury off A49 or A53. 3 m from village of Hodnet.

HODNET HALL GARDENS
(Mr & the Hon Mrs Heber-Percy)
nr Market Drayton   TF9 3NN   map **6** R17   &
Telephone: (01630) 685202
Fax: (01630) 685853

From the glorious daffodils of Spring to the magnificent roses of Summer, each season brings fresh delights to these award winning gardens. Over 60 acres of magnificent forest trees, sweeping lawns and tranquil pools ensure plentiful wildlife and brilliant natural colour within this beautiful setting.

Location: 12 m NE of Shrewsbury; 5½ m SW of Market Drayton, at junction of A53 to A442; M6 18½ m (junction 15) leading to A53 or M54 (junction 3).
Open: Beginning Apr-end Sept. Adults £2.80 child £1 OAP £2.30. Reduced rates for organ-ised parties of 25 or over. Season tickets on application. Free car and coach park.

Admission: Adults £2.60 OAPs £2.10 children £1 (1994 prices). Reduced rates for organ-ised parties of 25 or over. Season tickets on application. Free car and coach park.
Refreshments: Tea-rooms open daily during Gardens opening hours. *Parties to pre-book (menu on request). Gift shop, kitchen garden sales.*
Dogs allowed but must be kept on leads.

LUDFORD HOUSE
(Mr D.F.A. Nicholson)
Ludlow   SY8 1PJ   map **6** S17
Telephone: (01584) 872542
Fax: (01584) 875662

House dating back to 12th century.

Location: ½ m S of Ludlow, B4361 road.
Station(s): Ludlow.
Open: Grounds and exterior by written permission, with limited inspection of interior.
Admission: £3.
Refreshments: Hotels and Restaurants in Ludlow available.
Unsuitable for disabled.

LUDLOW CASTLE
(The Trustees of the Powis Castle Estate)
Castle Square, Ludlow   map **6** R17
Telephone: (01584) 873947 - Custodian or (01584) 873355 - Castle Ticket Office

Originally a Norman Castle of which the remains include the round nave of a Chapel with fine Norman doorways. Then a fortified Royal Palace and head-quarters of the Council of the Marches. An unusually complete range of medieval buildings still stands. Visitors can enjoy the large open space of the outer bailey, gift shop and exhibition gallery. Audio tape guides available.

Location: Castle Square, Ludlow.
Station(s): Ludlow
Open: Daily Feb 1-Apr 30 10.30-4, May 1-Sept 30 10.30-5, Oct 1-Dec 24 10.30-4. Closed January.
Admission: Adults £2.50, children £1.50, OAPs £2, family ticket £7.50, discounts for school parties by arrangement with the Custodian.
Refreshments: In Castle Square.
Events/Exhibitions: Craft Fair May 25-27; Ludlow Festival June 22-July 7.
Public car park off Castle Square. Suitable for the disabled with assistance.

MAWLEY HALL
Cleobury Mortimer map **14** S18

18th century house attributed to Francis Smith. Fine plasterwork and panelling.

Location: 1 m S of Cleobury Mortimer (A4117); 7 m W of Bewdley.
Open: Apr 16 to July 17th Tues & Wed 2.30-5. Visitors must give advance notice to Mrs R Sharpe, 43 Dover Street, London W1X 3RE. Tel (0171) 495 6702.
Admission: £3.

MOAT HOUSE
(Mr & Mrs C. P. Richards)
Longnor, nr Shrewsbury   SY5 7PP map **6** R17 △
Telephone: (01743) 718434
Fax: (01743) 718434

Fine example of a timber framed manor house of c1463. The hall exhibiting unique timber work and wooden masks, Surrounded by its moat of c1250.

Location: 8 m S of Shrewsbury E off A49 through village left into lane.
Open: Apr-Sept Thurs & Spring & Summer Bank Hols 2.30-5 other times by arrangement for parties of 20 plus.
Admission: £2.
Accommodation for four, dinner if pre booked, licensed, brochure available. No dogs. Not suitable for disabled.

SHIPTON HALL
(J.N.R.N. Bishop, Esq)
Much Wenlock   TF13 6JZ map **6** R17 △
Telephone: (01746) 785225

Delightful Elizabethan stone manor c.1587 with Georgian additions. Interesting Roccoco and Gothic plasterwork by T. F. Pritchard. Georgian stable block containing working pottery. Stone walled garden, medieval dovecote, and Parish Church dating from late Saxon period.

Location: In Shipton; 6 m SW of Much Wenlock junction B4376 & B4368.
Station(s): Craven Arms (10 M) Telford (14 M) Ludlow (14 M)
Open: Easter-end Sept Thurs Bank Holiday Suns and Mons (except Christmas and New Year) 2.30-5.30 also by appointment for parties of 20 or more any time of year.
Admission: House and Garden £2.50 children £1.50 special rate for parties.
Refreshments: Teas/buffets by prior arrangement.

STOKESAY CASTLE
Craven Arms map **6** R17
Telephone: (01588) 672544

A rare and wonderfully preserved example of a 13th century fortified manor house situated in peaceful countryside. The castle now stands in a picturesque group with its own splendid timber-framed Jacobean gatehouse and the parish church.

Location: 8 m from Ludlow; ¾ m S of Craven Arms on 3rd class Road off A49.
Station(s): Craven Arms (1 m).
Open: Apr 1-Sept 30 daily 10-6 Oct 1-31 daily 10-4, Nov 1-Mar 31 Wed-Sun 10-4.
Admission: Adults £2.50 concessions £1.90 children £1.30. Party bookings in advance.

UPTON CRESSETT HALL
(William Cash, Esq)
Bridgnorth map **14** R18
Telephone: (01746) 714 307
Fax: (01734) 714 506

Elizabethan Manor House and magnificent Gatehouse in beautiful countryside by Norman church. Unusually fine medieval timber work and interesting brick and plaster work; 14th century Great Hall.

Location: 4 m W of Bridgnorth; 18 m SE of Shrewsbury off A458.
Open: By appointment only. Parties welcome throughout the year.
Admission: Adults £2.50 children £1.
Accommodation: Self catering accommodation available in Gatehouse.

WALCOT HALL
(C.R.W. Parish)
Lydbury North, Nr Bishops Castle   SY7 8AZ map **6** R17
Telephone: 0171-581 2782
Fax: 0171-589 0195

Built by Sir William Chambers for Lord Clive of India. This Georgian House possesses a free-standing and recently restored Ballroom, stable yard with matching clock towers, extensive walled garden, in addition to its icehouse, meat safe and dovecote. There is a fine arboretum, noted for its rhododendrons and azaleas and specimen trees.

Location: 3 m E of Bishop's Castle, on B4385, ½ m outside Lydbury North.
Station(s): Craven Arms.
Open: Bank Hols Sun & Mon (except Christmas and New Year) May Sun Wed & Fri Jun Wed & Fri Jul & Aug Sun Sept Wed 2.15-4.30. Groups of 10 or more and other times, by appointment.

Admission: Adults £2.50 children (under 15) free.
Refreshments: Powis Arms; teas when available.
Accommodation: Holiday accommodation; 3 flats and Ground Floor Wing available all year.
Conferences: Magnificent ballroom: Licensed for Civil Weddings; Anniversaries; Celebrations; Conferences, with Estate suitable for Film and Photographic Locations etc. Suitable for disabled.

WENLOCK PRIORY
Much Wenlock map **6** R17
Telephone: (01952) 727466

The long history of Wenlock stretches back to the 7th century, although nothing visible remains of the religious house founded by St Milburge. After the Norman Conquest, a Cluniac priory was established, which came to be regarded as alien during the Hundred Years' War with France. Decorative arcading from the 12th century chapter house survives and some unusual features in the later, rebuilt church.

Location: In Much Wenlock.
Open: Apr 1-Sept 30 10-6 daily, 1-31 Oct 10-6 or dusk if earlier, daily Nov 1-Mar 31 (closed 1-2) Wed-Sun 10-4.
Admission: Adults £2 concessions £1.50 children £1. Price includes a Personal Stereo Guided Tour.

WESTON PARK
(Weston Park Foundation)
nr Shifnal   TF11 8LE map **14** R18 &
Telephone: (01952) 850207
Fax: (01952) 850430

Built 1671 and designed by Lady Wilbraham, contains a superb collection of antiques and paintings including works by Van Dyck, Lely and Gainsborough. Set in 1000 acres of classic 'Capability' Brown Parkland and formal gardens including restored Rose Garden, Italian Broderie. Fine Arboretum. Miniature Railway, Woodland Adventure Playground, Museum and Pets Corner. Horse Trials, Classical Concerts and other special events throughout the Summer. Conferences and private events all year.

Location: Entrance from A5 at Weston-under-Lizard, 6 m W of Junction 12, M6 (Gailey); 3 m N of Junction 3, M54 (Tong).
Station(s): Wolverhampton or Stafford.
Open: Easter: Apr 6th, 7th, 8th & 9th. May 4-June 9 weekends, Bank Hols and Whit week (May 25th-June 2nd). June 10-July 28 daily except Mons and Fri. July 29-Sept 1 open daily. Sept 2-15 open weekends. Park 11-7pm (last admission 5). House 1-5 (last admission 4.30).
Admission: House, Park and Gardens adults £5 children £3 OAPs £3.75. Park and Gardens adults £3.50 children £2 OAPs £2.50
Refreshments: Traditional country cooking in The Old Stables Tea-rooms and Licensed Bar. Restaurant service for pre-booked parties. Gourmet Dinners in the House on selected dates. Private functions incl. residential dinners and wedding receptions by arrangement.
Events/Exhibitions: Weston Park offers a full event organisation service with special events throughout the year.
Accommodation: 28 delightful bedrooms with bathrooms, 18 doubles, 7 twins and 3 singles.
Conferences: The Midlands' premier venue for meetings and conferences from 10-200 delegates. Dogs (on leads) welcome in Park.

WILDERHOPE MANOR   🦌 The National Trust
Longville   TF13 6EG map **6** R17 &
Telephone: (01694) 771363
Location: 7 m SW of Much Wenlock; ½ m S of B4371.

WROXETER (VIROCONIUM) ROMAN CITY   ENGLISH HERITAGE
map **6** R17
Telephone: (01743) 761330

Viroconium was the fourth largest city in Roman Britain and the largest to escape modern development. Deep beneath the exposed walls of the market-hall excavations are revealing a legionary fortress of the first century; while nearby the timber buildings of later settlers are being examined. The most impressive feature is the huge wall dividing the exercise yard from the baths.

Location: 5½ m (8.8 km) south east of Shrewsbury.
Open: Apr 1-Sept 30 10-6 daily, 1-31 Oct 10-6 or dusk if earlier, daily Nov 1-Mar 31 (closed 1-2) 10-4 Wed-Sun.
Admission: Adults £2.50 concessions £1.90 children £1.30.

SOMERSET

BARFORD PARK
(Mr & Mrs Michael Stancomb)
Enmore   TA5 1AG   map **3** U16
Telephone: (01278) 671269

Set in a large garden and looking out across a ha-ha to a park dotted with fine trees, it presents a scene of peaceful domesticity, a miniature country seat on a scale appropriate today. The well proportioned rooms, with contemporary furniture, are all in daily family use. The walled flower garden is in full view from the house, and the woodland and water gardens and archery glade with their handsome trees form a perfect setting for the stone and red-brick Queen Anne building.

Location: 5m W of Bridwater
Open: May-Sept by appointment.
Admission: Charges not available at the time of going to press.
Refreshments: Tea and Buffet Luncheons for groups, by arrangement.

BARRINGTON COURT   🦌 The National Trust
Nr Ilminster   TA19 0NQ   map **3** V17
Telephone: (01460) 241938
Location: In Barrington village, 5 m NE of Ilminster on B3168 visitors approaching from A303 follow signs for Ilminster town centre. (193: ST397182).

Butterfly Houses

can be found at the following properties included in Historic Houses Castles and Gardens:-

Berkeley Castle
Elsham Hall - Wild butterfly walkway
Syon House

THE BISHOP'S PALACE
(The Church Commissioners)
Wells   BA5 2PD   map **14** U17
Telephone: (01749) 678691 The Marketing Director; The Henderson Rooms
Fax: (01749) 678691

The fortified and moated mediaeval Palace unites the early 13th century first floor hall (known as The Henderson Rooms), the late 13th century Chapel and the now ruined Great Hall also the 15th century wing which is today the private residence of the Bishop of Bath and Wells. The extensive grounds, where rise the springs that give Wells its name, are a beautiful setting for borders of herbaceous plants, roses, shrubs, mature trees and the Jubilee Arboretum. The Moat is home to a collection of waterfowl and swans.

Location: City of Wells: enter from the Market Place through the Bishop's Eye or from the Cathedral Cloisters, over the Drawbridge.
Station(s): Bath, Bristol.
Open: The Henderson Rooms, Bishop's Chapel and Grounds Easter Sat-Oct 31 on Sun 2-6 Tues, Wed, Thurs Bank Holiday Mons and daily in Aug 10-6 also for exhibitions as advertised. As this is a private house The Trustees reserve the right to alter these times on rare occasions.
Admission: As advertised - guided and educational tours by arrangement with the Manager.
Refreshments: A limited restaurant service is available in the Undercroft unless prior bookings made.
Events/Exhibitions: Wedding receptions. Open-air theatre.
Conferences: Conferences and special events by arrangement with the Manager.

THE CHURCH HOUSE
(The Charity Commissioners)
Crowcombe

CLAPTON COURT GARDENS AND PLANT CENTRE
(Capt S J Loder)
Crewkerne   ♿
Telephone: (01460) 73220/72200
Beautiful 10 acre 'all seasons' garden in park-like setting.

COLERIDGE COTTAGE   The National Trust
Nether Stowey, nr Bridgwater   TA5 1NQ   map 3 U16
Telephone: (01278) 732662
Location: At W end of village on S side of A39; 8 m W of Bridgwater.

COMBE SYDENHAM COUNTRY PARK
Monksilver, Taunton   TA4 4JG   map 3 U16   Ⓢ
Telephone: (01984) 656284
Fax: (01984) 656273

Built in 1580 on the site of a monastic settlement, home of Elizabeth Sydenham, wife of Sir Francis Drake. Beautifully restored Courtroom and Cornmill with full working Bakery, Elizabethan style gardens, Deer Park, Children's play area. Woodland Walks with Alice Trail and The Ancient Trail of Trees. Trout Farm, beginners fly fishing school.

Open: Apr-Oct Park/Shop Sun-Fri 10-5. Farmshop sells smoked trout/pate, venison and freshly baked bread, also open Sat am. West wing of House Mon-Fri 1.30-4 evening tours of Private Rooms and supper by arrangement.
Admission: Adults £4.50 children £2.00. Free car/coach parking.
Refreshments: Country Park produce used for lunches, snacks and teas.

CROWE HALL
(Mr John Barratt)
Widcombe, Bath   BA2 6AR   map 3 V16
Telephone: (01225) 310322

Elegant George V classical Bath villa, retaining grandiose mid-Victorian portico and great hall. Fine 18th century and Regency furniture; interesting old paintings and china. 10 acres of romantic gardens cascading down hillside. Terraces, Victorian grotto, ancient trees.

Location: Approx ¼ m on right up Widcombe Hill. 1 m from Guildhall.
Open: Gardens only Suns Apr 21 and June 16 *for NGS*, Also Suns Mar 24 May 12 & 26 June 14. House and Gardens by appointment. Groups welcome.
Admission: Gardens only £1.50, House and Gardens £3.00.
Refreshments: Teas on opening days and by appointment.
Dogs welcome.

DODINGTON HALL
(Lady Gass, occupiers Mr and Mrs P Quinn).
nr. Nether Stowey, Bridgwater   map 3 U16
Telephone: (01278) 741400

Small Tudor Manor House on the lower slopes of the Quantock Hills. Great hall with oak roof. Carved stone fireplace. Semi-formal garden with roses and shrubs.

Location: ½ m from A39. 11 m from Bridgwater; 7 m from Williton.
Open: Sat and Sun 1-2 8-9 15-16 22-23 29-30 June. Donations for Charity.
Parking for 15 cars. Regret unsuitable for disabled.

DUNSTER CASTLE   The National Trust
Dunster, nr.Minehead   TA24 6SL   map 3 U16
Telephone: (01643) 821314
Location: In Dunster, 3 m SE of Minehead on A39.

EAST LAMBROOK MANOR GARDEN
(Mr & Mrs Andrew Norton)
East Lambrook Manor, South Petherton   TA13 5HL
Telephone: (01460) 240328
Fax: (01460) 242344

The Garden, created by the late Margery Fish, listed Grade 1.

Location: Off A303 2 m N of South Petherton.
Open: Mon-Sat 10-5, 1 Mar-31 Oct.
Admission: £2.

GAULDEN MANOR
(Mr & Mrs James Le Gendre Starkie)
Tolland, nr Taunton   TA4 3PN   map 3 U16   △ &
Telephone: (019847) 213

Small historic manor of great charm, a real lived in home.

Location: 9 m NW of Taunton signposted from A358 and B3224
Open: May 5-Sept 1 Sun & Thurs also Easter Sun and all Bank Hols 2-5.30pm.
Admission: Adults House and Garden £3.50 Garden only £1.75 Children £1.75. Parties on other days by prior arrangement.
Refreshments: Teas.
Plants for sale.

GLASTONBURY ABBEY
BA6 9EL   map 3 U17
Telephone: (01458) 832267

Traditionally the oldest Christian sanctuary in the British Isles, and the legendary burial place of King Arthur. The ruins of the Abbey buildings are set in 37 acres of beautiful Somerset parkland. The new Interpretation Centre, which includes a model of the Abbey as it might have been in the 16c, is worth a visit in itself. The Abbey Shop, Holy Thorn, Lady Chapel, Abbot's kitchen aand St. Patrick's Chapel all make your trip here worthwhile.

Open: Every day except Christmas Day 9.30 (9 in June, July and Aug) to 6 or dusk if earlier.
Admission: Adult £2.50 OAP/Student £2 Chd £1 Family (2+2) £5.50 Groups Adult/OAP/Student £2. Child (in aldult party) under 16 80p, all children under 5 free. Season tickets: Adult £8, OAP/chd under 16 £4.

HADSPEN GARDEN
(Nori and Sandra Pope)
Hadspen House, Castle Cary, Somerset   BA7 7NG
Telephone: (01963) 50939

HATCH COURT
(Dr and Mrs Robin Odgers)
Hatch Beauchamp, Taunton   TA3 6AA   map 3 V17   △ &
Telephone: (01823) 480120
Fax: (01823) 480058

Hatch Court is a most attractive and unusual Bath stone Palladian mansion built in 1755. It is surrounded by beautiful parkland with a herd of fallow deer. Still a very much lived in and loved family home, it contains a good collection of pictures, furniture, a unique semi-circular china room and a small military museum. The extensively restored gardens feature a spectacular working walled kitchen garden, the subject of recent TV programmes and magazine articles. Both house and gardens are shown by members of the present family and visitors are assured of a very warm personal welcome.

Location: 6 m SE of Taunton, M5 junction 25, off A358 Taunton-Ilminster.
Station(s): Taunton.
Open: House: Thurs 2-5 June 13-Sept 12. Garden: Mon-Thurs 10-5 Apr 15-Sept 30. Groups over 20 at any time throughout the year by prior appointment.
Admission: House & Garden: £3, 12-16 £1.00. Groups: £2.50 Garden: £1.50.
Refreshments: Home made teas when house is open. Licensed catering by prior arrangement.
Conferences: Full facilities for conferences, meetings, receptions, private functions, promotions and product launches.
The entire gardens and grounds are accessible to wheelchair users. Sales of unusual vegetable, produce and plant sales.

HESTERCOMBE HOUSE GARDENS
(Somerset County Council Fire Brigade)
Hestercombe House, Cheddon Fitzpaine   TA2 8LQ   map 3 U16
Telephone: (01823) 337222
Fax: (01823) 413030

A unique Edwardian garden designed by Sir Edwin Lutyen and Gertrude Jekyll. Restored to its former glory using the original Jekyllian planting schemes.

Location: 4 m north of Taunton, close to Cheddon Fitzpaine village.
Station(s): Taunton.
Open: All year Mon-Fri 9-5 May 1-Sept 31 Sat and Sun 12-5.
Admission: Adults £2.50 Children under 16 free. Parties by arrangement.
Conferences: Available

KENTSFORD HOUSE

(Mrs Wyndham. Occupier: Mr H Dibble)
Watchet   map **3** U16

House open **only** by written appointment with Mr H. Dibble.

Open: Gardens Tues and Bank Hols Mar 12-Aug 27.
Admission: Donations towards renovation of fabric.

LYTES CARY MANOR   The National Trust
nr Ilchester **A11 7HU** map **3** U17
Location: On W side of Fosse Way (A37); 2½ m N of Ilchester signposted on bypass (A303).

MILTON LODGE GARDENS

(Mr & Mrs David Tudway Quilter)
Wells map **14** U17
Telephone: (01749) 672168

Grade II listed terraced garden dating from 1906, with outstanding views of Wells Cathedral and Vale of Avalon. Mixed borders, roses, fine trees. Separate 8 acre early XIX Century arboretum,

Location: ½ m N of Wells. From A39 Bristol-Wells turn N up Old Bristol Road; free car park first gate on left.
Open: Garden and arboretum only Easter-end Oct daily (except Sat) 2-6. Parties and coaches by prior arrangement.
Admission: Adults £2 children (under 14) free. Open on certain Suns in aid of National Gardens Scheme.
Refreshments: Teas available Suns and Bank Hols Apr-Sept.
No dogs.

MONTACUTE HOUSE   The National Trust
Yeovil **TA15 6XP** map **3** U17
Telephone: (01935) 823289
Location: In Montacute village 4 m W of Yeovil on S side of A3088; 3 m E of A303.

ORCHARD WYNDHAM

(Mrs Wyndham)
Williton, nr Taunton **TA4 4HH** map **3** U16
Telephone: (01984) 632309
Fax: (01984) 633526

English Manor House. Family home for 700 years encapsulating continuous building and alteration from 14th to 20th centuries.

Location: 1 m from A39 at Williton.
Open: House and Gardens Thur and Fri in Aug 2-5. Guided tours only. Limited space within house. *To avoid disappointment please advance-book places on tour by telephone or fax.* Unsuitable for wheelchairs. Narrow access road suitable for light vehicles only.
Admission: Adults £3 children under 12 £1.

STOKE-SUB-HAMDON PRIORY   The National Trust
nr Montacute **TA4 6QP** map **3** V17
Location: Between A303 & A3088; 2 m W of Montacute between Yeovil & Ilminster.

TINTINHULL HOUSE GARDEN   The National Trust
nr. Yeovil **BA22 9PZ** map **3** V17 △
Telephone: (01935) 822545
Location: 5 m NW of Yeovil; ½ m S of A303 on outskirts Tintinhull village.

STAFFORDSHIRE

ANCIENT HIGH HOUSE

(Stafford Borough Council)
Greengate Street map **14** R18
Telephone: (01785) 223181 ext 353 or 240204
Fax: (01785) 240204

England's largest timber framed town house, built in 1595. Now has period room settings, shop, video theatre and the Museum of the Staffordshire Yeomanry.

Location: Centre of Stafford.
Open: Mon-Fri 9-5 Sat 10-4 Apr-Oct and 10-3 Nov-Mar.
Admission: Adult £1.50 Concessions £1.
Refreshments: Good variety of restaurants & cafes locally.
Events/Exhibitions: Series of temporary exhibitions plus special events and exhibitions.

BIDDULPH GRANGE GARDEN 🍂 The National Trust

Biddulph, Stoke-on-Trent   **ST8 7SD**   map **7** Q18
Telephone: (01782) 517999

A highly imaginative Victorian garden which brings together in 15 acres images and plants from all over the world. Included are the willow pattern garden of 'China', a topiary Egyptian Court, the Glen, Pinetum and Dahlia Walk.

Location: ½ m N of Biddulph, 3½ m SE of Congleton, 7 m N of Stoke-on-Trent. Access from A527 (Tunstall-Congleton road). Entrance off Grange Road.
Station(s): Kidsgrove 8 m Congleton, 2½ m. Stoke-on-Trent 7 m.
Open: 30 Mar-30 Oct Wed-Fri 12-6 Sat, Sun and Bank Holiday Mon 11-6 (last admission 5.30). Closed Good Fri. Pre-booked guided tours at 10, Wed, Thurs, Fri £5 (inc NT members); also open 2 Nov-22 Dec Sat & Sun 12-4.
Admission: £4 children £2 family ticket £10 (Nov and Dec half-price). Joint ticket with nearby Little Moreton Hall £6.
Refreshments: Tea-room and shop open same time as garden.
Access for disabled visitors is extremely difficult; unsuitable for wheelchairs. Please contact Garden Office for details.

CHILLINGTON HALL

(Mr & Mrs Peter Giffard)
nr Wolverhampton   **WV8 1RE**   map **14** R18   △
Telephone: (01902) 850236

Georgian house. Part 1724 (Francis Smith); part 1785 (Sir John Soane). Fine saloon. The lake in the Park is believed to be the largest ever created by 'Capability' Brown. The bridges by Brown and Paine, and the Grecian and Roman Temples, together with the eyecatching Sham House, as well as many fine trees and plantations add great interest to the four mile walk around the lake. Dogs welcome in grounds if kept on lead.

Location: 4 m SW of A5 at Gailey; 2 m Brewood; 8 m NW of Wolverhampton; 14 m S of Stafford. Best approach is from A449 (Junction 12, M6, Junction 2, M54) through Coven and follow signposts towards Codsall (no entry at Codsall Wood).
Open: June-Sept 14 Thurs (also Suns in Aug) 2.30-5.30 open Easter Sun & Suns preceding May and late Spring Bank Holidays 2.30-5.30. Parties of at least 15 other days by arrangement.
Admission: Adults £2.50 (Grounds only £1.25) children half-price.

DOROTHY CLIVE GARDEN

(Willoughbridge Garden Trust)
Willoughbridge, Nr. Market Drayton   **TF9 4EU**   map **7** R18   ♿
Telephone: (01630) 647237

8 acre woodland and rhododendron garden; shrub roses, water garden and a large scree in a fine landscape setting. Good herbaceous plantings are a summer feature: autumn colour. Spectacular waterfall, many interesting and less usual plants. Fine views.

Location: On A51 road midway between Nantwich and Stone and 3 m South of Bridgemere Garden World.
Open: Garden only Apr-Oct daily 10-5.30.
Admission: Adults £2.60 children £1.
Refreshments: Attractive tea-room and lawn open daily. Home baking. Free car park.

FORD GREEN HALL

(Stoke on Trent City Council)
Ford Green Road, Smallthorne   **ST6 1NG**   map **7** Q18
Telephone: (01782) 534771
Fax: (01782) 205033

A timber-framed farmhouse built for the Ford family in 1624, with eighteenth century brick additions. The house is furnished according to inventories of the 17th and 18th century to give a flavour of the domestic life of the Ford family. Regular performances of Early Music and other events; guided tours available.

Location: Smallthorne on B5051 Burslem-Endon Road.
Station(s): Nearest Stoke-on-Trent.
Open: Sunday-Thursday 1-5pm. Closed 25 December - 1 January.
Admission: Free.
Refreshments: Small tea-room.
Events/Exhibitions: Wide variety of events held throughout the year.
Small parties by prior arrangement.

HANCH HALL

(Mr & Mrs C Lee)
Lichfield
Telephone: (01543) 490308.

Original mansion built in the reign of Edward I. Seat of the Aston family until the end of the 16th century, then the Orms, staunch supporters of Charles 1st. Home of General William Dyott from 1817, then Sir Charles Forster in the 19th century. The present house which is lived in as a family home, exhibits Tudor, Jacobean, Queen Anne and Georgian architecture. Wealth of oak panelling; observation Tower, interesting collectinos. Pleasant gardens, trout pool, waterfowl. Tiny Chapel in grounds.

Location: 4 m NW of Lichfield on Uttoxeter Road (B5014).
Open: Apr 7 to Sept 29 1996. Suns only & Bank Hol Mon's 11-5 (last tour of house 4pm). Parties of 20 or more at other times by arrangement.
Admission: House & Gardens £3.50, Chdn £1.50. Reductions for parties of 20 or more. Free car park.
Refreshments: Tea-room in the 17th century stable block - which is open Tues, Thurs, Fri plus when house open. -Hot or cold meals by arrangement. Candlelight evenings - first week in Dec. Regret no dogs. No stiletto heels please inthe house. N.B. HANCH HALL ESTATE reserves the right to change days and hours of opening and to close all or parts of the Hall without prior notice.

IZAAK WALTON'S COTTAGE

(Stafford Borough Council)
Worston Lane, Shallowford, nr Stafford   map **7** R18
Telephone: (01785) 760278
Fax: (01785) 240204

Thatched, timber-framed cottage bequeathed to Stafford by Izaak Walton, author of the 'Compleat Angler'. Now has period room settings and a small fishing museum.

Location: Shallowford, off the A5013 5m N of Stafford.
Open: Tues-Sun 11-4.30 Apr-Oct.
Admission: Adults £1.50 Concessions £1.
Refreshments: Facilities at events.
Events/Exhibitions: Annual programme of events.

MOSELEY OLD HALL   🌿 The National Trust
Moseley Old Hall Lane, Fordhouses **WV10 7HY** map **14** R18 △ & Ⓢ
Telephone: (01902) 782808
Location: 4 m N of Wolverhampton mid-way between A449 & A460 Roads. Off M6 at Shareshill then via A460. Traffic from S via. M6 and M54 take junction 1 to Wolverhampton and Moseley is signposted after ½ m. Coaches via. A460 to avoid low bridge.

SANDON HALL

(The Earl of Harrowby)
Sandon, Stafford **ST18 0BZ** map **6** R18
Telephone: (01889) 508004

Neo-Jacobean ancestral home containing family museum, situated in the heart of Staffordshire amidst 400 acres of superb parkland and a notable arboretum.

Location: 5 miles NE of Stafford on A51. 10 mins from Junc.14 M6.
Open: Throughout the year to booked groups only.
Admission: Guided Tour £3. (Concessions £2.50) Gardens £1.50 (Concessions £1)
Refreshments: Tea & cakes or Ploughman's Lunch- advance booking essential.

> ### Sir Christopher Wren - architect
> ### (1632-1723)
>
> *Fawley Court*
> *Old Royal Observatory*
> *Winslow Hall*

SHUGBOROUGH   🌿 The National Trust
(Administered by Staffordshire County Council)
Stafford **ST17 0XB** map **14** R18 △ & Ⓔ Ⓢ
Telephone: (01889) 881388
Fax: (01889) 881323

Seat of the Earls of Lichfield. Architecture by James Stuart and Samuel Wyatt. Rococo plasterwork by Vassalli. Extensive parkland with neo-classical monuments. Beautiful formal gardens. Edwardian terraces and rose-garden. Guided garden and woodland walks. Working rare breeds farm. Restored Mill. Restored Victorian servants working areas.

Location: 6m E of Stafford on A513, entrance at Milford common 10 mins drive from M6 junction 13. Station: Stafford.
Open: House, County Museum Farm with Working Kitchens, Laundry and Corn Mill. Grade 1 Historic Garden Mar 23-Sep 29 daily inc. Bank Holiday Mons 11-5 site open all year round to pre-booked parties only from 10.30. The estate offers a superb range of tours and packages for schools and adult groups.
Admission: House £3.50 (reduced rate £2.50) County Museum £3.50 (reduced rate £2.50) Farm £3.50 (reduced rate £2.50) all-in ticket (House, County Museum and Farm) £8 (reduced rate £6) family all in ticket (2 adults and 2 reduced rates) £18 coach parties all-in ticket £6 or £2.50 per site (prices subject to change). Reduced rates available for children, OAPs, registered unemployed and children under 5 free. NT members free entry to house, reduced rate to County Museum and Farm. Party bookings for guided tours. Specialist tours and demonstrations available. School parties guided tour £2.00 per head per site (all 3 sites inc. of guide £5.00). Working school demonstrations Oct-East) £2.50 per head, per demo. When special events are held charges may vary.
Refreshments: Tea-rooms, restaurant.
Events/Exhibitions: Full programme of events available throughout the year. 'Lichfield at Home' Exhibition Mar-Sept in the Mansion.
Accommodation: Details of group and accommodation can be obtained from the Booking Officer.
Conference: Rooms available for hire throughout the year. Contact: Mrs Anne Wood. Promotion and Events Manager for details.
Guide Dogs admitted to House and County Museum. Site access for parking, picnic area, gardens, monuments and woodland trails £1.50 per vehicle. Coaches free. National Trust shop and toilets.

STAFFORD CASTLE
(Stafford Borough Council)
Newport Road, Stafford   map **14** R18
Telephone: (01785) 257698
Fax: (01785) 240204

The site of a Norman timber fortress, now covered by the ruins of a 19th century Gothic Revival building. The Visitor Centre contains an audio-visual display, model reconstructions and shop.

Location: Off the A518 Newport Road, SW of Stafford.
Open: Visitor Centre 10am-5pm Nov-Mar 10am-4pm. Closed Monday except Bank Holidays.
Admission: Adults £1.50 Concessions £1.
Refreshments: Facilities at events and during weekends.
Events/Exhibitions: Annual events programme on the Castle site. Temporary exhibitions in the Visitor Centre.

TAMWORTH CASTLE
(Tamworth Borough Council)
The Holloway, Tamworth   B79 7LR   map **14** R19
Telephone: (01827) 63563
Fax: (01827) 52769

Tamworth's sandstone castle is one of the few remaining shell-keeps in the country. Occupied at various periods between Norman and Victoran times, the castle's room settings include the Tudor chapel, great hall, Jacobean state apartments, Victorian suite, Norman exhibition, dungeon and haunted bedroom. Fine views from Tower roof weather permitting.

Location: In Tamworth; 15 m NE of Birmingham.
Station(s): Tamworth (¾ m).
Open: All the year weekdays 10-5.30 Suns 2-5.30 (Last adm 4.30) open Bank Hols. Closed Christmas Eve, Christmas Day & Boxing Day.
Admission: Adults £3.20 concessions £1.60 family ticket £8.
Events/Exhibitions: From April new Tamworth Story permanent exhibition and audio-visual on local transport.
Gift shop.

WHITMORE HALL
(Mr G.Cavenagh-Mainwaring)
Whitmore, nr Newcastle-under-Lyme   map **7** R18
Telephone: (01782) 680478/680235

Carolinian Manor House, owner's family home for over 800 years. Family portraits dating back to 1624. Outstanding Tudor Stable Block.

Location: 4 m from Newcastle-under-Lyme on the A53 Road to Market Drayton.
Open: Open 2-5.30 every Tues & Weds May-Aug inclusive (last tour 5).
Admission: Adults £2 *no reduction for parties* free car parking.
Refreshments: Mainwaring Arms Inn, Whitmore & also at Whitmore Art Gallery & Tea-rooms, Whitmore.
Not suitable for disabled. No wheelchairs available.

Sir Christopher Wren - architect
(1632-1723)
Fawley Court
Old Royal Observatory
Winslow Hall

SUFFOLK

AKENFIELD
Charsfield Woodbridge
Telephone: (0147337) 402

Half acre cottage garden.

BELCHAMP HALL
(M.M.J. Raymond, Esq)
Belchamp Walter, Sudbury   CO10 7AT
Telephone: (01787) 372744

Queen Anne period house with period furniture and 17th and 18th century family portraits.

BLAKENHAM WOODLAND GARDEN
Little Blakenham, nr Ipswich   map **5** S24

5 acre woodland garden with many rare trees and shrubs.

Open: 1 Mar-30 June every day except Sat 1-5.
Admission: £1. Free car park.

CHRISTCHURCH MANSION
(The Borough of Ipswich)
Christchurch Park, Ipswich   map **5** S25   △
Telephone: (01473) 253246/213761
Fax: (01473) 281274

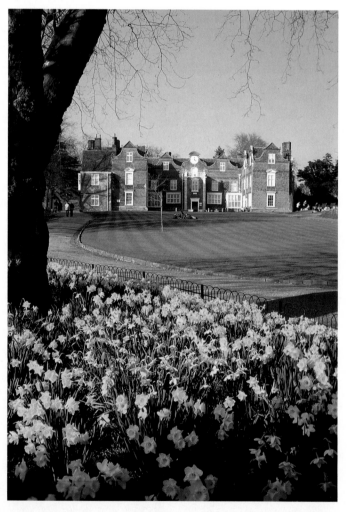

A fine Tudor house set in beautiful parkland. Period rooms furnished in styles from 16th to 19th century; outstanding collections of china, clocks and furniture. Paintings by Gainsborough, Constable and other Suffolk artists. Attached Wolsey Art Gallery shows lively temporary exhibition programme.

Location: In Christchurch Park, near centre of Ipswich.

Station(s): Ipswich (1¼ m).
Open: All the year Tues-Sat 10-5 (dusk in winter) Sun 2.30-4.30 (dusk in winter). Open Bank Hol Mons. Closed Dec 24 25 26 Jan 1 2 and Good Friday.
Admission: £2 (£1 concessions) Free to Ipswich residents.

EUSTON HALL
(The Duke and Duchess of Grafton)
Thetford   map **5** T25
Telephone: (01842) 766366

Euston Hall - Home of the Duke and Duchess of Grafton. The 18th century house contains a famous collection of paintings including works by Stubbs, Van Dyck, Lely and Kneller. The pleasure grounds were laid out by John Evelyn and William Kent, lakes by Capability Brown. 17th century parish church in Wren style. Watermill. Craft Shop. Picnic area.

Location: A1088; 3 m S Thetford.
Open: June 6-Sept 26 Thurs only 2.30-5 also Sun June 30 & Sept 1st 2.30-5.
Admission: Adults £2.50 children 50p OAPs £2. Parties of 12 or more £2 per head.
Refreshments: Teas in Old Kitchen.

FRAMLINGHAM CASTLE
ENGLISH HERITAGE
map **5** S25
Telephone: (01728) 724189

The present massive walls and their 13 towers were built by Roger Bigod, second Earl of Norfolk, on a site given to his father by Henry I. The ornamental brick chimneys were added in Tudor times when the arch of the entrance gateway was rebuilt. In 1636 the castle passed to Pembroke College, Cambridge, and in later years the great hall was converted to a poor-house and many of the buildings inside the walls were demolished. It was here, in 1553, that Mary Tudor learned she had become Queen of England.

Location: North side of Framlingham.
Open: Apr 1-Sept 30 10-6 daily Oct 1-Mar 31 10-4 daily.
Admission: Adults £2.50 concessions £1.90 children £1.30.

GAINSBOROUGH'S HOUSE
(Gainsborough's House Society)
Sudbury   CO10 6EU   map **4** S24
Telephone: (01787) 372958
Fax: (01787) 376991

Gainsborough's House is the birthplace of Thomas Gainsborough RA (1727-88). The Georgian-fronted town house, with an attractive walled garden, displays more of the artist's work than any other gallery. The collection is shown together with eighteenth-century furniture and memorabilia. Commitment to contemporary art is reflected in a varied programme of exhibitions throughout the year. These include fine art, craft, photography, printmaking, sculpture and highlights in particular the work of East Anglian artists.

Location: 46 Gainsborough Street, Sudbury.
Station(s): Sudbury (¼ m).
Open: Open all the year. 31 Apr-Oct Tues-Sat 10-5 Sun & Bank Hol Mons 2-5 Nov-Mar Tues-Sat 10-4 Sun and Bank Hol Mon 2-4 closed Mon Good Fri & between Christmas & New Year.
Admission: Adults £2.50 OAPs £2 students/children £1.25.

GUILDHALL OF CORPUS CHRISTI   The National Trust
Market Place, Lavenham   CO10 9QZ   map **5** T25
Telephone: (01787) 247646
Location: Market Place Lavenham, Sudbury.

HAUGHLEY PARK
(Mrs & Mrs R.J. Williams)
nr Stowmarket   IP14 3JY   map **4** S24
Telephone: (01359) 240205

Jacobean manor house. Gardens and woods, fine trees and shrubs.

Location: 4 m W of Stowmarket signed on A14 (previous A45) nr Wetherden (not Haughley).
Open: May-Sept Tues 3-6.
Admission: Adults £2 children £1.

Sir Joshua Reynolds
Portrait painter (1723-1792)
First President of the Royal Academy, knighted in 1769

His work can be seen in the following properties included in Historic Houses Castles and Gardens:-

Arundel Castle
Dalmeny House (Roseberry Collection of Political Portraits)
Elton Hall
Goodwood House
Ickworth House, Park & Garden
Kenwood, The Iveagh Bequest

Knole
Petworth House
Rockingham Castle
Saltram
Shalom Hall
Wallington House
Weston Park

HELMINGHAM HALL GARDENS
(The Lord & Lady Tollemache)
Ipswich   IP14 6EF   map **5** S25
Telephone: (01473) 890363

The Hall, which was completed in 1510, has been the home of the Tollemache family from that date to the present day. It is one of the finest houses of the Tudor period, surrounded by a wide moat with drawbridges raised every night. There are two superb gardens which extend to several acres all set in 400 acres of ancient park containing herds of Red and Fallow deer and Highland Cattle. The main garden is surrounded by its own moat and 1740 wall, with wide herbaceous borders and planted tunnels intersecting an immaculate kitchen garden; the second is a very special rose garden enclosed within high yew hedges with a Herb and Knot garden containing plants grown in England before 1750. English Heritage Grade I Garden.

Location: 9 m N of Ipswich on B1077.
Open: Gardens Only: Apr 28-Sept 8 Suns 2-6. In addition, Wed 2-5 for group bookings and individuals by appointment.*House not open to the public.*
Admission: Adults £3 children (15 and under) £1.50, OAPs £2.50 groups £2.50.
Refreshments: In the Coach House Tea-rooms. Cream teas.
Safari rides. Gift shop. Home-grown plants and produce for sale.

ICKWORTH HOUSE, PARK & GARDEN
❧ The National Trust
The Rotunda, Horringer   IP29 5AE   map **5** S24   ♿
Telephone: (01284) 735270
Location: 3 m SW of Bury St Edmunds on W side of A143.

IPSWICH MUSEUM
(Ipswich Borough Council)0
Ipswich   IP1 3QH   map **5** S25
Telephone: (01473) 213761/2
Fax: (01473) 281274

Geology and natural history of Suffolk; Mankind galleries covering Africa, Asia, America and the Pacific. 'Romans in Suffolk' gallery showing local archaeology. Temporary exhibitions in attached gallery.

Location: High Street, in town centre.
Station(s): Ipswich.
Open: Tues-Sat 10-5 closed Dec 24 25 26 Jan 1 2 closed Bank Holidays. Temporary exhibition programme.
Admission: Admission £1. Concessions 50p. Free to Ipswich residents.

KENTWELL HALL
(J. Patrick Phillips, QC)
Long Melford   CO10 9BA   map **5** S24
Telephone: (01787) 310207

For 25 years Kentwell has been the subject of a unique long term project to restore the House and its once fine Gardens. A prime purpose of the works has been to accentuate the House's 16th C features, without diminishing it as a family home. It offers a rare feeling of the 16th C with the service areas, Great Kitchen, Bakery, Dairy, Forge & usually fully equipped 16th C style. The Gardens are intimate, yet spacious with woodland walks. There is a fine moated Walled Garden including a Herb Garden and Potager. Kentwell is best known for its Award-Winning Re-Creations of Tudor Domestic Life when visitors may meet numerous 'Tudors' with dress, speech, activities & locations appropriate for the 16th C. These take place on selected week-ends between April & September. Also, Kentwell offers unique Tudor activity days when families may try various Tudor activities. Call the Info Line for details of current Tudor Events: (01891) 517475 (calls cost 39p per min cheap rate; 49p per min otherwise).

Location: Entrance on W of A134, N of Green in Long Melford; 3 m N of Sudbury.
Station(s): Sudbury (4 m).
Open: House Open: 12-5 Mar 10-June 15 Suns + selected days only; June 16-July 7 Sats & Suns only for Great Annual Re-Creation; July 10-Sept 22 daily; Oct Suns only. **Re-Creations Open:** 11-5 Great Annual Re-Creation June 16-July 7 Sats, Suns only, each Bank Hol week-end and other selected weekends & days throughout summer. Call Info Line for current events.
Admission: Inclusive tickets £4.75 adults £2.75 children £4 OAPs. Garden & Farm only: £2.75 adult £1.75 child £2.50 OAP. Special prices apply for Re-Creations & Activity days. (Children charged from 5 to 15).
Refreshments: Lunches and teas available.
Conferences:
No dogs beyond Avenue.

MELFORD HALL   ❧ The National Trust
Long Melford   CO10 9AH   map **5** S24   ♿
Telephone: (01787) 880286
Location: In Long Melford on E side of A134; 3 m N of Sudbury.

ORFORD CASTLE
map **5** S26
Telephone: (0139) 445 0472

No sooner had Henry II built this castle on the Suffolk coast than rebellion broke out (in 1173). The castle's powerful presence helped to uphold the King's authority and it continued to be an important royal residence for more than 100 years. In 1280 it was granted to the Earl of Norfolk for his lifetime, and from then on it remained in private hands. The design was very advanced for its time, and the keep, much of which remains, is unique in England. The outer wall of the castle, the last section of which collapsed in 1841, was punctuated by rectangular towers, an innovation that provided excellent cover for the defenders.

Location: In Orford.
Open: Apr 1-Sept 30 10-6 daily Oct 1-Mar 31 10-4 daily.
Admission: Adults £2 concessions £1.50 children £1. (Closed 1-2 throughout season).

OTLEY HALL
(Mr J G and Baroness Anne Mosesson)
Otley, nr Ipswich　IP6 9PA　map **5** S25　△
Telephone: (01473) 890264
Fax: (01473) 890803

Stunning 15th century Moated Hall (Grade 1) set in gardens and grounds of 10 acres, frequently described as 'one of England's loveliest houses'. Voted Oct 1994 by the AA as one of Britain's top 20 historic houses. Rich in history and architectural detail. Features of particular note are richly carved beams, herringbone brickwork, pargetting, linenfold and fresco-work. Otley Hall was built by the Gosnold family in around 1450 and was their home for 250 years. Some of the famous names and events connected with both the Gosnolds and the Hall are the Royal households of Elizabeth I, James I and Charles I; the Civil War (Colonel Robert Gosnold - Seige of Carlisle); the Virginia colonisation of 1607 - Bartholomew Gosnold, who settled and named Cape Cod and Martha's (Gosnold) Vineyard, and later founded Jamestown; Lady Jane Grey; Shakespeare. The Gardens are formal and informal, including part of a fascinating and historically important design by Francis Inigo Thomas (1866-1950) with canal mount, nutteries, croquet lawn, rose garden and moat walk.

Location: From A14 take Norwich/Diss junction (A140) and then follow B1078 to T-junction and follow sign for Otley (approx. 7 miles from Ipswich).
Open: General Public Open Days 1996: 7/8 Apr 26/27 May and 25/26 Aug 2-6pm.
Admission: Adults £4 children £2.50.
Refreshments: Cream teas on Open Days. Otley Hall is also open by appointment to groups for private guided tours throughout the year when Lunches or Afternoon Teas can be arranged in advance. Party bookings and coach parties welcomed.
Accommodation: The Hall, grounds and accommodation are available for private hire.
Conferences: Wedding receptions, corporate entertaining, film and photographic location. For further information please contact The Secretary, Otley Hall, Otley, Suffolk, IP6 9PA. Tel. (01473) 890264. Fax. (01473) 890803.

SOMERLEYTON HALL
(The Lord & Lady Somerleyton)
nr Lowestoft　map **4** S26　&

Somerleyton Hall is a perfect example of a House built to show off the wealth of the new Victorian aristocracy. The house was remodelled from a modest 17th century Manor House by the rich railwayman Sir Morton Peco. When he was declared bankrupt in 1863 his concoction of real brick white stone and lavish interiors was sold to another hugely successful businessman, carpet manufacturer Sir Francis Crossley. The present owner, Lord Somerleyton, is his great grandson.No expense was spared in the building or the fittings. Stone was brought from Caen and Aubigny and the magnificent carved stonework created by John Thomas (who worked on the Houses of Parliament) has been recently fully restoredIn the State Rooms there are paintings by Landseer, Wright of Derby and Stanfield, together with fine wood carvings by Willcox of Warwick and from the earlier house, Grinling Gibbons.The Oak Rooms retains its carved oak panelling and Stuart atmosphere, the rest is lavishly Victorian. Grandest of all is the Ballroom with its crimson damask walls reflected in rows of long white and gilt mirrors. Somerleyton's 12 acre gardens are justly renowned. The 1846 yew hedge maze is one of the few surviving Victorian mazes in Britain. The stable tower clock by Vuilliamy made in 1847 is the original model for a great clock to serve as the Tower Clock in the new Houses of Parliament, now world famous as Big Ben. Colour is added to the gardens by rhododendrons, azaleas and a long pergola trailing mauve, pink and white whisteria. Special features include a sunken garden; the Loggia Tea Room; glasshouses by Sir Joseph Paxton; an aviary; fine statuary.

Location: 5 m NW Lowestoft off B1074; 7 m Yarmouth (A143).
Station(s): Somerleyton (1½ m).

Open: House, Maze and Gardens, Easter Sun to and including October 1 Thursday, Sundays and Bank Holidays, with the additions of Tuesday and Wednesday in July and August. House open 2-5. Gardens 12.30-5. The house and gardens are available for guided tours for private parties or school groups. Details on application.
Admission: Adults £3.75 OAP £3.25 Children £1.75 Family ticket (2+2) £10.50. Group rates on application.
Refreshments: Luncheon and Teas in the loggia from 12.30.
Conferences: Suitable for conferences.
Suitable for receptions, fashion shows, archery, clay pigeon shooting, equestrian events, garden parties, shows, rallies, filming, wedding receptions. Details on request. Free car parking, sorry no dogs. Facilities for the disabled.

WINGFIELD OLD COLLEGE
(Ian Chance, Esq)
nr Eye　IP21 5RA　map **5** S25　△
Telephone: (01379) 384505
Fax: (01379) 384034

Founded in 1362 on the 13th century site of the Manor House by Sir John de Wingfield, a close friend of the Black Prince. Surrendered to Henry VIII in 1542 and seized by Cromwell's Parliament in 1649. Magnificent Medieval Great Hall. Mixed period interiors with 18th century neo-classical facade. Walled gardens and Topiary. Teas. Celebrated Arts and Music Season. Adjacent church with tombs of College founder and Benefactors, The Earls and Dukes of Suffolk.

Location: Signposted off B1118; 7 m SE of Diss.
Open: Easter Sat-Sept 25 Sats Suns & Bank Hols 2-6.
Admission: Adults £2.50 children £1.
Refreshments: Home-made teas.

SURREY

ALBURY PARK
(Country Houses Association)
Albury, Guildford　GU5 9BB　map **12** U22
Telephone: (01483) 202964

Country mansion by Pugin.

Location: 1½ m E of Albury off A25 Guildford to Dorking road.
Station(s): Stations: Chilworth (2 m); Gomshall (2 m); Clandon (3 m). Bus Route: Tillingbourne No 25 Guildford-Cranleigh
Open: May-Sept Weds & Thurs 2-5. Last entry 4.30.
Admission: £2.50 Children £1. Free car park.
No dogs admitted.

ASGILL HOUSE
(Asgill House Trust Ltd)
Richmond

BROMAGES BONSAI CENTRE
(D.N. Bromage)
St. Mary's Gardens, Worplesdon, Surrey　GU3 3RS　&
Telephone: (01483) 232893

Established 1922.

CLANDON PARK　🌿 The National Trust
nr Guildford　GU4 7RQ　map **12** U22　&
Telephone: (01483) 222482
Fax: (01483) 223479

This is a remarkable combination: A Palladian (1730s) house with its impressive marble hall; the Gubbay collection of porcelain, furniture and needlework; Ivo Forde collection of Meissen Italian Comedy Figures; the Museum of Queen's Royal Surrey Regiment and to cap it all, a Maori Meeting House in the garden. All this, and Clandon's celebrated restaurant.

Location: At West Clandon 3 m E Guildford on A247; S of A3 & N of A246.
Station(s): Clandon (1 m).
Open: House: 30 Mar-30 Oct, Sun-Wed and Good Fri 1.30-5.30, Sat 12-4, Bank Hol Mons 11-5.30. Last admission ½ hour before closing. Garden: Same days as house, plus weekends in Mar 12-5.30.
Admission: £4 Children half-price Family ticket £10. Parties (Mon-Wed only) £3.50.
Refreshments: Licensed Restaurant in house; lunches & teas 12.30-5.30. Limited advance booking available Tel (01483) 222502. Also open every weekend in March and pre-Christmas.
Events/Exhibitions: Telephone for details.
Shop. Picnic area. No dogs except on leads in car park and picnic area. Wheelchairs provided.

CLAREMONT
(The Claremont Fan Court Foundation Ltd)
Esher   KT10 9LY   map **12** U22
Telephone: (01372) 467841
Fax: (01372) 471109

Excellent example of Palladian style; built 1772 by 'Capability' Brown for Clive of India; Henry Holland and John Soane responsible for the interior decoration. It is now a co-educational school run by Christian Scientists.

Location: ½ m SW from Esher on Esher/Cobham Road A307.
Open: Feb-Nov first complete weekend (Sat and Sun) in each month 2-5.
Admission: Adults £2 children/OAPs £1 reduced rates for parties. Souvenirs.

CLAREMONT LANDSCAPE GARDEN
❧ **The National Trust**
Esher   KT10 9JG   map **12** U22   &
Telephone: (01372) 469421

One of the earliest surviving English landscape gardens, restored by the NT to its former glory. Features include a lake, island with pavilion, grotto, turf amphitheatre, view points and avenues. *House not National Trust property.*

Location: .5 SE of Esher on E side of A307. NB: no access from A3 by-pass.
Station(s): Esher (2 m) (not Suns); Hersham (2 m); Claygate (2 m).
Open: All year Jan-end Mar daily (except Mons) 10-5 or sunset if earlier. April-end Oct Mon-Fri 10-6 Sat Sun and BH Mons 10-7. Closed 10 July. 11-14 July closes 2. Nov-end Mar 1997 daily except Mon 10-5 or sunset if earlier. Last admission half hour before closing. Closed 25 Dec. Open 1 Jan 1-4. No coaches on Sunday.
Admission: Sun and Bank Hols £3 Mon-Sat £2(Children half-price). Parties by prior booking. Tel (01372) 469421. No reduction for parties.
Refreshments: Tea-room open 13 Jan-end Mar Sat and Sun 11-4.30 Apr-end Oct daily (except Mons) 11-5.30 Nov-Dec 15 daily (except Mons) 11-4. 19 Jan-end Mar 1997 Sat-Sun 11-4.30. Open Bank Hol Mons.
Events/Exhibitions: Phone for details.
Wheelchairs provided. Dogs allowed on leads Nov to Mar but **not** admitted Apr to end Oct. Braille guide available. Shop open as Tea-room.

COVERWOOD LAKES
(Mr & Mrs C G Metson)
Peaslake Road, Ewhurst
Telephone: (01306) 731103

Landscaped water and cottage gardens.

CROSSWATER FARM
(Mr & Mrs E. G. Millais)
Crosswater Lane, Churt, Farnham   GU10 2JN   map **12** U21
Telephone: (01252) 792698
Fax: (01252) 792526

6-acre woodland garden surrounded by acres of National Trust property. Plantsman's collection of Rhododendrons and Azaleas including many rare species collected in the Himalayas, and hybrids raised by the owners. Pond, stream and companion plantings. Plants for sale from adjoining Rhododendron nursery. (See Millais Nurseries entry in Garden Specialists section).

Location: Farnham/Haslemere 6 m. From A287 turn East into Jumps Road ½ m north of Churt village centre. After ¼ m, turn left into Crosswater Lane, and follow Nursery signs.
Open: May 1-June 2 daily 10-5. In aid of the *National Gardens Scheme* on May 25,26,27.
Admission: Adults £1.50 children free.
Refreshments: Teas available on NGS days.
No dogs.

FARNHAM CASTLE
(The Church Commissioners)
Farnham   map **12** U21   △
Telephone: (01252) 721194
Fax: (01252) 711283

Bishop's Palace built in Norman times by Henry of Blois, with Tudor and Jacobean additions. Formerly the seat of the Bishops of Winchester. Fine Great Hall re-modelled at the Restoration. Features include the Renaissance brickwork of Wayneflete's tower, and the 17th century chapel.

Location: ½ m N of Town Centre on A287.
Station(s): Farnham.
Open: All year round/Weds 2-4pm; parties at other times by arrangement. All visitors given guided tours. Centrally heated in winter.
Admission: Adults £1.20 OAPs/children/students 60p reductions for parties.
Conferences: Please contact Conference Organiser, Moya Doxsey.
Centrally heated in winter. Not readily accessible by wheelchair.

GODDARDS
(The Lutyens Trust)
Abinger Common, Dorking   RH5 6TH   map **12** U22
Telephone: (01306) 730487

Edwardian country house by Sir Edwin Lutyens, with Gertrude Jekyll garden, in beautiful setting on slopes of Leith Hill. Given to the Lutyens Trust in 1991 and now managed and maintained by The Landmark Trust. Closed for Restoration, due to re-open July 1996. For all enquiries telephone The Landmark Trust, Shottesbrooke, Maidenhead, Berkshire SL6 3SW (O1628) 825920.

Location: 4½ m SW of Dorking in Abinger Common.
Station(s): Dorking.
Open: By telephone appointment Apr-Oct.
Refreshments: Morning coffee, afternoon tea - functions and receptions by arrangement with the Administrator.
Conferences: Dauy conferences only.

GREATHED MANOR
(Country Houses Association)
Lingfield   RH7 6PA   map **12** U23
Telephone: (01342) 832577

Victorian Manor house.

Location: 2½ m SE of Lingfield on B2028 Edenbridge road, take Ford Manor road beside Plough Inn, Dormansland for final 1 m.
Station(s): Dormans (1½ m); Lingfield (1½ m). Bus Route: No. 429 to Plough Inn, Dormansland.
Open: May-Sept Weds & Thurs 2-5. Last entry 4.30.
Admission: £2.50 Children £1. Free car park.
No dogs admitted.

GUILDFORD HOUSE GALLERY

(Guildford Borough Council)
155, High Street, Guildford GU1 3AJ map **12** U21
Telephone: (01483) 444740
Fax: (01483) 444742

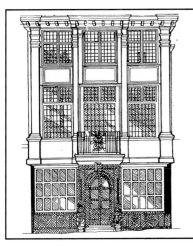

GUILDFORD HOUSE

Guildford House Gallery

155 High Street,
Guildford GU1 3AJ

Telephone:
01483 444740

Recently restored 17th century town house. Original fine carved staircase, plaster ceilings and wrought iron window fittings. Temporary exhibitions include historical and modern paintings of local and national importance, photography and craftwork.

Location: Centre of Guildford on High Street.
Station(s): Guildford ½ m.
Open: Tues-Sat 10-4.45 *Closed* Bank Hols.
Admission: Free.

Refreshments: Tea-room in old kitchen.
Events/Exhibitions: Temporary exhibitions and selections from the Borough's Collection - including pastel portraits by John Russell RA (1745-1806). Lectures and workshops. Leaflets available.
Accommodation: Meeting room for daytime use, up to 60 people.
Gallery shop with publications, cards and craftwork. Public car park nearby, none on site.

HATCHLANDS PARK   The National Trust

East Clandon GU4 7RT map **12** U22
Telephone: (01483) 222482

Hatchlands is an 18th century house with rich and inviting interiors. It houses the Cobbe Collection of early keyboard instruments, paintings and furniture. Small garden by Gertrude Jekyll and walks available in the Repton parkland.

Location: E of East Clandon on N side of Leatherhead/Guildford Road (A246).
Station(s): Clandon (2½ m), Horsley (3 m).
Open: 31 Mar-Oct 31 Tue Wed Thur Sun and Bank Hol Mons but also open Fri in Aug 2-5.30. Last admission 5. Park walks open 12.30-6.
Admission: £4 Children half-price Family ticket £10. Pre-booked parties £3.50. Park walks and grounds only £1.50.
Refreshments: Licensed restaurant and home-made teas 12.30-5.30 same days as house. Tel. (01483) 211120.
Events/Exhibitions: Please telephone for details.
Dogs permitted on leads in car park only. Wheelchair access to ground floor and part of the garden. Shop.

LITTLE HOLLAND HOUSE

(London Borough of Sutton)
Carshalton - See under Greater London.
Telephone: 0181- 770 4781
Fax: 0181-770 4666
Location: 40 Beeches Avenue, Carshalton B278 (opp Barrow Hedges Way).
Station(s): Carshalton Beeches B.R.
Open: First Sun in Month 1.30-5.30.
Admission: Free.

LOSELEY HOUSE

(Mr and Mrs James More-Molyneux)
Guildford GU3 1HS map **12** U21 △ &
Telephone: (01483) 304440

The Elizabethan country house with the friendly atmosphere. Built of stone from Waverley Abbey in a glorious parkland setting by an ancestor of the present owner and occupier. Queen Elizabeth I stayed here three times, James I once. Queen Mary visited in 1932. Panelling from Henry VIII's Nonsuch Palace. Fine ceilings, unique carved chalk chimney piece, inlaid cabinets, tapestries, needlework, but Loseley is a home, not a museum. Walled Gardens and Moat walk. Courtyard Restaurant in part of the old kitchens and courtyard of the house itself, offering morning coffees, light lunches and afternoon teas. Loseley Shop selling Loseley Produce and many attractive gifts and souvenirs. New for 1996 is Loseley Park Farms Education Centre where a traditional English Dairy Farm is at work.

Location: 2½ m SW of Guildford (take B3000 off A3 through Compton); 1½ m N of Godalming (off A3100).
Station(s): Farncombe (2 m) Guildford (3 m).
Open: Bank Hol Mon 27 May, and thereafter every Wed, Thurs, Fri & Sat, until Sat 31 Aug, also Bank Hol Mon 26 Aug 1996. Gardens, Restaurant & Shop 11-5, House Tours & Farm Visits 2-5.
Admission: Adult £3.50 Children £2 OAP/Disabled £3. Group rates for parties of 20 or more available on request.
Refreshments: Catering by Alexander Catering (est 1960).
Events/Exhibitions: Surrey Advertiser Motor Show 11/12 May, Craft Fair 31 May & 1/2 June, Performing Arts Outdoor Concert 29 June, Loseley Opera 23/25/26/27 July, Queen Elizabeth Foundation Classic Car Show 3/4 Aug, Christmas Food & Gift Fair 8/9/10 Nov, Christmas Fair 22/23/24 Nov.
Conferences: Facilities available.
Tithe Barn available for hire for weddings, company days, fun days, product launches, conferences.

THE OLD PALACE

(The Whitgift Foundation)
Old Palace Road, Croydon   map **12** U22 △
Telephone: 0181-668 3349 or 0181-688 2414

Seat of Archbishops of Canterbury since 871. 15th century Banqueting Hall and Guardroom, Tudor Chapel, Norman undercroft.

Location: In Croydon Old Town. Adjacent to Parish Church.
Station(s): East Croydon or West Croydon (few mins walk).
Open: Doors open at 2pm. Conducted Tours only (last tour commences 2.30) Mon 15 Apr-Sat 20 Apr, Mon 27 May-Fri 31 May, Mon 15 July-Sat 20 July, Mon 22 July-Sat 27 July.
Admission: Adults £4 children/OAPs £3 family £10. This includes afternoon tea served in the undercroft.
Car park. Souvenir shop. Parties catered for, apply 0181-668 3349 or 0181-688 2414. Unsuitable for wheelchairs.

PAINSHILL PARK

(Painshill Park Trust)
Portsmouth Road, Cobham KT11 1JE map **12** U22 △ &
Telephone: (01932) 868113 ansafone (01932) 864674
Fax: (01932) 868001

Painshill, contemporary with Stourhead & Stowe, is one of Europe's finest landscape gardens. It was created by The Hon Charles Hamilton, plantsman, painter, and brilliantly gifted designer, between 1738 and 1773. He transformed barren heathland into ornamental pleasure grounds and parkland of dramatic beauty and contrasting scenery, dominated by a 14 acre meandering lake fed from the river by an immense waterwheel. Garden buildings and features adorn the Park amongst magnificent shrubberies typical of the period: an extraordinary grotto, a Gothic temple, a ruined abbey, a Chinese bridge, a castellated tower, a Turkish tent, a mausoleum, and a working vineyard. Well maintained for 200 years in private ownership the Park was neglected after 1948 and sank into dereliction. In 1981 the Painshill Park Trust, a registered charity was formed to restore the gardens to their original splendour, raising the extensive funds needed for such an ambitious project. The Trust has made enormous progress and this masterpiece is re-emerging from the wilderness.

Location: W of Cobham on A245. 200 yards E of A3/A245 roundabout.
Station(s): Cobham.
Open: Apr 7-Oct 13 (Suns only) 11-5 (gates close 6). Pre-booked parties (min. 10) any day except Suns. Please ring (01932) 868113 for more information. Wide ranging Education programme - school parties welcomed, holiday activities organised and childrens parties catered for by arrangement with Painshill Park Education Trust, (01932) 866743. Full opening is expected during 1996. Telephone ansaphone (01932) 864674 to confirm opening arrangements.
Admission: Adults £3.50 OAPs/students/UB40s £3 children 5-16 £1 groups £2.80.
Refreshments: Light refreshments available.
Much of park accessible for disabled (wheelchairs available). Limited facilities and parking. No dogs please.

POLESDEN LACEY 🦋 The National Trust

nr Dorking RH5 6BD map **12** U22 &
Telephone: (01372) 458203 or 452048

Polesden Lacey is a peaceful country estate, set in the Surrey Downs. The house, and elegant Regency 'villa' was luxuriously furnished in Edwardian times by society hostess, The Hon. Mrs Greville. Her collection of furniture, paintings, porcelain and silver is remarkable. Walled rose garden and stunning landscape walks.

Location: 5 m NW of Dorking, reached via Great Bookham (A246) & then signed on road leading S (1½ m).
Station(s): Boxhill or Bookham (both 2½ m).
Open: Mar: Sat and Sun only 1.30-4.30. 3 Apr-end Oct Wed-Sun including Good Friday 1.30-5.30. Also open Bank Hol Mons and preceding Suns 11-5.30. Grounds open daily all year 11-6 or dusk if earlier.

Admission: £3 HOUSE £3 extra Children half-price. Pre-booked parties £5 weekdays only.
Refreshments: Licensed Restaurant in stableyard. Jan 13-end Mar: (light refreshments). Sats and Suns only 11-4.30. Apr-end Oct Weds-Suns and Bank Hol Mons 11-5. 5 Nov-Dec 20Wed-Sun 11-4.30. Special times before Christmas. Tel (01372) 456190.
Events/Exhibitions: Please telephone for details.
Wheelchairs admitted and provided. Shop open: 13 Jan-end of Mar: Sat & Sun only, 11-4.30. Apr to end Oct: Wed to Sun and BH Mon 11-6.00. Nov-23 Dec 11-4.30. July, Aug and Dec open 7 days a week. (Tel (01372) 457230.

RAMSTER

(Mr & Mrs Paul Gunn)
Chiddingfold
Telephone: (01428) 644422

Mature 20 acre woodland walk with rhododendrons and flowering shrubs.

Location: On A283 1½ m S of Chiddingfold.
Open: April 20-July 20 11-5.30
Admission: £2

RHS GARDEN WISLEY

(The Royal Horticultural Society)
Wisley, Woking GU23 6QB map **12** U22 &
Telephone: (01483) 224234

British gardening at its best in all its aspects. 250 acres of glorious garden. The Alpine Meadow, carpeted with wild daffodils in spring, Battleston Hill, brilliant with rhododendrons in early summer, the Heathers and autumnal tints together with the glasshouses, trials and model gardens are all features for which the garden is famous. But what makes **Wisley** unique is that it is not just beautiful to look at. As the showpiece of the Royal Horticultural Society, the Garden is a source of practical advice and a model of good horticulture to hundreds of thousands of visitors every year. It is probably the only garden in the world to give such a complete picture of different gardening styles and techniques.

Location: Wisley is just off M25 Junction 10, on A3. London 22 m Guildford 7m.
Open: The garden is open to the public Mon-Sat throughout the year (except Christmas Day) from 10-sunset (or 7pm during the summer). Sundays RHS Members only.
Admission: Adults £4.90 children under 6 yrs free children 6-16 £1.75. Groups of more than 10 Mon-Sat £3.75. Tickets for group visits must be obtained in advance of visit. RHS Members free. One person accompanying a blind or disabled person free.
Refreshments: Wisley's Terrace Restaurant and Conservatory Café inside the Garden are open throughout the year. (Please check in run up to Christmas).
Dogs not admitted (except guide dogs). Information centre. Shop and Plant sales centre.

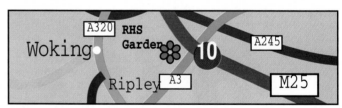

WHITEHALL

Cheam - See under Greater London. map **12** U22
Telephone: 0181-643 1236
Fax: 0181- 770 4666
Location: On A2043 just N of junction with A232.
Station(s): Cheam B.R.
Open: Apr-Sept: Tues-Fri & Sun 2-5.30; Sat 10-5.30. Oct-Mar: Wed, Thurs & Sun 2-5.30: Sat 10-5.30. Also open Bank Hol Mons 2-5.30. Closed from Dec 24-Jan 2 inc.
Admission: Adult 85p children 45p.
Refreshments: Tea-room.
Events/Exhibitions: Changing programme of events, fairs & exhibitions.

WINKWORTH ARBORETUM 🦋 The National Trust

Hascombe Road, nr Godalming GU8 4AD map **12** U21 &
Telephone: (01483) 208477

99 acres of trees and shrubs, world-renown for spectacular displays of Spring and Autumn colour. Two lakes and wonderful views.

Location: 2 m SE of Godalming on E side of B2130.
Station(s): Godalming (2 m).
Open: All year during daylight hours.
Admission: £2.50, Chd £1.25 Family ticket £6.25. No reduction for parties.*Coach parties by prior appointment in writing to* Head of Arboretum.
Refreshments: Apr 1-Nov 14 daily 11-5.30 (weather permitting) for light lunches and teas. Also open weekends in Mar and Nov-Xmas. Bookings with Concessionaire, Winkworth Arboretum (01483) 208265 when tea-room open.
Dogs must be kept under control. Limited wheelchair access.

EAST SUSSEX

ALFRISTON CLERGY HOUSE   The National Trust
Alfriston, nr Seaford   map **12** V23
Telephone: (01323) 870001
Location: 4 m NE of Seaford just E of B2108; adjoining The Tye & St Andrew's Church.

BATEMAN'S   The National Trust
Burwash   map **12** V23 △
Telephone: (01435) 882302

Built 1634. Rudyard Kipling lived here. Water-mill restored by the National Trust. Attractive garden, yew hedges, lawns, daffodils and wild garden.

Location: ½ m SW of Burwash on the Lewes/Etchingham Road (A265).
Open: Sat 30 Mar-end Oct, daily (exzcept Thurs & Fri but open Good Fri) 11-5.30pm. Last admission 4.30pm. Mill grinds corn each Sat at 2pm. Shop open as house.
Admission: House Mill & Garden Adults £4 Children £2 Family ticket £10. Pre-booked parties £3 Children £1.50.
Refreshments: Tea room: coffees, light lunches and teas, open as House.
Events/Exhibitions: Orchestral Concert with fireworks 3 Aug.
No dogs. Shop.

BATTLE ABBEY
ENGLISH HERITAGE
Battle   map **13** V24
Telephone: (01424) 773792

The Battle of Hastings, 1066 - the best-known date in English history. Battle Abbey was built by William the Conqueror as a thanksgiving for his victory, with the high altar on the spot where King Harold died. The church has yet to be fully excavated, but visitors may walk around the battlefield, and see the remains of many of the domestic buildings of the monastery and see an audio-visual show. An exhibition is open in the newly restored 14th century gatehouse re-creating the history of this famous monument. An Interactive Stereo Tour is available.

Location: Battle.
Open: Apr 1-Sept 30 10-6 daily Oct 1-Mar 31 daily 10-4.
Admission: Adults £3.50 concessions £2.60 children £1.80.

Sir Edwin Landseer Lutyens

Architect

His work can be seen at the following properties included in Historic Houses Castles and Gardens:-

Castle Drogo

Goddards

Great Dixter

Great Maytham Hall

Hestercombe House and Gardens

Knebworth

Lindisfarne Castle

BENTLEY HOUSE & GARDENS
Halland **BN8 5AF** map **12** V23 &
Telephone: (01825) 840573
Fax: (01825) 840573

Bentley House dates back to Tudor times and was built on land granted to James Gage by the Archbishop of Canterbury with the permission of Henry VIII. The family of Lord Gage was linked with Bentley from that time until 1904. The estate was purchased by Gerald Askew in 1937, and during the 1960's he and his wife, Mary, added two large double height Palladian rooms to the original farmhouse. The architect who advised them was Raymond Erith, who had previously worked on 10 Downing Street. The drawing room in the East wing contains mid 18th century Chinese wallpaper and gilt furniture, and the Bird room in the West wing contains a collection of wildfowl paintings by Philip Rickman. The Gardens at Bentley have been created as a series of 'rooms' divided by Yew hedges, one room leading into the next, specialising in many old fashioned roses including the Bourbons, the Gallicas and the Damask. Nearby six stone sphinxes stand along a broad grass walk where daffodils bloom in spring.

Location: 7 m NE of Lewes signposted on A22, A26 & B2192.
Open: Summer open daily 18 Mar-31 Oct 10.30-4.30 (last admissions) 5pm in July and Aug House opens 12 noon daily from 1 Apr. Winter open weekends only 10.30-4 (last admissions). House closed all winter, Estate closed throughout Dec & Jan.
Admission: Adults £3.90 OAPs/students £3 children (4-15) £2.30 Family ticket (2 adults+4 children) £11. Special rates for disabled (wheelchairs available). Parties of 11 or more - 10% discount. Adm price allows entry to House, Garden and Grounds, Wildfowl reserve, Motor Museum, Woodland Walk, Animal section, Children's adventure play area, Picnic area, Tearoom, Gift Shop and Education Centre with audio/visual.
Refreshments: Tea-Rooms on site (licensed).
Conferences: Civil wedding ceremonies.
Ample free parking. Dogs allowed in this area only. Special arrangements can be for parties outside normal hours. Please contact the Manager for details (01825) 840573.

BODIAM CASTLE   **The National Trust**
nr Robertsbridge   map **13** V24   &
Telephone: (01580) 830398
Fax: (01580) 830436

Built 1385-9, one of the best preserved examples of medieval moated architecture.

Location: 3 m S of Hawkhurst; 2m E of A21.
Open: 17 Feb-Sun 3 Nov daily 10-6 or dusk if earlier, 5 Nov-5 Jan Tues-Sun 10-dusk (closed 24-26 Dec, open New Year's Day). Last admission ½ hour before closing.
Admission: £2.70 Children £1.30 Family ticket £6.70. *Parties of 15 or more by prior arrangement.* £2 Children £1. Car park 50p. 1995 prices.
Refreshments: Restaurant as Castle from April, weekends only Nov & Dec, closes half hour before castle.
Events/Exhibitions: Medieval Spring Fair 5/6 May Jazz concert 29 June.
Museum. Audio visual. Shop. Dogs admitted in grounds only. Wheelchair access.

BRICKWALL HOUSE AND GARDENS
(Frewen Educational Trust)
Northiam, Rye   **TN31 6NL**   map **13** V24   △ &
Telephone: (01797) 252494 or Curator (01797) 223329
Fax: (01737) 252567

Home of the Frewen family since 1666. 17th century drawing room, superb plaster ceilings and family portraits. Grand staircase. The grounds contain a formal wall garden, topiary and an arboretum.

Location: 7m NW of Rye on B2088.
Open: Apr-Sept Sats and Bank Hol Mons 2-5 open at other times by prior arrangement with the curator.
Admission: £2.50

COBBLERS GARDEN
(Mr & Mrs Martin Furniss)
Crowborough. Telephone: 01892 655969

2 Acre sloping site designed by present owners since 1968 to display outstanding range of herbaceous and shrubs species and famous watergarden, giving all season colour. Subject of numerous articles and T.V. programmes. Now a very famous garden!

Open: Sun open days, see "National Garden Scheme "Yellow book. Groups welcome by appointment.
Admission £3.50 Chd £1 includes home made teas.

Lancelot 'Capability' Brown

Born 1716 in Northumberland, Capability Brown began work at the age of 16 in the vegetable gardens of Sir William and Lady Loraine at Kirharle Tower. He left Northumberland in 1739, and records show that he worked at Stowe until 1749. It was at Stowe that Brown began to study architecture, and to submit his own plans. It was also at Stowe that he devised a new method of moving and replanting mature trees.

Brown married Bridget Wayet in 1744 and began work on the estate at Warwick Castle in 1749. He was appointed Master Gardener at Hampton Court in 1764, and planted the Great Vine at Hampton Court in 1768. Blenheim Palace designs are considered amongst Brown's finest work, and the technical achievements were outstanding even for the present day.

Capability Brown died in February 1783 of a massive heart attack. A monument beside the lake at Croome Court was erected which reads "To the memory of Lancelot Brown, who by the powers of his inimitable and creative genius formed this garden scene out of a morass". There is also a portrait of Brown at Burghley.

Capability Brown was involved in the design of grounds at the following properties included in Historic Houses Castles and Gardens:

Audley End	*Longleat*
Berrington Hall	*Luton Hoo*
Bowood	*Moccas Court*
Burghley House	*Petworth House*
Burton Constable	*Sledmere House*
Charlecote Park	*Stowe (Stowe*
Chilham Castle Gardens	*School)*
(reputed)	*Syon House*
Clandon Park	*Warwick Castle*
Claremont	*Weston Park*
Chillington Hall	*Wimpole Hall*
Corsham Court	*Wrest Park and*
Fawley Court	*Gardens*
Highclere Castle	

CHARLESTON
(The Charleston Trust)
Firle, nr Lewes   map **12** V23   △
Telephone: (01323) 811265 (Visitor information) (01323) 811626 (Administration.)**Fax:** (01323) 811628

17/18th century farmhouse, the home of Vanessa and Clive Bell and Duncan Grant from 1916 until Grant's death in 1978. Virginia and Leonard Woolf 'discovered' Charleston in 1916, when her sister Vanessa was looking for a house in the country, 'If you lived there, you could make it absolutely divine' Virginia wrote prophetically. Vanessa Bell's household at Charleston was an unconventional and creative one, and was to become the focal point for a group of artists and intellectuals later to be known as 'Bloomsbury'. Walls, furniture and ceramics were decorated by the artists with their own designs, influenced by Italian fresco painting and post-impressionism. The walled garden has been restored as it was in its heyday, showing an artist's use of colour, shapes and textures.

Location: 6 m E of Lewes, on A27, between Firle and Selmeston.
Station(s): Lewes 6 m; Berwick 3 m.
Open: 1996 Apr 3-Oct 31: Admissions 2pm-5pm, Wed-Sun. Guided visits every open day except Sun. House closed Mon-Tues (except Bank Hols). July-August: 11.30am-5pm Wed-Sat, Sun 2pm-5pm. Nov-Dec: 2-4pm Sat-Sun only.
Admission: Adults £4.50 children £3 Connoisseur Days £6. Students/OAPs/UB40 concessions Wed, Thurs throughout the season.
Refreshments: Sats throughout season.
Events/Exhibitions: Charleston Festival 23-27 May; Changing programme of exhibitions throughout season.
Numbers in the House will be limited. No dogs. Coaches by prior appointment only. Contact Charleston Office at Farmhouse.

FIRLE PLACE
(Viscount Gage)
nr Lewes   BN8 6LP   map **12** V23   △
Telephone: (01273) 858335. **Fax:** (01273) 858043

Home of the Gage family since the 15th century, the original Tudor house was largely altered about 1730. The House contains a magnificent collection of European and British Old Masters. The pictures are further enhanced with French and English furniture by famous craftsmen. There is also a quantity of Sèvres porcelain of the finest quality. These are largely derived from the Cowper collection, and can be seen in a spacious family setting. A Connoisseurs house. There are items of particular interest to visitors from the USA through General Gage, Commander-in-Chief of the British Forces at the beginning of the War of Independence, and his wife Margaret Kemble of New Jersey. The House is set in parkland under the South Downs, 60 miles from London by road. Hourly rail service Victoria to Lewes, takes 65 minutes, thence by taxi (5 miles).

Location: 5 m SE of Lewes on the Lewes/Eastbourne Road (A27).
Station(s): Lewes (5 m, taxis available).
Open: May-Sept Wed Thurs & Sun also Easter, May, Spring & Summer Bank Hol Suns & Mons 2- with last tickets at 5. First Wed in month longer unguided Connoisseurs' tour of House with additional rooms. Exclusive Private Viewing Groups 25+ by arrangement.
Admission: Pre-booked group parties of 25 on Open Days (except first Wed in month) at reduced rate. Special exclusive viewings at other times of year for private parties over 25 by arrangement.*Party bookings in writing to Showing Secretary, Firle Place, nr Lewes, East Sussex BN8 6LP (01273) 858335.*
Refreshments: Licensed cold buffet luncheons 12-2. Sussex cream teas from 3, only on house open days. (Bookings (01273) 858307).
Events/Exhibitions: Various horse events, clay pigeon, archery etc.
Conferences: Receptions, concerts, corporate entertaining, country pursuits in Park.
Shop and contemporary pictures exhibition. Car park adjacent to house.

GLYNDE PLACE
(Viscount & Viscountess Hampden)
nr Lewes   BN8 6SX   map **12** V23   △
Telephone: (01273) 858224
Fax: (01273) 858224

Set below the ancient hill fort of Mount Caburn, Glynde Place is a magnificent example of Elizabethan architecture and is the manor house of an estate which has been in the same family since the 12th century. Built in 1579 of Sussex flint and Caen stone around a courtyard, the house commands exceptionally fine views towards Pevensey marshes and the South Downs. Amongst the collections of four hundred years of family living can be seen a fine collection of 17th and 18th century portraits of the Trevors and a room dedicated to Sir Henry Brand, Speaker of the House of Commons 1872-1884. The house is still the family home of the Brands and can be enjoyed as such.

Location: In Glynde village 4 m SE of Lewes on A27.
Station(s): Within easy walking distance of Glynde Station with hourly services to Lewes Brighton and Eastbourne.
Open: Easter Day and Easter Monday; May-Suns only and Bank Hols. June to Sept Weds, Thurs and Suns and Aug Bank Hol. Guided tours for parties (25 or more) can be booked on a regular open day (£2.50 per person) or on a non-open day when the tour will be guided by the owner (£5 per person)., Contact Lord Hampden on (01273) 858 224. House open 2pm and last admission 4.45.
Admission: Adults £3.25 children £1.50. Free parking.
Refreshments: Sussex cream teas in Georgian Stable Block. Parties to book in advance (as above). Exhibition of watercolours and prints by local artists and shop.
Events/Exhibitions: 'Harbert Morley and the Great Rebellion 1638-1660' the story of the part played by the owner of Glynde Place in the Civil War.
Conferences: House can be hired for weddings and parties. (Contact Lord Hampden).

HASTINGS CASTLE AND 1066 STORY
(Hastings Heritage Ltd)
Hastings
Telephone: (01424) 717963

Majestic ruins of England's first Norman castle.sound and scenic effects, and depicting the story of the Battle of Hastings, and the 900 year dramatic history of the castle.

KIDBROOKE PARK WITH REPTON GROUNDS
(The Council of Michael Hall School)
Forest Row   map **12** U13
Telephone: (01342) 822275
Fax: (01342) 826593

Sandstone house and stables built in 1730s with later alterations.

Location: 1 m SW of Forest Row, off A22, 4 m S of East Grinstead.
Open: Spring Bank Hol Mon (May 30) then Aug-Daily (inc Bank Hol Mon) 11- 6.
Admission: Apply to the Bursar during office hours.

LAMB HOUSE   🍂 The National Trust
Rye   map **13** V24
Telephone: (01892) 890651
Location: In West Street facing W end of church.

MONKS HOUSE   🍂 The National Trust
Rodmell   map **12** V23
Telephone: (01892) 890651
Location: 3 m SE of Lewes, in Rodmell village.

MOORLANDS
(Dr and Mrs Steven Smith)
Crowborough   map **12** U23
Telephone: (01892) 652474
Location: Friar's Gate. 2 m N of Crowborough. Approach via B2188 at Friar's Gate - take L fork signposted 'Crowborough Narrow Road', entrance 100 yards on left. From Crowborough crossroads take St. Johns Road to Friar's Gate.

PASHLEY MANOR GARDENS
(Mr & Mrs J.A. Sellick)
Ticehurst, Wadhurst   TN5 7HE   map **12** U23
Telephone: (01580) 200692
Fax: (01580) 200102

Pashley Manor Gardens, dating from 1550, stands in a well timbered park with magnificent views across to Brightling Beacon.

PEVENSEY CASTLE   ENGLISH HERITAGE 🔲
Pevensey   map **12** V23
Telephone: (01323) 762604

The walls that enclose this 10-acre site are from the 4th century Roman fort, Anderida. The inner castle, with its great keep, is medieval. With the fall of France in 1940, Pevensey was put into service again, after centuries of neglect. A Personal Stereo Guided Tour is available.

Location: Pevensey.
Open: Apr 1-Sept 30 10-6 daily Oct 1-31 10-4 daily Nov 1-Mar 31 (closed 1-2) Wed-Sun 10-4.
Admission: Adults £2 concessions £1.50 children £1.

PRESTON MANOR
(Borough of Brighton)
Brighton   map **12** V22
Telephone: (01273) 603005
Fax: (01273) 779108

A Georgian house built in 1738 and added to in 1905; the house of the Stanford family for nearly 150 years. The house is fully furnished, illustrating the upstairs and downstairs life of a rich gentry family and their servants. More than 20 beautifully restored rooms to explore over 4 floors from the servants quarters, kitchens and Butlers pantry in the basement to the day nursery, toy collections and attic rooms at the top of the house. Delightful grounds with walled garden, pets' cemetery and 13th parish church. Free parking.

Location: On main Brighton to London Road at Preston Park.
Station(s): Preston Park.
Open: All the year Mon 1-5 (Bank Hols 10-5) Tues-Sat 10-5 Sun 2-5 closed Good Fri Christmas & Boxing Day.

Admission: Charged. Reduced rates for parties, families, children and OAPs. Garden free.
Events/Exhibitions: Special Christmas events.
Conferences: Corporate hospitality available.
Parties by arrangement. Available for evening hire.

ROYAL PAVILION
Brighton   map **12** V22   ♿
Telephone: (01273) 603005

The Royal Pavilion, the famous seaside home of King George IV, has been justifiably termed "the most extraordinary palace in Europe". Originally a simple farmhouse, in 1787 architect Henry Holland created a neo-classical villa on the site. It was later transformed into its current Indian style by John Nash between 1815 and 1822. Decorated in the Chinese taste with an astonishingly exotic exterior, this Regency Palace is quite breathtaking. Magnificent decorations and fantastic furnishings have been re-created in the recent extensive structural and interior restoration programme. Throughout the building the main state rooms, apartments and suites have been returned to their original splendour, revealing dazzling colours and superb craftsmanship. The opening of the Yellow Bow Rooms in 1994 marked the completion of the final major stage of interior restoration. Originally the bedrooms of the Dukes of York and Clarence, brothers of George IV, the original 1821 decorative scheme of this suite of rooms has been painstakingly re-created. Following the successful restoration of the exterior of the Royal Pavilion, the surrounding gardens have now also been returned to as near as possible their appearance in 1826. Relaid to John Nash's elegant design, the picturesque gardens are a superb example of Regency planting schemes and a fitting setting for the magical Royal Pavilion. Plus award-winning floodlighting scheme.

Location: In centre of Brighton (Old Steine).
Station(s): Brighton (½ m).
Open: Daily throughout the year: June-Sept 10am-6pm Oct-May 10am-5pm. Closed 25/26 Dec.
Admission: Charged. Reduced rates for parties, families, children and OAPs.
Refreshments: Tea-room with balcony overlooking the gardens.
Conferences: State rooms available for evening hire plus daytime meeting space.
Ground floor accessible for the disabled. Pavilion Shop. Guided tours available. The Royal Pavilion is available for corporate entertaining, private hire and wedding ceremonies. For further information telephone Public Services on (01273) 603005.

SHEFFIELD PARK GARDEN   🍂 The National Trust

nr Uckfield   map **12** U23
Telephone: (01825) 790231
Fax: (01825) 791264

100 acre garden with series of lakes linked by cascades; famous for its rhodo-dendrons, azaleas and collection of rare trees and shrubs.

Location: Midway between East Grinstead & Lewes on E side of A275; 5 m NW of Uckfield.
Station(s): Sheffield Park (Bluebell Railway) .75; Uckfield 6 m.
Open: Mar; Sat and Sun only 11-4. 30 Mar-10 Nov; Tues-Sun and Bank Hol Mon 11-6 or sunset if earlier. 13 Nov-22 Dec, Wed-Sun 11-4. Last admission 1 hour before close.
Admission: Adults £4 Children £2 Family ticket £10. Pre-booked parties £3. *No reduction for parties on Sat Sun & Bank Hols.*
Refreshments: Tea-room (not NT) next to car park.
Events/Exhibitions: Twenties evening 22 June.
No dogs. Shop. Wheelchairs available.

WEST SUSSEX

APULDRAM ROSES

(Mrs D. R. Sawday)

Appledram Lane, Dell Quay, Chichester, West Sussex   map **12** V21   ♿
Telephone: (01243) 785769
Fax: (01243) 536973

Specialist Rose Nursery growing over 300 varieties of Hybrid Teas, Floribundas, Climbers, Ramblers, Ground Cover, Miniature and Patio Roses. Also a large selection of shrub roses both old and new. Mature Rose Garden to view. Field open during summer months. Suitable for disabled but no special toilet. One wheelchair available.

Location: 1 m SW of Chichester. A286 Birdham-Wittering road from Chichester. Turn right into Dell Quay Road and then right again into Apuldram Lane.
Open: Every day Jan 7 to Dec 23. Mon to Sat 9-5, Suns and Bank Hols 10.30-4.30. Parties can be taken around by prior arrangement with guided tour of roses June to Sept.
Admission: Charity box in garden.
Refreshments: Ice creams
Events/Exhibitions: Open evenings June 20 and 27 6.30-8.00
One wheelchair available. Ample car parking.

ARUNDEL CASTLE - See Opposite Page.

BERRI COURT

(Mr & Mrs J. C. Turner)

Yapton   map **12** V21
Telephone: (01243) 551663

3 acre garden of wide interest in centre of Yapton Village.

Open: Suns, Monds 31 Mar-1 Apr, May 12-13, June 23-24, Oct 27-28 or viewing by appointment.
Admission: Adults £1.50 in aid of National Garden Scheme (children free).
Dogs on lead.

BORDE HILL GARDEN

(Borde Hill Garden Ltd)

Haywards Heath   RH16 1XP   map **12** U22   ♿
Telephone: (01444) 450326
Fax: (01444) 440427

Large garden with woods and parkland of exceptional beauty. Rare trees and shrubs, herbaceous borders and fine views. Woodland Walk, water feature, pic-nic area by lake.

Location: 1½ m N of Haywards Heath on Balcombe Road. Brighton 17 m; Gatwick 10 m.
Station(s): Haywards Heath 1½ m.
Open: Daily Mar 18-Oct 1 10-6.
Admission: Adults £3.50 OAPs £3 children £1.50 family ticket £7.50 parties £3. Parkland admission £1 per person (not available during special events).
Refreshments: Licensed - morning coffee, lunches, cream teas and dinner; parties by arrangement.
Events/Exhibitions: Ring for details.
Conferences: Ring (01444) 441102 for details.
Children's Adventure Playground and trout fishing.

CHAMPS HILL

(Mr & Mrs David Bowerman)

Coldwaltham, nr Pulborough

27 acres of formal garden and woodland walks around old sandpits.

CHICHESTER CATHEDRAL

(The Dean & Chapter of Chichester)

West Street, Chichester   PO19 1PX   map **12** V21
Telephone: (01243) 782595
Fax: (01243) 536190

In the heart of the city, this fine Cathedral has been a centre of Christian worship and community life for 900 years and is the site of the Shrine of St Richard of Chichester. Its treasures range from Romanesque stone carvings to 20th century works of art by Sutherland, Feibusch, Procktor, Chagall, Skelton, Piper, and Ursula Benker-Schirmer. Treasury.

Location: Centre of city; British Rail; A27, A286.
Open: All year 7.30-7 (5 in winter except for those attending Evensong). Choral Evensong daily (except Wed) during term time and occasionally visiting choirs at other times. Ministry of welcome operates. Guided tours must be booked.
Admission: Free: suggested donations adults £2 children 50p.
Refreshments: Refectory off Cathedral Cloisters with lavatory facilities (including those for the disabled). Medieval Vicars' Hall (by prior arrangement).
Conferences: Meeting room available in the Vicar's Hall (for 100 people max).
Wheelchair access (one wheelchair available on application to Vergers). Loop system in the Cathedral. Touch and hearing centre for the blind and a braille guide. Guide dogs only. Gift shops in the Bell Tower and at 23 South Street. Parking in city car and coach parks.

COATES MANOR

(Mrs G H Thorp)

nr Fittleworth
Telephone: (01798) 865356

One acre garden, mainly shrubs and foliage of special interest.

Open: 20-21 Oct (1996) 11-5 or also by appointment.
Admission: Adults £1.50 children 20p in aid of the National Gardens Scheme.

COKE'S BARN

(Mr & Mrs Nigel Azis)

West Burton, nr Pulborough

¾ acre garden surrounding C17 barn.

DANNY

(Country Houses Association)

Hurstpierpoint   BN6 9BB   map **12** V22
Telephone: (01273) 833000

Elizabethan E-shaped house, dating from 1593.

Location: Between Hassocks and Hurstpierpoint (B2116) - off New Way Lane.
Station(s): Hassocks (1 m).
Open: May-Sept Weds & Thurs 2-5. Last entry 4.30.
Admission: £2.50 Children £1. Free car park.
No dogs admitted.

DENMANS GARDEN

(Mr John Brookes)

Denmans Lane, Fontwell, nr. Arundel   BN18 0SU   map **12** V21   ♿
Telephone: (01243) 542808
Fax: (01243) 544064

Unique 20th Century Garden artistically planted forming vistas with emphasis on colours, shapes and textures for all year interest; areas of glass areas for tender and rare species. John Brookes school of garden design in the Clock House where seminars available.

Location: Between Arundel and Chichester; turn off A27 into Denmans Lane (W of Fontwell racecourse).
Station(s): Barnham (2 m).
Open: Open daily throughout the year including all Bank Holidays except Christmas Day and Boxing Day 9-5. Coaches by appointment.
Admission: Adults £2.50 children £1.50 OAPs £2.25. Groups of 15 or more £1.95. (1995 prices)
Refreshments: Restaurant and shop open 10-5.
Plant centre. Gift Shop. No dogs. National Gardens Scheme.

Butterfly Houses

can be found at the following properties included in Historic Houses Castles and Gardens:-

Berkeley Castle
Elsham Hall - Wild butterfly walkway
Syon House

ARUNDEL CASTLE
(Arundel Castle Trustees Ltd)
Arundel   map **12** V21   &
Telephone: (01903) 883136

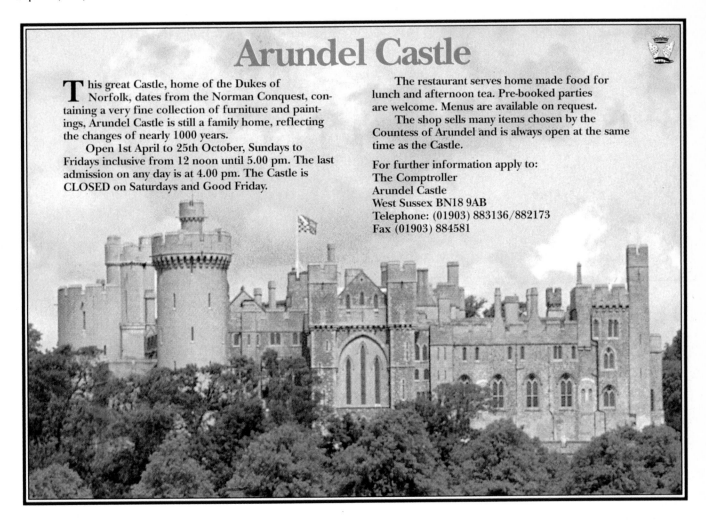

Arundel Castle

This great Castle, home of the Dukes of Norfolk, dates from the Norman Conquest, containing a very fine collection of furniture and paintings, Arundel Castle is still a family home, reflecting the changes of nearly 1000 years.

Open 1st April to 25th October, Sundays to Fridays inclusive from 12 noon until 5.00 pm. The last admission on any day is at 4.00 pm. The Castle is CLOSED on Saturdays and Good Friday.

The restaurant serves home made food for lunch and afternoon tea. Pre-booked parties are welcome. Menus are available on request.

The shop sells many items chosen by the Countess of Arundel and is always open at the same time as the Castle.

For further information apply to:
The Comptroller
Arundel Castle
West Sussex BN18 9AB
Telephone: (01903) 883136/882173
Fax (01903) 884581

HISTORIC HOUSES CASTLES & GARDENS

For further details on editorial listings or display advertising contact the

Editor: Deborah Valentine,
Windsor Court, East Grinstead House, East Grinstead, West Sussex RH19 1XA
Tel: (01342) 335794 Fax: (01342) 335720

GOODWOOD HOUSE

(Duke of Richmond)
Chichester   PO18 OPX   map **12** V21
Telephone: (01243) 774107
Fax: (01243) 774313

Goodwood is the ancestral seat of the Dukes of Richmond and Gordon. The magnificent state apartments of Goodwood House are filled with stunning treasures. There are paintings by Canaletto, Stubbs and Reynolds, a Sevres porcelain collection, rare French furniture and tapestries. The House also provides a spectacular setting for wedding receptions and private parties. A programme of refurbishment will restrict access to some of the state rooms on some open days during the year.

Location: 3½ m NE of Chichester, approach roads A283 & A286, A27. Aerodrome 1 m from House.
Open: House open days:Easter Sun and Mon (7 & 8 Apr) 2-5 and then Suns and Mons to 30 Sept plus Tues, Weds & Thurs in Aug. Closed on event days: 21,22 Apr; 12,13,19,20 May; 23,24 June; 1 Aug.
Admission: Thurs and Fri £7.50 per person, Sat £10 per person. Children and students half price.
Events/Exhibitions: Festival of Speed: 21/22/23rd June advance booking office (01243) 787766. Goodwood Racecourse 21/22/23rd May, 6/7th June (evening), 14th June (evening), 21st June (evening), 28th June (evening), 30-3 Aug, 24/25th Aug, 13/14th Sept, 25/26th Sept.
Accommodation: Goodwood Park Hotel, Golf and Country Club - reservations (01345) 123333/(01243) 775537.
Conferences: Licensed for Civil Weddings and functions throughout the year.
House suitable for wheelchairs (no steps); a wheelchair is available. For information concerning the Re-decoration of the State Apartments telephone (01243) 774107. For information about Goodwood Flying Club telephone (01243) 774656. For information about Goodwood Motor Circuit telephone (01243) 789660.

HAMMERWOOD PARK

(David Pinnegar, Esq)
nr East Grinstead   RH19 3QE   map **12** V23
Telephone: (01342) 850594
Fax: (01342) 850864

HAMMERWOOD PARK is said by visitors to be the most interesting house in Sussex. Built in 1792 as a temple of Apollo, the house was the first work of **Latrobe**, the architect of **The White House and The Capitol, Washington D.C., U.S.A.** Set in Reptonesque parkland on the edge of the Ashdown Forest,

the house is an early example of Greek Revival and was directly influenced by the French Revolution. In 1982 David Pinnegar purchased the house as a near ruin from the pop-group Led Zeppelin. Award winning restoration works have been completed and one of the most ambitious *trompe-l'oeil* decoration schemes of this century has recently been painted in the staircase hall. Just one room remains spectacularly derelict. Various collections include musical instruments and a copy of the **Elgin Marbles.** Guided tours by the owner and his family, luscious cream teas and musical evenings bring the house to life.

Location: 3½ m E of East Grinstead on A264 Tunbridge Wells; 1 m W of Holtye.
Station(s): East Grinstead
Open: Easter Mon-end Sept Wed Sat & Bank Hol Mons 2-5.30. Guided tour starts just after 2. Coaches (21 seats or more) by appointment. School groups welcome.
Admission: £3.50 Children £1.50.
Refreshments: Luscious cream teas in the Elgin Room.
Accommodation: B & B with a difference in an idyllically peaceful location only 20 minutes from Gatwick.
Conferences: Small events can be tailored to your requirements.

HIGH BEECHES GARDENS

(High Beeches Gardens Conservation Trust. Reg. non profit making Charity)
Handcross   RH17 6HQ   map **12** U22   △
Telephone: (01444) 400589

Help us to preserve these twenty acres of enchanting landscaped woodland and water gardens, with Magnolias, Camellias, Rhododendrons, and Azaleas, in Spring. In Autumn, this is one of the most brilliant gardens for leaf colour. Gentians and Primulas are naturalised, with Royal Fern and Gunnera in the Water Gardens. Four acres of natural Wildflower Meadows, Cowslips and Orchids.

Location: 1 m E of A23 at Handcross, on B2110.
Open: Gardens Only Mar 22 23 24 29 30 31 and Apr May June Sept and Oct daily except Wed 1-5. Coaches by appointment at all times, please.
Admission: Adults £3.00 per person. Accompanied children free. Groups by appointment, on any day, at any time. Special opening £3.50 per person. Guided, £4.50 per person inclusive.
Refreshments: Hot and cold drinks, ice cream and biscuits in Gate Lodge daily. Light lunches and teas on Event days, and by appointment for groups.
Events/Exhibitions: 10-5. Homemade Refreshments all day. Plants for sale. Daffodil Day. Marie Curie stalls, Apr 8. Bluebell Day. W.I. stall May 6. Azalea Day. W.I. stall May 27. Gentian Day working shire horses. W I. market and craft demonstrations Aug 18. Autumn Splendour Oct 13. Covered Bazaar, in aid of Aldingbourne Trust providing work and homes for those with learning disabilities.
Sadly, gardens not suitable for wheelchairs. Regret no dogs.

LEONARDSLEE GARDENS
(The Loder Family)
Horsham   RH13 6PP   map **12** U22
Telephone: (01403) 891212

One of the most beautiful gardens in the country. Fantastic setting of natural valley with 6 lakes. Famous for camellias & magnolias in April, glorious rhododendrons and azaleas in May, tranquil Summer foliage; brilliant Autumn tints.

Rock garden, Bonsai exhibition, Alpine house. Wallabies, Deer parks. Souvenirs & plants for sale.

Location: In Lower Beeding at junction of A279 & A281: 5 m SE of Horsham or 3 m SW of Handcross at bottom of M23.
Open: Apr 1-Oct 31 every day 10-6 (In May 10-8).
Admission: May adults £4.50 children £2 Apr & June-Oct adults £3.50 children £2.
Refreshments: Licensed Restaurant and Tea-room.
Not suitable for wheelchairs. No dogs please.

NEWTIMBER PLACE
(Andrew Clay, Esq)
Newtimber   BN6 9BU   map **12** V22   △
Telephone: (01273) 833104

Moated house - Etruscan style wall paintings.

Location: Off A281 between Poynings and Pyecombe.
Station(s): Hassocks 3 miles
Open: May-Aug incl Thurs 2.30-5 by appointment. Parties at other times by arrangement.
Admission: £2.
Refreshments: Tea parties only by prior arrangement.

NYMANS GARDEN   ❧ The National Trust
Handcross, nr Haywards Heath   RH17 6EB   map **12** U22   ♿
Telephone: (01444) 400321 or 400777

One of the most romantic gardens in Britain, with rare and beautiful plants, shrubs and trees from all over the world, including azaleas, rhododendrons, eucryphias, hydrangeas, magnolias, camellias and roses. Also, a walled garden, hidden sunken garden, pinetum, laurel walks and romantic ruins. Woodland walks now open.

Location: At Handcross just off London/Brighton M23/A23.
Station(s): Crawley 5½ m, Haywards Heath 6 m.
Open: 1 Mar-end Oct daily (except Mons & Tues) and open Bank Hol Mons 11-7 or sunset if earlier. Last adm 1 hour before closing.
Admission: £4.20 Children half-price. Parties of 15 or more £3.50 must book. Special joint party ticket which includes same day entry to Standen £6 available Wed-Fri. Family ticket £10.
Refreshments: Light lunches and teas in licensed tea-room. Weds-Sun Dec daily 11-5.
Dogs in car park only. Wheelchair available. Braille Guide. Shop and exhibition.

PALLANT HOUSE
9 North Pallant, Chichester   PO19 1TJ   map **12** V21
Telephone: (01243) 774557

Meticulously restored Queen Anne Townhouse with eight rooms decorated and furnished in styles from early Georgian to late Victorian. Also important displays of Bow Porcelain (1747-1775) and Modern British Art (1920-1980).

Location: Chichester City centre.
Open: All year Tues-Sat 10-5.15 (last admissions 4.45).
Admission: Adults £2.50 Students/Over 60s £1.70.
Refreshments: Available nearby.
Events/Exhibitions: Call for details.

PARHAM HOUSE AND GARDENS

(Parham Park Ltd. - Reg. Charity No. 276673)
Pulborough   RH20 4HS   map **12** V22   △
Telephone: (01903) 742021 info line 744888
Fax: (01903) 746557

The setting for "Haunted" starring Aidan Quinn, Kate Beckinsale and Anthony Andrews. Beautiful Elizabethan house with important collection of Elizabethan and Stuart portraits, furniture, carpets, tapestries and needlework. The flowers for the arrangements in the rooms are grown in the award-winning 11-acre gardens, which include a four-acre walled garden with herb and vegetable gardens.

Location: A283 Storrington-Pulborough road.
Station(s): Pulborough (Victoria line).
Open: Wed Thurs Sun and Bank Hol Mon. Afternoons from 3 Apr-31 Oct. Also the following Sats 15 June, 20th July and 24 Aug. Gardens and picnic area 1-6pm (12-6pm in July and Aug) House 2-6pm last admission 5pm.
Admission: House and Gardens adults £4.25 OAPs £3.75 children £1 Gardens only adults/OAPs £3 children 50p. Group rates for both guided Mon, Tues, Fri afternoons & Wed, Thurs mornings only. Unguided visits available on application to The Administrator.
Refreshments: Self service teas in Big Kitchen, some outside seating. Ice cream bike.
Events/Exhibitions: Parham House Garden Weekend - 20/21st July 1996.
Church, shop, plant sales (until the end of Sept). Picnic area conveniently close to large car park and House. Access for disabled to garden (House by special arrangement only); 2 wheelchairs available for loan.

PETWORTH HOUSE   ❦ The National Trust

Petworth   GU28 0AE   map **12** V23   ♿
Telephone: (01798) 342207
Fax: (01798) 342963

Perfect for a great day out, a magnificent house set within 700 acres of beautiful deer park, with lake and pleasure grounds landscaped by 'Capability' Brown. The State Rooms contain one of the most important collections of art in the country, including paintings by Turner, Van Dyck, Claude, Lely, Gainsborough and William Blake. Recently restored old kitchens in the Servants Block and full programme of exhibitions.

Location: In centre of Petworth 5½ m E of Midhurst.
Station(s): Pulborough 5 m.
Open: 30 Mar-end Oct daily except Mon and Fri. Open Good Fri and Bank Hol Mon 1-5.30 last adm 4.30. Pleasure grounds and car park 12-6. Deer Park open daily all year 8-sunset *closed* June 28-30 from 12 noon. Car park for visitors to House during open hours, 800 yds. Car park for Park only on A283, 1½ m N of Petworth.
Admission: £4.20 Children half-price Family ticket £10 Pre-booked parties of 15 or more £3.70. Deer park free.
Refreshments: Light lunches and teas in licensed tea-room 12-5 (last orders 4.30) same days as house.
Dogs under control in the park - no dogs in house or Pleasure Grounds. Shop. Wheelchairs provided. No prams or pushchairs in showrooms. Braille guide. Children's quiz.

SACKVILLE COLLEGE

(Patron Earl De La Warr)
East Grinstead   RH19 3AZ   map **12** U22   △
Telephone: (01342) 321930/326561

Jacobean Almshouses founded in 1609 and still in use. Common Room, Dining Hall, Chapel and Study. Original furniture.

Location: High Street, East Grinstead off A22.
Station(s): East Grinstead.
Open: June and July Wed-Sat 2-5 Aug each day 2-5.
Admission: Adults £1.50 children 75p parties by arrangement Apr-Oct.
Refreshments: Teas to order for parties.

SAINT HILL MANOR

Saint Hill, East Grinstead
RH19 4JY   map **12** U22
Telephone: (01342) 326711

Fine Sussex sandstone house built in 1792 and situated near the breathtaking Ashdown Forest. Saint Hill Manor's final owner, acclaimed author and humanitarian, L. Ron Hubbard lived for many years with his family. Under his direction extensive renovations were carried out uncovering exquisite period features hidden for over a century. Fine wood panelling, marble fireplaces, Georgian windows and plasterwork ceilings have been expertly restored to their original beauty. Outstanding features of this lovely house include a complete library of Mr. Hubbard's works, elegant Wintergarden, and the delightful Monkey Room housing John Spencer Churchill's 100 feet mural depicting many famous characters as monkeys, including his uncle Sir Winston Churchill. 59 acres of landscaped gardens, lake and woodlands.

Location: 2 m SW of East Grinstead on Saint Hill Road off A22.
Station(s): East Grinstead.
Open: All Year daily tours 1-5 or by appointment.
Admission: Free.
Refreshments: Tea room serving light refreshments.
Events/Exhibitions: Summer concerts on the terrace. Annual European Arts Festival and musical evenings throughout the year.
Parking for cars and coaches.

ST. MARY'S HOUSE AND GARDENS

(Peter Thorogood, Esq)
Bramber, nr Steyning BN44 3WE   map **12** V22
Telephone: (01903) 816205

Famous historic house in the downland village of Bramber. Built in 1470 by William Waynflete, Bishop of Winchester, founder of Magdalen College, Oxford. Classified (Grade 1) as 'the best example of late 15th Century timber-framing in Sussex'. Fine panelled rooms including the unique Trompe l'oeil 'Painted Room', decorated for the visit of Elizabeth I. The 'Kings Room' has connections with Charles II's escape to France in 1651. Rare 16th century painted wall leather. English furniture, ceramics, manuscripts and fine English costume -doll collection. The library houses important private collection of works by Victorian poet and artist Thomas Hood. Still a lived in family home, St.

Mary's was awarded the 'Warmest Welcome' Commendation by the S.E. Tourist Board. **GARDENS** Charming gardens with amusing topiary as seen on BBC TV. Features include an exceptional example of the Living Fossil Tree, Ginkgo Biloba, a magnificently tall Magnolia Grandiflora, and the mysterious ivy-clad Monk's Walk.

Location: 10 m NW of Brighton in village of Bramber off A283.
Station(s): Shoreham-by-Sea (4 m). Trains from London (Victoria).
Open: Easter Sun-last Sun in Sept Suns & Thurs & Bank Hol Mons 2-6. **Coach party bookings** morning or afternoon any other days by prior arrangement from Apr-Oct.
Admission: £3.80 OAPs £3.50 children £2. Reduced rates for parties £3.50 (25 or over). Free coach and car parking in grounds.
Refreshments: Homemade afternoon tea in the Music Room. Catering for parties by arrangement. Seating for up to 60.
Events/Exhibitions: Programme of concerts in our Victorian Music Room.
Conferences: Smaller day seminars.

STANDEN   The National Trust

East Grinstead   **RH19 4NE**   map **12** U22
Telephone: (01342) 323029

A family 'Arts and Crafts' inspired house and garden built just over 100 years ago. Wonderful collection of William Morris interiors - wallpapers, textiles, period furniture and paintings. The gardens have fine views across the Medway Valley.

Location: 2 m S of East Grinstead signposted from the Turners Hill road (B2110).
Station(s): East Grinstead (2 m).
Open: 23/24 & 30/31 Mar 1.30-4.30 last admission 4pm. Apr 1-end Oct Wed-Sun & Bank Hol Mons 12.30-6. Access may be restricted at busy times. Pre-booked parties Wed Thurs & Fri only telephone Property Manager.
Admission: House and Garden £4.50. Garden only £3. Children half price Parties £3.50. Special joint party ticket which includes entry to Nymans Garden £5.50 available Wed-Fri. Family ticket £11.25.
Refreshments: Light lunches and teas served from 12.30-5.00. March 1.30-4 (teas only).
Events/Exhibitions: Please phone for details.
Dogs admitted to car park & woodland walks only. Wheelchairs provided; disabled drivers may park near house with prior permission from Administrator. Shop. *No pushchairs or back-packs in house.*

WAKEHURST PLACE GARDEN   🌿 The National Trust
(Administered by Royal Botanic Gardens, Kew)
Ardingly, nr Haywards Heath   RH17 6TN   map 12 U22   ♿
Telephone: (01444) 892701 or (0181) 332 5066

A wealth of exotic plant species including many fine specimens of trees and shrubs. Picturesque watercourse linking several ponds and lakes. Heath garden and rock walk. Elizabethan Mansion.

Location: 1½ m NW of Ardingly on B2028.
Station(s): Haywards Heath 6 m. East Grinstead 6½ m.
Open: All the year Daily Nov-end Jan 10-4 Feb & Oct 10-5 Mar 10-6 Apr-end of Sept 10-7. Last adm ½ hour before closing. *Closed Christmas Day & New Year's Day.* Opening times may be subject to alteration. Please telephone 0181 332 5066 or 01444 892701 for up to date information.
Admission: Adults £4.50 children £2.50 concessions £3 family £12. *Visitors should check with Wakehurst Place for 1996 prices.*
Refreshments: Self service restaurant (not NT) open daily all year.
No dogs except guide dogs. Wheelchairs provided. Exhibition in Mansion. Book shop open (not NT).

THE WEALD AND DOWNLAND OPEN AIR MUSEUM
Singleton, nr Chichester   map 12 V21   △
Telephone: (01243) 811348

The Museum is rescuing and re-erecting historic Buildings from South-East England. The Collection illustrates the history of vernacular architecture in the Weald and Downland area. Exhibits include a Medieval Farmstead, Garden and History of Farming Exhibition centred on Bayleaf Farmhouse (above) Timber-framed Houses, a Tudor Market Hall, a 16th century Treadwheel. Farm Buildings include two 18th century Barns and a Granary, a Blacksmith's Forge, Plumber's and Carpenter's Workshops, a Village School and a History of Brickwork Exhibition. A 'Hands On' gallery explores building materials and techniques.

Location: 6 m N of Chichester on A286 just S of Singleton.
Open: Mar 1-Oct 31 daily 11-5 Nov 1-Feb 28 Wed Sat and Sun only 11-4 Dec 26-Jan 1 daily 11-4.
Admission: Charged. Parties by arrangement (group rates available).
Refreshments: Light refreshments during main season.

Giovanni Antonio Canale
- known as Canaletto
Born in Venice 1697, died 1768
Lived in England 1746 - 1755

His work can be seen in the following properties
included in Historic Houses Castles and Gardens:-

Alnwick Castle
Bowhill
Goodwood House
Upton House

WEST DEAN GARDENS
(The Edward James Foundation)
nr Chichester   PO18 0QZ   map 12 V21   ♿
Telephone: (01243) 818210 or (01243) 811301. **Fax:** (01243) 811342

Extensive downland garden in Lavant Valley with 300' pergola, water garden, herbaceous borders and bedding displays. 3 acre working walled kitchen garden with unusual vegetables, cut flowers, extensive fruit collection and 13 recently restored Victorian glasshouses including fruit, fern, orchid and tropical houses. Also tool and mower collection and thatched Apple Store. Park Walk (2¼ miles) through parkland and the peaceful 45 acre St Roches Arboretum with its extensive collection of trees and shrubs. House not open.

Location: 6 m N of Chichester on A286, nr Weald & Downland Open Air Museum.
Station(s): Chichester.
Open: Mar-Oct incl. daily 11-5 (last adm 4.30) parties by arrangement.
Admission: Adults £3 OAPs £2.50 children £1.50 pre-booked parties 20+ £2.50 per person.
Refreshments: Licesed restaurant.
Events/Exhibitions: Garden Fair 29-30 June. Chili Pepper Festival 11 Aug. Please phone for details.
Conferences: Facilities available. Please phone for details.
Coach and car parking. Sorry no dogs.

TYNE & WEAR

GIBSIDE   🌿 The National Trust
Gibside   NE16 6BG   map 9 N19
Telephone: (01207) 542255
Location: 6 m SW of Gateshead; 20 m NW of Durham between Rowlands Gill and Burnopfield.

SOUTER LIGHTHOUSE   🌿 The National Trust
Whitburn   SR6 7NH   map 9 N20
Telephone: 0191-529 3161
Location: 2½ m S of South Shields on A183, 5m N of Sunderland.

TYNEMOUTH CASTLE AND PRIORY   ENGLISH HERITAGE
map 9 M20
Telephone: 0191-257 1090

Two saints were buried within the walls of this Benedictine priory, established in the 11th century on the site of an earlier abandoned monastery. Two walls of the presbytery still tower to their full height and the 15th century chantry chapel has a splendid collection of roof bosses. A fortified gatehouse was added during the Border wars, which persuaded Henry VIII to retain the priory as a royal castle after the Dissolution. The headland remained in use for coastal defence until 1956, one restored battery is open to the public.

Location: Tynemouth.
Open: Apr 1-Sept 30 10-6 daily Oct 1-31 10-4 daily Nov 1-Mar 31 10-4 Wed-Sun.
Admission: Adults £1.50 concessions £1.10 children 80p.

WASHINGTON OLD HALL   🌿 The National Trust
Washington   NE38 7LE   map 9 N20   ♿
Telephone: 0191-416 6879
Location: In Washington on E side of Ave; 5 m W of Sunderland (2 m from A1); S of Tyne Tunnel, follow signs for Washington New Town District 4 & then village.

WARWICKSHIRE

ARBURY HALL

(The Rt Hon the Viscount Daventry)
Nuneaton   CV10 7PT   map **14** R20   △ &
Telephone: (01203) 382804
Fax: (01203) 641147

16th century Elizabethan House, gothicized late 18th century, pictures, period furniture etc. Park and landscape gardens. Arbury has been the home of the Newdegate family since the 16th century. For a country house the Gothic architecture is unique, the original Elizabethan house being Gothicised by Sir Roger Newdigate between 1750 and 1800, under the direction of Sanderson Miller, Henry Keene, and Couchman of Warwick. Beautiful plaster ceilings, pictures and fine specimens of period furniture, china and glass. Fine stable block with central doorway by Wren. Arbury Hall is situated in very large grounds and is about 1½ miles from any main road. Excellent carriage drives lined with trees. George Eliot's 'Cheveral Manor'.

Location: 2 m SW of Nuneaton off B4102.
Station(s): Nuneaton.
Open: Easter Sun-end Sept. Hall Sun & Bank Hol Mon 2-5.30 Gardens Sun & Mon 2-6 (last adm. 5). Arbury is an ideal venue for Corporate hospitality functions, promotions and as a film location etc. and the Dining Room is also available for exclusive luncheon and dinner functions. Wheelchair access ground floor only.
Admission: Hall and Gardens adults £3.50 children £2 Gardens adults £2 children £1 organised parties most days (25 or over) special terms by prior arrangement with Administrator. School parties also welcome. Free car park.
Refreshments: Available on all open days. Set meals arranged for parties.
Events/Exhibitions: Craft Fairs held twice a year. Motor Transport Spectacular and Warwickshire Country Show in early summer.
Conferences: Suitable for small conferences with capacity of 50 for seated meals and 120 for buffets. Marquees can also be provided for larger meetings.

Ghosts are in residence at the following properties included in Historic Houses Castles and Gardens:

Blickling Hall - *Anne Boleyn*

Breamore House - *Haunted picture - if touched, death on the same day*

East Riddleden Hall - *5 ghosts including ladyin Grey Hall Lady's Chamber*

Fountains Abbey & Studley Royal - *Choir of monks chanting in Chapel of Nine Altars*

Hinton Ampner - *Nocturnal noises*

Ightham Mote - *Supernatural presence*

Lindisfarne Castle - *Monk, and group of monks on causeway*

Lyme Park - *Unearthly peals of bells and lady in white, funeral procession through park*

Malmesbury House - *Ghost of a cavalier*

Overbecks Museum & Garden - *'Model' ghost in the Children's room (for them to spot)*

Rockingham Castle - *Lady Dedlock*

Rufford Old Hall - *Elizabeth Hesketh*

Scotney Castle Garden - *Man rising from the lake*

Sizergh Castle & Garden - *Poltergeist*

Speke Hall - *Ghost of woman in tapestry room*

Springhill - *Ghost of a woman*

Sudbury Hall - *Lady in Green, seen on stairs*

Tamworth Castle - *Haunted bedroom*

Treasurer's House - *Troop of Roman soldiers marching through the cellar*

Wallington House - *Invisible birds beating against the windows accompanied by heavy breathing*

Washington Old Hall - *Grey lady walking through corridors*

BADDESLEY CLINTON   🦋 The National Trust

Rising Lane, Lapworth, Knowle   B93 0DQ   map **14** S19   ♿
Telephone: (01564) 783294

A romantically sited medieval moated manor house, with 120 acres, dating back to the 14th century and little changed since 1634.

Location: ¾ m W of A4141 Warwick to Birmingham Road, nr Chadwick End; 7½ m NW of Warwick; 15 m SE of Birmingham.
Station(s): Lapworth (2 m) (not Suns).
Open: Mar 2-end of Sept Wed to Sun & Bank Hol Mon 2-6.*Closed Good Fri* Grounds and shop open from 12 noon. Oct Wed to Suns 2-5. Mar 5 Wed to Sun 2-6. Last admissions 30 mins before closing. Coach parties (not Sun) by prior arrangement. Timed tickets issued to control numbers in house.
Admission: £4.50 Children £2.25 grounds, shop & restaurant only £2.25. Family tickets £11.25.
Refreshments: Lunches and teas in licensed restaurant from 12.30-5.30 same days as house. Closed 2-2.30 (Oct 4.30). Also open Nov 1 to Dec 17 Wed to Sun 12.30-4.30.
Events/Exhibitions: Details from the Property Administrator.
No prams, pushchairs or back carriers in the house. No dogs. Wheelchair available. Shop. Restaurant.

Anthony Salvin (1799-1881)
Architect - trained under John Nash

His work can be seen in the following properties included in Historic Houses Castles and Gardens:-

Helmingham Hall Gardens
Muncaster Castle
Petworth House

CHARLECOTE PARK   🦋 The National Trust

Warwick   CV35 9ER   map **14** S19   △ ♿
Telephone: (01789) 470277

Originally built by the Lucy family, 1550s. Refurbished 1830s in Elizabethan Revival style. 'Capability' Brown Deer park.

Location: 5 m E of Stratford-upon-Avon on the N side of B4086.
Station(s): Leamington Spa No 18 bus.
Open: Apr to end Oct Fri to Tues 11-6 House closed 1-2.(*Closed* Good Friday. Last admission to house 5. Parties (including schools) by prior arrangement only. Evening guided tours for pre-booked parties Mons, May to Sept 7.30-9.30.
Admission: £4.40 Children £2.20 Family ticket £11. Full price for evening visits (incl. NT members). Group rate & introductory talk available weekdays only.
Refreshments: Morning coffee, lunches, afternoon teas in the Orangery Restaurant (Licensed) 11-5.30. Picnics in Deer park only
Events/Exhibitions: Details from the Property Administrator.
No dogs. Wheelchairs provided. Shop.

COUGHTON COURT

(Mrs Clare Throckmorton)
Alcester   B49 5JA   map **14** S19
Telephone: (01789) 400777 (01789) 762435 (visitor information)
Fax: (01789) 765544

Coughton Court has been the home of the Throckmortons since the fifteeth century and the family still live there today. The magnificent Tudor gatehouse was built around 1530 with the north and south wings completed ten or twenty years later. The gables and the first story of these wings are of typical mid-sixteenth century half-timber work. Of particular interest to visitors is the Throckmorton family history from Tudor times to the present generation. On view are family portraits through the centuries, together with furniture, porcelain, tapestries and other family memorabilia and recent photographs. A strong Roman Catholic theme runs through the family history as the Throckmortons have maintained their Catholic religion until the present day. The house has a strong connection with the Gunpowder Plot and also suffered damage during the Civil War. The house stands in 25 acres of gardens and grounds which also contain two churches and a lake. A new formal garden was constructed in 1992 with designs based on an Elizabethan knot garden in the courtyard. Further extensive gardens development plus new orchard and bog garden open in 1996. Visitors can also enjoy a specially created walk beside the River Arrow, returning to the house alongside the lake. Exhibitions of Gunpowder Plot and Childrens Clothes.

Location: 2 m N of Alcester on A435.
Station(s): Redditch.
Open: From Mar 16, Sat Sun 12-5 Easter Sat-Wed 12-5 (All Bank Hol Mons incl. Easter Mon 12-5 (closed Good Fri) May end Sept daily (except Thurs & Fri) 12-5 to Oct 20 Sat Sun 12-5. Last admissions to house 30 mins before closing. Evening Guided tours for pre-booked parties Mon-Wed Garden tours by appointment. Grounds open same days as house but 11-5.30 (5 in Oct). Coughton Court reserve the right to close at 4pm on Saturday.
Admission: Adults £4.95 children £2.50 family ticket £13.50 Grounds only £2.95. Parties by prior written arrangement no party rate or membership concessions for out-of-hours visits.
Refreshments: Restaurant open 11.30-5.30 for coffee, lunches and teas (licensed).

Events/Exhibitions: Gunpowder Plot Exhibition, Childrens' Clothes (open all season).Entrance included in admission.
Accommodation: Luxury accommodation available for select groups.
Conferences: Full range of corporate hospitality facilities including wedding receptions.
Shop and plant centre open as restaurant. Limited access for wheelchairs in house. Riverside walk and new garden suitable for wheelchairs. Dogs on leads and picnics in car park only. House, grounds, shop and restaurant managed by the family.

FARNBOROUGH HALL   The National Trust

nr Banbury   OX17 1DU   map **7** S20
Telephone: (01295) 690202

Home of the Holbech family since 1684 reconstructed in early 18th century. The house incorporates fine plasterwork and ancient sculpture. e mile terrace walk feature temples and obelisk.

Location: 6 m N of Banbury; ½ m W of A423.
Open: House, grounds and terrace walk Apr to end of Sept Wed and Sat 2-6. Also May 5/6, 2-6. Terrace Walk only Thurs & Fri 2-6. Last adm 5.30.
Admission: House, grounds and terrace walk £2.70 Garden and terrace walk £1.50. Terrace walk only Thurs & Fri £1. Children half-price. *No reductions for parties.* Parties by prior written arrangement only.
Dogs in grounds only, on leads. No indoor photography. Farnborough Hall is occupied and administered by Mr. & Mrs. G Holbech.

HONINGTON HALL

(B. Wiggin, Esq)
Shipston-on-Stour   CV36 5AA   map **7** S19   △
Telephone: (01608) 661434
Fax: (01608) 663717

Originally built by the Parker family in 1680. Contains fine 18th century plasterwork.

Location: 10 m S of Stratford-on-Avon; ½ m E of A3400.
Open: June July Aug Weds & Bank Hol Mons 2.30-5. Parties at other times by appointment.
Admission: Adults £2.75 children £1.

KENILWORTH CASTLE

map **14** S19
Telephone: (01926) 52078

One of the grandest ruins in England, this castle was made famous by Sir Walter Scott. Gone now is the great lake that once surrounded it, but still standing is the huge Noman keep with walls nearly 20ft (6m) thick in places. Inside the encircling walls built by King John are the remains of John of Gaunt's chapel and Great Hall, the Earl of Leicester's stables and gatehouse. The most splendid royal occasion took place in 1575 when Queen Elizabeth I was entertained lavishly by the Earl with music and dancing, fireworks and hunting, for 19 days.

Location: West side of Kenilworth.
Open: Apr 1-Sept 30 10-6 daily Oct 1-Mar 31 daily 10-4.
Admission: Adults £2.50 concessions £1.90 children £1.30.

LORD LEYCESTER HOSPITAL

(The Governors of Lord Leycester Hospital)
High Street, Warwick   CV34 4BH   map **14** S19   △
Telephone: (01926) 492797

In 1100 the chapel of St. James was built over the West Gate of Warwick and became the centre for the Guilds established by Royal Charter in 1383. In 1571 Robert Dudley, Earl of Leycester, founded his Hospital for twelve 'poor' persons in the buildings of the Guilds, which had been dispersed in 1546. The Hospital has been run ever since for retired or disabled ex-Servicemen and their wives. The buildings have been restored to their original condition including the Great Hall of King James, the Guildhall (museum), the Chaplain's Hall (Queen's Own Hussars Regimental Museum) and the Brethren's Kitchen. The Hospital, with its medieval galleried courtyard, featured in the BBC TV serial 'Pride and Prejudice'.

Location: W gate of Warwick (A46).
Station(s): Warwick (¾ m).
Open: All the year Tues-Sun 10-5 (summer) 10-4 (winter). Last admission 15 mins earlier. *Closed Mon, Good Fri & Christmas Day.*
Admission: £2.50 Children (under 14) £1.25 OAPs/Students £1.75. Free car park.
Refreshments: (Easter-Oct) morning coffee, light lunches, afternoon teas.
Conferences: Great Hall available including facilities for receptions, concerts, corporate entertainment, dinners, luncheons.

MIDDLETON HALL
(Middleton Hall Trust)
Tamworth, Staffordshire   B78 2AE   map **14** R19
Telephone: (01827) 283095

Grade 11* listed building. Birthplace of Francis Willoughby, the naturalist. Georgian West Wing. Medieval East Wing under restoration.

Location: on A4091 south of Tamworth.
Open: Easter-end Oct Sun Bank Hols Mon 2-5.30.
Admission: £1.20 Concessions 60p.
Refreshments: Refreshments.
Conferences: Private parties and conferences by arrangement.
Shop, walled gardens, lakes, craft centre.

Sir Peter Paul Rubens (1577-1640)
Knighted by Charles I in 1630

His work can be seen in the following properties included in Historic Houses Castles and Gardens:-

Sudeley Castle
Warwick Castle

PACKWOOD HOUSE   ❧ The National Trust
Lapworth   B94 6AT   map **14** S19
Telephone: (01564) 782024

Originally a sixteenth century house Packwood has been much altered over the years and today is the vision of Graham Baron Ash who recreated a Jacobean house in the 1920's and 30's. A fine collection of 16th century textiles and furniture. Important gardens with renowned herbaceous border and famous yew garden based on the serman on the mount.

Location: 2 m SE of Hockley Heath (which is on A3400) 11 m SE of Birmingham.
Station(s): Lapworth (1½ m); Dorridge (2 m).
Open: Apr to end of Sept Wed to Sun & Bank Hol Mons 2-6. Gardens 1.30-6.*Closed* Good Fri. Oct Wed to Suns 12.30-4.30. Last adm 30 minutes before closing.
Admission: £3.80 Children £1.90 Family tickets £9.50. Gardens only £2. Parties by prior written arrangement only.
Refreshments: Picnics welcome in car park and avenue opposite main gate.
Shop. No dogs. No prams in House. Wheelchair access to part of garden and ground floor. No sharp heeled shoes. No large bags.

RAGLEY HALL 🏛
(The Earl and Countess of Yarmouth)
Alcester   B49 5NJ   map **14** S19   △ &
Telephone: (01789) 762090
Fax: (01789) 764791

Built in 1680. Superb baroque plasterwork, fine paintings, china, furniture and works of art including the mural 'The Temptation'. Gardens, park and lake. Woodland trails, lakeside picnic areas. Superb Adventure Wood play-ground and maze for children. Sculpture Trail.

Location: 2 m SW of Alcester off the Birmingham/Alcester/Evesham Road (A435); 8 m from Stratford-upon-Avon; 20 m from Birmingham.
Station(s): Stratford-upon-Avon
Open: Apr 2-Oct 6 Park & Gardens open daily 10-6 (except Mon & Fri but open Bank Holiday Mons) House open daily except Mon and Fri 11-5 (open Bank Holiday Monday) Park open every day July & Aug.
Admission: House, Gardens & Park (includes Adventure Wood and Woodland Trails) £4.50 OAPs/group rate adults £4 children £3.50. Free car park.
Refreshments: Licensed Cafeteria open daily except Mon and Fri, please telephone for group reservations. Refreshments available in park. **Advance Bookings:** (at any time of the year). Coach parties welcome by arrangement. Lunches and teas - parties please write for menus. Private dinner parties for any number up to 150 can be arranged. For further information please contact: The Business Manager, Ragley Hall, Alcester,Warwickshire B49 5NJ. Telephone: Alcester (01789) 762090.
Events/Exhibitions: Open air concerts June 30-Aug 3; Game Fair Aug 17/18.
Conferences: Available for non-residential conferences and dinners. Activity days. Photographic locations.
Dogs welcome on leads in Park and on Woodland Trails, not in House, Gardens or Adventure Wood.

THE SHAKESPEARIAN PROPERTIES
Stratford-upon-Avon   map **14** S19 △
Telephone: (01789) 204016
Fax: (01789) 296083

Besides the world-famous attraction of **Shakespeare's Birthplace,** now enhanced by a fine permanent exhibition *William Shakespeare: His Life and Background,* and the picturesque **Anne Hathaway's Cottage at Shottery,** there are three other houses associated with Shakespeare and his family. **New Place/Nash's House**- the site and grounds of his last home with Elizabethan style knott garden, entered through Nash's House adjoining which contains fine Tudor furniture and displays on the history of Stratford. **Hall's Croft**- a delightful Elizabethan town house and walled garden, once the home of Shakespeare's daughter Susanna, married to the physician Dr. John Hall. Fine period furniture and exhibition about medical practice in Shakespeare's time. Tea room/restaurant. **Mary Arden's House, Wilmcote**- Tudor farmstead home of Shakespeare's mother in childhood, with outbuildings and grounds with extensive exhibits illustrating country life over 400 years. Rare breeds of sheep, cattle and poultry. Dovecote. Duck pond. Field Walk. Heart of England falconry displays all day. Cafe. **Open Daily all the year round except 24, 25, 26 December.**

UPTON HOUSE   🌿 **The National Trust**
Banbury OX15 6HT   map **7** S20 ♿
Telephone: (01295) 670266

17th century house remodelled 1927-29 containing one of the National Trust's finest collections of paintings and porcelain. Tapestries and 18th century furniture. Beautiful terraced garden descending to lakes and bog garden in deep valley.

Location: 1 m S of Edge Hill; 7 m NW of Banbury on the Stratford Road (A422).
Station(s): Banbury, 7 miles.
Open: 1 Apr-31 Oct Sat-Wed (inc BH Mon) 2-6. Closed Good Fri. Last admission 5.30.*Note: Entry to the House, is by timed tickets at peak times on Suns and Bank Hols, therefore delays are possible.* Motorized buggy with driver available for access to/from lower garden, manned by volunteers of the Banbury NT Association.
Admission: £4.80 Children £2.40 Family ticket £12. Garden only £2.40.
Refreshments: Tea-room in House.
Events/Exhibitions: Contact the Property Manager for details.
No indoor photography. Wheelchair available. Wheelchair access ground floor only. Shop.

William Kent (1685 - 1748)
Painter, architect, garden designer

His work can be seen in the following properties included in Historic Houses Castles and Gardens:-

> *Chiswick House*
> *Ditchley Park (decoration of Great Hall)*
> *Euston Hall*
> *Rousham House*
> *Stowe (Stowe School)*

WARWICK CASTLE
(Warwick Castle Ltd)
Warwick CV34 4QU   map **14** S19 △
Telephone: (01926) 406600
Fax: (01926) 401692

Come and relive history at the finest mediaeval Castle in England. From its soaring towers to the depths of the Dungeon, Warwick Castle epitomises the power and grandeur of the mediaeval fortress. For centuries Warwick Castle was home to the mighty Earls of Warwick, the most powerful noblemen in England. Experience the sights, sounds, and smell of the mediaeval household as it prepares for battle in 1471 in 'Kingmaker - a preparation for battle'. The 14th century Great Hall lies at the heart of the Castle along with the magnificent State Rooms containing an outstanding collection of furniture, tapestries and artefacts. The 'Royal Weekend Party 1898' recreates an actual weekend in 1898 when Victorian aristocracy met and dined in the elegant surroundings of the Castle.

Location: By road - 8 m from Stratford upon Avon and 1½ hours journey from London. Junction 15 of the M40 well signposted.
Station(s): Warwick (½ m); Leamington Spa (2 m).
Open: Every day (except Christmas Day) 10-6 (Apr-Oct) 10-5 (Nov- Mar).
Admission: Adults £8.75 Children (4-16 yrs incl.) £5.25 Seniors Citizens £6.25 Students £6.50 Family £24.50.
Refreshments: 2 Restaurants, 1 Cafe, Picnic areas and Barbecue Tent (Summer only).
Events/Exhibitions: Special events form Jousting to Foot Combat displays take place every weekend during the summer months and half term holidays.

WEST MIDLANDS

ASTON HALL
(Birmingham City Council)
Birmingham   map **14** R19 △
Telephone: 0121-327 0062

A fine Jacobean house built 1618-1635; home to the Holte family for 200 years.

BLAKESLEY HALL
(Birmingham City Council)
Birmingham   map **14** R19
Telephone: (0121) 783 2193

CASTLE BROMWICH HALL GARDENS
Birmingham   map **14** S19 ♿
Telephone: 0121-749 4100

The Gardens are a cultural gem and an example of the Formal English Garden of the 18th century.

COVENTRY CATHEDRAL AND VISITORS CENTRE
(Provost & Canons of Coventry Cathedral)
Coventry CV1 5ES
Telephone: (01203) 227597

Medieval cathedral ruins stands beside inspiring modern cathedral designed by Basil Spence.

HAGLEY HALL
(The Viscount Cobham)

nr Stourbridge DY9 9LG   map **14** S18   △
Telephone: (01562) 882408
Fax: (01562) 882632

The last of the great Palladian Houses, designed by Sanderson Miller and completed in 1760. The House contains the finest example of Rococo plasterwork by Francesco Vassali, and a unique collection of 18th century furniture and family portraits including works by Van Dyck, Reynolds and Lely.

Location: Just off A456 Birmingham to Kidderminster; 12 m from Birmingham within easy reach M5 (exit 3 or 4), M6 or M42.
Station(s): Hagley (1 m) (not Suns); Stourbridge Junction (2 m).
Open: 6-20 Apr closed 13 Apr. 25-28 May, 20 July-31 Aug daily 2-5.
Admission: Open for pre-booked parties by arrangement. For further details, please telephone.
Refreshments: Tea available in the House.
Conferences: Specialists in corporate entertaining and conferences throughout the year.

WIGHTWICK MANOR   The National Trust
Wightwick Bank, Wolverhampton WV6 8EE   map **14** R18   △ &
Telephone: (01902) 761108
Fax: (01902) 764663

Begun in 1887, the house is a notable example of the influence of William Morris, with many original Morris wallpapers and fabrics. Also of interest are Pre-Raphaelite pictures, Kempe glass and de Morgan ware. The 17-acre Victorian/Edwardian garden originally designed by Thomas Mawson has formal beds, pergola, yew hedges, topiary and terraces; woodland and two pools.

Location: 3 m W of Wolverhampton, up Wightwick Bank (off A454).
Open: 2 Mar-31 Dec; Thurs and Sat 2.30-5.30 (last entry 5). Admission by timed ticket. Guided groups through ground floor, freeflow upstairs. Minimum tour time approx 1hr.30mins. Also open Bank Hol Sat, Sun & Mon 2.30-5.30 (last entry 5) ground floor only, no guided tours. Open for pre-booked parties Wed & Thurs.
Admission: £4.80 children £2.40. Garden only £2.20.
Dogs in garden only, on leads.

Sir Anthony Van Dyck
Portrait and religious painter

Born in Antwerp 1599,
died in London 1641
First visited England in 1620,
knighted by Charles I in 1633

His work can be seen in the following
properties included in Historic Houses
Castles and Garden:-

Alnwick Castle	*Kingston Lacey*
Arundel Castle	*Petworth House*
Boughton House	*Southside House*
Breamore House	*Sudeley Castle*
Eastnor Castle	*Warwick Castle*
Euston Hall	*Weston Park*
Firle Place	*Wilton House*
Goodwood House	*Woburn Abbey*
Holkham Hall	

WILTSHIRE

AVEBURY MANOR & GARDEN   The National Trust
Nr Marlborough SN8 1RF   map **3** U19
Telephone: (01672) 539388
Location: 6 m west of Marlborough.

BOWOOD HOUSE & GARDENS
(The Earl and Countess of Shelburne)

Calne   map **3** U19   &
Telephone: (01249) 812102

Outstanding example of 18th century architecture, set in one of the most beautiful parks in the country, landscaped by 'Capability' Brown and not altered since his time. On display in the House is a remarkable collection of family heirlooms built up over 250 years, including Victoriana, Indiana, silver, porcelain, fine paintings and watercolours. Interesting rooms include Robert Adam's famous Library, Dr. Joseph Priestley's Laboratory where he discovered oxygen gas, and the Chapel. The 100 acre park contains many exotic trees, a 40 acre lake, Cascade, Grotto, caves and a Doric Temple, arboretum, pinetum, rose garden and Italian garden. For children, a massive Adventure Playground. For six weeks during May and June a separate garden of 50 acres features spectacular rhododendron walks.

Location: 2½ m W of Calne; 5 m SE of Chippenham. Immediately off A4 at Derry Hill village between Calne and Chippenham.
Open: House, Gardens & Grounds.   Mar 30-Oct 27 - Daily incl Bank Hols 11-6. Rhododendron Walks (entrance off A342 at Kennels Lodge) six weeks during May and June (depending on season) 11-6.
Admission: Free car park. £4.80 OAPs £4.10 children £2.60. Party rates (20 and over) £4.30 OAPs £3.60 children £2.30.
Refreshments: Licensed restaurant & Garden Tea-room. **Advance Bookings:** Coach parties welcome by arrangement. Lunches and Teas - please write for party menus and further information: The Estate Office, Bowood Estate, Calne, Wiltshire SN11 0LZ.
Conferences: Licensed for Civil Weddings.
No dogs.

BROADLEAS GARDENS (CHARITABLE TRUST)
(Lady Anne Cowdray)
Devizes   SN10 5JQ   map 14 U18
Telephone: (01380) 722035

A delightful garden where magnolias, camellias and rhododendrons flourish with exciting ground cover. Roses and rare perennials in other areas.

Location: 1½ m SW of Devizes on A360.
Open: Apr 1-Oct 31 Sun Wed & Thurs 2-6.
Admission: Adults £2.50 children (under 12) £1. Discount for parties.
Refreshments: Home-made teas on Sundays - also by prior arrangement.
Plants propagated for sale.

CHARLTON PARK HOUSE
(The Earl of Suffolk and Berkshire)
Malmesbury   map 14 U18

Jacobean/Georgian mansion, built for the Earls of Suffolk, 1607, altered by Matthew Brettingham the Younger, c. 1770.

Location: 1½ m NE Malmesbury. Entry only by signed entrance on A429, Malmesbury/Cirencester Road. No access from Charlton village.
Open: May-Oct Mon & Thurs 2-4 viewing of Great Hall, Staircase and saloon.
Admission: Adults £1 children/OAPs 50p.
Car parking limited. Unsuitable for wheelchairs. No dogs. No picnicking.

CORSHAM COURT
(Mr. & Mrs. H. Wallace (Curators)
Corsham   SN13 OBZ   map 14 T18   &
Telephone: (01249) 701610/701611
Fax: c/o (01249) 444556

Elizabethan (1582) and Georgian (1760-70) house, fine 18th century furniture. British, Spanish, Italian and Flemish Old Masters. Park and gardens laid out by 'Capability' Brown and Humphrey Repton. Contains one of the oldest and most distinguished collections of Old Masters and furniture.

Location: In Corsham 4 m W of Chippenham off the Bath Road (A4).
Station(s): Mainline to Paddington from Chippenham and Bath.
Open: Staterooms Jan 1-Nov 30 Daily except Mon and Fri 2-4.30. From Good Fri-Sept 30 2-6 (including Fri and Bank Hols) *Closed* Dec. Last adm 30 minutes before closing time. Other times by appointment. Parties welcome.
Admission: (incl gardens) £3.50 Children £2 Senior Citizens (U.K.only) £3. Parties of 20 or more by arrangement. Gardens only:£2 Children £1 Senior Citizens (U.K. only) £1.50.
Refreshments: Audrey's Tea-room Tel: (01249) 714931.

THE COURTS GARDEN   ❧ The National Trust
Holt   BA14 6RR   map 14 U18   &
Telephone: (01225) 782340
Location: 2½ m E of Bradford-on-Avon on S side of B3107; 3 m N of Trowbridge.

FITZ HOUSE GARDEN
(Mrs Mordaunt-Hare)
Teffont Magna, nr Salisbury
Telephone: (01722) 716257

Lovely hillside terraced gardens frame a listed group of beautiful ancient stone buildings.

GREAT CHALFIELD MANOR   ❧ The National Trust
nr. Melksham   SN12 8NJ   map 14 U18
Location: 2½ m NE Bradford-on-Avon via B3109, signposted in Holt village.

HAMPTWORTH LODGE
(Mr N. Anderson)
Landford, Salisbury   SP5 2EA   map 3 V19
Telephone: (01794) 390215
Fax: (01794) 390700

Rebuilt Jacobean Manor, with period furniture.

Location: 10 m SE of Salisbury, on the C44 road linking Downton on A338, Salisbury-Bournemouth to Landford on A36, Salisbury-Southampton.
Open: House and garden daily except Suns 1 Apr-4 May 1995 2.15-5. Conducted parties only 2.30 and 3.45. Coaches by appointment only 1 Apr-30 Sept. By appointment all year, 18 hole golf course (01794) 390155, Riding (01794) 390118.
Admission: £3 under 11 free. No special arrangements for parties, but about 15 is the maximum.
Refreshments: Downton, Salisbury; nil in house.
Car parking: disabled ground floor only.

HAZELBURY MANOR GARDENS
nr Box
Telephone: (01225) 812113

8 acres of Grade II landscaped formal gardens surrounding a charming 15th C fortified Manor House.

HEALE GARDENS, PLANT CENTRE AND SHOP
(Maureen Taylor)
Middle Woodford, Salisbury   SP4 6NT
Telephone: (01722) 73504

Comprehensive Plant Centre.

IFORD MANOR GARDENS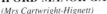
(Mrs Cartwright-Hignett)
Bradford-on-Avon   BA15 2BA
Telephone: (01225) 863146

Harold Peto's enchanting Italianate garden by River Frome - Grade 1.

Location: 7 m S of Bath via A35.
Open: Apr and Oct. June May Sept - Sat Sun Turs Wed Thurs 2-5.

LACOCK ABBEY   ❧ The National Trust
nr Chippenham   SN15 2LG   map 14 U18
Telephone: (01249) 730227
Location: In the village of Lacock; 3 m N of Melksham; 3 m S of Chippenham just E of A350.

LONGLEAT HOUSE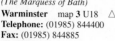
(The Marquess of Bath)
Warminster   map **3** U18 △
Telephone: (01985) 844400
Fax: (01985) 844885

Longleat House, built by Sir John Thynne in 1580, and still owned and lived in by the same family, was the first truly magnificent Elizabethan House to be built. Longleat was also the first Stately Home to be opened to the public in 1949. Throughout its existence, ancestors have commissioned alterations within the House; ceilings by Italian craftsmen, rooms and corridors by Wyatville, additional libraries to house the vast collection of rare books and of course, the beautiful parkland landscaped by 'Capability' Brown. In 1966 the late Lord Bath established the first drive through wild animal reserve outside Africa. It remains the model for safari parks throughout the world. Many other attractions have since been opened, making Longleat a full day's entertainment for all the family. Attractions include Victorian Kitchens, Lord Bath's Bygones, Dolls Houses, Lord Bath's Murals, Dr Who Exhibition, Butterfly Garden, Railway, World's Largest Maze, Pets Corner, Safari Boats, Historic Vehicle Exhibition, Adventure Castle for children and the Life and Times of Henry Lord Bath an exhibition of memorabilia on Edward VIII, Churchill and Hitler.

Open: Longleat House open all year (days and times may vary) please telephone before setting out. 16 Mar-3 Nov 10-6 remainder of year 10-4 Safari Park every day from 16 Mar-3 Nov (Last cars admitted 5.30 or sunset if earlier). All other attractions 16 Mar-3 Nov 11-6 dates and times may vary - please telephone before your journey.
Admission: Pre-booked School Parties and Tours of Safari Park and House welcome. Reduced rates for Party Bookings in advance. Helicopter landing facilities provided advance notice needed.
Refreshments: At the Cellar Cafe in the old vaults of Longleat House.
Specialist Tours and Seminars on request. Language tours also available.

LUCKINGTON COURT
(The Hon Mrs Trevor Horn)
Luckington SN14 6PQ map **14** T18 &
Telephone: (01666) 840205

Mainly Queen Anne with magnificent group of ancient buildings. Beautiful mainly formal garden with fine collection of ornamental trees and shrubs.

Location: 6 m W of Malmesbury on B4040 Bristol Road.

Open: All the Year Weds 2-5, Garden only. Open Sun 12 May, 2.30-5.*Collection box for National Gardens' Scheme*. Inside view by appointment 3 weeks in advance.
Admission: Outside gardens only £1. House £2.
Refreshments: Teas in garden or house (in aid of Luckington Parish Church).

LYDIARD PARK
(Borough of Thamesdown)
Lydiard Park, Lydiard Tregoze, Swindon, Wiltshire SN5 9PA map **3** T19 △ & Ⓔ
Telephone: (01793) 770401

Fully restored ancestral home of the St.John family, remodelled in the Georgian classical style in 1743.

MOMPESSON HOUSE   🌿 The National Trust
Salisbury SP1 2EL map **3** U19
Telephone: (01722) 335659
Location: In Cathedral Close on N side of Choristers' Green.

OLD SARUM
map **3** U19
Telephone: (01722) 335398

ENGLISH HERITAGE

On the summit of a hill north of Salisbury, huge ramparts and earth mounds are silhouetted against the skyline. Ancient Britons fortified the hill-top which was later inhabited by Romans, Saxons and Normans. Parts of an 11th century castle remain and the foundations of two successive cathedrals are marked on the grass.

Location: 2 m (3.2 km) north of Salisbury.
Open: Apr 1-Sept 30 10-6 daily Oct 1-Mar 31 10-4 daily.
Admission: Adults £1.70 concessions £1.30 children 90p.

OLD WARDOUR CASTLE
map **3** U18
Telephone: (01747) 870487

ENGLISH HERITAGE

The ruins stand in a romantic lakeside setting as a result of landscaping and planting in the 18th century. French in style and designed more for living than defence, the castle was built in 1393 by the fifth Lord Lovel, a campaigner in France. It was badly damaged in the Civil War and never repaired. The 18th century Banqueting House contains a small display about the 'Capability' Brown landscape.

Location: 2 m (3.2 km) south of Tisbury.
Open: Apr 1-Sept 30 10-6 daily Oct 1-31 10-4 daily Nov 1-Mar 31 (closed 1-2) Wed-Sun 10-4.
Admission: Adults £1.50 concessions £1.10 children 80p.

PHILIPPS HOUSE   🌿 The National Trust
Dinton SP3 5HJ map **3** U19
Telephone: (01722) 716208
Location: 9 m W of Salisbury; on N side of B3089.

PYTHOUSE
(Country Houses Association)
Tisbury SP3 6PB map **3** U18
Telephone: (01747) 870210

Palladian style Georgian mansion.

Location: 2½ m W of Tisbury; 4½ m N of Shaftesbury.
Station(s): Tisbury (2½ m).
Open: May-Sept Weds & Thurs 2-5. Last entry 4.30.
Admission: £2.50 Children £1. Free car park.
No dogs admitted.

"Playgrounds for the Children"

Belton House
Bowood
Drumlanrig (woodland playground)
Hever Castle
Kelburn (Secret Forest adventure course and stockade)
Longleat
Ragley Hall (adventure wood)
Weston Park
Wilton House

SHELDON MANOR

(Antony Gibbs ESQ Owner, Mrs Martin Gibbs Administration)
Chippenham SN14 0RG   map **14** U18   △ & Ⓔ Ⓢ
Telephone: (01249) 653120

Plantagenet Manor House, lived in as a family home for 700 years. There has been a house here since early Plantagenet times. The present Great Porch and Parvise above, dating from 1282, were built by Sir Geoffrey Gascelyn, Lord of the Manor and Hundred of Chippenham and were 700 years old in 1982. Sheldon is the sole survivor of a vanished medieval village. Succeeding generations and other families, notably the Hungerfords, have added to the beautiful house, its forecourt and surrounding buildings. All the house is lived in and it is shown by the family. There are good collections of early oak furniture, Nailsea glass, porcelain and Persian saddlebags. There are beautiful informal terraced gardens with ancient yew trees, water, interesting trees and shrubs and a connoisseur collection of old fashioned roses. Possibility of swimming in long stone pool; please enquire. Home-made lunches and cream teas served in the Barn or on the lawn. Visitors to Sheldon have found the food 'a major consideration'. 'In nominating an eating place with an intimate atmosphere, I could do no better than to recommend Sheldon'. Hugh Montgomery-Massingberd, Weekend Telegraph, July 11th, 1987. 'It was worth the whole trip for this.' - American visitor 1992. National Winner of the first Historic House Awards, given by the AA and the National Pensions Institute, in co-operation with the Historic Houses Association, for the privately-owned house open to the public which has best preserved its architectural integrity, character and furniture while remaining a lived-in family home.

Location: 1½ m W of Chippenham, signposted from A420; eastbound traffic also signposted from A4, E of Corsham (2½ m). M4 exit 17 4 m.
Station(s): Chippenham (2½ m).
Open: Open Easter Sun and Easter Mon then every Sun Thurs and Bank Hol to 6 Oct 12.30-6. House opens 2.
Refreshments: Home-made lunches & cream teas. Coaches welcome by appointment.
Conferences: Sheldon is delighted to host small conferences and corporate entertaining. Most of the property suitable for wheelchairs. Sheldon has made a speciality of wedding receptions.

STONEHENGE

ENGLISH HERITAGE

map **3** U19
Telephone: (01980) 624714

Built between 3100 and 1100 BC, this is Britain's most famous ancient monument and one of the world's most astonishing engineering feats. Many of the stones, some weighing 4 tons each, were brought from the Preseli Mountains in Wales to Salisbury Plain, there to be erected by human muscle power. Refreshments are available. Interactive Audio Tour available in six languages.

Location: 2 m (3.2 km) west of Amesbury.
Open: 16 Mar-31 June 9.30-6 daily, 1 June-31 Aug 9-7 daily, 1 Sept-15 Oct 9.30-6 daily, 16 Oct-15 Mar 9.30-4 daily.
Admission: Adults £3.50 concessions £2.60 children £1.80.

WILTON HOUSE

(The Earl of Pembroke)
Salisbury SP2 OBJ   map **3** U19   △
Telephone: (01722) 743115
Fax: (01722) 744447

The 17 minute film narrated by Anna Massey provides a dynamic introduction to the Earls of Pembroke and the 450 year history of the Estate. The Tudor origins of the House can still be seen in the tower which survived the 1647 fire and is now incorporated within the splendid 17th Century House, based on designs by Inigo Jones. Perhaps most famous of the State Rooms are the Single and Double Cube Rooms, with their fabulous painted ceilings. With early 19th Century additions by James Wyatt, Wilton House, over looking the majestic Palladian Bridge across the river Nadder provides a fascinating record of British history. Wilton House boasts, what is reputed to be, one of the best private art collections in Britain, with original paintings by Van Dyck, Reynolds, Breughel and Rubens amongst the 230 works of art on public show. Step back in time in the re-constructed Tudor Kitchen and the Estate's Victorian Laundry (in use until 1969). Relax in the 21 acres of landscaped parkland, including the walled rose garden with its Pergola, the water garden and, especially for children the massive adventure playground.

Location: Wilton 3 m W of Salisbury on A30.
Station(s): Salisbury.
Open: Apr 3-Nov 3 1996 7 days a week 11-6 (last admission 5).
Admission: Adults £6.20 OAPs £5.20 Children (aged 5-15) £3.80 under 5 free. All day family ticket (2+2) £16.20. Discounts for pre-booked parties and/or Grounds only admission only.
Refreshments: Licensed self-service restaurant. Open daily during the season 11-5.30pm. Hot lunches served 12-2pm.
Events/Exhibitions: 1996 featured exhibition - Victorian water-colours by Edwin Young. Please telephone for full events calender.
Conferences: Corporate hospitality facilities available for up to 120 guests.

NORTH YORKSHIRE

ALLERTON PARK

(The Gerald Arthur Rolph Foundation for Historic Preservation and Education)
nr. Knaresborough   map **7** O20
Telephone: (01423) 330927

The grandest of the surviving Gothic revival stately homes. Its Great Hall and Dining Room are considered amongst the finest carved wood rooms in England. Allerton Park, the ancestral home of Lord Mowbray (c. 1283), Segrave (c. 1283) and Stourton (c. 1448), the premier Baron in England, was enlarged by George Martin c.1850. Some interior rooms by J.C. Buckler and Benjamin Baud. Property owned by Frederick, Duke of York (brother to King George IV) in 18th century. The setting for the films 'Secret Garden' and Sherlock Holmes's 'The Sign of Four'. Private collection of mechanical music machines and luxury antique motor cars. World War II museum dedicated to Number 6 Group (RCAF).

Location: ¼ m E of A1 on York Road (A59); 14½ m W of York; 4½ m E of Knaresborough, 6 m N of Wetherby; 7 m S of Boroughbridge; 14 m N of Leeds.
Open: Easter Sun-end Sept and Bank Hol Mons 1-6, last house tour 5. Any other days by appointment for events or parties of 25 or more.
Admission: House Grounds and Car Museum and WWII Museum £4 (Includes guided tour of house) Students/OAPs/accompanied Children (under 16) £3. Parties (25 and over) £3.50. School groups £2. Free convenient car parking.
Refreshments: Tea rooms in WWII Museum.
Events/Exhibitions: House (all main rooms) and grounds available for conferences, civil weddings and receptions, filming, charity balls, concerts, car rallies, etc. Ballroom: dining 120 persons, theatre style 200. Dining Room: dining 80 persons, theatre style 120 persons. Great Hall for receptions and cocktails. Outside Marque unlimited capacity.
No dogs except guide dogs for the blind.

ASKE HALL

(The Marquess and Marchioness of Zetland)
Aske, Richmond   DL10 5HJ   map **7** O19
Telephone: (01748) 823222
Fax: (01748) 823252

The hall, nestling in Capability Brown parkland has been the family seat of the Dundas family for more than 200 years. It contains Georgian furniture, porcelain and pictures, many collected by Sir Lawrence Dundas who bought the hall in 1762.

Location: 2 m east of Richmond on the Gilling West Road (B6274).
Station(s): Darlington 13 miles away
Open: For parties of 15 or more by written appointment only. Week days only.
Admission: Adults £3.50.
Events/Exhibitions: Ongoing throughout the year.
Conferences: Suitable for up to a capacity of 100.

ASSEMBLY ROOMS

(De Blank Restaurants)
Blake Street   map **7** P20
Telephone: (01904) 637254

THE BAR CONVENT

(The Bar Convent Museum Trust)
York
Telephone: (01904) 643238

Impressive Georgian town house (1787) enclosing neo-classical Chapel (1769), both by Thomas Atkinson.

BENINGBROUGH HALL   The National Trust

nr York   map **7** O20   △ &
Telephone: (01904) 470666
Location: 8 m NW of York; 3 m W of Shipton (A19); 2 m SE Linton-on-Ouse; follow sign-posted route.

BOLTON ABBEY ESTATE

(Trustees of the Chatsworth Settlement)
Bolton Abbey, Skipton   BD23 6EX   △ & ⌂
Telephone: (01756) 710533
Fax: (01756) 710535
Location: On B6160 north from the roundabout junction with the A59 Skipton to Harrogate Road, 23 m from Leeds.

BROCKFIELD HALL

(Lord & Lady Martin Fitzalan Howard)
Warthill, York   YO3 9XJ   map **7** O21
Telephone: (01904) 489298

Small country house designed 1804 by Peter Atkinson. Dramatic round Hall and Staircase.

Location: 5m E of York off A166 or A64.
Open: Aug 1-31 1995 1-4 except Mon (Other times by appointment) tel: (01904) 489298.
Admission: Adults £2.50 children £1.

Thomas Gainsborough (1727-1787)

His paintings can be seen at the following properties included in Historic Houses Castles and Gardens:-

Arundel Castle
Bowhill
Christchurch Mansion
Dalmeny House
Elton Hall
Gainsborough's House
Ickworth Park & Garden
Firle Place
Kenwood, The Iveagh BequestKnowle
Parham House &
   Gardens
Petworth House
Shalom Hall
Upton House
Waddesdon Manor
Weston Park
Woburn Abbey

CASTLE HOWARD

(The Hon. Simon Howard)
York   YO6 7DA   map **7** 021
Telephone: (01653) 648333
Fax: (01653) 648462

In a dramatic setting between two lakes with extensive gardens and impressive fountains, this magnificent 18th Century Palace was designed by Sir John Vanbrugh in 1699. Undoubtedly the finest private residence in Yorkshire, it was built for Charles Howard, 3rd Earl of Carlisle whose descendants still live here. With its painted and gilded dome reaching 80ft into the Yorkshire sky, this impressive house has collections of antique furniture, porcelain and sculpture, while its fabulous collection of paintings is dominated by the famous Holbein portraits of Henry VIII and the Duke of Norfolk. Castle Howard has been open to the public since the day it was built. Interesting rooms include The Castle Howard Bedroom, Lady Georgiana's Bedroom and Dresssing Room, The Antique Passage, The Music Room, The Tapestry Room, The Museum Room, The Long Gallery and the Chapel. The Gardens are designed on a heroic scale covering 1,000 acres. They include memorable sights such as The Temple of the Four Winds, The Mausoleum, New River Bridge and the recently restored waterworks of the South Lake, Cascade, Waterfall and The Atlas Fountain. The walled garden has collections of old and modern roses. Nature Walks include those through Ray Wood with its unique collection of rare trees, shrubs, rhododendrons, magnolias and azaleas (in season). For children there is a superb lakeside Adventure Playground. Boat trips on the lake in a Victorian style launch in season (weather permitting).

Location: 15 m NE of York; 3 m off A64; 6 m W of Malton; 38 m Leeds; 36 m Harrogate; 22 m Scarborough; 50 m Hull.
Open: Daily Mar 15-Nov 3. House open from 11. Plant centre, rose gardens, grounds and cafeteria open from 10. Last admissions 4.30.
Admission: House & Garden: Adults £6.50 Child £3.50 OAP £5.50. Groups: (>12 persons) Adult £5.50 Child £3 OAP £5. Garden only: Adult £4 Child £2.
Refreshments: Cafeterias in House, Lakeside and Stable Courtyard. Licensed restaurant available for booked parties.
New shopping facilities in Stable Courtyard.

CLIFFORD'S TOWER

York map 7 O20
Telephone: (01904) 646940

York Castle, like the city itself, has had a long and turbulent history. Clifford's Tower was built on an earlier motte (or mound) in the 13th century. The tower is named after a Lancastrian leader from the Wars of the Roses, Sir Robert Clifford, who was defeated in 1322, and his body hung in chains from the tower.

Location: Near Castle Museum.
Open: Apr 1-Sept 30 daily 9.30-6, Oct 1-Mar 31 daily 10-4.
Admission: Adults £1.60 concessions £1.20 children 80p.

CONSTABLE BURTON HALL

(M. C. A. Wyvill, Esq)
Leyburn DL8 5LJ map 7 O19
Telephone: (01677) 450428
Fax: (01677) 450622

Extensive borders, interesting alpines, large informal garden. John Carr house completed in 1768.

Location: On A684, between Leyburn (3 m) & Bedale; A1 (7 m).
Open: Gardens Apr 1-Oct 20 daily 9-6 House opening dates not available at time of going to press.
Admission: Garden £2 Adults £1.50 OAPs and 50p Children under 16 (collecting box) House charges not available at time of going to press. Party rates by arrangement.

CRUCK COTTAGE CACTI

(Ronald J.A. Wood and Dorothy Wood)
Cliff Road, Wrelton, Pickering, North Yorkshire YO18 8PJ
Telephone: (01751) 72042

The Nursery is in a garden setting with a display area of mature cacti.

Lancelot 'Capability' Brown

Born 1716 in Northumberland, Capability Brown began work at the age of 16 in the vegetable gardens of Sir William and Lady Loraine at Kirharle Tower. He left Northumberland in 1739, and records show that he worked at Stowe until 1749. It was at Stowe that Brown began to study architecture, and to submit his own plans. It was also at Stowe that he devised a new method of moving and replanting mature trees.

Brown married Bridget Wayet in 1744 and began work on the estate at Warwick Castle in 1749. He was appointed Master Gardener at Hampton Court in 1764, and planted the Great Vine at Hampton Court in 1768. Blenheim Palace designs are considered amongst Brown's finest work, and the technical achievements were outstanding even for the present day.

Capability Brown died in February 1783 of a massive heart attack. A monument beside the lake at Croome Court was erected which reads "To the memory of Lancelot Brown, who by the powers of his inimitable and creative genius formed this garden scene out of a morass". There is also a portrait of Brown at Burghley.

EBBERSTON HALL

(W. de Wend Fenton, Esq.)
Scarborough

Palladian Villa of 1718 designed by the architect Colin Campbell.

FAIRFAX HOUSE

(York Civic Trust)
Castlegate, York map 7 P20
Telephone: (01904) 655543

An 18th century house designed by John Carr of York and described as a classic architectural masterpiece of its age. Certainly one of the finest townhouses in England and saved from near collapse by the York Civic Trust who restored it to its former glory during 1982/84. In addition to the superbly decorated plasterwork, wood and wrought iron, the house is now home for an outstanding collection of 18th century Furniture, and Clocks, formed by the late Noel Terry. Described by Christie's as one of the finest private collections of this century, it enhances and complements the house and helps to create a very special 'lived in' feeling. The gift of the entire collection by Noel Terry's Trustees to the Civic Trust has enabled it to fill the house with appropriate pieces of the period and has provided the basis for what can now be considered a fully furnished Georgian Townhouse.

Location: Centre of York, follow signs for Castle Area and Jorvik Centre.
Station(s): York 10 mins walk.
Open: Feb 20-Jan 6 Mon-Thurs and Sat 11-5 Sun 1.30-5 (last admission 4.30) closed Fri except during Aug. Special evening tours, connoisseur visits and receptions welcomed by arrangement with the Director.
Admission: Adults £3 OAPs/students £2.50 children £1.50 adult parties (pre-booked 15 or more) £2.50 children £1.25
Events/Exhibitions: 'Spiritous Liquors' exhibition Sept 1st to Nov 20th 1996.
Conferences: By arrangement with the Director.
Public car park within 50 yds. Suitable for disabled persons only with assistance (by telephoning beforehand staff can be available to help). A small gift shop offers selected antiques, publications and gifts. Opening times are the same as the house.

THE FORBIDDEN CORNER

(Mr C.R. Armstrong)
West House, Tupgill Park Estate, Coverdale, Nr Middleham   map **7** O19
Telephone: (01969) 640638

Hello there. As you can see I'm only a Tower but I'm only the first of a host of unusual things you will see in the "Forbidden Corner". If you think the characters which dwell above ground are strange wait until you go underground and see the Grotto. That's seriously worrying as it's much easier to get into than to get out of. An underworld creation of frenzied minds all set in beautiful Coverdale.

Location: From Middleham Market Place, take Coverham Road over Middleham Moor, past Coverham Church and through the big Estate Park Gates on right, signed Tupgill Park.
Open: Beginning Mar-end Oct every Sunday, Good Fri and Bank Hols 12-5 (last admission 4.30 (no rush). Other times by calling Doug & Margaret Weatherill on (01969) 640638.
Admission: Adults £3.50 children/OAP £2.

FOUNTAINS ABBEY & STUDLEY ROYAL

❧ The National Trust
Ripon   HG4 3DY   map **7** O19   ♿
Telephone: (01765) 601002/608888
Fax: (01765) 608889
Location: 2 m W of Ripon; 9 m W of Harrogate; NW of A61.

GEORGIAN THEATRE ROYAL

(The Georgian Theatre (Richmond) Trust Ltd)
Richmond   DL10 4DW   map **7** O19
Telephone: (01748) 823710
Fax: (01748) 823710

18th century Georgian Theatre.

Location: Victoria Road, Richmond.
Station(s): Darlington.
Open: Mar 31-Oct 31 (Museum) Mar-Dec (Theatre).
Admission: £1 (performance prices £12-£3).
Refreshments: Coffee-Bar (June-Sept).
Events/Exhibitions: Art exhibitions (Coffee bar) June-Sept.

HARLOW CARR BOTANICAL GARDENS

(Northern Horticultural Society)
Crag Lane   HG3 1QB   map **7** P19   △ ♿
Telephone: (01423) 565418
Fax: (01423) 530663
A 68 acre site established in 1948 by The Northern Horticultural Society as a centre for garden plant trials. Today the gardens offer a wide range of horticultural courses for amateurs as well as being a place of great beauty and repose. Extensive stream side plantings, rock gardens, bulbs, rhododendrons, heathers, alpines, fruit and vegetable trials. Hosts 5 National Collections, museum, model village, fern house, childrens play area. Restaurant. Manual and electric wheelchairs to loan. Guide dogs only. Plants and gift centre.
Location: 1½ m W of town centre on B6162 Otley Road.
Open: Daily from 9.30am. Last admission 6.00pm.
Admission: Adult £3.30, OAP £2.50, Parties of 20+ £2.50. Accompanied children free.
Events/Exhibitions: Held throughout the year, telephone for diary of events.

HELMSLEY CASTLE

map **7** O20
Telephone: (01439) 70442

Even in its ruined state, Helmsley Castle is spectacular. Begun by Walter Espec shortly after the Norman Conquest, the huge earthworks - now softened to green valleys - are all that remain of this early castle. The oldest stonework is 12th century. Like many English castles, Helmsley was rendered indefensible during the Civil War, when it belonged to the notorious George Villiers, Duke of Buckingham. It was abandoned as a great house when its owners built nearby Duncombe Park. The 17th century domestic buildings contains an exhibition about the castle.

Location: Helmsley.
Open: Apr 1-Sept 30 10-6 daily Oct 1-31 10-4 daily Nov 1-Mar 31 Wed-Sun 10-4.
Admission: Adults £2 concessions £1.50 children £1.

HOVINGHAM HALL

(Sir Marcus & Lady Worsley)
York   YO6 4LU   map **7** O21
Telephone: (01653) 628206
Fax: (01653) 628668

Palladian House designed c. 1760 by Thomas Worsley to his own design. Unique entry by huge Riding School. Visitors see family portraits and rooms in everyday use; also the extensive garden with magnificent yew hedges and dovecot and the private cricket ground, said to be the oldest in England.

Location: 20 m N of York on Malton/Helmsley Road (B1257).
Open: Open for parties of 15 or more **by written appointment only** Apr 16-Sept 26 1996 Tues Wed & Thurs 11-7.
Admission: Adults £3.00 children £1.50.
Refreshments: At the Hall by arrangement. Meals at The Worsley Arms, Hovingham.
Conferences: Facilities for up to 140.

MARKENFIELD HALL

(The Lady Grantley)
Ripon   HG4 3AD   map **7** O19

Fine example of English manor house 14th, 15th & 16th century buildings surrounded by moat.

Location: 3 m S of Ripon off the Ripon/Harrogate Road (A61). Access is up a road marked Public Bridleway Hell Wath Lane'.
Open: Apr-Oct Mon 10-12.30 and 2.15-5. Exterior only outside courtyard and moat all other days in May times as above.
Admission: Adults £2 children under 5 free. Exterior and outside courtyard free.

MIDDLEHAM CASTLE

map **7** O19
Telephone: (01969) 23899

The great days of Middleham were in the 14th and 15th centuries, when it was the stronghold of the mighty Neville family. After the death of Richard Neville - 'Warwick the Kingmaker' - in 1471, the castle was forfeited to the Crown and was the childhood home of Richard III. The dominant feature of the castle is the great keep, one of the largest in England. A replica of the famous Middleham jewel is on display.

Location: 2 m (3.2 km) south of Leyburn.
Open: Apr 1-Sept 30 10-6 daily Oct 1-31 10-4 daily Nov 1-Mar 31 (closed 1-2) Wed-Sun 10-4.
Admission: Adults £1.60 concessions £1.20 children 80p.

MOUNT GRACE PRIORY

map **7** O20
Telephone: (01609) 883494

These 14th century ruins provide a rare opportunity to study the plan of a Carthusian monastery, or 'charterhouse'. The Carthusian monks lived like hermits - in seclusion not only from the world, but from each other. They met together only in chapel, and for religious feasts. Every monk had his own cell - 21 in all - a tiny two-storey house with its own garden and workshop. And each cell had running water - a remarkable luxury in the Middle Ages. A fully restored cell with hand-carved furniture and exhibition gives a fascinating insight into the lives of the monks.

Location: 7 m (11⅓ km) north east of Northallerton.
Open: Apr 1-Sept 30 10-6 daily Oct 1-31 10-4 daily Nov 1-Mar 31 Wed-Sun 10-4. Last admission summer season 5.30, winter season 3.30.
Admission: Adults £2.40 concessions £1.80 children £1.20.

NEWBURGH PRIORY

(Sir George Wombwell, Bt)
Coxwold   Y6 4AS   map **7** O20
Telephone: (01347) 868435

One of the North's most interesting Historic Houses. Originally built in 1145 with alterations in 1568 and 1720-1760, the Priory has been the home of one family and its descendants since 1538. The house contains the tomb of Oliver Cromwell (his third daughter, Mary, was married to Viscount Fauconberg - owner 1647-1700). In the grounds there is a really beautiful Water Garden full of rare alpines, plants and rhododendrons. Afternoon tea is served in the original kitchen.

Location: 5 m from Easingwold off A19, 9 m from Thirsk.
Open: GROUNDS AND HOUSE Apr 2-June 28 Suns and Weds Easter Mon and Aug Bank Hol Mons HOUSE OPEN 2.30-4.45 GROUNDS 2-6 *Other days for parties of 25 or more by appointment with the Administrator.*
Admission: House and Grounds £3 Children £1 Grounds only £1.50 Children free.
Refreshments: In the Old Priory Kitchens.

Gertrude Jekyll
writer and gardener
(1843-1932)

Her designs were used at the following properties included in Historic Houses Castles and Gardens:-

Barrington Court
Castle Drogo
Goddards
Hatchlands Park
Hestercombe House and
    Gardens
Knebworth
Lindisfarne Castle

A collection of her tools can be found at Guildford Museum

NEWBY HALL & GARDENS

(R.E.J. Compton, Esq)
Ripon   HG4 5AE   map **7** O2O   ♿
Telephone: (01423) 322583
Fax: (01423) 324452

The family home of Mr and Mrs Robin Compton is one of Yorkshire's renowned Adam houses. It is set amidst 25 acres of award-winning gardens full of rare and beautiful plants. Famous double herbaceous borders with formal compartmented gardens including species rose garden, water and rock gardens, the Autumn garden and the tranquility of Sylvia's garden - truly a 'Garden for all Seasons'. Also holds National Collection of genus CORNUS. The contents of the house are superb and include an unique Gobelins Tapestry Room, a gallery of classical statuary and some of Chippendale's finest furniture. Other attractions are railway rides beside the river, adventure gardens for children, a woodland discovery walk, Newby shop and plants stall, and picnic area. Coach and car park free.

Location: 4m SE of Ripon on Boroughbridge Road (B6265). 3m W of A1; 14m Harrogate; 20m York; 35m Leeds; 32m Skipton.
Station(s): Harrogate or York.
Open: Apr 2-Sept 29 daily except Mons (but open Bank Holidays) from 11 and House open from 12. Full visitor information from the Administrator, The Estate Office, Newby Hall, Ripon HG4 5AE.
Admission: House & Garden adult £5.40, OAP £4.50, child/disabled £3.20. Gardens only adult £3.80 OAP £3.30, child/disabled £2.50. Also family rates & reduced price for groups.
Refreshments: Lunches & teas in the licensed Garden Restaurant.
Events/Exhibitions: Craft Fair June 8/9 Sept 7/8, Historic Vehicle Rally July 21.
Conferences: Function room for c.100.

NORTON CONYERS

(Sir James and Lady Graham)
Ripon HG4 5EH map **7** O19 △ &
Telephone: (01765) 640333 (house & garden).

Visited by Charlotte Brontë in 1839, Norton Conyers is an original of 'Thornfield Hall' in 'Jane Eyre', and a family legend was an inspiration for the mad Mrs Rochester. The building is late medieval with Stuart and Georgian additions. Family pictures, furniture, ceramics and costumes. The friendly atmosphere, resulting from over 370 years of occupation by the same family, has been noticed by many visitors. The 18th century walled garden, with Orangery and herbaceous borders, is 100 yards from the house. Pick your own fruit: intending pickers are advised to check beforehand.

Location: 4 m NW of Ripon nr Wath. 3 m from A1; turn off at the Baldersby Flyover, take A61 to Ripon, turn right to Melmerby.
Station(s): None.
Open: House and Garden open Bank Hol Sun & Mons; Sun 23 June-1 Sept; Mons in July; and daily 23-27 July 2-5pm.
Admission: £2.95, children (10-16) £2.50, OAPs £2.00. Prices for parties of 20 or more: on application. Garden free; donations are welcome.
Refreshments: Teas and light refreshments for booked parties. Teas served at charity openings of garden.
Dogs in grounds and garden only, (except guide dogs) and must be on a lead. Visitors are requested not to wear high-heeled shoes in the house. Photography by owners' written permission only.

NUNNINGTON HALL   🍂 The National Trust

nr Helmsley map **7** O21
Telephone: (01439) 748283
Location: In Ryedale; 4½ m SE of Helmsley; 1½ m N of B1257.

PICKERING CASTLE

ENGLISH HERITAGE

map **7** O21
Telephone: (01751) 474989

Most of the medieval kings visited Pickering Castle. They came to hunt deer and wild boar in the neighbouring forest. It was a sport of which they were inordinately fond, and the royal forests were zealously guarded. Romantics may like to speculate as to why Rosamund's Tower has been linked with 'Fair Rosamund', mistress of Henry II. They should, however, be aware that the tower was built in 1323, a century after the lady died.

Location: Pickering.
Open: Apr 1-Sept 30 10-6 daily Oct 1-31 10-4 daily Nov 1-Mar 31 (closed 1-2) Wed-Sun 10-4.
Admission: Adults £2 concessions £1.50 children £1.

RICHMOND CASTLE

ENGLISH HERITAGE

map **7** O19
Telephone: (01748) 822493

Surrounded on three sides by high moorland, Richmond Castle is in a strongly defensible position. However, the castle has seen little active service, which accounts for the remarkable amount of early Norman stonework that has survived. Built by Alan the Red, shortly after 1066, the castle went with the title 'Duke of Richmond' and has had many royal and powerful owners. The 100 foot high keep provides fine views over the ruins and surrounding countryside.

Location: Richmond.
Open: Apr 1-Sept 30 10-6 daily Oct 1-Mar 31 Wed-Sun (closed 1-2) 10-4.
Admission: Adults £1.80 concessions £1.40 children 90p.

RIEVAULX ABBEY

ENGLISH HERITAGE

map **7** O20
Telephone: (0143) 96 228

The fluctuating fortunes of the abbey may be read from the ruins. Within two decades of its foundation in 1131, Rievaulx - the first Cistercian monastery in the north - was vast, with 140 monks and 500 lay brothers. A costly building programme followed, and it is little wonder that by the 13th century the monastery was heavily in debt, and buildings were being reduced in size. By the Dissolution in the 16th century, there were only 22 monks. The church is a beautiful example of early English Gothic. New visitor centre with exhibition and shop.

Location: 3 m (4.8 km) north west of Helmsley.
Open: Apr 1-Sept 30 10-6 daily Oct 1-Mar 31 daily 10-4.
Admission: Adults £2.50 concessions £1.90 children £1.30.

RIEVAULX TERRACE   🍂 The National Trust

Helmsley map **7** O20 &
Telephone: (01439) 798340
Location: 2½ m NW of Helmsley on Stokesley Road (B1257).

Sir Joshua Reynolds

Portrait painter (1723-1792)

First President of the Royal Academy, knighted in 1769

His work can be seen in the following properties included in Historic Houses Castles and Gardens:-

Arundel Castle
Dalmeny House (Roseberry Collection of Political Portraits)
Elton Hall
Goodwood House
Ickworth House, Park & Garden
Kenwood, The Iveagh Bequest

Knole
Petworth House
Rockingham Castle
Saltram
Shalom Hall
Wallington House
Weston Park

RIPLEY CASTLE
(Sir Thomas Ingilby, Bt)
Ripley HG3 3AY map **7** O19 △ &
Telephone: (01423) 770152
Fax: (01423) 771745

Has been the home of the Ingilby family since early 14th century. Priests secret hiding place and Civil War armour. Fine furnishing, Anecdotal History. Extensive gardens. National Hyacinth and tropical plant collections, parkland walk.

Location: In Ripley 3½ m N Harrogate; 7½ m from Ripon.
Station(s): Harrogate (4 m)
Open: Castle and Gardens Apr May and Oct Sat & Sun 11.30-4.30 (also Good Friday and Bank Holidays 11-4.30) June and Sept Thurs Fri Sat & Sun 11.30-4.30 July and Aug daily 11.30-4.30. Parties of more than 15 people can arrange to visit the Castle and Gardens on any day of the year (except Christmas day) by arrangementment 10.30-7.30. Gardens only Mar, Thurs Fri Sat & Sun 11-4 Apr- Oct daily 11-5 Nov-Dec 23 daily 11-3.
Admission: Castle & Gardens adults £4parties over 25 people £3 OAPs £3 children (under 16 yrs) £2 parties over 25 children (under 16 yrs) £1.75. Gardens only adults £2.25 parties over 25 people £1.75 OAPs £1.75 children (under 16 yrs) £1 parties over 25 children (under 16 yrs) £1 family ticket (2 adults 2 children) £9.50 each additional child (under 16 yrs) £1.75. Garden Season Ticket £15.
Refreshments: Licensed restaurant and public bar (The Boar's Head Hotel) in village: Cromwell's Eating House in the Castle Courtyard, serving teas and refreshments. Party catering by arrangement.
Events/Exhibitions: Spring Flower Festival Apr 22-May 6; Homes and Gardens Magazine Grand Summer Fair June 6-9; North of England Hot Air Balloon Festival Aug 23-26.
Accommodation: 25 deluxe bedrooms at the Estate owned Boar's Head Hotel, 100 yards from the Castle in Ripley village. The Hotel is rated RAC****.
Conferences: Facilities for meetings up to 75 Theatre style. Dinners up to 66 in Castle, up to 800 in marquee adjacent to Castle.
Civil Weddings, activity days and launches/promotions catered for at Castle.

SCARBOROUGH CASTLE

Scarborough map **7** O22
Telephone: (01723) 372451

Standing on the massive headland between the North and South Bays, the castle commands magnificent views. There was a prehistoric settlement here, and a Roman signal station, but the first mention of the castle is in the 12th century, when it was seized by Henry II. During the Civil War the castle was besieged and changed hands several times. A hundred years later it was still in use to detain political prisoners - notably George Fox, founder of the Society of Friends (Quakers).

Location: East of town centre.
Open: Apr 1-Sept 30 10-6 daily Oct 1-Mar 31 daily 10-4.
Admission: Adults £1.80 concessions £1.40 children 90p.

SHANDY HALL

(The Laurence Sterne Trust)
Coxwold   YO6 4AD   map **7** O20   △
Telephone: (01347) 868465

Here in 1760-67 the witty and eccentric parson Laurence Sterne wrote *Tristram Shandy* and *A Sentimental Journey,* 'novels that jump clean out of the 18th century into the 20th', influencing Dickens, Goethe, Tolstoy, Balzac, Proust, Melville, Joyce, Virginia Woolf, and other great writers. Shandy Hall was built as a timber-framed open-hall in the mid-15th century, modernised in the 17th, curiously added to by Sterne in the 18th. It survives much as he knew it, almost as full of surprises and odd digressions as his novels, most of which he wrote in his little book-lined study. Not a museum but a lived-in house where you are sure of a personal welcome. Surrounded by a walled garden full of old-fashioned roses and cottage-garden plants. Also one acre wild garden in old quarry.

Location: 20 m from York via A19; 6 m from A19 at Easingwold; 8 m from Thirsk; 13 m from A1 at Dishforth.
Station(s): York.
Open: June-Sept Wed 2-4.30 Suns 2.30-4.30 any other day or time all year by appointment with Hon Curators. Gardens open everyday May-Sept 11-4.30 except Sat.
Admission: Adults £2.50 children (accompanied) half-price. Garden only £1.50.
Refreshments: Close by in village.
Events/Exhibitions: Paintings by local artists June-Sept. Annual memorial lecture. Book and handicrafts shop. Unusual plants for sale.

SION HILL HALL

(The H W Mawer Trust. Reg.d Charity No.502772)
Kirby Wiske, nr Thirsk   YO7 4EU   map **7** 020   △ &
Telephone: (01845) 587206
Fax: (01845) 587486

Charming Edwardian Country Mansion designed by York Architect Water Brierley- the 'Lutyens of the North'. The last country house built before the Great War and designated by the RIBA as being of outstanding architectural merit. This award winning mansion now houses the Mawer Collection of period furniture, porcelain, paintings and clocks- probably the most eclectic collection in the North; and period costume displays in room settings. Bird of Prey Centre in the Victorian walled garden. Flying demonstrations every day.

Location: Off A617; 6 m S of Northallerton, 4 m W of Thirsk, 8 m E of Al via A61.
Open: Mar 17-Oct 31. Hall Wed-Sun 12.30-4.30. Birds every day 10.30-5.30. Open Bank Hol Mons. Groups by arrangement at any time Feb-Nov.
Admission: Hall adults £3.50 concessions £3 children £1.50 group reductions. Birds of Prey additional charge.
Refreshments: Granary Tea-room 10.30-5.30. Visitor Centre/Shop 10.30-5.00.

SKIPTON CASTLE

Skipton   map **7** P18   △
Telephone: (01756) 792442

Guardian of the gateway to the Yorkshire Dales for over 900 years, this is one of the most complete and well-preserved medieval castles in England. The stronghold of the Cliffords from 1310, two Lords of Skipton went out to die on Roses battlefields. In the Civil War this was the last Royalist bastion in the North. Every phase of this turbulent history can be read in the Castle's stones, from the Norman gateway towers and entrance archway to the beautiful early Tudor courtyard build in the heart of the Castle by the 'Shepherd Lord'; there, in 1659, Lady Anne Clifford planted a yew tree (in whose shade you can sit today) to celebrate her completion of repairs after the Civil War. Thanks to her efforts, the Castle remains fully roofed - amply repaying a visit at any time of year.

Location: The Castle gateway stands at the head of Skipton's High Street. Skipton is 20 m west of Harrogate on A59, 26 m north-west of Leeds on A65.
Station(s): BR ½ m. buses; town centre.
Open: Every day (except 25 Dec) throughout the year, from 10am (Sundays 2pm). Last admissions 6pm (Oct to Mar 4pm).
Admission: Adults £3.40 with illustrated tour sheet. Over 60's £2.90 with illustrated tour sheet. Under 18's £1.70 with tour sheet and badge. Under 5's free! with badge. School parties £1.70 per head (teachers free).
Large coach and car park off nearby High Street.

STOCKELD PARK

(Mr and Mrs P.G.F. Grant)
Wetherby LS22 4AH map **7** P20   △
Telephone: (01937) 586101
Fax: (01937) 580084

This small country mansion is set amidst an extensive rural estate of farms, wood and parklands on the edge of the Vale of York and is one of the finest examples of the work of the celebrated architect James Paine and a splendid example of the Palladian style. Stockeld Park was built for the Middleton family during the period 1758-63 and purchased in 1885 by Robert John Foster. Mr Foster was the great grandson of John Foster who founded John Foster & Son based at the Black Dyke Mills. Visitors have an opportunity to see the house as it is lived in at present, together with furniture and pictures collected by the Foster family over many years.

Location: 2 m N of Wetherby; 7 m SE of Harrogate on A661.
Station(s): Nearest Harrogate then direct bus route approx. 7 m.
Open: Thurs only Apr 4-Oct 10.
Admission: Adults £2 children £1 OAPs £1.50.
Conferences: Film and photographic location - contact Estate office for further information.

THORP PERROW ARBORETUM

(Sir John Ropner)
nr Snape map **7** O19

Thorp Perrow, the country home of Sir John Ropner, contains the finest arboretum in the north of England. A collection of over 1,000 varieties of trees and shrubs including some of the largest and rarest in the country. It is also the home of four national collections - oak, ash, lime and walnut - and is becoming a popular attraction for all the family. The arboretum comprises 85 acres of landscaped grounds with a lake, grassy glades, tree trails and woodland walks. Thousands of daffodils carpet the ground in spring while the summer is noted for bold drifts of wild flowers and the autumn brings glorious and vibrant colour. Nature trail. Children's mystery trail. Tearoom and information centre. Plant centre. Electric wheelchair available.

Location: On the Well to Ripon Road, south of Bedale. O.S. map ref. SE258851. 4 m from Leeming Bar on A1.

Open: All year dawn-dusk. Guided tours available. Tel:(01677) 425323.
Admission: Adults £3 OAPs/children (5-16) £2. Free car and coach park.
Refreshments: Tea-room.
Picnic area. Toilets. Dogs permitted on leads.

TREASURER'S HOUSE   ❧ The National Trust

York map **7** P20
Telephone: (01904) 624247
Location: Behind York Minster.

WHITBY ABBEY

map **7** O21
Telephone: (01947) 603568

ENGLISH HERITAGE

Founded in 657 and presided over by the Abbess Hilda, Whitby was a double monastery for both men and women - a feature of the Anglo-Saxon church. This early history has been chronicled by the Venerable Bede, who tells us that here the poet Caedmon lived and worked. Destroyed by invading Danes in 867, the monastery was refounded after the Norman Conquest, but its exposed cliff-top site continued to invite attack by sea pirates. The building remains are from the later Benedictine monastery.

Location: E of Whitby Town Centre.
Open: Apr 1-Sept 30 10-6 daily, 1-31 Oct 10-6 or dusk if earlier, 1 Nov-31 Mar 10-4 Wed-Sun.
Admission: Adults £1.60 concessions £1.20 children 80p.

SOUTH YORKSHIRE

BISHOPS' HOUSE

(Sheffield City Museums)
Meersbrook Park, Norton Lees Lane S8 9BE map **15** Q20
Telephone: (0114) 2557701

Beautiful Tudor timber framed house with furnished rooms and permanent displays about life in Tudor and Stuart times. Exciting programme of temporary exhibitions and events.

Location: 2 m south of Sheffield on A61.
Open: Wed-Sat 10-4.30 Sun 11-4.30 open Bank Holidays.
Admission: Nominal charge.

BRODSWORTH HALL
Brodsworth   map **15** P20
Telephone: (01302) 722598

ENGLISH HERITAGE

The most complete example of a Victorian country house in England. A unique insight into a vanished way of life. But, as well as being an irreplacable document of High Victorian art and social history, Brodsworth is also an enchanting place, splendidly set in its Park and Garden.

Location: Brodsworth, S. Yorkshire, 6 m NW of Doncaster W of A1 between A635 & A638.
Open: 30 Mar-27 Oct Tues-Sun and Bank Hol Mons 1-6 (Gardens 12-6pm). Last admission 5.
Admission: Adults £4.20, concessions £3.20 children £2.10.

CANNON HALL
(Barnsley Metropolitan Borough Council)
Cawthorne   map **15** P19
Telephone: (01226) 790270

18th century house by Carr of York. Collections of fine furniture, paintings, glassware, art nouveau pewter and pottery. Also the Regimental Museum of the 13th/18th Royal Hussars. 70 acres of parkland. Walled garden with historic fruit trees.

Location: 5 m W of Barnsley on A635; 1 m NW of Cawthorne.
Open: All the year Tues-Sat 10.30-5 closed Mon (Open Bank Hol Mons) Suns 12-5.
Refreshments: Victorian kitchen cafe Sunday afternoons. Daily at farm cafe.

SHEFFIELD BOTANIC GARDENS
(Sheffield City Council)
Meersbrook Park, Brook Road   **S8 9FL**   map **15** Q20   △ & ⬚
Telephone: (0114) 2500500
Fax: (0114) 2552375

Designed in 1833 by Robert Marnock the original curator the Gardens are fine example of the Victorian *gardenesque* style. Occupying 19 acres in the south-west of the city the Gardens contain around 5,000 species of plants including the national collections of *Weigela and Diervilla*. The original layout is still largely intact including the straight promenade up to the "Paxton Pavilions", an important example of early metal and glass curvilinear structires. Listed as a Grade 2 garden by English Heritage the Gardens contain many interesting features including woodland garden, rock garden and pools. In addition to the pavilions there are a number of other listed buildings such as the 19C. Bear Pit, the Clarkehouse Road gateway (1836) and the Crimean War Memoral (1858)".

Open: Daily except Christmas day, Boxing day and New Years day.
Admission: Free.
Refreshments: Available for pre-arranged guided tours.
Events/Exhibitions: Aproximately 150 events/lectures held by the Friends of the Botanical Gardens and special horticultural societies.
Conferences: Room for 80 people in the lecture room and 50 in the new demonstration greenhouse.
On street at Clarkehouse or Thompson Road Entrances.

WEST YORKSHIRE

BAGSHAW MUSEUM
(Kirklees Metro Council)
Wilton Park, Batley   map **15** P19
Telephone: (01924) 472514

Victorian gothic mansion, Egyptian/Oriental displays. Rainforest study gallery.

Open: Mon-Fri 11-5 Sat-Sun 12-5.
Admission: Free.

Butterfly Houses

can be found at the following properties included in Historic Houses Castles and Gardens:-

Berkeley Castle
Elsham Hall - Wild butterfly walkway
Syon House

BRAMHAM PARK

(Mr & Mrs George Lane Fox)
Wetherby LS23 6ND   map **15** P20 △
Telephone: (01937) 844265
Fax: (01937) 845923

The house was created towards the end of the 17th century and affords a rare opportunity to enjoy a beautiful Queen Anne mansion containing fine furniture, pictures and porcelain - set in magnificent grounds with ornamental ponds, cascades, tall beech hedges and loggias of various shapes - unique in the British Isles for its grand vistas design stretching out into woodlands of cedar, copper beech, lime and Spanish chestnut interspersed with wild rhododendron thickets.

Location: 5 m S of Wetherby on the Great North Road (A1).
Open: Grounds Only Easter weekend May Day Weekend Spring Bank Hol weekend House & Grounds June 16-Sept 1 Sun Tues Wed & Thurs also Bank Hol Mon 1.15-5.30 last adm 5. 'Bramham Horse Trials' June 6-9 1996.
Admission: For charges and concessionary rates contact The Estate Office, Bramham Park, Wetherby, W. Yorks LS23 6ND Tel: (01937) 844265.
Refreshments: Picnics in grounds permitted.
The Red Lion in Bramham village offers bar meals and traditional Sunday lunches.

BRONTË PARSONAGE MUSEUM

Haworth, Keighley, West Yorkshire BD22 8DR   map **15** P15
Telephone: (01535) 642323
Fax: (01535) 647131

Once the home of the remarkable Brontë family, it is now an intimate museum cared for by thr Brontë Society. This small Georgian Parsonage has rooms furnished as in the Brontës' day, with displays of their personal treasures, their pictures, books and manuscripts. See where the writers of "Jane Eyre" and "Wuthering Heights" lived.

Open: Every day, except 15 Jan-9 Feb (96) and 24-27 December 10am-5pm, Apr-Sept 11am-4.30pm Oct-Mar.
Admission: Adults £3.80, plus range of concessions.

DEWSBURY MUSEUM

(Kirklees Metropolitan Council)
Crow West Park, Dewsbury   map **15** P19
Telephone: (01924) 468171

Refurnished mansion house, childhood displays, 1940s schoolroom.

Open: Mon-Fri 11-5 Sat-Sun 12-5.
Admission: Free.

EAST RIDDLESDEN HALL   ❀ The National Trust

Keighley   map **15** P19   ♿
Telephone: (01535) 607075
Location: 1 m NE of Keighley on S side of A650, on N bank of Aire.

Sir Peter Lely

(*PORTRAIT PAINTER*)

His paintings can be seen at the following properties included in Historic Houses Castles and Gardens:-

Aynhoe Park
Belton House
Breamore House
Browsholme Hall
Dalmeny House
Euston Hall
Goodwood House
Gorhambury
Kedleston Hall
Knole
Petworth House
Ragley Hall
Rockingham Castle
St Osyth Priory
Stanford Hall
Weston Park

HAREWOOD HOUSE AND BIRD GARDEN

(The Earl of Harewood)
Leeds LS17 9LQ   map **15** P19 Ⓢ
Telephone: (0113) 288 6331/288 6225
Fax: (0113) 288 6467

Harewood House, home of the Earl and Countess of Harewood, was designed for the Lascelles family by John Carr in 1759. The magnificent interior, created by Robert Adam, has superb ceilings and plasterwork and contains a fine collection of English and Italian paintings, Chippendale furniture and Sèvres and Chinese porcelain. New in 1995 were two dedicated Watercolour Rooms. In the grounds, landscaped by 'Capability' Brown, are lakeside and woodland walks, an internationally-renowned Bird Garden with 120 species, many endangered, and an outstanding Adventure Playground. Sir Charles Barry's parterre design on the Terrace has been restored to its original condition of intricate patterns made with box, bedding plants and white chippings. The Earl of Harewood is the son of the late Princess Mary, daughter of King George V, and is a cousin of Queen Elizabeth II. Princess Mary lived at Harewood for many years and some of her pictures and possessions are on display in her rooms. The Terrace Gallery shows a changing programme of contemporary art exhibitions.

Location: 7 m S of Harrogate; 8 m N of Leeds on Leeds/Harrogate road; Junction A61/659 at Harewood village; 5 m from A1 at Wetherby 22m from York. No. 36 bus from Leeds or Harrogate.
Station(s): Leeds or Harrogate.
Open: House, Grounds, Bird Garden and all Facilities Mar 16-Oct 27 daily. Gates open 10.00 House open 11.00. Concession rates for Coach parties, school parties welcome at all times. Bird Garden and Grounds open weekends Nov and Dec.
Admission: Charges and details of Special Event Admissions - including Car Rallies and Leeds Championship Dog Show available from Gerald Long, Visitors Information, Estate Office, Harewood, Leeds LS17 9LQ.
Refreshments: Cafeteria; Courtyard Suite; State Dining Room (private functions-max 50).
Conferences: Courtyard Functions Suite for Conferences/Product launches all year.

LEDSTON HALL
(G.H.H. Wheler, Esq)
nr Castleford   WF10 2BB   map **15** P20
Telephone: (01904) 610811
Fax: (01904) 610869

17th century mansion with some earlier work.

Location: 2 m N of Castleford off A656.
Station(s): Castleford (2¾ m).
Open: Exterior only May June July and Aug Mon-Fri 9-4. Other days by appointment.
Refreshments: Chequers Inn, Ledsham (1 m).

LOTHERTON HALL
(Leeds City Council)
Aberford   LS25 3EB   map **15** P20
Telephone: (0113) 281 3259
Fax: (0113) 260 2285

Modest late Victorian and Edwardian country house of great charm and character, formerly the home of the Gascoigne family. Fine collections of furniture, silver, pottery and porcelain, paintings, sculpture and costume, including many family heirlooms. Famouse period gardens; deer park and bird garden.

Location: 1 m E of A1 at Aberford on the Towton Road (B1217).
Open: Closed Mon. Open end Mar-end Oct. Tues-Sun 1pm-5pm.
Admission: Adults £2 children 50p OAPs/students £1 season ticket £4.75 (includes Temple Newsam, see below) pre-booked coach parties £1 Tel: (0113) 281 3259.
Refreshments: Café in stable block.

NOSTELL PRIORY   🌳 The National Trust
Wakefield   map **15** P20   ♿
Telephone: (01924) 863892
Location: 6 m SE of Wakefield, on N side of A638.

OAKWELL HALL
(Kirklees Metropolitan Council)
Birstall   WF19 9LG   map **15** P19   🏕
Telephone: (01924) 474926
Fax: (01924) 420536

Historic house, 17th century furnishings, country park, visitor centre.

Open: Mon-Fri 11-5 Sat-Sun 12-5.
Admission: Charges between 1 Mar-31 Oct. Please phone for details.
Refreshments: Oak Tree Cafe, light refreshments, restricted opening in winter.
Events/Exhibitions: Year round programme. Telephone for leaflet.
Conferences: Restored Oakwell barn and classroom available.

RED HOUSE
(Kirklees Metropolitan Council)
Gomersal, Cleckheaton   map **15** P19
Telephone: (01274) 872165

1830s period home, strong Bronte connections. Shop, exhibitions, garden.

Open: Mon-Fri 11-5 Sat-Sun 12-5.
Admission: Free.

SHIBDEN HALL
(Calderdale Metropolitan Borough Council)
Halifax   HG3 6XG   map **15** P19   △ ♿
Telephone: (01422) 352246 or (01422) 321455
Fax: (01422) 348440

Just outside Halifax, in its own landscaped park Shibden Hall provides an unusual place to visit. Built in about 1420, this half-timbered house reflects almost 600 years of occupation, with collections explaining how to build such a house to how people live in it. Famous owners include the diarist Anne Lister and her descendant, John Lister, antiquarian and philanthropist. Oak furniture, metalware and one of the earliest carriages are displayed, with an exciting events programme, shop, tea-room and activities in the park, making Shibden an excellent choice for a day out for everyone.

Location: 1½ m SE of Halifax on the Halifax/Hipperholme Road (A58).
Station(s): Halifax.
Open: Mar-Nov Mons-Sats 10-5 Suns 12-5 please telephone for winter opening.
Admission: Adults £1.50 children/OAPs 75p family ticket £4.50. Conducted tours after normal hours (Fee payable). Price correct at time of publication.
Refreshments: At the Hall.
Ground floor access for disabled.

TEMPLE NEWSAM HOUSE
(Leeds City Council)
Leeds   LS15 0AE   map **15** P20
Telephone: (0113) 264 7321
Fax: (0113) 260 2285

The magnificent Tudor-Jacobean house was the birthplace of Lord Darnley, husband of Mary Queen of Scots, and later became the home of the Ingram family, Viscounts Irwin. There are over 30 historic interiors (many newly restored) including a spectacular Picture Gallery, with superlative paintings, furniture (including the Chippendale Society collection), silver and ceramics. The thousand acre Capability Brown park (free) contains a home farm with rare breeds of animals, sensational displays of rhododendrons and azaleas (May and June), national collections of delphiniums and phlox (July and August), chrysanthemums (September) and roses (all summer).

Location: 5 m E of Leeds; 1 m S of A63 (nr junction with A641).
Station(s): Cross Gates (1¾ m).
Open: End Mar-end Oct. Tues-Sun 1pm-5pm. Nov-mid Mar Sat & Sun 12-4pm. Closed Mon.
Admission: Adults £2 children 50p OAPs/students £1 pre-booked coach parties £1.
Refreshments: Tea-room.

TOLSON MEMORIAL MUSEUM
(Kirklees Metropolitan Council)
Ravensknowle Park, Huddersfield   HD5 8DJ   map 15 P19
Telephone: (01484) 541455

Victorian mansion, local natural history, archaeology and social history.

Open: Mon-Fri 11-5 Sat-Sun 12-5.
Admission: Free.

WALES

CLWYD

BODELWYDDAN CASTLE
(Bodelwyddan Castle Trust)
Bodelwyddan, St Asaph   LL18 5YA   map 6 Q16
Telephone: (01745) 584060
Fax: (01745) 584563

Bodelwyddan Castle has been authentically restored as a Victorian Country House and contains a major collection of portraits and photography from the National Portrait Gallery. The collection includes works by many eminent Victorian Portraitists such as G. F. Watts, William Holman Hunt, John Singer Sargeant, Sir Edwin Landseer and Sir Thomas Lawrence. The portraits are complemented by furniture from the Victoria & Albert Museum and sculptures from the Royal Academy. An exhibition of Victorian Amusements and inventions features parlour games, puzzles and optical illusions - an extravaganza of Victorian fun, games and hands-on experience of the 19th century! The Castle is set in rolling parkland and gardens against the impressive backdrop of the Clwydian Hills. A programme of events takes place throughout the year. Winner of the Museum of the Year Award. Free audio guide and quiz sheet.

Location: Just off the A55 near St. Asaph (opposite the Marble Church).
Station(s): Rhyl.
Open: Mar 30-June 30 and Sept 7-Oct 31 daily except Fri 10*-5 July 1-Sept 6 daily 10*-5 Nov 1-Easter 1997 daily except Mon and Fri 11-4. Please telephone to check winter openings. *Castle galleries open at 10.30.
Admission: Castle and Grounds adults £4 (£2) OAPs/unemployed £3.50 (£2) children/students/disabled £2.50 (£1.50) family (2+3) £12 (£6.50). Grounds only price in brackets.
Refreshments: Tea-room.
Events/Exhibitions: Programme of temporary exhibitions, concerts and events throughout the year.
Evening visits welcome. Prior booking necessary. Suitable for disabled persons (wheelchairs available). Giftshop. Picnic Area. Woodland Walk. Gardens, Grounds and Childrens Play Areas.

BODRHYDDAN HALL
(Lord Langford)
Bodrhyddan, Rhuddlan   LL18 5SB
Telephone: (01745) 590414

A 17th Century country house with traces of an earlier building and additions, by William Eden Nesfield the famous Victorian architect. Notable features include an Egyptian mummy, armour and pictures. The Parterre was designed by Andrew Nesfield. Another garden has four ponds with ornamental duck, fish and picnic area.

Open: Tues & Thurs, June-Sept inclusive 2-5.30.
Admission: Adults £2 children under 16yrs £1 (house & garden). 10% reduction for parties of over 40.
Refreshments: Teas, meals by appointment.

CHIRK CASTLE   The National Trust
nr Wrexham   LL14 5AF   map 6 R16
Telephone: (01691) 777701
Location: ½ m from Chirk (on A5 trunk road) then 1½ m private driveway; 20 m NW of Shrewsbury 7 m SE of Llangollen.

ERDDIG   The National Trust
nr Wrexham   LL13 0YT   map 6 Q16   Ⓔ
Telephone: (01978) 313333
Location: 2 m S of Wrexham off A525 or A483.

EWLOE CASTLE
(Cadw: Welsh Historic Monuments)
nr Hawarden   map 6 Q16

Native Welsh castle with typical round and aspidal towers.

GYRN CASTLE   🏛
(Sir Geoffrey Bates, BT, MC)
Llanasa, Holywell   map 6 Q16
Telephone: (01745) 853500

Dating, in part, from 1700; castellated 1820. Large picture gallery, panelled entrance hall. Pleasant woodland walks and fantastic views to Mersey and Lake District.

Location: 26 m W of Chester (off A55); 4 m SE of Prestatyn.
Open: All the year-by appointment.
Admission: £4, parties welcome.
Refreshments: By arrangement.

PLAS NEWYDD AND THE LADIES OF LLANGOLLEN
(Glyndwr District Council)
Llangollen   LL20 8AW   map 6 R16
Telephone: (01978) 861314 (During opening hours) or (01824) 702201
Fax: (01824) 705026

Plas Newydd was the home of Lady Eleanor Butler and Miss Sarah Ponsonby, the 'Ladies of Llangollen' from 1780-1831. They eloped from Kilkenny, Ireland before settling in the enchanted spot of Llangollen. They became the centre of a personality cult which still draws visitors today as strongly as it did during the Regency period. The house retains some of the Gothic elements that they introduced, the gardens also possess the peace and tranquility that they sought.

Station(s): Nearest station Ruabon 7 miles
Open: 1 Apr-31 Oct Mon-Sun 10-5.
Admission: Adults £1.80 children 90p (1995 prices).
Events/Exhibitions: Permanent exhibition 'A Most Extraordinary Affair.'
Limited car parking.

VALLE CRUCIS ABBEY
(Cadw: Welsh Historic Monuments)
Llangollen   LL20 8DD   map 6 R16
Telephone: (01978) 860326

Lovely ruins of a 13th century Abbey set beside the Eglwyseg stream.

DYFED

CAREW CASTLE & TIDAL MILL
(Pembrokeshire Coast National Park)
Carew, Tenby   map **2** T13
Telephone: (01646) 651782
Fax: (01646) 651782

A magnificent Norman Castle - later Elizabethan residence. Royal links with Henry Tudor, setting for Great Tournament of 1507. The Mill is only restored tidal mill in Wales. Automatic talking points explaining milling process. Special exhibition, 'The Story of Milling'.

Location: 4 m east of Pembroke.
Station(s): Rail - Pembroke. Bus - Haverfordwest.
Open: Every day Easter-end Oct.
Admission: Entrance Carew Castle or Tidal Mill £1.50 dual ticket £2 children/OAPs special rate. School parties for both £1.20 per pupil. Teachers free.

CARREG CENNEN CASTLE
(Cadw: Welsh Historic Monuments)
Trapp   SA19 6UA   map **2** T14
Telephone: (01558) 822291

A 13th century castle dramatically perched on a limestone precipice.

CILGERRAN CASTLE
(Cadw: Welsh Historic Monuments)
Cilgerran   SA43 2SF   map **2** S13
Telephone: (01239) 615007

Picturesque remains that date essentially from the early 13th century.

COLBY WOODLAND GARDEN   The National Trust
Amroth   SA67 8PP   map **2** T13
Telephone: (01558) 822800/(01834) 811885
Location: NE of Tenby off A477; E of junction A477/A478.

DINEFWR PARK   The National Trust
Llandeilo   SA19 6RT   map **2** T14
Telephone: (01558) 823902
Fax: (01558) 822036
Location: A40 nr Llandeilo.

KIDWELLY CASTLE
(Cadw: Welsh Historic Monuments)
Kidwelly   SA17 5BQ   map **2** T14
Telephone: (01554) 890104

An outstanding example of late 13th century castle design.

LAMPHEY BISHOP'S PALACE
(Cadw: Welsh Historic Monuments)
Lamphey   SA71 5NT   map **2** T13
Telephone: (01646) 672224

Substantial remains of the medieval Bishops of St David's residence.

LLAWHADEN CASTLE
(Cadw: Welsh Historic Monuments)
Llawhaden   map **2** T13
Telephone: (01437) 541201

A fortified palace at the centre of a manorial estate belonging to the Bishops of St Davids.

PICTON CASTLE
(The Picton Castle Trust)
Haverfordwest   SA62 4AS   map **2** T13   △
Telephone: (01437) 751326

Occupied continuously since the 15th century by the Philipps family who are still in residence.

ST. DAVIDS BISHOP'S PALACE
(Cadw: Welsh Historic Monuments)
St Davids   SA62 6PE   map **2** T12
Telephone: (01437) 720517

A most impressive medieval Bishop's Palace within the Cathedral Close.

STRATA FLORIDA ABBEY
(Cadw: Welsh Historic Monuments)
Strata Florida   SY25 6BT   map **2** S15
Telephone: (01974) 831261

The ruins of this Cistercian abbey (1164) stand in a lovely valley.

TALLEY ABBEY
(Cadw: Welsh Historic Monuments)
Talley   map **2** T14
Telephone: (01558) 685444

A 13th century monastic site founded for the Premonstratensian Order.

TUDOR MERCHANT'S HOUSE   The National Trust
Tenby   map **2** T13
Telephone: (01834) 842279
Location: Quay Hill, Tenby.

MID GLAMORGAN

CAERPHILLY CASTLE
(Cadw: Welsh Historic Monuments)
Caerphilly   CF8 1JL   map **14** T16
Telephone: (01222) 883143

One of the largest medieval castles, water defences of 30 acres

COITY CASTLE
(Cadw: Welsh Historic Monuments)
Coity   map **3** T15
Telephone: (01656) 652021

An early Norman stronghold. In the Owain Glyndwr Uprising, the castle withstood a siege by the Welsh.

LLANCAIACH FAWR
(Rhymney Valley District Council)
Treharris   map **14** T16
Telephone: (01443) 412248

Step back in time to the year 1645 at this fascinating 17th Century Living Museum. Meet the servants of "Colonel" Edward Prichard as they guide you around this lovely manor house and gardens.
Location: .

SOUTH GLAMORGAN

CARDIFF CASTLE
(Cardiff City Council)
Cardiff   △

Begun 1090 on remains of Roman Fort. Rich interior decorations.

CASTELL COCH
(Cadw: Welsh Historic Monuments)
Tongwynlais, nr Cardiff   CF4 7JS   map **14** T16
Telephone: (01222) 810101

This late 19th century castle - a combination of Victorian Gothic fantasy and timeless fairytale.

WEST GLAMORGAN

MARGAM PARK
(West Glamorgan County Council)
nr Port Talbot Ⓢ
Telephone: (01639) 881635
Fax: (01639) 895897
Location: Easy access on A48 ¼ m from Exit 38 off M4 near Port Talbot.

NEATH ABBEY
(Cadw: Welsh Historic Monuments)
Neath SA10 7DW map **2** T15 ◨
Telephone: (01792) 812387

Originally founded 1130, the abbey was absorbed into the Cistercian order in 1147.

WEOBLEY CASTLE
(Cadw: Welsh Historic Monuments)
Llanrhidian, nr. Swansea SA3 1HB map **2** T14
Telephone: (01792) 390012

Picturesque fortified late medieval manor house.

GWENT

CAERLEON ROMAN FORTRESS
(Cadw: Welsh Historic Monuments)
Caerleon NP6 1AY map **14** T17
Telephone: (01633) 422518

Impressive remains of baths, amphitheatre, barracks and fortress wall.

TREDEGAR HOUSE
(Newport Borough Council)
Newport map **14** T17 △
Telephone: (01633) 815880

CHEPSTOW CASTLE
(Cadw: Welsh Historic Monuments)
Chepstow NP6 5EZ map **14** T17
Telephone: (01291) 624065

This strategic fortress is one of the earliest stone built castles.

CWRT PORTH HIR
(Coldbrook & Llanover Estate (WA))
Llanover

PENHOW CASTLE 🏛
(Stephen Weeks, Esq)
Nr Newport NP6 3AD map **14** T17 △ Ⓔ Ⓢ
Telephone: (01633) 400800
Fax: (01633) 400990

Penhow Castle is Wales' Oldest Lived-in Castle.

RAGLAN CASTLE 🍀
(Cadw: Welsh Historic Monuments)
Raglan NP5 2BT map **14** T17
Telephone: (01291) 690228

A 15th century castle with its tower, the 'Yellow Tower of Gwent'.

TINTERN ABBEY 🍀
(Cadw: Welsh Historic Monuments)
Tintern NP6 6SE map **14** T17
Telephone: (01291) 689251

Impressive ruins of Cistercian abbey 1131 set in the Wye valley.

One wing of the 16th century house survives, but Tredegar House owes its character to lavish 17th century rebuilding in brick. Ancestral home of the Morgan family, Lords of Tredegar. The 90 acre park includes gardens, lake, adventure play farm, carriage rides and craft workshops.

Location: SW of Newport; signposted from M4 junction 28, A48.
Station(s): Newport (2¾ m).
Open: Park open daily 6.15-Sunset. House and Attractions open Good Fri-Sept Wed-Sun and Public Hols and Tues school hols and weekends in Oct. House Tours every ½ hour from 11.30-4. House open at other times by appointment.
Admission: House and Walled Gardens adults £3.80 children/OAPs £3 family £10 coach and school parties welcome if booked in advance.
Refreshments: Lunch and teas at the Brewhouse Tea-room. Supper tours by arrangement.
Events/Exhibitions: Concerts and special events inside the House. Open air theatre, festivals and shows in the Park.
Conferences: Conference and meeting facilities, also wedding receptions and private functions by arrangement.

WHITE CASTLE

(Cadw: Welsh Historic Monuments)
Llantilio Crossenny   NP7 8UD   map **3** T17
Telephone: (0160085) 380

Imposing moated remains of 12th century castle by Henry II.

GWYNEDD

ABERCONWY HOUSE   The National Trust

Conwy   LL32 8AY   map **6** Q15
Telephone: (01492) 592246
Location: In the town at junction of Castle Street & High Street.

BEAUMARIS CASTLE (WORLD HERITAGE LISTED SITE)

(Cadw: Welsh Historic Monuments)
Beaumaris, Anglesey   LL58 8AP   map **6** Q14
Telephone: (01248) 810361

The last and largest of the castles built by King Edward I.

BODNANT GARDEN   The National Trust

Tal-y-Cafn   LL28 5RE   map **6** Q15
Telephone: (01492) 650460
Location: 8 m S of Llandudno & Colwyn Bay on A470; Entrance along Eglwysbach Road. Sign posted from A55 North Wales coastal route.

CAERNARFON CASTLE (WORLD HERITAGE LISTED SITE)

(Cadw: Welsh Historic Monuments)
Caernarfon   LL55 2AY   map **6** Q14
Telephone: (01286) 677617

Mighty medieval fortress built by King Edward I.

COCHWILLAN OLD HALL

(R.C.H. Douglas Pennant, Esq)
Talybont, Bangor   LL57 3AZ   map **6** Q14
Telephone: (01248) 364608

Fine example of medieval architecture (restored 1971).

Location: 3½ m Bangor; 1 m Talybont village off A55.
Open: Open by appointment.

CONWY CASTLE (WORLD HERITAGE LISTED SITE)

(Cadw: Welsh Historic Monuments)
Conwy   LL32 8AY   map **6** Q156
Telephone: (01492) 592358

Imposing medieval fortress built between 1283 and 1289.

CRICCIETH CASTLE

(Cadw: Welsh Historic Monuments)
Criccieth   LL52 0DP   map **6** R14
Telephone: (01766) 522227

Castle (1230) perched in a commanding position above Tremadog Bay..

GWYDIR UCHAF CHAPEL

(Cadw: Welsh Historic Monuments)
Llanrwst   map **6** Q15
Telephone: (01492) 640978

A 17th century chapel with elaborately painted ceilings and walls.

HARLECH CASTLE (WORLD HERITAGE LISTED SITE)

(Cadw: Welsh Historic Monuments)
Harlech   LL46 2YH   map **6** R14
Telephone: (01766) 780552

This magnificent castle was built by King Edward I in 1283.

PLAS BRONDANW GARDENS

Nr Penrhyndeudraeth   map **6** R14
Telephone: (01766) 771136

Created by Sir Clough Williams-Ellis, architect of Portmeirion, below his ancestral home. Italian inspired gardens with spectacular mountain views, topiary and folly tower.

Location: 2 m N of Penrhyndeudraeth. ¼ m off the A4085 on Croesor Road.
Open: Open all year daily 9-5.
Admission: Adults £1.50 children 25p.

TY'N Y COED   The National Trust

nr Penmachno   LL24 OPS   map **6** Q15
Telephone: (01690) 760229
Location: 1½ m S of Betws-y-Coed on the A5. NT car park approached via Penmachno Woollen Mills' car park.

WERN ISAF (FORMERLY ROSEBRIERS)

(Mrs P.J. Phillips)
Llanfairfechan   LL33 ORN   map **6** Q15
Telephone: (01248) 680437

Built in 1900 as his family home by H.L. North, one of the leading Arts and Crafts Architects in Wales.

Open: Sats and Suns 10.30 am - 4.00pm March, April August only.

POWYS

GREGYNOG

(The University of Wales)
Newtown   map **6** R16
Telephone: (01686) 650224
Fax: (01686) 650656

A Victorian mansion, in 750 acres of wooded parkland with extensive gardens, including one of the most striking displays of rhododendrons in Wales; the Western red cedar 'Zebrina' is probably the biggest tree of this variety in the U.K. Many walks in the grounds. The Hall has an exceptionally fine carved parlour dating to 1636, retained when the old hall was rebuilt in the 1840s. The works of art still remaining from the collections of the Davies sisters include two Rodin bronzes. On show also are books by the Gregynog Press, one of the best-known private presses of the 1920s and 30s, and by the present Gwasg Gregynog, where fine printing is still carried on. This is a working Press and visitors can only be accepted occasionally by prior appointment. Accommodation is sometimes available in the Hall, depending on the nature and size of the resident conference. Since 1963, The Hall has operated as an intercollegiate course and conference centre for the various colleges and institutions of the University of Wales. During the last week in June, an important annual Music Festival is held here.

Location: Near the village of Tregynon, 5 m N of Newtown, off B4389.
Station(s): Newtown
Open: Gardens always open. Hall Jun 1-Sept 30 Mon-Sat. Guided tours at 11 and 3. Hall and Gardens may very exceptionally have to be closed for a day.
Admission: £2.50 Guided tour to include morning coffee or afternoon tea. Children (under 15) half-price. Parties by arrangement. Free car parking.
Conferences: Contact the Warden for further details.
Suitable for disabled persons (no wheelchairs provided).

POWIS CASTLE   🌿 The National Trust

Welshpool   SY21 8RF   map **6** R16   ♿
Telephone: (01938) 554336
Location: 1 m S of Welshpool off A483; Pedestrian access from High Street (A490)

A beautiful castle in a beautiful setting.

TRETOWER COURT & CASTLE

(Cadw: Welsh Historic Monuments)
Crickhowell   NP8 2RF   map **3** T16
Telephone: (01874) 730279

One of the finest medieval houses in Wales.

IRELAND

ANNES GROVE GARDENS

(Mr and Mrs Patrick Grove Annesley)
Castletownroche
Telephone: (0122) 26145

Extensive Robinsonian woodland and riverside gardens with notable collection of rhododendrons and other exotica.

AYESHA CASTLE

(Mr & Mrs Aylmer)
Killiney, Co. Dublin
Telephone

A romantic 19th century Victorian Castle. Set in a naturally beautiful setting redolent of Ireland's past

BANTRY HOUSE

(Mr & Mrs Egerton Shelswell-White)
Bantry, Co. Cork   map **16** T4
Telephone: (027) 50047

Partly-Georgian mansion standing at edge of Bantry Bay, with beautiful views. Seat of family of White, formerly Earls of Bantry. Unique collection of tapestries, furniture etc. Terraces and Statuary in the Italian style in grounds.

Location: In outskirts of Bantry (½ m); 56 m SW of Cork.
Open: Open all year-Daily 9-6 *(open until 8 on most summer evenings).*
Admission: House & Grounds £3.00, Children (up to 14) accompanied by parents, free, OAPs/Students £1.75. Parties (20 or more) £2.25.
Refreshments: Tea room. Bed and Breakfast.
Events/Exhibitions: 1796 Bantry French Armada - (permanent exhibition).
Accommodation: Bed and Breakfast and dinner. Nine rooms en suite.
Conferences: Facilities available.
Craft shop.

BUNRATTY CASTLE AND FOLK PARK

(Shannon Heritage Ltd)
Bunratty, Co. Clare   map **16** R5
Telephone: 0161-361511
Fax: 0161-62523

Bunratty Castle and Folk Park is our main attraction. Craggaunowen Project: An Adventure in Time in the Bronze Age. During the Bronze Age, people protected themselves against marauding warriors by building their homes on lakes. The project includes: 'Ring Fort' a true reproduction of a Farmer's house, 'Crannog' constructed from wattles, reeds and mude, 'Brendan' the hide boat in which Tim Severin sailed from Ireland to the United States.

Open: Daily 9.30-5.30. June-Aug 9.30-7.00. Contact 361511 & 367178.
Admission: From 1 Apr 96. Adults £4.75 adult group £4.45. Child/Student £2.30. Child/Student £3.35. Family ticket (2 adults & 6 children) £11.50. Banq guest £3.35. Groups must consist of 10 persons or over.
Refreshments: Available.

CRAGGAUNOWEN - THE LIVING PAST

(The Hunt Museums Trust)
Kilmurry, Sixmilebridge, Co. Clare   map **16** R5

Craggaunowen, "Where Celtic Life is brought to life," is pleasantly situated in the wooded farmland of County Clare. The site consists of a mediaeval Tower House containing a display of furniture and reconstructed exhibits around the grounds. There are two iron-age dwellings - a lake dwelling and a ring fort - and the leather boat 'Brendan' sailed by Tim Severin from Ireland to Newfoundland. In the summer months displays and experiments are conducted on the techniques associated with milling, pottery making and weaving in the iron age.

Location: 3½ m E of Quin, 6 m N of Sixmilebridge. 15 m NW of Limerick.
Open: 10.00-18.00 daily mid Mar-Oct.
Admission: £3.90 Senior Citizens £2.75 Family ticket £10. Group rates available.
Refreshments: Tea, scones, porter cake available in tea-room.
Events/Exhibitions: 'Living Past Experience' dramatised images of Ancient Ireland, mid May to mid Sept.

CURRAGHMORE

Marquis of Waterford
Portlaw, Ireland   map **16** S8
Telephone: (051) 387102
Fax: (051) 387481

Magnificent home of the Marquis of Waterford and his ancestors since 1170. Outstanding arboretum.

Location: 14 miles from Waterford, 8 miles from Kilmacthomas, 5 miles from Carrick-on-Suir, 2 miles from Portlaw.
Open: Grounds and unique Shellhouse open Thur and Bank Hols 2-5. Easter-mid ct. Toilets. House, grounds and Shellhouse open to parties by appointmant Mon-Fri year round.

DUBLIN WRITERS MUSEUM

(Esther O' Hanlon, Curator)
18 Parnell Square, Dublin 1.   map **16** Q10
Telephone: (01) 8722077
Fax: (01) 8722231
Location: City centre - 5 mins walk from Tourist Information Office in O'Connell Street.

DUNGUAIRE CASTLE

Kinvara, Co. Galway   map **16** Q5
Telephone: Central reservations 061 360788. Free phone 1800 269899
Fax: 061 361020

Dunguaire was the stronghold of Guaire, King of Connaught in the 7th century. The 15th century Dunguaire Castle, now beautifully restored overlooks Galway Bay and gives an insight into the lifestyles of those that lived there. Dunguaire features mediaeval banquets nightly, May to September.

DUNKATHEL

Dunkathel, Glanmire   map **16** T6
Telephone: (021) 821014/821767
Fax: (021) 821023

DUNKATHEL is a fine late eighteenth century neo-classical mansion, built on high ground overlooking the beautiful Lee estuary, 3 miles/5½ km east of Cork city. The architect is thought to have been Hargreave, a pupil of Sardinian architect Davis Ducart. Built c 1790 Dunkathel has a finely proportioned interior with simple plasterwork, Adam chimney-pieces and a particularly elegant bifurcating staircase of Bath stone. In the hall stands a rare late nineteenth century orchestrion by Imhoff & Muckle which may be played on request. The house contains a unique collection of Victorian watercolours by Beatrice Gubbins, a former owner of the house. Dunkathel House is well known for its charming interior, the hall retains its 19th century decoration with marbled walls representing Siena and the ceiling depicting a skye scene.

Location: 3 m E of Cork.
Open: May 1-Oct 15. Wed-Sun 2-6.
Refreshments: By arrangement.

DUNLOE CASTLE HOTEL GARDENS

Beaufort, Killarney, Co. Kerry
Telephone: (0164) 44111 or (0164) 31900
Fax: (00353 64) 44583

The gardens at Dunloe Castle contain an extensive and interesting collection of plants, several of which are rarely, if at all, found elsewhere in Ireland. Each season brings its own specialities, camelias and rhododendron in spring, magnolias and sun roses in summer, Irish heaths and richly tinted leaves in autumn, are just a few of the many attractions. This combination of wild grandeur and garden exotica is situated in a setting of incomparable views of mountains and lakes.

Location: Situated adjacent to the Deluxe 140 bedroomed Hotel Dunloe Castle, off the main Killarney/Killorglin road, on the route to the Gap of Dunloe, approximately 8 km from Killarney.
Open: May 1 to end Sept.
Admission: Free. Catalogue of plants and trees available at hotel reception for £1.
Refreshments: Available at Hotel Dunloe Castle.

EMO COURT

Emo, Co Laois
Tel: (0502) 26573
The office of Public Works: Outstanding neo-classical house by James Gandon built in 1792 for the Earl of Portarlington. Extensive gardens with formal lawns, lake and woodland walks with a wealth of specimen trees and flowering shrubs. Park open every day during daylight hours, no charge.
Open: mid-June to mid-Sept 10am-6pm everyday. All visitors to the house must fo on a guided tour.
Admission: Adults £2, Group/Senior: £1.50, Child/Student: £1.00, Family: £5.

FERNHILL GARDEN

(Mrs Sally Walker)
Sandyford, Co. Dublin   map **16** Q10
Telephone: (01) 2956000

A Garden for all seasons, 200 years old in Robinsonian style with over 4,000 species and varieties of trees, shrubs and plants. Dogs not allowed.

Location: Sandyford, Co. Dublin.
Open: Tues-Sat 11-5 Sun 2-6 Mar-Nov inclusive.
Admission: Adults £2.50 OAPs £1.50 children £1.

THE GEORGE BERNARD SHAW BIRTHPLACE

33 Synge Street, Dublin 8   map **16** Q10
Telephone: (01) 4750854 (May-Oct) / 8722077
Fax: (01) 8722231

The famous playwright, essayist and Nobel prize winner for literature George Bernard Shaw, was born in the house on 26 July 1856.

GLIN CASTLE

(The Knight of Glin and Madam Fitz-Gerald)
Glin   map **16** R4   △ &
Telephone: (068) 34173/34112
Fax: (068) 34364

A Georgian Gothic castle with a series of battlemented folly lodges on lands held by the Knights of Glin for over 700 years. The interiors possess elaborate neo-classical plaster ceilings, a flying grand staircase and a notable collection of 18th century Irish mahogany furniture, family portraits and Irish landscapes. Formal gardens and walled kitchen garden.

Location: Situated on the N69 9km W of Foynes & 5km E of Tarbert Car ferry.
Open: May & June and other times by appointment. Tours, meals etc. can be arranged in the Castle. Please contact The Administrator, Mr Bob Duff (068) 34173.
Admission: £3 Group rate £2 Students £1.
Accommodation: Overnight stays arranged. Castle can be rented.
Conferences: Facilities for small groups.

JAPANESE GARDENS

(Irish National Stud)
Tully   map **16** Q9
Telephone: 00353 45521617
Fax: 00353 45522964

Created between 1906-1910, the Japanese Gardens symbolise the Life of Man from the Cave of Birth to the Gateway to Eternity. Special features include the Tea House, Bridge of Life and some very old bonsai trees.

Location: Co. Kildare 1 m from Kildare Town and 5 m from Newbridge.
Open: 12 Feb-12 Oct EVERYDAY 9.30-6.
Admission: Adults £5 Students/OAPs £3 Children under 12 years £2. Family 2 adults and 4 children under 12 years £10. Please note that it is one ticket for both the Irish National Stud and Japanese Gardens.
Refreshments: Restaurant and Gift Shop.
The path of life in the Japanese Gardens is unsuitable for disabled. The Irish National Stud is very suitable for disabled.

JOHNSTOWN CASTLE DEMESNE

(Teagasc Soils and Environment Centre)
Wexford   map **16** S10   △
Telephone: (053) 42888
Fax: (053) 42004

Grounds and gardens only. 50 acres of well laid out grounds, with artificial lakes and fine collection of ornamental trees and shrubs. Agricultural museum.

Location: 5 m SW of Wexford.
Open: All the year - Daily 9-5. Guidebook available at Castle. Although the grounds will continue to be open throughout the year, an admission charge will apply only from Apr 27-29 Sept 1996.
Admission: Car (and passengers) £2.50 coach (large) £17 coach (small) £9. Adults (pedestrians/cyclists) £1.50. Wedding parties for photography £17.
Refreshments: Coffee shop during July & Aug at museum.

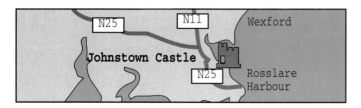

THE JAMES JOYCE TOWER

(Dublin Tourism)
Sandycove   map **16** Q10
Telephone: (01) 2809265/28722077

The Joyce Tower is a Martello tower, one of 26 built around Dublin in 1804 as defence against Napoleon. It has thick granite walls and a gun platform on the top. The building was lived in by James Joyce in 1904 and is described in his novel *Ulysses*. It now houses the James Joyce Museum and a modern exhibition hall has been added at ground floor level. The living-room upstairs, described in *Ulysses*, has recently been reconstructed.

Location: Sandycove Point on seafront 1 mile from Dun Laoghaire.
Station(s): Rail: Sandycove. Bus: No.8 to Sandycove.
Open: April-October Mon-Sat 10-1,2-5: Suns and Public Holidays 2-6.
Admission: Adults 18+ £2.20 concessions £1.70 Children (3-11) £1.20. Special reductions on application. 20+ rates on application.

KYLEMORE ABBEY

Kylemore, Connemara   map **16** P3
Telephone: (095) 41146, or shops (095) 41113
Fax: (095) 41123/41145

The only home of the Benedictine Nuns in Ireland. The Castle was acquired by the Nuns in 1920, and a precious heirloom was preserved, both for and on behalf of the people of Ireland, and visitors from all over the world. Built by Mr Mitchell Henry, MP for County Galway, and a native of Manchester. The Abbey is set amidst the lakes and mountains of Connemara in an area of outstanding beauty.

Location: Connemara, Co Galway.
Station(s): Galway.
Open: Easter-Halloween.
Admission: Adults £1.50 Families £3 Students-Senior Citizens £1.
Refreshments: Full self-service restaurant.
Events/Exhibitions: Visitors centre, history panels, exhibits, 11 mins video of the history. Craftshop.

LISMORE CASTLE GARDENS

(Trustees of the Lismore Estates)
Lismore, Co. Waterford   map **16** S7
Telephone: 00353 5854424
Fax: 00353 5854896

Beautifully situated walled and woodland gardens, containing a fine collection of camellias, magnolias and other shrubs. There is a remarkable yew walk.

Location: In town of Lismore; 45 m W of Waterford; 35 m NE of Cork.
Open: Open daily from the end of Apr-mid Sept.
Admission: Adults £2.50 children (under 16) £1.50 Reduced rates for groups of more than 20 - adults £2.25 children £1.30.

LOUGH RYNN ESTATE & GARDENS

Mohill, Co. Leitrim   map **16** P7

Formerly the home of the Earls of Leitrim, Lough Rynn makes for a wonderful stopping off point when travelling to or from the North West. Terraced 19th century gardens, extensive walks and nature trails, interesting Victorian rock garden and fernery, many 19th century buildings, castle ruins from 17th century, dolmen and crannog site. Craft shop, picnic area, plant sales, guided tours.

Location: R202 North from N4 at Dromod (Signposted).
Station(s): Dromod
Open: May 1 to Sept 1, 10-7.
Admission: £1.25, Chd 75p, Group rates on request.
Refreshments: Restaurant, fast food.

MALAHIDE CASTLE
(Maria Morgan, Curator)
Malahide, Co. Dublin   map **16** Q10
Telephone: (01) 8462184/8462516
Fax: (01) 8462537

One of Ireland's oldest and most historic castles.

MOUNT USHER GARDENS
(Mrs Madelaine Jay)
Ashford   map **16** Q10   ♿
Telephone: (0404) 40205/40116
Fax: (0404) 40205

The Gardens (20 acres) extend along the Vartry river in beautiful County Wicklow. They are laid out in the informal 'Robinsonian' style comprising rare plants, shrubs and trees, collected from many parts of the world.

Location: Ashford, 1 m from Wicklow on Dublin-Bray-Wexford Road.
Open: Mar 17 to Oct 31, open daily including Suns and Bank Holidays 10.30-6.
Admission: IR £3. OAPs/Students/Chd IR £2. Groups (20 +) IR £2.50, OAPs/Students/Chd IR £1.50.
Refreshments: Tea room at entrance, snacks, light lunches.
Car parking. Suitable for disabled. No wheelchairs provided. Shopping courtyard.

MUCKROSS HOUSE, GARDENS AND TRADITIONAL FARMS
Killarney, Co. Kerry   map **16** T4
Telephone: 00 353 64 31440
Fax: 00 353 64 33926

Muckross House, is a magnificent Victorian mansion and one of Ireland's leading stately homes. It is beautifully situated amidst the spectacular scenery of Killarney National Park. The House was built in 1843. The architect was Mr William Burn who built many houses for the nobility in England, including Knowsley for the Earl of Derby. The elegantly furnished rooms portray the lifestyles of the landed gentry, white downstairs in the basement one can experience the working conditions of the servants employed in the house. Skilled craft workers at Muckross House use traditional methods to produce high quality items of Weaving, Bookbinding and Pottery. The gardens of Muckross House are famed for their beauty world-wide. In particular they are noted for their fine collection of Rhododendrons and Azaleas, extensive water garden, and an outstanding rock garden hewn out of natural limestone **"Muckross Traditional Farms"**. **The latest development at Muckross House is an exciting outdoor representation of the lifestyles and farming traditions of a rural community of the 1930's. Three separate working farms, complete with animals, poultry and traditional farm machinery will help you relive the past.**

Location: 3½ m from Killarney on the Kenmare road.
Open: Daily all year 9-5.30 During July and Aug 9-7pm.
Admission: Adult IR £3.30 student IR £1.50. Group rates for 20 plus IR £2.20. Family ticket IR £8. Ditto for Muckross Traditional Farms. Substantial savings on joint tickets. Gardens free. Free car and coach parking.
Refreshments: Restaurant located in the old coach-house, serving teas, coffees, soup, sandwiches, pastries, hot and cold lunches. Wine licence.

NATIONAL BOTANIC GARDENS
(Office of Public Works)
Glasnevin, Dublin 9   map **16** Q10
Telephone: (01) 8374388
Fax: (01) 8360080

Founded 1795.

Location: 2 m city centre.

NEWBRIDGE HOUSE & TRADITIONAL FARM
Donabate, Co. Dublin   map **16** Q10
Telephone: (01) 8436534/5
Fax: (01) 8462537

Splendid 18th century manor.

POWERSCOURT GARDENS & WATERFALL
Enniskerry, Co. Wicklow   map **16** Q10
Telephone: (01) 2867676/7/8
Fax: (01) 2863561

Powerscourt is a magnificent example of an aristocratic garden laid out with taste and imagination.

STROKESTOWN PARK HOUSE
Strokestown, Co. Roscommon   map **16** P6
Telephone: (078) 33013
Fax: (078) 33712

Ancestral home of the Pakenham Mahon family.

TULLYNALLY CASTLE
(Thomas & Valerie Palceham)
Castlepollard, Co. Westmeath   map **16** P8   △ ♿
Telephone: (044) 61159 or (044) 61289
Fax: (044) 61856

Home of the Pakenhams (later Earls of Longford) since the 17th century; the original house is now incorporated in a huge rambling Gothick castle. Approximately 30 acres of woodland and walled gardens are also open to the public.

Location: 1½ miles outside Castlepollard on Granard Road.
Station(s): Mullingar.
Open: House open mid June-mid Aug 2-6 (Pre-booked groups admitted at other times). Gardens open May-Sept 2-6.
Admission: HOUSE AND GARDENS: £3.50 children £2 Groups £2.50. GARDENS ONLY: £2 children 50p.
Refreshments: Tea-room open mid June-mid Aug at weekends.

NORTHERN IRELAND

ARDRESS HOUSE   ❦ The National Trust
Co Armagh   map **16** O9   △ ♿
Telephone: (01762) 851236
Location: 7 m W of Portadown on Portadown/Moy Road (B28); 2 m from Loughgall intersection on M1.

THE ARGORY   ❦ The National Trust
Co Armagh   map **16** O9   △ ♿
Telephone: (01868) 84753

295 acre estate with neo-classical house, built c. 1820.

Location: 4 m from Moy on Derrycaw Road; 3 m from Coalisland intersection.
Open: Easter (Apr 14-18) Apr May June weekends and Bank Hols only July and Aug daily exc Tues 2-6 (open from 1 on Bank Hols). Last adm 5.15.
Admission: House and grounds £2.20 Children £1.10 groups £1.60 (after hours) £2.80. Car park £1.
Refreshments: Shop/tea-room open as house 2-6; Bank Holidays 1-6; weekdays July & Aug 3-5.

Wheelchairs provided - access to ground floor only. Dogs in grounds only on leads.

CASTLE COOLE   ❦ The National Trust
Co Fermanagh   BT74   map **16** O7
Telephone: (01365) 322690
Location: 1½ m SE of Enniskillen on Belfast/Enniskillen Road (A4).

CASTLE WARD 🍀 The National Trust

Co Down BT30 7LS map **16** O11 △ & Ⓢ
Telephone: (01396) 881204
Fax: (01396) 881729

Built by the first Lord Bangor in 1765 in a beautiful setting. Laundry museum. Strangford Lough Wildlife Centre in converted barn on edge of shore.

Location: 7 m NE of Downpatrick; 1½ m W of Strangford village (A25).
Open: Apr weekends and Good Fri-Sun after Easter (Apr 14-23) May-Aug daily (including Bank Hols) except Thurs 1-6. Sept-Oct weekends only. Estate and grounds open all year dawn to dusk daily. Shop and Restaurant open as house weekends and Bank Holidays 1-6 weekdays 1-5. Strangford Lough Wildlife Centre weekends and Good Fri-Sun after Easter Apr May June Sept weekends and Bank Holidays only July and Aug daily except Thurs 2-6.
Admission: House £2.60 Children £1.30 Groups £2 (after hours £3). Estate £3.50 per car Nov to end Mar £1.75 per car. Coaches Booked groups to house no charge others £10. Horses using bridlepath £5 per single horsebox.
Refreshments: Shop & tea-room open same days as house weekends and Bank Hols 1-6, weekdays 1-5.

DOWNHILL   🍀 The National Trust

Londonderry map **16** M9 &
Telephone: (01265) 848728
Location: 5 m W of Coleraine on Coleraine/Downhill Road (A2).

FLORENCE COURT   🍀 The National Trust

Co Fermanagh map **16** 07 △ &
Telephone: (01365) 348249 or 348788 (shop)
Location: 8 m SW of Enniskillen via A4 and A32; 1 m W of Florence Court village.

GRAY'S PRINTING PRESS   🍀 The National Trust

Strabane, Co. Tyrone BT82 8AU map **16** N8
Telephone: (01504) 884094
Location: In Main Street, Strabane.

HEZLETT HOUSE   🍀 The National Trust

Co Londonderry BT51 4RE map **16** M9 △
Telephone: (01265) 848567
Location: 4 m W of Coleraine on Coleraine/Downhill Coast Road (A2).

MOUNT STEWART HOUSE, GARDEN AND TEMPLE
🍀 The National Trust

Co Down BT22 2AD map **16** N11 △ &
Telephone: (012477) 88387/88487
Location: On E shore of Strangford Lough; 5 m SE of Newtownards; 15 m E of Belfast (A20).

ROWALLANE GARDEN   🍀 The National Trust

Saintfield, Co Down map **16** O11 &
Telephone: (01238) 510131 Northern Ireland Regional Office (01236) 510721
Fax: (01238) 511242

Beautiful gardens containing large collection of plants, chiefly trees and shrubs. Of particular interest in spring and autumn.

Location: 11 m SE of Belfast; 1 m S of Saintfield on the W of the Downpatrick Road (A7).
Open: Apr 1-end Oct Mon-Fri 10.30-6. Sat and Sun 2-6. Nov-end Mar 10.30-5 Mon-Fri. *Closed* Dec 25 and 26 Jan 1.
Admission: Easter-end Oct £2.50 Children £1.25 Parties £1.60 (after hours £2.80). Nov-end Mar £1.40 Groups 60p.
Refreshments: Tea-room Apr & Sept weekends only 2-6, Easter (Apr 5-9), daily 2-6, May-Aug daily 12.30-5.30.
Dogs admitted on leads, to indicated areas. Wheelchair access (1 provided).

SPRINGHILL   🍀 The National Trust

Moneymore, Co Londonderry BT45 7NQ map **16** N9 △ &
Telephone: (016487) 48210

House dating from 17th century. Magnificent oak staircase and interesting furniture & paintings. Costume museum. Cottar's kitchen.

Location: On Moneymore/Coagh Road (1 m from Moneymore).
Open: Apr weekends and Good Fri-Easter Tues (Apr 14-18) May June weekends and Bank Hols only July and Aug daily except Thurs. Sept weekends only 2-6.
Admission: House £2.20 Children £1.10 Groups £1.60 (after hours £2.80).
Refreshments: Shop and tea-room open as house.

WELLBROOK BEETLING MILL   🍀 The National Trust

Cookstown, Co. Tyrone map **16** N9
Telephone: (016487) 51735
Location: 3 m from Cookstown on Cookstown/Omagh Road.

SCOTLAND

BORDERS

NATIONAL TRUST FOR SCOTLAND

Last admissions to most NTS properties are 45 minutes before the advertised closing times. Other than guide-dogs for the blind and deaf, dogs are not generally permitted inside Trust buildings, walled and enclosed gardens or in the immediate area beside buildings which are open to the public. At a number of properties, special 'dog walks' are signposted.

ABBOTSFORD HOUSE

(Mrs P. Maxwell-Scott)
Melrose TD6 9BQ map **9** L17 & △
Telephone: (01896) 752043

The home of Sir Walter Scott, containing many historical relics collected by him.

Location: 3 m W of Melrose just S of A72; 5 m E of Selkirk.
Station(s): No railway.
Open: 3rd Mon of Mar-Oct 31 daily 10-5 Sun 2-5.
Admission: Adults £3 Children £1.50 Party rates Adults £2.20 Children £1.10.
Refreshments: Tea-shop.
Cars with wheelchairs or disabled enter by private entrance. Gift Shop.

AYTON CASTLE

Eyemouth TD14 5RD map **9** L18
Telephone: (0189 07) 81212
Fax: (0189 07) 81550

Victorian castle in red sandstone.

Location: 7 m N of Berwick-upon-Tweed on A1.
Station(s): Berwick-on-Tweed
Open: May-Sept Sun 2-5 or by appointment.
Admission: Adults £2 children (under 15) free.
Events/Exhibitions: occasionally.

BOWHILL   🏛

(His Grace the Duke of Buccleuch & Queensberry KT)
nr Selkirk TD7 5ET map **9** L17 △ & Ⓔ Ⓢ
Telephone: (01750) 22204
Fax: (01750) 22204

Border home of the Scotts of Buccleuch. Famous artists include Guardi, Canaletto, Claude, Gainsborough, Reynolds and Raeburn. Superb 17th/18th century French and 19th century British furniture and porcelain. Monmouth, Sir Walter Scott and Queen Victoria relics. For details of our specialist art courses, please tel: Buccleuch Heritage Trust Selkirk (01750) 22204. Restored Victorian kitchen. Visitor Centre with audio-visual programmes. Lecture Theatre. Exciting Adventure Woodland Play Area. Walks to historic Newark Castle and by lochs and rivers along nature trails.

Location: 3 m W of Selkirk on A708 Moffat-St. Mary's Loch road. Edinburgh, Carlisle, Newcastle approx 1½ hours by road.
Open: House July 1-July 31 daily 1-4.30. Country Park (includes Adventure Woodland Play Area and Nature Trails) Apr 27-late summer Bank Hol (UK) inclusive daily except Fri 12-5 (open Fridays in July with house), (last entry 45 mins before closing time). Open by appointment at additional times for museums and specialist or educational groups. Mountain bike hire (01721) 22515.
Admission: House and Grounds £4 parties over 20 £3.50, OAPs £3.50. Grounds only £1 (Wheelchair users and children under 5 free). Free car and coach parking.
Refreshments: Gift shop and licensed tea-room.
BOWHILL LITTLE THEATRE a lively centre for the performing arts. To join mailing list please write to the Administrator.

FLOORS CASTLE, KELSO

(The Duke of Roxburghe)
Roxburghe Estates Office, Kelso   **TD5 7SF**   map **9** L18
Telephone: (01573) 223333
Fax: (01573) 226056

Scotland's largest inhabited castle; built in 1721 by William Adam and remodelled by Playfair; outstanding collection of French furniture, stunning tapestries and works of art. Beautiful Chinese and European porcelain and a unique Victorian collection of birds.

Location: N of Kelso.
Station(s): Berwick-on-Tweed.
Open: Easter weekend until the end of Sept: daily 10.00-4.30pm. Oct: Sun & Weds 10.00-4.00pm.
Admission: Adults £3.90 OAPs £3.50 children (5-16) £2.20 family £10.60. Party rates on request.
Refreshments: Restaurant and coffee shop.
Events/Exhibitions: Pipe bands and Highland Dancers on Sundays throughout the year.
Accommodation: Accommodation at nearby Sunlaws House Hotel.
Conferences: Facilities available including dinners, receptions, product launches and outdoor events.
Free parking, walled garden, woodland walks and garden centre.

THE HIRSEL GROUNDS & DUNDOCK WOOD

(Lord Home of The Hirsel, KT)
Coldstream   **TD12 4LP**   map **9** L18   &
Telephone: (01890) 882834/882965
Fax: (01890) 882834

Snowdrops, aconites and daffodils in Spring in grounds. Fantastic rhododendrons and azaleas May/June Dundock wood and grounds. Herbaceous borders and roses in summer. Marvellous Autumn colouring. Picnic area. Parking. Playground. Homestead museum. Centre for art and crafts.

Location: W of Coldstream on A697.
Open: Grounds all reasonable daylight hours throughout the year. Crafts & Museum 10-5 weekdays 12-5 Sat & Sun.
Admission: Parking charge only.
Refreshments: Tea-rooms all year.
Events/Exhibitions: Craft Fairs May and November.

MANDERSTON

(Lord and Lady Palmer)
Duns, Berwickshire   **TD11 3PP**   map **9** L18
Telephone: (01361) 883450
Fax: (01361) 882010

The swan-song of the great classical house. Georgian in its taste but with all the elaborate domestic arrangements designed for Edwardian convenience and comfort. Superb classical yet luxurious rooms and the only silver staircase in the world, in a house on which the architect was ordered to spare no expense. The extensive 'downstairs' domestic quarters are equally some of the grandest of their type. Biscuit Tin Museum. Outside, the grandeur is continued. See the most splendid stables and picturesque marble dairy. 56 acres of formal woodland garden and lakeside walks.

Location: 2 m E of Duns on A6105; 14 m W of Berwick upon Tweed.
Station(s): Berwick-upon-Tweed
Open: May 9-Sept 29 Sun & Thurs only 2-5.30pm + Bank Hol Mons 27 May and 26 Aug 2-5.30pm. Parties at any time of year by arrangement.
Admission: Charges not available at time of going to press.
Refreshments: Tea-room, Cream Teas.
Events/Exhibitions: By arrangement.
Accommodation: By arrangement.
Conferences: By arrangement.
Gift Shop.

MELLERSTAIN

(The Mellerstain Trust)
Gordon, Berwickshire   **TD3 6LG**   map **9** L17
Telephone: (01573) 410225

Scotland's famous Adam mansion. Beautifully decorated and furnished interiors. Terraced gardens and lake. Gift shop.

Location: 9 m NE of Melrose; 7 m NW of Kelso; 37 m SE of Edinburgh.
Open: Easter weekend (Apr 5-8) then May-Sept daily except Sats 12.30-5pm (last adm 4.30). Groups at other times by arrangement.
Admission: Charges not available at time of going to press *special terms for organised parties by appointment, apply Curator* Free parking.
Refreshments: Tea rooms.
Events/Exhibitions: June 2 - Vintage Car Rally; July 27-29 - Craft Festival; Permanent Exhibition - Antique Dolls and Toys.

MERTOUN GARDENS

(His Grace the Duke of Sutherland)
St Boswells, Roxburghshire   **TD6 0EA**   map **9** L17
Telephone: (01835) 823236
Fax: (01835) 822474

26 acres of beautiful grounds with delightful walks and river views. Fine trees, herbaceous plants and flowering shrubs. Walled garden and well-preserved circular dovecot.

Location: 2 m NE of St Boswells on the B6404.
Station(s): Berwick
Open: Garden only Sat and Sun and Mon on Public Holidays only Apr-Sept 2-6 (last entry 5.30) parties by arrangement.
Admission: Adults £1 children 50p.
Refreshments: Dryburgh Abbey Hotel, Buccleuch Arms Hotel, St Boswells. No dogs. Car parking.

PAXTON HOUSE

(The Paxton Trust)
Paxton, nr Berwick-upon-Tweed   **TD15 1SZ**   map **9** L18   & △
Telephone: (01289) 386291
Fax: (01289) 386660

Scotland's most perfect Palladian country mansion. Built for a daughter of Frederick The Great. Designed by the Adam family and furnished by Chippendale and Trotter. Restored Regency picture gallery the largest in a Scottish country house (outstation of National Galleries of Scotland). Gardens. Riverside Walks. Adventure Playground. Tearoom. Gift Shop.

Location: 5 m from Berwick-upon-Tweed on B6461, signed from A1.
Station(s): Berwick-upon-Tweed 5 m.
Open: Daily Good Fri-Oct 31. House noon-5 Grounds 10-5 last tour of house 4.15.
Admission: £4 grounds only £1.75 family ticket £10. Parties catered for.
Refreshments: Morning coffee, light lunches, afternoon teas, Licensed.
Events/Exhibitions: Changing programme - ring for details.
Conferences: Reception room, gallery available for functions (inc conferences).
Car parking. Suitable for disabled persons. Wheelchairs available. School parties welcome.

PRIORWOOD GARDEN

(The National Trust for Scotland)
Melrose   map **9** L17
Telephone: (01896) 822493

Garden featuring flowers suitable for drying. Shop and Trust visitor centre.

Location: In Melrose.
Open: 1 Apr-(or Good Friday if earlier)-30 June and 1-30 Sept, Mon-Sat 10-5.30 Sun 1.30-5.30; 1 July-31 Aug Mon-Sat 10-6.30 Sun 1.30-6.30 1 Oct-24 Dec Mon-Sat 10-4 Sun 1.30-4. NTS shop in Abbey Street 9 Jan-31 Mar Mon-Sat 12-4; Apr-24 Dec, Mon-Sat 10-5.30, Sun 1.30-5.30 closed 28 Oct-5 Nov for stocktaking.
Admission: £1.00. Groups should pre-book.

ROBERT SMAIL'S PRINTING WORKS ♟

(The National Trust for Scotland)
Tweeddale   map **15** L16
Telephone: (01896) 830206

The buildings contain vintage working machinery, including a 100-year-old printing press which was originally driven by water wheels. The Victorian office is on display complete with its acid-etched plate-glass windows and examples of historic items printed in the works.

Location: In Innerleithen High Street, 30 m S of Edinburgh.
Open: 1 May-30 Sept Mon-Sat 10-1 and 2-5. Sun 2-5.
Admission: Adult £2.10 child/concession £1.40 adult party £1.70 child/school party £1 family £5.60.

Humphrey Repton (1752-1815)

Artist and garden designer

His work can be seen at the following properties
included in Historic Houses Castles and Gardens:-

Corsham Court

Uppark

Sezincote

THIRLESTANE CASTLE
(Thirlestane Castle Trust)
Lauder, Berwickshire   TD2 6RU   map **9** L17
Telephone: (01578) 722430
Fax: (01578) 722761

Described as one of the oldest and finest Castles in Scotland, Thirlestane has its roots in an original 13th century fort overlooking the Leader Valley. The main keep was built in 1590 by the Maitland family who have lived in the Castle for over 400 years; it was extended in 1670 and again in 1840. The Restoration Period plasterwork ceilings are considered to be the finest in existence. The family nurseries now house a large collection of historic toys and children are encouraged to dress up. Visitors see the old kitchens, pantries and laundries as well as the Country Life Exhibitions portraying day to day life in the Borders through the centuries. Grounds, picnic tables, woodland walk, gift shop and tea room.

Location: 28 m S of Edinburgh off A68 - follow signs on all main approach roads.
Open: Easter 5-12 Apr incl. May June and Sept Mon Wed Thurs and Sun only. July and Aug daily except Sat Castle 2-5 (last adm 4.30) Grounds 12-6.
Admission: £4 party rate £3 family ticket (parents and own children only) £10. Booked party tours at other times by arrangement. Free car park.
Refreshments: Tea-room.

TRAQUAIR
(Mrs Flora Maxwell Stuart)
Innerleithen   EH44 6PW   map **15** L16   △
Telephone: (01896) 830323
Fax: (01896) 830639

A house full of beauty, romance and mystery. Rich in associations with Mary Queen of Scots, the Jacobites and Catholic persecution. Priest's room with secret stairs. The world-famous Traquair House Ale is brewed in the 18th-century brewhouse. Extensive grounds, craft workshops and maze.

Location: 1 m from Innerleithen; 6 m from Peebles; 29 m from Edinburgh at junction of B709 & B7062 (40 minutes by road from Edinburgh Airport, 1½ hours from Glasgow).
Station(s): Edinburgh Waverley - 1 hour.
Open: 6 Apr-Sept 30 daily 12.30-5.30 (July and Aug 10.30-5.30) Oct Fri-Sun 2-5. Last adm 5. Grounds May-Sept 10.30-5.30.
Admission: Adults £3.80 children £1.80 OAPs £3.30 family £10.
Refreshments: Home cooking at the 1745 Cottage Tea Room from 12 pm.
Events/Exhibitions: New High Gallery in House with rotating exhibitions.
Accommodation: 2 rooms B&B and Holiday flat to rent.
Conferences: Suitable for small conferences, weddings, meetings, lunches and dinners.
Gift Shop, Antique Shop. Traquair Fair 3/4th August. Sheep and Wool Day Sun 28th July. Needlework Weekend 14th & 15th September.

CENTRAL

CALLENDAR HOUSE
(Falkirk District Council)
Callendar Park, Falkirk   FK1 1YR   map **15** L15

Imposing mansion within attractive parkland with a 900 year history. Facilities include a working kitchen of 1825 where costumed interpreters carry out daily chores including cooking based on 1820's recipes. Exhibition area, "Story of Callendar House" plus two temporary galleries, with regularly changing exhibitions. There is also a history research centre, gift shop and Georgian tea-shop at the Stables.

Location: To the east of Falkirk Town Centre on Callendar Road (A803).
Station(s): Within walking distance of Falkirk High and Grahamstone Stations.
Open: Jan-Dec Mon-Sat 10-5 Apr-Sept Sun 2-5 open all Public Hols.
Admission: Adults £1.60 children and OAPs 80p.
Refreshments: Delicious home baking available in the Tea Shop.
Events/Exhibitions: Annual Programme.
Accommodation: Readily available throughout the district.

DUMFRIES & GALLOWAY

ARBIGLAND GARDENS
(Captain and Mrs J. B. Blackett)
Kirkbean

Built in the 18th century, the house is set amongst woodland, formal and water gardens.

CARLYLE'S BIRTHPLACE
(The National Trust for Scotland)
Ecclefechan   map **8** L13
Telephone: (01576) 300666

Thomas Carlyle was born here in 1795. Mementoes and MSS.

Location: 5 m SE of Lockerbie on the Lockerbie/Carlisle Road (A74).
Station(s): Lockerbie.
Open: May 1-Sept 30 Fri-Mon 1.30-5.30 (last admission 5). Other times by appointment.
Admission: Adult £1.60 child/concession £1 adult party £1.30 child/school party £1 family £4.20.
Refreshments: Ecclefechan Hotel.

CASTLE KENNEDY GARDENS
(The Earl and Countess of Stair)
Stranraer   DG9 8BX   map **8** M13
Telephone: (01776) 702024
Fax: (01776) 706248

World famous gardens, set in 75 acres of landscaped terraces and mounds between two lochs. Outstanding displays of Rhododendrons, Azaleas, Embothriums, Eucryphia. Surrounded by breathtaking scenery. Many original specimens from Hooker expeditions. Also only known Monkey Puzzle avenue. Plant Centre selling plants produced from garden stock.

Location: 5 m E of Stranraer on A75 opposite Castle Kennedy village.
Open: Easter to Sept - Daily 10-5.
Admission: Charged. Disabled free. Reduction for groups over 20.
Refreshments: Light refreshments only. Hotels Eynhallow, Castle Kennedy & Stranraer.

CRAIGDARROCH HOUSE
(J. H. A. Sykes)
Moniaive   DG3 4JB   map **8** M15
Telephone: (01848) 200202

William Adam house built for Annie Laurie.

Location: 2 miles west of Moniaive on B729.
Open: All July 2-4pm.
Admission: £2.
Please note: no public conveniences.

SCOTLAND'S BORDER

HERITAGE

TRAQUAIR · NEAR PEEBLES

OLDEST INHABITED HOUSE IN SCOTLAND

BOWHILL · NEAR SELKIRK

INTERNATIONALLY RENOWNED ART COLLECTION

ABBOTSFORD · NEAR MELROSE

HOME OF SIR WALTER SCOTT

THIRLESTANE CASTLE · LAUDER

UNSURPASSED 17TH CENTURY CEILINGS

FLOORS CASTLE · KELSO

SCOTLAND'S LARGEST INHABITED CASTLE

*S*pectacular Houses, Castles, Parks and Gardens, all within a 50 mile radius in one of the most scenic areas of Scotland.

PAXTON HOUSE · NEAR BERWICK UPON TWEED

BUILT FOR A KING'S DAUGHTER

THE HIRSEL · COLDSTREAM

COUNTRY PARK, MUSEUM AND CRAFTS

MELLERSTAIN · NEAR GORDON

SCOTLAND'S FINEST ADAM MANSION

MANDERSTON · DUNS

THE SWAN-SONG OF THE GREAT CLASSICAL HOUSE

Please send me more information, including details of the 10% saving
with a Scotland's Border Heritage Pass.

NAME ....

ADDRESS ....

....

.... POSTCODE ....

Return to: The Administrator, SBH Hawthornbank, High Cottages,
                 Walkerburn, EH43 6AZ.   Tel/Fax: 01896 870277

DRUMLANRIG CASTLE GARDENS AND COUNTRY PARK
(Home of the Duke of Buccleuch & Queensberry KT)
nr Thornhill map **8** M13 △ & Ⓢ
Telephone: (01848) 330248 and (01848) 331682 (24 hr answering service). Country Park: (01848) 331555

1680/90 pink sandstone castle with outstanding art treasures - Leonardo, Rembrandt, Holbein - 300 year old silver chandelier & Louis XIV furniture, Bonnie Prince Charlie relics. Extensive grounds and woodland include gardens, adventure play area, nature trails and picnic sites. Tearoom and giftshop. Working craft studios, lecture room and cycle hire. Bird of Prey Centre.

Location: 18 m N of Dumfries; 3 m N of Thornhill off A76; 16 m from A74 at Elvanfoot; approx 1½ hrs by road from Edinburgh, Glasgow & Carlisle.
Open: Sat 27 Apr-Mon 26 Aug, 11-5. Last entry to castle 4.15. Castle closed Thurs. Guided tours operate at times early season. Restricted route in castle 12-14 July.
Admission: Prices not available at time of going to press.
Refreshments: Lunches, Afternoon Teas and snacks at above times.
Events/Exhibitions: Horse driving trials 12-14 July.

RAMMERSCALES
(M A Macdonald, Esq)
Lockerbie map **8** M16
Telephone: (0138) 781 0229

Georgian manor house dated 1760 set on high ground with fine views over Annandale. Pleasant policies and a typical walled garden of the period. There are Jacobite relics and links with Flora Macdonald retained in the family. There is also a collection of works by modern artists.

Location: 5 m W of Lockerbie (M6/A74); 2½ m S of Lochmaben on B7020.
Open: Last week of July, 1st 3 weeks Aug. 2-5 daily (except Sats)
Admission: Adults £5.00 Children/OAP's £2.50.

THREAVE GARDEN
(The National Trust for Scotland)
nr Castle Douglas map **8** N15 &
Telephone: (01556) 502683

The Trust's School of Horticulture. Gardens now among the major tourist attractions of SW Scotland. Visitor centre. Magnificent springtime display of some 200 varieties of daffodil, Trust shop, Restaurant, Exhibition. Ramp into garden for wheelchairs.

Location: 1 m W of Castle Douglas off A75.
Open: All year daily 9.30-Sunset. Visitor Centre, Exhibition and Shop 1 Apr-31 Oct daily 9.30-5.30.
Admission: Adult £3.60 child/concession £2.40 adult party £2.90 child/scholl party £1 family £9.60.
Refreshments: Restaurant daily 10-5.
Events/Exhibitions: 'Lilies, Lamas and Leeches' on plant collectors.
Accommodation: Holiday cottages on Threave estate-apply to NTS.

FIFE

BALCARRES
(Balcarres Trust)
Colinsburgh map **9** K17
Telephone: (01333) 340206

16th century house with 19th century additions by Burn and Bryce. Woodland and terraced garden.

Location: ½ m N of Colinsburgh.
Open: Woodlands and Lower Garden Feb 12-28 Apr 1-June 23 (daily except Suns) West Garden June 10-23 (Daily except Suns) 2-5 *House not open except by written appointment* and Apr 22-May 7 (except Suns).
Admission: Gardens Only Adults £2.50 OAPs/children £1.50 House £4.
Car park. Suitable for disabled persons, no wheelchairs provided.

BALGONIE CASTLE
(The Laird of Balgonie)
by Markinch, Fife KY7 6HQ
Telephone: (01592) 750119

Family 'lived in' castle with one of the finest 14th c.Towers in Scotland. Banquets/Wedding Receptions for 50. One of Scotland's most romantic wedding chapels.

CULROSS PALACE, TOWN HOUSE & STUDY

(The National Trust for Scotland)
Culross   map **15** K15
Telephone: (01383) 880359

Outstanding survival of Scottish 17th century burgh architecture carefully restored for 20th century living. Early 17th century palace of Sir George Bruce, and garden with contemporary plantings. Induction loop for the hard of hearing.

Location: 12 m W of Forth Road Bridge, off A985.
Station(s): Dunfermline.
Open: Palace: Apr 1-Sept 30, daily 11-5 (last admission 4). Town House and Study, same dates 1.30-5 and weekends in Oct, 11-5. Groups at other times by appointment. Tearoom (in Bessie Bar Hall), dates as Town House, 10.30-4.30.
Admission: Combined ticket (Palace, Study and Town House), adult £3.60, child/concession £2.40 adult party £2.90 child/school party £1.00 family £9.60.
Refreshments: Tea-room.
Events/Exhibitions: In Town House.

FALKLAND PALACE & GARDEN

(Her Majesty the Queen. Hereditary Constable, Capt & Keeper: Ninian Crichton Stuart. Deputy Keeper: The National Trust for Scotland)
Fife   map **9** K16
Telephone: (01337) 857397

Attractive 16th century Royal Palace, favourite retreat of Stuart kings and queens. Gardens now laid out to the original Royal plans. Town Hall, Visitor Centre, Exhibition and Shop. Original Royal Tennis court built in 1539. Ramp into garden for wheelchairs.

Location: In Falkland, 11 m N of Kirkcaldy on A912.
Station(s): Kirkcaldy
Open: 1 Apr-31 Oct Mon-Sat 11-5.30, Sun 1.30-5.30.
Admission: Palace and Garden: adult £4.10 child/concession £2.70 adult party £3.30 child/school party £1 family £10.90 (these charges include entrance to Town Hall exhibition). Garden only: adult £2.10 child/concession £1.40 adult party £1.70 child/school party £1. Scots Guards and memebers of the Scots Guards' Association (wearing the association's badge) admitted free.
Refreshments: Bruce Arms, Falkland.
Events/Exhibitions: At Royal Tennis court
Accommodation: Holiday flat in village-apply to NTS.
Conferences: Open by appointment.
Visitor centre and Trust shop. Display in Town Hall.

HILL OF TARVIT

(The National Trust for Scotland)
nr Cupar   map **9** K17
Telephone: (01334) 653127

Mansion house remodelled 1906. Collection of furniture, tapestries, porcelain and paintings. Gardens.

Location: 2½ m SW of Cupar A916.
Station(s): Cupar (2½ m).
Open: House: Good Fri-Easter Mon and 1 May-30 Sept daily 1.30-6.30; Weekends in Oct 1.30-5.30 (last admission 4.45). Tearoom, same dates, but opens 12.30. Gardens and grounds: 1 Apr-31 Oct daily 9.30-7pm 1 Nov-31 Mar daily 9.30-4.
Admission: House and garden: adult £3.10 child/concession £2 adult party £2.50 child/school party £1 family £8.20. Garden only: £1 (honesty box).

KELLIE CASTLE AND GARDEN

(The National Trust for Scotland)
Fife   map **9** K17   ♿
Telephone: (01333) 720271

Fine example of 16th-17th century domestic architecture of Lowland Scotland. Victorian walled garden with wheelchair access. Nursery, video, adventure playground, picnic area, shop.

Location: 3 m NNW of Pittenweem on B9171.
Open: Castle: Good Fri-Easter Mon and 1 May-30 Sep, daily 1.30-5.30; weekends in Oct 1.30-5.30 (last admission 4.45). Garden and grounds 1 Apr-31 Oct daily 9.30-7, 1 Nov-31 Mar, daily 9.30-4.
Admission: Castle and garden: adult £3.10 child/concession £2 adult party £2.50 child/school party £1 family £8.20. Garden only £1 (honesty box).
Refreshments: Tea-room.
Gardens only suitable for the disabled. A/V presentation with induction loop for the hard of hearing.

GRAMPIAN

ARBUTHNOTT HOUSE AND GARDEN

(The Viscount of Arbuthnott)
Arbuthnott House, Laurencekirk   map **11** H18
Telephone: (01561) 361226

Arbuthnott family home for 800 years. Formal 17th century garden on unusually steep slope with grass terraces, herbaceous borders and shrubs.

Location: On B967 between A90 and A92 25 miles south of Aberdeen.
Open: Gardens open all year 9-5. House open on May 26,27. July 14,15,28,29. Aug 24,26. Sept 12.
Admission: House £3. Gardens £1.50.
Refreshments: Available at Grassic Gibbon Centre in village.
Events/Exhibitions: Self-catering accommodation tel (01561) 320417.

BALMORAL CASTLE
(Her Majesty the Queen)
nr Ballater

BRAEMAR CASTLE
(Captain A A C Farquharson of Invercauld Trusts)
Braemar, Aberdeenshire   AB35 5XQ   map **11** H16 △
Telephone: (013397) 41219
Fax: (013397) 41252

Built in 1628 by the Earl of Mar. Attacked and burned by the celebrated Black Colonel (John Farquharson of Inverey) in 1689. Repaired by the government and garrisoned with English troops after the rising of 1745. Later transformed by the Farquharsons of Invercauld, who had purchased it in 1732, into a fully furnished private residence of unusual charm. L-plan castle of fairy tale proportions, with round central tower and spiral stair. Barrel-vaulted ceilings, massive iron 'Yett', and underground pit (prison). Remarkable star-shaped defensive curtain wall. Much valuable furniture, paintings and items of Scottish historical interest.

Location: ½ m NE of Braemar on A93.
Open: Easter-late Oct daily 10-6 except Fri.
Admission: Adults £2 children £1 special rates for groups and OAPs. Free car and bus park.
Refreshments: In Braemar.

Butterfly Houses

can be found at the following properties included in Historic Houses Castles and Gardens:-

Berkeley Castle
Elsham Hall - Wild butterfly walkway
Syon House

BRODIE CASTLE
(The National Trust for Scotland)
nr Nairn Moray   map **11** G15 &
Telephone: (01309) 641371
Fax: (01309) 641600

Ancient seat of the Brodies, burned in 1645 and largely rebuilt, with 17th/19th century additions. Fine furniture, porcelain and paintings. Audio-taped guide for the blind.

Location: Off A96 between Nairn & Forres.
Station(s): Forres (4½ m).
Open: Castle Apr 1(or Good Fri if earlier)-Sept 30 Mon-Sat 11-5.30 Sun !.30-5.30; weekends in Oct, Sat 11-5.30, Sun 1.30-5.30 (last admission 4.30). Other times by appointment. Grounds all year daily 9.30-sunset.
Admission: Adult £3.60 child/concession £2.40 adult party £2.90 child/school party £1 family £9.60. Grounds only (outwith summer season's published opening times): £1 (honesty box).
Refreshments: Tea-room.
Accommodation: Holiday house in grounds -apply to NTS.

CASTLE FRASER
(The National Trust for Scotland)
Sauchen   map **11** H18
Telephone: (01330) 833463

One of the most spectacular of the Castles of Mar. Z-plan castle begun in 1575 and completed in 1636. Formal garden.

Location: Off A944 4 m N of Dunecht. 16 m W of Aberdeen.
Open: Castle: Good Fri-Easter Mon, 1 May-30 June and 1-30 Sept daily 1.30-5.30 1 July to 31 Aug daily 11-5.30 weekends in Oct 1.30-5.30 (last admission 4.45). Tearoom dates as castle but opens 12.15 in Sept. Garden: all year, daily 9.30-6; grounds, all year, daily 9.30-sunset.
Admission: Castle: adult £3.60 child/concession £2.40 adult party £2.90 child/school party £1 family £9.60. Garden and grounds: adult £1.60 child/concession £1 adult party £1.30 child/school party £1.
Refreshments: Tea-room
Accommodation: Holiday flat in castle-apply NTS.
Picnic area, children's adventure playground.

CRAIGSTON CASTLE

(Mrs Urquhart of Craigston)
Turriff   map **11** G18
Telephone: (01888) 551228

Early 17 th century, unfortified castle with Adam wings and an 18th century library.

Location: 40 miles NW from Aberdeen.
Station(s): Aberdeen.
Open: By written appointment only and 25 days per annum (advetised in local press).
Admission: £3.00

CRATHES CASTLE & GARDEN

(The National Trust for Scotland)
Banchory   map **11** H18   △ ໔
Telephone: (01330) 844525
Fax: (01330) 844797

Fine 16th century baronial castle. Remarkable early painted ceilings. Beautiful gardens provide a wonderful display all year. Great yew hedges from 1702. Children's adventure playground.

Location: 3 m E of Banchory on A93; 15 m W of Aberdeen.
Station(s): Aberdeen.
Open: 1 Apr-31 Oct daily 11-5.30. Garden and Grounds all year, daily 9.30-sunset.
Admission: Castle, adult £1.60, child/concession £1. Combined ticket, adult £4.10, child/concession £2.70, adult party £3.30, child/school party £1, family £10.90. Grounds only/walled garden only, adult £1.60, child/concession £1, adult party £1.30, child/school party £1.
Refreshments: Shop and licensed Restaurant.

DRUM CASTLE

(The National Trust for Scotland)
nr Aberdeen   map **11** H18
Telephone: (01330) 811204

The oldest part of the historic Castle, the great square tower - one of the three oldest tower houses in Scotland - dates from the late 13th century. Charming mansion added in 1619. Garden of historic roses.

Location: 10 m W of Aberdeen, off A93.
Station(s): Aberdeen.
Open: Castle: Good Fri-Easter Mon and 1 May to 30 Sep daily 1.30-5.30; weekends in Oct 1.30-5.30 (last admission 4.45). Garden same dates daily 10-6. Grounds, all year, daily 9.30-sunset.
Admission: Castle, garden and grounds adult £3.60 child/concession £2.40 adult party £2.90 child/school party £1 family £9.60. Garden and grounds only adult £1.60 child/concession £1 adult party £1.30 child/school party £1.
Refreshments: Tea-room.

DRUMMUIR CASTLE & WALLED GARDEN

(L.A. Gordon-Duff)
Drummuir   AB55 3JE   map **11** G16
Telephone: (01542) 810332
Fax: (01542) 810302

Built in 1848 by a Duff and home of the Duff family since then. 60ft high Lantern Tower. Castellated Victorian Gothic style with fine plasterwork, and interesting family portraits, artifacts and other paintings. Organic walled garden. Plants for sale.

Location: Half way between Keith and Dufftown (5 m) off B9014.
Station(s): Keith.
Open: Tours at 2 and 3 on Aug 25 and 31 Sept 1 and 8-29 inc.
Admission: OAPs/Children £1.50. Others £2
Free car park.

DUFF HOUSE

Banff   AB45 3SX   map **11** G17
Telephone: (01261) 818181
Fax: (01261) 818900

One of Scotland's most significant mansions, designed by William Adam in 1735 for William Duff MP, later Lord Braco and first Earl of Fife. Recently restored to its former grandeur by Historic Scotland, Duff House now operated as an outstation of the National Galleries of Scotland. Important collection of paintings, furniture and works of art. Set in eight acres of beautiful parkland with woodland walks leading to the family mausoleum, Ice house and Bridge of Alvah.

Location: Banff.
Open: 26 Apr-30 Sept 10-5pm closed Tues. 1 Oct-31 Mar 10-5pm Thurs-Sun Closed Mon Weds. Closed 25/26 Dec 1/2 Jan.
Admission: Adults £2.50, concessions £1.
Refreshments: Cafe.
Access by lift to gallery floors for Disabled Visitors. Gift Shop and Cafe. For further information and coach bookings call (01261) 818181.

FASQUE

(The Gladstone Family)
Fettercairn AB30 1DJ map **11** H17
Telephone: (01561) 340202 or (01561) 340569
Fax: (01561) 340325

1809 Home of the Gladstone family with a full complement of furnishings and domestic articles little changed for 160 years. A wonderful example of 'Upstairs-Downstairs' family life. Deer Park. Church. Picnic Site.

Location: 1 m N of Fettercairn on the B974 Cairn O Mount pass road; 34 m Aberdeen and Dundee; 17 m Stonehaven; 12 m Montrose; 18 m Banchory. Part of The Victorian Heritage Trail.
Open: House open May 1-Sept 30 every day 11-5.30 with last entry at 5.
Admission: Adults £3 OAPs £2.50 children £1. Parties welcome. Morning and evening opening for parties by arrangement.
Refreshments: By arrangement.
Events/Exhibitions: Various.
Welcome. Available for all functions - Entrance Hall, Dining Room, Drawing Room and Library available.

FYVIE CASTLE

(The National Trust for Scotland)
Fyvie map **11** H18
Telephone: (01651) 891266

The oldest part of the castle dates from the 13th century and its five great towers are the monuments to the five families who owned the castle. The building contains the finest wheel stair in Scotland and a magnificent collection of paintings.

Location: Off A947, 8 m SE of Turriff, 25 m NW of Aberdeen.
Open: 1 Apr-30 Jun and 1-30 Sep daily 1.30-5.30 1 Jul-31 Aug daily 11-5.30 weekends in Oct 1.30-5.30. Grounds all year daily 9.30-sunset.
Admission: Castle: adult £3.60 child/concession £2.40 adult party £2.90 child/school party £1 family £9.60. Grounds only £1 (honesty box).
Refreshments: Tea-room.
Permanent exhibition - Castles of Mar.

HADDO HOUSE

(The National Trust for Scotland)
nr Methlick   map **11** H18 △ &
Telephone: (01651) 851440

Georgian house designed in 1731 by William Adam. Home of the Gordons of Haddo for over 500 years. Terraced gardens.

Location: 4 m N of Pitmedden; 19 m N of Aberdeen (A981 & B999).
Station(s): Aberdeen.
Open: House: Good Fri-Easter Mon and 1 May-30 Sept daily 1.30-5.30; weekends in Oct 1.30-5.30 (last admission 4.45). Shop and Stables Restaurant: 1 Apr-30 Sept daily 11-5.30; weekends in Oct 11-5.30. Shop closed 26/27 Oct for stocktaking. Garden and Country Park, all year, daily 9.30-sunset.
Admission: Adult £3.60 child/concession £2.40 adult party £2.90 child/school party £1 family £9.60. Garden only (outwith summer season's published opening times), £1 (honesty box).
Refreshments: Restaurant open daily 11-5.30.
Events/Exhibitions: Permanent exhibition of James Giles paintings.
Accommodation: Holiday flats in grounds-apply to NTS.
Wheelchair access.

LEITH HALL AND GARDEN

(The National Trust for Scotland)
Kennethmont   map **11** H18 &
Telephone: (01464) 831216

Home of the Leith family from 1650. Jacobite relics, and major exhibition of family's military collection. Charming garden.

Location: 1 m W of Kennethmont on B9002; 34 m NW of Aberdeen.
Open: House and tearoom: Good Fri-Easter Mon and 1 May-30 Sept daily 1.30-5.30; weekends in Oct 1.30-5.30 (last admission 4.45). Garden and grounds all year daily 9.30-sunset.
Admission: House: adult £3.60 child/concession £2.40 adult party £2.90 child/school party £1 family £9.60. Garden and grounds only: adult £1.60 child/concession £1, child/school party £1.
Refreshments: Tea-room.
Picnic area.

PITMEDDEN GARDEN

(The National Trust for Scotland)
Udny   map **11** H18 &
Telephone: (01651) 842352

Reconstructed 17th century garden with floral designs, fountains and sundials. Display on the evolution of the formal garden. Museum of Farming Life.

Location: 14 m N of Aberdeen on A920.
Station(s): Aberdeen.
Open: 1 May-30 Sept daily 10-5.30.
Admission: Garden and Museum: adult £3.10 child/concession £2 adult party £2.50 child/school party £1 family £8.20.
Refreshments: Tea-room.
Events/Exhibitions: Visitor Centre.
No dogs in garden please.

HIGHLANDS

CAWDOR CASTLE

(Countess Cawdor)
nr Inverness   IV12 5RD   map **11** G15
Telephone: (01667) 404615
Fax: (01667) 404674

The 14th century Keep, fortified in the 15th century and impressive additions, mainly 17th century, form a massive fortress. Gardens, nature trails and splendid grounds. Shakespearian memories of Macbeth. The most romantic castle in the Highlands.

Location: S of Nairn on B9090 between Inverness and Nairn.
Station(s): Nairn 5 miles. Inverness 14 miles.
Open: May 1-Oct 13 daily 10-5.30 (last adm 5).
Admission: Adults £4.70 children (aged 5-15) £2.50 OAPs and disabled £3.70 parties of 20 or more adults £4.20 and 20 or more children (aged 5-15) £2.00 family ticket (2 adults and up to 5 children) £13.00. Gardens, grounds and nature trail only £2.50. Blind people, no charge.
Refreshments: Licensed restaurant (self-service); Snack bar.
Gift shop. Book shop. Wool shop. Picnic area.9-hole golf course. Nature Trails. No dogs allowed in Castle or Grounds.

THE DOUNE OF ROTHIEMURCHUS

Inverness-shire   PH22 1QH   map **11** H15
Telephone: (01479) 810858
Location: Inverness-shire.

DUNROBIN CASTLE

(The Sutherland Trust)
Golspie, Sutherland KW10 6SF   map 11 G15
Telephone: (01408) 633177/633268
Fax: (01408) 633800 - Office (01408) 634081 - Castle

The most northerly of Scotland's great castles, the ancient earldom of Sutherland being created about 1235. Remodelled in 1845 by Sir Charles Barry and re-designed by Sir Robert Lorimer after a fire in 1915. Fine furniture, notable paintings, china, family memorabilia. Rooms decorated with flowers from the gardens. Victorian museum in grounds. The castle is set in fine woodlands overlooking the sea, with magnificent gardens, one of the few remaining formal parterres in the French style with a definite Scottish flovour.

Location: ½ m NE of Golspie on A9.
Station(s): Dunrobin Castle Station (200 metres).
Open: Easter - 31 May Mon-Sat 10.30-4.30, Sun 1-4.30. 1 June-30 Sept 10.30-5.30, Sun 12-5.30. Suns during July and Aug 10.30-5.30. 1-mid Oct same times as May. Last admissions ½ hour earlier.
Admission: Adults £4.50 party rates £4.20 OAPs £2.80 children £2.30 party rates £2.10 family tickets £11. Open all year round for pre-booked groups.
Refreshments: Tea-room.
Events/Exhibitions: 18 Aug - Vintage Car Rally.

DUNVEGAN CASTLE

(John MacLeod of MacLeod)
Isle of Skye map 10 H9 △
Telephone: (01470) 521206
Fax: (01470) 521205

Dating from the 13th century and continuously inhabited by the Chiefs of MacLeod. Fairy flag. Licensed restaurant; two craft and souvenir shops; castle water garden; audio-visual theatre; clan exhibition; items belonging to Bonnie Prince Charlie; loch boat trips; famous seal colony; pedigree highland cattle fold.

Location: Dunvegan village (1 m); 23 m W of Portree on the Isle of Skye.
Station(s): Kyle of Lochalsh 50 mins.
Open: Mon 18 Mar-Thurs 31 Oct Mon-Sat 10-5.30. Last admission 5. Sun gardens craft shop and restaurant open all day 10-5.30. Castle open 1-5.30. Last admission 5pm.

Admission: Adults £4 Children £2.20 parties OAPs students £3.60. Gardens only Adults £2.50 Children £1.50.
Refreshments: Fully licensed restaurant.
Events/Exhibitions: Annual music festival.
Accommodation: Self catering cottages within grounds.
Loch cruises aboard the motor vessel "Macleod of Macleod" seats 35 passengers - Department of Marine Transport Licensed - Fully insured. Also visit our exclusive woolen shop "The St Kilda Connection".

EILEAN DONAN CASTLE

(Conchra Charitable Trust)
Wester Ross map 10 H12 △
Telephone: (0159 985) 202

13th century Castle. Jacobite relics - mostly with Clan connections.

Location: In Dornie, Kyle of Lochalsh; 8 m E of Kyle on A87.
Station(s): Kyle or Lochalsh.
Open: Easter-Oct 26 daily (inc Suns) 10-5.30.
Admission: £2.50
Conferences: Weddings.

INVEREWE GARDEN

(The National Trust for Scotland)
Poolewe, Wester Ross map 10 G11 ♿
Telephone: (01445) 781200
Fax: (01445) 781497

Remarkable garden created by the late Osgood Mackenzie. Rare and sub-tropical plants.

Location: 7 m from Gairloch; 85 m W of Inverness, A832.
Open: Garden: 1 Apr-31 Oct daily 9.30-9pm; 1 Nov-31 Mar, daily 9.30-5. Visitor Centre and shop: 1 Apr-31 Oct, dailly 9.30-5.30.
Admission: Acult £3.60 child/concession £2.40 adult party (including cruise party £2.90 child/school party £1 family £9.60.
Refreshments: (Licensed) restaurant open during same period, open at 10 and closes at 5.00.
Ranger Naturalist Service. For disabled: Half garden, greenhouse, toilets, wheelchair available. Guided walks with gardener Apr 1-Oct 31. Mon-Fri at 1.30pm.

LECKMELM GARDENS
(Mr. & Mrs. Peter Troughton)
Ullapool

An arboretum founded in 1870'on shores of Loch Broom.

HUGH MILLER'S COTTAGE
(The National Trust for Scotland)
Cromarty   map **11** G4
Telephone: (01381) 600245

Birthplace (10 Oct 1802) of Hugh Miller, stonemason, eminent geologist, editor and writer. Furnished thatched cottage built 1698 by his great-grandfather contains an interesting exhibition on his life and work. Captioned video programme. Cottage garden.

Location: In Cromarty 22 m from Invernes A832.
Open: 1 May-30 Sept Mon-Sat 10-1 and 2-5.30, Sun 2-5.30.
Admission: Adult £1.60 child/concession £1 adult party £1.30 child/school party £1 family £4.20.

LOTHIAN

AMISFIELD MAINS
(Lord Wemyss' Trust)
nr Haddington   map **9** L17
Telephone: (01875) 870201
Fax: (01875) 870620

Georgian farmhouse with 'Gothick' Barn and Cottage.

Location: Between Haddington & East Linton on A1 Edinburgh/Dunbar Road.
Open: Exteriors only. By appointment, Wemyss & March Estates, Estate Office, Longniddry, East Lothian EH32 0PY.

ARNISTON HOUSE
(Mrs A. Dundas-Bekker)
Gorebridge, Midlothian   EH23 4RY   map **15** L16
Telephone: (01875) 830238
Fax: (01875) 830573

William Adam house commissioned by the Dundases in 1726. The family have owned Arniston since 1571 and still live there. Set in acres of outstanding Adam landscaping with views to the Moorfoot hills much loved by Sir Walter Scott it was the hunting ground of King David in the 1100's. The Dundases rose to great legal heights in the 18th century and boast two Lord Presidents of the Court of Session, and Henry Dudas, 1st Viscount Melville, was Cabinet Minister and close friend of Sir William Pitt. Arniston contains portraits of the generations of the family from the 16th century up to the present day by artists including Ramsay and Raeburn. Also are fine examples of Adam architecture, stucco work, furniture and other fascinating contents. Arniston has been beset by dry rot problems and has been involved , grant aided by 'Historic Scotland', in an extensive restoration programme over the years which still continues. 1994-95 the John Adam dining room, gutted in 1957, reinstated.

Location: On B6372 between Gorebridge and Temple 1 mile from A7 and half an hour's drive from Edinburgh's city centre.
Open: July-15 Sept 1996. Sun Tues and Thurs from 2-5. Guided tours. Pre-arranged groups welcome throughout the year.
Admission: £3. Grounds free
Refreshments: Home baked teas.

ARTHUR LODGE
(S.Roland Friden)
60 Dalkeith Road, Edinburgh   EH16 5AD   map **15** L16
Telephone: 0131-667 5163

A Neo Grecian dream of a country gentleman's residence in Town (Thomas Hamilton 1827). Set in a beautiful garden and imaginatively restored and decorated, an exquisite and surprising private residence.

Open: June-July Wed and Sat Aug-Sept Wed only. Tours 2.15 3.15 and 4.15 or by appointment.
Admission: £3.00 concessions £2.00.

BEANSTON
(Lord Wemyss' Trust)
nr Haddington   map **9** L17
Telephone: (01875) 870201
Fax: (01875) 870620

Georgian farmhouse with Georgian Orangery.

Location: Between Haddington & East Linton on A1 Edinburgh/Dunbar Road.
Open: Exteriors only. By appointment, Wemyss & March Estates, Estate Office, Longniddry, East Lothian EH32 0PY.

DALKEITH COUNTRY PARK

(Duke of Buccleuch and Queensberry KT)
Dalkeith EH22 2NA   map **15** L16
Telephone: (0131) 663 5684 / 665 3277

Magnificent former home of the Dukes of Buccleuch. 800 acres of parkland dominated by Dalkeith Palace, the last remaining Dutch influenced Palladian house in the area. Extensive parkland first enclosed as deer parks by Charles I in 1637 still retain many fascinating features. Traces of a former lime avenue, manmade caves and tunnels, an amphitheatre and woodland walks can still be seen, reflecting the former glory of Dalkeith Park. The remains of the 12-sided conservatory of 1832 dominates what would have been an elaborate parterre designed by William Gilpin. The Victorian ice house is open for special guided tours with a ranger. Plunge into pitch darkness in this perfectly preserved building. Children thrill to our exciting woodland adventure play area including aerial ropeways, highlevel walkways, giant slides, wildwest fort and entertainment for all ages. Ancient scottish farm animals, events and Clydesdale horses all go toward making Dalkeith a place not to miss. A ranger service operates at Dalkeith to help people enjoy the beauties of the countryside and the work of a country estate. Guided walks, talks and special school activities are available year round by arrangement. Cafeteria & shop in our new Visitor Centre open Spring 1996.

Location: Off Dalkeith High Street A68.
Station(s): Edinburgh Railway / Dalkeith Bus.
Open: 1/4/95 to 31/10/95. 10-6.
Admission: 1995 all entrants £1.50. Family tickets and group discounts on request.
Refreshments: Cafeteria.
Events/Exhibitions: See annual programme.
Conferences: Corporate entertainment.

Ghosts are in residence at the following properties included in Historic Houses Castles and Gardens:

Blickling Hall - *Anne Boleyn*

Breamore House - *Haunted picture - if touched, death on the same day*

East Riddleden Hall - *5 ghosts including ladyin Grey Hall Lady's Chamber*

Fountains Abbey & Studley Royal - *Choir of monks chanting in Chapel of Nine Altars*

Hinton Ampner - *Nocturnal noises*

Ightham Mote - *Supernatural presence*

Lindisfarne Castle - *Monk, and group of monks on causeway*

Lyme Park - *Unearthly peals of bells and lady in white, funeral procession through park*

Malmesbury House - *Ghost of a cavalier*

Overbecks Museum & Garden - *'Model' ghost in the Children's room (for them to spot)*

Rockingham Castle - *Lady Dedlock*

Rufford Old Hall - *Elizabeth Hesketh*

Scotney Castle Garden - *Man rising from the lake*

Sizergh Castle & Garden - *Poltergeist*

Speke Hall - *Ghost of woman in tapestry room*

Springhill - *Ghost of a woman*

Sudbury Hall - *Lady in Green, seen on stairs*

Tamworth Castle - *Haunted bedroom*

Treasurer's House - *Troop of Roman soldiers marching through the cellar*

Wallington House - *Invisible birds beating against the windows accompanied by heavy breathing*

Washington Old Hall - *Grey lady walking through corridors*

DALMENY HOUSE
(The Earl of Rosebery)
South Queensferry   **EH30 9TQ**   map **15** L16   △ &
Telephone: 0131-331 1888
Fax: 0131-331 1788

Family home of the Earls of Rosebery, magnificently set in beautiful parkland on the shores of the Firth of Forth, 7m from the centre of Edinburgh. Scotland's first Gothic Revival house, designed in 1814 by William Wilkins. Rothschild Collection of 18th century French furniture and decorative art. Portraits by Reynolds, Gainsborough, Raeburn and Lawrence. Goya tapestries. Napoleonic Collection assembled by Prime Minister, the 5th Earl. Woodland garden with superb rhododendrons and azaleas.

Location: 3 m E of South Queensferry; 7 m N of Edinburgh signposted off A90.
Open: July and Aug incl Sun 1-5.30 Mon 12-5.30 Tues 12-5.30. Special parties also welcome at other times by arrangement with Administrator.
Admission: Adults £3.50 senior citizens £3 students £2.80 children 10-16 years £1.80 (under 10 years free). Groups (min 20) £2.80.
Refreshments: Light lunches and home-made teas.
Events/Exhibitions: Fashion shows, product launches, shows, filming, shooting and small meetings.
Public Transport: From St. Andrew Sq Bus Station to Chapel Gate (1 m from house). Disabled facilities available.

GOSFORD HOUSE
(Lord Wemyss' Trust)
East Lothian   **EH32 0PX**   map **9** L17
Telephone: (01875) 870201
Fax: (01875) 870620

GOSFORD HOUSE, LONGNIDDRY

Robert Adam designed Central Block, and Wings, later demolished. 1800 roof recently restored; part burnt (military occupation) restored 1987. Two Wings, rebuilt 1890, William Young. North Wing now roofless, South Wing is family home and contains famous Marble Hall (Staffordshire Alabaster). Parts of South Wing and Central Block open. Fine collection of paintings and works of art. Surrounding gardens redeveloping. Extensive policies, artificial ponds; geese and other wildfowl breeding.

Location: On A198 between Aberlady & Longniddry; NW of Haddington.
Station(s): Longniddry (2½ m).
Open: June and July Wed Sat and Sun 2-5.
Admission: Adults £2.50 children 75p.
Refreshments: Hotels in Aberlady.
Wemyss & March Estates, Longniddry, East Lothian EH32 OPY.

THE GEORGIAN HOUSE
(The National Trust for Scotland)
No. 7 Charlotte Square, Edinburgh   **EH2 4DR**   map **15** L16   Ⓢ
Telephone: 0131-225 2160

The north side of Charlotte Square is classed as Robert Adam's masterpiece of urban architecture. The main floors of No. 7 are open as a typical Georgian House. Audio-visual shows. Shop.

Location: In Edinburgh city centre.
Station(s): Edinburgh Waverly.
Open: Apr 1-Oct 31 Mon-Sat 10-5 Sun 2-5.
Admission: (incl. audio-visual): adult £3.60 child/concession £2.40 adult party £2.90 child/school party £1 family £9.60.

HARELAW FARMHOUSE
(Lord Wemyss' Trust)
nr Longniddry   map **9** L17
Telephone: (01875) 870201
Fax: (01875) 870620

Early 19th century 2-storey farmhouse built as an integral part of the steading. Dovecote over entrance arch.

Location: Between Longniddry and Drem on the B1377.
Open: Exteriors only. By appointment. Wemyss and March Estates, Estate Office, Longniddry, East Lothian EH32 OPY.

GLADSTONE'S LAND
(The National Trust for Scotland)
Edinburgh   map **15** L16
Telephone: 0131-226 5856

Built 1620 and shortly afterwards occupied by Thomas Gledstanes. Remarkable painted wooden ceilings; furnished as a typical 'Old Town' house of the period. Shop.

Location: 477B Lawnmarket, Edinburgh.
Station(s): Edinburgh Waverley.
Open: Apr 1-Oct 31 Mon-Sat 10-5 Sun 2-5.
Admission: Adult £2.60 child/concession £1.70 adult party £2.10 child/school party £1 family £6.90.
Accommodation: Holiday flat above property-apply to NTS.

HOPETOUN HOUSE

(Hopetoun House Preservation Trust)
South Queensferry, nr Edinburgh   map **15** L16 Ⓢ
Telephone: 0131-331 2451

Home of the Marquess of Linlithgow. Fine example of 18th century Adam architecture. Magnificent reception rooms, pictures, antiques.

Location: 2 m from Forth Road Bridge nr South Queensferry off A904.
Open: Daily 10-5.30 from Apr 1 to Oct 2 inclusive. (Last admission 4.45).The house is also available for private evening functions throughout the year. Enquiries to Administrator's Office 031-331 2451.
Admission: £3.80, party rates £3.10, OAPs £3.10, Chd 5-16 yrs £1.90, Chd party rates £1.70. Grounds only: £2.00, Chd 60p. Family tickets £10.50, grounds only £5.00. Free parking.
Refreshments: Licensed restaurant and snack bar in Tapestry Room.
Gift shop. Deer park. Picnic areas. Free Ranger service. 3 Nature Trails (including one specifically aimed at children). Roof top viewing platform with magnificent views of the Forth and the Bridges.

Thomas Gainsborough (1727-1787)

His paintings can be seen at the following properties included in Historic Houses Castles and Gardens:-

Arundel Castle	*Knowle*
Bowhill	*Parham House &*
Christchurch Mansion	*Gardens*
Dalmeny House	*Petworth House*
Elton Hall	*Shalom Hall*
Gainsborough's House	*Upton House*
Ickworth Park & Garden	*Waddesdon Manor*
Firle Place	*Weston Park*
Kenwood, The Iveagh	*Woburn Abbey*
Bequest	

THE HOUSE OF THE BINNS

(The National Trust for Scotland)
by Linlithgow   map **15** L15 △
Telephone: (01506) 834255

Historic home of the Dalyells. Fine plaster ceilings. Interesting pictures. Panoramic viewpoint.

Location: 3½ m E of Linlithgow off A904.
Station(s): Linlithgow.
Open: House: 1 May-30 Sept daily except Fri 1.30-5.30 (last admission 5pm). Parkland 1 Apr-31 Oct daily 9.30-7; 1 Nov-31 Mar daily 9.30-4 (last admission 30 mins before closing time).
Admission: Adult £3.10 child/concession £2 adult party £2.50 child/school party £1 family £8.20. Visits by guided tours only. Members of the Royal Scots Dragoon Guards, successors of 'The Greys' in uniform are admitted free.

INVERESK LODGE GARDEN

(The National Trust for Scotland)
Inveresk   map **15** L16
Telephone: 0131-665 1855

Attractive terraced garden, with large selection of plants.

Location: In Inveresk village; 6 m E of Edinburgh off A1.
Station(s): Musselburgh (1m).
Open: 1 Apr-30 Sept Mon-Fri 10-4.30 Sat/Sun 2-5, 1 Oct-31 Mar Mon-Fri 10-4.30 Sun 2-5.
Admission: £1 Honesty Box.

LAURISTON CASTLE
(City of Edinburgh District Council)
Edinburgh   map **15** L16   △

A beautifully furnished Edwardian home, associated with John Law (1671-1729), founder of first bank in France.

Location: Cramond Road South, Davidsons Mains, 4½ m from GPO, Edinburgh.
Open: Castle all year Apr-Oct daily (except Fri) 11-1 and 2-5 Nov-Mar Sat and Sun only 2-4 guided tours only (last tour 40 mins before closing time) Grounds daily 9-dusk.
Admission: Adults £2 children £1.

Anthony Salvin (1799-1881)
Architect - trained under John Nash

His work can be seen in the following properties included in Historic Houses Castles and Gardens:-

Helmingham Hall Gardens
Muncaster Castle
Petworth House

LENNOXLOVE
(His Grace the Duke of Hamilton)
Haddington   **EH41 4NZ**   map **9** L17
Telephone: (01620) 823720
Fax: (01620) 825112

Lennoxlove, home of the Duke of Hamilton, is a house with a three-fold interest; its historic architecture, the association of its proprietors with the Royal House of Stewart and the famous Hamilton Palace collection of works of art, including the Casket, ring and Death Mask of Mary Queen of Scots. Formerly Lethington Tower, ancient home of the Maitlands. The Lime Avenue, known as Politician's Walk, was laid out by William Maitland, Secretary of State to Mary Queen of Scots.

Location: 1½ m S of Haddington on B6369; 18 m E of Edinburgh off A1.
Open: Easter weekend then May-Sept Wed Sat & Sun 2-5 at other times by appointment (minimum charge £30); apply to Estate Office, Lennoxlove, Haddington (01620 823720).
Admission: Adults £3 children £1.50 pre-booked parties (15 or more - minimum charge £30) £2 children £1 price includes guided tour of House, entry to gardens and parking.
Refreshments: Tea-room.
Conferences: Select business conferences, residential or non-residential, and film and photograph location, etc. For further information contact The Factor, Lennoxlove, Haddington. East Lothian EH41 4NZ (Tel. 01620 822156, Fax 01620 825112).

MALLENY GARDEN
(The National Trust for Scotland)
Balerno   map **15** L16
Telephone: 0131-449 2283

A delightfully personal garden with a particularly good collection of shrub roses. National Bonsai Collection for Scotland.

Location: In Balerno, off A70.
Station(s): Edinburgh Haymarket.
Open: 1 Apr-31 Oct, daily 9.30-7; 1 Nov-31 Mar, daily 9.30-4.
Admission: £1 Honesty box.
No dogs in garden please.

PALACE OF HOLYROODHOUSE
(The official residence of HM The Queen in Scotland)
Edinburgh   **EH8 8DX**   map **15** L16
Telephone: 0131-556 7371

Throughout history, Holyrood has been the scene of turbulent and extraordinary events, yet the Palace retains a modern appeal appropriate to a Royal residence still in regular use.

PRESTON MILL
(The National Trust for Scotland)
East Linton   map **9** L17
Telephone: (01620) 860426

The oldest mill (16th century) of its kind still working and only survivor of many on the banks of the Tyne. Popular with artists. Renovated machinery.

Location: 5½ m W of Dunbar, off A1.
Station(s): Dunbar.
Open: 1 May-30 Sep Mon-Sat 11-1 and 2-5.30 Sun 1.30-5.30; weekends in Oct 1.30-4 (last admission 20 mins before closing, morning and afternoon).
Admission: Adult £1.60 child/concession £1 adult party £1.30 child/school party £1 family £4.20.

PRESTONHALL
(Major J.H. Callander (WA)
Pathhead   map **9** L17

Built in 1791, in 70 acres of parkland with fine architecture and interiors.

STEVENSON HOUSE
(Trustees of the Brown Dunlop Country Houses Trust)
Haddington   EH41 4PU   map **9** L16
Telephone: (01620) 823376 Mrs J.C.H Dunlop

A family home for four centuries, of charm and interest and dating from the 13th century when it belonged to the Cistercian Nunnery at Haddington, but partially destroyed on several occasions, and finally made uninhabitable in 1544. Restored about 1560 and the present house dates mainly from this period, with later additions in the 18th century. Fine furniture, pictures etc.

Location: 20 m approx from Edinburgh; 1½ m approx from A1; 2 m approx from Haddington. (See Historic House direction signs on A1 in Haddington.)
Open: July-mid-Aug Thur Sat & Sun 2-5. Guided tours take at least 1-1½ hours 3 pm. Other times by arrangement only. GARDENS and Walled Kitchen Garden are open daily Apr-Oct.
Admission: £2 OAPs £1.50 Children under 14 £1. Special arrangement parties welcome. GARDENS 50p only payable into Box on House Garden entrance gate.
Refreshments: Appointment parties morning coffee etc at Stevenson. Nearest hotels and restaurants are in Haddington, i.e. 2 m from Stevenson.
Car parking. Suitable for wheelchairs in garden only.

ORKNEY ISLANDS

BALFOUR CASTLE
Shapinsay, Orkney Islands   KW17 2DY   map **11** D17
Telephone: (01856) 711282
Fax: (01856) 711283

Balfour Castle was built in 1848

Location: 1/4 mile from sea, on island 20 mins by Ro-Ro ferry from Kirkwall- capital of Orkney. In private grounds, woods, gardens.
Station(s): Thurso-Scottish mainland. Kirkwall airport 4 miles.
Open: On Suns & Weds May-Sept. Guided tours of the walled garden and Castle by members of the resident family.
Admission: Inclusive price for return boat fare, tour of Castle and Gardens and home baked tea. £12.80 Adults £6.40 Children.
Events/Exhibitions: Weddings, private parties, musical evenings, lunches, visits of Cruise liners.
Accommodation: 8 bedrooms, most en-suite. Large rooms, canopy, 4 poster beds. Original furnishings. £68 per night includes bed, breakfast & dinner and VAT.
Conferences: Small private meetings can be arranged- approx 30-40.

STRATHCLYDE

ARDUAINE GARDEN
(The National Trust for Scotland)
Argyll   map **8** K11
Telephone: (01852) 200366

Outstanding 18 acre garden on a promontory bounded by Loch Melfort and the Sound of Jura. Nationally noted for rhododendrons and azalea species, magnolias and other rare trees and shrubs.

Location: A816, 20 m S of Oban and 17 m N of Lochgilphead.
Station(s): Oban.
Open: All year daily 9.30-sunset.
Admission: Adult: £2.10 Child/Concession £1.40 Adult Party £1.70 Child/School Party £1 Family £5.60.

BACHELORS' CLUB
(The National Trust for Scotland)
Tarbolton   map **8** L13
Telephone: (01292) 541940

17th century thatched house where Burns and his friends formed their club in 1780. Period furnishings.

Location: In Tarbolton village 7½ m NE of Ayr (off A758).
Station(s): Ayr.
Open: Good Fri-Easter Mon and May 1 to Sept 30 daily 1.30-5.30; weekends in Oct 1.30-5.30. Other times by appointment.
Admission: Adult £1.60 child/concession £1 adult party £1.30 child/school party £1 family £4.20.

BALLOCH CASTLE COUNTRY PARK
Balloch
Telephone: (01389) 58216

Balloch Castle is a 200 acre Country Park situated on the bonnie banks of Loch Lomond. Folk say that it is one of the finest Parks in the whole of the country and who are we to argue. Steeped in history and with breathtaking views over Loch Lomond, this ancient seat of the Lennox offers the visitor a chance to blend the wild, natural beauty of Scotland with the formal glory of ornamental gardens and splendid trees of former estate days. The present Balloch Castle, now the Visitor Centre, was built in 1808 and is built in the "castle-gothic" style of architecture and was one of the first of its type built in Scotland. We look forward to seeing you

Location: SE shore of Loch Lomond off A82 for Balloch or A811 for Stirling
Admission: Free for both Visitor Centre and Country Park
For information contact Loch Lomond Park Authority (01389) 758216

BLAIRQUHAN CASTLE AND GARDENS
(James Hunter Blair)
Straiton, Maybole, Ayrshire KA19 7LZ map **8** M13
Telephone: (01655) 770239
Fax: (01655) 770278

Magnificent Regency castellated mansion approached by a 3m private drive beside the river Girvan. Walled gardens and pinetum. Picture gallery.

Location: 14m S of Ayr off A77. Entrance Lodge is on B7045 ½ m S of Kirkmichael.
Open: July 14-Aug 11 *not Mons.*
Admission: £3 Children £2.50 OAPs £2. Parties by arrangement at any time of year.
Refreshments: Tea in castle.
Car parking. Wheelchairs - around gardens and principal floor of the castle.

BRODICK CASTLE, GARDEN AND COUNTRY PARK
(The National Trust for Scotland)
Isle of Arran map **8** M13
Telephone: (01770) 650100
Fax: (01770) 302312

Historic home of the Dukes of Hamilton. The castle dates in part from the 13th century. Paintings, furniture, objets d'art. Formal and woodland gardens, noted for rhododendrons. Country park.

Location: 2m N of Brodick pierhead on the Isle of Arran.
Station(s): Ardrossan Harbour and Claonaig in Kintyre (& hence by Caledonian MacBrayne ferry). Ferry enquiries to Caledonian MacBrayne. Tel. Gourock (01475) 650100.
Open: Castle 1 Apr (or Good Fri if earlier) to 31 Oct daily 11.30-5pm (last admission 4.30). Reception Centre and shop (dates as castle) open 10-5; restaurant 11-5. Garden and Country Park, all year, daily 9.30-sunset.
Admission: Castle and garden: adult £4.10 child/concession £2.70 adult party £3.30 child/school party £1 family £10.90. Garden only: adult £2.10 child/concession £1.40 adult party £1.70 child/school party £1.
Refreshments: Restaurant. (Self-service in Castle). Dates as Castle, daily 11-5.
Accommodation: Holiday flats in castle- apply to NTS.
Car park free. Ferry from Ardrossan (55mins) to Brodick. Connecting bus, pier to castle (2 miles). Ferry enquiries to Caledonian MacBrayne; tel Gourock (01475) 650100.

BURNS COTTAGE
Alloway

Thatched cottage in which Robert Burns was born, 1759. Museum with Burns' relics.

Location: 1.5M SW of Ayr
Open: Open all year

CULZEAN CASTLE, GARDEN AND COUNTRY PARK
(The National Trust for Scotland)
Maybole map **8** M13 △ & ⑤
Telephone: (01655) 760274
Fax: (01655) 760615

One of the finest Adam houses in Scotland. Spacious policies and gardens. Adventure playground.

Location: 12 m SW of Ayr just off A719.
Station(s): Maybole (4m)
Open: Castle, Visitor Centre and Shops 1 Apr-31 Oct daily 10.30-5.30. Country Park, all year daily 9.30-sunset.
Admission: Castle: adult £3.50 child concession £1.80 family £9.70; Country Park adult £3 child/concession £1.50 adult party £2.50 school coaches £20 family £7.50. Combined ticket castle and country park: adult £5.50 child/concession £3 adult party £4.50 child/school party £2.50 family £15. Enquiries and all party bookings: tel Kirkowald (01655) 760269.
Refreshments: Licensed restaurant. Open 10.30-5.30.
Events/Exhibitions: In Visitor Centre.
Accommodation: Holiday flats in castle and grounds - apply to NTS.

DUART CASTLE
(Sir Lachlan Maclean)
Isle of Mull, Argyll **PA64 6AP** map **8** K11 △
Telephone: (01680) 812309

Duart Castle is built on a cliff dominating the Sound of Mull. Home of the Chief of Clan Maclean. Panoramic views from 13th Century Keep built by 5th Chief Lachlan Lubanach. Dungeons and exhibitions.

Location: Duart is 3 m from Craignure, off the A849, on the way to Iona.
Open: May-Mid Oct daily 10.30-6.
Admission: Adults £3.30 OAPs £2.20 student £2.75 family ticket £8.25.
Refreshments: Tea-room with home baking.
Shop.

GREENBANK GARDEN

(The National Trust for Scotland)
Glasgow   map **15** L14   ♿
Telephone: 0141-639 3281

Walled garden, woodland walk and policies. Wide range of plants, flowers and shrubs. Regular garden walks and events. Best seen Apr-Oct. Attractive series of gardens, extending to 2½ acres, surrounding Georgian house. Special garden and greenhouse for the disabled, together with special gardening tools.

Location: Flenders Road, near Clarkston Toll.
Station(s): Clarkston (1¼ m).
Open: All year daily 9.30-sunset, except 25/26 Dec and 1/2 Jan. Shop and tearoom: 1 Apr (or Good Fri if earlier) to 31 Oct daily 11-5. House: 1 Apr-31 Oct Sundays only 2-4 (subject to functions in progress).
Admission: Adult £2.60 child/concession £1.70 adult party £2.10 child/school party £1 family £6.90.
Refreshments: Tea-room.
No dogs in garden please.

THE HILL HOUSE

(The National Trust for Scotland)
Helensburgh   map **8** K13
Telephone: (01436) 673900

Overlooking the estuary of the River Clyde the house is considered to be the finest example of the domestic architecture of Charles Rennie Mackintosh. Commissioned in 1902 and completed in 1904 for the Glasgow publisher Walter W Blackie. Special display about Charles Rennie Mackintosh.

Location: In Upper Colquhoun Street, Helensburgh; NW of Glasgow via A814.
Station(s): Helensburgh.
Open: Apr 1-Oct 31 daily 1.30-5.30.
Admission: Adult £3.60 child/concession £2.40 adult party £2.90 child/school party £1 family £9.60.
Refreshments: Tea-room open 1.30-4.30.

HUTCHESONS' HALL

(The National Trust for Scotland)
Glasgow   map **15** L14
Telephone: 0141-552 8391
Fax: 0141-562 7031

Described as one of the most elegant buildings in Glasgow's city centre, the Hall was built in 1802-5 to a design by David Hamilton.

Location: 158 Ingram Street, nr SE corner of George Square.
Station(s): Glasgow Central or Glasgow Queen Street.
Open: Information Centre, shop and function hall, all year (except public holidays and 24 Dec-3 Jan), Mon-Sat 10-5 (hall on view subject to functions in progress). Shop closed for stocktaking 1/2 Nov and 24 Dec-8 Jan.
Admission: Free. Groups must pre-book.
Conferences: Apply to the NTS Travel Trade Dept.
Shop: Mons to Sats 10-5.

INVERARAY CASTLE

(The Trustees of the 10th Duke of Argyll)
Inveraray   PA32 8XE   map **8** K12   △ ♿
Telephone: (01499) 302203
Fax: (01499) 302421
Location: ¾ m NE of Inveraray on Loch Fyne 58 m NW of Glasgow.

KELBURN CASTLE AND COUNTRY CENTRE

(The Home and Park of the Earls of Glasgow on the Firth of Clyde)
Largs   KA29 0BE   map **8** L13
Telephone: (01475) 568685
Fax: (01475) 568121

Historic home of the Boyle family, later Earls of Glasgow, Kelburn is situated on the picturesque North Ayrshire coast. Kelburn Castle dates from 1200 and features four architectural styles: a Norman Keep, James VI Tower House, William and Mary Mansionhouse and Victorian Wing. There are romantic walks, waterfalls and gorges in Kelburn Glen; Gardens, Horse Riding, Kelburn Story Exhibition, Family Museum, Adventure Courses, Children's Play Areas, Pets Corner, Nature Centre, Gift Shop and The Secret Forest, a natural wood filled with unusual follies. Birds of Prey displays (May-Sept).

Location: On the A78 two miles south of Largs. 45 mins from Glasgow.
Station(s): Largs. Free minibus service at 11.45 am and 1.45 pm daily July-Aug.
Open: Country Centre Apr-Oct Daily 10-6. Castle July-Aug. Riding Centre year round. Grounds only Oct-Apr.
Admission: Adults £4 Child/OAP/Student £2.50. Group Rates. Winter prices Adult £1.75. Child/OAP £1. Castle Adm £1.50
Refreshments: Licensed Restaurant, Cafe.

MOUNT STUART HOUSE AND GARDENS

(The Mount Stuart Trust)
Rothesay, Isle of Bute   PA20 9LR   map **8** L12
Telephone: (01700) 503877
Fax: (01700) 505313

Open to the public for the first time in 1995: Scottish Tourism Oscar Winner 1995 ancestral home of the Marquesses of Bute; one of Britain's most spectacular High Victorian Gothic houses; fabulous interiors, art collection and architectural detail; extensive grounds with stunning woodland and shoreline walks; exotic gardens, Victorian kitchen garden; mature Victorian Pinetum.

Location: 5½ m south of Rothesay pierhead on Isle of Bute.
Station(s): Glasgow Airport: 50 mins drive/train to Wemyss Bay. Rail Stations: Glasgow Central and Wemyss Bay (British Rail: (0141) 204 2844). Frequent ferry service from Wemyss Bay (Caledonian MacBrayne: (01475) 650 100). Regular bus service from Rothesay Pier.
Open: May-end Sept 11.00-17.00 (16.30 last admission). Mon, Wed, Fri, Sat & Sun. Gardens open 10.00-17.00 (16.30 last admission). Gardens open Sat/Sun Apr and Oct.
Admission: House and garden: Adult £5.50, Child £2.50, Family £15. Garden only: Adult £3, Child £2, family £8 Season ticket £15. Concession and group rates given.
Pre-booked house/gardens/ranger guided tours available on application.

SORN CASTLE

Sorn, Mauchline   map **8** M14
Telephone: (01505) 612124 (Cluttons)

Dating from the 14th century in impressive setting on sandstone cliff over the River Ayr with attractive woodland walks. Further details from Cluttons.

Location: 4 m E of Mauchline on B743.
Open: Jul 20-Aug 17 2-5 or by appointment. Grounds Apr 1-Oct 30.
Admission: £3.50.
Accommodation: Available- contact Cluttons.

SOUTER JOHNNIE'S COTTAGE

(The National Trust for Scotland)
Kirkoswald   map **8** M13
Telephone: (01655) 760671

Thatched home of the original Souter in Burns' 'Tam o' Shanter' Burns relics. Life-sized stone figures of the Souter, Tam, the Innkeeper and his wife, in restored ale house in the cottage garden.

Location: In Kirkoswald village 4 m W of Maybole on A77.
Station(s): Maybole.
Open: Good Fri-Easter Mon and 1 May-30 Sept daily 1.30-5.30; weekends in Oct 1.30-5.30 (last admission 5). Other times by appointment.
Admission: Adult £1.60 child/concession £1 adult party £1.30 child/school party £1 family £4.20.

THE TENEMENT HOUSE
(The National Trust for Scotland)
Glasgow map **15** L14
Telephone: 0141-333 0183

A restored first floor flat in a Victorian tenement building, built 1892, presents a picture of social significance. A second flat on the ground floor provides reception, interpretative and educational facilities.

Location: No 145 Buccleuch Street, Garnethill (N of Charing Cross).
Station(s): Charing Cross.
Open: 1 Mar-31 Oct daily 2-5.
Admission: Adult £2.60 child/concession £1.70 adult party £2.10 child/school party £1 family £6.90.

TOROSAY CASTLE AND GARDENS
(Mr Christopher James)
Craignure, Isle of Mull PA65 6AY map **8** J11
Telephone: (01680) 812421
Fax: (01680) 812470

Early Victorian house by David Bryce, still a family home, surrounded by 12 acres of terraced and contrasting informal gardens, all offset by dramatic West Highland scenery.

Location: 1½ m SE of Craignure by A849, by Forest Walk or by N.G. Steam Railway.
Station(s): Oban.
Open: Castle mid Apr-mid Oct 10.30-5.30 (last adm 5). Gardens Summer 9-7 Winter sunrise to sunset. Parties at other times to Castle by appointment only.
Admission: Castle £3.50 also concession rates. Garden only adults £2 children (5-16)/OAPs/students £1.50 (honesty box when castle closed). Free car park.
Refreshments: Home baked teas in Castle.
Events/Exhibitions: See local press.
Accommodation: Self catering cottages.
Conferences: No.
Dogs on lead in Gardens only. Gardens and tearoom only suitable for wheelchairs. Local Craft Shop.

WEAVER'S COTTAGE
(The National Trust for Scotland)
Kilbarchan map **15** L13
Telephone: (01505) 705588
Location: In Kilbarchan village; 12 m SW of Glasgow off A737.

TAYSIDE

ANGUS FOLK MUSEUM
(The National Trust for Scotland)
Glamis map **9** J16
Telephone: (01307) 840288

Row of 19th century cottages with stone-slabbed roofs, restored by the Trust. Adapted to display the Angus Folk Collection, one of the finest in the country. Agricultural collection displayed in farm steading opposite.

Location: In Glamis village; 12 m N of Dundee off A94.
Station(s): Forfar
Open: Open: Good Fri to Easter Mon and 1 May to 30 Sep, daily 11-5; weekends in Oct, 11-5 (last admission 4.30).
Admission: Adult: £2.10 Child/Concession £1.40 adult parties £1.70 School parties 80p. Family £5.60.

BARRIE'S BIRTHPLACE
(The National Trust for Scotland)
Kirriemuir map **9** J16
Telephone: (01575) 572646

Contains mementoes of Sir James Barrie. Exhibition features Peter Pan and other works of Barrie.

Location: No 9 Brechin Road, in Kirriemuir.
Station(s): Forfar (6m).
Open: Good Fri-Easter Mon and 1 May-30 Sept, Mon-Sat 11-5.30, Sun 1-30-5.30 weekends in Oct, Sat 11-5.30 Sun 1.30-5.30 (last admission 5pm).
Admission: Adult £1.60 child/concession £1 adult party £1.30 child/school party £1 family £4.20.
Refreshments: Airlie Arms Hotel. Coffee and tea in house.
Events/Exhibitions: See above.
Accommodation: Holiday house nearby - apply to NTS.

BARRY MILL
(The National Trust for Scotland)
Carnoustie map **9** J17
Telephone: (01241) 856761

This 19th century meal mill works on a demonstration basis. Displays highlight the important place the mill held in the community.

Location: 2 m NW of Carnoustie.
Open: Good Fri-Easter Mon and May 1-Sept 30, daily 11-5 weekends in Oct 11-5.
Admission: Adult £1.60 child/concession £1 adult party £1.30 child/school party £1 family £4.20.

BLAIR CASTLE
Blair Athol
Telephone: (01796) 481207

Scotland's most visited historic house is home for the 10th Duke of Atholl and the Atholl Highlanders, Britain's only private army.

BRANKLYN GARDEN
(The National Trust for Scotland)
Perth map **9** K16
Telephone: (01738) 625535

One of the finest gardens of its size in Britain (2 acres).
Location: In Perth on Dundee Road (A85).
Station(s): Perth.
Open: Mar 1-Oct 31: daily 9.30-sunset.
Admission: Adult £2.10 child/concession £1.40 adult party £1.70 child/school party £1 family £5.60.
Events/Exhibitions: Display in summmerhouse.

CASTLE MENZIES
(Menzies Charitable Trust)
Weem PH15 2JD   map **8** J15
Telephone: (01887) 820982

Magnificant example of a 16th century fortified house, seat of the Chiefs of Clan Menzies, situated in the beautiful valley of the Tay. It was involved in the turbulent history of the Central Highlands and here 'Bonnie Prince Charlie' rested on his way to Culloden in 1746.

Location: 1½ m from Aberfeldy on B846.
Open: Apr-mid Oct weekdays 10.30-5 Suns 2-5.
Admission: Adults £2.50 children £1 OAPs £2 family concessions. Reductions for parties by prior arrangement.
Refreshments: Tea-room.
Events/Exhibitions: 9-11 Aug Clan Menzies Gathering.

DRUMMOND CASTLE GARDENS
(Grimsthorpe & Drummond Castle Trust Ltd)
Muthill, Crieff   PH5 2AA   map **8** K15
Telephone: (01764) 681257
Fax: (01764) 681550

The gardens of Drummond Castle first laid out in the early 17th century by John Drummond, 2nd Earl of Perth, are said to be among the finest formal gardens in Europe. A spectacular view can be obtained from the upper terrace, overlooking a magnificent example of an early Victorian Parterre in the form of a St. Andrew's cross. The multi faceted sundial by John Mylne, Master Mason to Charles 1 has been the centre piece since 1630 - featured recently in United Artists "Rob Roy".

Location: Entrance 2 m south of Crieff on Muthill Road A822.
Open: Daily 2-6 (last admission 5) May-Oct - and Easter weekend.
Admission: Adults £3 OAPs £2 children £1.50. Coach parties and disabled by prior arrangement.

GLAMIS CASTLE
(The Earl of Strathmore and Kinghorne)
Glamis   DD8 1RJ   map **9** J16   △
Telephone: (01307) 840393/242
Fax: (01307) 840733

Family home of the Earls of Strathmore and Kinghorne and a royal residence since 1372. Childhood home of H.M. Queen Elizabeth The Queen Mother and birthplace of H.R.H. The Princess Margaret. Legendary setting of Shakespeare's play 'Macbeth'. Five-storey L shaped tower block dating from 15th century, remodelled 1606, containing magnificent rooms with wide range of historic pictures, furniture, porcelain etc.

Location: Glamis.
Open: 31 Mar-28 Oct 1996 (last admission 4.45).
Admission: Adults £4.70 OAPs £3.60 children 5-16 £2.50 family £13. Party rates £4.30 OAPs £3.20 children 5-16 £2.20 min number 20. Grounds only adults £2.20 children/OAPs £1.10.
Refreshments: Licensed Restaurant at the Castle.
Ample bus and car parking. Picnic area, Shops, Garden and Nature Trail. Further details available from The Administrator, Tel: (01307) 840393/242. Fax: (01307) 840733.

HOUSE OF DUN

(The National Trust for Scotland) ·
Nr Montrose   map **9** J17
Telephone: (01674) 810264

Georgian house overlooking the Montrose Basin, built in 1730 for David Erskine, Lord Dun, to designs by William Adam. Exuberant plasterwork in the saloon.

Location: 4 m W of Montrose.
Station(s): Montrose.
Open: House and shop: Good Fri-Easter Mon and 1 May-30 Sept daily 1.30-5.30; weekends in Oct 1.30-5.30 (last admission 5). Garden and grounds, all year, daily 9.30-sunset.
Admission: House: adult £3.10 child/concession £2 adult party £2.50 child/school party £1 family £8.20. Garden and grounds only £1 (honesty box).
Refreshments: Restaurant open at 12.30. Dates as above.

MEGGINCH CASTLE GARDENS

(Captain Drummond of Megginch and Lady Strange)
Errol   **PH2 7SW**
Telephone: (01821) 642222
Fax: (01821) 642708

Gardens of 15th century Castle, 1000 year old yews, walled kitchen garden and 'Astrological Garden'.

Location: 8 m E of Perth on A90.
Open: Apr-Oct on Weds, Aug every day 2-5.
Admission: Adult £2 child £1.

MONZIE CASTLE

Crieff, Perthshire   **PH7 4HD**   map **8** K15
Telephone: (01764) 653110

Built in 1791. Destroyed by fire in 1908. Rebuilt and furnished by Sir Robertt Lorimer.

Location: 2 miles north east of Crieff.
Open: May 18-June 16 1996 inclusive 2-5. By appointment anytime.
Admission: Adults £3 children £1 groups £2.50.

SCONE PALACE

(Rt Hon the Earl of Mansfield)
Perth   **PH2 6BD**   map **9** K16
Telephone: (01738) 552300
Fax: (01738) 552588

This medieval palace was Gothicised for the third Earl of Mansfield in the early 19th century. Superb collections of French furniture, china, ivories, clocks, Vernis Martin vases and objets d'art. Magnificent trees.

Location: 2 m NE of Perth on the Braemar Road (A93).
Station(s): Perth (2½ m).
Open: Good Fri-mid Oct Mon-Sun 9.30-5.
Admission: Palace and Grounds: adults £4.70 party rate £4.20 OAPs £3.90 party rate £3.60 children £2.60 party rate £2.30 family ticket £13.50 Grounds only: adults £2.35 children £1.30. Free car park.
Refreshments: Coffee shop. Old Kitchen Restaurant (licensed). Home baking. State Room dinners.
Events/Exhibitions: Both in the Palace and very extensive parklands.
Conferences: Mostly in the Winter season.
Shops. Picnic park. Playground.

STOBHALL

(Earl of Perth)
Guildtown, Perth   map **9** J16

Gardens and Policies, Chapel with 17th century painted ceiling.

Location: 8 m north of Perth on A93.
Open: Mid May-mid June 1-5.
Admission: Adults £2 children £1.

The Garden Specialists
in Great Britain and Ireland

A selection of nurseries specialising in rare of uncommon plants

♿ Denotes the major part of the property is suitable for wheelchairs

---

ARCHITECTURAL PLANTS
(Angus White)
Cooks Farm, Nuthurst, Horsham, West Sussex   RH13 6LH   map **12** U22
Telephone: (01403) 891772
Fax: (01403) 891056

Hardy Exotics - evergreen trees and shrubs with big, spiky and frondy leaves, including conservatory plants. Many extremely rare. Please send for free catalogue.
Location: Behind Black Horse pub in Nuthurst, 5 m S of Horsham, West Sussex.
Station(s): Horsham.
Open: Mons-Sats 9-5.

AYLETT NURSERIES LTD

(Mr R.S. Aylett)
North Orbital Road (A414), St Albans, Hertfordshire   map **12** T22   ♿
Telephone: (01727) 822255

Aylett Nurseries of St. Albans is a well known family business with a reputation of high quality plants and service. Famous for its dahlias - having been awarded a Gold Medal by the Royal Horticultural Society every year since 1961. Spacious planteria contains a profusion of trees, shrubs, herbaceous plants and many more! In the spring our greenhouses are full of geraniums, fuchsias, hanging baskets and many other types of bedding plants. Facilities also include garden shop, coffee and gift shop, houseplants, florist, garden furniture. From the middle of October do not miss our Christmas Wonderland.
Location: 2 m out of St. Albans, 1 m from M10 and M1, M25 and A1.
Station(s): St. Albans- Thames Link
Open: Mon to Fri 8.30-5.30, Sats 8.30-5, Suns 10-4 and Bank Hols 9-5. *Closed* Christmas Day, Boxing Day and Easter Sunday. Parties with pre advice please.
Admission: Free.
Refreshments: Dahlia coffee shop serves light lunches, homemade cakes, creamy gateaux. Coffee, tea and soft drinks.
Events/Exhibitions: Dahlia Festival- last two weekends in September.
Suitable for disabled visitors. Five wheelchairs available.

BLACKTHORN NURSERY
(Mr & Mrs A.R. White)
Kilmeston, Alresford, Hampshire   SO24 ONL
Telephone: (01962) 771796

Specialist nursery growing a wide range of alpines and rock plants.

BLAKENEY HOUSE NURSERIES LTD
Osier Grounds;Denton, Canterbury, Kent   CT4 6NP
Telephone: (01227) 831800
Fax: (01227) 831883

Conifer specialists, wholesalers and distributors of hardy nursery stock.

BODIAM NURSERY
(Richard Biggs)
Ockham House, Bodiam, Robertsbridge, East Sussex   TN32 5RA   map **13** V24
Telephone: (01580) 830811/830649

Set beside fine old oasthouse and Queen Anne house in unspoilt countryside. Spectacular view of Bodiam Castle just across the River Rother. Enormous selection of heathers (over 200), Acers, shrubs (over 700), climbers, conifers, alpine and herbaceous plants, many unusual, propagated and grown here. Sizes from tinies for the economy minded to specimens for 'instant gardening'. Acres of plants in pots.
Location: 11 m from Hastings, 3 m from Hurst Green which is on the A21. Follow signs for Bodiam Castle. Nursery is just across the river valley from the Castle.
Station(s): Etchingham (5 m).
Open: Every day 9-7 (sunset in winter).

BODNANT GARDEN NURSERY LTD
Tal Y Cafn, Nr. Colwyn Bay, Clwyd   LL28 5RE   ♿
Telephone: (01492) 650460
Fax: (01492) 650448

Bodnant Garden Nursery is famous for its unusual trees and shrubs. We propagate over 800 species and varieties of flowering and foliage shrubs, including rhododendrons, azaleas, magnolias and camellias. The many thousands of plants produced in our own propagation units by experienced staff are available to purchase, either by personal selection or our efficient mail order service.
Location: 8 m S of Llandudno and Colwyn Bay on the A470, just off the A55 Coastal Expressway.
Open: Daily (excl. Christmas Day) 9.30-5.
Admission: Free.
Refreshments: Morning coffee, light lunches and afternoon teas are available Apr-Sept. Car parking. Ramps for disabled.

J.W. BOYCE
(Mr Roger Morley)
Bush Pasture, Fordham, Ely, Cambridgeshire   CB7 5JU   map **7** S23
Telephone: (01638) 721158

Specialists in garden seeds for over 80 years. Specialising in the production of pansy seed and plants. Also over 1000 items of seed which includes a wide range of separate colours for cut flowers, bedding and drying. Also old and unusual vegetables. Seed list free on request: Telephone above number, or write to J. W. Boyce, Bush Pasture, Carter Street, Ely, Cambs CB7 5JU.

BURNCOOSE NURSERIES AND GARDEN
(C H Williams)
Gwennap, Redruth, Cornwall   TR16 6BJ   map **2** W12   ♿
Telephone: (01209) 861112
Fax: (01209) 860011

The Nurseries are set in the 30-acre woodland gardens of Burncoose. Some 12 acres are laid out for nursery stock production of over 2000 varieties of ornamental trees, shrubs and herbaceous plants. Specialities include camellias, azaleas, magnolias, rhododendrons and conservatory plants. The nurseries are widely known for rarities, and for unusual plants. Full mail order catalogue £1 (posted).
Location: 2 m SE of Redruth on the main A393 Redruth to Falmouth road between the villages of Lanner and Ponsanooth.
Station(s): Redruth.
Open: Mon-Sat 9-5 Sun 11-5 Gardens and tea-rooms open all year.
Admission: Nurseries free Gardens £1.
Refreshments: Light refreshments in tea-rooms.

THE COTTAGE HERBERY

(Mrs Kim Hurst)
Mill House, Boraston, Nr. Tenbury Wells   WR15 8LZ
Telephone: (0158 479) 575

Large collection of herbs, aromatics, scented foliage and cottage garden plants.

DEACONS NURSERY (H.H.)

(Grahame and Brian Deacon - Partners)
Moor View, Godshill, Isle of Wight   PO38 3HW   map 5 V20
Telephone: (01983) 840750/(01983) 522243. (24 hours (01983) 840750)
Fax: (01983) 522243

Specialist national fruit tree growers. Trees and bushes sent anywhere so send NOW for FREE catalogue. Over 250 varieties of apples on various types of rootstocks from M27 (4ft), M26 (8ft), to M25 (18ft). Plus Pears, Peaches, Nectarines, Plums, Gages, Cherry, soft fruits and an unusual selection of Family Trees. Many special offers. Catalogue always available, 30p stamp please. Many varieties of grapes, dessert and wine, plus hybrid hops and nuts of all types.

Location: Godshill - a picturesque village visited by all. Deacons Nursery is in Moor View off School Crescent (behind the only school).
Open: Summer Mon-Fri 8-4 winter Mon-Fri 8-5 Sat 8-1.

FAMILY TREES

PO Box 3, Botley, Hampshire   SO32 2HQ   map 5 V20
Telephone: (01329) 834812

Fruit for the connossieur in wide variety. Trained tree specialists; also standard and extra large Ornamental trees and old roses; hedgerow and woodland trees. Free mail order catalogues (and nursery location) from Family Trees, PO Box 3, Botley, Hampshire SO3 2EA.

Location: See map in free catalogue.
Station(s): Botley 2½ m.
Open: Mid Oct-mid Apr Wed and Sat 9.30-12.30.
Admission: No charge. Minimum order £35 overseas £300.

G. REUTHE LTD

(C. Tomlin & Mrs P. Kindley)
Crown Point Nursery, Sevenoaks Rd, Ightham, Nr. Sevenoaks, Kent   TN15 OHB
Telephone: Reg. Office: Starborough Nursery (01732) 865614

Rhododendron and Azalea Specialists including many unusual and specie rhododendrons.

HADDONSTONE SHOW GARDEN

The Forge House, Church Lane, East Haddon, Northampton   NN6 8DB
map **14** S20 &
Telephone: (01604) 770711
Fax: (01604) 770027

See Haddonstone's classic garden ornaments in the beautiful setting of the walled manor gardens - including urns, troughs, fountains, statuary, bird baths, sundials and balustrading. Featured on BBC Gardeners World, the garden is on different levels with shrub roses, ground cover plants, conifers, clematis and climbers.

Location: 7 miles NW of Northampton off A428.
Open: Mon-Fri 9-5.30 closed weekends, Bank Holidays and Christmas period.
Admission: Free.
Groups must apply in writing for permission to visit.

THE HERB AND HEATHER CENTRE

West Haddlesey, Nr. Selby, North Yorkshire   YO8 8QA
Telephone: (01757) 228279

The nursery has herb, heather and conifer display gardens, and specialises in herbs and heathers.

THE HERB FARM AND SAXON MAZE

Sonning Common, Reading   RG4 9NJ   map 12 T21
Telephone: (01734) 724220

Specialist herb nursery with herb garden filled with culinary, medical and aromatic plants. Restored 18th century timber frame barn houses, a unique shop filled with all manner af things herbal (from toothpastes to table mats)! Also visit the Saxon maze, a Beech hedge maze planted in 1991. An intriguing puzzle for all the family.

Location: 4 m N of Reading on B481.
Station(s): Reading.
Open: Every day except Mon 10-5 also open on Bank Hol Mons.
Admission: Free. 60p for maze. Parties by arrangement.
Refreshments: Coffee shop.

JUNGLE GIANTS BAMBOO NURSERY

(Michael John Brisbane)
Plough Farm, Wigmore, Nr. Leominster, Herefordshire   HR6 9UW &
Telephone: (01568) 86708

LANGLEY BOXWOOD NURSERY

(Mrs Elizabeth Braimbridge)
Rake, Nr Liss, Hampshire   GU33 7JL   map 12 U21 &
Telephone: (01730) 894467
Fax: (01730) 894703

This small nursery in a beautiful setting specialises in box-growing, offering a chance to see together a unique range of old and new varieties, hedging, topiary, specimens and rarities. Some taxus also. Descriptive list available (4 x 1st class stamps).

Location: On B2070 (old A3) 3 m S of Liphook.
Open: Notify by telephone first.

MILLAIS NURSERIES

(David Millais)
Crosswater Farm, Churt, Farnham, Surrey   GU10 2JN   map 12 U21
Telephone: (01252) 792698
Fax: (01252) 792526

Growers of one of the finest ranges of Rhododendrons and Azaleas in the country, including many rare species from the Himalayas, and a good selection of new American hybrids. Specialist advice. Mail Order Catalogue available £1 (please send 4x1st class stamps). Display garden also open (see Crosswater Farm).

Location: Farnham/Haslemere 6 m. From A287 turn E into Jumps Road ½ m N of Churt village centre. After ¼ m, turn into Crosswater Lane, and follow Nursery signs.
Open: Tues-Fri 10-5. Sats in Oct Nov Mar Apr, and daily in May.

PERHILL NURSERIES

(Baker Straw Partnership)
Worcester Road, Great Witley, Worcestershire   WR6 6JT   map 14 S18 &
Telephone: (01299) 896329
Fax: (01299) 896990

Specialist growers of 2,500 varieties of alpines, herbs and border perennials. Many rare and unusual. Specialities include penstemons, salvias, osteospermums, dianthus, alpine phlox, alliums, campanulas, thymes, helianthemums, diascias, lavenders, artemesias, digitals and scented geraniums.

Location: 10 m NW of Worcester on main Tenbury Wells Road (A443).
Open: Every day Feb 1-Oct 15 9-6 closed Oct 16-Jan 31 except by appointment.

PERRYHILL NURSERIES

(Mrs S M Gemmell)
Hartfield, East Sussex   TN7 4JP   map 12 U23
Telephone: (01892) 770377
Fax: (01892) 770929

The Plant Centre for the discerning gardener, with the widest range of plants in the South East of England. Old fashioned and shrub roses a speciality, also herbaceous plants. Trees, shrubs, rhododendrons, alpines, fruit trees and bushes, bedding plants in season. No mail order. Catalogues £1.65 inc. postage.

Location: 1 m N of Hartfield on B2026.
Open: Mar-Oct 9-5 Nov-Feb 9-4.30 seven days a week.

SAMARÈS HERBS-A-PLENTY

(Richard Adams)
Samarès Manor, St. Clement, Jersey   JE2 6QW   map **3** Y18   ⛬ △
Telephone: (01534) 870551
Fax: (01534) 68949

Specialist Herb and Hardy Perennial Nursery situated in the grounds of Samarès Manor. Extensive range of culinary, fragrant and medicinal herbs including many variegated and ornamental forms. Specialist range of hardy perennials including plants for shade, ground cover and wet conditions. Availability list on request. Herb shop, craft centre, farm animals, herb gardens, tours of Manor.

Location: 2 m E of St. Helier on the St. Clements Inner Road.
Open: Daily 10-5 Apr-Oct.
Admission: Charge for gardens. No charge for Nursery.
Refreshments: Tea garden and restaurant.
Accommodation: Self-catering holiday flats available.

SEAFORDE NURSERY AND BUTTERFLY HOUSE

(Patrick Forde)
Seaforde, Downpatrick, Down   map **16** O11   ⛬
Telephone: (01396) 811225
Fax: (01396) 811370

Over 600 trees and shrubs, container grown. Many Camellias and Rhododendrons. National collections of E. ucryphius. Tropical Butterfly House with hundreds of free flying butterflies. Also open beautiful gardens and maze.

Location: On A24 Ballynahinch to Newcastle Road.

Open: Easter to end Sept: Mon to Sat 10-5; Sun 2-6. Nursery only: Sept to Easter, 10-5.
Refreshments: Tea rooms.

STAPELEY WATER GARDENS

Stapeley, Nantwich, Cheshire   map **6** Q17
Telephone: (01270) 628628
Location: 1 m S of Nantwich on the A51 to Stone, signposted from Jct 16 on the M6.

TREHANE CAMELLIA NURSERY

(Miss Jennifer Trehane)
Stapehill Road, Hampreston, Nr. Wimborne, Dorset   BH21 7NE
Telephone: (01202) 873490
Fax: (01202) 873490

Britain's leading Camellia Specialists.

WAITHMAN NURSERIES

(Reginald Kaye Ltd)
Lindeth Road, Silverdale Carnforth, Lancashire LA5 0TY
Telephone: (01524) 701252

'Plant Hunters Paradise in Silverdale.' Specialists in Meconopsis, Hellebores, Orientalisis sees strains, hardy ferns. Large range of unusual alpines, herbaceous, shrubs, climbers. -Visitors welcome.

Location: 4m W of Carnforth, A6 (Jct 35 M6) Siton Lindeth Rd, Silverdale.
Open: Tues-Sat 10-5, Sun 2-5 March-Aug.

Lancelot 'Capability' Brown

Born 1716 in Northumberland, Capability Brown began work at the age of 16 in the vegetable gardens of Sir William and Lady Loraine at Kirharle Tower. He left Northumberland in 1739, and records show that he worked at Stowe until 1749. It was at Stowe that Brown began to study architecture, and to submit his own plans. It was also at Stowe that he devised a new method of moving and replanting mature trees.

Brown married Bridget Wayet in 1744 and began work on the estate at Warwick Castle in 1749. He was appointed Master Gardener at Hampton Court in 1764, and planted the Great Vine at Hampton Court in 1768. Blenheim Palace designs are considered amongst Brown's finest work, and the technical achievements were outstanding even for the present day.

Capability Brown died in February 1783 of a massive heart attack. A monument beside the lake at Croome Court was erected which reads "To the memory of Lancelot Brown, who by the powers of his inimitable and creative genius formed this garden scene out of a morass". There is also a portrait of Brown at Burghley.

Capability Brown was involved in the design of grounds at the following properties included in Historic Houses Castles and Gardens:

Audley End	*Claremont*	*Petworth House*
Berrington Hall	*Chillington Hall*	*Sledmere House*
Bowood	*Corsham Court*	*Stowe (Stowe School)*
Burghley House	*Fawley Court*	*Syon House*
Burton Constable	*Highclere Castle*	*Warwick Castle*
Charlecote Park	*Longleat*	*Weston Park*
Chilham Castle Gardens (reputed)	*Luton Hoo*	*Wimpole Hall*
Clandon Park	*Moccas Court*	*Wrest Park and Gardens*

Supplementary List of Properties
Open by Appointment Only

The list of houses in England, Scotland and Wales printed here are those which are usually open 'by appointment only' with the owner, or open infrequently during the summer months. These are in addition to the Houses and Gardens which are open regularly and are fully classified. Where it is necessary to write for and appointment to view, see code (WA), *denoted owner/address if this is different from the property addresses.

The majority of these properties have received a grant for conservation from the government given on the advice fo the Historic Buildings Councils. Public buildings, almshouses, tithe barn, business premises in receipt of grants are not usually included, neither are properies where the architectural features can be viewed from the street.

AVON

BIRDCOMBE COURT
(Mr.& Mrs. P.C. Sapsed WA)
Wraxall, Bristol, Avon

EASTWOOD MANOR FARM
(Mr A.J. Gay)
East Harptree

PARTIS COLLEGE
(The Bursar (WA)
Newbridge Hill, Bath   BA1 3QD
Telephone: (01225) 421532

THE REFECTORY
(Rev. R Salmon)
The Vicarage
Telephone: (01934) 833126

WOODSPRING PRIORY
(WA)
Kewstoke, Weston-Super-Mare
*The Landmark Trust, Shottesbrooke, nr. Maidenhead, Berks SL6 3SW.

BEDFORDSHIRE

THE TEMPLE
(The Estate Office (WA)
Biggleswade

WARDEN ABBEY
(WA)
nr. Biggleswade
*The Landmark Trust, Shottesbrooke, nr. Maidenhead, Berks SL6 3SW

BERKSHIRE

HIGH CHIMNEYS
(Mr & Mrs S. Cheetham (WA)
Hurst, Reading
Telephone: (01734) 34517

ST. GABRIEL'S SCHOOL
(The Headmaster)
Sandleford Priory, Newbury
Telephone: (01635) 40663

BUCKINGHAMSHIRE

BISHAM ABBEY
(The Director)
Marlow
Telephone: (016284) 76911

BRUDENELL HOUSE
(Dr H. Beric Wright (WA)
Quainton, Aylesbury   HP22 4AW

CHURCH OF THE ASSUMPTION
(Friends of Friendless Churches)
Hardmead, Newport Pagnell
Telephone: (01234) 39257
For key apply to H. Tranter, Manor Cottage, Hardmead, by letter or phone (0234) 39257.

IVER GROVE
(Mr & Mrs T. Stoppard (WA)
Shreding Green, Iver

REPTON'S SUBWAY FACADE
(WA)
Digby's Walk, Gayhurst
Telephone: (01908) 551564
*Mr. J.H. Beverly, The Bath House, Gayhurst.

CAMBRIDGESHIRE

THE CHANTRY
(Mrs T.A.N. Bristol (WA)
Ely, Cambridge

THE CHURCH OF ST JOHN THE BAPTIST
(Friends of Friendless Churches)
Papworth St. Agnes
For key apply to Mrs. P. Honeybane, Passhouse Cottage, Papworth St. Agnes, Camb. by letter or phone (01480) 830631

THE KING'S SCHOOL, ELY
(WA)
Ely   CB7 4DB
Telephone: (01353) 662837
Fax: (01353) 662187
Bursars Office, The King's School, Ely.

LEVERINGTON HALL
(Professor A. Barton (WA)
Wisbech   PE13 5DE

THE LYNCH LODGE
(WA)
Alwalton, Peterborough
*The Landmark Trust, Shottesbrooke, nr. Maidenhead, Berks SL6 3SW.

CHESHIRE

BEWSEY OLD HALL
(The Administrator (WA)
Warrington

CROWN HOTEL
(Prop. P.J. Martin)
High Street, Nantwich   CW5 5AS
Telephone: (01270) 625283
Fax: (01270) 628047

CHARLES ROE HOUSE
(McMillan Group Plc (WA)
Chestergate, Macclesfield   SK11 6DZ

SHOTWICK HALL
(Tenants: Mr & Mrs G.A.T. Holland)
Shotwick
Telephone: (01244) 881717
*Mr.R.B. Gardner, Wychen, 17 St. Marys Road, Leatherhead Surrey. By appointment only with the tenants Mr and Mrs G.A.T. Holland

TUDOR HOUSE
Lower Bridge Street, Chester
Telephone: (01244) 20095

WATERGATE HOUSE
(WA)
Chester
Telephone: (01352) 713353
*Ferry Homes Ltd. 49 High St. Holywell, Clwyd CH8 9TF.

CLEVELAND

ST CUTHBERT'S CHURCH & TURNER MAUSOLEUM
(Kirkleatham Parochial Church Council)
Kirkleatham
Telephone: (01642) 475198 Mrs R.S. Ramsdale (01642) 485395 Mrs. D. Cook, Church Warden.

CORNWALL

THE COLLEGE
(WA)
Week St Mary
*The Landmark Trust, Shottesbrooke, nr. Maidenhead, Berks SL6 3SW.

TOWN HALL
(Camelford Town Trust)
Camelford

TRECARREL MANOR
(Mr N.H. Burden)
Trebullett, Launceston
Telephone: (01566) 82286

CUMBRIA

COOP HOUSE
(WA)
Netherby
*The Landmark Trust, Shottesbrooke, nr. Maidenhead, Berks SL6 3SW.

PRESTON PATRICK HALL
(Mrs J.D. Armitage (WA)
Milnthorpe   LA7 7NY
Telephone: (0153) 956 7200
Fax: (015395) 67200

WHITEHALL
(WA)
Mealsgate, Carlisle   CA5 1JS
*Mrs. S. Parkin-Moore 40 Woodsome Road,
London NW5 1RZ

DERBYSHIRE

ELVASTON CASTLE
(Derbyshire County Council)
nr. Derby   DE72 3EP
Telephone: (01332) 571342

10 NORTH STREET
(WA)
Cromford
*The Landmark Trust, Shottesbrooke, nr.
Maidenhead, Berks SL6 3SW.

SWARKESTONE PAVILION
(WA)
Ticknall
*The Landmark Trust, Shottesbrooke, nr.
Maidenhead, Berks SL6 3SW.

DEVON

BINDON MANOR
(Sir John & Lady Loveridge WA)
Axmouth

BOWRINGSLEIGH
(Mr & Mrs M.C. Manisty (WA)
Kingbridge

ENDSLEIGH HOUSE
(Endsleigh Fishing Club Ltd)
Milton Abbot, nr. Tavistock
Telephone: (01822) 870248
Fax: (01822) 870502

HARESTON HOUSE
(Mrs K.M. Basset)
Brixton   PL8 2DL
Telephone: (01752) 880426

THE LIBRARY
(WA)
Stevenstone, Torrington
*The Landmark Trust, Shottesbrooke, nr.
Maidenhead, Berks SL6 3SW.

SANDERS
(WA)
Lettaford, North Bovey
*The Landmark Trust, Shottesbrooke, nr.
Maidenhead, Berks SL6 3SW.

THE SHELL HOUSE
(Endsleigh Fishing Club Ltd)
Endsleigh, Milton Abbott
Telephone: (0182) 287248
Fax: (0182) 287502

SHUTE GATEHOUSE
(WA)
Shute Barton, nr. Axminster
*The Landmark Trust, Shottesbrooke, nr.
Maidenhead, Berks SL6 3SW.

TOWN HOUSE
(Tenant Mr & Mrs R.A.L. Hill)
Gittisham, Honiton
Telephone: (01404) 851041
*Mr. & Mrs. R.J.T. Marker.

WORTHAM MANOR
(WA)
Lifton
*The Landmark Trust, Shottesbrooke, nr.
Maidenhead, Berks SL6 3SW.

DORSET

BLOXWORTH HOUSE
(Mr T.A. Dulake (WA)
Bloxworth

CLENSTON MANOR
Winterborne, Clenston, Blandford Forum

HIGHER MELCOMBE
(Mr M.C. Woodhouse (WA)
Dorchester   DT2 7PB

MOIGNES COURT
(Mr A.M. Cree (WA)
Owermoigne

SMEDMORE HOUSE
Kimmeridge, Dorset   BH20 5PG

STAFFORD HOUSE
(Mr & Mrs Richard Pavitt)
West Stafford, Dorchester, Dorset
Telephone: (01305) 263668

WOODSFORD CASTLE
(WA)
Woodsford, Nr Dorchester
*The Landmark Trust, Shottesbrooke, nr.
Maidenhead, Berks SL6 3SW.

COUNTY DURHAM

THE BUILDINGS IN THE SQUARE
(Lady Gilbertson (WA)
1 The Square, Greta Bridge   DL12 9SD
Telephone: (01833) 27276

ESSEX

**BLAKE HALL, BATTLE OF BRITAIN
MUSEUM & GARDENS**
(Mr R. Capel Cure, owner)
Chipping Ongar   CM5 0DG
Telephone: (01277) 362502

**CHURCH OF ST ANDREWS AND
MONKS TITHE BARN**
(Harlow District Council)
Harlow Study & Visitors Centre, Netteswellbury Farm,
Harlow   CM18 6BW
Telephone: (01279) 446745
Fax: (01279) 421945

GRANGE FARM
(Mr J. Kirby)
Little Dunmow   CM6 3HY
Telephone: (01371) 820205

GREAT PRIORY FARM
(Miss L. Tabor)
Panfield, Braintree   CM7 5BQ
Telephone: (01376) 550944

THE GUILDHALL
(Dr & Mrs Paul Sauven)
Great Waltham
Telephone: (01245) 360527

OLD ALL SAINTS
(Mr R. Mill)
Old Church Hill, Langdon Hills   SS16 6HZ
Telephone: (01268) 414146

RAINHAM HALL
(The National Trust: tenant Mr D. Atack
Rainham

RAYNE HALL
(Mr & Mrs R.J. Pertwee (WA)
Rayne, Braintree

THE ROUND HOUSE
(Mr M.E.W. Heap)
Havering-atte-Bower, Romford   RM4 1QH
Telephone: (01708) 728136

GLOUCESTERSHIRE

ABBEY GATEHOUSE
(WA)
Tewksbury
*The Landmark Trust, Shottesbrooke, nr.
Maidenhead, Berks SL6 3SW.

ASHLEWORTH COURT
(Mr H.J. Chamberlayne)
Gloucester
Telephone: (01452) 700241

ASHLEWORTH MANOR
(Dr & Mrs Jeremy Barnes (WA)
Ashleworth, Gloucester   GL19 4LA
Telephone: (01452) 700350

BEARLAND HOUSE
(The Administrator (WA)
Longsmith Street, Gloucester   GL1 2HL
Fax: (01452) 419312

CASTLE GODWYN
(Mr & Mrs J. Milne (WA)
Painswick

CHACELEY HALL
(Mr W.H. Lane)
Tewkesbury
Telephone: (01452) 28205

CHELTENHAM COLLEGE
(The Bursar)
The College, Bath Road, Cheltenham   GL53 7LD
Telephone: (01242) 513540

THE COTTAGE
(Mrs S.M. Rolt (WA)
Stanley Pontlarge, Winchcombe   GL54 5HD

EAST BANQUETING HOUSE
(WA)
Chipping Camden
*The Landmark Trust, Shottesbrooke, nr.
Maidenhead, Berks SL6 3SW.

FRAMPTON COURT 1730 & GOTHIC
Orangery 1750 (WA)
(Frampton Court Estate)
Frampton-on-Severn, Gloucester   GL2 7EU
Telephone: (01452) 740267 (home) or (01452) 740698
(office)
*Apply to Mrs. Clifford (0452) 740267 home
(0452) 740698 office.

**MINCHINHAMPTON MARKET
HOUSE**
(Mr B.E. Lucas)
Stroud
Telephone: (01453) 883241

THE OLD VICARAGE
('Lord Weymyss' Trust)
The Church, Stanway
Telephone: (01386) 584469

*Apply to Stanway House, Stanway, Cheltenham

ST MARGARET'S CHURCH
(The Gloucester Charities Trust)
London Road, Gloucester
Telephone: (01452) 23316

By appointment with the Warden. Tel: (01831) 470335

TYNDALE MONUMENT
(Tyndale Monument Charity)
North Nibley　GL11 4JA
Telephone: (01453) 543691

Keys available as per notice at foot of Wood Lane.

GREATER MANCHESTER

CHETHAM'S HOSPITAL AND LIBRARY
(The Feoffees of Chetham's Hospital & Library)
Manchester　MS 1SB
Telephone: 0161-834 9644
Fax: 0161-839 5797

SLADE HALL
(Manchester & District Housing Assn. (WA)
Slade Lane, Manchester　M13 0QP

HAMPSHIRE

CHESIL THEATRE (FORMERLY 12TH CENTURY CHURCH OF ST PETER CHESIL)
(Winchester Dramatic Society)
Chesil Street, Winchester, SO23 0HU
Telephone: (01962) 867086

THE DEANERY
(The Dean & Chapter)
The Close, Winchester　SO23 9LS
Telephone: (01962) 853137
Fax: (01962) 841519

HOUGHTON LODGE GARDENS
(Captain & Mrs M.W. Busk)
Stockbridge　SO20 6LQ
Telephone: (01264) 810177/(01264) 810502
Fax: (01264) 388072

MANOR FARM HOUSE
(Mr S.B. Mason)
Hambledon
Telephone: (01705) 632433

MOYLES COURT
(Headmaster, Moyles Court School (WA)
Moyles Court, Ringwood　BH24 3NF
Telephone: (01425) 472856

HEREFORD & WORCESTER

BRITANNIA HOUSE
(The Alice Ottley School)
The Tything, Worcester

Apply to the Headmistress.

CHURCH HOUSE
(The Trustees)
Market Square, Evesham

GRAFTON MANOR
(Mr J.W. Morris, Lord of Grafton)
Bromsgrove
Telephone: (01527) 31525

NEWHOUSE FARM
(The Administrator (WA)
Goodrich, Ross-on-Wye

THE OLD PALACE
(The Dean & Chapter of Worcester (WA)
Worcester

Apply to Diocesan Secretary.

SHELWICK COURT
(WA)
Hereford

*The Landmark Trust, Shottesbrooke, nr. Maidenhead, Berks. SL6 3SW.

HERTFORDSHIRE

HEATH MOUNT SCHOOL
(The Abel Smith Trustees)
Woodhall Park, Watton-at-Stone, Hertford SG14 3NG
Telephone: (01920) 830286
Fax: (01920) 830357

NORTHAW PLACE
(The Administrator)
Northaw
Telephone: (01707) 44059

KENT

BARMING PLACE
(Mr J. Peter & Dr. Rosalind Bearcroft)
Maidstone
Telephone: (01622) 727844

BEDGEBURY NATIONAL PINETUM
(Foresty Enterprise)
nr Goudhurst　map 3 U23
Telephone: (01580) 211044
Fax: (01580) 212523

FOORD ALMSHOUSES
(The Clerk to the Trustees (WA)
Rochester

MERSHAM-LE-HATCH
(The Hon. M.J. Knatchbull)
nr. Ashford　TN25 5NH
Telephone: (01233) 503954
Fax: (01233) 611650

Apply to tenant - The Directors, Caldecott Community.

NURSTEAD COURT
(Mrs S.M.H. Edmeades-Stearns)
Meopham
Telephone: (01474) 812121

OLD COLLEGE OF ALL SAINTS
Kent Music Centre, Maidstone
Telephone: (01622) 690404

Apply to Regional Director.

THE OLD PHARMACY
(Mrs Peggy Noreen Kerr)
6 Market Place, Faversham　ME13 7EH

PROSPECT TOWER
(WA)
Belmont Park, Faversham

*The Landmark Trust, Shottesbrooke, nr. Maidenhead, Berks SL6 3SW.

YALDHAM MANOR
(Mr & Mrs J. Mourier Lade (WA)
Kemsing, Sevenoaks　TN15 6NN
Telephone: (01732) 761029

LANCASHIRE

THE MUSIC ROOM
(WA)
Lancaster

*The Landmark Trust, Shottesbrooke, nr. Maidenhead, Berks SL6 3SW.

PARROX HALL (WA)
(Mr & Mrs H.D.H. Elletson (WA)
Parrox Hall, Preesall, nr. Poulton-le-Fylde　FY6 ONW
Telephone: (01253) 810245
Fax: (01253) 811223

LEICESTERSHIRE

LAUNDE ABBEY
(The Rev. Graham Johnson)
East Norton

THE MOAT HOUSE
(Mrs H.S. Hall)
Appleby Magna
Telephone: (01530) 270301

OLD GRAMMAR SCHOOL
Market Harborough
Telephone: (01858) 462202

*The Market Harborough Exhibition Foundation, 18 Springfield Street, Market Harborough, LE16 8BD

STAUNTON HAROLD HALL
(Ryder-Cheshire Foundation)
Ashby-de-la-Zouch
Telephone: (01332) 862798

LINCOLNSHIRE

BEDE HOUSES
Tattershall

THE CHATEAU
(WA)
Gate Burton, Gainsborough

*The Landmark Trust, Shottesbrooke, nr. Maidenhead, Berks SL6 3SW.

EAST LIGHTHOUSE
(Cdr. M.D. Joel RN (WA)
Sutton Bridge, Spalding　PE12 9YT

FULBECK MANOR
(Mr J.F. Fane (WA)
Grantham　NG32 3JN
Telephone: (01400) 272231

HARLAXTON MANOR
(University of Evansville (WA)
Grantham

HOUSE OF CORRECTION
(WA)
Folkingham

*The Landmark Trust, Shottesbrooke, nr. Maidenhead, Berks SL6 3SW.

THE NORMAN MANOR HOUSE
(Lady Netherthorpe (WA)
Boothby Pagnell

PELHAM MAUSOLEUM
(The Earl of Yarborough)
Limber, Grimsby

SCRIVELSBY COURT
(Lt. Col. J.L.M. Dymoke MBE.,DL (WA)
Scrivelsby Court, Nr. Horncastle   LN9 6JA
Telephone: (01507) 523325

LONDON

ALL HALLOWS VICARAGE
(Rev. R. Pearson)
Tottenham, London   N17

69 BRICK LANE
(The Administrator (WA)
London   E1

24 THE BUTTS, 192,194,196,198,202,204-224 CABLE STREET
(Mrs Sally Mills (WA)
London

11-13 CAVENDISH SQUARE
(Heythrop College (WA)
London

CELIA AND PHILLIP BLAIRMAN HOUSES
(The Administrator (WA)
Elder Street, London   E1

CHARLTON HOUSE
(London Borough of Greenwich (WA)
Charlton Road, Charlton, London   SE7 8RE
Telephone: 0181-856 3951

CHARTERHOUSE
(The Governors of Sutton Hospital (WA)
Charterhouse Square, London   EC1

17/27 FOLGATE STREET
(WA)
London   E1

36 HANBURY STREET
(WA)
London   E1

HEATHGATE HOUSE
(Rev Mother Prioress, Ursuline Convent)
66 Crooms Hill, Greenwich, London   SE10 8HG
Telephone: 0181-858 0779

140,142,166,168 HOMERTON HIGH STREET
(WA)
London   E5

HOUSE OF ST BARNABAS-IN-SOHO
(The Warden of the House (WA)
1 Greek Street, Soho, London   W1V 6NQ
Telephone: 0171-437 1894

KENSAL GREEN CEMETERY
(General Cemetery Company)
Harrow Road, London   W10 4RA
Telephone: 0181-969 0152
Fax: 0181-960 9744

69/83 PARAGON ROAD
(WA)
London   E5

RED HOUSE
(Mr & Mrs Hollamby) (WA)
Red House Lane, Bexleyheath

SUNBURY COURT
(The Salvation Army)
Sudbury-on-Thames
Telephone: (01932) 782196

88/190 THE CRESCENT
(WA)
Hertford Road, London   N9

VALE MASCAL BATH HOUSE
(Mrs F. Chu)
112 North Cray Road, Bexley   DA5 3NA
Telephone: (01322) 554894

WESLEY'S HOUSE
(The Trustees of Methodist Church)
47 City Road, London   EC1Y 1AU
Telephone: 0171-253 2262
Fax: 0171-608 3825

MERSEYSIDE

THE TURNER HOME
(Mr R.A. Waring RGN.,CGN)
Dingle Head, Liverpool
Telephone: 0151-727 4177

NORFOLK

ALL SAINTS' CHURCH
(Norfolk Churches Trust)
Barmer
Keyholder - No 5 The Cottages.

ALL SAINTS' CHURCH
(Norfolk Churches Trust)
Cockthorpe
Keyholder - Mrs. Case at farmhouse.

ALL SAINTS' CHURCH
(Norfolk Churches Trust)
Dunton
Key of Tower at Hall Farm.

ALL SAINTS' CHURCH
(Norfolk Churches Trust)
Frenze
Keyholder - Mrs. Alston at farmhouse.

ALL SAINTS' CHURCH
(Norfolk Churches Trust)
Hargham
Keyholder - Mrs. Clifford, Amos, Station Road, Attleborough.

ALL SAINTS' CHURCH
(Rector, Churchwardens and PCC)
Weston Longville   NR9 5JU
Key holder - Rev. J P P Illingworth.

ALL SAINTS' CHURCH
(Norfolk Churches Trust)
Snetterton
Keyholder - at Hall Farm.

BILLINGFORD MILL
(Norfolk County Council)
Scole

6 THE CLOSE
(The Dean & Chapter of Norwich Cathedral (WA)
Norwich

FISHERMEN'S HOSPITAL
(J.E.C. Lamb FIH Clerk to the Trustees)
Great Yarmouth
Telephone: (01493) 856609

GOWTHORPE MANOR (WA)
(Mrs Watkinson)
Swardeston   NR14 8DS
Telephone: (01508) 570216

HALES HALL
(Mr & Mrs T. Read (WA)
London   NR14 6QW
Telephone: (0150) 846395

HOVETON HOUSE
(Sir John Blofeld)
Wroxham, Norwich   NR12 8JE

LATTICE HOUSE
(Mr & Mrs T. Duckett (WA)
King's Lynn
Telephone: (01553) 777292

LITTLE CRESSINGHAM MILL
(Norfolk mills and Pumps Trust)
Little Cressingham, Thetford, Norfolk
Telephone: (01953) 850567

LITTLE HAUTBOIS HALL (WA)
(Mrs Duffield)
nr Norwich   NR12 7JR
Telephone: (01603) 279333
Fax: (01603) 279615

THE MUSIC HOUSE
(The Warden)
Wensum Lodge, King Street, Norwich
Telephone: (01603) 666021/2
Fax: (01603) 765633

NORWICH CATHEDRAL CLOSE
(WA)
Norwich
3,4,27,31,32,34,35,40,The Close. Contact Cathedral Steward's Office Messrs. Percy Howes & Co. 3 The Close, Norwich.

THE OLD PRINCES INN RESTAURANT
20 Prince Street, Norwich
Telephone: (01603) 621043

THE OLD VICARAGE
(Mr & Mrs H.C. Dance)
Crown St. Methwold, Thetford, Norfolk   IP25 ANR

ST. ANDREW'S CHURCH
(Norfolk Churches Trust)
Frenze
Keyholder - Mrs. Alston at farmhouse opposite.

ST. CELIA'S CHURCH
West Bilney
Keyholder - Mr Curl, Tanglewood, Main Road, West Bilney

ST. MARGARET'S CHURCH
(Norfolk Churches Trust)
Morton-on-the-Hill   NR9 5JS
Keyholder - Lady Prince-Smith at The Hall.

ST. MARY'S CHURCH
(Norfolk Churches Trust)
Dunton

ST. PETER'S CHURCH
(Norfolk Churches Trust)
The Lodge, Millgate, Aylsham   NR11 6HX
Keyholder - Lord & Lady Romney, Wesnum Farm or Mrs. Walker Pockthorpe Cottages.

STRACEY ARMS MILL
(Norfolk County Council)
nr Acle
Telephone: (01603) 611122 ext 5224

THE STRANGERS' CLUB
22,24 Elm Hill, Norwich
Telephone: (01603) 623813

THORESBY COLLEGE
(King's Lynn Preservation Trust (WA)
Queen Street, King's Lynn   PE30 1HX

WIVETON HALL
(D. MacCarthy (WA)
Holt

NORTHAMPTONSHIRE

COURTEENHALL
(Sir Hereward Wake Bt,M.C. (WA)
Northampton

DRAYTON HOUSE
(L.G. Stopford Sackville (WA)
Lowick, Kettering   NN14 3BG
Telephone: (01832) 732405

THE MONASTERY
(Mr & Mrs R.G. Wigley (WA)
Shutlanger   NN12 7RU
Telephone: (01604) 862529

PAINE'S COTTAGE
(Mr R.O. Barber (WA)
Oundle

WESTON HALL
(Mr & Mrs Francis Sitwell (WA)
Towcester

NORTHUMBERLAND

BRINKBURN MILL
(WA)
Rothbury
*The Landmark Trust, Shottesbrooke, nr. Maidenhead, Berks SL6 3SW.

CAUSEWAY HOUSE
(WA)
Bardon Mill

CRASTER TOWER
Col J.M. Craster, Miss M.D. Craster, Mr F. Sharratt (WA)
Alnwick

HARNHAM HALL
(Mr J. Wake)
Belsay

MORPETH CASTLE
(WA)
Morpeth
*The Landmark Trust, Shottesbrooke, nr. Maidenhead, Berks SL6 3SW.

NETHERWITTON HALL
(Mr J.C.R. Trevelyon (WA)
Morpeth   NE61 4NW
Telephone: (01670) 772219
Fax: (01670) 772332

NOTTINGHAMSHIRE

WINKBURN HALL
(Mr R. Craven-Smith-Milnes)
Newark   NG22 8PQ
Telephone: (01636) 636465
Fax: (01636) 636717

WORKSOP PRIORY CHURCH & GATEHOUSE
The Vicarage, Cheapside
Telephone: (01909) 472180

OXFORDSHIRE

26/7 CORNMARKET STREET AND 26 SHIP STREET
(Home Bursar)
Jesus College, Oxford
Shop basement by written appointment Laura Ashley Ltd. 150 Bath Rd. Maidenhead, Berks SL6 4YS.

HOPE HOUSE
(Mrs J. Hageman)
Woodstock

THE MANOR
(Mr & Mrs Paul L. Jaques (WA)
Chalgrove   OX44 7SL
Telephone: (01865) 890836
Fax: (01865) 891810

MONARCH'S COURT HOUSE
(Mr R.S. Hine (WA)
Benson

RIPON COLLEGE
(The Principal (WA)
Cuddesdon

30/43 THE CAUSEWAY
(Mr & Mrs R. Hornsby)
39/43 The Causeway, Steventon

SHROPSHIRE

BROMFIELD PRIORY GATEHOUSE
(WA)
Ludlow
Telephone: (01628) 825925
*The Landmark Trust, Shottesbrooke, nr. Maidenhead, Berks SL6 3SW.

HALSTON
(Mrs J.L. Harvey (WA)
Oswestry

HATTON GRANGE
(Mrs P. Afia (WA)
Shifnal

LANGLEY GATEHOUSE
(WA)
Acton Burnell
Telephone: (01628) 825925
*The Landmark Trust, Shottesbrooke, nr. Maidenhead, Berks SL6 3SW.

MORVILLE HALL
(The National Trust (tenant Mrs. J.K. Norbury (WA)
Bridgenorth   WV16 5NB

OAKLEY MANOR
(Shrewsbury & Atcham Borough Council)
Belle Vue Road, Shrewsbury   SY3 7NW
Telephone: (01243) 231456
Fax: (01243) 271598

ST. WINIFRED'S WELL
(WA)
Woolston, Oswestry
*The Landmark Trust, Shottesbrooke, nr. Maidenhead, Berks SL6 3SW.

STANWARDINE HALL
(P.J. Bridge)
Cockshutt, Ellesmere
Telephone: (01939) 270212

SOMERSET

COTHELSTONE MANOR AND GATEHOUSE
(Mrs J.E.B. Warmington (WA)
Cothelstone Manor, Cothelstone, nr Taunton   TA4 3DS
Telephone: (01823) 432200

FAIRFIELD
(Lady Gass)
Stogursey, Bridgwater   TA5 1PU
Telephone: (01278) 732251
Fax: (01278) 732277

GURNEY MANOR
(WA)
Cannington
Telephone: (01628) 825925
*The Landmark Trust, Shottesbrooke, nr. Maidenhead, Berks SL6 3SW.

THE OLD DRUG STORE
(Mr & Mrs E.J.D. Schofield (WA)
Axbridge

THE OLD HALL
(WA)
Croscombe
*The Landmark Trust, Shottesbrooke, nr. Maidenhead, Berks SL6 3SW.

THE PRIEST'S HOUSE
(WA)
Holcombe Rogus, nr. Wellington
*The Landmark Trust, Shottesbrooke, nr. Maidenhead, Berks SL6 3SW.

STOGURSEY CASTLE
(WA)
nr Bridgewater
*The Landmark Trust, Shottesbrooke, nr. Maidenhead, Berks SL6 3SW.

WEST COKER MANOR
(Mr & Mrs Derek Maclaren)
West Coker, Somerset   BA22 9BJ
Telephone: (01935 86) 2646

WHITELACKINGTON MANOR
(Mr E.J.H. Cameron)
Dillington Estate Office, Illminster   TA19 9EQ
Telephone: (01460) 54614

STAFFORDSHIRE

BROUGHTON HALL
(The Administrator) (WA)
Eccleshall

DUNWOOD HALL
(Dr. R. Vincent-Kemp FRSA)
Longsdon, Nr. Leek   ST9 9AR
Telephone: (01538) 385071

THE GREAT HALL IN KEELE HALL
(Registrar, University of Keele (WA)
Keele

INGESTRE PAVILION
(WA)
nr Stafford
*The Landmark Trust, Shottesbrooke, nr. Maidenhead, Berks SL6 3SW.

OLD HALL GATEHOUSE
(Mr R.M. Eades)
Mavesyn Ridware
Telephone: (01543) 490312

THE ORANGERY
(Mrs M. Philips)
Heath House, Tean, Stoke-on-Trent   ST10 4HA
Telephone: (01538) 722212

PARK HALL
(Mr E.J. Knobbs (WA)
Leigh

TIXALL GATEHOUSE
(WA)
Tixall, Nr Stafford
*The Landmark Trust, Shottesbrooke, nr. Maidenhead, Berks SL6 3SW.

SUFFOLK

THE DEANERY
(The Dean of Bocking)
Hadleigh IP7 5DT
Telephone: (01473) 822218

DITCHINGHAM HALL
(The Rt Hon Earl Ferrers)
Ditchingham, Bungay

THE HALL
(Mr & Mrs R.B. Cooper) (WA)
Great Bricett, Ipswich

HENGRAVE HALL CENTRE
(The Warden)
Bury St Edmunds IP28 6LZ
Telephone: (01284) 701561

MARTELLO TOWER
(WA)
Aldeburgh
*The Landmark Trust, Shottesbrooke, nr. Maidenhead, Berks SL6 3SW.

MOAT HALL
(Mr J.W. Gray)
Woodbridge IP13 9AE
Telephone: (01728) 746317

THE NEW INN
(WA)
Peasenhall
*The Landmark Trust, Shottesbrooke, nr. Maidenhead, Berks SL6 3SW.

NEWBOURNE HALL
(John Somerville Esq. (WA)
Woodbridge

WORLINGHAM HALL
(Viscount Colville of Culross (WA)
Beccles

SURREY

CROSSWAYS FARM
(Mr C.T. Hughes (tenant) (WA)
Abinger Hammer

GREAT FOSTERS HOTEL
(Mr J. E. Baumann (Manager)
Egham TW20 9UR
Telephone: (01784) 433822

ST. MARY'S HOMES CHAPEL
Church Lane, Godstone
Telephone: (01883) 742385

EAST SUSSEX

ASHDOWN HOUSE
(The Headmaster)
Ashdown House School, Forest Row RH18 5JY
Telephone: (01342) 822574
Fax: (01342) 824380

LAUGHTON TOWER
(WA)
Lewes
*The Landmark Trust, Shottesbrooke, nr. Maidenhead, Berks SL6 3SW.

WEST SUSSEX

CHANTRY GREEN HOUSE
(Mr & Mrs G.H. Recknell)
Steyning
Telephone: (01903) 812239

THE CHAPEL, BISHOP'S PALACE
(Church Commissioners)
The Palace, Chichester

CHRIST'S HOSPITAL
(WA)
Horsham
Telephone: (01403) 211293

NORTHUMBERLAND

CAPHEATON HALL
(Mr J. Browne-Swinburne (WA)
Newcastle upon Tyne NE19 2AB

WARWICKSHIRE

BATH HOUSE
(WA)
Walton, Stratford-on-Avon
*The Landmark Trust, Shottesbrooke, nr. Maidenhead, Berks SL6 3SW.

BINSWOOD HALL
(North Leamington School) (WA)
Binswood Avenue, Leamington Spa CV32 5SF
Telephone: (01926) 423686

FOXCOTE
(Mr C.B. Holman (WA)
Shipton-on-Stour

NICHOLAS CHAMBERLAIN'S ALMSHOUSES
(The Warden)
Bedworth
Telephone: (01203) 312225

NORTHGATE
(Mr R.E. Phillips) (WA)
Warwick CV34 4JL

ST. LEONARD'S CHURCH
(WA)
Wroxall
Mrs. J.M. Gowen, Headmistress, Wroxall Abbey School, Warwick CV35 7NB.

WAR MEMORIAL TOWN HALL
(The Secretary, Mr D.R. Young)
27 Henley St, Alcester B49 5QX
Telephone: (01789) 765198

WILTSHIRE

CHINESE SUMMERHOUSE
Amesbury Abbey, Amesbury
Telephone: (01980) 622957

FARLEY HOSPITAL
(The Warden)
Church Road, Farley SP5 1AH
Telephone: (01722) 712231

MILTON MANOR
(Mrs Rupert Gentle)
The Manor House, Milton Lilbourne, Pewsey SN9 5LQ
Telephone: (01672) 563344
Fax: (01672) 564136

OLD BISHOP'S PALACE
(The Bursar, Salisbury Cathedral School)
1 The Close, Salisbury
Telephone: (01722) 322652

THE OLD MANOR HOUSE
(Mr J. Teed) (WA)
2 Whitehead Lane, Bradford-on-Avon

ORPINS HOUSE
(Mr J. Vernon Burchell (WA)
Church Street, Bradford-on-Avon

THE PORCH HOUSE
(Mr Tim Vidal-Hall (WA)
6, High Street, Potterne, Devizes SN10 5NA

NORTH YORKSHIRE

BEAMSLEY HOSPITAL
(WA)
Skipton
*The Landmark Trust, Shottesbrooke, nr. Maidenhead, Berks SL6 3SW.

BROUGHTON HALL
(H.R. Tempest Esq.)
Skipton BD23 3AE
Telephone: (01756) 792267
Fax: (01756) 792362

BUSBY HALL
(Mr G.A. Marwood (WA)
Carlton-in-Cleveland

CALVERLEY OLD HALL
(WA)
Nr. Leeds
*The Landmark Trust, Shottesbrooke, nr. Maidenhead, Berks SL6 3SW.

CAWOOD CASTLE
(WA)
nr. Selby
*The Landmark Trust, Shottesbrooke, nr. Maidenhead, Berks SL6 3SW.

CHAPEL AND COACH HOUSE
Aske, Richmond

THE CHURCH OF OUR LADY AND SAINT EVERILDA
(WA)
Everingham
Telephone: (01430) 860531

THE CULLODEN TOWER
(WA)
Richmond
*The Landmark Trust, Shottesbrooke, nr. Maidenhead, Berks SL6 3SW.

THE DOVECOTE
(Mrs P. E. Heathcote)
Forcett Hall, Forcett, Richmond
Telephone: (01325) 718226

HOME FARM HOUSE
(Mr G. T. Reece (WA)
Old Scriven, Knaresborough

MOULTON HALL
(The National Trust (tenant Hon. J.D. Eccles) WA)
Richmond

THE OLD RECTORY
(Mrs R.F. Wormald (WA)
Foston, York

THE PIGSTY
(WA)
Robin Hood's Bay
*The Landmark Trust, Shottesbrooke, nr. Maidenhead, Berks SL6 3SW.

WEST YORKSHIRE

FULNECK BOYS' SCHOOL
(I.D. Cleland B.A. M.Phil Headmaster (WA)
Pudsey

GRAND THEATRE & OPERA HOUSE
(Warren Smith, General Manager)
46 New Briggate, Leeds LS1 6NZ
Telephone: (0113) 245 6014
Fax: (0113) 246 5906

HORBURY HALL
(D.J.H. Michelmore Esq.)
Horbury, Wakefield
Telephone: (01924) 277552

TOWN HALL
(Leeds City Council)
Leeds
Telephone: (0113) 2477989

WESTON HALL
(Lt. Col. H.V. Dawson (WA)
nr Otley LS21 2HP

WALES

CLWYD

FFERM
(Dr M.C. Jones-Mortimer)
Pontblyddyn, Mold CH7 4HN
Telephone: (01352) 770876

GATEHOUSE AT GILAR FARM
(Mr P.J. Warbourton-Lee (WA)
Pentrfoclas

GOLDEN GROVE
(N. R. & M. M. J. Steele-Mortimer(WA)
Llanasa, Nr Holywell, Clywd CH8 9NE
Telephone: (01745) 854452
Fax: (01745) 854547

HALGHTON HALL
(Mr J.D. Lewis (WA)
Bangor-on-Dee, Wrexham

LINDISFARNE COLLEGE
(The Headmaster (WA)
Wynnstay Hall, Ruabon
Telephone: (01978) 810407

PEN ISA'R GLASCOED
(Mr M.E. Harrop)
Bodelwyddan LL22 9DD
Telephone: (01745) 583501

PLAS UCHAF
(WA)
Llangar, Nr Corwen
*The Landmark Trust, Shottesbrooke, nr. Maidenhead, Berks SL6 3SW.

DYFED

MONKTON OLD HALL
(WA)
Pembroke
*The Landmark Trust, Shottesbrooke, nr. Maidenhead, Berks SL6 3SW.

TALIARIS PARK
(Mr J.H. Spencer-Williams (WA)
Llandeilo

UNIVERSITY OF WALES LAMPETER
(Prof. Keith Robbins)
Lampeter SA48 7ED
Telephone: (01570) 422351
Fax: (01570) 423423

WEST BLOCKHOUSE
(WA)
Haverfordwest, Dale
*The Landmark Trust, Shottesbrooke, nr. Maidenhead, Berks SL6 3SW.

SOUTH GLAMORGAN

FONMON CASTLE
(Sir Brooke Boothby Bt)
Fonmon Castle, Barry CF6 9ZN
Telephone: (01446) 710206
Fax: (01446) 711687

GWENT

BLACKBROOK MANOR
(Mr & Mrs A.C. de Morgan)
Skenfrith, nr. Abergavenny NP7 8UB
Telephone: (01600 84) 453
Fax: (01600 84) 453

CASTLE HILL HOUSE
(Mr T. Baxter-Wright (WA)
Monmouth

CLYTHA CASTLE
(WA)
Abergavenny
*The Landmark Trust, Shottesbrooke, nr. Maidenhead, Berks SL6 3SW.

GREAT CIL-LWCH
(Mr J.F. Ingledew (WA)
Llantilio Crossenny, Abergavenny NP7 8SR
Telephone: (01600) 780206

KEMYS HOUSE
(Mr I.S. Burge (WA)
Keyms Inferior, Caerleon

LLANVIHANGEL COURT
(Mrs D. Johnson (WA)
Abergavenny NP7 8DH

OVERMONNOW HOUSE
(Mr J.R. Pangbourne (WA)
Monmouth

3/4 PRIORY STREET
(Mr H.R. Ludwig)
Monmouth

TREOWEN
(John Wheelock)
Wonastow, Monmouth NP5 4DL
Telephone: (01600) 712031

GWYNEDD

THE BATH TOWER
(WA)
Caernarfon
*The Landmark Trust, Shottesbrooke, nr. Maidenhead, Berks SL6 3SW.

CYMRYD
(Miss D.E. Glynne (WA)
Cymryd, Conwy LL32 8UA

DOLAUGWYN
(Mrs S. Tudor WA)
Towyn

NANNAU
(Mr P. Vernon (WA)
Dolgellau

PENMYNYDD
(The Rector of Llanfairpwll (WA)
Alms Houses, Llanfairpwll

PLAS COCH
(Mrs N. Donald)
Llanedwen, Llanfairpwll
Telephone: (01248) 714272

POWYS

ABERCAMLAIS
(Mrs J.C.R. Ballance (WA)
Brecon

ABERCYNRIG
(Mrs W.R. Lloyd (WA)
Brecon

1 BUCKINGHAM PLACE
(Mrs Meeres (WA)
1 Buckingham Place, Brecon   LD3 7DL
Telephone: (01874) 623612

3 BUCKINGHAM PLACE
(Mr & Mrs A. Whiley (WA)
3 Buckingham Place, Brecon   LD3 7DL

MAESMAWR HALL HOTEL
(Mrs M. Pemberton, Mrs. I. Hunt)
Caersws
Telephone: (01686) 688255

NEWTON FARM
(Mrs Ballance (WA) to Mr. D.L. Evans, tenant)
Brecon

PEN Y LAN
(Mr J.G. Meade)
Meifod, Powys   SY22 6DA
Telephone: (01938) 500202

PLASAU DUON
(Mr E.S. Breese)
Clatter

POULTRY HOUSE
(WA)
Leighton, Welshpool
*The Landmark Trust, Shottesbrooke, nr. Maidenhead, Berks SL6 3SW.

RHYDYCARW
(Mr M. Breese-Davies)
Trefeglwys, Newtown   SY17 5PU
Telephone: (01686) 430411
Fax: (01686) 430331

YDDERW
(Mr D.P. Eckley (WA)
Llyswen

SCOTLAND

BORDERS

OLD GALA HOUSE
(Ettrick & Lauderdale District Council)
Galashiels
Telephone: (01750) 20096

SIR WALTER SCOTT'S COURTROOM
(Ettrick & Lauderdale District Council)
Selkirk
Telephone: (01750) 20096

WEDDERLIE HOUSE
(Mrs J.R.L. Campbell (WA)
Gordon   TD3 6NW
Telephone: (0157) 874 0223

DUMFRIES & GALLOWAY

BONSHAW TOWER
(Dr J.B. Irving) (WA)
Kirtlebridge, Lockerbie   DG11 3LY
Telephone: (01461) 500256

CARNSALLOCH HOUSE
(The Leonard Cheshire Foundation)
Carnsalloch, Kirkton   DG1 1SN
Telephone: (01387) 254924
Fax: (01387) 257971

KIRKCONNELL HOUSE
(Mr F. Maxwell Witham)
New Abbey, Dumfries
Telephone: (0138) 785-276

FIFE

BATH CASTLE
(Mr Angus Mitchell)
Bogside, Oakley   FK10 3RD
Telephone: 0131-556 7671

THE CASTLE
(Mr J. Bevan (WA)
Elie

CASTLE OF PARK
(WA)
Glenluce, Galloway
*The Landmark Trust, Shottesbrooke, nr. Maidenhead, Berks SL6 3SW.

CHARLETON HOUSE
(Baron St. Clair Bonde)
Colinsburgh
Telephone: (0133 334) 249

GRAMPIAN

BALBITHAN HOUSE
(Mr J. McMurtie)
Kintore
Telephone: (01467) 32282

BALFLUIG CASTLE
Mr Mark Tennant (WA)
Grampian
30 Abbey Gardens, London, Greater London, NW8 9AT.

BARRA CASTLE
(Dr & Mrs Andrew Bogdan (WA)
Old Meldrum

CASTLE OF FIDDES
(Dr M. Weir)
Stonehaven
Telephone: (01569) 740213

CHURCH OF THE HOLY RUDE
St John Street, Stirling

CORSINDAE HOUSE
(Mr R. Fyffe) (WA)
Sauchen by Inverurie, Inverurie   AB51 7PP
Telephone: (01330) 833295
Fax: (01330) 833629

DRUMMINOR CASTLE
(Mr A.D. Forbes (WA)
Rhynie

ERSKINE MARYKIRK - STIRLING YOUTH HOSTEL
St. John Street, Stirling

GARGUNNOCK HOUSE
(Gargunnock Estate Trust (WA)
Stirling

GORDONSTOUN SCHOOL
(The Headmaster (WA)
Elgin Moray

GRANDHOME HOUSE
(D.R. Paton Esq.)
Aberdeen
Telephone: (01224) 722202

GUILDHALL
(Stirling District Council)
Municipal Buildings, Stirling
Telephone: (01786) 79000
Also JOHN CAWANE'S HOUSE contact above telephone number.

OLD TOLBOOTH BUILDING
(Stirling District Council)
Municipal Buildings, Stirling
Telephone: (01786) 79000

PHESDO HOUSE
(Mr J.M. Thomson (WA)
Laurencekirk

THE PINEAPPLE
(WA)
Dunmore, Airth, Stirling
*The Landmark Trust, Shottesbrooke, nr. Maidenhead, Berks SL6 3SW.

TOLBOOTH
(Stirling District Council)
Broad Street, Stirling
Telephone: (01786) 79400

TOUCH HOUSE
(Mr P.B. Buchanan (WA)
Stirling   FK8 3AQ
Fax: (01786) 464278

HIGHLANDS

EMBO HOUSE
(Mr John G. Mackintosh)
Dornoch
Telephone: Dornoch 810260

LOTHIAN

CAKEMUIR
(Mr M.M. Scott (WA)
Parthhead, Tynehead, Lothian   EH3Y 5XR

CASTLE GOGAR
(Lady Steel-Maitland)
Edinburgh
Telephone: 0131-339 1234

FORD HOUSE
(F.P. Tindall OBE (WA)
Ford

FORTH ROAD BRIDGE
(The Bridgemaster)
South Queensferry
Telephone: 0131-319 1699

LINNHOUSE
(Mr H.J. Spurway (WA)
Linnhouse, Livingston   EH54 9AN
Telephone: (01506) 410742
Fax: (01506) 416591

NEWBATTLE ABBEY COLLEGE
(The Principal)
Dalkeith   EH22 3LL
Telephone: 0131-663 1921
Fax: 0131-654 0598

PENICUIK HOUSE
(Sir John Clerk Bt (WA)
Penicuik

ROSEBURN HOUSE
(Mr M.E. Sturgeon (WA)
Murrayfield

TOWN HOUSE
(East Lothian District Council)
Haddington
Telephone: Haddington 4161

SHETLAND ISLES

THE LODBERRIE
(Mr Thomas Moncrieff)
Lerwick

STRATHCLYDE

ASCOG HOUSE
(WA)
Rothsa
*The Landmark Trust, Shottesbrooke, nr. Maidenhead, Berks SL6 3SW.

BARCALDINE CASTLE
(Roderick Campbell esq. (WA)
Benderloch

CRAUFURDLAND CASTLE
(J.P. Houison Craufurd Esq.)
Kilmarnock   KA3 6BS
Telephone: (01560) 600402

DUNTRUNE CASTLE
(Robin Malcolm of Poltalloch (WA)
Lochgilphead

KELBURN CASTLE
(The Earl of Glasgow (WA)
Fairlie, Ayrshire   KA29 0BE
Telephone: (01475) 568685 - Country Centre; (01475) 568204 - Kelburn Castle
Fax: (01475) 568121 - Country Centre; (01475) 568328 - Kelburn Castle

NEW LANARK
(New Lanark Conservation Trust)
New Lanark Mills, Lanark   ML11 9DB
Telephone: (01555) 661345
Fax: (01555) 665738

THE PLACE OF PAISLEY
(Paisley Abbey Kirk Session)
Paisley Abbey, Abbey Close, Paisley   PA1 1JG
Telephone: 0141-889 7654

SADDELL CASTLE
(WA)
Campbeltown, Argyll

*The Landmark Trust, Shottesbrooke, nr. Maidenhead, Berks SL6 3SW.

TANGY MILL
(WA)
Campbeltown, Kintyre, Argyll

*The Landmark Trust, Shottesbrooke, nr. Maidenhead, Berks SL6 3SW.

TANNAHILL COTTAGE
(Secretary, Paisley Burns Club)
Queen Street, Paisley
Telephone: 0141-887 7500

TAYSIDE

ARDBLAIR CASTLE
(Laurence P.K. Blair Oliphant)
Blairgowrie   PH10 6SA
Telephone: (01250) 873155

CRAIG HOUSE
(Charles F.R. Hoste)
Montrose
Telephone: (01674) 722239

KINROSS HOUSE
(Sir David Montgomery Bt) (WA)
Kinross

MICHAEL BRUCE COTTAGE MUSEUM
(Michael Bruce Trust)
Kinnesswood

THE PAVILION, GLENEAGLES
(J. Martin Haldane of Gleneagles) (WA)
Gleneagles, Auchterarder   PH3 1PJ

TULLIEBOLE CASTLE
(The Lord Moncreiff)
Crook of Devon

UNIVERSITIES

CAMBRIDGE

NOTE: Admission to *Colleges* means to the *Courts,* not to the staircases and students' rooms. All opening times are subject to closing for College functions etc. on occasional days. *Halls* normally close for lunch (12-2) and many are not open during the afternoon. *Chapels* are closed during services. *Libraries* are not usually open, special arrangements are noted. *Gardens* do not usually include the Fellows' garden. *Figures* denote the date of foundation, and existing buildings are often of later date. *Daylight hours -* some colleges may not open until 9.30 am or later and usually close before 6 pm - many as early as 4.30 pm. All parties exceeding 10 persons wishing to tour the college between Easter and October are required to be escorted by a Cambridge registered Guide. All enquiries should be made to the Tourist Information Centre, Wheeler Street, Cambridge CB2 3QB. **Terms:** *Lent:* Mid-January to Mid-March. *Easter:* April to June. *Michaelmas:* 2nd week October to 1st week December. Examination Period closures which differ from one college to another now begin in early April and extend to late June. Notices are usually displayed. **Visitors and especially guided parties should always call at the Porters' Lodge before entering the College.**

CHRIST'S COLLEGE *(1505)*
Porter's Lodge, St. Andrew's Street   CB2 3BU
Telephone: (01223) 334900
Fax: (01223) 334967
Open: The College is closed to all visitors from early May-mid June(Exams). At other times it is open as follows:- mid June-early Oct daily 9.30-noon, for the rest of the year daily 9.30-dusk. Chapel daily dawn till dusk. Library by appointment with Librarian. Fellows' Garden Mon-Fri 10.30-12.30, and 2-4 when college open. (Closed Bank Hols, Easter break and weekends).

CLARE COLLEGE *(1326)*
Trinity Lane
Open: Hall Monday to Sat 9-12 (usually). Chapel Daily (usually). Library by prior arrangement with the Librarian. Gardens daily: 12-4.30. An entry fee of £1.50 will be charged for each visitor between Mid Mar and 1st October.

CORPUS CHRISTI COLLEGE *(1352)*
Porter's Lodge, Trumpington Street   CB2 1RH
Telephone: (01223) 338000
Fax: (01223) 338061
Open: Opening times shown at Porter's Lodge.
Closed to large groups mid April-mid June during examinations

DOWNING COLLEGE *(1800)*
Downing College, Regent Street   CB2 1DQ
Telephone: (01223) 334800
Fax: (01223) 467934
Open: College Gardens daily daylight hours, Chapel: Term-daily, vacation - by appointment. Hall closed to the public. Library by arrangement only.

EMMANUEL COLLEGE *(1800)*
Porter's Lodge, St. Andrew's Street   CB2 3AP
Telephone: (01223) 334200
Fax: (01223) 334426
Open: College Daily 9-6. Hall 2.30-5. Chapel 9-6 both daily except when in use. Library only by prior application to Librarian. Gardens & Paddock Daily 9-6 or dusk if earlier. Fellows' Garden Not open to visitors. (Closed for annual holidays, variable).

GONVILLE & CAIUS COLLEGE *(1348)*
Porter's Lodge, Trinity Street   CB2 1TA
Telephone: (01223) 332400
Open: College & Chapel Daily daylight hours. Library By appointment with Librarian. Closed during exams from early May to mid June and for short periods each day. Times shown at Porter's Lodge.

JESUS COLLEGE *(1496)*
Porter's Lodge, Jesus Lane   CB5 8BL
Telephone: (01223) 339339
Open: College daily 9-5.30. Hall closed to the public.
The college is closed to the public from 1 Apr-mid June. Groups of over 20 must make special visit arrangements in writing to the Domestic Bursar.

KING'S COLLEGE *(1441)*
Porter's Lodge, King's Parade   CB2 1ST
Telephone: (01223) 331212
Fax: (01223) 331315
Open: Out of term weekdays 9.30-4.30 Suns 10-5. Adults £2.50 students/child (12-17) £1.50 (chidren under 12 free) cost includes Chapel during term time the Chapel is open weekdays 9.30-3.30 Suns 1.15-2.15 5-

5.30 (Terms are from early Jan-mid Mar, late Apr-mid June, most of July and early Oct-Early Dec) from late Apr-mid June grounds are closed. Further information may be obtained from the Cambridge Tourist Information Centre on (01223) 322640 or the Tourist Liason Officer at the College (01223) 331212.

MAGDALENE COLLEGE *(1542)*
Porter's Lodge, Magdalene Street
Open: College & Chapel Daily 9-6.30 (except during exams). Hall Daily 9.30-12.30 (except during exams). Gardens Daily 1-6.30 (except during exams). Pepys Jan 15-Mar 16 weekdays 2.30-3.30 Apr 23-Aug 31 weekdays (not Suns) 11.30-12.30 2.30-3.30.

NEWNHAM COLLEGE *(1871)*
Sidgwick Avenue
Open: College & Gardens Daily during daylight hours. College and gardens closed May 1-mid June.

PETERHOUSE *(1284)*
Porter's Lodge, Trumpington Street   CB2 1RD
Telephone: (01223) 338200
Fax: (01223) 337578
Open: Guided parties of not more than 12. Chapel daily. Hall mornings only during term. Gardens Daily 10-5 (no dogs).

QUEENS' COLLEGE *(1448)*
Porter's Lodge, Silver Street   CB3 9ET
Telephone: (01223) 335511
Fax: (01223) 335566
Open: Open daily 1.45-4.30 & also 10.15-12.45 during July, Aug & Sept & for guided parties of not more than 20. Adm. charge.

SIDNEY SUSSEX COLLEGE *(1596)*
Porter's Lodge, Sidney Street   CB2 3HU
Telephone: (01223) 338800
Fax: (01223) 338884
Open: *College* Daily, during daylight hours. *Hall & Chapel*

ST. CATHARINE'S COLLEGE *(1473)*
Porter's Lodge, Trumpington Street
Open: College & Chapel Daily during daylight hours. (Closed May & June. Chapel Hall Closed to the public.

ST. JOHN'S COLLEGE *(1511)*
Tourist Liaison Office, St. John's Street   CB2 1TP
Open: *College* Daily 10.30 until 5.30. (Closed May & June). *Hall* Closed to the public. Admission charge July - October and March - April. £1 Adult, 50p Child/OAPs, £2 family ticket. Admission includes Guide leaflet.

TRINITY COLLEGE *(1546)*
Porter's Lodge, Trinity Street
Open: 10-6.
Admission: Adults £1.50 children/OAPs 75p families £3. UB40 form holders - free.

CONDUCTED TOURS IN CAMBRIDGE Qualified badged, local guides may be obtained from: Tourist Information Centre, Wheeler Street, Cambridge CB2 3QB. Tel: (01223) 322640 or Cambridge Guide Service, 2 Montague Road, Cambridge CB4 1BX. We normally obtain the Passes and make all negotiations regarding these with the Tourist Office, so separate application is not needed. We have been providing guides for English, Foreign language and special interest groups since 1950. We supply couriers for coach tours of East Anglia, visiting stately homes etc. As an alternative to the 2 hour walking tour we can now offer half hour panoramic in clients' coach (provided there is an effective public address system) followed by a 1.5 hours tour on foot, or 1 hour panoramic only, special flat rate for up to 55 people.

UNIVERSITIES

OXFORD

NOTE: Admission to *Colleges* means to the Quadrangles, not to the staircases and students' rooms. All opening times are subject to closing for College functions etc., on occasional days. *Halls* normally close for lunch (12-2) . *Chapel* usually closed during services. *Libraries* are not usually open, special arrangements are noted. *Gardens* do not usually include the Fellows' garden. *Figures* denote the date fo foundation, and existing buildings are often of later date.
Terms: *Hilary:* Mid-January to Mid-March. *Trinity:* 3rd week April to late June. *Michaelmas:* Mid October to 1st week December. **Visitors and especially guided parties should always call at the Porters' Lodge before entering the College.**

ALL SOULS COLLEGE *(1438)*
Porter's Lodge, High Street   OX1 4AL
Open: College Weekdays: 2-4.30. (2-4pm Oct-Mar).

BALLIOL COLLEGE *(1263)*
Porter's Lodge, Broad Street
Open: Hall Chapel & Gardens Daily 2-5. Parties limited to 25.

BRASENOSE COLLEGE *(1509)*
Radcliffe Square
Open: Hall Chapel & Gardens Tour parties: Daily 10-11.30 2-5 (summer) 10-dusk (winter). Individuals 2-5. College closed 11.30-2.

CHRIST CHURCH *(1546)*
St. Aldate's, Enter via Meadow Gate   OX1 1DP
Telephone: (01865) 276499
Open: Cathedral daily 9-4.30 (winter) 9-5.30 (summer). Hall daily 9.30-12, 2-5.30 adm £3 chd £2 Picture Gallery weekdays 10.30-1 2-4.30 adm £1 Meadows daily 7-dusk hall published hours occasionally curtailed for College or Cathedral events.
Tourist Information: (24 hrs) (01865) 276499

CORPUS CHRISTI COLLEGE *(1517)*
Porter's Lodge, Merton Street
Open: *College, Chapel & Gardens* Term and vacations - daily 2-45.

EXETER COLLEGE *(1314)*
Porter's Lodge, Turl Street   OX1 3DP
Telephone: (01865) 279600
Fax: (01865) 279630
Open: College & Chapel, Fellows' Garden term and vacations daily 2-5. (except Christmas and Easter).

HERTFORD COLLEGE *(1284,1740 & 1874)*
Porter's Lodge, Catte Street   OX1 3BW
Telephone: (01865) 279400
Fax: (01865) 279437
Open: Quadrangle & Chapel Daily 10-6. Closed for a week at Christmas and during exam periods. Parties restricted to 10 people

JESUS COLLEGE *(1571)*
Turl Street
Open: *College, Hall & Chapel* Daily 2.30-4.30. *Library* special permission of librarian. (closed Christmas and Easter holidays).

KEBLE COLLEGE *(1868)*
Porter's Lodge, Parks Road
Open: *College & Chapel* Daily 10-7 (or dusk if earlier).

LADY MARGARET HALL *(1878)*
Porter's Lodge, Norham Gardens
Open: College & Gardens daily 2-6 (or dusk if earlier). Visitors must call at The Lodge before walking around the grounds. Access to the buildings is not permitted. The Chapel is open to the public.

LINCOLN COLLEGE *(1427)*
Porter's Lodge, Turl Street
Open: *College & Hall* weekdays 2-5. Suns 11-5. *Wesley Room   All Saints Library* Tues & Thurs 2-4.

MAGDALEN COLLEGE *(1458)*
High Street, Oxford   OX1 4AU
Telephone: (01865) 276000
Fax: (01865) 276103
Open: College Chapel Deer Park & Water Walks daily 2-6 June-Sept 11-6. Parties limited to 25.

MANSFIELD COLLEGE *(1886)*
Porter's Lodge, Mansfield Road
Open: *College* Open May, June & July, Mon to Sat 9-5. Interior of Chapel and Library may be viewed by prior appointment.

MERTON *(1264)*
Merton Street   OX1 4JD
Telephone: (01865) 276310
Fax: (01865) 276361
Open: Chapel & Quadrangle Mon-Fri 2-4 Oct-Jun: Sat & Sun 10-4. Mon-Fri 2-5 Jul-Sept: Sat & Sun 10-5. Old Library Mon-Sat 2-4 admission £1. Apply Verger's office.
Library not open on Saturdays Nov-Mar.

NEW COLLEGE *(1379)*
New College Lane
Open: Hall, Chapel, Cloister, Gardens daily. Oct-Easter, in Holywell Street Gate (2-4) Easter-early Oct, in New College Lane Gate (11-5, £1).

NUFFIELD COLLEGE *(1937)*
Porter's Lodge, New Road
Open: College only Daily 9-5

ORIEL COLLEGE *(1326)*
Oriel Square   OX1 4EW
Telephone: (01865) 276555
Fax: (01865) 276532
Open: College Daily 2-5. (closed Christmas and Easter holidays and mid Aug to mid Sept)

PEMBROKE COLLEGE *(1624)*
Porter's Lodge, St. Aldate's
Open: *College, Hall, Chapel & Gardens* Term - daily on application to the Porter's Lodge. Closed Christmas and Easter holidays and occasionally in Aug.

THE QUEEN'S COLLEGE *(1340)*
High Street   OX1 4AW
Telephone: (01865) 279120
Fax: (01865) 790819
Open: Hall Chapel Quadrangles & Garden Open to public by appointment or through Oxford Guild of Guides.

ST. EDMUND HALL *(1270)*
Queen's Lane   OX1 4AR
Telephone: (01865) 279000
Open: *College, Old Hall, Chapel & Garden* Daily, daylight hours. *Crypt or St. Peter in the East* On application to Porter.

ST. JOHN'S COLLEGE *(1555)*
St. Giles' Oxford   OX1 3JP
Telephone: (01865) 277300
Fax: (01865) 277435
Open: College & Garden Term & Vacation - daily 1-5 or dusk if earlier. Guided parties must obtain permission from Lodge. Hall & Chapel Summer 2.30-4.30. Apply Porter. Closed during conferences & college functions.

TRINITY COLLEGE *(1554)*
Main Gate, Broad Street   OX1 3BH
Telephone: (01865) 279900
Fax: (01865) 279898
Open: Hall Chapel & Garden daily 2-5 (summer) 2-dusk (winter).Opening hours may vary - visitors should check in advance.

TRINITY HALL *(1350)*
Trinity Lane   CB2 1TJ
Telephone: (01223) 332531
Fax: (01223) 462116
Open: College, Chapel & Gardens Daily during daylight hours except during examination period (end April to mid June). Library - apply beforehand to College Librarian.

UNIVERSITY COLLEGE *(1249)*
Porter's Lodge, High Street   OX1 4BH
Open: *College, Hall & Chapel* Term 2-4.

WORCESTER COLLEGE *(1714)*
Porter's Lodge, Worcester Street   OX1 2HB
Telephone: (01865) 278300
Fax: (01865) 278387
Open: College & Gardens Term daily 2-6. Vacation daily 9-12 and 2-6. Hall & Chapel Apply Lodge.

GUIDED WALKING TOURS OF THE COLLEGES & CITY OF OXFORD Tours conducted by the Oxford Guild of Guides. Lecturers are offered by the Oxford Information Centre, morning for much of the year, afternoon , tours daily. For tour times please ring (01865) 726871. Tours are offered for groups in English, French, German, Spanish, Russian, Japanese, Polish and Serbo-Croat. Chinese by appointment. The most popular tour for groups, Oxford Past and Present, can be arranged at any time. The following special interest tours are available in the afternoon only: Alice in Oxford; Literary Figures in Oxford; American Roots in Oxford; Oxford Gardens; Modern Architecture in Oxford; Architecture in Oxford (Medieval, 17th Century and Modern); Oxford in the Civil War and 17th Century. Further details are available from the Deputy Information Officer.

INDEX TO PROPERTIES
OFFERING ACCOMMODATION

Weston Park
　　nr Shifnal　TF11 8LE
　　Telephone: (01952) 850207
　　Fax: (01952) 850430
　　Accommodation: 28 bedrooms with bathrooms, 18 doubles, 7 twins and 3 singles.　114

STAFFORDSHIRE
Shugborough
　　Stafford　ST17 0XB
　　Telephone: (01889) 881388
　　Fax: (01889) 881323
　　Accommodation: Details of group accommodation can be obtained
　　from the Booking Officer　119

SUFFOLK
Otley Hall
　　Otley, nr Ipswich　IP6 9PA
　　Telephone: (01473) 890264
　　Fax: (01473) 890803
　　Accommodation: The Hall, grounds and accommodation are available for private hire.　123

SURREY
Guildford House Gallery
　　155, High Street, Guildford　GU1 3AJ
　　Telephone: (01483) 444740
　　Fax: (01483) 444742
　　Accommodation: Meeting room for daytime use, up to 60 people.　125

WEST SUSSEX
Goodwood House
　　Chichester　PO18 OPX
　　Telephone: (01243) 774107
　　Fax: (01243) 774313
　　Accommodation: Goodwood Park Hotel, Golf and Country Club
　　- reservations (01345) 123333/(01243) 775537.　134

Hammerwood Park
　　nr East Grinstead　RH19 3QE
　　Telephone: (01342) 850594
　　Fax: (01342) 850864
　　Accommodation: B & B with a difference in an idyllically peaceful
　　location only 20 minutes from Gatwick.　134

WARWICKSHIRE
Coughton Court
　　Alcester　B49 5JA
　　Telephone: (01789) 400777 (01789) 762435 (visitor information)
　　Fax: (01789) 765544
　　Accommodation: Luxury accommodation available for select groups.　140

NORTH YORKSHIRE
Ripley Castle
　　Ripley　HG3 3AY
　　Telephone: (01423) 770152
　　Fax: (01423) 771745
　　Accommodation: 25 deluxe bedrooms at the Estate owned Boar's Head
　　Hotel, 100 yards from the Castle in Ripley village. The Hotel is rated RAC****.154

IRELAND

Bantry House
　　Bantry, Co. Cork
　　Telephone: (027) 50047
　　Accommodation: Bed and Breakfast and dinner. Nine rooms en suite.　165
Glin Castle
　　Glin
　　Telephone: (068) 34173/34112
　　Fax: (068) 34364
　　Accommodation: Overnight stays arranged. Castle can be rented.　165

SCOTLAND

BORDERS
Floors Castle, Kelso
　　Roxburghe Estates Office, Kelso　TD5 7SF
　　Telephone: (01573) 223333
　　Fax: (01573) 226056
　　Accommodation: Accommodation at nearby Sunlaws House Hotel.　170
Manderston
　　Duns, Berwickshire　TD11 3PP
　　Telephone: (01361) 883450
　　Fax: (01361) 882010
　　Accommodation: By arrangement.　170

Traquair
　　Innerleithen　EH44 6PW
　　Telephone: (01896) 830323
　　Fax: (01896) 830639
　　Accommodation: 2 rooms B&B and Holiday flat to rent.　172

CENTRAL
Callendar House
　　Callendar Park, Falkirk　FK1 1YR
　　Telephone: (01324) 612134
　　Accommodation: Readily available throughout the district.　172

DUMFRIES & GALLOWAY
Threave Garden
　　nr Castle Douglas
　　Telephone: (01556) 502683
　　Accommodation: Holiday cottages on Threave estate-apply to NTS.　174

FIFE
Falkland Palace & Garden
　　Fife
　　Telephone: (01337) 857397
　　Accommodation: Holiday flat in village-apply to NTS.　175

GRAMPIAN
Brodie Castle
　　nr Nairn Moray
　　Telephone: (01309) 641371
　　Fax: (01309) 641600
　　Accommodation: Holiday house in grounds -apply to NTS.　176

Castle Fraser
　　Sauchen
　　Telephone: (01330) 833463
　　Accommodation: Holiday flat in castle-apply NTS.　176
Haddo House
　　nr Methlick
　　Telephone: (01651) 851440
　　Accommodation: Holiday flats in grounds-apply to NTS.　178

HIGHLANDS
Dunvegan Castle
　　Isle of Skye
　　Telephone: (01470) 521206
　　Fax: (01470) 521205
　　Accommodation: Self catering cottages within grounds.　179

LOTHIAN
Gladstone's Land
　　Edinburgh
　　Telephone: 0131-226 5856
　　Accommodation: Holiday flat above property-apply to NTS.　182

ORKNEY ISLANDS
Balfour Castle
　　Shapinsay, Orkney Islands　KW17 2DY
　　Telephone: (01856) 711282
　　Fax: (01856) 711283
　　Accommodation: 8 bedrooms, most en-suite. Large rooms, canopy, 4 poster beds.
　　Original furnishings. £68 per night includes bed, breakfast & dinner and VAT.　185

STRATHCLYDE
Brodick Castle, Garden and Country Park
　　Isle of Arran
　　Telephone: (01770) 650100
　　Fax: (01770) 302312
　　Accommodation: Holiday flats in castle- apply to NTS.　186
Culzean Castle, Garden and Country Park
　　Maybole
　　Telephone: (01655) 760274
　　Fax: (01655) 760615
　　Accommodation: Holiday flats in castle and grounds - apply to NTS.　186
Sorn Castle
　　Sorn, Mauchline
　　Telephone: (01505) 612124 (Cluttons)
　　Accommodation: Available- contact Cluttons.　187
Torosay Castle and Gardens
　　Craignure, Isle of Mull　PA65 6AY
　　Telephone: (01680) 812421
　　Fax: (01680) 812470
　　Accommodation: Self catering cottages.　188

TAYSIDE
Barrie's Birthplace
　　Kirriemuir
　　Telephone: (01575) 572646
　　Accommodation: Holiday house nearby - apply to NTS.　188

INDEX TO PROPERTIES LICENSED
FOR CIVIL MARRIAGES

INDEX TO PROPERTIES

INDEX TO PROPERTIES
OPEN ALL YEAR

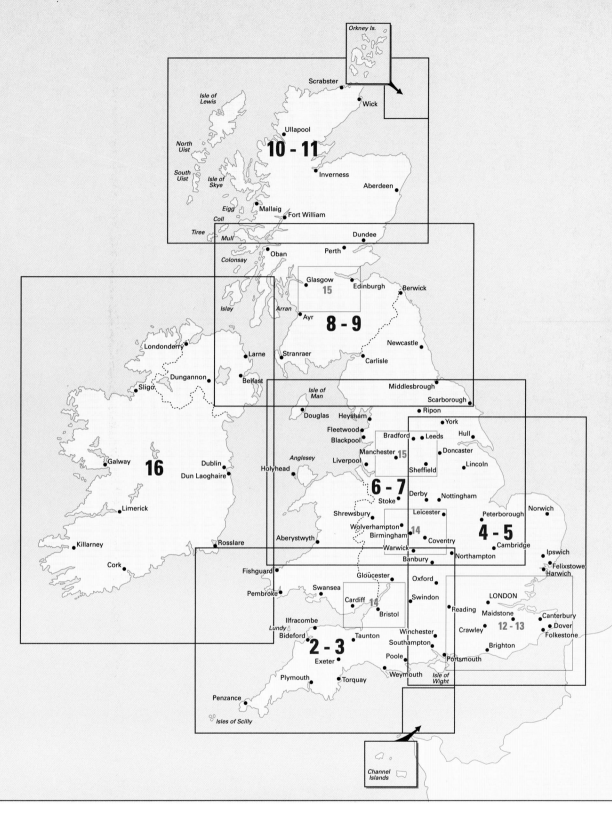

Orkney Is.

Scrabster
Wick

Isle of
Lewis

Ullapool

North
Uist

10 - 11

Inverness

South
Uist

Isle of
Skye

Aberdeen

Eigg
Mallaig
Fort William
Coll

Tiree
Mull

Dundee

Colonsay
Oban
Perth

Glasgow
15
Edinburgh
Berwick

Islay
Arran
Ayr

8 - 9

Newcastle

Londonderry

Larne
Stranraer
Carlisle

Dungannon
Belfast

Middlesbrough

Sligo

Isle of
Man

Scarborough

Douglas
Heysham
Ripon

York

Fleetwood
Bradford
Leeds
Hull

Blackpool
Manchester
15
Doncaster

Liverpool
Sheffield
Lincoln

Anglesey

Galway

Dublin
Holyhead

6 - 7

Derby
Nottingham

16
Dun Laoghaire
Stoke

Shrewsbury
Leicester
Peterborough
Norwich

Limerick
Wolverhampton
14
Coventry

Aberystwyth
Birmingham

4 - 5
Cambridge

Killarney
Warwick
Ipswich

Rosslare
Banbury
Northampton
Felixstowe

Cork
Fishguard
Gloucester
Harwich

Oxford

Pembroke
Swansea
Norwich

Cardiff
14
Swindon
LONDON

Bristol
Reading
Maidstone
Canterbury

Ilfracombe
Crawley
Dover

Lundy
Winchester
12 - 13
Folkestone

Bideford
Southampton
Brighton

2 - 3
Poole
Portsmouth

Exeter
Weymouth
Isle of
Wight

Plymouth
Torquay

Penzance

Isles of Scilly

Channel
Islands

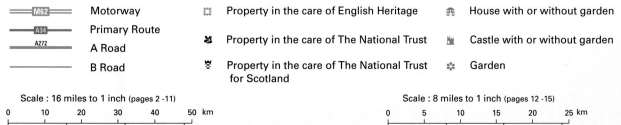

Wexford

10 Rosslare Harbour
Greenore Pt.

11

12

13

14

6

15
Strata Florida
Abbey

S

Carnsore Pt.

Tregaron

Aberaeron

New Quay

ST. GEORGE'S CHANNEL

Aberporth

Cardigan

Cilgerran Castle

Goodwick

Fishguard

St. David's Hd.
St. Davids
Bishop's Palace
St.
David's

T

St. Brides Bay

Haverfordwest

Milford
Haven

Pembroke

Lamphey
Bishop's
Palace

Llandysul

Lampeter

A487

DYFED

Llanybydder

Newcastle Emlyn

Llandovery

A40

Talley Abbey

Llandeilo

Llangadog

A40

Letterston

Llandissilio

Carmarthen

Dinefwr Park

Carreg
Cennen
Castle

Llawhaden Castle

Whitland

A40

A48

Ammanford

WEST
GLAMORG

Picton Castle

A4076

Narberth

Laugharne

Kidwelly
Castle

Pontardulais

Pontard

Carew Castle & Tidal Mill

Neyland

A477

Colby Woodland
Garden

Kidwelly

A4138

M4

Clydach

Nea

Tudor Merchant's House

Burry Port

Gorseinon

Tenby

Llanelli

Carmarthen
Bay

Swansea
Port Talbot

Weobley
Castle

Margam

Port Eynon

Swansea
Bay

Porthc

Bristol Chann

Lynton

Ilfracombe

Combe
Martin

Woolacombe

U

Braunton

Arlington Court

Barnstaple
or
Bideford Bay

Appledore

Barnstaple

A361

Bideford

Taw

South
Molton

Hartland Pt.
Hartland Abbey

Great
Torrington

A39

A377

Chulmlei

RHS Garden
Rosemoor

A386

Torr

Kilkhampton

Bude

Stratton

Holsworthy

Hatherleigh

North
Tawton

DEV

V

Tamar

Okehampton

A30

A386

Boscastle

Tintagel Castle
Tintagel - The
Old Post Office

A39

A395

Launceston

Endsleigh
House

Cas

Camelford

Long Cross
Victorian Gardens

Prideaux Place

Padstow

St. Tudy

Pencarrow

Gunnislake

Tavistock

Ashburton

Wadebridge

A388

The Garden
House
Buckland Abbey

Buckfastleigh

A39

Bodmin

A30

Callington

Cotehele

A386

High Cross
House

A3

Newquay

St. Columb
Major

A38

Lanhydrock

Liskeard

A38

Saltash

Hemerdon
House

Totnes
Castle

A392

Lostwithiel

A390

Antony Woodland Garden

Plympton

Ivybridge

A38

Trerice

Antony
Saltram House

Perranporth

Tregrehan

East
Looe

Torpoint

PLYMOUTH

St. Agnes

Fowey

Mount Edgcumbe
House & Park

Flete

W

St. Ives

Camborne

Redruth

A30

Probus

A390

St.
Austell

Trewithen House
and Gardens

Caerhays Castle Gardens

Overbecks
Museum
& Garden

Truro

A39

Trelissick
Garden

Burncoose
Nurseries & Garden

Hayle

Penryn

St. Mawes Castle

Bolt
Head

Trengwainton Garden

St. Michael's
Mount

Godolphin
House

Falmouth

St. Mawes
Pendennis Castle

St. Just

Penzance

Glendurgan
Garden

Falmouth
Bay

Sennen

Newlyn

A394

Helston

Land's End

Porthleven

Trelowarren
House & Chapel

Mount's
Bay

Tresco

Isles Of Scilly

X

St. Mary's

Lizard Pt. Lizard

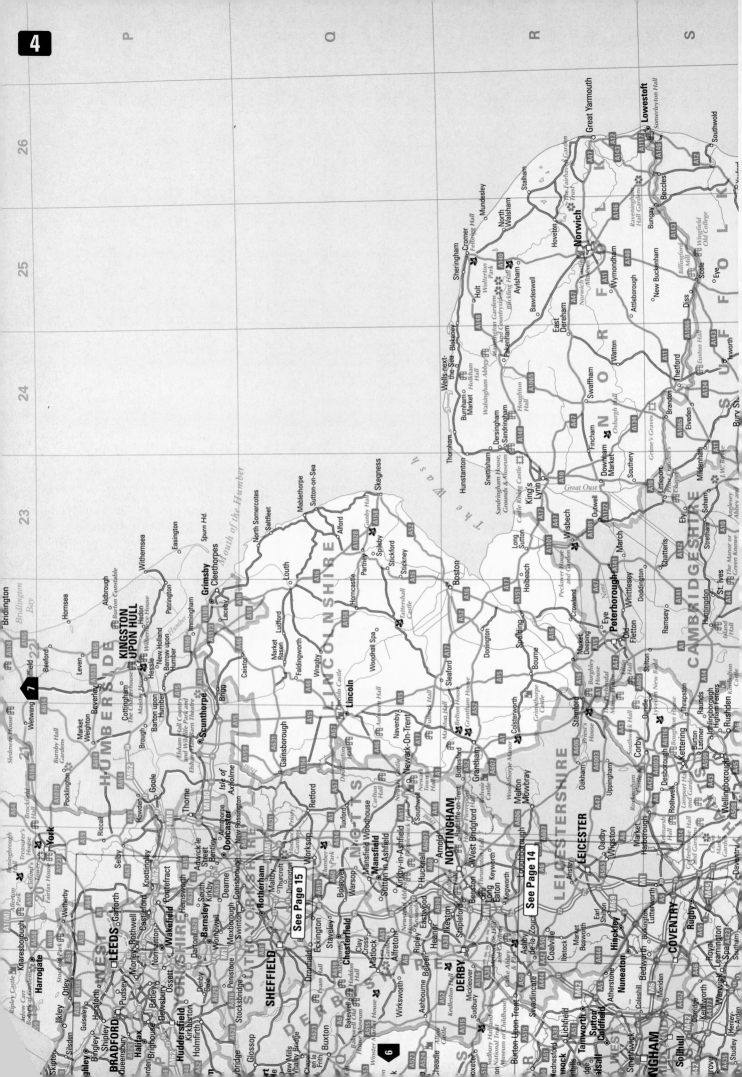

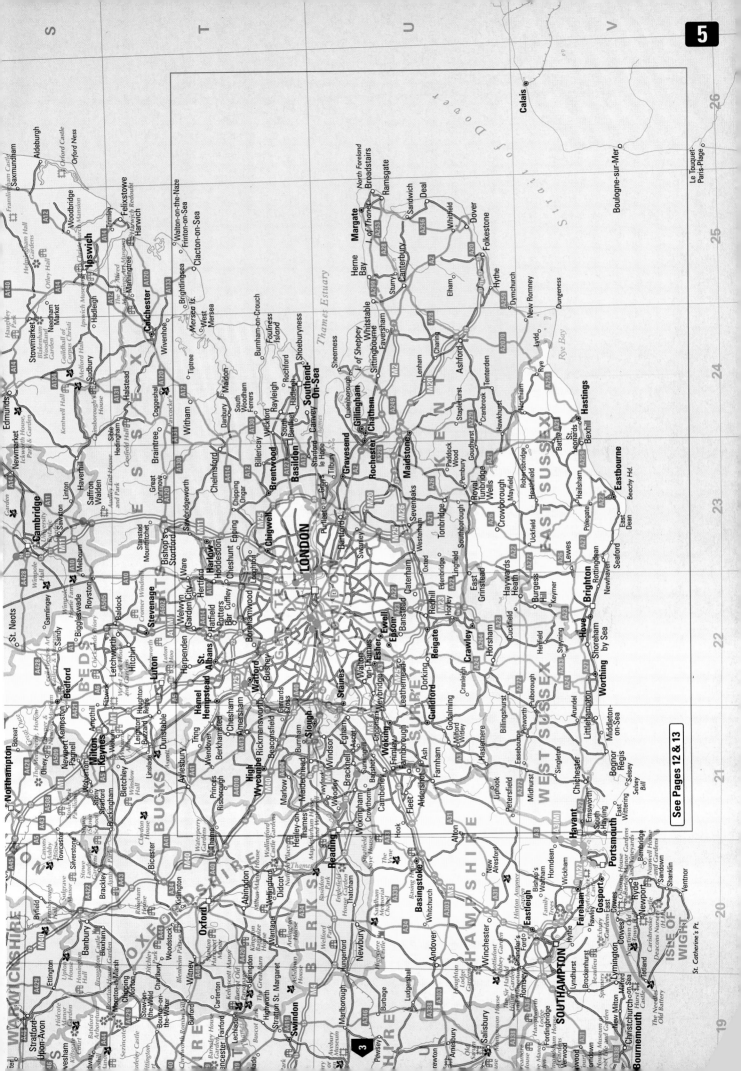

See Pages 12 & 13

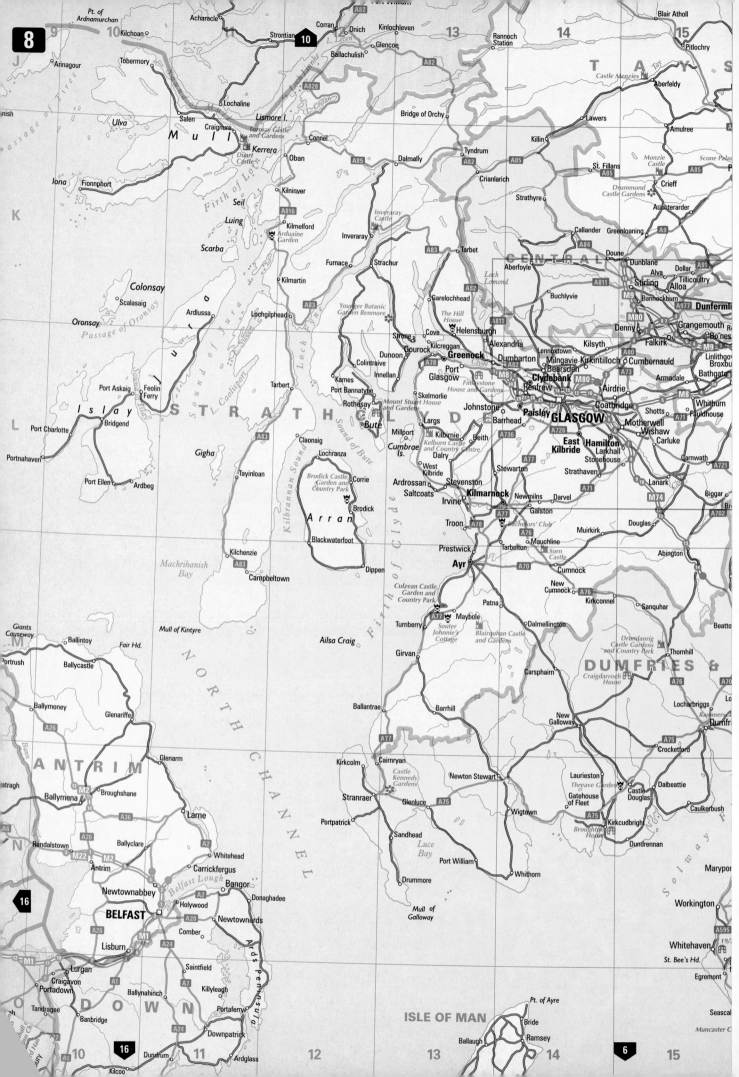

7   8   9   10   11   12   13

E

**WESTERN
ISLES**

Butt of Lewis
Port Nis

Barabhas
Siabost   Tolastadh bho
Thuath
F   Broad Bay

Great
Bernera   Port Nan Giuran
Stornoway
Eye
Peninsula
Gearraidh
na h-Aibhne

Lewis
Baile Ailein

Scarp

Huisinis

West L. Tarbert

Taransay   Tairbeart
(Tarbert)
Sound of Taransay   East L. Tarbert
Scalpay
Pabbay   Harris
Berneray
G   Roghadal

North Uist   Loch nam
Madadh
(Lochmaddy)
Clachan
na Luib
Baleshare
Grimsay
Benbecula
Wiay

Tobha Mor
South
Uist
Loch Baghasdail
(Lochboisdale)
H

Eriskay

Barra
Bagh a Chaisteil
(Castlebay)
Vatersay

Sandray

Barra Hd.
J

Cape
Wrath

Durness

Eriboll

Laxford Bridge
Eddrachillis   Kinloch   Altnaha
Bay   Kylestrome
Inchnadamph

Enard Bay   Lochinver
Reiff   Ledmore

Rosehall
Strathkanaird

Gruinard Bay   Ullapool   Inver

Aultbea
Melvaig   Ardessie
Inverewe   Braemore
Garden   Poolewe   A835
L. Gairloch   Gairloch
Kilmaluag
L. Torridon
Uig   Rona   Kinlochewe   Garve
L.   Achnasheen
Snizort   Torridon   Contin
Shieldaig   Muir of Or

Dunvegan   Carbost   Coulags
Castle   Skye   Raasay   Lochcarron
Dunvegan   Portree   HIGHLAN
Cannich   Drumnadrochi
L. Bracadale   Scalpay   L. Carron
Kyle of   Eilean Donan
Sligachan   Lochalsh   Castle
Kyleakin   A887
Broadford   Kyle of Alsh   Invermo
Kylerhea   Glenelg
Shiel Bridge
Soay   L. Hourn   Fort Augustus
Cuillin Sound   Sound of Sleat   A87
Canna   Armadale   Invergarry
Rhum
Mallaig
Eigg   Spean
Bridge   A86
Sound of Arisaig   Lochailort   Corpach
Muck   A830
Pt. of   Fort William
Ardnamurchan   A82
Corran   Kinlochleven
Kilchoan   Acharacle   Onich
Coll   Strontian   Glencoe
L. Leven   Ballachulish   A82
Arinagour   Tobermory   Rann
Stati
Tiree   A828   8
Scarinish   Salen   Lismore I.   Bridge of Orchy
Ulva   Craignure   Torosay Castle
and Gardens   Connel
Mull

Stromness   **Mainland**   Gritley
St. Mary's
Scapa Flow   Burray
Hoy   South Ronaldsay
Burwick
Pentland Firth
Stroma
John o' Groats
Duncansby Head
Scrabster   Thurso   Dunnet   Freswick
A882
Bettyhill   Melvich   Halkirk   Reiss
Tongue   Dalhalvaig   Mybster   A882   Wick
A895   Kinbrace   Thrumster   A9
Lybster
Latheron
Dunbeath
Helmsdale
A9
Lairg   Brora
Dunrobin Castle   Golspie
Bonarbridge   Clashmore   Dornoch
Kincardine   *Dornoch Firth*
Tain   Portmahomack

Papa Westray
Westray
Sanday
Rousay   Eday
Egilsay   Stronsay
The Barony   Wyre   *Stronsay Firth*
Gairsay
Finstown   *Balfour Castle*   Shapinsay
Stromness   Kirkwall
O R K N E Y
Mainland
St. Mary's   Gritley
Scapa Flow
Hoy   Burray
South Ronaldsay
Burwick
Pentland Firth
Stroma
John o' Groats
Scrabster   16   Duncansby Head   17
Thurso   Dunnet   Freswick

Moray Firth
Alness   Invergordon   *Hugh Miller's Cottage*
Evanton   Cromarty
Cromarty Firth
Dingwall   Nairn   *Brodie Castle*   Forres
Fortrose
North Kessock   A96   *Cawdor Castle*   Ferness
Balloch
Inverness
A9   Tomatin   Grantown-on-Spey
A95
Boat of Garten
Aviemore   *The Doune of Rothiemurchus*
A9
Kingussie
Newtonmore   *Spey*
A9
Dalwhinnie

Burghead   Branderburgh   Lossiemouth   Findochty   Portknockie   Cullen   Portsoy   Macduff   Fraserburgh
Buckie   A98   Banff
Elgin   Fochabers   *Duff House*   A98
A96   *Spey*   Aberchirder   Turriff   *Craigston Castle*   A952   St. Fergus
A941   Keith   New Deer   Mintlaw   Peterhead
Rothes   A96   *Buchan Ness*
Charlestown of Aberlour   *Drummuir Castle & Walled Garden*   Huntly   *Fyvie Castle*   *Haddo House*   A92
Dufftown   *Pitmedden Garden*   Ellon
Leith Hall and Garden   Oldmeldrum   Newburgh
Rhynie   **G R A M P I A N**   Inverurie   A92
Strathdon   *Don*   *Castle Fraser*   Kintore   *Don*   Dyce
Bridge of Don
Westhill   **Aberdeen**
Drum Castle   Cults
Crathes Castle & Garden   Peterculter
Crathie   Aboyne   *Dee*   Banchory   A93   A90
Braemar Castle   Ballater
Braemar   *Dee*   *Arbuthnott House and Garden*   Stonehaven
A93
Fasque   A90
Spittle of Glenshee   Laurencekirk   Inverbervie
A92
St. Cyrus
Blair Atholl   Brechin   Montrose
A93   *Barrie's Birthplace*   *House of Dun*
Pitlochry   Kirriemuir
A90
Castle Menzies   **T A Y S I D E**   Alyth   *Angus Folk Museum*   Forfar
Aberfeldy   Blairgowrie   Rattray   *Glamis Castle*   Arbroath
Lawers   Amulree   Coupar Angus   Carnoustie
Burrelton   A92
Stobhall   *Tay*   **Dundee**   *Barry Mill*
Killin   Monifieth
Tayport

18   19   20
D   E   F   G   H   J

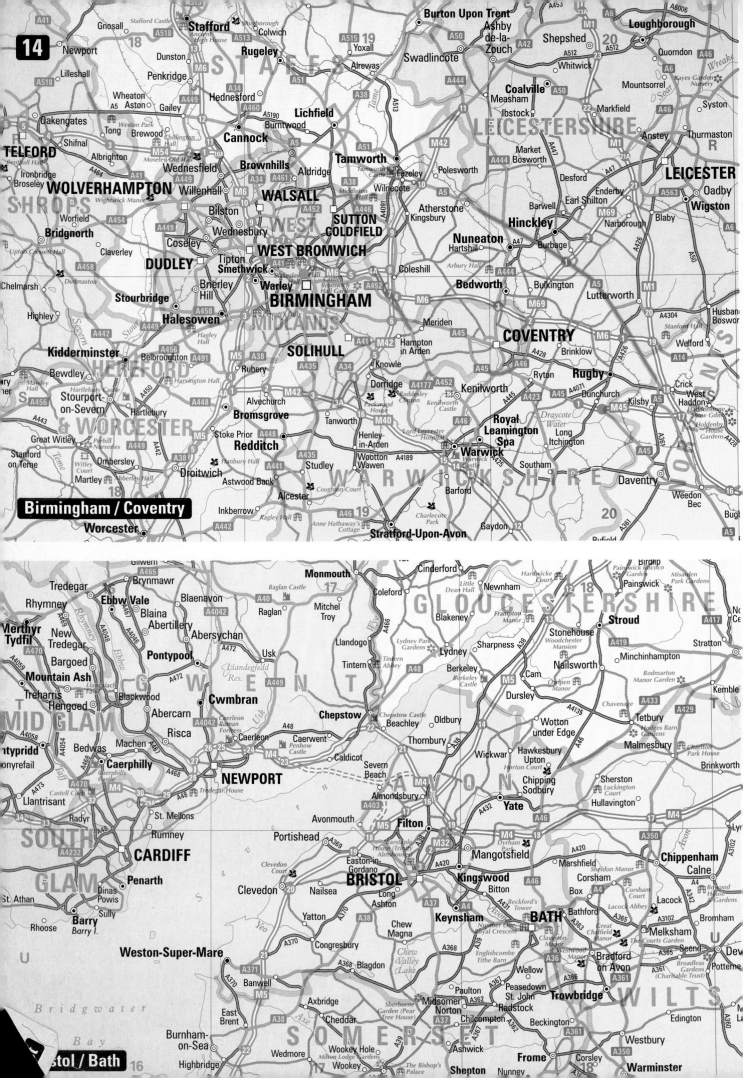

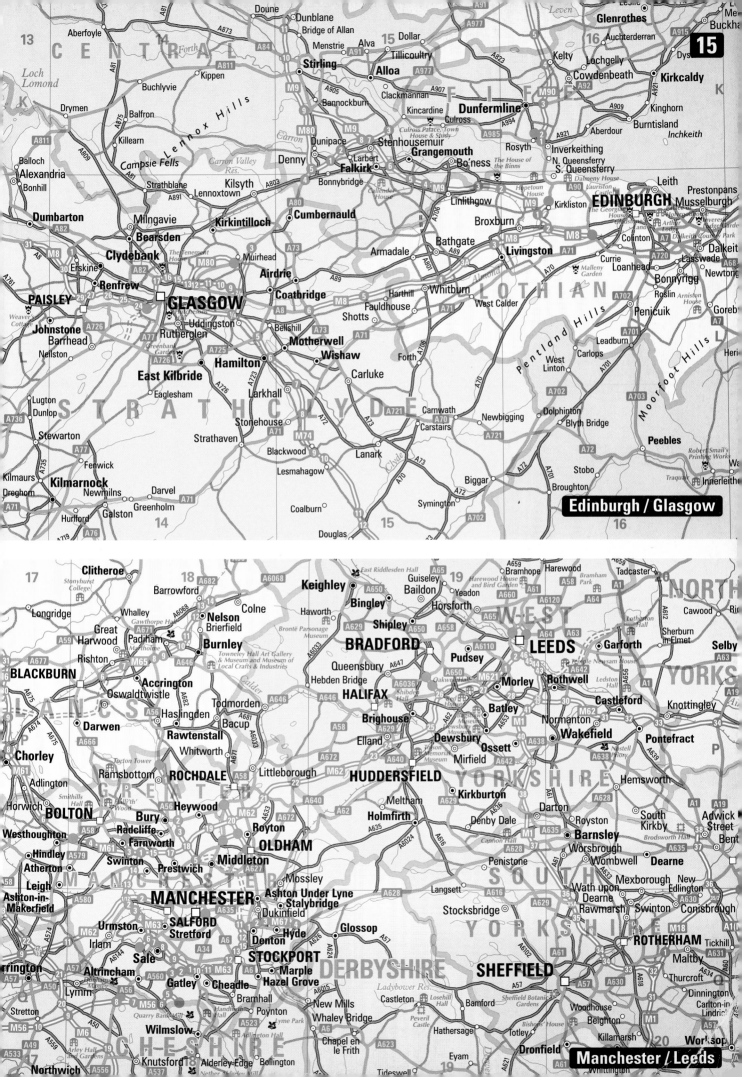

Edinburgh / Glasgow

Manchester / Leeds